HUME

HUME
A RE-EVALUATION

Edited by
DONALD W. LIVINGSTON
&
JAMES T. KING

New York
FORDHAM UNIVERSITY PRESS
1976

Printed in the United States of America

To the Members of
THE HUME SOCIETY

Acknowledgments

The idea of this collection grew out of the Hume conferences held in Illinois during the early 'seventies. From these congenial conferences The Hume Society was founded in 1974. The editors and, indeed, all Hume scholars are indebted to Professors Páll S. Árdal, Robert F. Anderson, Nicholas Capaldi, Antony Flew, Ronald J. Glossop, Donald Gotterbarn, Thomas Hearn, Peter Jones, David Norton, Terrence Penelhum, Wade L. Robison, Keith E. Yandell, and Farhang Zabeeh for their support of the early conferences and for their work in establishing The Hume Society. The editors are especially grateful to Professors Ernest Campbell Mossner, Páll S. Árdal, and Peter Jones who read the entire manuscript and made many helpful suggestions. A special debt is owed to Mr. Robert Miller for his prompt and careful editorial assistance.

Abbreviations

Citations of Hume's works appear, for the most part, in parentheses in the body of the text. Such references are to the standard editions listed below. Other citations of Hume, as well as scholarly references, appear in footnotes.

A   *An Abstract of a Treatise of Human Nature*, edd. J. M. Keynes and P. Sraffa (Cambridge, 1938).

D   *Dialogues Concerning Natural Religion*, ed. Norman Kemp Smith (New York, 1947).

EHU, EPM   *An Enquiry Concerning Human Understanding* and *An Enquiry Concerning the Principles of Morals*, ed. L. A. Selby-Bigge (Oxford, 1902).

Essays   *Essays Moral, Political, and Literary* (Oxford, 1966).

L   *A Letter from a Gentleman to His Friend in Edinburgh*, edd. E. C. Mossner and J. V. Price (Edinburgh, 1967).

LDH   *The Letters of David Hume*, ed. J. Y. T. Grieg, 2 vols. (Oxford, 1932).

NHR   *The Natural History of Religion*, ed. H. E. Root (Stanford, 1957).

NLDH   *New Letters of David Hume*, edd. R. Klibansky and E. C. Mossner (Oxford, 1954).

T   *A Treatise of Human Nature*, ed. L. A. Selby-Bigge (Oxford, 1888).

CONTENTS

Introduction

Donald W. Livingston
Northern Illinois University

It is now generally agreed that Hume is one of the great philosophers of the modern period. But this was not always so, and even now it is not clear in exactly what way Hume should be thought of as a great philosopher. During his lifetime, he was appreciated mainly for the *Essays* and as an historian. *The History of Great Britain* was widely read and became a classic after his death, passing through at least 167 posthumous editions. And it was not seriously challenged until Macaulay's *History of England* appeared in 1849. Even so, it continued to be read and taught down to the early-twentieth century.

Hume's philosophical writings, however, were generally viewed by his contemporaries as sceptical. But we should distinguish between two sorts of scepticism: one is virtuous and is used as a dialectical foil against which truth is illuminated; the other is vicious and destructive of reason and truth. In the popular mind of his contemporaries, Hume was seen as the latter sort of sceptic. In a letter to Andrew Millar, William Warburton wrote of Hume's thought that "there are vices of the *mind* as well as of the body: and I think a wickeder mind, and more obstinately bent on public mischief, I never knew." [1] James Beattie dealt with Hume's philosophical works in *The Nature and Immutability of Truth, In Opposition to Sophistry and Scepticism* (1770) which was extremely popular, going through eleven editions in the first decade. Beattie agreed that "scepticism, where it tends to make men well-bred, and good natured, and to rid them of pedantry and petulance . . . is an excellent thing. And some sorts of scepticism there are, that really have this tendency." But Hume's is not among them: "Mr. Hume, more subtle, or less reserved, than any of his predecessors, hath gone to still greater lengths in the demolition of common sense. . . ." [2] John Stuart Mill read Hume in a similar way: "Hume possessed powers of a very high order; but regard for truth formed no part of his character. He reasoned with surprising acuteness; but the object of his reasonings was, not to obtain truth, but to show that it is unattainable. His mind, too, was completely enslaved by a taste for literature . . . that literature which without regard for truth or utility, seeks only to excite emotion." [3] Essentially the same interpretation has continued into the twentieth century. John H. Randall writes of Hume's philosophy that it is "extremely acute, and malicious

1

throughout. Just because he had no real interest in either science or religion, no deep feeling for the values involved, he was able to be utterly consistent in the pricking of metaphysical bubbles, both scientific and theological. . . ." [4] And Prichard writes of the *Treatise*: "of course there is a great deal of cleverness in it, but the cleverness is only that of extreme ingenuity or perversity, and the ingenuity is only exceeded by the perversity." [5] The most recent and defensible interpretation of Hume as a subversive sceptic has been proposed by D. C. Stove:

> The overall impression made by Hume's philosophy on its readers has always been remarkably uniform; and it has been the kind which they have tried to express by calling it "sceptical," or "negative," or "critical," or "destructive." Hume has appeared to his readers as pre-eminently a *subverter* of natural or common sense beliefs . . . and no one, I think, before the present century, ever saw any reason to dissent from that verdict. There is, indeed, room and need for a *precise* account of what his characteristic scepticism consists in. But as to the broad fact, opinion has been uniform and emphatic.[6]

From the very first, however, there was another view, running parallel to the above, which saw Hume as a virtuous sceptic. Thomas Reid offered the first serious criticism of Hume's philosophy in the *Inquiry into the Human Mind* (1764). Reid took Hume's work to be a reduction to absurdity of a philosophical hypothesis which began in modern times with Descartes but had antecedents, he thought, stretching back at least as far as Plato: "The hypothesis I mean, is, that nothing is perceived but what is in the mind which perceives it. . . ." [7] Reid, however, found Hume's scepticism to be in the interest of truth and illuminating because it showed in the clearest way the absurdity of the principles from which it followed. In a respectful letter, he complimented Hume on the integrity and courage of mind to follow to the bitter end the "principles commonly received among philosophers" (principles which Reid had also accepted), allowing their absurdity to be made manifest and enabling a new start in philosophy to begin.[8] It was from Reid that we get the interpretation of Hume as the great and somewhat noble sceptic who must be answered. Reid's respectful confession to Hume that he had brought to light the perverse idealism in his own soul is paralleled by Kant's famous confession that Hume had awakened him from his dogmatic slumbers. Kant also viewed Hume as a great sceptic, working in the interest of philosophic truth and went out of his way to defend him as such. By 1838 Sir William Hamilton could write that "Hume . . . is author, *in* a sort, of all our subsequent philosophy. For out of Reid and Kant, mediately or immediately, all our subsequent philosophy is evolved; and the doctrines of Kant and Reid are both . . . attempts to find for philosophy deeper foundations than those which he had so thoroughly subverted." [9] The Absolute Idealists in Britain continued this sort of interpretation. T. H. Green republished Hume's philosophical works in 1874–75 and worked out what was then the longest and most careful study of Hume's philosophy. Like Reid, Green took Hume to be the last and most lucid figure in a bankrupt tradition, calling him "the last great English philosopher." Green writes: "Adopting the premises and method of Locke, he cleared them of all illogical adaptations to popular belief, and experimented with them on the body of professed knowledge, as one only could do who had neither any twist of vice nor any bias for doing good, but was a philosopher because he could not help it." [10] It was Absolute Idealists such as Green who presented the interpretation of Hume as a phenomenalist working with radically disconnected sensory atoms who had to be, not *answered*, as Reid and Kant had thought, but *refuted* in the light of idealist doctrines of continuity, internal relations, and absolute coherence.

With the collapse of Absolute Idealism and the rise of empirically and scientifically oriented philosophies such as Logical Atomism and Logical Positivism, Hume's supposed atomistic phenomenalism began to appear more congenial. And A. J. Ayer records how the Vienna Circle in its manifesto of 1929 officially included Hume as a founder: "those who stand closest to the Vienna Circle in their general outlook are Hume and Mach. It is indeed remarkable how much of the doctrine that is now thought to be especially characteristic of logical positivism was already stated, or at least foreshadowed, by Hume." [11] The Logical Positivists were the first philosophical movement to treat Hume publicly as not being a sceptic of any sort, vicious or virtuous, but as one of the few great philosophers of the past whose essential doctrines are, with some contemporary polishing, true.

Proponents of the three above interpretations typically assumed that there were no exegetical problems with the Humean text. Hume, after all, was known for analytical clarity and as a master of English style. The only problem seemed to be that of assessing the value of what he had said. However, one must keep in mind that the *Treatise* was not widely read. It was published in three volumes of a thousand copies in 1739–40, and it sold so slowly that the publisher was still advertising it in 1756. The next edition appeared in 1817, and it was not published again until the Green and Grose edition of 1874–75. But it was not until Selby-Bigge's editions of the *Treatise* (1888) and of the *Enquiries* (1893) that the Humean *text* began to be seen as a special problem. In the Introduction to the *Enquiries*, Selby-Bigge warned that "Hume's philosophic writings are to be read with great caution. His pages, especially those of the *Treatise*, are so full of matter, he says so many different things in so many different ways and different connexions, and with so much indifference to what he has said before, that it is very hard to say positively that he taught, or did not teach, this or that particular doctrine. . . . This makes it easy to find *all* philosophies in Hume, or, by setting up one statement against another, *none* at all." [12] This sort of thing cannot be said of the text of any other great modern philosopher. The gradual recognition that Hume's writings require special exegetical effort opened up the twofold question of how to read those writings and what philosophical value might they have. This latter question could, of course, give rise to scepticism about whether Hume's writings really have *any* philosophical value. A. E. Taylor expressed this doubt at the conclusion of his Leslie Stephen lecture as a "haunting uncertainty as to whether Hume was a really great philosopher or only 'a very clever man.' " [13]

In 1941 Norman Kemp Smith published *The Philosophy of David Hume,* the first book-length study on Hume devoted entirely to the problem of exegesis. Limiting himself mainly to the *Treatise*, Kemp Smith concluded that Hume should be read not as a sceptic, virtuous or otherwise, but as one who had worked out a highly original naturalistic defense of common sense beliefs along with a criticism of dogmatic metaphysics. The sceptical interpretation of the text had assumed that the entire structure of Hume's thought is *ad hominem* and that he himself had nothing to say. But if Kemp Smith is right, Hume is a philosopher with something to teach which has yet to be fully appreciated.

The general outline of the Kemp Smith thesis was widely accepted and is the framework in which most work on Hume is done today, though the interpretations of Hume mentioned above are still very much alive. The Hume literature since Kemp Smith falls into two classes. Most of it is exegetical. Kemp Smith's thesis was limited to a study of the structure and origins of the *Treatise*, but there was also the problem of how to read and connect the other texts: the two *Enquiries*, the *Dialogues Concerning Natural Religion*, the *Essays Moral, Political, and Literary*, *The Natural History of Religion*, the "Dissertation on the Passions," and *The History of Great Britain*. The work is by no means complete. Most Hume scholarship still congregates around the epistemological and ontological problems raised in Book I of the *Treatise*, and even here there is a fairly limited selection of topics. Hume is, of course, appreciated as a moral philosopher and as a philosopher of religion, but neither his moral philosophy nor his philosophy of religion has received the in-depth analysis which Professor Stove, for example, has brought to his formulation of the problem of induction.[14] Very little has been done on Hume's work in aesthetics and on his quite extensive social and political thought. The other sort of literature which the Kemp Smith interpretation made possible is that which attempts the further *philosophical* development of Hume's insights. And this raises the question of whether eventually some sort of "Humean" outlook on a wide range of philosophical issues might arise. There have been Platonists, Kantians, Hegelians, and Wittgensteinians who have cultivated and extended the ideas of their teachers. Whether there can be anything like a Humean school of thought depends on how scholars construct the text and what philosophers can find there which is fruitful. Both processes are under way and have accelerated remarkably since Kemp Smith's thesis was laid out in 1941. Since then, twenty-four book-length studies in English have appeared on Hume's work, eighteen of which were published in the last fifteen years.

In the light of this remarkable interest in Hume, it seems fitting to present, on the bicentennial of Hume's death, a volume of essays by established and new Hume scholars which might help to focus and encourage the study of Hume's thought. All but four of the nineteen essays were written or reworked especially for the volume and have not been previously published. Some of the essays are close studies of the text; others deal with the philosophical issues Hume raises, either by criticizing his doctrines or by developing his insights further. All the interpretations mentioned above are represented in fresh form along with new interpretations the classification of which is best left to the reader.

The essays cover the full range of Hume's thought including his historical work. But they are unified by two main questions: What is the nature and limit of Hume's scepticism, and, in the light of an answer to this question, what are the positive doctrines of his philosophy and what value do they have? The modern problem of scepticism began with the "Pyrrhonian crisis" of the late-sixteenth and early-seventeenth centuries which challenged all existing norms in every area of life: religious, scientific, moral, and political. The power and influence of this crisis can be seen in the popularity of Montaigne's melancholy *Apology for Raimond Sebond* (1576) and in Descartes' project to refute total scepticism by assuming its truth and reducing it to absurdity, an attempt in which, as Professor Popkin has argued, he perished, becoming a sceptic *malgré lui*.[15] Sceptical anxiety continued into Hume's time. The questions of despair which he asked at the end of the sceptical ordeal which concludes Book I of the *Treatise* were addressed to a state of mind he thought his readers would share:

> Where am I, or what? From what causes do I derive my existence, and to what condition shall I return? Whose favour shall I court, and whose anger must I dread? What beings surround me? and on whom have I any influence, or who have any influence on me? I am confounded with all these questions, and begin to fancy myself in the most deplorable condition imaginable, inviron'd with the deepest darkness, and utterly depriv'd of the use of every member and faculty" [T 269].

By the nineteenth century, Nietzsche had given a different conceptual shape to this sceptical anxiety, which he called the problem of "nihilism," and proposed as its solution the "transvaluation of values." Similarly, in the twentieth century a literary philosopher like Albert Camus could propose the philosophy of "the absurd" as a condition of reason and value, a condition celebrated artistically in the "theater of the absurd."

From the first, the Pyrrhonian challenge to all authority had revolutionary social and political consequences. One of the first to call for total revolution against all existing social and political norms was Jean Meslier (1678–1729), who has been aptly described as a "left-wing Cartesian." [16] Meslier ended his *Testament* for total revolution on a note of metaphysical despair: "I shall finish this with nothingness; but then I am hardly anything more than nothing, and soon I shall be nothing." [17] Two centuries later, Bruno Bauer, a left-wing Hegelian, was to call for a "revolution against everything positive" and for the "terrorism of the true theory." And in a letter to Ruge, Marx echoed the same attitude of metaphysical revolution: "What we must accomplish is the ruthless critique of everything that exists." [18] Although the Pyrrhonian challenge has undergone considerable modification since the sixteenth century, it continues to determine the structure and tone of many philosophical problems, and it is against this background that we must try to understand the nature of Hume's scepticism and the philosophy he built around it.

The essays gathered for this volume fall conveniently into six groups. The first group deals with the nature of Hume's scepticism and his conception of reason, the second with Hume's views on the rationality of religious belief; the third examines some of the positive doctrines which constitute Hume's naturalistic and common sense philosophy. Closely related to this third group is a set of essays dealing with Hume's views on the nature of time and tradition and the role these concepts play in his epistemology, political philosophy, and historical writing. The fifth group examines Hume's aesthetic and moral philosophy, and the last group deals with the influence of Hume's political thought on the American Founders. I shall introduce the essays in this order, devoting a section to each group.

I

To many commentators, Hume's philosophy has appeared a strange mixture of scepticism and an immodestly optimistic ambition to secure the sciences on a foundation of certainty. Commentators like Kemp Smith who view Hume as a naturalist have tried to resolve this apparent conflict by arguing that Hume's scepticism is aimed at eliminating rationalistic metaphysics and building the sciences on a system of unavoidable nature beliefs. To do this, Hume had to show that the rationalistic demand to justify our natural beliefs (particularly causal beliefs and beliefs in the existence of natural objects) is impossible. Having shown that there is no concept of reason which could justify the system of natural beliefs, Hume then proposes an alternative conception of reason (built on analytic and causal judgments) which operates coherently within the system of natural beliefs. Wade L. Robison, however, in "David Hume: Naturalist and Meta-sceptic," argues that although Hume is a naturalist, he is also a sceptic and one of a special sort. Robison argues, in effect, that Hume shows and believed himself to have shown that reason is incoherent *within* the system of natural beliefs: "what Hume has discovered is that the human mind is *essentially incoherent*." We are, nevertheless, constrained to have natural beliefs and to form a system of natural beliefs even though we know these beliefs are incoherent. This reading suggests that Hume's solution to the Pyrrhonian crisis is *aesthetic*: human reason within the system of natural beliefs is essentially comic. And, as in comedy, Hume's solution, paradoxically, affirms and celebrates what it finds absurd. In this case, reflection on the incoherence of reason within the system of natural beliefs is a condition for understanding what we mean by nature and what it means to understand it. There is an interesting parallel here in Christian theology. Christian theologians may be taken to hold that the spiritual life of man cannot be understood without belief in such fundamental doctrines as the Trinity and the Incarnation, doctrines which certainly appear to be incoherent. Rationalistic theologians argue that the incoherence is only apparent and that the doctrines are merely *paradoxical*. Fideistic theologians argue that the doctrines really are incoherent and are to be thought of as *mysteries*, belief in which is necessary for understanding. Similarly, on Robison's reading (though he himself does not say so) Hume may be interpreted as a secular fideist, holding that certain natural beliefs are in themselves incoherent but necessary for understanding.

The most important set of natural beliefs we have are *inductive* beliefs, and Hume's famous sceptical challenge to justify these beliefs has come to be known as the problem of induction. C. D. Broad considered this problem the "scandal" of modern philosophy insofar as no consensus had been reached about its solution. In his essay "Why Should Probability Be the Guide of Life?" D. C. Stove argues that many twentieth-century philosophers of science have confused Hume's inductive scepticism with scepticism about statements of logical probability. He quotes W. C. Salmon, for instance, as contending that the theory of logical probability provides "no basis for expecting the probable rather than the improbable" and so "fails to qualify as a 'guide of life.'" According to Stove such scepticism is common in contemporary philosophy of science where there is reluctance to assess the probability of scientific conclusions in relation to their evidence. We have become, Stove says, "probability numb." This state of affairs is due, he thinks, to the legacy of Hume's celebrated problem of induction. But, Stove argues, Hume had no concept of the theory of logical probability, and in any case inductive scepticism is not probability scepticism since there are probability arguments which are not inductive. Behind Hume's inductive scepticism is the principle of *inductive fallibilism*: that the conclusion of the best inductive argument may be false even though its premises are true. Philosophers of science such as Carnap and his followers have made this non-deducibility thesis the whole meaning of inductive inference and have tended to worry about it to the exclusion of every other feature of scientific inference. It is this sceptical mood, brought on by an obsession with inductive fallibilism, which has insensibly spilled over into probability scepticism. Stove contends, however, that probability scepticism is incoherent because it presupposes an assessment of probability as a condition for raising the sceptical question. He concludes that Hume's influence on the philosophy of science and on twentieth-century intellectual culture generally has been pernicious. Although inductive fallibilism is the most influential and profound of Hume's non-deducibility theses, two others have had an almost equal negative influence: the non-deducibility of "ought" from "is" and the non-deducibility of factual propositions from necessary truths. These three theses, in Stove's view, have weakened scientific, religious, and moral confidence respectively and have been at the bottom not only of the "probability-numbness in our present philosophy of science, but of the far wider phenomenon of 'modern nervousness.'"

Granted that Hume's philosophy may have had some such negative influence on our intellectual culture, the question remains whether the negative theses in question are really in Hume's work or whether they have been read into it by a rationalistic mind which is morbidly vulnerable to scepticism of any kind. In short, the supposed destructive Humean legacy may be just the melancholy realization that the rationalistic program of early modern philosophy (which was a response to the Pyrrhonian crisis) is impossible, a point which Hume's whole philosophy appears designed to show.

If so, then the question to be asked is whether Hume perished in the attempt or whether he was sufficiently emancipated from rationalistic *and* sceptical preconceptions to have offered a fresh approach. Whatever the answer, a deeper understanding of the rationale of Hume's philosophy appears necessary for an adequate understanding of our contemporary intellectual condition.

Just as Stove argues that probability scepticism is incoherent, Farhang Zabeeh in "Hume's Problem of Induction: An Appraisal" argues that the problem of inductive scepticism is incoherent. The traditional formulation of the problem is how one can be justified in claiming that unobserved cases will resemble observed ones. Zabeeh holds that the concept of an "observed case" presupposes inductive inferences; so unless induction is generally justified there cannot be any "observed cases" to support the sceptical question. The problem of induction, then, is absurd because it is possible only if induction is justified. Zabeeh contends that the problem of induction was never at home in Hume's philosophy; it in fact arises only because of certain phenomenalistic assumptions which are built into his epistemology of impressions and ideas. The problem of induction has persisted mainly because of the strong phenomenalistic outlook which has dominated later forms of empiricism, requiring that knowledge be built on something having no inductive structure, such as incorrigible sense data, basic propositions, protocol sentences, and the like. But, in the end, Hume abandoned phenomenalism for the system of natural beliefs within which he recognized that "there is no problem of induction." Working within this system, Hume was the first to recognize the need to develop an "*a posteriori* logic of induction." As a naturalist, then, Hume solved the general problem of induction by pointing out that there is really no such problem, the only problem being that of codifying and improving actual inductive practices.

Combining the results of Stove's and Zabeeh's essays, we may say that probability scepticism and inductive scepticism are problems which belong more to twentieth-century philosophy of science than to Hume's own philosophy; they are generated by a rationalistic obsession with inductive fallibilism and a phenomenalistic epistemology, neither of which Hume shared.

Páll S. Árdal in "Some Implications of the Virtue of Reasonableness in Hume's *Treatise*," agrees with Zabeeh that the main point of Hume's scepticism is to *reconstruct* the concept of reason within the system of natural beliefs rather than to eliminate it as Robison's essay may suggest. One traditional view of reason opposes it to passion and imposes on us the duty of governing our passions by reason. In a famous passage, however, Hume holds that "Reason is, and ought only to be the slave of the passions, and can never pretend to any other office than to serve and obey them" (T 415). Reason here is the understanding of analytic and factual truths and, for Hume, such understanding alone can never be a motive to action. It is in this sense that Hume says elsewhere that reason is "inert" and can never oppose our passions. In other passages, however, reason is presented as a *calm passion* which *can* oppose passion: "that *reason*, which is able to oppose our passion . . . [is] nothing but a general calm determination of the passions, founded on some distant view or reflexion" (T 583). It is this conception of reason which Árdal finds peculiarly Humean, and whatever else may be said of it, it is a conception of reason which radically breaks with the tradition which opposes reason to passion (something Hume's other conception of reason as inert does not do), for here Hume is building the concept of reason into the concept of passion. But how precisely are we to think of reason as a structure of passion? For Hume the passions are normatively structured by the concepts of virtue and vice, and on Árdal's reading, we are to think of "that *reason*, which is able to oppose our passion" as a *virtue*. Reason is the virtue of being *reasonable*, that is, of taking a universal and objective point of view. Reason so understood is subject to Hume's general theory of the virtues and, like all Humean virtues, is approved of because it serves human ends and purposes. This conception of reason can operate within the system of natural beliefs even if that system, on some other concept of reason, is incoherent as a whole.

II

No discussion of Hume's scepticism would be complete without some appreciation of his views on the rationality of religion. Although Hume had a special interest in religion and wrote extensively on it, his views have not appeared entirely clear. On the one hand he seems to have rejected religious belief as rationally untenable. We have observed Stove's remark that one of Hume's non-deducibility theses that necessary propositions cannot entail factual propositions (which rules out all forms of the ontological argument) has led to a weakening of "religious confidence." Even more devastating, perhaps, is Hume's well-known criticism of the more popular theistic argument from design. On the other hand, Hume himself remarks in *The Natural History of Religion* that the "whole frame of nature bespeaks an intelligent author; and no rational inquirer can, after serious reflection, suspend his belief a moment with regard to the primary principles of Theism and Religion" (NHR 21). Keith E. Yandell in "Hume on Religious Belief" argues that, appearances to the contrary, Hume's position on the rationality of religion is consistent. The key to his analysis is a distinction which Hume makes between the origin of religion in reason and its ground in human nature. For Hume, there is no foundation in reason for religion, but, equally, there is no foundation in reason for belief in the causal principle and in the existence of natural objects (a point thoroughly discussed in Robison's essay). But just as there is an origin in human nature for these beliefs, so there is an origin in human nature for what Yandell calls the "minimally theistic belief" that the order of nature is due, as Hume says, to an "intelligent author."

Yandell contends that this belief, for Hume, is due to a "propensity of reason" where reason is understood as a "wonderful instinct of the soul" (compare this with Árdal's analysis of reason as a virtue). The propensity is triggered whenever men are able to reflect calmly on the apparent order in nature. In this sense only is "minimal theism" reasonable. It is not reasonable in the sense of being certified by either deductive or inductive argument. As a propensity of reason, minimal theism is not as invariant as, for example, the propensity to belief in the causal principle, and is more susceptible to corruption by education and other variables. But it is, nonetheless, an original propensity of the mind which Hume does not pretend to explain and which, as he says in *The Natural History of Religion*, "may be considered as a kind of mark or stamp which the divine workman has set upon his work . . ." (NHR 75). Yandell's interpretation suggests that Hume's views on religious belief are, in some way, fideistic, an interpretation parallel to the fideistic analysis of the system of natural beliefs which we found suggested in Robison's essay.

One important contribution of Yandell's essay is to have distinguished Hume's two questions about religion: its foundation in reason as distinct from its foundation in human nature. The first question is the main subject of the *Dialogues Concerning Natural Religion*; the second is the main subject of *The Natural History of Religion*. Most commentators have asked the first question and have, therefore, concentrated on the *Dialogues* to the neglect of the *Natural History*. The merit of Yandell's essay is to have shown the importance of the second question and, hence, of the *Natural History* for an adequate understanding of Hume's views on religion. George J. Nathan's essay "The Existence and Nature of God in Hume's Theism" deals with the more traditional first question raised in the *Dialogues* and so may be read as a complement to Yandell's essay.

The received interpretation of the *Dialogues* is that Hume argues for the impossibility of a causal argument for the existence and nature of God. Nathan argues, however, that this interpretation is sound only if we accept as Hume's sole conception of causation "the standard analysis" (that a cause is a constant-conjunction of like events along with a habit of expectation that the conjunction will continue). Nathan contends that in the *Dialogues* and in other works Hume affirms a broader notion of causality which entails a doctrine of *ultimate* causation which is used to support the "philosophical theism" of the *Dialogues*. Hume, on this reading, believes in the existence of causal powers and dispositions, and regularly refers to them in his own explanations, and, indeed, holds that no causal explanation is adequate unless it identifies the proper causal power. Unlike causes understood as constant-conjunctions, causal powers cannot be experienced, and so Hume is forced to admit that we have no idea of them, where "idea" is understood to mean "image." But on Nathan's interpretation, although Hume holds that talk about causal powers is *empirically* meaningless, he also holds that descriptions of causal powers are intelligible and are presupposed in all scientific explanation. (For supporting views that Hume thought terms could be meaningful even if they do not refer to an idea, see the essays by Livingston and Capaldi, and Jones's essay on Hume and Wittgenstein; for a contrary view, see the essay by Flew.) Nathan documents the empirical and analytical criteria which Hume lays down for the conception and discovery of causal powers or what he sometimes calls "principles." Among these criteria is the idea that particular constant-conjunction causes are to be explained by general principles which, in turn, are to be explained by more general principles until the most general principle of all is reached. Nathan argues that, in the *Dialogues*, Hume means to identify the ultimate causal principle or power with God, conceived only as the intelligent principle of order in the world. Hume took this conception of God to be what is rationally defensible in the theistic tradition. But it is at variance with that tradition insofar as it entails that God be a principle, not a particular being, and, hence, not a person. For Hume, the need to frame an imaginary conception of God as a person is not a demand of reason but has its rationale in propensities of human nature, which brings us back to a consideration of Hume's second question about religion raised in Yandell's essay: What ground do religious beliefs have in human nature, whether they be rationally justified or not?

III

The dominant interpretation of Hume's philosophy as a whole is that it is a form of *phenomenalism*. Indeed, Hume's philosophy is often taken as an especially clear paradigm of *radical* empiricism, the program of explicating our understanding of the world in terms of ontologically disconnected phenomenal entities. This interpretation is challenged by Nathan's thesis that a doctrine of logically unobservable causal powers is internal to Hume's philosophy, and it is challenged also in a number of other ways by most of the essays in this volume. Robert F. Anderson in "The Location, Extension, Shape, and Size of Hume's Perceptions" argues that Hume embraced the thesis that some perceptions are located in the brain, a view which appears remarkably similar to the contemporary identity theory of mind and body. Anderson shows that Hume believed in the possibility of physiological explanations of mental states, and he examines some tentative physical explanations which Hume offers of the association relations.

Nicholas Capaldi in "Hume's Theory of the Passions" makes a similar point, arguing that Hume conceives of the passions as the "conscious tip of a more basic physiological process," the operation of which he thinks is, at present, largely unknown. According to Capaldi, Hume's philosophy is explicitly and consistently governed by a common sense criterion of what exists which includes a public world of dispositions, bodies, and other selves. Capaldi exhibits this structure of Hume's philosophy by a systematic examination of the passions and the public world they presuppose, taking seriously Hume's claim (T 8) that the main point of the *Treatise* is to examine the nature of the passions and the constitutive role they play in the structure and understanding of common life. A particularly interesting point in Capaldi's study is the thesis that the account of the self in Books II and III of the *Treatise* is consistent with the account in Book I. This has been far from obvious. In Book I, Hume seems to offer a purely phenomenalistic account of the self: the self appears to be just a "bundle of perceptions." But, in Books II and III, the self appears as a thoroughly public entity having the properties of body as well as mind and possessing character and dispositions as well as impressions and ideas.

That Hume's philosophy is and was intended to be a critical common sense philosophy is defended also by Peter Jones in "Strains in Hume and Wittgenstein." Like Anderson and Capaldi, Jones stresses the material foundations of Hume's philosophy, paying special attention to Hume's conception of man as a social animal. For Hume reason is a social phenomenon (compare this with Árdal's analysis of reason as a virtue). Human beings, like other animals, learn at first by means of reaction, imitation, and reinforcement; in this way certain habits are developed which can be displaced only partly by subsequent education. According to Jones, Hume recognized that "Doubt and scepticism cannot precede initial training because they are attitudes that logically presuppose a natural background." To reason at all, then, presupposes a background of beliefs framed in habit, custom, and tradition. On this reading, we may say that Hume's thought emerges as a modern version of the Augustinian and medieval principle *credo ut intelligam* as opposed to the modern Cartesian principle *dubito ut intelligam*. But whereas for Augustine the tradition which is the logical background of thought is a sacred one, for Hume it is a natural one, what Jones calls the "secular *a priori*." The task of the philosopher is to uncover critically the fundamental beliefs and practices which constitute the natural and historical tradition. The tradition frames what we do in the widest sense of "do," and our understanding of what we do is often obscured by misuse of language and faulty analogies brought about by philosophical pretensions to constitute the norms of reason and practice *a priori*. All these themes occur in Wittgenstein's later work (especially in *On Certainty*) which is often seen as antithetical to Hume's philosophy mainly because of the popular interpretation of Hume as a phenomenalist and sceptic.

IV

Another essay which argues against the phenomenalist interpretation and stresses the categorical role of tradition in Hume's thought is Donald Livingston's "Hume's Historical Theory of Meaning." Hume's "first principle" is a theory of meaning which explicates meaning as a relation between present and *past* existences. In this, Hume differs from later empiricists: phenomenalism explicates meaning in terms of actual or possible *present* experiences; pragmatism explicates meaning in terms of a relation between *present* and *future* experiences; and logical empiricism (and most forms of idealism as well) hold that past tense expressions must be recast into a *tenseless* idiom. Hume's theory is the only *past-entailing* theory of meaning in the empirical tradition. The other theories all entail that expressions purportedly about the past are either meaningless or must be recast into some non–past-tense idiom. They are all inadequate insofar as they make impossible past-entailing concepts such as "is a father," "is a U. S. senator," "is in accord with English Common Law," concepts which logically apply to the present on condition that certain sentences about the *past* are true. Most theories of meaning in the empirical tradition have been designed to account for the language of theoretical science which is not in any obvious way a past-entailing language. But the language of common life, being woven out of traditions, customs, and habits, is *essentially* past-entailing. So whatever difficulties there may be in Hume's past-entailing theory of meaning, it is a better account of the language of common life and history than the alternatives in the empirical tradition. If this analysis is right, then there is a conceptual foundation in Hume's deepest principle for a philosophically tradition-laden interpretation of thought and reality.

The philosophical conservatism grounded in Hume's theory of meaning and understanding provides broad conceptual support for his conservative social and political philosophy. Sheldon S. Wolin in "Hume and Conservatism" discusses the conservative structure of Hume's political philosophy and shows how it differs from other forms of conservatism. As a political movement and as a philosophy, conservatism began as a criticism of the ideas informing the French Revolution, which was viewed as the natural result of the Enlightenment confidence in reason to fathom and reconstruct the ground of social and political order. Conservatism from the first was not so much a defense of the *ancien régime* as an attack on the intrusion of rationalistic metaphysics into the social and political affairs of common life. Early conservatives, such as Burke, sought to defend the traditions of common life by treating them as *sacred* and invoking a mysterious providence to explain their authority. Hume's conservatism, however, developed out of the very analytical and empirical materials of the Enlightenment which Hume used to "whittle down" the claims of reason (see the essays by Robison and Árdal). It is a conservatism based on a concept of tradition certified by analytical and empirical reason alone and without benefit of a sacred providence.

The essays by Jones, Livingston, and Wolin point out in different ways the special qualitative and normative character of *past* time for Hume's epistemology and political philosophy, and this raises the general question of Hume's views on the nature of time. Antony Flew in "Infinite Divisibility in Hume's *Treatise*" examines Hume's analysis of the ideas of space and time in Book I, Part II of the *Treatise*. There has been little commentary on this part of the *Treatise*, which is generally agreed to be one of its least satisfactory parts. There Hume holds the counter-intuitive theses that the parts of space and time cannot be infinitely divisible and that the indivisible points composing space and time cannot themselves have extension and duration respectively. On Flew's reading, Hume is thereby committed to "a very drastic and pervasive form of atomism" which is incompatible with "any stock pictures of Hume—including his own." The point of Flew's essay is to uncover empathetically the rationale of Hume's problems in order to appreciate how he could think these conclusions are solutions to them.

Another essay dealing with Hume's conception of time is James Noxon's "Remembering and Imagining the Past." Noxon discusses Hume's attempt to distinguish between memory and imagination on the one hand and historical narratives and fictional narratives on the other. Hume offers two criteria for distinguishing ideas of memory from those of imagination, a phenomenal one in terms of introspectible intrinsic qualities and an epistemological one in terms of truth conditions. These two criteria are combined in a causal account of memory beliefs: that the phenomenal distinguishing features of memory experiences are attributable to the past events which cause them. Noxon argues that Hume uses this analysis of memory belief as a model to account for the distinction between historical and fictional narratives, an account which leads to paradoxical conclusions. Among other things, Hume was forced by the phenomenal criterion to view memory and imagination on a continuum, with imagination conceived as a kind of false memory. Applying this analysis to history and fiction, he was compelled to view fiction as false history (thereby failing to appreciate the difference between aesthetic and historical credibility) and to seek for an impossible phenomenal–causal certification of historical beliefs. Noxon argues that memory–imagination and history–fiction are different, not in degree, but in kind; by working through the rationale of Hume's errors, he proposes what he considers to be a more adequate criterion for making the relevant distinctions. (For another discussion of Hume's views on the structure of historical narration, see Livingston.)

No examination of Hume's conception of the nature of time and the past would be complete without some discussion of his monumental *History of England*. Constant Noble Stockton in "Economics and the Mechanism of Historical Progress in Hume's *History*" argues that the *History* is an integral part of the "science of man" which Hume began in the *Treatise*. One important area in this science is economics, a field in which Hume made founding contributions. The economic theory is worked out mainly in the *Essays* and is applied to the *History* to explain the mechanism of historical change. Stockton discusses the origin of the idea of economic history, contending that Hume was the first to work out a coherent economic interpretation of historical events and that his methods resemble more closely those of twentieth-century "cliometricians" than those of nineteenth-century historians. Stockton shows how Hume uses economic materials from the *Essays* in the *History* to analyze and explain historical events. These include discussions of historical demography, theory of money, government fiscal problems (such as taxation, national expenditure, and national debt), the issue of mercantilism and economic liberty, wages, prices, inflation, and economic cycles. These discussions not only throw light on the economic interpretation of the *History*; they also serve to clarify Hume's intentions in the *Essays*. The guiding causal narrative in the *History* is that economic developments lead to social developments which provide the condition for political, constitutional, and higher cultural developments, a view which appears inconsistent with such essays as "Of the Rise and Progress of the Arts and Sciences" where Hume seems to hold that the political constitution of a nation provides the condition for its economic and cultural development. Stockton suggests that on the relation of economic development to social, political, and cultural development, Hume takes a position similar to Marx's. Just how the two interpretations differ, and why, would be an interesting and timely study.

Hume's *History* is usually considered independently of his philosophical work. The main contribution of Stockton's essay is that it presents the

History as an illuminating and integral part of Hume's philosophical program to contruct a science of man which not only includes history but is itself profoundly historical. Moreover, as a theoretician of the mechanism of historical change, Hume is seen to deserve a place in the tradition of philosophy of history alongside such founders as Vico, Turgot, Hegel, and Marx.

v

In the Introduction to the *Treatise,* Hume promised to write a treatise on "Criticism" which would show how aesthetic experience and the norms for aesthetic judgment are grounded in human nature. This promise was partially fulfilled in later essays such as "Of the Delicacy of Taste and Passion," "Of the Standard of Taste," and "Of Tragedy," and in scattered remarks in the two *Enquiries.* Together these constitute a comprehensive aesthetic theory which is among the most interesting and neglected parts of Hume's philosophy. In "Cause, Reason, and Objectivity in Hume's Aesthetics," Peter Jones discusses Hume's views on the nature of beauty, the nature of judgments of beauty, and the conditions for a proper response to works of art. Beauty itself is a "power" in an object which when perceived from a certain disciplined viewpoint (which we may call the aesthetic point of view) produces in a normal viewer a pleasurable sentiment. The objectivity of aesthetic judgments, for Hume, is empirical and is secured by the basic physiological fact that men's internal sentiments are much the same in similar circumstances and by the public character of aesthetic language. Beyond this uniformity, aesthetic judgments are modified by historical circumstances and the extent to which a society has developed the discipline of the aesthetic point of view. Aesthetic judgment is located in a tradition in which an aesthetic language has been formed which registers what our aesthetic sentiments are and ought to be. One of the main points of art criticism is to modify and extend this language by new experiences and by a more careful analysis of the causal conditions which give rise to aesthetic sentiments. For Hume, the enjoyment of art through aesthetic discourse is a social and rational activity which increases the level both of our knowledge and of our humanity.

Jones's essay provides a reading of Hume's aesthetic theory as a project governed by the objective standards of a common human psychology expressed in public aesthetic language rather than the phenomenalistic program of charting private mental states. In an interesting discussion, Jones examines Hume's attempt to distinguish between a bad critic and an aesthetic pretender, the latter being one who has mastered the public criteria of aesthetic judgment but does not have the inner sentiment. The Humean concept of the aesthetic pretender is possible only on the condition that the criteria for aesthetic judgment are public. In presenting Hume as an objectivist in aesthetics, Jones's essay is another move away from the phenomenalistic and sceptical interpretation of Hume's philosophy.

The structure of Hume's moral theory parallels very closely his aesthetic theory insofar as both are grounded on a theory of sentiment. Just as Jones's essay stresses the importance of aesthetic language in Hume's aesthetic theory, so James T. King's "The Place of the Language of Morals in Hume's Second *Enquiry*" and Ronald J. Glossop's "Hume, Stevenson, and Hare on Moral Language" stress the importance of moral language in Hume's moral theory. Both are further challenges to the phenomenalistic interpretation of Hume's philosophy. King discusses the difference between Hume's approach to moral philosophy in Book III of the *Treatise* and in the *Enquiry Concerning the Principles of Morals*, arguing that the latter is philosophically superior. The project of the *Treatise* is to explain the principles of morals by deriving them empirically from the psychological mechanisms of the passions. This *Treatise* approach has been the favorite reading of those who view Hume's moral philosophy as phenomenalistic, and although King does not read Hume in this way, he does allow that the psychological analysis of morals in the *Treatise* is open to serious objections, the most serious of which is the account of how sentiments are corrected to achieve a moral point of view. (For another discussion of difficulties in the *Treatise* account, see Capaldi's essay.) In the *Enquiry*, however, the epistemic ground of Hume's moral theory is the language of morals in common use. It is only by reference to this language that a judgment or sentiment might be denominated as moral (as opposed to non-moral), and it is this language also which comprises the general principles of approval and disapproval which we apply in judging a trait or deed to be moral. King argues that the shift in Hume's interests from the analysis of moral sentiments (understood as perceptions) in Book III to a concern with the analysis of moral language and historical institutions in the *Enquiry* is an advance because it avoids the scepticism inherent in the introspective approach of Book III while preserving its psychological insights.

Ronald Glossop's "Hume, Stevenson, and Hare on Moral Language" also views Hume's moral theory as essentially requiring an analysis of moral language, a reading which places Hume in the context of contemporary Anglo-American moral philosophy. Two of the foremost recent writers on ethics, Stevenson and Hare, have found in Hume a precursor of their own theory. Glossop argues, however, that Hume's theory not only is different from that of Stevenson and Hare but is a more adequate account of moral language. Against Stevenson, he contends that moral terms reflect a general rather than a personal point of view and that, in recognizing this and in relating morality to the general welfare, Hume presents a better analysis of moral expressions. One main principle of Hare's ethics is what he calls "Hume's law," that "ought" cannot be deduced from "is." Glossop offers a qualified naturalist interpretation of Hume's ethics and defends it against Hare's antinaturalism by arguing that the naturalist definition of virtue (any quality of character which arouses a sentiment of approbation in an informed, disinterested spectator) is essentially commendatory, and that Hare's challenge that the naturalist definition comprise no terms having evaluative meaning is simply illegitimate, deriving from a false dichotomy between descriptive and evaluative meaning. Glossop admits that "ought" cannot be deduced from "is" but contends that Hume was concerned with the *origins* of morals in human nature and intended to frame a connection between "is" and "ought" which proceeds by sentiment rather than by reason and that in this Hume is essentially correct. Glossop offers an interpretation of Hume as a case of the *disinterested spectator* approach to ethics, citing several passages where Hume insists on the objectivity and impartiality of moral judgment. He grants that in the end the disinterested spectator is an "ideality," but argues that the reference of the language of morals to that ideality is necessary to preserve the objectivity of moral judgment (compare this with Árdal's analysis of reason as a virtue).

VI

Hume died on August 25, 1776, shortly after the American colonies had declared independence from Great Britain. But the idea and historical ideal of being "American" was available some time before the Declaration. In a letter to Baron Mure in 1775, Hume confessed ". . . I am an American in my Principles, and wish we woud let them alone to govern or misgovern themselves as they think proper . . ." (LDH II 303). But what does it mean to have principles which are "American"? Hume's own political principles were decidedly conservative, as the essay by Sheldon S. Wolin shows. He was, especially in later years, bitterly opposed to the "fantastical system of liberty" defended by some of the Whigs of his own day, and he may well have considered the Declaration of Independence with its appeal to ahistorical natural rights to be a case of such fantasy. Certainly Thomas Jefferson found little in Hume's political thought to agree with. In "Hume and Jefferson on the Uses of History," Craig Walton shows how Jefferson used his influence to suppress Hume's influential *History of England* in the new republic and at his own University of Virginia. Jefferson apparently thought that the Whig interpretation of history as a progressive series of precedents for popular sovereignty and republicanism was an essential belief for the welfare of the fledgling republic. Since Hume's *History* is contrary to the Whig interpretation, Jefferson viewed it as a conceptual menace to the nation. Walton quotes, from a letter to John Adams, Jefferson's complaint that "This single book has done more to sap the free principles of the English Constitution than the largest standing army," and once again in a letter to the publisher William Duane he writes that "this book . . . has undermined free principles of the English government, has persuaded readers of all classes that there were usurpations on the legitimate and salutary rights of the crown, and has spread universal toryism over the land." Walton shows that Jefferson's attack on Hume's *History* is due not merely to national stress but to a fundamentally different philosophical outlook on human nature and history.

But if Hume's political thought did not sit well with the author of the Declaration of Independence, it had a seminal influence on one of the main architects of the United States Constitution. Douglass Adair's " 'That Poli-

tics May Be Reduced to a Science': David Hume, James Madison, and the
Tenth *Federalist*" discusses the influence Hume had on Madison in solving
what appeared to the Framers to be a constitutional dilemma. Montesquieu
had taught, and it was a popular belief, that republican forms are limited
to small territories and that monarchy alone is workable in large territories
or empires. Hume examined this thesis in "Of the Idea of a Perfect Commonwealth," and having concluded that it is not empirically impossible
for an empire to have republican form, he went on to describe the structure of such a government. Adair argues that Madison saw in this essay a
ready-made conceptual framework with which to solve the constitutional
dilemma, a framework which roughly corresponded to actual social and
political realities in America. The result was the tenth *Federalist* paper
which proposed a federal union of republics having varying degrees of
independence. Adair discusses other ways in which Hume influenced
Madison and in general how the unique social and political philosophy
of the Scottish Enlightenment influenced the mind of the Framers. The
works of such thinkers as Hume, Francis Hutcheson, Adam Smith, Thomas
Reid, Lord Kames, and Adam Ferguson had become the standard textbooks
of the colleges of the late colonial period. Hume's role in the Scottish Enlightenment and its influence on the origins of American social and political
thought are issues which have not yet been adequately discussed. But it
already appears that if Hume was an American in his principles, it is also
true that many of the Framers had taken their principles from Hume and
the Scottish Enlightenment.

The contrary attitudes of Jefferson and Madison to Hume's philosophy
has mythical significance for an understanding of American social and political order. The Declaration and the Constitution are founding documents
of that order. Americans of radical sentiment have tended to see the meaning
of American order in the rationalistic Declaration with its doctrine of
natural rights and its claim to moral authority. American conservatives have
tended to rally around the more sceptical Constitution with its historically
grounded system of checks and balances. The essays by Walton and Adair
suggest that an appreciation of Hume's philosophy is internal to an adequate understanding of the philosophical and historical significance of both
documents and, hence, to the continuing debate about the meaning of
American order.

NOTES

1. William Warburton, *A Selection from Unpublished Works*, ed. Francis Kilvert (London, 1841), pp. 309–10.
2. James Beattie, *Essay on Truth*, 8th ed. (London, 1812), pp. 448, 213.
3. John Stuart Mill, review of Brodie, *History of the British Empire*, in *The West-
minster Review*, 2 (1824), 34.
4. John H. Randall, Jr., "David Hume: Radical Empiricist and Pragmatist," *Freedom
and Experience: Essays Presented to Horace M. Kallen*, edd. Sidney Hook and Milton R.
Konvitz (Ithaca & New York, 1947), pp. 293–94.
5. Harold A. Prichard, *Knowledge and Perception* (Oxford, 1950), p. 174.
6. D. C. Stove, "Hume, the Causal Principle, and Kemp Smith," *Hume Studies*, 1,
No. 1 (1975), 21.

7. *The Works of Thomas Reid*, ed. Sir William Hamilton (Edinburgh, 1863), p. 96.

8. Ibid., pp. 91–92.

9. Ibid., p. 91.

10. *The Works of Thomas Hill Green*, ed. R. L. Nettleship, 3 vols. (London, 1906), I vii, 2.

11. *Logical Positivism*, ed. A. J. Ayer (Glencoe, 1959), p. 4.

12. *Enquiries Concerning the Human Understanding and Concerning the Principles of Morals*, ed. L. A. Selby-Bigge, 2nd ed. (Oxford, 1902), p. vii (emphasis added).

13. A. E. Taylor, *David Hume and the Miraculous* (Cambridge, 1927), p. 54.

14. D. C. Stove, *Probability and Hume's Inductive Scepticism* (Oxford, 1973).

15. Richard H. Popkin, *The History of Scepticism from Erasmus to Descartes* (New York, 1964).

16. Gerhart Niemeyer, *Between Nothingness and Paradise* (Baton Rouge, 1971), p. 8.

17. *Le Testament de Jean Meslier*, ed. C. Rudolf, 3 vols. (Amsterdam, 1864), III 398.

18. Quoted in Niemeyer, *Between Nothingness and Paradise*, pp. 81, 82.

I

David Hume: Naturalist and Meta-sceptic

WADE L. ROBISON
Kalamazoo College

> Do you come to a philosopher as to a *cunning man*, to learn
> something by magic or witchcraft, beyond what can be known
> by common prudence and discretion?
>
> "The Sceptic"

HUME'S SCEPTICAL CLAIMS and Newtonian pretensions thread his philosophical works. His final advertisement in *An Abstract of a Treatise of Human Nature* is that "if any thing can intitle the author [himself] to so glorious a name as that of *inventor*, 'tis the use he makes of the principle of the association of ideas" (A 31). As "these [associations]," he says, "are the only ties of our thoughts, they are really *to us* the cement of the universe . . ." as gravity is the cement of the natural world (A 32; see also T 12–13). Their discovery is thus of "vast consequence . . . in the science of human nature" (A 32) and requires, Hume claims, that "*we . . . alter from the foundations the greatest part of the sciences*" (A [4]). The optimism of these remarks, with their vision of a future new science, is not even cautious, and yet they occur after an analysis of causation which Hume sums up by saying that "the philosophy contain'd in this book is very sceptical, and tends to give us a notion of the imperfections and narrow limits of human understanding" (A 24).

This curious pairing of sceptical claims with a positive program of the association of ideas has traditionally been explained by separating Hume's philosophical achievements from his psychological concerns.[1] In this view his scepticism is the result of a rigorous application of the empiricist principle combined with an assumption that what we experience is limited to our own impressions and ideas. Since we experience no necessary connection between a cause and its effect and no enduring and independent substances, either material or immaterial, we have no ideas, and hence no knowledge, of causation or of external objects or ourselves *as* such substances. On the other hand, it is assumed, the appeal to the principle of the association of ideas serves a psychological function. It is an hypothesis to explain the phenomenon that while some of our thoughts follow each other randomly, others follow in a manner "not entirely without rule and method" (T 283). The hypothesis is a simple one. The objects we experience can bear to each other a myriad of relations. They resemble each other; they can be contiguous, identical, similar in quality and quantity, contrary, and so on. Our observation of objects in some of these relations has no bearing on the manner in which our thoughts proceed, or so the theory runs. But our observation of them in others does:

> The rule, by which [our thoughts] proceed, is to pass from one object to what is resembling, contiguous to, or produc'd by it. When one idea is present to the imagination, any other, united by these relations, naturally follows it, and enters with more facility by means of that introduction [T 283].

The point of this appeal to associations of ideas, what Hume calls natural relations, is wholly psychological, it is claimed. That is, Hume is proposing an hypothesis to explain a psychological phenomenon. In this traditional view, therefore, Hume's writings must be divided into two parts, one philosophical and one psychological, and the curious pairing of scepticism and positive pretensions is to be explained by Hume's diverse concerns: they bear no necessary connection.

This explanation, however, presupposes a limitation upon Hume's appeal to the principles of association: they have no philosophical point. But that is not true. When Hume analyzes judgments of "beauty and deformity, virtue and vice" (*Essays* 168, note), he draws as his general thesis that "Objects have absolutely no worth or value in themselves" (*Essays* 169). One consequence is that "it is not from the value or worth of the object which any person pursues, that we can determine his enjoyment, but merely from the passion with which he pursues it, and the success which he meets with in his pursuit" (*Essays* 169). But the more important consequence is that judgments of value must be analyzed partly in terms of the passions of their makers. The comparison Hume draws is with "that famous doctrine, . . . 'That tastes and colours, and all other sensible qualities, lie not in the bodies, but merely in the senses.' The case is the same," he claims, "with beauty and deformity, virtue and vice" (*Essays* 168, note). In short, certain of our judgments do not have the general form we might mistakenly think they have. They appear to assert that certain objects have certain properties —as in "That book is red" or "*The Sting* is a good movie"—but they in fact assert that certain subjects have certain passions "produced by an object" (*Essays* 166). Hume puts the point not so clearly in terms of judgments as in terms of the ontological status of beauty and worth: these, he says, "are merely of a *relative* nature, and consist in an agreeable sentiment . . ." (*Essays* 166; emphasis added). They are relative both to the object which produces them and "to the peculiar structure and constitution of that mind" (*Essays* 166) in which they are produced.

When we turn to other judgments such as causal ones, for example, the general move is the same. We say that hitting a ball with a bat causes the ball to move. We are apparently asserting that some relation holds between the ball and the swinging of the bat such that when the bat moves through the air at a certain rate and comes into contact with the ball, which is free to move, the ball is caused to move. But, in fact, Hume claims, such judgments are not to be analyzed in that way. They are certainly relative, but relative in the way judgments of worth and value are relative. They depend upon "the peculiar structure and constitution" of the mind, and, as we shall see in Section III, natural relations are an integral part or consequence of that structure and an integral part of the analysis of such judgments. To put the matter briefly here, the judgment that hitting a ball with a bat causes the ball to move is to be analyzed in terms of three conditions: the observation "a sufficient number of instances" of the contiguity and successiveness of a ball's moving and a bat's moving (T 165); the constitution of the mind which makes the observation; and the production, because of that observation and constitution, of a propensity of the mind to conceive of the ball's moving when thinking of the bat's hitting it and to believe that the ball will move when seeing the bat's hitting it. This mental propensity is a natural relation of causation. Its existence can explain why some of my perceptions succeed each other as they do, why I think of one thing after thinking of another or believe something after seeing something else. But Hume's theory of the association of ideas is not simply meant to be explanatory of a psychological phenomenon. Hume is claiming that unless we have such a propensity, we shall not make such a causal judgment at all. In short, Hume's Newtonian pretensions have a philosophical point: how are certain empirical judgments possible? They are possible, Hume is claiming, only if some of our thoughts are tied together by some natural relations.

If we cannot even make certain judgments unless certain of our thoughts are related by the principle of association, the traditional splitting off of Hume's psychological from his philosophical concerns is mistaken. Somehow the two must be bound together. For clearly the proper analysis of such judgments as that *a* causes *b* is as much a philosophical concern as an analysis of aesthetic judgments, and if that analysis requires an appeal to certain psychological principles if we are to understand the meaning of such judgments, then those principles, whatever their separate psychological function, have a philosophical point.

Kemp Smith claimed precisely that when he argued that the traditional view is mistaken because, by failing to understand the point of Hume's appeal to psychological principles, it cast him as a sceptic.[2] In Kemp Smith's view, Hume is no sceptic at all. He *appears* to be because he holds that if any beliefs in empirical matters are to be reasonable, they must be in accord with the empiricist principle, which he thinks is the only principle of reason in such matters, and because he rigorously applies the empiricist principle to show that by it our fundamental beliefs in causation and in external objects and the self as substances cannot be justified. To this extent the traditional view is correct. But the point of Hume's apparent scepticism is only to show, Kemp Smith claims, that we ought to reject the request for a showing that those beliefs are justified. We hold them anyway, and the proper *philosophical* task is to account for why we do. To put the point in a contemporary idiom: since justification must come to an end somewhere, what it ends with cannot be justified, but only explained. Hume's appeal to psychological principles is thus part of a philosophical response to the philosophical query of how certain judgments are possible.

In Kemp Smith's view, and mine as well, Hume is a naturalist. He is concerned with, as it were, the natural history of the human mind, with how we come to hold certain beliefs or make certain judgments, and necessary to that history is an explanation of the mind's basic structure and of the objective conditions which, when combined with that structure, produce the basic beliefs we have. Hume's philosophy is thus meant to be essentially *descriptive*. Its point is no different from that of any other descriptive enterprise: by the persuasiveness of its conception and the accuracy of its detail, it is to allow us to come to understand what we had not understood. And its source of knowledge is no different either. Philosophers are not after the "mysteries of reality," and they are not cunning men who somehow have special access to any such mysteries or special abilities to overcome the constraints either of nature or of human nature. Their concern is rather with such facts as that we all judge that grass is green or that heat causes wax to melt, and they account for such ordinary judgments using ordinary skills with "common prudence and discretion."

It is a mistake, however, to suppose that Hume, being a naturalist, is not a sceptic. For, first, however causal judgments are analyzed, there are normative criteria for making them, and it is one of the persistent features of Hume's philosophical works that he uses those criteria to assess judgments made by ordinary persons and philosophers alike. Whatever the difficulties of detailing Hume's criteria, this kind of scepticism is straightforward enough to require no special treatment here. I shall bring it up briefly in Sections II and IV. Second, Hume is committed to some form of inductive scepticism by explicit arguments in the *Abstract* and the *Enquiry* and by implicit assumptions in the *Treatise*. Again, whatever the difficulties, Hume's commitment has often enough been documented and detailed to require no special treatment here. We shall examine it briefly in Section II. It is Hume's commitment to a third sort of scepticism which I wish to pursue. For, as I shall argue, Hume's main sceptical point is not that certain concepts do not or cannot apply to experience, but that even though they do not apply, we *must* apply them. He is, as it were, a meta-sceptic: in describing the natural operations of the human mind to account for why we make judgments which are unreasonable by the empiricist principle, Hume discovered that the mind's essential nature is such that we must make such unreasonable judgments. This scepticism clearly emerges from his analysis of judgments regarding external objects, and we shall examine that briefly in Section IV. But its main elements are present in his analysis of causal judgments. In Section I we shall look at the stage Hume sets in the *Treatise* for what he calls the problem of causation, and in Section III we shall lay out his solution and the consequent scepticism which, I suggest, he *discovered* in giving his naturalistic description. It is a scepticism, as we shall see, which, were it true, would be devastating to our pretensions of rationality.

1 · THE STAGE-SETTING IN THE *Treatise*

A first move in determining what a cause is is to examine clear cases where we say that one thing causes another. Hume begins his long discussion of causation in the *Treatise* in this way, asking us to "cast our eye on any two objects, which we call cause and effect . . ." (T 75). He discovers little, and the significance of that failure can be seen by examining what Locke discovers regarding two cases in which we say that one thing causes another, the case in which we say, e.g., that one moves one's arm and the case in which we say, e.g., that one billiard ball causes another to move.

Locke says of the latter case that

> when the Ball obeys the stroke of a Billiard-stick, it is not any action of the Ball, but bare passion: Also when by impulse it sets another Ball in motion, that lay in its way, it only communicates the motion it had received from another, and loses in it self so much, as the other received; . . . we observe it only to transfer, but not produce any motion.[3]

Locke thinks the situation different when we turn from external objects to ourselves. When we reflect "on what passes in our selves," we find, he says, "that barely by willing it, barely by a thought of the Mind, we can move the parts of our Bodies, which were before at rest." [4] The two causal situations are different, Locke claims, because when we see the second billiard ball receive motion from the first, we come to the idea of something's being capable of receiving change: that is the idea of passive power. When we move our arms, we come to the idea of something's producing something else: that is the idea of active power. The difference Locke is getting at is that in the volition case, but not in the billiard ball case, there is the *production* of something: something new is created, in the volition case something distinct in kind from thought, viz., a motion in a body, one's arm. As Hume puts it, with the occurrence of the motion in the arm we have, as it were, "a real creation; a production of something out of nothing . . ." (EHU 68). There is first an act of will, and then a motion in a body. The two are different in kind, one being "a thought of the mind," the other a mode of body, and we observe no connection or link between the two which could account for "the manner, in which this operation is performed . . ." (EHU 68). The point is a general one for Locke about the relation of mind and matter. Whether one considers cases where mind acts on matter, as in the volition situation, or cases where matter acts on mind, as in cases of sensation where, e.g., a knife causes pain by cutting into flesh, Locke thinks the case is the same: there is the production of something new, but we have no understanding of how that production occurs.

The case is quite otherwise with regard to the billiard balls. When one moving ball hits another and sets it in motion, there is only, Locke thinks, the transfer of motion. If the second ball moved on with an additional spurt or if it changed color, for example, we would then have a situation similar to the volition situation: there would be the production of something new. But what we in fact observe, Locke claims, is nothing different from motion in the second ball, no more or less motion in the second ball than was transferred to it from the first, and the transfer of the motion from the one ball to the other. There is observed no production of anything. There is just a transfer, and this transfer, being observable, is intelligible to us.

Locke may thus be viewed as making two general points. First, it is active causation which is really causation. For to say truly that *a* is the cause of *b*, *b* must be produced by *a*. A necessary condition for such production is that *b* be distinct from *a*. It is this latter condition which Locke thinks is not satisfied in the billiard ball situation, for, on his analysis, if *a* is truly to be said to have caused *b*, *b* must be either different in kind, as when motion occurs in a body after an act of will, or different in quantity or quality, as would happen were a billiard ball to move with a greater quantity of motion than was transferred to it by an object it came into contact with. But when the one billiard ball (passively) causes the other to move, it is only transferring its motion to the other. The motion of the second ball is not numerically different from the motion of the first: it is the very same motion transferred to a different object. The motion of the one billiard ball thus does not, for Locke, truly cause the second billiard ball to move. For causation to occur, there must be the production of something distinct from the cause.

The other general point is that there is a disparity in our causal judgments. In just those situations in which there is production, we find that we observe no connection between *a* and *b* which could account for *how a* produces *b*: there is no intelligibility where there is production. This is the case when we make causal judgments regarding the interaction of mind and matter. And in just those situations where there is an intelligible relation between *a* and *b*, we find that there is no production. This is the case when we make causal judgments regarding the interaction of bodies. We may hypothesize with Boyle, for example, that a body is black because it is of such a texture that it yields to the beams, or particles, of light

> in like manner as to a ball, which thrown against a Stone or Floor, would Rebound a great way Upwards, but Rebounds very Little or not at all, when it is thrown against Water, or Mud, . . . because the Parts yield, and receive into themselves the Motion, on whose account the Ball should be Reflected Outwards.[5]

Its texture *causes* it to "Dead the Beams of Light." [6] And yet, if the motion of the beams is only received, passively, by the parts of the black body, the texture does not *produce* a deadening of the beams. There is intelligibility, but no production, and so no causation.

We are thus faced with a curious disparity: in just those cases where we seem to understand what is happening, what we understand is not the production of anything and so, on Locke's terms, not truly causal at all, and in just those cases where there is production, we do not understand how it occurs. This disparity is certainly awkward for the new science, for its coherence would seem to rest upon the possibility of its judgments being both causal and intelligible. But, more importantly, if there is no production where there is intelligibility and no intelligibility where there is production, there is the dangerous threat of a general scepticism: how can intelligible causal judgments be possible?

It is Hume who makes this threat a real one. When, at the beginning of his discussion of causation in the *Treatise*, he examines "any two objects, which we call cause and effect," he finds, to rehearse the familiar, less than Locke does. When one billiard ball strikes another, Hume thinks that one observes contact between the two: the first touches the second before the second moves. That relation is contiguity in space. The two are observed to be contiguous in time as well, for we observe that the second moves immediately after the first comes in contact with it: there is neither hesitation nor anticipation. Hume thus says that

> whatever objects are consider'd as causes or effects, are *contiguous*; and . . . nothing can operate in a time or place, which is ever so little remov'd from those of its existence [T 75].

They are also successive. That they are contiguous in time implies that they are, of course. But these relations are the only relations Hume discovers when he examines the billiard ball case: nothing is seen to be passed from one object to the other. "Some philosophers," he says, referring, we may assume, to Locke at least, "have imagin'd that there is an apparent cause for the communication of motion, and that a reasonable man might immediately infer the motion of one body from the impulse of another . . ." (T 111). But this is a mistake due, he claims, to the *"resemblance* betwixt the cause and effect, which . . . binds the objects in the closest and most intimate manner to each other, so as to make us imagine them to be absolutely inseparable" (T 111–12). The motion of the one billiard ball so resembles that of the other—in being motion and in being of a certain quantity—that one can easily mistake the two motions for one transferred from ball to ball. But, in fact, there is perceivable no transfer, Hume claims, no communication of motion, and so, Hume concludes,

> Having thus discover'd or suppos'd the two relations of *contiguity* and *succession* to be essential to causes and effects, I find I am stopt short, and can proceed no farther in considering any single instance of cause and effect. . . . 'Tis in vain to rack ourselves with *farther* thought and reflexion upon this subject. We can go no *farther* in considering this particular instance [T 76–77].

In short, the one kind of causal situation which Locke thinks it intelligible how *b* should occur because *a* occurs, Hume finds unintelligible. There is observed just *a* and then *b* occurring in *a*'s immediate spatial and temporal vicinity.

In regard to the interaction of mind and matter, the situation is essentially the same. There is one difference: namely, that when *a* or *b* is a mental event, like an act of will, or a sensation, like pain, they will be contiguous only in time. They will not be contiguous in space. That is why, when Hume first introduces contiguity, he says that we may "consider the relation of CONTIGUITY as essential to that of causation; at least . . . till we can find a more proper occasion to clear up this matter, by examining what objects are or are not susceptible of juxtaposition and conjunction" (T 75). He later argues that some perceptions are not susceptible of spatial relations and thus cannot be considered as spatially contiguous with anything else (T 235ff.). But his conclusion is not that therefore they cannot be causes or effects. He rather thinks that they can be, but that for a to be a cause or b to be an effect, it is not essential that a and b be spatially contiguous. It is for this reason that he leaves out spatial contiguity as an essential in the definition of the causal relation he gives in the *Enquiry*.[7] His intentions are made clear in the *Treatise* not only by his hedging his introduction of spatial contiguity, but also by his warning his readers that his extended analysis of causation and, thus, the two definitions which he gives of causation at its end are in terms of causal situations in which a and b are susceptible of spatial relations:

> tho' the ideas of cause and effect be deriv'd from the impressions of reflexion as well as from those of sensation, yet for brevity's sake, I commonly mention only the latter as the origin of these ideas; tho' I desire that whatever I say of them may also extend to the former. Passions are connected with their objects and with one another; no less than external bodies are connected together. The same relation, then, of cause and effect, which belongs to one, must be common to all of them [T 78].

Hume is thus asserting that though there is a difference between the two kinds of causal situation which Locke considers, it is not an essential difference. Whether one is concerned with external objects or with the mind's interaction with them, one observes only that the cause and its supposed effect are successive and temporally contiguous.

This is an advance over Locke's analysis just because the disparity has been removed: the world presents itself to us as of one piece. This is, of course, just what we should hope would happen when we make causal judgments, viz., that the same conditions are satisfied in each case no matter what the nature of the items being judged causally related. But the fulfillment of that hope in the way Hume fulfills it carries a devastating loss. For though in Locke's view at least part of the world is intelligible, in Hume's view the world presents itself as of one *unintelligible* piece. For we do not observe what Locke thought we had to in order to observe a causal relation. We do observe distinct occurrences in any situation we call causal, but we observe no link between any of those occurrences to account for why some occur after and contiguous to others. We observe no *production* of b by a.

Hume takes this to be an obvious, though arguable, fact discoverable by examining "any two objects, which we call cause and effect." This examination covers less than three full pages of text in the *Treatise*, and Hume uses it to raise a problem he does not bring to its denouement until almost one hundred pages later. The problem, as he puts it, is that

> An object may be contiguous and prior to another, without being consider'd as its cause. There is a NECESSARY CONNEXION to be taken into consideration; and that relation is of much greater importance, than any of the other two above-mention'd [T 77].

There are objects which are contiguous and successive which are *not* called, or "consider'd," cause and effect. What is needed, Hume says, is a necessary connection, and only with that, he goes on to claim, will we have "a compleat idea of causation" (T 77). But not just anything will do as a necessary connection. It will not do to "pretend to define a cause, by saying it is something productive of another" (T 77). That simply gives "a synonimous term instead of a definition" (T 77), and it clearly does not guarantee that a cause and its effect really are connected. To give such a guarantee we must perceive a connection. Only in that way will we "discover the nature of this necessary connexion" (T 77). In short, Hume thinks we must define a cause in terms of impressions, one of which is that of a necessary connection,[8] and he thus conceptualizes the problem he thinks he faces as that of "find[ing] the impression, or impressions, from which its idea may be deriv'd" (T 77).

As we shall see, it is this conceptualization of the problem which structures Hume's nearly one hundred pages of analysis in the *Treatise*. But two points need to be clarified at this stage. One is that there are two problems Hume eventually claims to solve. One he does not mention in his conceptualization of the problem, and that is that we make causal inferences in some situations where we can observe only contiguity and succession, but not in others. The other problem is raised explicitly, and that is that we call, or consider, only some such situations causal. The problem in both cases is that of accounting for our distinctions: what in addition to contiguity and succession is required in each case? As we shall come to see, Hume thinks that both these problems are solved by the discovery of an impression of a necessary connection.

This raises the other point which requires clarification: why does Hume conceptualize the problem as one of finding a necessary connection and why does he require for that finding that there be an impression of such a connection? It is not obvious, on the one hand, that the missing element need be a necessary connection between a cause and its effect, and, on the other hand, it is not clear why, in order to come to call some situations causal (or to make causal inferences), we need an impression of a necessary connection.

In conceptualizing the problem as he does, Hume is assuming at least two things which are true. He is assuming, first, that we all make causal judgments. We do this in a multitude of ways where we are committed, by our actions, to an assumption that one thing, e.g., eating, is causally related to another, surviving. Hume is also assuming, correctly, that when we call (or judge) one thing a cause and another an effect, we are saying more than that the two are contiguous and successive.[9] The problem is, what more are we saying? What Hume is assuming, I suggest, is that we all suppose, as Locke did, that in order for *a* to cause *b*, *b* must be not only distinct from *a*, but also *produced* by it. That is, we all suppose there has to be a "real intelligible connexion betwixt" the two such that given *a*, *b* must occur (T 168). We make this supposition, Hume is claiming, when we call a situation causal. But if so, the discovery that no such connection is observed in any situation we call causal creates a compelling problem. For if this is to be an intelligible supposition, then what we are supposing must be observable: by the empiricist principle, we cannot make intelligible what we cannot have impressions of. So either we must find an observable link we have somehow missed, or we must conclude that we are supposing what we cannot make intelligible. Our inability to observe any link in any causal situation obviously sets the stage for the latter possibility. It comes as a real threat, and that is why Hume sets finding an impression of a necessary connection as the problem he must solve. For only with such a find, he thinks, can he show how intelligible causal judgments are possible.

II · INDUCTIVE SCEPTICISM

Hume's stage-setting is in fact more than that, for in the setting up of what he takes to be his problem, Hume has *already* made a sceptical point. He has done so by surreptitiously appealing to an argument which surfaces only from time to time in the *Treatise* and in no way structures his presentation there. At one point Hume claims that

> If we be possest . . . of any idea of power in general, we must also be able to conceive some particular species of it; and . . . be able to place this power in some particular being, and conceive that being as endow'd with a real force and energy, by which such a particular effect *necessarily* results from its operation [T 161; emphasis added].

But to conceive such a necessary connection between any two objects "wou'd amount to a demonstration," he argues, "and wou'd imply the absolute impossibility for the one object not to follow, or to be conceiv'd not to follow upon the other: Which kind of connexion has already been rejected in all cases" (T 161–62). It was rejected when it was claimed that a cause and its effect are contiguous and rejected as well when it was claimed that they are successive. For to claim of any items that they are contiguous or successive is to imply that they are distinct from each other: each can exist without the existence of the other.[10] The motion in the second billiard ball is *not* the same motion the first ball had, but a numerically distinct motion, though of the same kind and of the same quantity as the motion of the first ball. As Hume baldly puts it in the *Enquiry*, "Motion in the second Billiard-ball is a quite distinct event from motion in the first . . ." (EHU 29). But if so, there can be no demonstration of a necessary connection between any two such items, for there cannot be any such necessary connection.

What we were unable to observe in any causal situation was thus guaranteed by Hume's request that we "cast our eye on any *two* objects, which we call cause and effect." For we observe no production of *b* by *a* because a necessary condition for such production is that *a* and *b* be distinct. If they are distinct, then each can exist without the other's existing. But if so, there is no way that the occurrence of the one can produce, or necessarily bring into existence, the other. We cannot both get what is necessary for production and production.

One sceptical consequence is that we cannot know, from the occurrence of any one item, that any other will occur. It is not just that we cannot know *what* the effect will be; we cannot even know that there will be an effect. This is not a particularly startling consequence when one realizes that it depends upon a rather high standard of knowledge. But a second sceptical consequence is startling. For Hume thinks that we are in no better position even after experience that a particular kind of item has always been followed by the occurrence of another particular kind of item. This is a startling consequence just because, though we are inclined to agree that Adam could not know or even suspect that water will suffocate when he first sees it, it is natural to think that after some experience with water he will know that if he sticks his head face down in it for an extended period of time, he will drown. Yet Hume is denying that what we naturally think is justified. For what we observe are *particular* events, e.g., that *a* is contiguous and prior to *b*, that *a'* is contiguous' and prior' to *b'*, that *a''* is contiguous'' and prior'' to *b''*, and so on.[11] Each of these conjunctions is itself a distinct complex event, i.e., each can exist without the existence of another conjunction. And if each conjunction is so distinct, then the occurrence of one conjunction is of no relevance, Hume is claiming, to the occurrence of another: we cannot know from the occurrence of one that any other will occur. So when we observe another object, *a'*, similar to *a*, we are in no better position, despite our observation of similar conjunctions of objects similar to *a* and *b*, to know that a *conjunction* will occur, and not just *a'*. Hume's sceptical point, which depends upon the fact that the world presents itself to us in distinct parts, is that we cannot know, either with or without experience, that an effect will follow upon what we perceive as a cause.

This inductive scepticism depends upon what we may call the Separability Principle: whatever is distinguishable is separable (see, e.g., T 16).[12] Hume commits himself to such a version of this principle that if any two entities are distinguishable, then it is at least true that each can exist without the other's existing and that both can exist without continuing in the same relations with each other. It follows from this principle and from what Hume takes to be the observable fact that any cause and its effect are distinguishable because they are, e.g., temporally successive that any cause can occur without its supposed effect's occurring and any effect can occur without its supposed cause's occurring and that both can exist without being causally related at all. I shall not analyze this argument here, and I shall not pursue the role the Separability Principle plays in it and, in particular, whether or not it is appealed to in order to create the supposedly

observed "fact" that any cause and its effect are distinguishable.[13] For
whether or not my particular reconstruction of its basic form is accurate,
there is, I think, little disagreement among commentators that Hume accepts some such argument and makes some such sceptical point. My concern
is with the failure to see anything else in Hume but that sort of sceptical
point. For there is more.

First, that point does not follow merely from the way the world presents
itself to us: there is a definition of knowledge assumed. That definition
makes it appear that Hume is simply claiming that induction is not deduction, and the sceptical point may thus appear trivial and Hume's scepticism
innocuous. But Hume concludes that since no effect of human reason can
discover any necessary connection between a cause and its effect,

> the utmost effort of human reason is to reduce the principles, productive of
> natural phenomena, to a greater simplicity, and to resolve the many particular
> effects into a few general causes, by means of reasonings from analogy, experi-
> ence, and observation [EHU 30].

Correctly or incorrectly, what Hume draws from his sceptical point is a
conception of the limited function of human nature, but a conception
which gives philosophers hope: we may improve our ability for such reduction and resolution by carefully laying out rules for reasoning. Hume does
this to some extent in all his works, but especially in the *Dialogues*, and, as
I shall argue briefly in Section IV, he appeals to those rules to draw sceptical
conclusions; that is, he argues that certain beliefs we hold and certain claims
philosophers make are not reasonable. To ignore such sceptical arguments
is to ignore vast sections of Hume's philosophical work and, in particular,
to ignore almost entirely Hume's scepticism concerning religion—from the
attack on belief in miracles to that in God. Yet to make these sceptical arguments it is necessary to claim more than that we cannot know certain
propositions because they cannot be deduced from propositions we do know.
It is to claim that even where such (deductive) knowledge is not possible,
reasonable distinctions can be made between different causal inferences and
thus between the reasonableness of beliefs which rely upon those inferences.
Hume made such distinctions in the *Treatise* (T 124).

Second, and more importantly, the assumption that Hume's scepticism
concerning causation is simply inductive scepticism rests upon a conceptualization of Hume's concern which, in regard to the *Treatise* at any rate,
is mistaken; that is, that in claiming that "an object may be contiguous and
prior to another, without being consider'd as its cause," Hume is saying that
those two relations are not sufficient to distinguish causal relations from
casual regularities and that the problem is thus to find some additional
feature or criterion for *a*'s truly causing *b*—a necessary connection or whatever. It is assumed, that is, that the problem Hume is fretting with is the
problem of determining the necessary and sufficient conditions for *a* to
cause *b*. Since the only additional feature which seems both available and
appropriate is invariable conjunction, Hume has been thought to hold
the Uniformity Thesis: *a* is the cause of *b* if, and only if, *a* and *b* are con-

tiguous and successive and every object (event, or whatever) relevantly similar to *a* is contiguous and successive to an object relevantly similar to *b*.[14] But the addition of invariable conjunction to the features necessary for *a* to cause *b* makes knowledge that *a* causes *b* impossible for us. In this conceptualization of his problem, therefore, Hume is setting the stage for the problem of induction, his statement of his problem (at T 77) becomes a recognition of the consequence of his previous sceptical point, and his scepticism concerning causation amounts to no more than inductive scepticism.

If it does, then it is a scepticism dependent upon the nature of the world. It is not *our* fault that we lack such knowledge. It is because the world presents itself in discrete events that we have difficulties, and the scepticism which results from that fact affects at most our expectations, not our critical and rational capacities. It leaves untouched the human mind: we humans could have such knowledge if only the world were different or presented itself differently. Hume's inductive scepticism is, in short, not about *us*.

Or, perhaps more accurately, it is about us only in the sense in which it illustrates Locke's admonition that philosophy ought to be used "to prevail with the busy Mind of Man, to be more cautious in meddling with things exceeding its Comprehension; . . . and to sit down in a quiet Ignorance of those Things, which, upon Examination, are found to be beyond the reach of our Capacities." [15] For since inductive scepticism makes no claim about the basic coherence of the human mind, but only points out its inability to predict because of the nature of the world, Hume can point that out, and we can still safely sit down to do what is within our capacities. Hume's scepticism, on this view, is simply a reminder for the human mind "to stop," in Locke's phrase, "when it is at the utmost Extent of its Tether." [16]

But Hume's scepticism is more than a cautious reminder. When he proceeds in the *Treatise* to pose what he conceives of as the problem of causation, he does so without any apparent awareness that he has already committed himself to a sceptical position regarding induction and inference, and when he draws his sceptical conclusions in Section XIV of Part II of Book I, he does not tie them up with induction or with the issue of what must be true for *a* truly to cause *b*. He ties them up with another set of issues regarding our *calling* one thing a cause and another an effect. And those sceptical conclusions *do* concern the basic coherence of the "Mind of Man." To make this clear it is necessary to examine Hume's analysis of how causal judgments can be intelligible.

III · Hume's scepticism concerning causal judgments

When Hume sums up his analysis in Section XIV, he says, first, that causal judgments are not made intelligible by what we observe in any single instance in which we make a causal judgment. It is not "from any one instance [of a supposed causal relation], that we arrive at the idea of cause and effect . . ." (T 162). This is a summation of the stage-setting: we only perceive a and b to be contiguous and successive in any one instance.

Second, he says, he has discovered that when "we observe several instances, in which the same objects are always conjoin'd together, we immediately conceive a connexion betwixt them, and begin to draw an inference from one to another" (T 163). What Hume is referring to is his discovery of "a new relation betwixt cause and effect," viz., a constant conjunction (T 87). What he discovered was that "any two objects, which we call cause and effect," bear similar relations of contiguity and succession which similar objects have been observed to bear. When we call a a cause and b an effect, there is not just a conjunction, i.e., a contiguity and succession of a and b; there has also been observed a set of similar conjunctions, i.e., constant conjunction. When there is such a set of similar conjunctions of objects similar to a and b, it is observed, and the similarities are noted and remembered, then, and apparently only then, two consequences occur:

(1) "we immediately conceive a connexion betwixt" the two, and
(2) we "begin to draw an inference from one to the other."

That we do either of these after we have observed the constant conjunction of similar objects is extremely puzzling. For, first, how can we *conceive* a connection between the two *now* when all we have discovered is that what we do conceive between the two, viz., contiguity and succession, are repeated each time we perceive the two? Where does the extra conception come from? What possible impression could be its source? Second, how is it that we begin to infer one from the other when, again, we are in no better position than we were before? If contiguity and succession are not sufficient either to allow us to infer or to justify our inferring b from a, how can the repetition of contiguity and succession between *other* (however similar) objects account for our inferring b from a?

These problems arise from the difficulty of accounting for our particular causal judgments: we make them *anyway*, even though any two objects we call cause and effect are observed to be only contiguous and successive. One question concerns how we do so: what is the mechanism which facilitates the inference from a to b? The other concerns what we can mean when we say two objects are cause and effect. When we make a causal judgment, we mean more than that two objects are contiguous and successive: what, if anything, provides that extra meaning? Hume thinks the answer to *both* these questions depends upon a single discovery, viz., the source of the idea of necessity which he thinks we have.

That source is not constant conjunction, he says, but an effect which the observation of constant conjunction has upon the mind. Constant conjunction is not the source of our idea of necessity because it neither allows us to discover nor produces a new relation between a cause and its effect. All we discover is the repetition of contiguity and succession, and that repetition of conjunctions does not alter any conjunction to produce a new relation between the conjuncts (T 163–64). It is rather that "the *observation* of this resemblance [i.e., constant conjunction] produces a new impression *in the mind . . ."* (T 165). It is the existence of this impression which accounts for both (1) and (2).

It accounts for (2) because it is, Hume says, "a propensity . . . to pass from an object to the idea of its usual attendant . . ." (T 165). That is, when we have observed "a sufficient number of instances" the constant conjunction of objects similar to *a* and *b*, then, upon the perception of another object similar to *a*, say *a**, a propensity is activated to produce a perception of *b*, or of a previously observed object similar to *b*, say *b**. If our perception of *a** is an impression, i.e., if we actually *observe a**, then our perception of *b** is a belief, i.e., it is an enlivened idea; and if our perception of *a** is an idea, i.e., if we happen to think of *a**, then our perception of *b** is simply an idea and not a belief that *b** will occur. In short, what the observation of the constant conjunction of similar objects does is to produce a propensity, or "determination of the mind" as Hume sometimes calls it (see, e.g., T 165), to conceive of or believe in the occurrence of an object similar to *b* upon the perception of an object similar to *a*. The propensity connects perceptions; it is a natural relation; [17] and its existence explains why some of our thoughts succeed others as they do. It explains the psychological phenomenon that we, e.g., think of smoke after thinking of a fire, believe that the second billiard ball will move after seeing it hit by the first, and so on. But Hume also has in the propensity an answer to one of the questions his stage-setting posed for him. For if we discover only contiguity and succession in any situation we call causal, then it must be true that "our conclusions from . . . experience are *not* founded on reasoning, or any process of the understanding" (EHU 32). Yet we draw causal conclusions. The explanation for our doing so is that there are such natural relations, or propensities of the mind.

But we do not simply infer an effect from the perception of a cause. We also "call the one object, *Cause*; the other *Effect*" (EHU 75). It is possible that

> when we speak of a necessary connexion betwixt objects, and suppose, that this connexion depends upon an efficacy or energy, with which any of these objects are endow'd; in all these expressions, *so apply'd*, we have really no distinct meaning, and make use only of common words, without any clear and determinate ideas [T 162].

But, Hume claims, " 'tis more probable, that these expressions do here lose their true meaning by being *wrong apply'd*, than that they never have any meaning . . ." (T 162). What is their meaning? It is to be discovered, for Hume, in an impression or set of impressions from which the idea associated with them is derived. And that impression has been discovered: it is a propensity of the mind, which Hume identifies with an "internal impression, or impression of reflexion" (T 165).[18] Such a propensity can thus be the source of an idea. What is more, such a propensity is a kind of necessary connection. For, first, given its existence, there is the production of a perception of *b**, say, *because of* the occurrence of the perception of *a**: the perception activates the propensity to *produce* the perception of *b**. The perceptions are thus connected in the way Locke insisted they had to be to be causally related. Second, it produces the perception *necessarily*, for when we observe a*, we are *determined* to conceive of or believe in the occurrence of b*. We cannot help but flinch when we perceive a ball about to strike us. The activation of the relevant mental propensity and its operation once activated are not matters within our control. We cannot prevent ourselves from having perceptions, and if the relevant past observations have occurred, such perceptions will activate the relevant propensities no matter what our wishes may be. Though some of our thoughts are within our control, some are not. Those are the ones which succeed each other "with rule and method," and their succession is mediated by propensities whose operation, as Hume puts it, is "irresistible" (T 225). We thus have with the existence of such a propensity a source for an idea of necessary connection.

This is what Hume says, claiming that "the idea of necessity arises from some impression" and that the impression which gives rise to it is that propensity, it being "the essence of necessity" (T 165). For it is not

> possible for us ever to form the most distant idea of it [i.e., necessity], consider'd as a quality in bodies. Either we have no idea of necessity, or necessity is nothing but that determination of the thought to pass from causes to effects and from effects to causes, according to their experienc'd union [T 165–66].

The mental determination, or propensity, thus serves two different functions. As Hume says,

> Necessity . . . is the effect of this observation [of the constant conjunction of similar objects], and is nothing but an internal impression of the mind, or a determination to carry our thoughts from one object to another [T 165].

The propensity both connects perceptions and is itself a perception. It is *as a propensity, or determination*, that it accounts for "our inference from one to the other" (T 165). It is, Hume says, "only so far as [causation] is a *natural* relation, and produces an union among our ideas, that we are able to reason upon it, or draw any inference from it" (T 94). And it is *as an impression* that it provides us with an idea of necessity and so apparently solves the problem with which Hume began (at T 77): this impression is a source of an idea of necessary connection to give us "a compleat idea of causation."

But the idea we have is *not* the idea of *a causing b*. The impression, or propensity, is not essential to causal relations. Being a natural relation, it is a relation dependent upon and consequent to the operations of the understanding.[19] It thus provides a connection of the wrong sort to hold between a cause and its effect: it can only connect a *perception* of a cause with a *conception of or belief in* its effect. It is not the *effect* which our perception of the cause produces, but a *perception* of the effect, and it is not the *cause* which produces that, but a *perception* of the cause. In claiming that the natural relation of causation is the source of our idea of necessary connection, Hume thus is not claiming that it is a necessary connection essential to any causal relation. He is not claiming that *it* enters into a situation in which *a* causes *b*. He is rather claiming that it is essential to causal *judg-*

ments. He is claiming that it enters into any situation in which there are "any two objects, which we *call* cause and effect"; that since "an object may be contiguous and prior to another, without being *consider'd* as its cause," it is the extra condition which accounts for why we *do* consider the object a cause.

He is claiming that the proper analysis of causal judgments will give a display like those for aesthetic judgments and judgments concerning sensible qualities. There are three elements in that analysis. There is what is objective, or observable. For causal judgments these are the philosophical relations Hume says are implied by causation, viz., "contiguity, succession, and constant conjunction" (T 94). These, he says, are "operations of nature . . . independent of, and antecedent to the operations of the understanding" (T 168), and it is our observing them and remembering them which is necessary for us to come to call one object a cause and another an effect (see T 87). In Hume's long analysis in the *Treatise*, he limits himself, as we saw, to those objects susceptible of spatial relations, but, as was indicated, there is nothing in the nature of his analysis which prevents the philosophical relations of contiguity, succession, and constant conjunction from holding between entities not susceptible of spatial relations. There is nothing, that is, which precludes the possibility of our making causal judgments concerning, e.g., passions. What is *objective* is not what belongs to *objects*. It is what we observe, what is "independent of, and antecedent to" what we add to the situation, and Hume thinks we can observe our passions, feelings, and thoughts as well as entities capable of spatial relations. Second, there is "the peculiar structure and constitution of that mind" in which the impression of determination is produced. This structure Hume refers to by the phrase "the operations of the understanding," and what I suggest he has in mind are the underlying mental dispositions which, together with the observation of the relevant "operations of nature" regarding *a* and *b* and objects similar to *a* and *b*, produce, to use Hume's word (T 165), that propensity, or impression, to have a perception of *b* upon perceiving *a*. That propensity, or impression, is the third element, and, like the impressions of "beauty and deformity, virtue and vice," it is both relative to the objective situation which produces it and to the structure of the mind in which it is produced.

To claim that these three elements feature in the analysis of causal judgments is to claim that causal judgments must exist and can exist only when these elements are present. Or, more accurately, it is to claim this of what we may call clear cases of causal judgments. For it is true that we (including philosophers) sometimes claim that some object causes another (e.g., that God causes the world to exist) when these conditions are not satisfied. But these are not clear cases of causal judgments: they are cases of judgments which *purport* to be causal. *Saying* that "*a* causes *b*" is not *judging* that the two are causally related. The clearest cases, in fact, are those which do not reach the level of explicit assertion. We are judging causally when we get out of bed without checking the floor to see if it, like ourselves, withstood the night, when we eat our cereal for nourishment, drink our orange juice to quench our thirst, and so on. These are the paradigm cases of causal judgment for Hume, and of these he claims that they must exist and can exist only when the relevant operations of nature combined with the operations of the understanding produce an internal impression, or determination of the mind. For if there is a constant conjunction of objects similar to a and b, i.e., if the objective conditions for making causal judgments are present, then, unless that constant conjunction is observed and remembered, there are no clearly causal judgments about a and b or any similar objects. And even if that constant conjunction is observed and remembered, if, for some reason, there is no triggering of the underlying mental dispositions necessary to produce the mental propensity, there are no clearly causal judgments. They come into existence only if there is a constant conjunction, observed and remembered, triggering those operations of the understanding to produce a mental determination, or impression. When those conditions are satisfied, we then must think that a causes b when we perceive a or some similar object, and we then can say, in a clear case of a causal judgment, "a causes b."

What we can *mean* when we say that is, Hume thinks, far different from what (he thinks) we think we mean. For when we say that a causes b, what (he thinks) we think we mean is what Locke meant, that there is an object, a, which is prior to another object, b, that a and b are contiguous, and that a *produces* b, i.e., is so connected with it that upon a's occurrence, b occurs *because* a has occurred. But, Hume claims, we cannot mean quite that. For, first, we can only mean what we can think. That is, if we assert, e.g., "a causes b," then our assertion is meaningful only insofar as there are ideas associable with our words. But we have no impression of any connection between a and b and so no idea associable with "a causes b" which could allow us to mean that a produces b. So, since we cannot think that a produces b, we cannot mean that when we say or think that a causes b. All we can think about a single instance of a and b is that a and b are contiguous and successive, and, as Hume says when he sets up the problem of causation, we surely mean to say more than that when we judge that a and b are causally related. And, in fact, we do mean more than that. For, second, we mean what we do think, and when we judge that a causes b, what we think, i.e., what is in our minds, are perceptions of a and b—perceptions that they are contiguous and successive—and a mental determination between the perceptions of them. That is, what our words "a causes b" are associated with are impressions of the contiguity and succession of a particular a and b and the impression, or determination, of the mind. So, what we mean, and all we can mean, when we say or judge that a causes b is that some natural relation exists between contiguous and successive perceptions.

When we make causal judgments, we are thus saying something intelligible. But we are not saying what we think we are saying. We are misled by the form of our causal judgments just as we are misled by predications of some sensible qualities. When we say that a ball is red, by the new science we are asserting that the qualities which the ball has, when observed by beings with the particular sensory apparatus which we have, produce in us a certain impression, or sensation. Our judgment, which is in form dyadic, is in reality triadic, and we are one of the relata: some sensible qualities are dependent upon us. In the same way, when we say *a* causes *b*, we are not saying that there is a connection between distinct objects, but that what relations there are between those objects, when observed by beings with our particular mental constitution, produce a propensity, or internal impression. Our causal judgment, which is in form dyadic, is intelligible as a causal judgment only if it is in reality triadic with the propensity in us as one of the relata. The connection we (and Locke) suppose exists between causal objects or events really exists only between some of our perceptions: it is in us, and not perceived between the objects.

This conclusion is *so far* innocent of sceptical implications. First, it does not by itself imply that there are no necessary connections in nature. Hume's explicit argument is that we observe no such connection in any single case, but it does not follow from our not having any impression of any such connection that no such connection exists.[20] We know, in fact, that Hume is committed to claiming that no such connection *can* exist. That claim follows from his appeal to the Separability Principle and the argument he constructs around that appeal, but that argument is an addition *drawn from scattered remarks* in the *Treatise*. It does not structure his presentation, which in fact ignores that additional move. Hume ends his analysis of causation by saying that necessity itself is nothing but an impression. And this, he says, appears "a gross absurdity" since it appears

> to remove [power] from all causes, and bestow it on a being, that is no ways related to the cause or effect, but by perceiving them . . . [T 168].

In short, he makes the same claim about necessity which he makes about "beauty and deformity, virtue and vice." For in regard to them he makes not only a claim about what we mean when we utter such judgments as that a painting is beautiful or that a man is wicked, but also a claim about what they are: they are nothing but impressions. Whatever one may think about this claim in regard to those qualities, it clearly is not true of necessity without at least the additional argument dependent upon the Separability Principle. But Hume does not give that additional argument. Instead he shifts his ground when one objects, arguing that though one may attempt to respond by talking of a necessity which exists independently of the reaction of a mind to the conjunctions it observes, "we do not understand our own meaning in talking so . . ." (T 168). Hume shifts, that is, from the ontological question to considerations of meaning, and argues, in effect, that the claim that any such necessary connection exists is meaningless. When we say, "*a* causes *b*," we either must mean nothing or be really saying that there is an impression, or determination, in a mind. This follows from his theory of meaning, but it does not follow from that that there are no necessary connections in nature.

The second way in which Hume's conclusion about the intelligibility of causal judgments is innocent of sceptical implications comes out with a comparison of judgments concerning sensible qualities. If it is true that, e.g., red is relative to us in that an object is not red in itself, but has such other properties that, under certain conditions and to certain observers, it will appear red, the discovery of that fact ought not in itself to lead to scepticism about such sensible qualities. If one thinks it does, it can only be because one assumes that the mere fact of their relativity to observers makes some sort of difference—to the security of their existence or of what they supposedly depend upon, to the security of our knowledge of them, or to the nature of our conduct and action regarding such things as, say, requests for "the red ticket." But without some *further* arguments drawing consequences of that relativity, the mere fact of that relativity makes no such difference: things are still judged red; we judge them red truly or falsely depending upon whether certain specifiable conditions are satisfied or not, and we act the same after the discovery of their relativity as before, stopping at red lights, looking askance at our bloodshot eyes in the mirror, and so on. As Hume puts it in "The Sceptic," discovering that sensible qualities are relative to us does not take anything from their reality (see *Essays* 168, note). The problem created by such a discovery is not in itself a sceptical problem, but a problem of conflict between scientific progress and previous prejudices. After all, if such qualities are relative to observers, we ought to know that fact. In the same way, if the necessity we suppose exists between a cause and its effect is really an impression in the mind of some observer, then we ought to know that fact, and the only problem so far posed is between what was previously claimed about that necessity and what is now claimed.

It is certainly *frustrating* to have Hume tell us, to put the matter linguistically, that when we say, "*a* causes *b*," we cannot get outside the framework of the mind's reaction to what is objective and still say something meaningful, but there is no reason because of that to think that we cannot use some other word to talk of what is objective in situations in which we call one object "cause" and another "effect" or to think that we cannot co-opt "cause" for that. There is more than a hint of these possibilities in Hume, in fact, and one should not be misled by frustration into scepticism.

But, in fact, Hume's claim about what we can mean by saying "*a* causes *b*" is not innocent of sceptical implications. Hume begins with situations in which there are "any two objects, which we call cause and effect," and with the supposition that in those situations we all suppose that the one object produces the other. But, first, this is contradictory. Hume thinks that "an object may be contiguous and prior to another, without being consider'd as its cause," but that when we do consider it as a cause, we suppose that it is distinct from its effect and yet is so related to it that it produces it or, in other words, so related that upon its occurrence, the effect must occur. And that is to suppose that of two distinct objects, one cannot exist without the existence of the other. Yet the mere fact that the objects are two, or the mere fact that the objects are contiguous and successive, is enough to show that they are distinct in such a way that each can exist without the existence of the other. In other words, Hume conceives us to be saying of two objects which we suppose are distinct that they are not distinct because one produces the other. That is a contradiction. And, second, even if it were not, it is not meaningful, for we observe no such production and thus have no impression of it from which an idea could be derived to give meaning to our supposition. The supposed connection of production is thus inconceivable because it cannot exist and because, even if it could, we have no impression of it. To suppose that such a connection exists when we call two objects cause and effect is thus, to put it mildly, a serious mistake.

It is a mistake we make, Hume claims, because

> we transfer the determination of the thought to external objects, and suppose [a] real intelligible connexion betwixt them; [though] that [is] a quality, which can only belong to the mind that considers them [T 168].

This is an understandable mistake. For the determination of the thought seems to have all the essential features of the supposed connection except that it does not hold between a cause and its effect, and it is easy to understand how we could make it and not notice it. Only a philosopher could be expected to discern the diverse elements which go into causal judgments and to see whether any mistake has occurred. But if it is a mistake, it is a mistake which is discoverable: Hume discovered it. And if it is a mistake, presumably we ought not to make it. Yet Hume apparently thinks we cannot help but make it.

He distinguishes in regard to causation three opinions, "that of the vulgar, that of a false philosophy, and that of the true . . ." (T 222). The vulgar, "in their common and careless way of thinking . . . imagine they perceive a connexion betwixt such objects as they have constantly found united together" and "are apt to fancy . . . a separation to be in itself impossible and absurd" (T 223). The philosophers discover that the vulgar err and "that there is no known connexion among objects" (T 223), but instead of "concluding . . . that we have no idea of power or agency, separate from the mind, and belonging to causes," they seek "for this connexion in matter" (T 223). "The just conclusion" is that of the true philosophy, and had philosophers fallen upon it, Hume claims,

> they wou'd have return'd back to the situation of the vulgar, and wou'd have regarded all these disquisitions with indolence and indifference [T 223].

This is an incredible ending. One would expect Hume to remark that the philosophers should not have sought for the connection in matter and to admonish that, given the uselessness of the search, they should strive not to suppose an intelligible connection between a cause and its effect. What accounts for Hume's curious resignation?

He does think that we cannot draw causal inferences without mental propensities: some tie is needed between distinct events, and the propensity of the mind provides the only link. He also thinks that the inferences based on such propensities are not within our control. We cannot change the discrete way the world presents itself to us, and we cannot change or control the underlying operations of the understanding. These, he says, "are permanent, irresistible, and universal" and such that "upon their removal human nature must immediately perish and go to ruin" (T 225). The creation of the mental propensities is not within our control, and once they exist, their activation is not within our control:

> this operation of the mind, by which we infer like effects from like causes, and *vice versa*, is so essential to the subsistence of all human creatures [that nature has secured it] by some instinct or mechanical tendency, which may be infallible in its operations . . . [EHU 55].

But what of the supposition of a conceivable connection? After all, it is one thing, after perceiving a cause, to infer, because of a mental propensity, that an effect will occur and quite another to suppose that that mental propensity holds between the cause and its effect. The two acts are distinct, and each can thus exist without the other's existing. It is thus not necessary to make the supposition of a conceivable connection in order to make causal inferences, however necessary and irresistible they may be, and the true philosophy knows that there is and can be no such connection. But having discovered what he takes to be the truth about our supposition, Hume is so far from suggesting solutions to set us free that he proposes as the *philosophical* solution "indolence and indifference."

The reason for this proposal, I suggest, is that Hume thinks the supposition is also not within our control. He gives no explanation for why it is not, no analysis in terms of mental stimuli, dispositions, or propensities. He simply asserts as a fact that

> when one particular species of event has always, in all instances, been conjoined with another, we make no longer any scruple of foretelling one upon the appearance of the other, and of employing that reasoning, which can alone assure us of any matter of fact or existence. We then call the one object, *Cause*; the other, *Effect*. We suppose that there is some connexion between them; some power in the one, by which it infallibly produces the other, and operates with the greatest certainty and strongest necessity [EHU 74–75].

Hume thinks, I suggest, that the "true philosophy" recognizes that we can change neither the world nor the essential features of ourselves, and its insight, what makes it the true philosophy rather than the false, is that, having recognized that, it accepts the consequence: there is nothing philosophers can do.

As luck would have it, Hume thinks, even if philosophers could do something, there is no reason for them to and good reason for them not to. For as things now stand, Hume claims, there is a harmony between us and the world, nature having "implanted in us an instinct, which carries forward the thought in a correspondent course to that which she has established among external objects . . ." (EHU 55). This is a point Hume makes which clearly applies to our drawing causal inferences, but we also suppose that an intelligible connection ought to make no difference. What has been discovered is that causal judgments are relative to the way we are as well as to the way the world is. We are ignorant of the basis of the harmony between the world and us (EHU 55), and we obviously have no guarantee that it will not suddenly cease. But it exists. Given its existence, there is no need for any alteration either in ourselves or in the world, and its discovery clearly makes no difference to the fact that it exists.

What it does make a difference to is our conception of our condition. What distinguishes the true philosophy from the vulgar situation is that the vulgar are ignorant of what an analysis of causal situations reveals. The sceptical impact of that revelation is best seen by comparison with the scepticism usually attributed to Hume. That has been of two sorts. First, it has been claimed, quite rightly as we saw in Section ɪɪ, that Hume denied that we have any justification for making causal inferences. According to this view, his scepticism is scepticism about our knowledge of unobserved events and of regularities and general causal principles, and the problem he poses is the problem of induction. The conception of our condition implied by this view is that we humans are limited beings, unable to come to knowledge beyond what we can immediately perceive. Second, it has been claimed, quite rightly as we have just seen, that Hume denied that when we say "*a* causes *b*," we are saying what we might normally think we are saying. According to this interpretation, his scepticism is scepticism about such general metaphysical categories as that of causation, and the problem is that metaphysicians utter nonsense. We all do, as we have seen, but in this view only that of the metaphysicians is dangerous, for they have the view that what they are saying makes sense and they draw inferences from their claims. The conception of our condition implied by this view is that we humans make mistakes. But that we thus err and that we are limited beings are not particularly exciting theses. They are true, and Hume certainly believes them to be true, but to believe that they are all he believed about our condition is to make another mistake.

That we are limited beings and that we err are consistent with our essential rationality. For the former blames the world far more than it blames us, and the latter, though it blames us for making causal judgments when we ought not to, does not imply that we cannot stop: no one is *required* to be a metaphysician. It is not our essential nature which is put into question on either conception. Yet it is Hume's view that we are of such a nature that we *must* suppose the existence of a connection which we do not perceive and which cannot exist. We *must* suppose the existence of an inconceivable connection. This is not a matter to be solved by detailed analysis of rules for causal inference. It is not a matter to be solved by toasting books of metaphysics in the flames. These solutions give philosophers hope. But what Hume has discovered is that the human mind is *essentially incoherent*, that it is of such a nature that even after discovering that it has no perception of any connection between a cause and its effect and that there cannot be any such connection, it continues to suppose that there is such a connection. This is not a matter to give a philosopher hope. It is a matter to be recognized, contemplated, and accepted with philosophical indolence and indifference.

IV · JUDGMENTS REGARDING EXTERNAL OBJECTS

This general view of the nature of Hume's conception of the human condition, and so his general view of the nature of scepticism, would be more persuasive if it were backed, on the one hand, by a detailing of how his two definitions of the causal relation fit his analysis of causal judgments [21] and, on the other, by a careful study of his analyses of moral and aesthetic judgments. What needs to be shown is that he everywhere uses as his model the analysis embodied in "that famous doctrine, . . . 'That tastes and colours, and all other sensible qualities, lie not in the bodies, but merely in the senses.' " But even with such backing, the conclusions I have drawn about the essential incoherence of the human mind are not as plausible as they might be in regard to causation for two different reasons.

First, we certainly can separate our making causal inferences from our supposing a necessary connection between a cause and its effect, and Hume has given us no reason for thinking the second in any way essential to the first. But it is the supposition which gives rise to the sceptical conclusions. Second, Hume himself does not seem at the point of his analysis to be cognizant that he has done anything new and unusual in regard to scepticism. He certainly knows that what he is saying is striking and paradoxical. He thus has his reader exclaim,

> What! the efficacy of causes lie in the determination of the mind! As if causes did not operate entirely independent of the mind, and wou'd not continue their operation, even tho' there was no mind existent to contemplate them, or reason concerning them [T 167].

But that is consistent with his realization that his analysis runs counter to the usual interpretation of causal judgments. He does not pursue or apparently even consciously recognize the sceptical consequences of his claim that we suppose the existence of what is inconceivable. The matter is quite otherwise, I think, with regard to his analysis of judgments concerning external objects. There Hume's consciousness of what he was doing caught up with his discoveries, and he first became aware of how sceptical what he was saying was. That is the explanation for his famous lament at the end of the Section "Of scepticism with regard to the senses" in which he says

> I begun this subject with premising, that we ought to have an implicit faith in our senses, and that this wou'd be the conclusion, I shou'd draw from the whole of my reasoning. But to be ingenuous, I feel myself *at present* of a quite contrary sentiment . . . [T 217].

The reason for this self-consciousness on his part is, I suggest, that in analyzing our judgments regarding external objects he laid out what was missing in his analysis of causal judgments, viz., the mechanism in terms of stimuli, underlying dispositions, and mental propensities.

What that mechanism must account for is why we make such judgments as, e.g., that the tomatoes in the garden are ripening. Hume thinks that we normally suppose, in making such judgments, the existence of objects which exist independently of our perception of them and continue to exist even when they are not perceived. What he discovered, as I have elsewhere argued,[22] is that necessary to that supposition are two propensities of the mind.

The first is the propensity "which makes us reason from causes and effects . . ." (T 266). This propensity is created by the constancy of some of our perceptions. Some come constantly conjoined, and, as we saw, our perception of that constancy produces particular mental propensities to conceive or believe in particular effects upon perceiving particular causes. These mental propensities are necessary for the supposition of external objects because, without some causal inferences, we have no way of going beyond what is currently observed (T 73–74). It is a causal inference that makes us suppose that *something* exists which we are not now perceiving. But such inferences are not enough to account for our supposition of external objects. For if we infer "justly and regularly," to use Hume's phrase (T 266), we can only infer another perception, and perceptions, philosophers know, do not exist independently of our perception of them (T 210–11, 228–31). Therefore to account for our supposition of external objects something more is required.

That something more is a second propensity which is activated by the first. There are complications in Hume's analysis, but what he claims is that when we reason justly from causes and effects, the mind continues unreasonably on its way as "a galley put in motion by the oars, carries on its course without any new impulse" (T 198). The explanation seems to be that the mind can only make causal inferences and make them "justly and regularly" by supposing that some perceptions exist unperceived. Assuming the proper constant conjunctions, the perception of a^*, say, will activate the relevant propensity to produce another perception, the idea of or belief in b^*. Whether or not that is a just inference will depend upon the existence of what we have an idea of or belief in, viz., b^*. We can only check whether we have a causal or a casual regularity by checking the inference, and that means having an impression of b^*. But if we only made inferences we could check, we would make few, if any. For the constancy of our impressions is continually interrupted: we blink, turn our heads, are inattentive, and so on. We all know, for instance, that when we discover a newspaper on our porch, someone has put it there, but the number of times we have observed a *conjunction* of the two is small indeed. We *suppose* a constancy we have not observed to distinguish causal from casual regularities, and indeed, though I shall not argue the point here, Hume thinks we suppose such a constancy in order to have enough to allow us to reason causally at all. We fill the many gaps to create the constancy necessary for causal inference. But to suppose such constancy is to suppose, Hume thinks, the existence of perceptions which are unperceived, and that is to suppose the existence of external objects.

Hume thinks that an unreasonable supposition for two reasons. First, he thinks we have no idea of anything which exists independently of our perceiving it (e.g., T 234), and we are thus supposing the existence of what is inconceivable. Second, the inference necessary to the supposition cannot be a causal one, but Hume thinks that in regard to empirical matters one can *reason* only causally. The inference we make he thus thinks unreasonable. Yet we must make it in order to reason causally.

It is this latter point which Hume picks up in the conclusion of Book I of the *Treatise*. He says that

> 'Tis this principle [i.e. the imagination], which makes us reason from causes and effects; and 'tis the same principle, which convinces us of the continu'd existence of external objects, when absent from the senses. But tho' these two operations be equally natural and necessary in the human mind, yet in some circumstances they are directly contrary, nor is it possible for us to reason justly and regularly from causes and effects, and at the same time believe the continu'd existence of matter [T 266].

There is a conflict because we cannot reason causally without doing more than reasoning causally. We thus cannot be reasonable in regard to empirical matters without making an unreasonable supposition. It is this fact which explains Hume's lament at the end of the Section "Of scepticism regarding the senses" and his closing remark there that "Carelessness and in-attention alone can afford us any remedy" (T 218). After all, if we cannot reason at all regarding empirical matters without being unreasonable, and if the operations of the mind which produce this result are "equally natural and necessary," then there is nothing a philosopher can do about it.

What he can do is to make us understand how pretentious is our claim to be the rational animal by describing our inherent incoherence and by subjecting to rational scrutiny the many judgments we make which purport to be causal. In emphasizing Hume's account of how certain empirical judgments are possible, we must not forget how much of his philosophical labor was expended in attacking such supposed causal inferences as that God exists or that He is all good. But this sort of attack on our pretensions to rationality can be met, to use Locke's phrase, by shortening the tether of our minds so it infers only what it can "justly and regularly" infer. But if we must make some causal inferences and if to make them we must be unreasonable, then we can, as philosophers, only follow Hume's advice and do "what is commonly done; which is, that this difficulty is seldom or never thought of . . ." (T 268). There is no philosophical solution.

NOTES

1. I have in mind primarily the group of Scottish philosophers starting with Thomas Reid, but the interpretation is widely held today by persons who find Hume's psychology deploring, but are sympathetic to his philosophical views.

2. Norman Kemp Smith, "The Naturalism of Hume," *Mind*, 30, N.S. 14 (April and October 1905), 149–73, 335–47.

3. John Locke, *An Essay Concerning Human Understanding*, ed. Peter N. Nidditch (Oxford, 1975), p. 235.

4. Ibid.

5. Robert Boyle, *Experiments and Considerations Touching Colours* (New York, 1964), p. 119.

6. Ibid., p. 118.

7. For another view of the relation between the definitions Hume gives in the *Treatise* and the *Enquiries*, see Selby-Bigge's introduction to his edition of the *Enquiries*, pp. xv–xvi.

8. For Hume a definition is a real, ostensive definition. It is a real definition because what is being defined is not a word, but an idea; and it is ostensive because it is being defined in terms of the impressions which go to make it up, and these impressions we must be acquainted with to understand (see, e.g., T 277 and EHU 62–63).

9. I am assuming a distinction between *judging that p* and *saying that p*. This is not a distinction Hume makes, but there is no difficulty imposing it on his views. For there are obviously a great many ways one can display one's judgment that p without saying that p. I shall, however, often use saying that p as a clear case of judging that p.

10. I intend *not* to imply that this is the only sense in which causal objects are distinct.

11. Hume is a nominalist who holds that everything which exists is a particular. Constant conjunction is thus not a relation which holds between kinds of entities, but a set of particular relations holding between particular entities.

12. I have ignored here for simplicity's sake the role of the auxiliary principle that whatever is distinct is distinguishable (see, e.g., T 18). Its addition would complicate the presentation and not change the basic structure of the argument.

13. The point of the disclaimer is that it does not follow from the fact that a and b are themselves distinguishable, and therefore separable, that their *qualities* are distinguishable and separable. The motion of the one ball may be transferred to the other even if the balls can each exist without the other's existing. Some added premiss is needed here to guarantee the implication that the qualities are distinguishable and separable. The Separability Principle itself does not, I would argue, give us a criterion for distinguishability, but it is not clear what Hume thinks does, and I shall bypass the issue here.

14. It is a common assumption that Hume defines causation in this way. Someone who argues for this common assumption is J. A. Robinson (see his "Hume's Two Definitions of 'Cause,'" *Philosophical Quarterly*, 12, No. 47 [April 1962], 162–71; repr. in *Hume: A Collection of Critical Essays*, ed. V. C. Chappell [Garden City, 1966], 129–47).

15. Locke, *Essay Concerning Human Understanding*, pp. 44–45.

16. Ibid., p. 45.

17. It is not its being a relation between perceptions which makes it a natural relation. See note 19.

18. On this identification, Robert Paul Wolff says, "Hume is not saying here that the impression arises from the transition or is conjoined with the transition or is dependent upon the transition; he is saying that the impression *is* the transition" ("Hume's Theory of Mental Activity," *Philosophical Review*, 69, No. 3 [July 1960], 289–310; repr. in *Hume*, ed. Chappell, pp. 99–128, at 112).

19. Natural relations are not to be distinguished from philosophical relations on the basis that they hold between particular sorts of entities—namely, perceptions—between which philosophical relations do not hold. For although natural relations hold only between perceptions philosophical relations can hold between them as well. Perceptions succeed one another, and succession is a philosophical relation. What I suggest, though I shall not argue for it here, is that natural relations are distinguished by their causes. They come into being because certain observations trigger certain underlying dispositions of the mind to produce them.

20. See my "Hume's Ontological Commitments," *Philosophical Quarterly*, 26, No. 102 (January 1976), 39–47.

21. I have argued, in an unpublished paper entitled "Hume's Two Definitions of Cause," that the backing is available.

22. For a detailed analysis of Hume's views regarding judgments about external objects, see my "Hume's Scepticism," *Dialogue*, 12, No. 1 (March 1973), 87–99.

2

Why Should Probability Be the Guide of Life?

D. C. Stove
The University of Sydney

I

> Q1: Why should one believe a proposition H which is certain in relation to one's total evidence E?

Because (A1), necessarily, if one's total evidence E is true, then every proposition H which is certain in relation to E is true.

LET US ASSUME that **A1** is an appropriate and adequate answer to the question **Q1**. I do not think it is, and it seems obvious to me that there is even something seriously wrong with the question itself. But many philosophers think otherwise, and I intend to proceed on their assumption for the first half of this essay.

Now consider the question, analogous to **Q1**:

> Q2: Why should one believe a proposition H which is probable but not certain in relation to one's total evidence E (since any such H may be false)?

Is there an adequate answer to **Q2** which is analogous to **A1**?
One possible answer to **Q2** is:

Because (A2), necessarily, if one's total evidence E is true, then every proposition H which in relation to E has probability $= \frac{x}{y}$ (where $x > 0 < 1$, but may be close to 1) has probability $= \frac{x}{y}$ in relation to E.

What **A2** says is true, but it does not seem an adequate answer to **Q2**, and perhaps not even an appropriate one. It is, rather, a repudiation of that question. The proviso it contains, that E be true, is clearly redundant. And once that is omitted it is evident, if it was not so before, that **A2** simply says that one should believe what is probable in relation to one's total evidence because it is probable in relation to one's total evidence. But that seems too short a way with the dissenter who asks **Q2**. I do not deny that there is something seriously wrong with **Q2**; on the contrary, it seems obvious to me that there is. But, then, there is also something seriously wrong with "Why should one respect what is sacred?"—yet that question can have merit. It does not always deserve to be repudiated with "One should respect what is sacred because it is sacred." But as an answer to **Q2**, **A2** seems to be no better than that.

A second possible answer to **Q2** is:

Because (**A2'**), necessarily, if one's total evidence E is true, then every proposition H which in relation to E has probability $= \frac{x}{y}$ (where

$\frac{x}{y} > 0 < 1$, but may be close to 1) has (simple) probability $= \frac{x}{y}$.

This is not an adequate answer. The conception of simple probability—that is, of the probability of a proposition in itself, as contrasted with the conception of the probability of a proposition in relation to another proposition—is a mysterious one in itself, and to give this answer to **Q2** would be to invite in its place another question which would prove harder still to answer, viz.:

Why should one believe a proposition H which is (simply) probable but not certain (since any such H may be false)?

But in any case it is disastrous to *connect* the simple or one-placed conception of probability with the two-placed conception, in the way in which **A2'** does, as the following well-known argument shows.

"Tex is rich" has probability $= .9$ in relation to "$\frac{9}{10}$ths of Texans are rich and Tex is a Texan"; and it has probability $= .1$ in relation to "$\frac{1}{10}$th of Texan philosophers are rich and Tex is a Texan philosopher." The former conjunction might be my total evidence, the latter yours. Both could be true. If they are, then given **A2'**, it would follow that "Tex is rich" has (simple) probability both $= .9$ and $= .1$.

A third possible answer to **Q2** is:

Because (**A2''**), necessarily, if one's total evidence E is true, then a proportion $= \frac{x}{y}$ of the propositions H which each have probability $= \frac{x}{y}$ in relation to E are true.

This seems an appropriate answer, and perhaps would even be adequate if true. But it is not true. "There are just 100 tickets in Lottery L_1, and L_1 is fair, and I hold just one ticket in L_1" might be true and might be my total evidence E. The only proposition H which in relation to this E has probability $= \frac{1}{100}$ is "I win L_1." But it is not only not necessary, it is impossible, that in this unit-class of propositions a proportion $= \frac{1}{100}$ should be true.

The case is no different where the number of propositions H each having probability $=\frac{x}{y}$ in relation to E is such as to allow the possibility of a proportion $\frac{x}{y}$ of them to be true. My total evidence E might be true, and might be such that the only propositions H each having probability $=\frac{x}{y} > 0 < 1$ in relation to it were the hundred hypotheses "I win Lottery L_1," "I win Lottery L_2," and so on, to "I win Lottery L_{100}." Common sense says "You can't win them all," and so says a certain immemorial distortion of classical probability-theory; and so says A2″. But of course I *can* win them all, or none, or any other proportion, and what A2″ says is false. This is really excessively obvious, and is of course no more than almost every reputable writer on probability has always allowed. At the same time, it is necessary to insist on it, because there is a permanent temptation to distort the Law of Large Numbers so as to make it testify to the contrary.

That there is no adequate answer to **Q2** does not of course follow from the fact that the three answers I have now considered are inadequate. Nevertheless, this alarming conclusion is already looming up, because there is, in fact, in the answers to **Q2** already found wanting, at least an approach to exhaustiveness. To explain.

What is wanted is an answer to **Q2** which differs from **A1** in some respects (viz., those required by its being an answer to a question about probability rather than about certainty), but which also preserves some features of **A1** intact.

One feature of **A1** which any answer to **Q2** must preserve is the beginning "(Because) *necessarily*. . . ." To begin an answer to **Q2** with "(Because) it is probable though not certain in relation to our total evidence that . . ." would be inadequate for an obvious reason. To begin it with "(Because) it is (simply) probable that . . . " would be inadequate for other obvious reasons; among them, the inviting of the already-mentioned question which is the simple-probability analogue of **Q2**. To begin our answer with "(Because) it is a scientific law that . . . ," or with "(Because) to date it has always turned out that . . . ," or, in general, with "(Because) contingently . . ." would be to renounce all hope of finding an answer to **Q2** analogous to **A1**. For it would be to admit at the outset that, whereas it is of course necessarily true that one should believe what is certain in relation to one's total evidence, it is simply *not* necessarily true that one should believe what is probable but not certain in relation to that evidence. If this were to be admitted, then the only proper response to **Q2** would be, not to try to answer it in analogy with **A1**, but to reject the question as containing a most serious *suggestio falsi*, and one to which **Q1** seems to contain no counterpart.

A second feature of **A1** which must be regarded as fixed also for the answer to **Q2** is its continuing with "(Because) (necessarily) *if E is true then*. . . ." Or, at any rate, I must regard this feature as fixed. This is simply because, although it is hard to complete an answer to **Q2** which contains this proviso, without this proviso I simply have no idea at all of the way an answer to **Q2** might go after "Because necessarily. . . ."

Now **A1** ran thus: "Because, necessarily, if E is true, then *every* H (which stands in the specified relation to E) is *true*." Well, with the first seven words fixed, as being needed also in our answer to **Q2**, and with the specified relation varied from certainty to probability, what possibilities remain for making other variations of **A1** suitable for an answer of **Q2**? There seem to be only two. One could leave the (final) "true" intact but vary the "every" along the proportion-dimension. That is what **A2″** did. Or one could leave the "every" intact, and try to vary the "true"—and how else but along the simple-probability dimension? That is what **A2** did. Either course, as we have seen, is radically objectionable. But, as far as I can see, there are no other variations which could be made at either of these two places, and no other place at which any variation could be made. That is why I said that in the answers to **Q2** already found wanting there is at least an approach to exhaustiveness.

Our negative results, therefore (taken along with the assumption made in favour of **A1** at the outset), suggest the conclusion that whereas there is an adequate answer to **Q1**, viz., **A1**, there is none at all to **Q2**.

This conclusion is alarming. For one thing, it would seem to involve us in Hume's notorious scepticism concerning induction. All inductive arguments are fallible; that is, it is possible for their conclusions to be false even though their premises be true. Consequently the conclusion of an inductive argument is at best probable, never certain, in relation to the premises. But we now seem unable to answer someone who asks us why one should believe conclusions which are probable but not certain, and hence unable to answer someone who asks us why one should believe the conclusion of any inductive argument. And is not this to be unable to answer Hume's inductive scepticism?

The conclusion that **Q1** is adequately answered by **A1** while **Q2** is not answerable in any analogous way seems especially alarming for those philosophers who adhere to the Keynes–Carnap theory of probability, the "logical-probability" theorists; or perhaps only for them. For **A1** answers **Q1** in terms of the truth-frequency among propositions H which are certain in relation to E; whereas no answer of the **A2″** type, that is, no answer in terms of the truth-frequency among propositions H which are probable in relation to E, appears to be available for **Q2**. This lack of symmetry would seem to show that the logical theory of probability provides "no basis for expecting the probable rather than the improbable . . . and [that it] lacks predictive content and thus fails to qualify as a 'guide of life.' " [1]

This suspicion is confirmed by certain remarks of Keynes himself, at the scattered points in *A Treatise on Probability* where he touches on what is in effect my **Q2**. Keynes's answer to **Q2** appears to be the "repudiationist" answer **A2** above. A conclusion which is probable but not certain in relation to one's total evidence has—such seems to be Keynes's view—"*nothing to recommend it but its probability.*" [2] This is cold comfort indeed, and the contrast between this answer to **Q2** and the answer **A1** to **Q1** is painfully marked. Probability, then, is to be, like virtue according to the Stoic doctrine, its own reward. Stoic doctrine indeed, of which the plain English is that there is *no* reward for believing what is probable! For believing what is certain in relation to one's total evidence, by contrast, A1 holds out the reward, concrete though conditional, of truth.

II

What I have done in Section 1 above is to give my own version of an argument which Professor Wesley Salmon, if I have understood him rightly, has several times advanced.[3] I should stress that this version is my own, and therefore may contain some inadvertent misrepresentation.

In the present section I will try to show that in two important respects Salmon has misconceived the conclusion to which his argument points. In the next section I return to examine the starting point of the argument, the questions Q2 and Q1.

Salmon appears to think, as I have indicated, that the difficulty of answering Q2 in analogy with A1 is a difficulty especially for, or perhaps only for, the theorists of logical probability. But it should be obvious that this is not so. There is absolutely nothing in the argument of the preceding section which depends in any way at all on any thesis which is peculiar to the theorists of logical probability. (In particular, their thesis that assessments of the probability of one proposition in relation to another are non-empirical propositions has played no part whatever in the argument, either overtly or covertly.) This is something which the reader can easily verify for himself by referring back to Section 1.

In order to be exposed to the difficulty of answering Q2 on lines analogous to A1, one does not need to be a logical-probabilist, or even a philosopher. All one does need to be, in fact, is someone who thinks that one *should* believe what is probable though not certain in relation to all the evidence one has. And who thinks that? Why, nearly everyone. The difficulty which Salmon has brought to light then, if it is a genuine one, is equally a difficulty for everyone, and certainly not only or especially for one tiny group of philosophers.

A second and much more important misconception which Salmon entertains, if I have understood him rightly, is that the difficulty of finding an answer to Q2 which is analogous to A1 "is Hume's problem of induction once again." [4] It is nothing of the kind.

An inductive argument, according to the main stream of philosophical usage, is simply an argument from observed to unobserved instances of some empirical predicates. Now, in that conception, it is important to notice, there is nothing which precludes the conclusion of an inductive argument from being certain in relation to the premisses; and, indeed, nothing whatever about the degree of probability which the conclusion of an inductive argument can or cannot have in relation to the premisses. Equally, in the conception of an argument whose conclusion is (at best probable but) not certain in relation to the premisses, there is nothing to tell us that there

is any *inductive* argument which falls under that conception. If, then, someone who asks **Q2** wishes to bring inductive arguments within the scope of
his question, it will be necessary for him to do what was done in the third-
last paragraph of Section I, viz., to *state* that the conclusion of an inductive
argument is at best probable, never certain, in relation to the premises.

Now, this proposition, despite what Carnap, Edwards, and many others
have implied to the contrary, is not a triviality like "Bachelors are un-
married." It is a logico-philosophical thesis, and an extremely important
one: the thesis of "inductive fallibilism" as I call it. I think indeed that
this thesis is true, as most philosophers now think; though it has not always
been thought so.[5] But even if it were not true, we would have no less need
to answer **Q2**, and no less difficulty in doing so, than we have as things are.
Let us suppose that arguments from observed to unobserved instances of
empirical predicates are all such that their conclusions are certain in relation to their premises. Clearly, that is not going to make the possible
answers to **Q2** any more numerous, or any less defective, than we have
found them to be! That supposition would deprive us of what is perhaps
our most important class of *examples* of arguments whose conclusions are
not certain in relation to their premises; but that is all it would do. And
that would be no fatal deprivation. When we wished to illustrate **Q2**, we
could simply draw all our examples from some non-inductive class of fallible arguments. This is in fact what I did do above. The lottery arguments,
and the arguments about Tex, are arguments none of whose conclusions
are certain in relation to their premises; but none of them is inductive.
They belong, on the contrary, to what was formerly, and aptly, called
"direct" probability, as expressly distinguished from "inverse" or "inductive" probability. (In particular they were examples of what may aptly be
called "Bernoullian" arguments.)

The question **Q2** which we have found difficulty in answering, then, is
far from being about inductive arguments only, or about them especially,
because it is not necessarily about them at all. It is safe to assume that on
the other hand Hume's scepticism about inductive arguments *is* necessarily
about inductive arguments. Consequently, the difficulty of answering **Q2**,
whatever it is, is at any rate *not* the difficulty of answering Hume's inductive
scepticism.

This is still putting the matter much too mildly.

Hume's inductive scepticism, it is reasonable to assume, is some proposition, some thesis or other. **Q2** on the other hand is not a proposition but a
question.

More important still: Hume's inductive scepticism, as I have tried to
show in detail elsewhere,[6] is actually a version of the thesis that the conclusions of inductive arguments, in relation to their premises, *are not
probable*.[7] Now, the mental state which that thesis expresses is very different
from that which is expressed by the question **Q2**, and even incompatible
with it. For the mental state behind **Q2** is that of someone who concedes
that sometimes a proposition H is probable though not certain in relation
to his total evidence E, and who could with perfect consistency admit that

some of these cases happen to be ones in which the argument from E to H is inductive; but who then goes on to ask, concerning all such cases (inductive or not) indifferently, why he should believe any such H since any such H may be false. It is surely obvious that this person is maintaining a different position from that of someone who just denies that the conclusions of inductive arguments ever are probable in relation to their premises.

But I do not need to rely only on indirect arguments, for the matter before us has a straightforward textual side. If we are to be persuaded rationally that Q2 is an expression of Hume's inductive scepticism, it can only be by references to Hume's text which are sufficient to sustain that attribution. Although Salmon, if I understand him rightly, does attribute Q2 to Hume, he gives no such references; indeed he gives no references which are even intended specifically to support that attribution. A sufficient reason is that no such references could be given. Not only is Q2 not an expression of Hume's inductive scepticism, it is not an expression of anything whatever to be found in Hume's writings. The attribution of Q2 to him is simply a glaring instance of a bad habit of twentieth-century philosophers, of which I have elsewhere collected some other examples, of fathering on Hume things which are no more than the sprouts of their own brains.[8]

How this particular cuckoo's egg can ever have looked at home in the Hume nest is hard for anyone with any feeling for the history of thought to imagine. Hume's inductive scepticism is clear, and straightforward, and a thesis; and in these and many other respects it manifestly "belongs" where it actually occurs, viz., at the centre of the Scottish Enlightenment of the eighteenth century. Q2, on the other hand, has a contrived and morbid air which stamps it as a question which equally belongs where *it* actually occurs, viz., in the mid-twentieth century and nowhere else.

It will be worthwhile briefly to enlarge on the state of mind which Q2 expresses, and to ask after its probable cause. And here, despite what I have said above, I think it is true, *causally* speaking, that Hume's philosophy of induction will be found at the bottom of the matter.

The *ground* on which Q2 is asked—and I have incorporated this in the question all along—is that any H which is probable but not certain in relation to one's evidence E *may be false*. Yet that, of course, was given in the question, since to say that H may be false is just another way of saying that H is not certain in relation to E. It was equally given in the question, on the other hand, that the Hs in question *are* probable in relation to E. But this part of the data is simply lost on a person who asks Q2 in earnest. He is someone who can think only of the other part, the possibility that H is false. "Still, I *may* win all the lotteries," "Still, the sun *may* not rise"—these are the thoughts which occupy his mind to the exclusion of all else. This questioner is someone anaesthetised to probability, hyperaesthetised to possibility: he is "probability-numb."

This sounds like a rather strange mental state, and certainly a distilled expression of this state, such as Q2, is not to be met with every day. Yet the state itself seems to me to be not really an unfamiliar one nowadays.

Salmon's question, though new, has not lacked other philosophers to second it. But much more than that, large areas of probability-numbness seem to me to exist at present in our intellectual culture generally. The philosophy of science is one such area. The feature of scientific arguments on which nowadays we are most anxious to insist, and for many of us the sole feature on which we are at all eager to insist, is their fallibility: the permanent possibility that the conclusions may be false even though all the empirical evidence for them be true. We know that by concentrating so exclusively as we do on this feature, we open the door to an extreme irrationalism about science (Feyerabend's for example), which we do not particularly welcome. But still, on the whole, we stay numb to any aspect of scientific inference except its fallibility. A more complete contrast with the philosophers of science of 1876 or of 1776, could scarcely be imagined; for where they characteristically made too favourable an assessment of the probability of scientific arguments, and prized scientific conclusions chiefly for their supposed certainty, we characteristically avoid making *any* assessment of the probability of those arguments, and prize scientific conclusions for—what reason is not quite clear. And what brought this change about was not that we quietly outgrew "the search for certainty"; though we think we did, which is why that phrase is now found so incomparable a soporific. No, we are separated in our philosophy of science from the nineteenth and eighteenth centuries rather by this: that we suffered sudden certainty-*deprivation*, and are to this day still in the resulting state of shock, a state in which mere probabilities leave one cold.

And who brought on the shock? Who taught twentieth-century philosophers of science, what their predecessors saw only fitfully or dimly or not at all, that even the best inferences from empirical evidence to scientific conclusions are incurably fallible? Taught it to us with such overwhelming force, I may add, that by 1950 it was often made, what it never was before, part of the *meaning* of the phrase "inductive inference," that it be possible for the conclusion to be false and premises true; and even made, by Carnap [9] and most of his followers, the *whole* meaning of "inductive inference"?

Why, David Hume of course; with the assistance of Einstein, who (though himself an avowed Humean fallibilist) enabled philosophy to teach by example, and that example, the most resounding of all. And what philosophy was irresistibly taught by the ending of the *pax Newtoniana*? Not Hume's inductive *scepticism*, although naturally in the ensuing period of turbulence a few *esprits forts* have been found willing to embrace even that. It was Hume's inductive *fallibilism*.

This seems to me to be the historical key to Q2. It is the realisation that *whatever* the weight of empirical evidence in its favour, any scientific theory *may* be false—it is that *possibility*, brooded on to the exclusion of every other feature of scientific inference—which has brought Q2 before us. This strange and novel question is a delayed effect of the intellectual earthquake set off early in the twentieth century by Hume and Einstein, a faint tremor reaching us from that great but distant subsidence of scientific confidence, and now amplified by morbidly nervous philosophic ears. Such at any rate appears to me to have been the aetiology of **Q2**.

Inductive fallibilism is only one of Hume's profound and influential *non-deducibility theses*. Two others are: the non-deducibility of factual propositions from necessary truths ("There can be no demonstrative arguments for a matter of fact and existence"), and the non-deducibility of "ought" from "is." But non-deducibility theses are especially abundant in his philosophy, and are, in fact, chiefly what give it its negative or destructive character. That his philosophy *is* of a predominantly destructive character I take to be as obvious to Hume's readers now, even after the efforts of Professor Kemp Smith to portray it in an opposite light,[10] as it always was before. Indeed, when I consider the immense destructive effects which have actually been wrought, by the three theses just mentioned, on scientific confidence, religious confidence, and moral confidence, respectively, I wonder whether the philosophy of Hume is not at the bottom, not just of probability-numbness in our present philosophy of science, but of the far wider phenomenon of "modern nervousness," of which Freud advanced a different and singularly improbable explanation.[11]

To recapitulate. The difficulty of answering **Q2** in analogy with **A1** is not a difficulty only or especially for the logical theory of probability. Nor is this difficulty "Hume's problem of induction once again." No doubt someone who asks **Q2** in earnest can rightly be called a sceptic of *some* kind. But his kind of scepticism is not Hume's, if only because it has no necessary connection at all with inductive arguments. His kind of scepticism need not even extend to inductive arguments, though it may do so. It will do so, if he is an inductive fallibilist (and is consistent). But even if it does, his scepticism about inductive arguments will still be quite different from Hume's scepticism about them; for Hume's consists in denying that their conclusions ever are probable in relation to their premises, whereas the **Q2** kind of scepticism could admit that some such conclusions are probable in relation to their premises, but goes on to ask, in effect, "So what?"

But at best all this shows only that Salmon has misinterpreted the difficulty of answering **Q2** in analogy with **A1**. We have yet to dispose of that difficulty itself.

III

The answer **A1** to **Q1** states a necessary connection between certainty in relation to evidence, and truth; and hence it ensures a certain truth-frequency among some of our conclusions. Clearly, what Salmon and indeed all of us would *like* most, by way of an answer to **Q2**, is something similar for the case of probability: that is, an answer which states a necessary connection between probability in relation to evidence, and truth, and which therefore ensures a certain truth-frequency among some of our other conclusions. An answer of this *type* has, of course, already been canvassed above, viz., **A2″**. But **A2″** stated only a very simple form which the desired connection might take, and anyway **A2**" was false. What is wanted is something which, like **A1**, states a necessary *truth*; only, one connecting probability with truth.

This, which I shall call "Salmon's desideratum," is so natural a one that it will be worthwhile to prove that it cannot be satisfied. It cannot, because its satisfaction would be inconsistent with the satisfaction of another, and genuine, desideratum for an adequate answer to **Q2**.

Suppose **Q2** were given an answer which, although true, was such that it never, when added to one's total evidence E, raised to certainty the probability of any H which was not certain in relation to E alone. Such an answer would not be adequate. For such an answer, if it were added to the total evidence E of the questioner in particular, would *ex hypothesi* leave every proposition H which was not certain in relation to his E before not certain still. Now, our questioner's ground for asking why he should believe an H which is probable but not certain in relation to his E was that any such H may be false. But any H of his which before might have been false still might be false after he has added to his E an answer to **Q2** such as we are at present supposing. Given such an answer, then, our questioner, unless he were just inconsistent, would have to renew his original question **Q2**. But if an answer to one's question, when added to one's total evidence, leaves one with exactly the same ground for asking the question as one had before, it is inadequate. On the other hand, an adequate answer to **Q2** must be such that there is at least some H and some E such that while H is probable but not certain in relation to E, H *is* certain in relation to E plus that answer.

But this desideratum and Salmon's cannot be met together. Any E in relation to which some H has probability < 1 is consistent, and any H which in relation to some consistent E has probability < 1 and > 0 is contingent. Hence H must be contingent and E consistent in order to satisfy the first part of the desideratum just stated. But then the second part of that desideratum cannot be satisfied along with Salmon's. For it is impossible to raise to certainty the probability of a contingent proposition H by adding, to consistent evidence E, a necessary truth connecting probability with truth, or by adding any necessary truth whatever. (To suppose otherwise would be to suppose that with N necessarily true, H contingent, and E consistent, it is possible that (*i*) $P(H/E) < 1 > 0$ and (*ii*) $P(H/E.N) = 1$. But if (*i*) is true, then the conditional E ⊃ H is neither necessarily true nor necessarily false, hence must be contingent; while if (*ii*) is true, that contingent proposition is certain in relation to N alone, which is impossible.)

It will be worthwhile to illustrate what this argument shows, and best to do so by reference to the special case of inductive arguments. The argument shows this: that if we *could* get an answer to **Q2** of the type which Salmon and the rest of us would most like, viz., a truth stating a necessary connection between probability and truth, this answer, even when we added it to our total evidence E, would leave every single inductive conclusion H which was not certain before not certain still. All our generalisations and predictions from experience, in other words, even the most probable ones, would *still have nothing to recommend them except their probability!*

The same argument also proves a more general result: that two of the desiderata for an adequate answer to Q_2 are inconsistent. These are: the desideratum that an answer to Q_2 be a necessary truth; and the desideratum that it be sufficient, when added to some E, to make certain some H which in relation to E alone was not so.

This consideration ought at least to incline us to the view that Q_2 is a question to be repudiated rather than answered. I can render this view more acceptable still by pointing out a certain defect in *all* the answers we have considered to Q_2, and another one in that question itself.

In Section 1 I said that an adequate answer to Q_2 must, after "Because necessarily," continue ". . . if E is true . . ."; though I admitted that I had said this only because I could conceive of no other way in which an adequate answer could continue.

I now point out, however, that even if one could complete in an otherwise adequate way an answer beginning so, the result would be at most *half* of an answer to Q_2. For the obligation to believe what is probable in relation to one's total evidence E is not confined to the cases in which E is true. It subsists also and equally where E is false. A second arm of an answer is required, therefore, one which begins ". . .; and if E is false. . . ." But now, I think it will be agreed, no one has any idea at all how to complete the part of an answer to Q_2 which begins in that way. Least of all does anyone know how to complete it in terms of the *truth-frequency* among Hs probable in relation to E. (For nothing can be said *a priori* and in general about the truth-frequency among propositions probable though not certain in relation to false E.) And even if this could be done, the result would still be not quite the kind of answer which is required. For the obligation to believe what is probable though not certain in relation to one's total evidence E has really nothing at all to do with the truth *or* the falsity of E. An answer to Q_2, accordingly, should take account, not of both, but of neither of those cases. Yet no one, I think it will be agreed, has any idea how an answer to Q_2 which takes no account of the truth-value of E might run. Least of all does anyone know how an answer which is in terms of the truth-frequency among Hs might run, once the truth-value of E is disregarded. (For nothing can be said *a priori* and in general about the truth-frequency among propositions probable though not certain in relation to an E which is of unspecified truth-value.)

If all this is so, then we really have no idea how to answer Q_2 at all.

The question itself, moreover, contains a *suggestio falsi* of the most serious kind. It suggests that always, when one believes what is probable though not certain in relation to one's total evidence, one believes as one should, and it asks why this is so. But it is *not* so. What is true is that if H has probability $= \dfrac{x}{y}$ in relation to one's total evidence E, where $\dfrac{x}{y} > 0 < 1$, one should have in H a degree of belief which is a fraction $= \dfrac{x}{y}$ of one's degree of belief in E. But if, for example, H has probability $= .9$ in relation to my E, and I have in H a degree of belief which is a fraction > 1, or $= .8$, say, of my degree of belief in E, then while indeed I believe *what* I should, viz., H, it is by no means true that I believe *as* I should. Nor is this false suggestion only of peripheral importance in the present context. On the contrary. The very thing which assessments of probability do, and which no other propositions do, is to characterise certain *degrees* of belief as rational, and others as not, as distinct from characterising just some *beliefs* as rational, or not.

It would be necessary, in order to free **Q2** from this *suggestio falsi*, to reformulate the question as follows:

Q2′: Why should one have, in a proposition H which has probability $= \dfrac{x}{y}$ in relation to one's total evidence E (where $\dfrac{x}{y} > 0 < 1$, but may be close to 1), a degree of belief which is a fraction $= \dfrac{x}{y}$ of one's degree of belief in E?

And, now, to *this* question what answer could possibly be given, except some repudiationist one? What could one say to the questioner, except, in the spirit of Keynes and of **A2**, "You *told* us why one should! Because H has probability $= \dfrac{x}{y}$ in relation to E."

But neither is **A1** an adequate, even if it is an appropriate, answer to **Q1**. It is at best *half* of such an answer. For the obligation to believe what is certain in relation to one's total evidence E is not confined to the cases in which E is true. It subsists also and equally where E is false. A second arm of an answer is required, therefore, one which begins ". . .; and if E is false. . . ." But, now, I think it will be agreed, no one has any idea at all how to complete the part of an answer to **Q1** which begins in that way. Least of all does anyone know how to complete it in terms of the truth-frequency among Hs certain in relation to E. (For nothing can be said *a priori* and in general about the truth-frequency among propositions certain in relation to false E, except that it is < 1.) And even if this could be done, the result would still be not quite the kind of answer which is required. For the obligation to believe what is certain in relation to one's total evidence E has really nothing at all to do with the truth *or* the falsity of E. An answer to **Q1**, accordingly, should take account not of both but of neither of those cases. Yet no one, I think it will be agreed, has any idea how an answer to **Q1**, which takes no account of the truth-value of E, might run. Least of all does anyone know how an answer which is in terms of the truth-frequency among Hs might run, once the truth-value of E is disregarded. (For nothing can be said *a priori* and in general about the truth-frequency among propositions certain in relation to an E which is of unspecified truth-value.)

If all this is so, then we really have no idea at all how to answer **Q1**, either.

But that very question, like **Q2**, contains in addition a *suggestio falsi* of the most serious kind. It suggests that always when one believes what is certain in relation to one's total evidence, one believes as one should, and asks why this is so. But it is not so. What is true is that if H has probability $= \dfrac{x}{y} = 1$, i.e., is certain, in relation to one's total evidence E, one should have in H a degree of belief which is a fraction $= \dfrac{x}{y} = 1$ of one's degree of belief in E. But if, for example, H has probability $= 1$ in relation to my E, and I have in H a degree of belief which is a fraction > 1, or $= .8$, say, of my degree of belief in E; then while indeed I believe *what* I should, viz., H, it is by no means true that I believe *as* I should. Nor is this false suggestion only of peripheral importance in the present context. On the contrary. The very thing which assessments of probability do (assessments of probability $= 1$ or certainty among them), and which no other propositions do, is to characterise certain *degrees* of belief as rational, and others as not; as distinct from characterising just some *beliefs* as rational, or not.

It would be necessary, in order to free **Q1** from this *suggestio falsi*, to reformulate the question as follows:

Q1′: Why should one have, in a proposition H which has probability $= \dfrac{x}{y} = 1$, i.e., is certain, in relation to one's total evidence E, a degree of belief which is a fraction $= \dfrac{x}{y} = 1$ of one's degree of belief in E?

To *this* question, it will be evident, the original answer **A1** is not only not adequate, but not even appropriate. And what answer could possibly be given to **Q1′**, any more than to **Q2′**, except a repudiationist one? "You told us why one should. Because H is certain in relation to E."

To summarise. An adequate answer to **Q2** could not be a necessary truth connecting probability with truth.

An adequate answer to **Q2** would have to satisfy inconsistent conditions.

The answer **A1** to **Q1**, and all of the possible answers to **Q2** analogous with **A1**, are inadequate, in not reflecting the fact that the obligations to believe what is certain and to believe what is probable in relation to all one's evidence are both independent of the truth-value of that evidence; and it does not seem possible to remedy this defect in either case.

Both **Q1** and **Q2** contain serious *suggestiones falsi*, the avoidance of which would turn these questions into **Q1′** and **Q2′**, *neither* of which is a question admitting of a substantial answer any more than does "Who wrote the novels Scott wrote?" or "What number is three?" Thus the contrast between the apparent answerability of **Q1** and the apparent unanswerability of **Q2** disappears along with those questions themselves.

IV

But someone who asked my original question **Q2** might well mean by it something quite different from the question which in Section III we have seen reason to repudiate. I can think of three such things that Q_2 might mean. In this final section I discuss these.

"Why should one believe . . ." sometimes means the same as "What evidence is there for believing. . . ." Consequently Q_2 might mean: "What evidence is there for believing any of those propositions H which are probable though not certain in relation to one's total evidence E?"

This is clearly a very foolish question. I do not accuse any actual person of having intended to ask it. Yet I am not sure that some of the modishly "sceptical" questions I have seen in print—though usually arbitrarily confined to the special case of induction, and almost always groundlessly fathered on Hume—did not mean the above (perhaps among other meanings). Anyway Q_2, if it ever does mean this, deserves to be answered even more unsympathetically than on any other interpretation of it. For the answer to the above question is clearly just: "E!" And to an *inductive* scepticism, in particular, which was of this degenerate variety, the correct answer would consist just in a report of past experience.

A person might ask Q_2 with, as it were, invisible scare-quotes around the word "probable": he might be wondering whether what *passes with us* for probable really is so. Thus a second possible meaning for Q_2 is this: "Prove that the propositions $P(H/E) = \frac{x}{y} (0 < \frac{x}{y} < 1)$, which are naturally or usually *believed*, are true."

It must be admitted that there are cases, that is, particular values of H, E, and $\frac{x}{y}$, for which this demand cannot be satisfied at a given time, and even that there may be cases for which it cannot be satisfied at any time. A particular "natural" assessment of probability $P(H/E) = \frac{x}{y}$ may be, although natural, false; and on that account permanently incapable of proof. Another particular assessment $P(H/E) = \frac{x}{y}$ may be true as well as natural, and yet be temporarily or permanently incapable of being proved, either through our ignorance or stupidity, or because this particular assessment of probability is simply one of those which cannot be derived from anything else whatever.

Yet it is certain, too, that there are cases even at the present time, in which the above demand can be satisfied. How much can in fact be done in the way of such proofs is much less well known among philosophers than it deserves to be.

Consider for example the following assessment of the probability of a certain Bernoullian inference:

(A) P(a is red/Just two out of a, b, and c are red) = $\frac{2}{3}$.

It is an eminently natural assessment. But it might be thought, and has in fact been thought by good philosophers, to be one of those natural assessments of probability which are destined to remain permanently underived from anything else. Yet one of the things which Carnap made known in

1950 was that that is not so; that on the contrary (A) can easily be derived from extraordinarily weak premises of just the following two kinds.

(B) P(a is red and b is red and c is not red/T) < 1

and

(C) P(a is red/T) = P(b is red/T),

where T is some tautology.[12] So if our questioner were to demand a proof, for example, that the natural assessment of probability (A) is also a true assessment, then his demand could be satisfied at present, and with the greatest *éclat*. (For even the most inveterate opponent of what Carnap calls "inductive logic" will not contest the truth of premises of either the (B) or the (C) kind. The symmetry of individual constants [that is, their uniform exchangeability *salva probabilitate*], which is sufficient for (C), is so indispensably necessary even for deductive logic that no one could afford to deny (C). And (B) is a non-deducibility thesis of the most obvious possible kind, and hence a proposition which the more hardened a "deductivist" one is, the more one will heartily affirm.)

A demand for proofs of the truth of natural assessments of probability, then, is in some cases able at some times to be met, though in other cases or at other times it will not be able to be. Whether or not it can be met in a given case will depend partly on the state of our knowledge, and partly on which particular natural assessment a proof is demanded for.

This shows, however, that the above demand is a perfectly fair and limited demand, which does not express any kind of scepticism whatever about assessments of probability. It is as innocuous as a demand, say, that natural *arithmetical* beliefs be proved to be true: a demand which no doubt can be met in some cases at some times though not in all, and which expresses no kind of scepticism about arithmetical propositions.

The question Q2, therefore, if and when it means just this demand, is likewise perfectly innocuous. It expresses no kind of scepticism about assessments of probability, and, hence, need occupy us here no further.

What *would* express a kind of scepticism would be a demand that *every* assessment made of the probability of one proposition in relation to another be proved. It is certainly impossible to satisfy *this* demand. For an assessment of the probability of one proposition in relation to another can be validly derived only from premises which themselves include other assessments of the probability of propositions in relation to others. It must not be supposed that there is anything sinister in this. The same is true not only of the kind of probability which we are here concerned with, but of any kind of probability at all. For example, assessments of "factual" probability or of long-run relative-frequency (Carnap's "probability $_2$") can be validly derived only from premises which themselves include other assessments of factual probability or of long-run relative-frequency. Still, it *is* true of the probability of one proposition in relation to another, as well as of all other kinds of probability. And a demand that every assessment made of this kind of probability be proved would therefore be, in effect, a demand that no assessments of this kind of probability ever be made at all.

Just that, though, is clearly a third possibility as to what Q_2 might mean. Earlier I compared Q_2 with "Why should one respect what is sacred?" Now that question *might* mean: "Why should I not just stop ascribing sacredness to anything? What (intellectual) trouble would I get into if I simply let the concept of the sacred drop out of my life?" Well, similarly Q_2 might mean: "Why should I not just stop assessing the probability of propositions in relation to others? What (intellectual) trouble would I get into if I simply let this concept of probability drop out of my life?"

This question about the sacred seems to me to be not only perfectly proper; I do not believe its challenge can be met. *No* intellectual trouble results if one drops the concept of the sacred, and one should drop it. The above question about probability, too, is perfectly proper; but its challenge can be met. The intellectual trouble which a poser of Q_2 gets into, if Q_2 means this challenge, is no less than inconsistency.

My poser of Q_2, it will be recalled, asked that question on a specific ground: the ground that any H probable but not certain in relation to his total evidence E may be false. But now, what does his "H . . . *may be false*" mean? Not, for example, what in another context it might mean: that H is not a necessary truth. No, that H may be false clearly means here that the falsity of H is possible in *relation to E*. But to say that is no different from saying that the probability of H in relation to E is < 1. And to say that is to make a certain assessment of the probability of one proposition in relation to another. If, therefore, someone who asked my Q_2 meant by it a proposal to refrain from making assessments of the probability of propositions in relation to others, then his proposal would be inconsistent with the ground on which he makes it. For that ground itself consists of assessments of the probability of propositions in relation to others; assessments, namely, of the $P(H/E) < 1$ kind.

"But there is a great deal of difference," Professor Popper for one would object here, "between assessments of probability of the $P(H/E) < 1$ kind, and those of the $P(H/E) = \frac{x}{y}$ kind, where $0 < \frac{x}{y} < 1$. The former are completely innocent, and can even be discovered to be true by means of empirical counter-examples. It is the latter kind of assessment alone which one should refrain from making. For that kind is admitted by Carnap to rest in the end on intuition; and one should not rely on intuition. If your charge of inconsistency were correct, one could not so much as point out a fallacy —and that is all that making the $P(H/E) < 1$ kind of assessment comes to —without getting oneself implicated in the number-magic of so-called inductive logic. But this is absurd." [13]

Unfortunately for this reply, assessments of the kind Popper objects to, $P(H/E) = \frac{x}{y}$ where $0 < \frac{x}{y} < 1$, are in some cases *derivable from* assessments of kinds he does not object to. The derivability of (A) above from premises just of the (B) and (C) kinds is an example. But more importantly still, with trifling exceptions, reliance on intuition is required in learning the truth *even of assessments of the $P(H/E) < 1$ kind*.

It will be possible to learn the truth of $P(H/E) < 1$ purely empirically: if

E and H are constants (i.e., if $P(H/E) < 1$ assesses the probability of a concrete argument, not of every member of a certain *class* of arguments); if E is true; if E is observational; if not-H is true; if not-H is observational; if E-and-not-H is observational. For then it will be possible to discover that E-and-not-H is *possible*, by discovering empirically that it is true. But if any one of the above exceedingly restrictive conditions fails, then it will not be possible to learn the truth of $P(H/E) < 1$ empirically.

For example, it is impossible to learn, from experience alone, even so meagre a fragment of elementary logical truth as:

(D) P(x is a present member of the Politburo/All present members of the Politburo are men and x is a man) < 1.

Observational counter-examples do of course exist, to the class of arguments every member of which is correctly assessed by (D) as being fallible. Indeed, they abound, since each man not a present member of the Politburo is one such counter-example. But the truth of (D) could not be learnt just by observing one or any number of those counter-examples. Such observation would not teach us the truth of (D) unless it were supplemented by knowledge of the *symmetry of individual constants*. We all do have such knowledge, of course. But no one will maintain that this knowledge is empirical.[14]

If even so small and uninteresting a non-deducibility thesis as (D) cannot be learnt without at least some reliance on intuition, still less can large and interesting ones be learnt without it. The non-deducibility theses of Hume, for example, mentioned earlier, and the thesis of inductive fallibilism among them, certainly cannot be learnt without it. Those assessments, and almost every other assessment of the $P(H/E) < 1$ kind, are quite as empirically inaccessible as assessments of the $P(H/E) = \frac{x}{y}$ kind where $0 < \frac{x}{y} < 1$.

The inconsistency which I pointed out above, then, cannot be escaped by pleading that assessments of probability of the $P(H/E) < 1$ kind are "only little ones." They are only little ones, in the sense that $P(H/E) < 1$ is a far weaker proposition than, for example, $P(H/E) = \frac{2}{3}$. But, still, assessments of probability are what they are, and with the trifling exceptions noticed above, the truth of $P(H/E) < 1$ can be learnt only in the same non-empirical way as the truth of $P(H/E) = \frac{2}{3}$.

Q2, if it means the first of the things considered in this section, is foolish; if it means the second, it is innocuous; if it means the third, it is inconsistent. And these are all the things I have been able to think of that Q2 might mean, if it were not the question which we saw reason in Section III to repudiate.

The inconsistent position which was discussed a moment ago as a possibility is at least perilously close to the *actual* position of most contemporary philosophers of science, if what was said of the latter in Section II is true. I said there that these philosophers systematically refrain from assessing (though especially from assessing favourably) the probability of scientific conclusions in relation to their evidence, and that the historical *cause* of their so refraining is chiefly the influence of Hume's inductive fallibilism. Now, if that is true, then all that would be needed to make their position the inconsistent one which was discussed above is that inductive fallibilism (as well as being the cause of it) should be taken as a *ground* for not assessing the probability of scientific conclusions in relation to their evidence. For that would be, again, to take certain assessments of probability, of the $P(H/E) < 1$ kind, as a ground for not assessing probabilities.

Well, *is* the truth of inductive fallibilism ever taken as a ground for not assessing probabilities in contemporary philosophy of science? It seems to me to be constantly so taken. I am not aware, for example, of any *ground* of the Popperians' hostility to the Carnapians' proposal to assess the probability of inductive arguments, except in the end just this, that inductive arguments *are* fallible! But I will not lengthen an already long essay by trying now to document this accusation. It will be safe, though, to speak hypothetically: *if* the mere possibility of a false conclusion with true premisses is widely taken as a ground for not assessing the probability of scientific arguments, then our current philosophy of science contains a massive inconsistency. We would be no better than, in fact we would be exactly like, another group of contemporary irrationalists, the antinomian pantheists, to whom, grotesquely, nothing is sacred, *on the ground that everything is*. And just as those persons, while thinking they have dispensed with the concept of the sacred, are secretly those who are most intoxicated with it, so we, while thinking we never assess the probability of scientific arguments, would secretly be in fact the persons who most constantly and even obsessively do so.

NOTES

1. W. C. Salmon, *The Foundations of Scientific Inference* (Pittsburgh, 1967), p. 79.

2. J. M. Keynes, *A Treatise on Probability* (London, 1921), p. 322; emphasis added.

3. See Salmon, *Foundations*, pp. 48–49, 74–79; "Symposium on Inductive Evidence," *American Philosophical Quarterly*, 2 (1965), 265–70, 277–80; "The Justification of Inductive Rules of Inference," in *The Problem of Inductive Logic*, ed. Imre Lakatos, Studies in Logic and the Foundations of Mathematics No. 2 (Amsterdam, 1968), pp. 24–43.

4. Salmon, *Foundations*, p. 79; see also p. 52. The same is said in Salmon, "Justification," 33.

5. I have tried to trace some of the historical fortunes of this thesis in D. C. Stove, *Probability and Hume's Inductive Scepticism* (Oxford, 1973), chap. 8.

6. Ibid., chaps. 2–4.

7. Hume's inductive scepticism, if I have understood it rightly, is an assessment of probability belonging to the comparative kind which Keynes called "judgments of irrelevance." In particular it is the thesis that for all tautological E, and for all E′ and H such that the argument from E′ to H is inductive, $P(H/E.E') = P(H/E)$. That is, it asserts that the conclusions of inductive arguments are not even more probable, in relation to their premisses, than they are in relation to tautological evidence alone. This is clearly a very unfavourable assessment of the probability in question, and inconsistent with describing the conclusions of inductive arguments as being, in relation to their premisses, "probable" in any sense of that vague but still unmistakably *favourably*-evaluative word. (Much as, if a man is not even taller than the average man, he is *a fortiori* not "tall.")

8. For other examples, see Stove, *Probability*, pp. 125–32. To these might be added the following, from Salmon, *Foundations*, p. 52 (emphasis added): *"As Hume has shown,*

we have no reason to suppose that probable conclusions will often be true and improbable ones will seldom be true."

That is sheer invention masquerading as history. And unfortunately this is a variety of mischief which is far easier to do than to undo. What indeed can one do against such a thing, except give it a flat denial? I say, then, that Hume did not show what Salmon here says he showed; that he never attempted to show it; that it never occurred to him to attempt to show it.

Between Salmon's assertion and my counter-assertion, the matter now rests entirely with the texts. In order to prove the truth of his assertion and the falsity of mine, all Salmon needs to do, though also what he must do, is to put before us those passages in which Hume showed what he is here claimed to have shown.

For Salmon, or anyone who wishes on his behalf to accept this challenge, perhaps the least unpromising place to start, would be Book I, Part III, Section XI, Paragraph VIII of the *Treatise*—though Salmon has never referred to that passage, or, indeed, to the *Treatise* at all. But they should also be warned that up to the present no writer on Hume has been able to get out of that paragraph any clear philosophical matter at all, let alone anything important. The same is true, indeed, of this baffling Section XI as a whole (apart from the two introductory paragraphs and interspersed repetitions of material from earlier sections of Book I, Part III).

9. See R. Carnap, *Logical Foundations of Probability* (Chicago, 1962), p. 580 (Glossary, under "inductive inference") and *passim*. This twentieth-century change in the meaning of "inductive" has had several effects, all bad. One is the trivialisation of the thesis of inductive fallibilism. Another is the disastrous misnaming, by Carnap, of the general theory of the probability of one proposition in relation to another as "inductive logic." See Stove, *Probability*, chaps. 7, 8, and chap. 1, pp. 21–23.

10. See N. Kemp Smith, *The Philosophy of David Hume* (London, 1964).

11. See S. Freud, " 'Civilised Sexual Morality and Modern Nervousness,' " *Collected Papers*, trans. Joan Riviere (London, 1924), II 76–99.

12. In other words (A) holds as given only that our assessments of probability are, in Carnap's terminology, both "regular" and (with respect to individual constants) "symmetrical." This is the foundation of Carnap's proof that (his versions of) the classical "Theorems" associated with the name of Bernoulli hold "for any regular symmetrical confirmation-function." See Carnap, *Logical Foundations of Probability*, chap. 8.

13. The words here are my own, but the views are a summary of those expressed by Popper in his "Theories, Experience and Probabilistic Intuitions," in *Problem of Inductive Logic*, ed. Lakatos, pp. 286–87, 296–97.

14. Popper writes: "I have had students who thought that 'All men are mortal; Socrates is mortal; thus Socrates is a man' was a valid inference. Yet they realised the invalidity of this rule when I discussed with them a counter-example (arising from calling my cat 'Socrates')," ibid., p. 297. It appears then that Popper taught these students that one can learn from a counter-example that every instance of "All F are G and x is G, so x is F" is invalid. If so, he taught them two falsities. For $G = red$, $F = coloured$, for example, "$P(x$ is F/All F are G and x is G$) < 1$" is false. And even if it were true, its truth would not be learnable from a counter-example, for various reasons, among them the one mentioned in the text: the empirical inaccessibility of the symmetry of individual constants.

3

Hume's Problem of Induction: An Appraisal

FARHANG ZABEEH
Roosevelt University

FOR MORE THAN ONE HUNDRED YEARS philosophers of various persuasions such as Kant, Mill, Russell, Broad, Reichenbach, Popper, and many others were seriously troubled by the scandal which Hume's problem of induction was supposed to be.[1] Since then all sorts of strategies have been used for the solution, dissolution, or reformulation of that problem, though none has received universal acceptance.

A partial explanation for this sorry state of affairs is that no one has undertaken the task of examining with care all that Hume wrote on the whole issue of induction and causal inference and their underlying principles—i.e., the presuppositions of this supposed problem.

This essay provides an informal systematization of Hume's numerous assertions and arguments, often puzzling and sometimes conflicting, about the general and particular problems of induction, against the metaphysical nature of causation and the alleged presuppositions of the laws of nature, and of his positive arguments, which are a concatenation of some factual and conceptual material on various features of inference, inductive logic, probability, and the psychology of belief-formation.

I shall then attempt an appraisal of these negative and positive arguments in the light of some recent work and with the hope that those who suffered through "the tragic problem of induction," [2] may find at the end their due reward, "calm of mind, all passion spent."

Hume's arguments are couched within a traditional and a partly original prescriptive philosophical language. To translate this philosophical language into familiar vocabulary is the first step toward systematization of his arguments. The systematization will make the hidden assumptions of his framework explicit and will exhibit the justification of each step of the arguments. We shall see, at the end, how some of these unquestioned assumptions contributed to the persistence of the puzzlement and how their removal may dissolve at least the general problem of induction and end the continuous demand for justification of the inductive method.

Let us notice that the very word "induction," which was used by Bacon and Locke, does not appear, except accidentally, in Hume's text.[3] Instead of "induction," the term often used is "inference" or "probable arguments" or "reason from experience," which is contrasted with "demonstrative" or deductive argument. However, "inference" and "reason" are used in many different ways. One of our tasks is to distinguish between the different senses of such key terms insofar as they are germane to the issue.

I · SYSTEMATIZATION

We begin our systematization by abstracting from Hume's text certain fundamental assertions and assumptions which are used throughout and which constitute a background theory. These may be translated into three theses: Semantic, Syntactic, and Pragmatic. To avoid the charge of arbitrariness, evidence will be cited when necessary.

1. The Semantic Thesis

T1. Significant indicative sentences [4] have truth or probability value; such sentences are either factual (F) or conceptual (C).[5]

T2. Factual or conceptual sentences are reducible to "basic propositions"; [6] basic propositions denote sense data (or their corresponding ideas). (*Reduction* is to be taken as an epistemological search for the origin of concepts or beliefs similar to Locke's backward "historical, plain method.")

T3. Basic propositions are the ultimate premises of the logical reconstruction of our knowledge- or belief-claim.

T4. There are two distinct methods for truth-value assignment. Truth value for (F)-type sentences can be obtained either by direct inspection, in case they are basic propositions, or by induction, in case they are not. It can be obtained for (C)-type sentences either by direct inspection, in case they are basic, or by deduction from certain conceptual relations in conjunction with certain rules.

T4 can be further explained thus:

Let S be any significant indicative sentence of the form

$$(x)\ (y)\ [xRy]$$

Substitute in the brackets "3" for 'x', "=" for 'R' and "2 + 1" for 'y'
We obtain S_1: $3 = 2 + 1$

Since S_1 expresses a mathematically true relation between relata (substituting "$\neq$" for '=' in S_1 turns S_1 to falsehood), then S_1 belongs to (C)-type sentences.

S_1 expresses a mathematically true relation discoverable either by direct inspection, i.e., by finding "repugnancy or contradiction in denying the judgment . . . as long as our idea remains the same" (T 69) or by an appeal to a mathematical principle "in which we can carry on a chain of reasoning to any degree of intricacy." Hume provides a criterion or truth condition for numerical equality in terms of one–one correlation of sets (T 71).

Now substitute "arsenic" for 'x', "causes" for 'R', and "death" for 'y' in the brackets. We obtain S_2: Arsenic causes death; since the denial of S_2 is not self-contradictory, S_2 belongs to (F) type.[7]

2. *The Syntactic Thesis*

T5. The structure of reasoning is inferential. Given that P is the case, Q is inferrible from P.

T6. There are two sorts of inference or reasoning: cognitive and non-cognitive, i.e., psychological, or what Russell called "animal inference."[8] In cognitive inference P and Q are replaceable by sentences; in non-cognitive, by sense data or objects.

T7. There are at least two fundamental sorts of cognitive inferences, i.e., deductive or inductive. For any cognitive inference R, there exists only a finite class of premises substitutable for P.

T8. In the domain of deductive inference, the move from P to Q is valid if and only if P and $\bar{Q}$ is logically impossible, i.e.,

$$P \to Q \longleftrightarrow - (P \wedge \bar{Q})$$

In the domain of inductive inference the move from P to Q is not valid, since it is logically possible that P and $\bar{Q}$.

T9. It is logically necessary that Q if and only if Q is a theorem of a deductive system containing P as an axiom.[9] If so, the ascription of *de dicto* modality to Q is in order, i.e.,

$$P \to Q \longleftrightarrow \square Q$$

De dicto modalities are time-independent.

T10. It is inductively necessary that Q if and only if Q is derivable from P and P is a conjunction of (F)-type sentences containing laws of science or statistical generalizations plus initial conditions. If so, ascription of *de re* modality to Q is in order, i.e.,

$$P \to \boxed{\text{I}}\, Q$$

De re modalities are time-dependent.

In each case the necessity ascribed to Q is of the sort called by medieval logicians *necessitas consequentis*, i.e., what is necessary is the consequent of the conditional and not the whole conditional.[10]

T11. Causal inference is a sub-class of inductive inference such that P and Q contain different spatio-temporal variables. **T11** could be further explained thus:

Let
$$(1)\; Fa_{t1} \wedge Ga'_{t2}$$
$$(2)\; Fb_{t3} \wedge Gb'_{t4}$$
$$(3)\; Fc_{t5} \wedge Gc'_{t6}$$

be a set of conjunction of (F)-type sentences reporting occurrence of certain events at certain times t where 1 is a positive integer, we obtain

$$(4)\ (x)\ (Fx \rightarrow (\exists y)\ Gy)$$

Now we observe $(5)\ Fd_{t7}$

We conclude $(6)\ \boxed{\text{r}}\ (\exists y)\ Gy_{tn}$

But since the necessity of (6) is relative to the necessity of (4), and (4) is not logically necessary, so (6). Hence the invalidity of causal inference. Putting it another way: since the time variable is injected into the premises and the conclusion of the causal inference, and since the argument from the concomitance of events at some time to their recurrence at any time is invalid (by **T9**), causal inference is invalid.[11]

3. The Pragmatic Thesis

T12. Our knowledge of (F)- and (C)-type sentences is either intuitive or inferential. (F)-type sentences are known *a posteriori*. (C)-type sentences are known either intuitively or *a priori*.

T13. Basic propositions are known intuitively and are indubitable.

T14. Non-cognitive inferences are functions of "the union of ideas," and this produces a strong conviction in the inferrer.[12]

T15. It is reasonable to believe in the conclusion Q of an inductive argument if one believes in P, and P contains sentences expressing laws of nature or "strongest probabilities" or "the superior number of past experiments" (T 136), and Q is derived from P.[13]

T16. It is unreasonable to believe that P, i.e., laws of nature, the strongest probabilities, or even "full proof," could never be weakened by a contrary experiment or be falsified by future events.[14]

T17. It is unreasonable to believe in a report of the violation of "the most establish'd laws of nature" by "the Deity or an invisible agent," i.e., in miracles. The probability Pr of the violation of laws L under the following initial conditions i, e.g., a divine agency, testimony of a biased witness (it is highly probable that the witness is self-deceived or deluded), that is, a miracle M, is less than the probability of the laws of nature under initial conditions i_1, and the report of neutral observers, etc., thus:

$$[Pr(i,m) < Pr(i_1,L) \leqq Pr(i,m)]$$

Hume makes use of his semantic and syntactic theses in arguing against, first, the causal maxim; second, the general principle of induction; and third, some particular causal arguments. We shall see how some of these theses are the main source of the puzzles about the nature of induction and of certain unmitigated scepticisms about the rationality of scientific beliefs —in spite of the other sorts of arguments against "superstition of every kind or denomination" (T 271). The pragmatic thesis served him to establish his positive theory on the nature of beliefs and the criteria for identifying well-founded beliefs.

i.—*Criticism of the Causal Maxim*

The causal maxim was used in support of theology; and the general principle of induction or causation served in support of the validity of inductive inference as a super-law covering all the natural laws. Hume attempts to prove the baselessness of both. The double-edged sword of scepticism in his hand struck both the theologians and the natural philosophers (the Cartesians and the Newtonians)—those who tried to prove God's existence by postulating the necessity of cause and those who substituted "the most establish'd laws of nature" for God's will, e.g., the deists. The intention of the great secular philosophers seems to be that by weakening the thesis of the inevitability and absolute certainty of natural laws one also weakens, even more so, the theological systems which are grounded on the causal maxim. If it could be shown that the belief in the uniformity of nature or the claim that "Nature is governed by immutable laws which she never transgresses" (Galileo) is unsupportable, or that the Newtonians' over-confidence in the universal applicability of the laws of motion—a projection of certain observed regularities in our idiosyncratic region of the universe to the entire cosmos—is unfounded, it could also be shown that there is no support at all for the rational foundation of theology. So writes Hume:

> While we cannot give a satisfactory reason, why we believe, after a thousand experiments, that a stone will fall, or fire burn; can we ever satisfy ourselves concerning any determination, which we may form, with regard to the origin of worlds, and the situation of nature, from, and to eternity? [EHU 162].

The causal maxim is stated in three different forms:

(1) " 'Tis a general maxim in philosophy, that *whatever begins to exist, must have a cause of existence*" (T 78).

(2) It "is not from knowledge or any scientific reasoning, that we derive the opinion of the necessity of a cause to every new production . . ." (T 82).

(3) ". . . *Ex nihilo, nihil fit,* by which the creation of matter was excluded . . ." (EHU 164, note).

Hume argues, first: The maxim is not a conceptual truth, because if it were, its denial would be self-contradictory, which it is not, by **T4**;

second: The modal operator "necessity" (or "must") is misapplied, since there is neither logical nor inductive necessity that

$$(x) \, (x \text{ is an event} \rightarrow \Box \text{ or } \boxed{\text{I}} \, (\exists \, y) \text{ such that } y \text{ causes } x)$$

by **T9** and **T10**;

third: The maxim is not a law of science of the causal kind. All that experience suggests is "that such particular causes must *necessarily* have

(1) " 'Tis a general maxim in philosophy, that *whatever begins to exist,* tence has a beginning must have a cause;

fourth: It is logically possible that P if P is "There is an event without a cause" that is, "$-\Box\bar{p}$," by **T8**; "Not only the will of the supreme Being may create matter; but, for aught we know *a priori*, the will of any other being might create it . . ." (EHU 164, note).

Hume shows not only that the maxim is unsupportable by deductive or inductive reason, but also that none of the purported deductive justifications offered by Hobbes, Spinoza, Clark, and Locke is valid. It was Hume's refutation of the causal maxim which awakened Kant from his "dogmatic slumber." Kant feared that the destruction of this paradigm of a metaphysical principle may leave no place for any future metaphysics. "Since the origin of metaphysics, so far as we know its history, nothing has ever happened which might have been more decisive to the fortune of the science than the attack made upon it by David Hume." [15]

As is well known, Kant's solution of Hume's argument against the causal maxim (and the principle of induction), though meant to be a rational justification of science, was itself based on his dogmatic assumptions concerning that *a priori* nature and universal validity of Aristotelian logic, Euclidean geometry, and Newtonian mechanics.

ii.—*Criticism of the General Principle of Induction*

Immediately after the rejection of the causal maxim, there appears another problem. "The next question, then, shou'd naturally be, *how experience gives rise to such a principle?* But as I find it will be more convenient to sink this question in the following, *Why we conclude, that such particular causes must necessarily have such particular effects, and why we form an inference from one to another?*" (T 82). This is the problem of justification of induction which appears first in the causal context and later in a more general form: "*why from this experience we form any conclusion beyond those past instances, of which we have had experience*" (T 91).

Hume assumes that if there is an answer to his questions (the questions about the justification of a particular causal inference and about the justification of a particular inductive inference) it should be by an appeal to the very general principle, call it "PI," "*that instances, of which we have had no experience, must resemble those, of which we have had experience, and that the course of nature continues always uniformly the same*" (T 89).

Now suppose PI in fact justifies the inference from causal law to its instances, or from instances back to causal laws and thereby makes the inference deductively valid, may we not take the question a step further to ask what justifies the principle itself?

Hume did not deny the legitimacy of this second-order question but has produced strong objections against any argument in support of the answer to it, arguing that no deductive or inductive defense of the principle of induction is possible. Hume's argument is as follows:

(1) The principle cannot be supported by an appeal to the rule of deductive inferences, by **T8** and **T9**; i.e., to affirm the antecedent and deny the consequent of a report of a causal sequence is logically possible. "We can at least conceive a change in the course of nature . . ." (T 89). The principle cannot be supported by appeal to inductively supported regularities or frequencies without circularity.

(2) Since "probability is founded on the presumption of a resemblance

betwixt those objects, of which we have had experience, and those, of which we have had none; . . . therefore 'tis impossible this presumption can arise from probability" (T 90).

We can summarize the conclusions of Hume's arguments:

1: The metaphysical belief in the necessity of a cause for every event or class of events is unsupportable, that is

$$(x) \ (x \text{ is an event or class of events} \rightarrow (\exists M) \ x \text{ is caused by M})$$

is not provable.

2: However, even a more guarded belief in the necessity of a cause or causes for an event or set of events likewise is unsupportable; that is

$$(\exists x) \ (X \text{ is an event} \rightarrow \Box \ (\exists y) \ x \text{ is caused by y})$$

is not provable.

3: PI cannot be used as a meta-covering law such that in conjunction with a covering law, it could make the inference valid, since PI itself is not supportable by reason.

4: Hume's question about the ground for an inductive inference from "particular causes" or "this experience" or "those past instances" to "particular effects" or future experience or instances has not been answered at this point.

The assumption that such an inference is valid is rejected, but this question "Why do we make such invalid inferences?" at this juncture remains unanswered, though, as we shall see, Hume does provide some answers to his own question.

iii.—*Criticism of Some Particular Causal Inference*

Hume sometimes criticizes a particular inductive inference with the intention of weakening our confidence in certain "established" regularities. For example, he points out how the existence of certain hidden variables, i.e., "hidden causes," sometimes changes the deep structure of a material object without causing change in its surface qualities.

> In vain do you pretend to have learned the nature of bodies from your past experience. Their secret nature, and consequently all their effects and influence, may change, without any change in their sensible qualities. This happens sometimes, and with regard to some objects: Why may it not happen always, and with regard to all objects? [EHU 38].

Similar arguments are produced to show that even the most solid inductive inferences may turn out to be mistaken: e.g., a sudden earthquake may arise and tumble my house, my best friend may be seized with a sudden and unknown frenzy and stab me (EHU 91). These arguments are not of the same sort adduced for proving the invalidity of any inductive argument on the ground of the logical possibility of change in the course of nature. Rather, the arguments are *a posteriori*, inasmuch as they start with premises about some discovered anomalies. It is argued that since the existence of these anomalies does disturb our confidence in some established regularities, it is in vain to pretend that we can discover nature's secret by experience.

Before we consider Hume's positive contribution to the formation of inductive belief and the rules to be used for the improvement of inductive inference, it is proper to make some assessments of his negative theses.

II · AN APPRAISAL

The arguments against the metaphysical principle of causation, the possibility of validating a causal inference by appeal to a meta-covering law, i.e., PI, and the validity of inference from a particular causal law, are all unobjectionable.

The use of theses **T8**, **T9**, and **T10** for destruction of these arguments is correct and subtle, and these theses, though themselves vague and informal, are not incompatible with "the establish'd laws" of modal logic and the covering-law model of explanation.

There are, however, two important questions which should be raised (a) with regard to a supposed answer to Hume's question about justification of induction by appeal to PI, and (b) with regard to his question about the justification of a particular causal inference. Let us start with (a).

After Hume raises the question about whether there is any reason to conclude, "that such particular causes must necessarily have such particular effects," he writes "If reason determined us, it would proceed upon that principle," i.e., PI, which is stated in various names:

"*that instances, of which we have had no experience, must resemble those, of which we have had experience, and that the course of nature continues always uniformly the same*" (T 89);

"that the future will resemble the past . . ." (EHU 37);

"that like causes, in like circumstances, will always produce like effects" (A 15).

The question is whether in fact the mixture of such seemingly similar assumptions is ever made in prediction or retrodiction based upon induction. We need to separate the big assumption about the uniformity of nature from the more guarded assumption of the continuation of certain established regularities under certain specifiable conditions.

The assumption of the uniformity of nature, if ever made, is made to guarantee the validity of an inference from a causal law which, however, is entirely vacuous. Indeed it is like another empty assumption, i.e., "the religious hypothesis," the argument to the effect that the universe has a purposive order. It was Hume's insight that since any change is compatible with the providential design, and since "No new fact can ever be inferred from the religious hypothesis; no event foreseen or foretold . . ." (EHU 146), that assumption is utterly empty. In like manner the empty assumption of the uniformity of the course of nature cannot support our inference with regard to a particular prediction.

To the question whether such an assumption was made by the natural philosophers in Hume's time, there may be a positive answer, and, if so, Hume's warning about the unavailability of this assumption is in order. Scientists do not simply project every earthly regularity into the entire cosmos, however, even if some philosophers (with the exception of the starry-eyed cosmologists) think that they do.

The other assumption is about the continuity of certain causal laws. Such an assumption has the force of a *ceteris paribus* clause or the force of statements of initial conditions in prediction and explanation. Without specification of these initial conditions, even the classical laws of mechanics are inapplicable. We know that the range of the applicability of the classical laws of mechanics is limited, e.g., speed must not approach the speed of light, the quantities must not approach the quantities of elementary particles, temperature must not get too close to absolute zero. The assumption of the continuity of certain confirmed and non-exceptional causal laws under certain specified conditions does in fact justify our prediction and explanation, though the assumption of the continuity of any regularity under all possible conditions does not. Indeed, Hume himself seems to agree that such inferences are "just" or are "justly" done. Thus he writes "One who concludes somebody to be near him, when he hears an articulate voice in the dark, *reasons justly and naturally*; tho' that conclusion be deriv'd from nothing but custom . . ." (T 225; emphasis added), and "Heat and light are collateral effects of fire, and the one effect may *justly be inferred* from the other" (EHU 27; emphasis added).

Such inferences are based upon the experience of a constant and invariable connection between causes and effects or properties of natural kinds. "Were there nothing to bind them together, the inference would be entirely precarious" (EHU 27).

Where Hume disagrees with such justification of an inductive inference is with the implicit use of "reason" as a ground of justification. Hume sometimes speaks as if the use of "reason" and of "inference" in its cognitive sense should be dropped altogether and be replaced by a psychological concept of "habit or custom"—habits then are explained by the principle of association (T 97).

These suggestions are confusing (and produced confusion) especially when Hume himself provides a better ground for inductive inference than a conditioned reflex or an animal inference.

Let us look with a sterner eye through Hume's questioning eye. His persistent questions are:

"*Why we conclude, that such particular causes must necessarily have such particular effects* . . ." (T 82);

"*why from this experience we form any conclusion beyond those past instances, of which we have had experience*" (T 91); and

"what is the nature of that evidence which assures us of any real existence and matter of fact, beyond the present testimony of our senses, or the records of our memory" (EHU 26)?

In all these questions what is challenged is the reason for our inference (either deductive or inductive) from P to Q. It was assumed that we do know the antecedent P of the conditional P then Q. But our knowledge-claim to the consequent Q is questioned. That is, it is easily assumed that

(1) we do know certain causal sequences;

(2) we do know something about the experience of the moment and about some past experiences similar to the experience of the moment;

(3) we can correctly speak of such experiences and such causal sequences.

Hume's basis for belief in (1), (2), and (3) are his theses **T3**, **T7**, and **T13**; that is, the theses that basic propositions are the ultimate premisses of the logical reconstruction of our knowledge- or belief-claim—that there are a finite number of premisses in every cognitive inference, and that basic propositions are known intuitively and are indubitable. There is, however, no compelling reason to believe that there are such things as basic propositions which are known by mere direct inspection and thus indubitable and which are the ultimate premisses of our knowledge. This is so because our knowledge of such propositions presupposes conceptualization; i.e., certain experiences belong to certain linguistic categories.

Here the semantic principle is at work; that is, in order for me to speak about any object or event, let that object or event be an experience itself or the name of that experience. I must use its name or its description. I cannot use the object or event itself.[16] However, to do this is to transcend the experience by conceptualizing it, and to conceptualize it is to make an inductive inference.

If this is the case about the antecedent: *"this instance or experience"* and *"those past experiences,"* it is also the case about the consequent: *"such particular effects and conclusions beyond those past instances"* (since "instance" must mean instance of some causal law or regularity). Without a rudiment of semantic and syntactic regularities, we cannot speak of knowing any particular causes or experiences of the present or the past.

The well-worn idea of Humean phenomenalists that sense-data statements are incorrigible "except linguistically" is the point at issue. But do admit the exception, and no sentences remain incorrigible, for the reason that sentences are made of words, and the relation between words and sense data is contingent. Hence we should give up Hume's presupposition about the incorrigibility and indubitability of the premisses of an inductive argument, even if this move requires giving up radical empiricism which is a large portion of Hume's epistemology. Consider Russell's suggestion about basic propositions: "most object-words are condensed induction; this is true of the word 'dog.' We must avoid such words, if we wish to be merely re-cording what we perceive. To do this is very difficult, and requires a special vocabulary." [17]

However, why "most object-words"? Indeed, if we use any words, "even a special vocabulary," we have to transcend the given phoneme if we wish to use it as a word. This argument is Kantian inasmuch as it is compatible with Kant's view that knowledge presupposes the use of concepts and that in using concepts we unify or "contract" our perceptions. But the very use of concepts necessitates the existence of a language, and there cannot be any language without rules, and the use of rules requires, among other things, inductive inference. Learning language, like learning other techniques, is receiving cultural inputs by instruction from an institution, even though it also requires a genetic background or innate disposition. So it seems that here the general Lamarckian explanation of adaptation as the result of direct instruction given through repetition by the environment to an aim-seeking organism has force if we substitute "culture" for "environment" and "human" for "organism."

But instruction—that is, learning from others—is not just learning by the mere repetition of associating ideas with symbols.

Learning language requires the use of words, and that requires making cognitive inference from certain semantic and syntactic regularities. This would be the case even if there could be a private language, i.e., someone *ex nihilo* inventing and using his own language. Still, so impoverished a monologue stands in need of some conceptualization.

Conceptualization is a name for what Hume calls "formation of ideas." Hume observes that the passive association of ideas is checked, on the level of cognitive activity, by certain conventional restraints. He notes that in learning general terms—e.g., "square," "figure," "government," "conquest," etc.—we need to "fix the meaning of the word" so that "we may avoid talking nonsense . . . and may perceive any repugnance among the ideas. . . ." The "custom, which we have acquir'd of attributing certain relations to ideas, still follows the words, and makes us immediately perceive the absurdity of that proposition [that in the war the weaker have always recourse to conquest] . . ." (T 22, 23).

Hume does not have a theory about the trinomial relation of impressions, ideas, and language. But when he uses "idea" not as a mere "copy" of an impression but as a concept, as he often does, he notices the role which language plays in cognitive activities. He speaks, for example, about "certain characters and letters present either to our memory or senses; which characters we likewise remember to have been us'd as the signs of certain ideas . . ." (T 83); and about certain conventional usage, "a certain form of words" like the expression "I promise" which when used under certain conditions are binding (T 523); or about "the general language" of morals (which is contrasted with "the language of self-love") when used for moral evaluation (EPM 222).

This oblique awareness of the operation of such linguistic "customs" in geometry and morality is revealed also in the idea that the learner may misapply the customary rules. In a passage under the title "Of the inference from the impression to the idea," he notes the possibility of mistake in the inference from impression to idea—a mistake which is a common feature of every inference: "When we pass from a present impression to the idea of any object, we might possibly have separated the idea from the impression, and have substituted any other idea in its room" (T 87).

Thus it seems that Hume sees that the formation of concepts and the use of words are corrigible, but having an experience is not since "the only thing, that can stop them [our inferences], is an impression of the memory or senses, beyond which there is no room for doubt or enquiry" (T 83).

However, since speaking about "particular causes," "this experience . . . and those past instances," and "the present testimony of our senses, or the records of our memory" presupposes learning conceptual lessons, we should give up questioning only the conclusion of an inductive argument and leaving its premises alone as if they are unquestionably yielding. Since the premises of an inductive argument are exactly in the same position as the supposed unwarranted conclusion, and since the sceptical doubt about induction could not arise unless we grant these inductively laden premises, and since to accept these premises is to deny by implication the falsity of the sceptical conclusion, we conclude that the general problem of induction is a pseudo-problem. We give up therefore Hume's theses T_3, T_7, and T_{13}, and with them the general problem of induction.

Note that we *could* stop the infinite regress of justifying the premises of an inductive argument by *deciding* to accept sense-data sentences as those needing no further justification. If we do so, we should also accept the method of induction because without it sense-data statements could not be known, asserted, and utilized.

There are some strong arguments against blocking the regress via sense data. One is Popper's: "That theories or expectations are built into our very sense organs shows that the epistemology of induction breaks down even before having taken its first step. It cannot start from sense data or perceptions and build our theories upon them, since there are no such things as sense data or perceptions which are not built upon theories (or expectations, that is, the biological predecessors of linguistically formulated theories)." [18]

It seems that not only does the epistemology of induction break down even before taking its first step (as Popper rightly states), but also its logic—because in each case, the background of inductive inference, either the psycho-biological background of animal inference or the socio-cultural and conceptual background of cognitive inference, was not taken into the epistemology and methodology of our knowledge. The ghost of the Cartesian solipsists seeking certitude, but looking in the wrong place, haunted the empiricists from Locke to Hume, Russell, Moore, Ayer, and Carnap. Hume, however, does consider the psycho-biological background of noncognitive inference and its role in belief-formation, the theory considered by his followers as philosophical evasion!

To see the importance of the background theory, let us consider for a moment a supposed autonomous domain of knowledge; namely, the deductive sciences. The undeniable contribution of Hume to the traditional problem of induction is his argument against the validity of inductive inference. In so arguing, Hume takes for his model the structure of valid inference and shows, by an appeal to that model, the invalidity of induction. (Even though that very model was later subjected to some sceptical attack of a very dubious kind.[19])

Pursuing Hume's use of that model, we shall see some noteworthy similarities between deductive and inductive inferences. By showing that deductive systems are not free from background theory, we hope to remove a certain unmitigated scepticism, which is still in vogue, concerning the vulnerability and indefensibility of any inductive inference.

In recent times certain deductive systems have been axiomatized. In an axiomatization certain primitive concepts are singled out as basic for the definition of other concepts and certain sentences are taken as axioms—deriving other sentences of the system by deduction. Axiomatization reveals hidden assumptions which could not be justified within the system itself.

The step from axiomatization to formalization of a deductive system is taken when these background assumptions, including logic, the meaning of primitives, etc., are transmitted into the system itself. But even a pure formalized system is not free from a semantic background when the issue is the meaning of sentences and the interpretation of the system.[20]

Aristotle, long before the construction of formalized systems and the recognition of background assumptions and, hence, of the limitations of the system, observed the limits of his own deductive logic. The limitation of his system was revealed when Aristotle observed that though valid syllogisms are reducible to some basic ones, and hence their validity could be justified, there is no way of justifying within the system those basic syllogisms or some of the basic laws employed in the reduction, e.g., the law of contradiction. He tried then to provide some pragmatic justification, e.g., showing the indispensability and the utility of the law of contradiction.

In modern logic there is a consistency proof, but in the end an inconsistent system in which every formula is derivable cannot be useful.[21] The point of this disgression about deductive systems is that in a particular deductive system an inference may be justified by an appeal to the axioms or the rules of inference of that system (even though here there are known limitations, e.g., not every truth is provable within a deductive system). It makes no sense, however, to ask for justification of the axioms or of the inference rules within the system, or for justification of the system as a whole or of the method of deduction. By analogy it makes no sense at all to ask for the justification of induction as such.

Induction, like deduction itself, is a method of justifying beliefs. The method itself could not be justified though it could be improved upon. Since it is sensible to ask whether a theorem is proven by *modus tollens* or by mathematical induction, it makes sense to ask whether an inference in a domain of science is obtained by enumerative induction or by one crucial experiment. As we check and correct the reliability of our instruments of testing or even of our senses when we suspect their normal functioning, so we check the correctness of our inference by seeing whether the sample is fair, the experiment biased, or relevant facts discarded. Also it is sensible to axiomatize our intuitions about rational action in the face of uncertainty, to formulate canons of induction, correct the logic of induction, e.g., by observing why some regularities are projectable and why others are not, and prevent inductive inconsistencies.[22] Still using the analogy: it makes sense to observe the background of the inductive method by noting the psychological and biological conditions of man in the pursuit of knowledge —just as it makes sense to observe behind the abstraction of the Euclidian system the existence of concrete geometrical information, or to observe behind the abstractions of Aristotle's logic concrete cases of correct reasoning.

The temptation to provide an answer to Hume's non-sense question was so strong that varieties of solutions were offered, sometimes for the general problem of justifying induction and at other times for solutions to other puzzles of inductive inference. It led to Kant's synthetic *a priori* justification of science, to Keynes' principle of limited variety, to Russell's postulates for validation of scientific method, to Feigel's vindication of induction as a policy well adopted to achieve certain aims, and to Popper's denial that induction is the method of science.

But each solution has been challenged by critics on various grounds, and none has received universal acceptance. What was not challenged was the very existence of the general problem of induction.

Let us now consider (*b*) and provide some answer to the criticism of particular inductive inference.

The so-called inductive fallibilism is the application of **T8** to causal or inductive inferences which is made in science and ordinary prediction. It is argued that since it is logically possible for the course of nature to be otherwise, the argument from P to Q is invalid (if P stands for (*F*)-type sentences reporting the occurrence of an event at time t_1 and Q stands for the same type sentences but states the occurrence of an event at time t_2). So it is. We all agree with Hume that neither "the sun will not rise tomorrow" nor "that it will rise" is "demonstratively false" (EHU 26) by **T8**.

Hume's argument from the failure of a particular inductive inference to the conclusion for the unreliability of induction is itself invalid. It moves from saying that an object x at time *t* has a property *a* (*a* is anomalous behavior) to the conclusion that

(x) (x is an object → x could have *a* at all times)

to a further conclusion that it is "in vain [to] pretend to have learned the nature of bodies from your past experience" (EHU 38).

Remembering that the very existence of anomalies is established by induction, we can see that the argument does not have any force against induction as such. The existence of irregularities will not force us to give up making inferences; rather, we shall continue to make them, just as before—let the course of nature be as risky as the wheel of fortune. So even in the face of anomalies, we do not give up seeking explanations, for the very reason that such a search is conducive to our animal existence and to the growth of knowledge. Rather than give up the inductive method, we try to explain the anomalies by auxiliary hypotheses having inductive supports. The existence of anomalies is also cited by Popper as an argument against induction. Popper in fact uses some of Hume's examples in order to cast doubt on our reliance upon induction.

That "the sun will rise tomorrow" and that "other bread must also nourish me" are falsified when negative instances such as "the midnight sun" or "a case of poisoned bread" are cited.

Popper then states that Hume "believed that induction by repetition was logically untenable—that rationally, or logically, *no amount* of observed instances can have the slightest bearing upon unobserved instances. This is Hume's negative solution of the problem of induction, a solution which I fully endorse." [23] Nonetheless Popper himself is the first to see how auxiliary hypotheses lead to theoretical triumph when their postulation does not decrease the testability of the system and when they themselves are tested independently of the general theory. To Hume's sceptical thesis *"That even after the observation of the frequent or constant conjunction of objects, we have no reason to draw any inference concerning any object beyond those of which we have had experience . . ."* (T 139), we retort that we have every *reason* to draw inferences if certain other conditions (apart from constant conjunction) are satisfied, among them elimination of "superficial accident" and "the repetition of experiment beyond the given and past experiences" as mentioned by Hume himself in other contexts.

We may use Philo's argument (Hume's) against Hume. "That a stone will fall, . . . that the earth has solidity, we have observed a thousand and a thousand times; and when any new instance of this nature is presented, we draw without hesitation the accustomed inference. The exact similarity of the cases gives us a perfect assurance of a similar event; and a stronger evidence is never desired nor sought after" (D 144). On the contrary. We have *no reason* at all to believe that just as no sequence of luck in a game of chance is evidence that the next bet will win, so no causal sequence of events is evidence for their recurrence. The astronomical improbability that a regular concomitance of events is pure coincidence like a game of pure chance increases when we realize (1) that the very idea of chance or randomness presupposes some notion of order—i.e., randomness is relative to order and is defined in terms of "incompressibility of information into a formula" with resultant unpredictability; (2) that the search for a causal explanation begins after we rule out pure chance. In parapsychology, for example, only after finding that the odds against performing certain acts by chance are about a million to one (for example, forecasting the roll of a die inside a box 95 out of 100 times) do we look for a possible explanation of that feat.

The problem of the scope and the limit of projectable regularities, and the problem about positive and negative confirmation of properties, are problems within the logic of induction and should not be confused with the general problem of induction. To repeat: it is quite unreasonable to believe on the basis of Hume's prescriptive epistemology that since "all events seem entirely loose and separate," and since "all impressions are internal and perishing existences," therefore every combination of events is a like possibility. Indeed in such a disjointed universe no positive inference could be made.

Hume himself contrasted the *a priori* or the logical possibility of the occurrence of events with the *a posteriori* occurrence of causes and effects, which is a legitimate ground for inference. "If we reason *a priori*, anything may appear able to produce anything. The falling of a pebble may, for aught we know, extinguish the sun; or the wish of a man control the planets in their orbits. It is only experience, which teaches us the nature and bounds of cause and effect, and enables us to infer the existence of one object from that of another" (EHU 164).

We should be aware that Hume, having identified "rational" with "demonstrative," insists that there is no rational foundation, "no reason," for inference from causes to effects and vice versa—though there is *natural* and *habitual* ground.

Hume's epistemological frame of impression–idea is the background for his sceptical arguments about induction. Outside this background and within his theory of natural belief, in which the existence of the "external universe" and the existence of instincts and habits were taken as a matter of course, there is no problem of the justification of induction, and Hume himself does not believe that any justification of induction is needed (though he did not see the senselessness of raising the problem, or the absurdity of saying that we have "no reason" to draw inferences transcending experience). To that extent the judgment of Strawson stands: "It is said that there is a problem of induction, and that Hume posed it; it must be added that he solved it." [24]

III · HUME'S POSITIVE CONTRIBUTION

"[P]hilosophical decisions are nothing but the reflections of common life, methodized and corrected" (EHU 162).

The author of the so-called problem of induction is also the author of the psycho-logical theory of inference, and the methodology of belief-justification. In a passage in the *Abstract*, Hume prides himself on having taken Leibniz' advice; [25] i.e., on having paid some attention to "probabilities, and those measures of evidence on which life and action intirely depend" (A 8) and which have been neglected in the "common systems of logic" (A 7). Hume shares Bacon's suspicion of the utility of logic and Locke's disbelief in its autonomy. The autonomy of logic, even of God, is one of the rationalists' dogmas. Locke sees otherwise. "God has not been so sparing to Men to make them barely two-legged Creatures, and left to *Aristotle* to make them Rational. . . ." [26] Hume goes farther and tries to establish that "divine reason" itself is the by-product of certain natural and habitual dispositions shared by humans and animals.

While providing all kinds of reasons for the thesis that reason cannot be supported by reason (and, moreover, that reason alone cannot cause action), he also tries to provide some answer to the question: how is it that it is nonetheless "reasonable" to believe (and act) in some regularities and "unreasonable" to do otherwise, i.e., not to believe in those regularities or to suspend judgment?

Hume's answer to this question is complex. First, he appeals to a certain innate disposition operating in humans and animals; i.e., he gives a sort of biological explanation for the causes of behavior or even of "action." Secondly, he also considers a psychological explanation for belief-formation and expectation in terms of the law of association of ideas and as a result of repetition. Thirdly, he formulates some rules for judging causes and effects and appeals to some criteria for separating reasonable from unreasonable beliefs, **T15** and **T16**.

The biological conjecture is revealed in such passages as "reason is nothing but a wonderful and unintelligible instinct in our souls, which carries us along a certain train of ideas . . ." (T 179).[27] And again: "It seems evident, that men are carried, by a natural instinct or prepossession, to repose faith in their senses; and that, without any reasoning, or even almost before the use of reason, we always suppose an external universe, which depends not on our perception, but would exist, though we and every sensible creature were absent or annihilated. Even the animal creation are governed by a like opinion . . ." (EHU 151). The psychological theses of inference, non-cognitive **T6** and **T14**, are offered as a substitution for cognitive inference (though critical reflection may improve animal inference).

The speculative theory of the association of ideas is offered as an explanation for inference, i.e., how an inference is made. The biological side of our nature is reinforced by the observation of invariable frequencies, and is weakened by negative instances. We have found as a consequence of observed invariable frequencies that "fire warms or water refreshes" and that such beliefs are conducive to our survival; "it costs us too much pains to think otherwise" (T 270).

We may paraphrase Hume by saying that animal as well as human survival requires prediction. Prediction is an inference from certain regularities, those discovered regularities which are conducive to our survival. We see therefore that induction, which is nothing more than a method of inference, is essentially *natural* rather than *rational* activity—though like some of our natural activities, it is also a methodized activity.

But Hume does not stop with the explanation of the nature of the non-cognitive inference, since he sees clearly that he cannot defend on this ground alone the credibility of scientific beliefs, and attack the credibility of natural religion and superstitions, which was one of the expressed intentions of his philosophical inquiries. Hence we find in his work various moves toward the construction of a methodological theory.

Hume notes that neither what Russell called "animal inference" in non-cognitive activities, nor what Bacon called "induction by simple enumeration" in cognitive and theorizing activities, is adequate for explaining our ordinary actions or the enterprise of science.

That "all probable reasoning is nothing but a species of sensation" (T 103) is true enough, but it is not enough to tell us why on the basis of these probabilities we project some and not other regularities. Frequencies of experiments could give us a reason for projection. When "we transfer the past to the future, the known to the unknown, every past experiment has the same weight, and . . . 'tis only a superior number of them, which can throw the ballance on any side" (T 136).[28] But he also realized, with Bacon, that we should torture nature to get her secrets.

There is no phænomenon in nature, but what is compounded and modify'd by so many different circumstances, that in order to arrive at the decisive point, we must carefully separate whatever is superfluous, and enquire by new experiments, if every particular circumstance of the first experiment was essential to it. These new experiments are liable to a discussion of the same kind; so that the utmost constancy is requir'd to make us persevere in our enquiry, and the utmost sagacity to choose the right way among so many that present themselves [T 175].[29]

Along with this line, in the *Enquiries*, after discussing reason in animals, he provides some answers to a would-be questioner. "Since all reasoning concerning facts or causes is derived merely from custom, it may be asked how it happens, that men so much surpass animals in reasoning, and one man so much surpasses another?" (EHU 107, note). He then lists nine criteria which supposedly demarcate a Newton from a brute. The gist of the rules is that man is able to expand his experience by using language, generalize from experiments, and form rules for prediction and inference. Like Bacon, he sees that with due caution we can make an inference from a single experiment, i.e., an *experimentum crucis* (EPM 219; see also T 131).[30]

Hume's venture into inductive logic is not incompatible with his psycho-biological explanation of belief-formation. The subordination of the logic of induction to biological and habitual causes of inference is not a commitment to psychologism, a reduction of logic to psychology. Rather, it is based on observing the operation of non-cognitive inference and formulating some rules in order to improve upon it. Hume's explanation about the natural foundation of inductive inference is an empirical thesis. It is a first step toward a psychological theory of learning. However, the very idea has been echoed by many philosophers of our time. Thus Ramsey writes "It is true that if anyone has not the habit of induction, we cannot prove to him that he is wrong, but there is nothing peculiar in that. If a man doubts his memory or his perception we cannot prove to him that he is wrong: but there is nothing peculiar in that they are trustworthy." [31]

There is an old charge about Hume's inconsistency in believing in the invalidity of induction while trying to distinguish between rational and irrational beliefs. Thus Broad writes: "Hume has told us that he can find no logical ground for induction. . . . All that he professes to do is to tell us that we actually do make this transition, and to explain psychologically how it comes about. Now, this being so, I cannot see how Hume can distinguish between our variously caused beliefs about matters of fact, and call some of them justifiable and others unjustifiable." [32]

However, we can vindicate Hume by showing that belief in the invalidity of induction is compatible with the belief that two arguments may be of unequal degrees of conclusiveness even though both are invalid.

On this issue Strawson defends Hume against the charge of holding two inconsistent beliefs. "Was it inconsistent in Hume, then, to frame some rules for judging of causes and effects? It was not. For Nature does not always force our hand (our mind): and it is a requirement of Reason that our beliefs should form a coherent system. Committed by Nature to the 'basic canons' of induction, we are led by Reason to elaborate our procedures and policies. On this basis Reason is, and ought to be, the slave of the passions." [33] To this defense, Popper objects that, although he agrees fully with Hume's destructive argument against induction, he disagrees with "Hume's answer to the psychological problem [which], in spite of its persuasiveness, is quite mistaken." "I hold that neither animals nor men use any procedure like induction, or any argument based on the repetition of instances. The belief that we use induction is simply a mistake. It is a kind of optical illusion." [34]

Hume does not commit himself to such a simple-minded theory of induction, induction as a result of mere repetition on a non-cognitive level, or as a consequence of induction by simple enumeration on a cognitive level. Hume considered the biological and cultural background of belief-formation and the role of experimentation, even of a single experiment, in the construction of theories. This is one issue which we have tried to settle in this essay by looking at his arguments in their entirety. Hume, after creating (for others) a pseudo-problem of the justification of induction—a problem the solution of which engaged the minds of many philosophers—provides us with a compelling explanation of the mechanism and logic of inductive inference. We know now, after two hundred years, that neither Hume's bio-psychological conjectures nor his logic of induction is adequate. But it was to his credit that he replaced the discredited causal maxim of the theologians, the unsupportable inductive principle of the natural philosophers, and the dogma of the immutability of the laws of science, with a testable psychological theory and an *a posteriori* logic of induction.

NOTES

1. This allegation is Broad's and is used in imitation of Kant's saying about another scandal, i.e., the lack of proof for the existence of the external world. "There is a skeleton in the cupboard of Inductive Logic, which Bacon never suspected and Hume first exposed to view. . . . May we venture to hope . . . that Inductive Reasoning, which has long been the glory of Science, will have ceased to be the scandal of Philosophy?" (C. D. Broad, *Ethics and History of Philosophy* [New York, 1957], pp. 142–43).

2. The phrase is D. C. Williams'.

3. I have found only two instances in which the word is used, and in each case the word is used non-essentially: "I conclude, by an induction which seems to me very evident . . ." (T 628), and "Whether we attain the knowledge of them [the general foundation of Morals] by a chain of argument and induction, or by an immediate feeling . . ." (EPM 170).

4. For detail, see chap. 1, "The Principle of Meaning," in Farhang Zabeeh, *Hume: Precursor of Modern Empiricism*, 2nd rev. ed. (The Hague, 1973).

5. In various places in the *Treatise*, this is expressed by distinction between two sorts of relations, i.e., "separable" and "inseparable" relations between relata. In the *Enquiry*, the same view is expressed by a distinction between Matters of Fact and Relations of Ideas.

6. The expression is Ayer's and is used by Russell as "Those statements about matters of fact that appear credible independently of any argument in their favour" (*An Inquiry into Meaning and Truth* [London, 1948], p. 17). The idea of the reduction of ideas to impressions, or of belief to experience, is carried over throughout. The idea of a basic proposition is expressed by: "The only existences, of which we are certain, are perceptions, which being immediately present to us by consciousness, command our strongest assent, and are the first foundation of all our conclusions" (T 212). Likewise, the theses T2, T3,

and **T7** are supportable by: " 'Tis impossible for us to carry on our inferences *in infinitum*; and the only thing, that can stop them, is an impresssion of the memory or senses, beyond which there is no room for doubt or enquiry" (T 83).

7. In many places in the *Treatise*, a distinction is made between "demonstrative reasoning" and "causal." Similarly, in the *Enquiry*; e.g., "All reasonings may be divided into two kinds, namely, demonstrative reasoning, or that concerning relations of ideas, and moral reasoning, or that concerning matter of fact and existence" (EHU 35). "No negation of a fact can involve a contradiction. . . . The case is different with the sciences, properly so called [demonstrative sciences]" (EHU 164). "Such an inference wou'd amount to knowledge, and wou'd imply the absolute contradiction and impossibility of conceiving any thing different. But as all distinct ideas are separable, 'tis evident there can be no impossibility of that kind" (T 87).

8. Russell, *Inquiry into Meaning and Truth*, p. 244.

9. ". . . the necessity, which makes two times two equal to four, or three angles of a triangle equal to two right ones . . ." (T 166). "Nor is less certain of the future event than if it were connected with the objects present to the memory or senses, by a train of causes, cemented together by what we are pleased to call a *physical* necessity" (EHU 91). ". . . the necessity or power, which unites causes and effects . . ." (T 166).

10. "$\boxed{\Gamma}$" denotes *de re* modality. Hume speaks of "*hypothetical* arguments, or reasonings upon a supposition" which could be traced back, in case of "reasonings concerning causes and effects" to some impressions, and in case of demonstration to "comparison of ideas" (T 83, 84). It is tempting to read into Hume the modern idea that mathematical truths are analytic; but for Hume the axioms are not analytic, only the theorems are. For the detail, see Appendix, "Hume on Pure and Applied Geometry," in Zabeeh, *Hume*, pp. 200–15.

11. "[W]e define a cause to be *an object precedent and contiguous to another, and where all the objects resembling the former are plac'd in a like relation of priority and contiguity to those objects, that resemble the latter* . . ." (T 172). It is also indicated by Hume's use of "instance" and "effect" which by implication stand in need of a law or law-like regularities, since "instance" is instance of a law, and an "effect" is an event which is covered by a causal regularity.

12. ". . . that *belief* is something felt by the mind . . ." (EHU 49).

13. Philo's argument in the *Dialogue*: "That a stone will fall . . . we have observed a thousand and a thousand times; and when any new instance of this nature is presented, we draw without hesitation the accustomed inference" (D 144); also in "reason[ing] justly and naturally" and in not doing so (T 225); and the whole argument in "Of Miracles" in the *Enquiry* (EHU 109–31).

14. "[T]here is no probability so great as not to allow of a contrary possibility; because otherwise 'twou'd cease to be a probability, and wou'd become a certainty" (T 235). "All our reasonings concerning fact are of the same nature [cause and effect]. And here it is constantly supposed that there is a connexion between the present fact and that which is inferred from it. *Were there nothing to bind them together, the inference would be entirely precarious.* . . . nor can our reason, unassisted by experience, ever draw any inference concerning real existence and matter of fact" (EHU 26–27; emphasis added).

15. Immanuel Kant, *Prolegomena to Any Future Metaphysics*, trans. J. P. Mahaffy (London 1889), p. 7.

16. See Alfred Tarski, "The Semantic Concept of Truth," in *Readings in Semantics*, edd. Farhang Zabeeh et al. (Urbana, 1974), pp. 675–711.

17. Russell, *Inquiry into Meaning and Truth*, p. 152.

18. K. R. Popper, "Epistemology Without a Knowing Subject," *Logic, Methodology and Philosophy of Science III*, edd. B. van Rootselaar and J. F. Staal, Studies in Logic and the Foundations of Mathematics (Amsterdam, 1968), pp. 333–73 at 368–69.

19. For criticism of that, see Farhang Zabeeh, "Hume's Scepticism with Regard to Deductive Reason," *Ratio*, 2, No. 2 (February 1960), 134–43.

20. See Charles Parson, "Informal Axiomatization, Formalization and the Concept of Truth," *Synthese*, 27 (1974), 27–47.

21. See Arend Heyting, "Intuitionistic Views on the Nature of Mathematics," *ibid.*, 79–91.

22. See Carl G. Hempel, *Inductive Inconsistencies* (New York, 1965). Carnap also sees that the old problem of the justification of induction should be replaced by "inductive logic, the role of rationality in the foundation of inductive logic, and finally the epistemological question of the source of our insights about validity in inductive logic. . . . When I speak here about justification, I do not have in mind the grand old problem of justification discussed so much since Hume's time. I think it has become clear in recent years that the old problem is not the right way of asking the question" (Rudolf Carnap, "Inductive Logic and Inductive Intuition," *The Problem of Inductive Logic*, ed. Imre Lakatos, Studies in Logic and the Foundations of Mathematics No. 2 [Amsterdam, 1968], pp. 258–67 at 258).

23. Karl Popper, "My Solution of Hume's Problem of Induction," *The Philosophy of Karl Popper*, ed. Paul Arthur Schilpp, The Library of Living Philosophers No. 14, 2 vols (La Salle, 1974), II 1013–23 at 1018.

24. P. S. Strawson, "On Justifying Induction," *Philosophical Studies*, 9, Nos. 1–2 (January–February 1958), 20–21.

25. "I have more than once said that we should have a *new kind* of logic, which would treat degrees of probability" (*Leibniz*, ed. P. P. Weiner [New York, 1951], chap. 16).

26. John Locke, *An Essay Concerning Human Understanding*, ed. Peter H. Nidditch (Oxford, 1975), p. 671.

27. Hence it is wrong to assume that empiricism of Hume's sort is incompatible with the belief in innate disposition. It is said, for example, that "The fundamental axiom of empiricism—*nihil in intellectu quod non prius in sensu*—is of course mistaken. Animals *inherit* information (for example, on how to build nests or what to sing) in the form of a sort of chromosomal tape recording" (Peter Medawar, "Hypothesis and Imagination," *Philosophy of Karl Popper*, ed. Schilpp, I 274–90 at 290n2).

28. Here it seems that Hume would not deny Carnap's statement "that two arguments may be of unequal degrees of conclusiveness, even though both are invalid." The contrary is stated by D. S. Stove, *Probability and Hume's Inductive Scepticism* (Oxford, 1973), p. 119. But in Hume's work there is no hint at the objective theory of probability (in spite of various talk about arguments which may "admit of no doubt or uncertainty" and so amount to "proofs"). Degree of conclusiveness, for Hume, is not, like validity, a logical property of an argument; rather, it is a subjective degree of belief. Some inductive conclusions are stronger than others in virtue of their power to induce conviction. And when we project some uniformities, we do not do so merely because they have a strong objective probability-property: "if the transference of the past to the future were founded merely on a conclusion of the understanding, it cou'd never occasion any belief or assurance" (T 139).

29. I see no evidence for the remark "On the other hand, and quite inconsistently, Hume also asserted that no causal uniformity can be an object of reasoning or operate upon the mind in any way 'but by means of custom'"; or for "[Hume] seems obsessed with the kind of causal influencing of the mind that is analogous to what logicians like Bacon called induction by simple enumeration, and ignores altogether the kind of causal influencing that is analogous to induction by variation of circumstances" (L. Jonathan Cohen, *The Implications of Induction* [London, 1970], pp. 125, 126).

Again, I see no textual supports for J. W. N. Watkins' assertion that "The conjunction of Hume's psychological claim with his logical point means that *sanity and science demand a robust and systematic illogicality*" ("Hume, Carnap and Popper," *Problem of Inductive Logic*, ed. Lakatos, pp. 271–82 at 272). Or, for that matter, for Popper's rephrasing of that assertion: "what Watkins alluded to was the fact that the rationalist Hume turned into an irrationalist because despite his great logical discovery that induction is irrational, Hume failed to reconsider his (psychological and methodological) view that we must, and do, depend on induction" (K. R. Popper, "Theories, Experience, and Probabilistic Intuitions," ibid., pp. 285–303 at 288).

30. Popper, believing that Hume's positive theory is a simple frequency theory, assumes that whatever Hume said about learning from a single experiment "was merely his attempt to explain away unfavorable facts which threatened his theory" ("Hume's Explanation of Inductive Inference," *Conjecture and Refutations* [New York, 1962], p. 42). But see the following: "What we have found once to follow from any object, we conclude will for

ever follow from it; and if this maxim be not always built upon as certain, 'tis not for want of a sufficient number of experiments, but because we frequently meet with instances to the contrary; . . . we are oblig'd to vary our reasoning . . . and take into consideration the contrariety of events" (T 131).

31. F. P. Ramsey, *The Foundations of Mathematics*, ed. R. R. Braithwaite (London, 1931), pp. 196–97.

32. C. D. Broad, "Hume's Theory of the Credibility of Miracles," *Proceedings of the Aristotelian Society*, 17 (1916–17), 77–94 at 91. More incredible is Lazerowitz' interpretation of Hume's thesis and a psychoanalytical explanation for the genesis of the alleged thesis: "Hume's position that the past provides no rule for the future can be seen to lend itself to the interpretation that it gives hidden expression to a disposition to doubt. Hume's view about what the past cannot teach us is not a theory about how nature works; rather it reveals a tendency in him to fall prey to doubt" (Morris Lazerowitz, "The Problem of Justifying," *Psychoanalysis and Philosophy*, ed. C. Hanly [New York, 1970], p. 210).

33. Strawson, "On Justifying Induction," 21.

34. Popper, "My Solution of Hume's Problem of Induction," 1019, 1015.

4

Some Implications of the Virtue of Reasonableness in Hume's *Treatise*

Páll S. Árdal
Queen's University
Kingston, Ontario

I

WHAT PLACE DOES HUME GIVE to reason in his *Treatise*? This question has puzzled me for a long time, and I have concluded that there is no simple or short answer to be given to it. I have therefore approached the problem indirectly through the examination of a set of related concepts, such as conformity to reason, reasoning, truth, and reasonableness. It should be understood that in this essay I am not aiming at an exhaustive analysis of these concepts; nor am I unaware of the fact that Hume does not explicitly refer to the virtue, or virtues, of reasonableness. Hume's silence on this topic may seem embarrassing to me in view of the fact that my main purpose is to give substance to the claim that a clear conception of the virtue, or virtues, of reasonableness is of central importance for the proper understanding of at least some aspects of Hume's epistemology. My thesis would indeed be vulnerable were it not understood as a claim about what Hume is implicitly committed to rather than as a statement of what he explicitly and deliberately argues for. Indeed, Hume may have been only dimly aware of the view I am claiming to find in his work.

II

In a frequently quoted passage Hume insists that "Reason is, and ought only to be the slave of the passions, and can never pretend to any other office than to serve and obey them" (T 415). In spite of the fact that Hume elsewhere insists that reason is entirely inert, the slave passage clearly suggests that reason can influence conduct. Let us begin by considering the ways in which Hume thinks the slave (reason) can serve the master (passion), even though it *alone* can never furnish a motive to action. Here we must remind ourselves that Hume believes the "understanding exerts itself after two different ways, as it judges from demonstration or probability; as it regards the abstract relations of our ideas, or those relations of objects, of which experience only gives us information" (T 413). I shall consider the two functions of the understanding only with regard to their influence upon action. My justification for this is that the virtue of reasonableness, to which I want to draw attention, is, like most, if not all, other virtues, revealed in action.[1]

Hume takes pure mathematics as an example of reasoning about the relations between ideas, and points out that in doing pure mathematics our reasoning has no influence on behaviour. It must of course be understood that a man may use his mathematical skills to achieve ends, such as the obtaining of an office through the passing of a test. But here it is presupposed that the person in question wants the post, so that the reasoning influences conduct only as the slave of a desire.

More important is the function of applied mathematics, which, unlike the case I have just mentioned, is explicitly discussed by Hume. He draws attention to the enormous aid to action to be drawn from mechanics and accountancy. But, again, the mathematical reasoning of a civil engineer building a dam influences people's conduct only because they want to build a dam. A man who makes up his accounts to find out his debts will be spurred to action by the result only if he *wants* to pay his debts, or has some other purpose to which the reasoning is relevant. Again, reason is the slave of a desire.

Reasoning and individual judgments concerning matters of fact may influence conduct by showing us the means to an end we already desire. But we may also come to desire an end we had not desired previously when we see how it can be obtained. We may not have sought the object because we thought it entirely beyond our reach. Discovering how it may be obtained may lead to an active quest to obtain it. We may also discover that an object we seek does not exist, or is unobtainable, and this obviously would modify our conduct. In a somewhat similar fashion we may desire an object, such as an apple, because we think it is delicious. When we discover that it is rotten, our interest in obtaining it ceases. In all these cases change in the content of our beliefs influences our behaviour, either through showing how our already existing desires or passions can or cannot be satisfied, or through revealing something which arouses or extinguishes our desires. In each case the reasoning or individual judgment does not, by itself, modify conduct; assistance from desires or passions is needed.

One further way in which reason may have a practical effect must be mentioned. Hume thinks that human beings have a passion which he describes as curiosity, or the love of truth, and to that joy of reasoning he ascribes the origin of his philosophy.[2] A man who enjoys reasoning will obviously be more likely to engage in it than one who does not enjoy it. Here, then, tasting the pleasures of reasoning may help to determine what we do.

We have seen that reason can in certain ways influence our conduct when, understood as reasoning or judgment, it aids passions or desires. It furnishes no separate "motive to any action of the will" (T 413)—to use Hume's expression—but it is not yet entirely obvious why Hume should describe it as completely inert. To see clearly why Hume should insist upon the total inertness of reason one must turn one's attention to his claim that reason can be equated with truth or the discovery of truth.

III

Hume stresses at the beginning of the section "Of the Influencing Motives of the Will" that philosophers and ordinary people have often represented human life as a struggle between reason, a divine, infallible faculty, and blind, unruly passions. To live as one ought is to follow reason rather than the passions. This picture is to Hume deeply misconceived, although, as we have seen, there is a sense in which reason can have a practical function as the servant of desires and passions. To be sure, a superficial reading of the slave passage may suggest that one ought to be guided by reason rather than by passions. But this cannot be correct. Since reason unaided is inert, it needs the assistance of passions and cannot furnish an alternative guide to them. Reason by itself cannot provide a motive to the will. Now, this is a somewhat startling contention which Kant later attempted to refute. But the reader of Hume's *Treatise* is likely to be even more dumbfounded when he discovers Hume's considerations in support of this claim. Reason, he tells us, is inert, because truth, or its discovery, is inert, and reason is nothing but truth, or the discovery of truth. How can reason be equated with an event, such as a discovery? How can it be said to be the same as truth, if truth is, as Hume contends, an agreement "to the *real* relations of ideas, or to *real* existence and matter of fact" (T 458)?

Hume describes reason as a discovery both in Book II (T 414) and in Book III (T 458), and in each case the claim is made in the context of his argument that reason is entirely inert. His assertion that "Reason is the discovery of truth or falsehood" (T 458) can thus hardly be an accident or a lapse. An explanation of this claim must thus be found in some other of his doctrines or presuppositions.

One need not be too surprised to find Hume abandoning talk about an infallible faculty of reason, for a great deal of his *Treatise* consists in an attempt to explain human experience without an appeal to hidden powers; and a faculty is clearly a hidden power. One can *say*, Hume thinks, that anything which is inconsistent with truth or is self-contradictory is contrary to reason; but one must always remember that faculty talk is fundamentally misleading,[3] and that the reason which, according to the traditional view, we were supposed to take as our guide was conceived of as an infallible faculty. If we follow it in preference to the solicitations of desires and passions, we cannot go wrong. Thus an erroneous judgment cannot be the work of reason. Hume's characterisation of reason as truth, or the discovery of truth, is forced upon him if he is to avoid talking in terms of faculties. One may compare this characterisation with his contention that the will is an impression and that there is no distinction between power and the exercise of power. Here one cannot think of the power as distinct from the performances which in faculty language are supposed to *show* it. Hume's description of the will as an impression rather than as a power or faculty and his attempt at reducing the concept of power to the concepts of possibility and probability also point to the conclusion that he did not consider the concept of a mental power, or a faculty, a basic, unanalysable one. It is also difficult to see how talk about faculties can be reconciled with what he says about the nature of the self as a system of perceptions.

All the surprising contentions I have drawn attention to can be explained only by Hume's desire to avoid committing himself to the existence of faculties. It must of course be admitted that Hume often does express himself in language which appears to imply their existence, but this can be explained by the fact that ordinary language makes it difficult to avoid talking in this way without giving an impression of paradox.

In general, I take it to be a sound principle of philosophical scholarship to seek an explanation of the surprising statements a philosopher makes, particularly when they seem to follow a certain pattern. To take one's cue from a contention which anyone could be expected to make, independently of a special theory, when one is attempting to establish a philosopher's doctrine would of course tend to make all philosophers' views appear much the same. I am revealing the principle I have been following in my interpretation of a crucial aspect of Hume's thought so that the reader may judge its merits. It is in the light of the rejection of faculties that we must understand the claim that " 'Tis not contrary to reason to prefer the destruction of the whole world to the scratching of my finger" (T 416). This simply means that doing so is neither self-contradictory nor inconsistent with a true proposition. Neither actions nor persons can have these characteristics; only propositions and beliefs can be in contradiction with other propositions or beliefs and not conform to reality. Passions and actions have no representative characteristics and consequently cannot conform, or fail to conform, to reality.

Hume admits that actions may be indirectly reasonable or unreasonable in that they may be based upon *false* beliefs. If I desire an apple because it has an especially attractive taste, my desire is unreasonable if the apple has a rotten taste. If I take the wrong means to a desired end, my action is also unreasonable since it is based upon false belief. But strictly speaking it is the belief which is unreasonable (false) in both cases.

Although Hume's view that false beliefs are unreasonable is intelligible in light of his interpretation of the alleged infallibility of the faculty of reason, there is no doubt that the use he makes here of "reasonable" and "unreasonable" is out of tune with the ordinary meaning of these terms. We consider beliefs and actions reasonable or unreasonable by reference to the strength of the evidence the agent has in support of them. Thus it would be reasonable for me to believe an apple to be a good one if I bought it at a store which has consistently sold good food, including apples. Although the firm may have slipped up in this one instance, my action, in being based upon a false belief, has not thereby been made unreasonable. On the other hand, it would be unreasonable for me to make a proposal of marriage on the basis of information given to me by a fortuneteller, although the resultant union may turn out extremely well. In these cases there is, of course, a true belief related to the reasonable action and a false one to the unreasonable action. The customer's belief in the strength of the evidence is a true belief and the suitor's belief in the reliability of the fortuneteller is a false one. But a man need not be unreasonable in relying on such unreliable evidence as fortunetelling. The person may have been genuinely deceived about the possibility of the powers claimed by the fortuneteller. To show that a person has been deceived about the reliability of certain kinds of evidence is not sufficient to warrant the conclusion that he was unreasonable in acting on beliefs based upon this evidence. Whereas omniscient beings cannot be deceived, reasonable beings can.

IV

In this section I want to illustrate how Hume's use of "reason" as equivalent to "truth" is connected with his polemic against those rationalists who had argued that the immorality of actions consisted in their falsehood.[4] The doctrine is most often associated with William Wollaston's *The Religion of Nature Delineated* (1722), but passages can be found in the writings of John Balguay and Samuel Clarke which seem to express a similar view. The following quotations from Wollaston's work may serve as a reminder of what the doctrine was:

> I lay this down then as a fundamental maxim, *that whoever acts as if things were so, or not so, doth by his acts declare, that they are so, or not so*; as plainly as he could by words, and with more reality. And if the things are otherwise, his acts contradict *those propositions*, which assert them to be as they are.[5]

And, in support of the contention that failing to keep a promise contradicts the proposition that the promise was made, he writes as follows:

> if one proposition imports or contains that which is *contrary* to what is contained in another, it is said to *contradict* this other, and denies the existence of what is contained in it. Just so if one act imports that which is *contrary* to the import of another, it contradicts this other, and *denies its existence*. In a word, if A by his actions denies the engagements, to which he hath subjected himself, his actions deny them; just as we say, Ptolemy by his writings denies the motion of the earth, or his writings deny it.[6]

It should now be clear that reason as truth is entirely inert. It is the content of our beliefs, what we believe, which influences conduct, and not the fact that the beliefs are true. If truth is equated with virtue, and truth does not admit of degrees, then, presumably, it follows that all virtues are equal. This to Hume is an unacceptable consequence of the doctrine we are considering, but I shall omit any mention of its merits or demerits, for, in the main, Hume gives a slightly different interpretation of Wollaston's doctrine.

Hume for the most part does not take Wollaston to be maintaining that virtue consists in truth. He attributes to him the rather different doctrine that to be virtuous is to cause beliefs in true propositions and that vice is behaviour which causes beliefs in false propositions. Although this interpretation of Wollaston is doubtful, I do not propose to discuss it in detail; rather, I want to draw attention to Hume's main criticism of the doctrine, for this will lead quite naturally to a consideration of the special notion of reasonableness which I particularly want to stress in this essay. In what, Hume asks, does the merit in belief in true propositions as such consist? Wollaston leaves the matter entirely unexplained, but Hume thinks that it should be explained and that he is in a position to do so.

Hume rejects the contention that knowing or believing truths has intrinsic value. Thus it can be argued that we would be better off if no one knew or believed certain truths. An example does not come readily to mind for it would have to involve exceptional circumstances. But would there really be any value in knowing or believing in advance the inevitable destruction of the world within a limited period of time? What would be the compensating factor for the distress such knowledge or belief would cause if, as I am assuming, no escape from the disaster is possible? It is a great deal easier to find examples to illustrate that it need not be valuable for individual people to know or believe particular truths. Thus a person may have no right to pry into the private affairs of another. Malicious prying is generally not thought to be admirable. And may it not be argued that there are occasions when an exaggerated idea of one's own abilities may lead to greater achievement than a realistic appraisal of them would? It is not clear what value lies in beliefs or knowledge used for thoroughly evil purposes, but all these limitations to the value of knowledge and true belief do nothing to change the fact that they are in general of value because they serve human ends and purposes and contribute to the enjoyment of life. To possess a "quality of mind or character" which facilitates the acquisition of true belief and knowledge is valuable. The quality thus is a virtue, in Hume's sense of that term, and we must now explain what is involved in saying this.

The following passage reveals the essence of Hume's view about the nature of judgments of virtue:

> An action, or sentiment, or character is virtuous or vicious; why? because its view causes a pleasure or uneasiness of a particular kind. In giving a reason, therefore, for the pleasure or uneasiness, we sufficiently explain the vice or virtue. To have the sense of virtue, is nothing but to *feel* a satisfaction of a particular kind from the contemplation of a character. The very *feeling* constitutes our praise or admiration. We go no farther; nor do we enquire into the cause of the satisfaction. We do not infer a character to be virtuous, because it pleases: But in feeling that it pleases after such a particular manner, we in effect feel that it is virtuous. The case is the same as in our judgments concerning all kinds of beauty, and tastes, and sensations. Our approbation is imply'd in the immediate pleasure they convey to us [T 471].

Hume's meaning seems to me to be beyond question. A man who has the sense of virtue has special kinds of feelings when he contemplates the character of those we call virtuous or vicious. What we in ordinary life talk of as thinking that a man is virtuous or vicious, that objects are beautiful or ugly, or that a sensation is exquisite, thrilling, etc., really amounts to having certain peculiar kinds of feelings. Having the feelings constitutes valuing. The pleasures derived from different causes are specifically different: the pleasures of music are not of the same kind as the pleasures of drinking good wine. This is indeed reflected in the way we characterise the respective values: we do not call wine harmonious or music flavourful. Although Hume's account of taste and beauty is undoubtedly interesting, we must here confine ourselves to what he thinks constitutes the evaluation of actions and, in particular, qualities of mind and character.

v

In order to understand Hume's account of the feelings which constitute the evaluation of actions and personal qualities, one must distinguish between two basic problems he tries to deal with: (1) how can evaluations of this kind be made intelligible without an appeal to special powers and faculties? and (2) how could the rationalists and, indeed, many if not most, ordinary people mistake for thoughts the passions which constitute evaluations?

In Book II Hume discusses at length the nature and causal explanation of four passions he calls indirect: love, hatred, pride, and humility. These passions, like others, are described as simple and indefinable. It turns out that love and hatred really are favourable and unfavourable reactions to others, and that pride and humility are favourable and unfavourable reactions to ourselves. Whatever makes a person proud must be a pleasing quality which belongs either to him or to someone closely related to him. Whatever makes an individual love another person must be a pleasing quality belonging to, or closely related to, that person. If one substitutes "displeasing" for "pleasing," one would have the conditions which give rise to humility and hatred, respectively. The passions denoted by the ordinary use of "love," "hatred," "pride," and "humility" are a subclass of the indirect passions to which Hume refers in using these terms. He is thus not inconsistent in claiming both that approval and disapproval are ". . . nothing but a fainter and more imperceptible love and hatred" and that those passions are unique and thus different from ordinary love and hatred.[7]

We must now ask for the nature of the causal conditions which differentiate approval and disapproval from love, hatred, pride, and humility as normally understood. These latter passions are naturally biased, whereas approvals and disapprovals would seem to have to be unbiased if they are to justify saying that a person is an evil person, a good man, a just man, a courageous man, or to attribute to him any other virtue or vice. Hume must now explain how we come to adopt an objective point of view and thus overcome the natural bias of our passions. Thus in stressing how differently we feel about persons on the one hand and inanimate objects on the other, he says:

> Nor is every sentiment of pleasure or pain, which arises from characters and actions, of that *peculiar* kind, which makes us praise or condemn. The good qualities of an enemy are hurtful to us; but may still command our esteem and respect. 'Tis only when a character is considered in general, without refer-

ence to our particular interest, that it causes such a feeling or sentiment, as denominates it morally good or evil. 'Tis true, those sentiments, from interest and morals, are apt to be confounded, and naturally run into one another. It seldom happens, that we do not think an enemy vicious, and can distinguish betwixt his opposition to our interest and real villainy or baseness. But this hinders not, but that the sentiments are, in themselves, distinct; and a man of temper and judgment may preserve himself from these illusions [T 472].

Here and in many other passages Hume insists that the sentiments which make us praise and blame, the moral sentiments, are unique. Although a person may mistake his love and hatred for approval and disapproval, and therefore show in his value judgments bias in favour of friends and against enemies, this bias can be avoided if people are careful enough; for love really is distinct from approval and hatred from disapproval. The trick is to strive towards becoming a "man of temper and judgment," and we must now consider how this is to be achieved.

In the last part of Book III Hume attempts to explain why we try to overcome the natural bias of our passions. He attributes the requirement of impartiality to reason and notes that it is by no means always successful. We do not always follow the "determination of our judgment." But note that he immediately adds to this an apparent concession to the power of reason. "This language will be easily understood, if we consider what we formerly said concerning that *reason*, which is able to oppose our passion; and which we have found to be nothing but a general calm determination of the passions, founded on some distant view or reflexion" (T 583). Reason is here clearly not equated with truth or its discovery. It is by no means inert and consists in certain calm passions.

The calm passions are on the whole more known by their effects than by their immediate feeling. They thus resemble attitudes more than they do occurrent emotions, such as violent anger or terror. This is, of course, not to be understood to mean that approvals and disapprovals may not involve great conscious emotional upheaval: a person can be violently upset by the thought of great injustice and not only by personal injuries. What characterizes the so-called calm passions is that they, generally speaking, do not involve great inner conscious turbulence as feelings. It is this calmness of the calm passions, in which approvals and disapprovals consist, which has led to the common mistake that the moral sentiments are thoughts which can be true or false. Although it is easier to see Hume's point if one remembers that to him the difference between thought and feeling is one of vivacity and liveliness and not one of kind, there are of course difficulties about this doctrine which it would unfortunately take too long to discuss in this essay.

The distant view or reflexion which is needed for the calm passions to arise is forced upon us by the fact that our biased passions lead to all kinds of conflict. Although man is not selfish by nature, he has greater concern for himself than for any other one person and is biased in favour of those with whom he is closely concerned. Because men discover the disadvantages for social life of this bias, a tacit understanding to abide by certain rules and to adopt common viewpoints in looking at objects we are concerned with develops. This tacit convention is reflected in the fact that we talk of good and bad actions, things, and people in addition to expressing our mere likes and dislikes of them. And when these linguistic devices themselves are considered, they have obvious value in furthering communication, which in turn helps to reduce friction and to make life more commodious for all. We therefore, on reflection, approve of those who make proper use of them. The making of objective judgments, and the use of language for expressing them, are comparable to the artificial virtues. In each case a convention is explained by showing that it can intelligibly have arisen from the motives of confined benevolence and self-interest, and we approve of those who adhere to these conventions because of the utility of general adherence to them. In each case, too, isolated instances may not have value: it is sometimes beneficial to mislead people and to break the rules of justice, although the general scheme is to be treasured to such an extent as to make these exceptions rare. We likewise adopt common standpoints in assessing size, colours, and other perceptible qualities of objects because of the utility this has. Assessments both of the qualities of mind and character (virtues) and of the perceptible qualities of objects are, of course, extremely important in securing successful action. Once the objective way of speaking has been adopted, and we talk about real colours, size, hardness, tastes, etc., adherence to the common criteria for speaking in this way is approved of on reflection, for precisely the same reason we approve of the artificial virtues, i.e., their utility.

The passions of approval and disapproval, in which evaluations consist, are calm because they arise under conditions which remove the person from any special interests in the object assessed and involve discounting special characteristics of the assessor which might be shared by few, if any, other people. Furthermore, when a certain pattern of evaluation has been settled, people pronounce upon values without having any detectable emotional reaction at all. One is carried immediately into one's verbal assessments because of the habit which has led to objects of a certain kind having come to be valued, and unfavourable attitude having been developed to others. People follow a general rule in their overt evaluations without having a detectable emotion on each occasion.

We can now see that the rationalists mistake certain calm passions for thoughts. It is these passions we express when we condemn as unreasonable the man who prefers the destruction of the whole world to the scratching of his finger. These calm passions constitute what we call approval and form a subclass of the so-called indirect passions: love, hatred, pride, and humility. These passions have people as their natural objects, and consequently approval and disapproval always have persons as their objects; actions come to be morally assessed only in so far as they are indications of some quality of mind or character in the agent.

It is only towards the end of Book III that Hume explains how we come to adopt the objective point of view which is a necessary condition for the unique passions of approving and disapproving as opposed to those of loving and hating. We sympathize with the effects which the qualities of mind or character of an agent normally would have, and this leads us to approve or disapprove of any person to whom the beneficial or pernicious quality belongs. One must remember that Hume preferred to take his list of virtues from the ancients rather than from *The Practice of Christian Grace, or The Whole Duty of Man.*[8] His account in the *Treatise* deals with valuable characteristics of the mind or character of persons and is not to be understood as an explication of the nature and origin of virtues in the narrower sense given to this term today. Thus both wit and intelligence are virtues to him, and this leaves the door wide open for the inclusion of reasonableness as a virtue, and that in more senses than one. The man who prefers the destruction of the whole world to the scratching of his finger either totally lacks the capacity for viewing situations from an objective point of view, or lacks concern for others. The man who prefers his own total ruin to prevent the least uneasiness to a completely unknown Indian lacks prudence and a sense of proportion.

VI

It is important to see that the concept of reasonableness we are now concerned with is quite different from the concepts of judgment, reasoning, and truth; nor can this account of reasonableness be understood as a subjectivist analysis of truth. Such an interpretation has recently been advanced by W. H. Walsh. "True belief," says Walsh, "is just belief in which the feeling of conviction occurs appropriately." [9] Then follows an account of how, from our objective point of view, we react to some beliefs as appropriate and others as inappropriate. To me this reaction indicates approval of the belief, but this approval is not necessarily equivalent to thinking the belief true. Walsh, following Kemp Smith, reads into Hume a Hutchesonian account of judgment, from which he thinks it follows that Hume was committed to a subjectivist analysis of *truth*. He writes as follows:

> According to Hutcheson, beauty and goodness are not objective characteristics of things or actions, but qualities that they have when contemplated by an observer; to put it crudely, they are subjective. An attempt to transfer the Hutchesonian account of moral and aesthetic judgments to judgments about matter of fact and existence involves inevitably saying that there is something similarly subjective about truth. That Hume never does this explicitly must be admitted. But that his whole account of the understanding committed him to this conclusion seems to me quite obvious.[10]

Unfortunately Hume says little about truth, but his typical references to it are not, as Walsh indeed notes, in conformity with the subjective analysis of truth which Walsh attributes to him. Hume, in fact, maintains that "Truth is of two kinds, consisting either in the discovery of the proportions of ideas, consider'd as such, or in the conformity of our ideas of objects to their real existence" (T 448). And we are also told that contradiction to truth or reason consists "in the disagreement of ideas, consider'd as copies, with those objects, which they represent" (T 415). Passions cannot be contrary to truth because they are original existences which are not taken to point beyond themselves. Only ideas or beliefs which are taken to represent reality can be thought of as true or false. I think Hume is simply accepting what we normally think about the truth of our beliefs. Our beliefs are true if the world is as we believe it to be. This seems also to have been the Cartesian view of truth in so far as Descartes thought that we needed to know the existence of a non-deceiving deity to be able to trust that our ideas correspond to reality. I believe Hume to maintain that, if one discounts relations between ideas, with which we are not concerned in this essay, the concept of truth essentially involves the notion of correspondence. He did not give a special analysis of truth, but rather thought that as a criterion of the adequacy of our beliefs in certain metaphysical contexts it had been over-emphasised by previous philosophers. Thus we should not be attempting to establish the truth of both the propositions that the world exists continuously and that it exists independently of our perceptions. If we do allow ourselves to doubt these propositions, there is no way in which we can establish their *truth*. If we consider establishing their truth a precondition for justified belief, we cannot be saved from total scepticism.

It is of course a debatable point whether Hume is consistent. Can he claim that passions as impressions are original existences, and therefore neither true nor false, whereas thoughts and beliefs have a representative capacity in virtue of which *they* may be true or false? It seems that this clashes with his repeated insistence that the difference between ideas and impressions is one of degree and not of kind, and that belief is simply a vivid impression or an idea. For one thing to have a representative capacity and for another to lack it seems to indicate a difference in kind rather than in degree. But this possible inconsistency in Hume's thought does not seem to me to affect the main point of this essay. Truth as correspondence (and this seems to be the way Hume conceives of it) is of little consequence as a criterion of the adequacy of our beliefs when compared with the concept of reasonableness. To be reasonable is to possess a virtue which serves human ends and purposes and of which men consequently approve.

VII

It is not always sufficiently stressed that Hume begins the section "Of Scepticism With Regard to the Senses" as follows: "We may well ask," he says, "*What causes induce us to believe in the existence of body?* but 'tis in vain to ask, *Whether there be body or not?* That is a point, which we must take for granted in all our reasonings" (T 187). Hume is here attempting to make psychologically intelligible our belief in a continuously and independently existing world of objects. He wants to make it absolutely clear that he does not consider it his business as a philosopher to attempt to establish by reasoning the existence of such a world.

Hume rejects the view that the senses reveal the world to us as independent and continuous. They cannot reveal it as independent because they reveal it only as *perceived*, and they cannot reveal it as existing continuously because our sense experience is interrupted. He clearly emphasises that we may "conclude with certainty, that the opinion of a continu'd and of a distinct existence never arises from the senses" (T 192).

Hume denies equally emphatically that we come to our belief in a continuous, independently existing world by inference. The understanding, rather, leads us to believe that our natural tendency to take our perceptions to be objects is mistaken. This aspect of Hume's view was stressed by Wade L. Robison in an interesting paper entitled "Hume's Scepticism." [11] Robison maintains that since being reasonable is by definition "reasoning only from cause and effect," we are doomed to be unreasonable, since we cannot but believe in a world of independently and continuously existing objects, and this very belief of ours is shown to be false when we reason from causes to effects. (Notice that Robison seems to think that believing what is false entails being unreasonable.) Indeed, Hume concludes that "reason neither does, nor is it possible it ever shou'd, upon any supposition, give us an assurance of the continu'd and distinct existence of body" (T 193). By "reason" he here means "reasoning" and, in light of Hume's account of causal reasoning, which is the species of reasoning relevant in this context, one can understand why he should deny the possibility that such reasoning can lead us beyond the limits of our experience. Hume, indeed, insists that our belief in a world of bodies is due to the imagination, and that no philosophical speculation, such as the view that bodies are the permanent unknown causes of our fleeting perceptions, can long shake the view of the vulgar that what we perceive exists continuously and independently, as we perceive it. And we must not forget that the class of the vulgar includes all men most of the time, not excluding philosophers when they are not engaged in speculative enterprises.

When Hume compares the philosophical system of objects as causes of perceptions with the vulgar view that perceptions, in the sense of what we perceive, sometimes are objects, he maintains that the vulgar view is to be preferred. It is, according to him, perfectly possible that what is perceived may exist independently of being perceived. Indeed, we must take some of our perceptions to be objects, and though "this opinion be false" he says, "'tis the most natural of any, and has alone any primary recommendation to the fancy" (T 213). Notice that Hume does not say here that the belief that our perceptions exist unperceived is false, only that it *may be* false. At other times he seems to claim that those beliefs are false. But how could we, on his own principles, claim to *know* that our perceptions do not exist unperceived. To claim such knowledge would be to go beyond what can be learned from any possible experience.

VIII

It is questionable whether Robison is right when he claims in his article that Hume *defines* "reasonableness" as "arguing justly and regularly from causes and effects," although Hume may *sometimes* use the term with this meaning. But it should now be clear that to say of a person that he is reasonable is to pass upon him a value judgment, and one must therefore interpret both the reasonableness of a belief in a world of objects, and the reasoning justly from causes to effects, in terms of Hume's general view about the nature of value judgments. One could say that Hume is changing the question from "How, if at all, can we establish the truth of our belief that there is a continuously, independently existing world of objects?" to "Is it *reasonable* for us to believe in such a world?" We may be reasonable in holding a belief whether the belief be true or not. One cannot of course continue to believe that p, after one concludes that p is false or likely to be false. This explains why "carelessness and in-attention" (T 218) are the only remedy when our philosophical reasoning leads us to conclude that the beliefs of the vulgar are quite likely to be false. But notice that inattention is a "remedy." The reason for this is that a belief in a continuously and independently existing world is both a necessary and useful presupposition for the possibility of action and communication.

In Book III Hume distinguishes between virtues according to the main source of their value. We may approve of qualities of mind because they are pleasing to the person himself or to others, or useful to the person himself or to others. We approve of the person who is guided by past regularities, or causal inferences, because he will be less often thwarted in his enterprises. In a similar way his belief in a continuously and independently existing world will enable him to make sense of other people's sense reports. You can understand why your typewriter is not on your desk if a person tells you that he observed someone carrying it out of your office.

But Hume also seems to think that we should approve of the activities of the philosopher who comes to quite different conclusions from the vulgar. The philosopher may conclude from such experiments as that of the double image, when you press your eyeball, that our perceptions are not continuous independent existences, but fleeting and perishing ones. But notice that the approval is determined by the fact that there are people who feel that they would be "loser[s] in point of pleasure" (T 217) if they did not abandon the attitude of the vulgar to the world. Hume, indeed, as we have seen, says that the pleasure of philosophical speculation "is the origin of my philosophy" (T 271). It is thus reasonable for someone like Hume to engage in philosophical speculation, but when the conclusions of these speculations are inconsistent with the vulgar view of the world, the latter is quite reasonably retained for all practical purposes. When you leave your study and engage your friends in a game of backgammon, philosophical doubts are not only necessarily but also rightly forgotten. "Here then I find myself absolutely and necessarily determin'd to live, and talk, and act like other people in the common affairs of life" (T 269). Although in this passage Hume is emphasising what we necessarily must believe, it should be noted that, on my interpretation, Hume neither *confuses* the necessity of a belief in a world of objects with its justifiability nor does he *fail to raise* the question of its justification. The call of philosophy as well as of practical life is strong, since

'tis almost impossible for the mind of man to rest, like those of beasts, in the narrow circle of objects, which are the subject of daily conversation and action, we ought only to deliberate concerning the choice of our guide, and *ought to prefer that which is safest and most agreeable*. And in this respect I make bold to recommend philosophy, and shall not scruple to give it the preference to superstition of every kind or denomination [T 271; emphasis added].

Perhaps characterising both the vulgar and the philosopher as each in his own way reasonable can help us to understand why Hume should in Book I totally reject the distinction between primary and secondary qualities, while in Book III he describes this distinction as a great discovery. He may be wanting to stress that a scientist may be quite reasonable in treating secondary qualities as merely subjective, but that this should not alter the ways of the vulgar in taking these qualities really to belong to objects, for this way of looking at things helps people to get on perfectly satisfactorily in their daily affairs.

It is surely not an accident that towards the end of the third and final book of the *Treatise* Hume should draw a parallel between the reason why we find it useful to distinguish between "liking" and "thinking good" on the one hand and "appearing" and "being so," in the case of perceptual judgments, on the other. Basically we approve of and call reasonable people who are guided by these distinctions, because it enables them to avoid confusion and to promote their own as well as the general interest; the distinctions in both cases greatly facilitate communication by language, and this serves people's interests in general. When an object is said to be red, and not only to seem red, certain information is supposedly conveyed which is independent of the special peculiarities of the speaker, and the special (perhaps peculiar) conditions under which he has viewed the object. A similar difference exists between "John is a good person" and "I like (love) John." [12]

It may seem wildly implausible to use the favourable results of a belief as a criterion for the reasonableness of holding it. Surely many false beliefs have favourable consequences: a timid man might never have entered upon a worthwhile enterprise if he had realised the obstacles in his way. I do not think that Hume wants to deny this any more than he wants to deny the usefulness of an isolated act of injustice. It is the general fundamental presumption of a continuously and independently existing world which is here at issue. Belief in such a world is inevitable and desirable in quite the same way as the rules of justice are inevitable and desirable. Hume is always careful to distinguish the psychological explanation from the justification of an evaluation, though many readers of his work have failed to see this. Thus, causal inferences are essential for successful action, and it is impossible for us to avoid arguing from causes to effects and effects to causes. Francis Chilton Bayley [13] has drawn attention to the importance to Hume of a pragmatic criterion for the justification of beliefs. Among other passages he quotes the following one from Hume's *Enquiry Concerning Human Understanding*:

Had not the presence of an object, instantly excited the idea of those objects, commonly conjoined with it, all our knowledge must have been limited to the narrow sphere of our memory and senses; and we should never have been able to adjust means to ends, or employ our natural powers, either to the producing of good, or avoiding of evil [EHU 55].

Although we cannot prove that all events have a cause any more than we can prove that there is an independently continuously existing world of objects, it is the general disposition to hold these beliefs which is beneficial, and our tendency to sympathise with all who may benefit from such a disposition may lead us to approve of it. Sympathy, from an objective point of view, with the usual effects of a disposition, leads us to approve of its cause in this case as in all other cases.

IX

To conclude: I have been arguing that Hume does not have a special subjective theory of truth. Although the ordinary concept of truth serves us perfectly well in our day-to-day practical affairs, the most fundamental question to be asked about some of our metaphysical beliefs is not "Are they true?" but rather "Are we reasonable in holding them?" Reasonableness, in this sense, is a virtue, and the account of our approval of this virtue must therefore follow the pattern which Hume lays down for the explanation of all virtues. We approve of people's beliefs in so far as they serve human ends and purposes and avoid confusion, for confusion is a most unpleasant condition.

I believe my interpretation helps to explain Hume's ambivalent attitude towards the value of the distinction between primary and secondary qualities. It also makes sense of his apparent praise of the beliefs about the external world both of the vulgar and of the philosopher. I furthermore think that the place I have given to reasonableness as a virtue may help us to see why Hume should argue against superstition on the ground of its pernicious consequences for human life. Religious errors (in that they tend to have bad effects upon behaviour) are dangerous, whereas errors in philosophy are merely ridiculous. The preference of sanity to madness can also be explained in terms of the adverse effects of madness both upon the madman himself and upon other people.

I am aware of the fact that I cannot easily reconcile all that Hume writes in his *Treatise* with my interpretation. But it seems plain to me that if Hume had been asked "Is reasonableness a virtue?" he would, to remain consistent, have had to answer "Of course it is." In our attempt to understand reasonableness we must therefore take full account of what follows from the analysis of judgments of virtue which he offers. It is my firm belief that, although I have in this essay only scratched the surface of this tangled issue, digging deeper will lead to an improved understanding of some fundamental aspects of Hume's philosophy.

NOTES

1. I express myself in this guarded fashion to allow for the fact that those virtues immediately pleasing to the person himself qualify as virtues independently of their tendency to lead to certain kinds of behaviour. Thus a person who tends to experience

the pleasant passions is on that account virtuous. It goes without saying that such a person is also likely to behave in a cheerful manner and to spread happiness around him. This would be an additional reason for approving of those who possess a cheerful temper.

2. Rachael M. Kydd seems to overlook this when in contrasting Hume with Spinoza she writes: "For Hume seems to have thought that the passion which prompts us to reason is always a passion for some particular end or for happiness. According to him, we desire to reason in order to discover the ways in which our other desires may be fulfilled, while Spinoza on the other hand maintains that we desire to reason *for its own sake*" (*Reason and Conduct in Hume's Treatise* [London, 1946], p. 156). Hume's view seems to be that, while it is true that the desire to reason and to seek truth for its own sake may not be universal, some people undoubtedly do possess this desire.

3. In his *A Faculty Theory of Knowledge* (Lewisburg, 1971; p. 31), George Stern writes: "The aim of the *Enquiry*, then, is to develop a faculty theory of knowledge. . . ." Stern does not argue for the conclusion that this was also the aim of the *Treatise*. It is beyond the scope of this essay to examine Stern's interpretation of the first *Enquiry*, but I have no doubt that it will be challenged. Here I must make it suffice to suggest that it is most implausible to claim that Hume was in the *Treatise* arguing for "a faculty theory of knowledge."

4. Hume's rejection of the rationalism of his predecessors is discussed in my introduction to the Fontana Philosophy Classics edition of Books II and III of the *Treatise* (London, 1972).

5. *British Moralists: 1650–1800*, ed. D. D. Raphael, 2 vols. (Oxford, 1969), I 243.

6. Ibid., 242.

7. For a criticism of the way in which I expressed myself upon this topic in *Passion and Value in Hume's Treatise* (Edinburgh, 1966), see Thomas K. Hearn, Jr., "Árdal on the Moral Sentiments in Hume's *Treatise*," *Philosophy*, 48, No. 185 (July 1973), 288–92. I believe the way I express myself here is an improvement upon the version which Hearn attacks, and avoids at least some of the confusion with which he charges me. *Passion and Value* contains a much fuller statement than can be attempted here of the passions in Hume's account of the evaluation of qualities of mind or character.

8. Though this work was first published anonymously in 1658, the author was probably Richard Allestree (1619–81). See *Hume's Dialogues Concerning Natural Religion*, ed. Norman Kemp Smith (Edinburgh, 1935), p. 5, and "An Account of My Last Interview with David Hume, Esq.," *Private Papers of James Boswell*, edd. Geoffrey Scott and Frederick A. Pottle (New York, 1931), XII 227–32 (included in ibid., pp. 76–79).

9. W. H. Walsh, "Hume's Concept of Truth," *Reason and Reality*, Royal Institute of Philosophy Lectures Vol. 5, 1970–71 (London, 1972), 99–116 at 112. As far as I know, Walsh is the first person to express in print the view that Hume's account of value judgments is relevant for the interpretation of his epistemology. I independently came to the same conclusion in my commentary on a paper by Wade L. Robison in May 1972 (note 11).

10. Ibid., p. 113.

11. Robison's paper was delivered at the meeting of the Western Division of the American Philosophical Association in May 1972, and has since been published in *Dialogue*, 12, No. 1 (March 1973), 87–99. The essence of the current essay was contained in my commentary on that paper, and a somewhat extended version of it was read at the Second Hume Conference at Northern Illinois University in November 1973.

12. The point made here must, I believe, be accepted by those who advocate a different account from mine of the nature of judgments of virtue in Hume's *Treatise*.

13. *The Causes and Evidence of Beliefs: An Examination of Hume's Procedure* (Mount Hermon, 1936), p. 73.

II

5

Hume on Religious Belief

KEITH E. YANDELL
The University of Wisconsin
Madison

THERE IS NO UNIVERSAL CONSENT as to what view of religion Hume embraced.[1] He himself seems to vacillate hopelessly. On the one hand, he solemnly writes that the "whole frame of nature bespeaks an intelligent author; and no rational enquirer can, after serious reflection, suspend his belief a moment with regard to the primary principles of genuine Theism and Religion" (NHR 21). This claim is repeated often in his treatment of religion as an historical phenomenon, and appears again (in a qualified version) as the avowed conclusion of the *Dialogues*:

> If the whole of natural theology, as some people seem to maintain, resolves itself into one simple, though somewhat ambiguous, at least undefined proposition, *that the cause or causes of order in the universe probably bear some remote analogy to human intelligence* . . . what can the most inquisitive, contemplative, and religious man do more than give a plain, philosophical assent to the proposition, as often as it occurs; and believe that the arguments, on which it is established, exceed the objections which lie against it? [D 227].

The speaker is Philo, who, throughout the *Dialogues*, has been the constant and insightful critic of all endeavors to establish the truth of religious claims. Even he finds belief in an intelligence-resembling cause or causes of natural order simply inescapable.

On the other hand, no volume in the literature has subjected the argument from design to more extended and acute criticism than Hume's *Dialogues*. No criticism of the ontological argument has been more widely accepted than his dictum that "Whatever we conceive as existent, we can also conceive as non-existent" (D 189).[2] The argument from contingent to necessary being, or from contemporary events to a First Cause, plainly cannot be successful if the principle that every event must have a cause is

I should like to thank Professor Julius Weinberg, my late friend and colleague, and Professors Marvin Fox and Jon Moline for their comments on an earlier version of this paper. This paper was written in part under a National Endowment for the Humanities grant (No. F-72-529).

nothing more than a "natural belief"—i.e., a belief which we can neither escape having nor rationally justify.[3] Hume's critique of the claim that the causal principle is self-evident is too well known to require comment.[4] Furthermore, no argument from eternal moral truths or from man's rational–moral nature can be mounted if morality is founded, as Hume insists, on sentiment rather than on reason.[5] What, then, can Hume of all men mean by the remarks quoted in our opening paragraph? Is it any wonder that he concludes his study of the natural history of religion with an apparent confession of failure?

> The whole [of religion] is a riddle, an ænigma, an inexplicable mystery. Doubt, uncertainty, suspence of judgment appear the only result of our most accurate scrutiny, concerning this subject [NHR 76].

Since the "terrible David" has expressed himself so ambiguously, appearing as apparent apologist for the claims of religion [6] but also as its most avid critic, and since he seems to confess unequivocally his own final puzzlement, can we do more than record his inconsistencies and note his failure?

It is the thesis of this paper that, in spite of appearances, Hume has spoken with clarity to those who have ears to hear. It is patently true that in one sense, or at one level, he has expressed himself with studied ambiguity on a topic which is laden with emotional overtones and is frequently regarded as having intimate ties with everyday morality. I shall attempt to show that, equally patently, he has tipped his hand in just those places and in just that manner which anyone familiar with his methods of writing might have expected.

If this is so, a word of explanation is required as to why commentators have not been more frequently aware of it. One influential assumption which has often led Humean commentators astray is that the key to Hume's view on religion lies in discovering who, in the *Dialogues*, speaks for Hume. Remarkable variety can be found among competent commentators as to the answer to this question.[7]

Nonetheless, it is easily shown that no one participant always speaks for Hume. No argument is really needed to show that Demea does not, and his championing of the claims that there is "some ultimate cause, that is *necessarily* existent . . ." (D 188) and that we "Finite, weak, and blind creatures . . . ought to humble ourselves in his august presence, and, conscious of our frailties, adore in silence his infinite perfections . . ." (D 141) are not, I think, claims which competent students of Hume will identify with Hume's own position. What Pamphilus refers to as "the rigid inflexible orthodoxy of Demea" (D 128) is not Humean orthodoxy, though it may certainly be doubted that Demea's position is in fact that of orthodox Christian belief.

Notoriously, it is more plausible to identify Philo or Cleanthes as always being Hume's spokesman. Cleanthes, however, expresses one view of the relation of religion and morality whereas Hume, clearly in his own name, expresses quite another in the *Natural History*. Thus Cleanthes says:

> Religion, however corrupted, is still better than no religion at all. The doctrine of a future state is so strong and necessary a security to morals, that we never ought to abandon or neglect it. For if finite and temporary rewards and punishments have so great an effect, as we daily find: How much greater must be expected from such as are infinite and eternal? [D 219–20].

But it is too well known to require detailed comment that the dependence of morality on religion, either for rational justification or for conative or affective backing, is a theme neither of the relevant portions of the *Treatise* (Book I, Part III) nor of the relevant *Enquiry*. Hume's own view of the relation of religion and morality is discussed in the *Natural History* (NHR 70–73), and that discussion is in effect repeated by Philo in the *Dialogues* as a response to Cleanthes' recently quoted remarks (D 219ff.). So it seems that Cleanthes does not always speak for Hume.

Neither does Philo. Early in the *Dialogues*, he holds that suspense of judgment concerning religious belief is possible (D 35–36), but later joins Cleanthes in denying this (D 216). Clearly, he cannot "speak for Hume" in both places. Furthermore, in the *Natural History* it seems clear that Hume himself agrees with the view which Philo first holds and then abandons in the *Dialogues* (NHR 75–76).

On the other hand, it seems clear that every one of the three participants sometimes "speaks for Hume." Philo does so, for example, when he contends that all religion corrupts "except the philosophical and rational kind" (D 220).[8] So does Cleanthes when he queries "Whence can any cause be known but from its known effects?" (D 199).[9] And so does Demea when he argues that the special sort of simplicity sometimes ascribed to God is inconsistent with God's also being an intelligence.[10] In sum, if to "speak for Hume in the *Dialogues*" is to say what Hume has said in his own name elsewhere, no one of our three participants always succeeds, or always fails, in so speaking. Hence it seems wisest to proceed on what is in any case surely the safest assumption, namely, that it is the *Dialogues* itself which serves as Hume's "spokesman," and to inquire into the significance of the *Dialogues* in the context of the whole of Hume's writings on relevant matters. For present purposes, this requires a closer look at his companion piece on religion—namely, *The Natural History of Religion*—than is usually given in attempts to understand the *Dialogues*.

Underlying the assumption that some *one* participant in the *Dialogues* must always "speak for Hume" is the more fundamental thesis that it is in the *Dialogues* that one must seek for Hume's position. I believe this thesis to be mistaken for reasons which will take up the remainder of this paper, and that a different approach must be taken if we are to determine what Hume's views on religion were and why he believed them to be correct. I suggest that *The Natural History of Religion* contains the key to Hume's position, and that the *Dialogues* must be read in the light of the *Natural History*. Or, to be more accurate, the *Natural History* expresses straightforwardly theses which the *Dialogues* expresses only by implication.[11]

The correctness of this particular approach to Hume's views on religion can be fully justified only by a detailed analysis of the relevant portions of the *Dialogues* and the *Natural History*. I shall turn to this analysis shortly. Nonetheless, certain considerations can be offered in its favor even before this analysis is begun. Hume's introductions are important, functioning as contour maps of the intellectual terrain to be traversed in the work being introduced. This is notoriously true of the introduction to the *Treatise*, where Hume remarks:

> 'Tis evident, that all the sciences have a relation, greater or less, to human nature; and that however wide any of them may seem to run from it, they still return back by one passage or another. Even *Mathematics, Natural Philosophy, and Natural Religion*, are in some measure dependent on the science of MAN; since they lie under the cognizance of men, and are judged of by their powers and faculties [T xix].

Hume's insistence that "the science of man is the only solid foundation for the other sciences" and that "the only solid foundation we can give to this science itself must be laid on experience and observation" (T xx) governs the development of the *Treatise*. From our experiences and observations, and the principles and propensities which comprise human nature, the entire structure of human belief arises. It would be strange indeed in the light of Hume's insistence on the centrality of the science of man if the question of religious belief were not related in some explicit manner to human nature. This would be the case even if Hume had not, in the passage just quoted, explicitly listed natural religion (though not natural theology) as having "a relation to human nature." The crucial issue, then, must be "How, for Hume, is religious belief related to human nature?" It is by answering this question—not the comparatively superficial one about "Who in the *Dialogues* speaks for Hume?"—that we can properly determine Hume's views on religion.

Hume opens his *Natural History of Religion* by distinguishing "two questions . . . which challenge our attention, to wit, that concerning [religion's] foundation in reason, and that concerning its origin in human nature" (NHR 21). The *Dialogues* are mainly concerned with the first question, although we shall see that the last part of the *Dialogues*, which has caused such consternation among commentators,[12] deals with the second. The *Natural History* but touches on the first question and concentrates on the second. Therefore it is the *Natural History* which one must regard as Hume's *locus classicus* with respect to his views concerning religion, for it is there that he most fully relates religion to human nature.[13]

I have stressed, then, that the fundamental question to ask in attempting to understand Hume's views on religion is "How is religious belief related to human nature?" This question leads us immediately into the doctrines of the *Natural History* where he writes "The whole frame of nature bespeaks an intelligent author . . ." (NHR 21).[14] Nonetheless, belief in an author of nature is not absolutely universal, and even where such belief prevails there is no single account of the nature of the author. Given these facts, Hume suggests a conclusion:

It would appear, therefore, that this preconception springs not from an original instinct or primary impression of nature, such as gives rise to self-love, . . . since every instinct of this kind has been found absolutely universal in all nations and ages, and has always a precise determinate object, which it inflexibly pursues [NHR 21].[15]

It follows that the "first religious principles must be secondary; such as may easily be perverted by various accidents and causes, and whose operation too, in some cases, may, by an extraordinary concurrence of circumstances, be altogether prevented" (NHR 21).[16] What is denied in this passage is less to be stressed than what is affirmed: namely, that there are "religious first principles" built into human nature, though not so indelibly and lucidly imprinted that they may not be blurred or erased. Nor is this passage unique.

The universal propensity to believe in invisible, intelligent power, if not an original instinct, being at least a general attendant of human nature, may be considered as a kind of mark or stamp, which the divine workman has set upon his work . . . [NHR 75].[17]

If all men have this propensity to minimal theism, what interferes with its operation? The answer to this question is implicit in the distinction between religion's "foundation in [human] reason" and its "origin in human nature." It is Hume's contention that acceptance of theism is a product of man's *rational* capacities; the propensity to theism is a propensity of reason.[18]

[N]o *rational* enquirer can, after serious reflection, suspend his belief a moment with regard to the primary principles of genuine Theism and Religion [NHR 21; emphasis added].

The mind rises gradually, from inferior to superior. . . . Nothing could disturb this natural process of thought, but some obvious and invincible *argument* . . . the order and frame of the universe, *when accurately examined,* affords such an argument . . . [NHR 24; emphasis added].[19]

Whoever learns by *argument,* the existence of invisible intelligent power, must *reason* from the admirable contrivance of natural objects, and must suppose the world to be the workmanship of that divine being, the original cause of all things [NHR 38; emphasis added; see also NHR 74].

As a propensity of reason,[20] the propensity to minimal theism is a less fundamental portion of human nature than are propensities of the imagination. Propensities of the imagination, which in Hume's view give rise to beliefs in external objects and causal connections,[21] have these features: (*a*) they are universally efficacious in bringing about the beliefs toward which they are propensities; and (*b*) the belief to which they give rise is always the *same* belief with little or no variation. In line, however, with reason's role in Hume as the "slave of the passions," the propensity to minimal theism is often thwarted or perverted by other propensities. It is worth noting that the only (though not unimportant) difference between the minimal theism mentioned here and that of Part XII concerns the greater caution of the latter which speaks of a cause (or causes) of order bearing *some remote analogy* to intelligence, not as intelligent *simpliciter.*

It is worth a brief detour to note an interesting parallel between Hume's treatment of belief in the external world and in causal connections, and his treatment of minimally theistic belief. Belief in the external world and in causal connections is sustained in the face of conflict between the set of reasons offered for the one belief and the set of reasons offered for the other, as well as the inherent insufficiency of either set to establish its own conclusion (T 215, 231, 266).[22] Hume says:

> my natural propensity, and the course of my animal spirits and passions reduce me to this indolent belief in the general maxims of the world. . . . I must yield to the current of nature. . . . These are the sentiments of my spleen and indolence; and indeed I must confess, that philosophy has nothing to oppose to them. . . . In all the incidents of life we ought still to preserve our scepticism. If we believe, that fire warms, or water refreshes, 'tis only because it costs us too much pains to think otherwise [T 269, 270].

Just so, in the case of religious belief,

> Doubt, uncertainty, suspence of judgment appear the only result of our most accurate scrutiny, concerning this subject. But such is the frailty of human reason, and such the irresistible contagion of opinion, that even this deliberate doubt could scarcely be upheld; did we not enlarge our view, and opposing one species of superstition to another, set them a quarrelling; while we ourselves, during their fury and contention, happily make our escape into the calm, though obscure, regions of philosophy [NHR 76].

Our beliefs in each case are determined by "nature" (our innate propensities), which we cannot escape in the first case, but can with difficulty escape in the second, so that absence of religious belief (i.e., "suspence of judgment") is possible. System is necessary (NHR 29), but not a religious system.[23]

Returning to our exposition of the *Natural History*: one factor (not a propensity) which, Hume claims, thwarts the propensity to minimal theism at lower stages of mental evolution is a law of progression in thought from the lower to the higher. Much at least of his argument that monotheism is late in the history of religion rests on the *a priori* claim that the earlier stages of human thought are too crude to have seized upon anything so rarified (NHR 23).[24] This claim, however, is peripheral to our present interests.

Another factor is more relevant. There is, Hume asserts, a quite different source of religious belief from the actualization of a propensity of reason. Put succinctly: men are unaware of the causes which control their fate, but are filled with hope and fear about these causes. This combination of ignorance, hope, and fear unites with other natural propensities to create religious beliefs other than simple minimal theism:

> in all nations, which have embraced polytheism, the first ideas of religion arose not from a contemplation of the works of nature, but from a concern with regard to the events of life, and from the incessant hopes and fears, which actuate the human mind [NHR 27; see also NHR 28, 29].

Hume lists several natural propensities, besides that toward minimal theism, which operate to produce religious belief.

[The] imagination, perpetually employed on the same subject [the unknown causes of human destiny], must labour to form some particular and distinct idea of them [NHR 29].

Men would not be led to raise questions as to the causes of their pleasures and pains "were it not for a propensity in human nature, which leads into a system, that gives them some satisfaction" (NHR 29).[25] Thus there is a propensity to seek a satisfying system of interpretation for the events of human life.

There is also a universal propensity of mankind to "conceive all beings like themselves, and to transfer to every object, those qualities, with which they are familiarly acquainted . . ." (NHR 29). This propensity to anthropomorphize both deities and natural objects is not assigned to any "faculty."

There is still another propensity to concentrate our attention on perceivable objects.

And thus, however strong men's propensity to believe invisible, intelligent power in nature, their propensity is equally strong to rest their attention on sensible, visible objects; and in order to reconcile these opposite inclinations, they are led to unite the invisible power with some visible object [NHR 38].

Thus Hume in attributing to men a propensity to minimal theism is by no means ascribing to man's rational capacities the primary role in producing religious belief. Most religious beliefs, in his view, arise from a combination of ignorance, hope, and fear working in correlation with propensities quite distinct from the propensity to minimal theism. We have seen that these other propensities include a propensity to anthropomorphize the deity or deities, ascribing literal human passions to the object of religious devotion, thus both making the invisible, intelligent power less intelligent and also corrupting the moral influence of belief in such a power (NHR 51–52). Also noted was a propensity to concentrate on sensible objects, thus making the intelligent power visible (NHR 40). The net result is to produce religious beliefs which are farther from those of minimal theism than are the beliefs of avowed atheists (NHR 32–33). Thus while all men seek a satisfactory system, thereby manifesting a propensity of the imagination, following the propensity of reason toward minimal theism is only one case of providing content to such a system. Although, with certain qualifications, minimal theism is the best way of providing such content, it is not the most widely influential, being easily perverted and subjugated to propensities whose products are less noble where its operation is not altogether prevented.[26]

With the influence of these various propensities in mind, we can now return to the propensity to minimal theism with which we began. Given that for Hume reason is an "instinct of the soul," [27] given also that a detailed critique of the traditional attempts to justify theism of *any* sort has been offered in Parts I through IX of the *Dialogues*, it is plausible to suggest the following analysis of Hume's "natural theology passages." What Hume means when he says that "the order and frame of the universe affords [obvious and invincible] argument . . ." (NHR 24) for the existence of an intelligent, invisible author of its design [28] is merely this: that when men note the (at least apparent) design in nature, a propensity (of reason) to ascribe this design to an intelligent author is triggered insofar as other, competing propensities do not thwart it. In no stronger sense than this is belief in minimal theism "justified." Indeed, its *foundation in human reason is nil*, for here *justification* is in question. Its *origin in human nature* is simply the propensity which, under favorable conditions, and upon appropriate stimulus, gives rise to the belief.[29] This account is, I believe, plainly compatible with the doctrines of the *Natural History* and is indeed precisely what that essay intends to make clear.

One who supposes that Hume thought the argument from design a success [30] in justifying the mitigated conclusion that the cause or causes of order in nature bear some remote analogy to human intelligence, in the sense of proving it to be more probably true than its denial, faces the obvious difficulty of making Hume more oblivious to the force of his powerful critique of that argument, at least in every formulation which he considers, than I at least would suppose possible for so astute a philosopher. But those who yield to this temptation face other difficulties as well. If Hume accepted some version of the argument from design, presumably that version has one essential premiss of the form *Since artifacts and natural objects are similar effects, they have similar causes,* and another of the form *Natural objects manifest order.*[31] Obviously enough, the latter premiss entails *At least some natural object exists,* and presumably the relevant rationale for the former is the claim that *Like causes have like effects, and conversely.* To accept an argument is, of course, to accept its premisses as true, or as more likely true than their competitors. This, in turn, is to accept whatever those premisses entail, and whatever must be true if those premisses are known to be true. But notoriously Hume does not think that either the causal principle (*Every event must have a cause*) or the causal maxim (*Like effects, like causes* in the formulation here relevant) are either known to be true or known to be more likely true than their denials (T 78ff.). Nor did he think it was known to be true or known to be more likely true than not that there exist any natural objects (T 231).

He does of course, as I suggested earlier, suppose that these beliefs are "natural" and so inescapable, and in the course of the *Dialogues* Philo grants Cleanthes both the causal principle (D 142) and the causal maxim (D 165–66). I suspect Hume has Philo do so because: (a) his critical say on these points is reserved for the *Treatise*; (b) it is a much more effective critique of the design argument if one can grant these theses and show that the argument still fails; and (c) as a man of common sense, Philo will ultimately have to accept them anyway. But to "accept" these claims "as a man of common sense," or in any other way which can properly be ascribed to Hume, is to grant that we cannot doubt the claims (save perhaps in moments of philosophic reflection), or perhaps doubt that they are more likely true than their competitors, not to grant that they are known to be true or known to be more likely true than their competitors. Similar remarks apply, I think, to the claim that there are natural objects, which is not questioned at all in the *Dialogues*.

One who maintains, then, that Hume accepts the argument from design, in any version which appears in the *Dialogues* or in any version which requires as essential premisses the causal principle and/or maxim and the thesis that there are natural objects (and what version of the design argument will not?) must also maintain that Hume accepts as known, or known to be more likely true than not, just those premisses. This interpretation of Hume, I should think, suffers from at least one defect—namely, it contradicts what Hume himself is notorious for having clearly maintained with respect to causality and the external world. Or it assumes that Hume forgot, or did not hold, those views when he wrote the *Dialogues*. And with that we have, I think, gone well beyond the bounds of reasonable interpretation. But if this is correct, then "at face value" interpretation of the "natural theology" passages in Hume will not do; he does not—not even in those passages— sanction the design argument. How then are we to read them? Just in the way I have suggested, with the appeal to the *Natural History* and the propensity-account of religious belief which it offers. If this interpretation also makes sense of Part XII, we may take its Humean orthodoxy as established, and this is the question we must now investigate.[32]

A surprising switch *seems* to occur in Part XII of Hume's *Dialogues*. Philo, throughout the first eleven dialogues, has been the severe critic of all attempts to defend religion rationally. The critique of the argument from design has come mainly from his lips. Cleanthes states the crucial objection to the ontological argument, but does so saying that he will "not leave it to PHILO . . . to point out the obvious weakness of this metaphysical reasoning" (D 189). The implication is that Philo concurs, but that the refutation is so easy that his vast critical talents are not necessary. This role of adamant critic of natural theology makes it all the more shocking to hear from Philo a statement of faith. No interpretation of the *Dialogues* is even plausible unless it accounts for this apparent alteration in Philo's sentiments.

What is crucial, however, is that no alteration of sentiments has occurred. Rather, the topic has changed. Hume emphasizes this by having Demea, the champion of "rigorous orthodoxy," leave the scene. Demea's major positive contribution to the discussion has been to emphasize the incomprehensibility of God (D 141–42, 158–59).[33] Hume exploits this emphasis for his own purposes in a manner shortly to be discussed. Philo, however, agrees at this point with Demea against Cleanthes. Thus a representative of an important part of Demea's position which Hume weaves into the final section is present after Demea's departure.[34] Hence no genuine loss is sustained when alteration of theme is underlined by the departure of one of the discussants. Philo explicitly points out the change of topic in his "confession of faith." He makes his confession, not as a sceptic, but as a man of common sense.

> I must confess . . . that I am less cautious on the subject of natural religion than on any other; both because I know that I can never, on that head, corrupt the principles of any man of common sense, and because no one, I am confident, in whose eyes I appear a man of common sense, will ever mistake my intentions [D 214].

Minimal theism, having no rational justification, will not be destroyed by arguments purporting to show that it has none. Just as our beliefs in causation and in external objects [35] are not demolished by a recognition that these beliefs are utterly unfounded, so belief in minimal theism remains unscathed after a similar recognition.

Philo's role as critic of natural theology makes him an all the more appropriate spokesman for natural religion. He identifies himself as such a spokesman in no indefinite terms.

> You, . . . CLEANTHES, with whom I live in unreserved intimacy . . . are sensible, that, notwithstanding the freedom of my conversation, and my love of singular arguments, no one has a deeper sense of religion impressed on his mind, or pays more profound adoration to the divine Being, as he discovers himself to reason, in the inexplicable contrivance and artifice of nature [D 214].

The sciences "lead us insensibly" [36] to acknowledge a first intelligent author without any intention of establishing such a position. In the passages which follow, Philo offers us once again the "argument from design" which has been so thoroughly criticized in the preceding dialogues by Philo himself, but its purpose here is merely to point to data which can serve to trigger an innate propensity. He does not endeavor to establish any conclusions about the truth or falsity of the resultant belief.

The religious hypothesis is also supported by Cleanthes who defends it in a manner most revealing to anyone who comes to the *Dialogues* with the *Natural History* in mind:

> A false, absurd system, human nature, from the force of prejudice, is capable of adhering to with obstinacy and perseverance: But no system at all, in opposition to a theory, supported by strong and obvious reason, by natural propensity, and by early education, I think it absolutely impossible to maintain or defend [D 216].

Cleanthes relates belief in the "religious hypothesis" to human nature by means of a "natural propensity." The reference to "strong and obvious reason" is to be seen as indicating the (at least apparent) design which triggers the propensity, leading us insensibly to have a belief in an intelligent author.[37] On this much, Philo can and does agree. Furthermore, for both Philo and Cleanthes, this propensity is part of man's rational capacity.[38]

In the past several paragraphs I have made use of the terms "natural theology" and "natural religion," and I had best make clear my understanding and use of these terms. Natural theology is the attempt to establish, by argument(s), that a particular set of theistic claims are true. By analogy, natural atheology is the attempt to establish, in a similar manner, that these claims are false. Hume is neither a natural theologian nor a natural atheologian. Rather, he argues in the *Dialogues* that certain familiar endeavors in natural theology fail. By itself, this feature of Hume's writings no more shows that he himself rejects (or even thinks he can reject) all such beliefs than his critique of our reasonings concerning the external world, or cause and effect, shows that he himself rejects (or even thinks he can reject) belief that there are external objects which bear causal connections to one another. None of these beliefs—in an Author of Natural Order, an external world, or causal connection—has for Hume any foundation in human reason along the lines of being either self-evident or defensible by cogent arguments.

Natural religion (for Hume) is, I take it, the set of theistic beliefs which are produced by the passions and propensities he discusses in the *Natural History*. The set is of course open-ended, for as the causes and contents of human hopes and fears, and encounters with order, vary, so will the particular beliefs to which the propensities (triggered by these hopes, fears, and experiences) give rise. It is natural religion which provides the topic of Part XII, while natural theology has been the main concern of the first eleven parts. Still, Hume calls them dialogues "concerning natural religion," and given the concluding part and his introductory comments, this seems appropriate. In the introduction he has the young Pamphilus discuss the sort of topic with respect to which dialogic style is appropriate, which he takes to be

> Any point of doctrine, which is so *obvious*, that it scarcely admits of dispute, but at the same time so *important*, that it cannot be too often inculcated . . . Any question of philosophy, on the other hand, which is so *obscure* and *uncertain*, that human reason can reach no fixed determination with regard to it; if it should be treated at all; seems to lead us naturally into the style of dialogue and conversation. . . . Happily, these circumstances are all to be found in the subject of NATURAL RELIGION. What truth so obvious, so certain, as the *being* of a God . . . What truth so important . . . But in treating of this obvious and important truth; what obscure questions occur, concerning the *nature* of that divine Being . . . [D 127, 128].[39]

Here, natural religion is made to concern both the *being* and the *nature* of God, and is not distinguished from natural theology. But of course the beliefs Hume in the *Natural History* says are produced by passions and propensities concern both matters—being and nature—and in saying that "human reason has not reached any determination" concerning the divine nature Pamphilus is saying that natural theology has failed. Hume's conviction that disputes concerning competing conceptions of God are "verbal" has the effect of reducing genuine theological dispute to the question as to whether or not God exists (a point said not to be open to dispute). So, in effect, natural theology has no legitimate office (having no foundation in human reason). Natural religion has nonetheless (a secondary) origin in human nature, and so it is among the natural phenomena which anyone who wishes to be "thoroughly acquainted with the extent and force of human understanding, and [to] explain the nature of the ideas we employ, and of the operations we perform in our reasonings" (T xix) must concern himself. This concern manifests itself particularly in Part XII of the *Dialogues*, whereas the previous parts were mainly concerned to show the failure of natural theology to place any theistic belief on a firm rational foundation. This shift of concern explains the (merely apparent) shift of contentions.[40]

It might be suggested that this interpretation makes things *too* definite. Did not Hume himself confess at the end of the *Natural History* that the "whole is a riddle, an ænigma, an inexplicable mystery. Doubt, uncertainty, suspence of judgment appear the only result of our most accurate scrutiny, concerning this subject" (NHR 76)? How can anyone claim that Hume's views are clearly this, or that, when he himself confesses failure?

My answer is to distinguish the question as to what Hume's conclusions were from the different question as to whether Hume was (or ought to have been) satisfied with them. Condemned to a conflict of propensities which are relevant to religious belief, man's state is, if Hume is correct, less than enviable. Either blind belief which is destructive of morality or blind belief which is not: such is man's destiny with respect to religious belief. For should the propensity to deism be wed with, say, the propensity to concentrate on sensible objects, religious beliefs arise which are detrimental to morality.[41]

It is important in this connection to remember that according to Hume man is no better off with respect to his beliefs in an external world and in causal connections between the objects of that world. Hume writes in "Of the Modern Philosophy" that

> there is a direct and total opposition . . . betwixt those conclusions we form from cause and effect, and those that persuade us of the continu'd and independent existence of body. When we reason from cause and effect, we conclude, that neither colour, sound, taste, nor smell have a continu'd and independent existence. When we exclude these sensible qualities there remains nothing in the universe, which has such an [external and independent] existence [T 231].

Nonetheless we believe in an external and independent world. Thus our "natural beliefs" conflict: by reasoning from our natural belief in causal connections, we are led to the conclusion that our natural belief in an external world is false, and yet we cannot reject either belief save in the short-lived heat of philosophic reflection.

In the Appendix to the *Treatise* Hume admits that although he had hoped that his "theory of the intellectual world" would be "free from those contradictions, and absurdities, which seem to attend every explication, that human reason can give of the material world" he finds that "upon a more strict review of the section concerning *personal identity*, . . . I neither know how to correct my former opinions, nor how to render them consistent" (T 633). It is, I believe, in the light of these confessions, as well as with regard to the view of religious belief which we have discussed, that we must understand the enigma passage. For surely it is not hard to see why Hume finds the matter of religion "an inexplicable mystery." The reason is simply that natural religion, as well as mathematics and natural philosophy, must rest on the "one sound foundation"—the science of man.[42] Given the results of investigating the explanation which human reason, he thinks, must give of beliefs concerning the material and intellectual worlds, excluding religious belief, one also finds "an inexplicable mystery" which makes Hume "plead the privilege of a sceptic, and confess, that this difficulty is too hard for my understanding" (T 636). If the enigma passage casts doubt upon the claim that the present interpretation presents Hume's views on religious matters, then the passages quoted in these concluding paragraphs cast equal doubt on the claim that the comments made by Hume in the *Treatise* express his own views about the "material" and "intellectual" worlds.[43] Rather, I should think, the passages from the *Treatise* and the *Natural History* show that in the last analysis it is man himself who is for Hume "a riddle, an ænigma, an inexplicable mystery." [44]

NOTES

1. James Noxon ("Hume's Agnosticism," *Philosophical Review*, 73, No. 3 [1964], 248–61; repr. in *Hume: A Collection of Critical Essays*, ed. V. C. Chappell [Garden City, 1966], pp. 361–83) goes so far as to say that "David Hume has left his readers to wonder about his personal convictions on the great questions of religion" (*Hume*, p. 361). He qualifies this only by the assertion that Hume does tell us that disputes in natural theology are only "verbal."

2. Nonetheless, it seems to be little more than a begging of the question against the ontological arguer.

3. On natural belief in Hume, see Norman Kemp Smith, *The Philosophy of David Hume* (London, 1941), pp. 409–11, 443–64, 485–96.

4. Hume's critique appears in Book I, Part III, Sections III and IV of *A Treatise of Human Nature*. For a clear statement of the view Hume attacks, see John Locke's first Letter to Bishop Stillingfleet (1697), the relevant portion of which is reproduced in *Problems in Philosophical Inquiry*, edd. J. R. Weinberg and K. E. Yandell (New York, 1971), p. 163.

5. This point did not escape Kant's notice: Hume "overlooked the positive injury which results, if reason be deprived of its most important prospects, which can alone supply to the will the highest aim for all its endeavor" (*Prolegomena to Any Future Metaphysic*, ed. Paul Carus [La Salle, 1902], p. 5n). Kant's "answer to Hume" is to restore to reason "its most important prospects." See the Preface to the second edition of the *Critique of Pure Reason*. Hume's claim that reason is not the source of morality is made in Book II, Part I, Sections I and II of the *Treatise*. On this aspect of Kant's "answer to Hume," see my *Basic Issues in the Philosophy of Religion* (Boston, 1970), chap. 5.

6. He even sometimes appears as advocate for the thesis that religion rests securely on revelation. See D 227.

7. Norman Kemp Smith, for example, in the introduction to his edition of the *Dialogues*, says that ". . . Philo, from start to finish, represents Hume . . ." (D 59); Antony Flew agrees (*Hume's Philosophy of Belief* [London, 1961], p. 216). But A. Seth Pringle-Pattison (*The Idea of God in Recent Philosophy* [Oxford, 1920], pp. 155ff.) regards Cleanthes as Hume's spokesman, and Charles Hendel concurs (*Studies in the Philosophy of David Hume* [Indianapolis, 1963], pp. 267ff.). See Noxon, "Hume's Agnosticism," *Hume*, ed. Chappell, pp. 367, 369, for further references, and compare the remarks of Pamphilus to Hermippus which introduce the *Dialogues*. So far as I know—and for obvious reasons—no one has suggested that it is Demea who is Hume's sole mouthpiece.

8. Compare D 220 with NHR 70–73.

9. Compare D 199 with EPM 141.

10. Compare D 158 with T 240ff.

11. The *Dialogues* and the *Natural History* were evidently written during the same period (1749–51), although the *Natural History* was published, along with other works, in 1757 while the *Dialogues* were posthumously published in 1779 in accordance with Hume's wishes. It would not do to argue that Hume's "great care" in ensuring that the *Dialogues* be published shows that they express his "real" views; what reason is there to doubt that he would have been equally careful to see that the *Natural History* would be published had it not already been in print? See D 87–96, Appendix C.

12. Noxon ("Hume's Agnosticism," *Hume*, ed. Chappell, p. 367) speaks of "the complete reversal of standpoint made by Philo in the twelfth and final dialogue," and quotes

T. E. Jessop as saying "The conclusion [i.e., Dialogue 12] being disconnected from the argued content of the *Dialogues*, I shall ignore it" ("Symposium: The Present-Day Relevance of Hume's *Dialogues concerning Natural Religion*," *Proceedings of the Aristotelian Society*, Suppl. vol. 18 [1939], 220). We shall see that there is neither reversal nor discontinuity of argument. Wollheim believes it would "be a mistake to look for any way of removing or resolving all the inconsistencies that appear in Hume's writings on religion, and of extracting from them a rigorous and unified doctrine" (*David Hume on Religion*, ed. Richard Wollheim [New York, 1963], p. 17). I shall try to show that Hume has a unified, consistent view of religion, and that to think otherwise is a mistake.

13. This, not the fact that only one of the works is in dialogue form, is their crucial difference.

14. It is worth noting that, for Hume, religion has a natural history just as do, say, reptiles.

15. Note that Hume here describes belief in an "intelligent author" as a "preconception" and a "first principle," suggesting thereby that justification by arguments is neither available nor appropriate.

16. At D 155, Cleanthes remarks, "Some beauties in writing we may meet with, which seem contrary to rules, and which gain the affections, and animate the imagination, in opposition to all the precepts of criticism, and to the authority of the established masters of art. And if the argument for theism be, as you [Philo] pretend, contradictory to the principles of logic: its universal, its irresistible influence proves clearly, that there may be arguments of a like irregular nature. Whatever cavils may be urged; an orderly world, as well as a coherent, articulate speech, will still be received as an incontestable proof of design and intention." As the *Natural History* makes clear, Hume holds the propensity to deism not to be "universal" or "irresistible," and of course Hume knew not everyone finds the design argument acceptable. Perhaps (as Professor Deanna McMahon suggested in conversation) the "irregularity" of the argument is, for Hume, in some way related to the secondary status of the propensity.

17. I shall speak of "belief in invisible, intelligent power" as "minimal theism."

18. Using "propensity of reason" here as a not altogether felicitous contrastive term to "propensity of imagination." See note 20.

19. Men cannot, however, make this accurate examination until the evolution of mind progresses to a fairly advanced state. See below.

20. In two ways which do not materially affect my exegesis, the locutions "propensity of reason" and "propensity of imagination" are problematic. One concerns the ambiguity of "imagination" in the *Treatise*. In one sense, it is the faculty by which we repeat our impressions at a degree of vivacity "somewhat intermediate betwixt an impression and an idea," and in this respect it contrasts with memory (T 8; see also T 86, 628). In another, more important sense, it is tantamount to "human nature" which can separate "all simple ideas" and unite them again "guided by some universal principles" of association (T 10). In this latter sense, it is "affected by" (T 371) general rules and extends "custom and reasoning beyond the perceptions" (T 198). Indeed, Hume can say ". . . the understanding, that is, . . . the general and more establish'd properties of the imagination" (T 267). The other difficulty lies in the fact that both the *imagination* qua *faculty/ imagination* qua *human nature* and the *reason/imagination* (and, hence, the *propensity of reason/propensity of imagination*) distinctions are to be viewed as simply marking gradations on a continuum. Thus, when "the imagination" converts an idea into an impression of sympathy (T 317), it both acts as a faculty of creating impressions (not here, however, as merely repeating them, or as producing an impression of "intermediate" vivacity), and acts in a way similar to its production of belief. And reason, while it (under the name "reflection") is contrasted with imagination (T 215; see also T 231, 266), is also said to be "a wonderful instinct in the soul" (T 179). Furthermore the "memory, senses, and understanding are . . . all of them founded on the imagination, or the vivacity of our ideas" (T 265). Again, inductive reasoning is a "species of sensation" (T 103, 179; see also T 183 with T 371*n* and D 150–51).

21. Propensities explicitly ascribed to the imagination at T 215 concerning "continu'd and uninterrupted existence" and at T 93 concerning "customary transition from causes

to effects and effects to causes." That (a) and (b) *are* features of propensities of the imagination is clear, I think, from that fact that belief in causality and objects so patently fit
the pattern described in (a) and (b) and are produced by propensities of the imagination.

22. Hume tells us that reason opposes the view that something remains permanent
through a series of resembling perceptions, that our reasoning from cause and effect is
incompatible with our reasoning to "the continu'd and independent existence of objects";
but he adds that we nonetheless retain both of these beliefs. (See note 4.) He adds (T 270)
that it is only where reason is connected with a propensity that it produces assent. For
a fuller discussion of this issue, see Robert P. Wolff, "Hume's Theory of Mental Activity,"
Philosophical Review, 69, No. 3 (July 1960), 289–310; repr. in *Hume*, ed. Chappell,
pp. 99–128.

23. At D 216, where Philo says that no suspense of judgment in these cases is possible,
he speaks as a man of common sense, "yielding to the course of nature."

24. This explains his cavalier dismissal of counter-examples.

25. Such belief systems are "rational" for Hume, if at all, not in the sense that those
who accept them have reason to think them true, but only in the sense that no one can
rightly be *blamed* for having them.

26. On the moral superiority of minimal theism, and the qualifications, see D 220–24
and NHR 74–76 (General Corollary). This "moral superiority" cannot be interpreted in
any way inconsistent with the claim that minimal theism provides no basis for inference
"that affects human life, or can be the source of any action or forbearance . . ." (D 227).
Its superiority is mainly negative (it leads to fewer instances of grossly immoral behavior
than any alternative) and motivational. (On motivation, see especially NHR 75.) See
R. E. Braithwaite, *An Empiricist's Analysis of the Nature of Religious Belief* (Cambridge,
1956) for a not dissimilar view. Braithwaite's view, in turn, is discussed in an exchange
between the present author and Professor Kai Nielsen in "Empiricism and Theism,"
"Comments on 'Empiricism and Theism': A Defense of Braithwaite," and "A Reply to
Nielsen's Comments," *Sophia*, 7, No. 3 (October, 1968), 3–11, 12–17, 18–19; repr. in *God,
Man and Religion*, ed. Keith E. Yandell (New York, 1973), pp. 230–43.

27. See note 20, and the passages cited there.

28. Hume in such passages speaks as a "man of common sense," thus "speaking with the
vulgar."

29. Note that the power believed in is not said to have created the world or to be
providential.

30. No reading of Hume can take every Humean passage at face value. I hope my
reading takes him at face value everywhere in which good reason for not doing so is
lacking. What follows is an argument which appeals to systematic considerations and endeavors to show that there *is* good reason not to take Hume's "natural theology passages"
quite at face value.

31. I am not concerned with the exact formulation of these equally essential premisses;
what I claim about the particular formulations here given will apply, *mutatis mutandis*,
to any others which might replace them but serve the same function in yielding the desired conclusion.

32. There are, of course, other scattered passages in the Humean corpus which are also
relevant. But I shall have to be content here with stating my conviction that they too can
be read along the lines suggested in this paper. For a discussion of Hume's views on religion which discusses these passages and concentrates on the *Treatise* and *Enquiries*, see
Marvin Fox's brilliant "Religion and Human Nature in the Philosophy of David Hume,"
in *Process and Divinity*, edd. William L. Reese and Eugene Freeman (La Salle, 1964),
pp. 561–77. T 179, 250, and 633, together with EHU 141, seem to me to be particularly
important passages relevant to the theses of this paper.

33. At the end of Part XI, Demea, just before departing, criticizes Cleanthes "who
would measure every thing by a human rule and standard" (D 212). He adds that Philo is
"a more dangerous enemy" than Cleanthes. One reason for this, I take it, is that Cleanthes
allows some proof of God's existence, but Philo allows none (see D 143). More basic is
the danger that Philo's theology is *purely* negative.

34. Demea is perhaps too much neglected as a forerunner of or "preparer for" positions

Hume will weave into Part XII; he too professes to be a "man of common sense" with respect to the "being of God" (D 141) and complains insightfully that Cleanthes' religion is but "slight fabric" (D 179).

35. Our belief in particular causal connections is ostensibly in a different boat. Hume offers rules by which to judge causal inferences, prefacing his account of these rules by saying "Since . . . 'tis possible for all objects to become causes or effects to each other, it may be proper to fix some general rules, by which we may know when they really are so" (T 173ff.).

36. See the use of similar terms in Hume's account of how the mind is made to "pass with facility from one to the other" of a series of resembling perceptions and thus to posit one object (T 202). This "smooth passage" or "easy transition" is practically automatic when triggered by resembling appearances (T 203ff.).

37. Philo's response to Cleanthes (D 216ff.) raises another crucial question when Philo calls the dispute between theist and atheist "merely verbal." This is a topic in itself, the clue to which is to be found in the discussion (D 217) of a "species of controversy, which . . . is involved in perpetual ambiguity . . ." (D 217). See the Introduction by "Pamphilus" to the *Dialogues*.

38. Each also agrees that pure or abstract ("philosophical") theism is morally superior to theism of a more anthropomorphic sort (see D 220, 223, 224). Nevertheless, "pure" theism is rare (D 223). This discussion gives evidence for identifying the propensity to theism as a propensity to minimal theism, as the theism of the *Natural History* is given the same sort of moral superiority as that of the minimal theism of the *Dialogues* (see NHR 74–76 [General Corollary]). In addition, both are propensities of reason relevant to religious belief. It is worth remembering that the *Dialogues* and the *Natural History* were written concomitantly, though the former was revised twice (in 1761 and in 1776, the year of Hume's death).

39. It is worth noting that Pamphilus is made to say that he is "a mere auditor" (D 128) because of his youth, and so one must be careful in identifying Hume's views with those Pamphilus expresses. For example, he says "the *being* of a God . . . is . . . the surest foundation of morality . . ." (D 128)—a view which we know, from both the *Treatise* and the *Natural History*, is not Hume's. It is inevitable that one will take what confirms one's own view as Pamphilus' speaking for Hume, and what does not as resulting from Pamphilus' being a neophyte. My point here is simply that one can take seriously everything Pamphilus says, save when he directly contradicts what Hume has explicitly said elsewhere, on the interpretation which this paper defends. It would, by the way, be mistaken to suppose that Pamphilus ever says that human reason discovers it to be obvious that God exists.

40. There is a shift of contentions within the *Dialogues* concerning whether suspense of judgment in religious matters is possible. Philo says it is (D 135–36), but later says it is not (D 216–17). Pamphilus says it is not, and Cleanthes has all along declared it is not.

41. See the passages cited in note 38.

42. See the entire Introduction to the *Treatise*.

43. Of course, John O. Nelson thinks Hume did repudiate the *Treatise*; see "Two Main Questions Concerning Hume's *Treatise* and *Enquiry*," *Philosophical Review*, 81 No. 3 (July 1972), 333–50. But see Phillip D. Cummins, "Hume's *Disavowal of the Treatise*," ibid., 82, No. 3 (July 1973), 371–79. Wade L. Robison's "Hume's Scepticism" (*Dialogue*, 12, No. 1 [March 1973], 87–99) notes the unity of Hume's view of the principles of the imagination in the *Treatise* and the *Enquiry Concerning Human Understanding* (compare T 225 with EHU 42, 47).

44. This paper has not dealt with the autobiographical and biographical material relevant to the question of Hume's private views regarding religion, since its concern is simply Hume's philosophic arguments and his theory of human nature insofar as they are relevant to the origin and possible justification of religious belief. On Hume's personal views, which are fully compatible with the present interpretation, see E. C. Mossner, *The Forgotten Hume* (New York, 1943), esp. pp. 181ff., and *The Life of David Hume* (Austin, 1954), chaps. 39 and 40; Kemp Smith's Introduction, Appendices, and Supplement to his edition of the *Dialogues*. Professor Arthur Holmes, in conversation, has noted an interest-

ing similarity between Hume's view that there is a propensity to theism and Calvin's claim that all men have a "seminal knowledge" of God. See his *Institutes of the Christian Religion*, Book I, Chapter III, and Kemp Smith's Introduction, D 1–8.

As I have indicated, Hume was neither natural theologian nor natural atheologian with regard to the design argument. He might be construed as arguing for the proposition *If God exists, He is not omnibenevolent* in Parts X and XI of the *Dialogues*, and hence as being to that degree an atheologian; nonetheless, I think that even here he limits himself to maintaining that one who accepts the principles to which the design arguer appeals, will find as good reason for believing that the source of order is not omnibenevolent as he has for believing that there is a source of order which is intelligent. On Hume's treatment of the problem of evil, see Nelson Pike, "Hume on Evil," *Philosophical Review*, 72 (1963), 180–97; repr. in *God and Evil*, ed. N. Pike (Englewood Cliffs, 1964), pp. 85–102. On Hume's treatment of miracles, see the present writer's "Miracles, Epistemology and Hume's Barrier," *International Journal for Philosophy of Religion*, 7, No. 3 (Autumn 1976).

6

The Existence and Nature of
God in Hume's Theism

GEORGE J. NATHAN
Brock University

IN HUME's *Dialogues Concerning Natural Religion,* the narrator, Pamphilus, sets the tone of the ensuing discussion by remarking that, although it is obvious and indisputable that God exists, questions concerning his nature are involved in obscurity and uncertainty. Both Demea and Philo in Part II echo these sentiments, maintaining that it is "unquestionable and self-evident" that God exists. But they go beyond Pamphilus' claim in alleging that God's nature is not only obscure but incomprehensible. This view is opposed only by Cleanthes, who puts forth the position that a proof for the existence of God is required. This proof, he says, can be provided only by the *a posteriori* argument from design, which, in addition, establishes that the nature of God is similar to that of the human mind and intelligence.

To those well acquainted with Hume's conclusions in the *Treatise* and the first *Enquiry,* it would seem that Cleanthes speaks for Hume insofar as he regards the existence of God as being, like any other matter of fact, demonstrable only by an argument from cause and effect. Moreover, in the Humean causal scheme, every effect is produced by a prior cause, which is in turn produced by some other prior cause, and so on. As Cleanthes put it, "in tracing an eternal succession of objects, it seems absurd to inquire for a general cause or first Author" (D 190). We should expect, then, to find Hume in accord with Cleanthes by denying the possibility of a first cause because of its incompatibility with his theory of causation. It is disconcerting, however, to note that on two occasions Hume avows his belief that God is the first cause. In *A Letter to a Gentleman,* he proclaims that he is "far from pretending to deny . . . *God's being the first Cause and prime Mover of the Universe*" (L 29). The same contention, less ambiguously expressed, occurs in the essay "On the Immortality of the Soul": "every effect implies a cause, and that another, till we reach the first cause of all, which is the Deity . . ." (*Essays* 600). These two passages, although far from providing conclusive evidence that Hume believed in a God who is a first cause, must be taken seriously. In fact, as I shall argue on grounds entirely separate from these passages, Hume did think that there is a first or original cause and that it is self-evident that this cause exists. I shall also explain why he thought this and why he considered the nature of God to be obscure and even incomprehensible. Finally, I shall make some brief comments about what of God's nature we can discover.

My procedure in making good on these intentions requires careful attention to Hume's theories of causation (in Section I), causal inference (Section II), and causal explanation (Section III). In Section I, I distinguish two kinds of different, but related, causes. The first I call, following popular terminology, "Humean causes" or, alternatively, "particular causes." These causes are the particular objects which are mentioned in Hume's two definitions of cause. In contrast to these is a second type of cause, which I join Hume in calling "principles" or, alternatively "general causes." These are not particular objects but rather powers which such objects possess to produce certain effects in certain circumstances in virtue of their essential natures. These principles are the causal mechanisms (which need not be mechanical) which engender the phenomena or effects in the visible world. Most often such principles are not, as such, observable, but are known by their effects. The intrinsic nature of the most basic principles is entirely unknown to us. Nevertheless, principles may be identified by the observable regularities they produce among particular causes and effects.

Building on this distinction between two types of causes, in Section II I attempt to ascertain the nature of causal inference. To put it briefly: I argue that Hume believes two types of causal inferences to be possible: (1) an inference from a particular Humean cause to a particular Humean effect, which inference is licensed by our observation of regular sequences between two species of objects; an inference from one *object* to another must conform to this pattern; (2) an inference from observed regularities among objects to the principles or powers which produce them; such inferences do not require the observation of any principles.

In Section III, I examine Hume's theory of causal explanation in the light of the discussion in the preceding sections. I argue that the theory of causal explanation which Hume employs throughout his works does not (except in a subsidiary way) employ either Humean causes or a covering-law model to account for the behavior of objects. Rather, it enjoins recourse to certain principles or general causes which may be subsumed under others still more general until the most general available to human knowledge are reached. Principles or general causes, then, provide the ultimate scientific explanation of the experienced phenomena. Moreover, because principles are intrinsic natures or essences of objects, they also provide the ultimate metaphysical grounds for all observable occurrences.

Given the foregoing accounts of causation, causal inference, and causal explanation, it becomes apparent (as I point out in Section IV) that Hume is committed to the view that there is a first cause, or first principle of order in the universe, which is not a particular being but rather the ultimate macro-principle. As such it shares with all other principles the characteristic of incomprehensibility, i.e., of being something of which we have no idea. I conclude with a brief discussion of Hume's attitudes toward other traditionally ascribed attributes of God. Hume's concern, I argue, is not so much to establish a new theology as it is to rebut superstition.

I

There can be no disputing the centrality of the concept of causality to all of Hume's works. It has been, perhaps more than any other topic in Hume's philosophy, the subject of numerous discussions and analyses. Yet, strangely enough, the problem of causality as it bears on the *Dialogues Concerning Natural Religion* has never been very closely examined, in spite of the fact that the notion of causality found there is somewhat of an anomaly. It is my contention that the chief obstacle to an adequate understanding of Hume's *Dialogues* lies in the prevalence of a misconceived and consequently misconstrued analysis of Hume's concept of causality. In fact, it is but a slight exaggeration to say that only Parts I and II of the *Dialogues* are intelligible when they are interpreted in the light of the traditional view of the Humean causal nexus. Moreover, the basis of the dispute between Philo and Cleanthes must remain opaque unless it is realized that more than one notion of cause is being used by the disputants. Indeed it could justifiably be claimed that one of the major, if not the major, points of the Philo–Cleanthes argument is to reveal the inadequacy of so-called "Humean" causes in an investigation of the existence and nature of God.

In order to fill in the bare bones of this somewhat abstractly stated thesis, in this section I shall try to give a coherent account of Hume's claims about causality. In subsequent sections I shall aim at spelling out the intrinsic importance which the concept of causality as thus delineated bears to the *Dialogues*.

The account of causality with which most students of Hume are familiar is that encapsulated in the famous two definitions of cause in the *Treatise*:

> We may define a CAUSE to be "An object precedent and contiguous to another, and where all the objects resembling the former are plac'd in like relations of precedency and contiguity to those objects, that resemble the latter."

> "A CAUSE is an object precedent and contiguous to another, and so united with it, that the idea of the one determines the mind to form the idea of the other, and the impression of one to form a more lively idea of the other" [T 170].

There are other passages, however, which lead us to believe that these definitions do not provide us with a complete account of Hume's view of causality. In these passages Hume speaks of hidden powers or forces in nature, which powers are the "true springs and causes of every event" (NHR 28).

> It must certainly be allowed, that nature has kept us at a great distance from all her secrets, and has afforded us only the knowledge of a few superficial

qualities of objects; while she conceals from us those powers and principles on which the influence of those objects entirely depends. Our senses inform us of the colour, weight, and consistence of bread; but neither sense nor reason can ever inform us of those qualities which fit it for the nourishment and support of a human body [EHU 32–33].

[W]e are ignorant of those powers and forces, on which the regular course and succession of objects totally depends [EHU 55].

[T]he particular powers, by which all natural operations are performed, never appear to the senses . . . [EHU 42].

We are placed in this world, as in a great theatre, where the true springs and causes of every event are entirely concealed from us . . . [NHR 28].

The scenes of the universe are continually shifting, and one object follows another in an uninterrupted succession; but the power or force, which actuates the whole machine, is entirely concealed from us, and never discovers itself in any of the sensible qualities of body. We know, that, in fact, heat is a constant attendant of flame; but what is the connexion between them, we have no room so much as to conjecture or imagine [EHU 63–64].

It may seem, at first glance, that here Hume is not merely offering us further information about causes, but also making claims about causes which are at variance with his explicit definitions. According to the definitions, causes are items which are observable and thus not the least bit concealed. But secret causes are not observable at all. How, then, can Hume call them causes in any sense when they are plainly not objects of one kind observed to have been in constant conjunction with objects of another kind? Moreover, even if some sense can be attached to the notion of hidden causes, how according to Hume can we know of their existence? Hume denies that they are known by the senses or reason. Seemingly, then, the only alternative mode of knowledge would be that of causal inference. But this, too, seems to be ruled out. Because causal inference requires observation of *both* cause and effect, plainly if the cause is never observed, causal inference is rendered impossible. There are then three problems which have emerged from a brief consideration of these passages: (1) reconciling Hume's claims about hidden causes or powers with his definitions of cause; (2) explaining exactly what Hume took a hidden cause to be; (3) explaining how knowledge of such hidden features of the world can be gotten when Hume's epistemology appears to rule out any such possibility. The remainder of the present section will be devoted to the first two problems; Section II will deal with the third.

The problem of reconciling Hume's assertions about hidden powers with his two definitions of cause is not nearly so difficult as it may appear to be. Instead of assuming, as is only natural, that Hume is talking about two kinds of objects, the observable and the non-observable, we should be better advised to think of him as talking about one type of object, the observable, but from two different but related perspectives. In brief, when Hume formulates his two definitions of cause, he is attempting to establish empirical criteria for the application of the term "cause" to certain observable objects. He is trying to answer the question: "In virtue of what relations in which this thing stands is it called 'a cause'?" However, when Hume refers to hidden powers or forces or causes, he is not intending to single out a new class of objects. Rather, he is alluding to the nature or essence of those same observable objects in virtue of which they stand in those relations.

Let me document these claims in further detail. When Hume asks us to "cast our eye on any two objects, which we *call* cause and effect . . ." (T 75; emphasis added), he discovers that "there is no one quality, which universally belongs to all beings, and gives them a *title to that denomination* [viz., "cause" or "effect"]" (T 75; emphasis added). By "quality" Hume understands "known quality" (see T 77). He soon comes to realize that the relevant feature which entitles us to call objects "causes" or "effects" is the relation of constant conjunction:

> Thus we remember to have seen that species of object we call *flame*, and to have felt that species of sensation we call *heat*. We likewise call to mind their constant conjunction in all past instances. Without any farther ceremony, we call the one *cause* and the other *effect*, and infer the existence of the one from that of the other [T 87].

> Contiguity and succession are not sufficient to make us *pronounce* any two objects to be cause and effect, unless we perceive, that these two relations are preserv'd in several instances [T 87; emphasis added].

It is clear that Hume is addressing himself to the question: Why are objects called "causes" or "effects"? It is also clear that part of the answer to this question is that they are so called because we have perceived them to stand in the relation of constant conjunction and identify them as causes or effects precisely because of our recognition of this fact. Hume has found, then, one of the criteria in terms of which we apply the expression "cause." This first criterion forms Hume's first definition of "a cause." Nevertheless, Hume indicates (T 87–88) that his account of causality as thus far developed has not fully unpacked our notion of causality, since we consider necessary connexion to be an essential element in it, and there is no trace of necessity in the first criterion. As is well known, Hume finally locates the desired necessary connexion in the guise of that impression of reflection which is the determination of the mind to pass from the idea of the object called "cause" to the idea of the object called "effect," or from the impression of the one to the lively idea of the other. This determination is caused by the observance of constant conjunctions between two species of objects. A complete account of causality is now assured, allegedly, insofar as an account of the element of necessary connexion has been produced.

The details of Hume's attempts can be bypassed here. What is important to note is that Hume took two elements, constant conjunction and the determination of the mind, to be essential to ascriptions of causality. Because both are necessary they must be included in the definitions of cause. The first definition notes that an object is to be called a cause if it stands in a relation of constant conjunction to other objects. The second notes that it is to be so called if it stands in a certain relation to the mind. In other words, the definitions incorporate two types of relational criteria for the ap-

plication of the term "cause": relations of the object to other objects and of
the object to the mind. The application of both criteria will, of course, pick
out the same objects, for there can be no object which we can tell satisfies
the first criterion which does not also satisfy the second, and conversely. The
reason for this is that we tell that the first criterion is satisfied by observing
constant conjunctions; and because the observing of constant conjunctions
causes the determination of the mind, it is causally impossible for the cause
(the observation) to exist without the existence of the effect (the determination of the mind), and, conversely, the effect cannot exist without its cause.

In moving from this topic to the next, which deals with the explanation of
the nature of secret or hidden powers, a helpful means of making the transition lies in noting that Hume himself in both the first *Enquiry* (EHU 76–
77) and the *Treatise* (T 170) expressed dissatisfaction with his definitions of
cause. It will prove instructive to find out the reasons for this attitude.

In both texts, Hume confesses that the definitions might be considered to
be defective because, as he puts it, "both these definitions be drawn from
circumstances foreign to the cause . . ." (EHU 77). What he has in mind
here is, presumably, that we think an object *is* a cause in virtue of some
qualities or features of the object itself. Yet, it is *called* "a cause," not because of any of its qualities, but rather because of another object, the effect,
to which it is related. Hume thinks, then, that a perfect definition, if one
could be provided, would "point out that circumstance in the cause, which
gives it a connexion with its effect" (EHU 77). In other words, Hume is
maintaining that, ideally, a definition of "a cause," i.e., the criteria for the
application of that term, should point out that feature or circumstance of
the object which makes it stand in certain relations to other "extraneous"
objects. Providing such a definition is, of course, beyond Hume's powers
since, as he admits (T 77), it is not because of any of the *known qualities* of
objects that a cause is necessarily connected with its effect, and hence it is
not because of their known qualities that they can be called "causes." Nevertheless, Hume has left it an open question whether objects *are* causes because of some of their *unknown* qualities. We must now examine his attitude towards this possibility.

It has been noted already that Hume believed that there are hidden
"powers" and "principles" in nature, which powers or principles are responsible for all changes which we observe. Up to now we have referred to these
factors as powers or forces or causes, using the various terms indifferently.
To be accurate, though, we should be aware that Hume is almost always
careful to refer to these mysterious factors as "powers" or "forces" or "principles" reserving the term "cause" for the *object* which *has* the power or
force (see, e.g., EHU 32–33, 36–37, 54–55).[1] When he does refer to "secret
causes" (as, e.g., at T 132) what he usually has in mind are *objects* "hid by
reason of their minuteness or remoteness" (T 132), i.e., objects which are
very small or very far away. Hume, then, in his precise and usually consistent use of these technical terms, intends a distinction to be drawn between
powers and causes, i.e., between powers and the objects which are the bearers of powers. What remains to be discovered now is what these powers are

and what connection they have with the unknown qualities of the objects we call causes. As we shall see, the connection is most intimate.

In an important footnote in the *Enquiry* Hume makes explicit what he takes a power to be:

> When we consider the *unknown* circumstance of an object, by which the degree or quantity of its effect is fixed and determined, we call that its power: And accordingly, it is allowed by all philosophers, that the effect is the measure of the power [EHU 77, note].

Clearly, a power is an unknown circumstance of an object. But this passage is misleading insofar as it suggests that this circumstance accounts for only the quantitative features of the effect and not for any of its qualities. I do not think Hume ordinarily does or wants to construe the notion of power so narrowly. Rather, he construes it more broadly as "that very circumstance in the cause, by which it is enabled to produce the effect . . ." (EHU 67–68), an account which would permit us to think of the power as responsible for both qualitative and quantitative features of the effect. Interpreting the notion of power in this fashion is obviously preferable. Still, certain difficulties remain. The "broad" construction of powers, as exemplified in the above passage, makes mention of a "circumstance" in the cause, but not of a hidden circumstance. But we can gather from Hume's numerous claims to the effect that powers are hidden, that if powers are circumstances of causes, then powers are hidden circumstances of causes. The objects we call causes are causes in virtue of their powers, that is to say, in virtue of some of their unknown qualities, even though they are called causes, not because of those qualities, but rather because of the relation of constant conjunction in which they stand with respect to other objects.

Having penetrated this far into Hume's notion of power, we need to learn still more about these mysterious hidden qualities. Hume is, I think, prepared to offer us a bit more information when he tells us what must be known about objects if we are to know of their powers: we must know their *natures*.

> But if by consciousness we perceived any power or energy in the will, we must know this power; we must know its connexion with the effect; we must know the secret union of soul and body, and *the nature of both these substances*; by which the one is able to operate, in so many instances, upon the other [EHU 65; emphasis added].

> It must be allowed, that, when we know a power, we know that very circumstance in the cause, by which it is enabled to produce the effect: For these are supposed to be synonimous. We must, therefore, know both the cause and effect, and the relation between them. But do we pretend to be acquainted with the *nature* of the human soul and the *nature* of an idea, or the aptitude of the one to produce the other? [EHU 67–68; emphasis added].

> The command of the mind over itself is limited, as well as its command over the body; and these limits are not known by reason, or any acquaintance with the *nature* of cause and effect, but only by experience and observation, as in

all other natural events and in the operation of external objects [EHU 68; emphasis added].

To be directly acquainted with a power is to be acquainted with the natures of those objects designated causes and effects. Because the union of cause and effect depends upon the natures of *both* objects, it is slightly misleading to suppose, as has been done so far, that the power of an object always depends exclusively on features intrinsic to it. The truth of the matter is that, in the case of interactions, for example, the powers manifested depend at least as much on the nature of the object acted upon as they do on the agent, which brings us to a very important point. To assert that powers are merely the natures of objects is to say something which appears to be utterly trivial. It sounds remarkably like talk about the dormitive power which opium possesses because its nature is such as to put people to sleep. Such talk is, indeed, empty, and so would Hume's about "natures" be were it not for the fact that in speaking of the nature or powers of opium we are alluding to certain structural features of opium which, when opium is ingested by a man, form the generative mechanism whereby sleep is brought about. This allusion to a generative mechanism is what absolves such talk about the nature and power of opium from the charge of emptiness. To ascribe a power to an object is in part to suppose that there is some such generative mechanism without making any claims to knowledge of what it is or how it operates, but leaving open the possibility that it might be discovered. This, I believe, is very close to Hume's position on powers, for, speaking of the variations in command which the mind has over itself at different times, he inquires:

Can we give any reason for these variations, except experience? Where then is the power, of which we pretend to be conscious? Is there not here, either in a spiritual or material substance, or both, some *secret mechanism or structure of parts*, upon which the effect depends, and which, being entirely unknown to us, renders the power or energy of the will equally unknown and incomprehensible? [EHU 68–69; emphasis added].

The fact that Hume speaks about a mechanism or structure of parts which might pertain to a *spiritual* substance alerts us to avoid the error of thinking that a causal mechanism must be either mechanical or physical. In any event, whether they be physical or spiritual, these generative mechanisms are what form the powers or natures of objects.

Hume, I think, wants to go even further than this in an important way. He notices that there are in nature regularities of various kinds, which seems to indicate to him that there are *kinds* of powers. But if there are kinds of powers, there must also be kinds of generative mechanisms, and this Hume does think to be the case. In the *Enquiry* he lists a few of them: "Elasticity, gravity, cohesion of parts, communication of motion by impulse" (EHU 30). In the *Dialogues*, he lists four more: reason, instinct, generation, and vegetation (D 178). All of these Hume refers to as "principles" or, alternatively, "general causes" (D 178; EHU 30). He regards them as "prob-

ably the ultimate causes and principles which we shall ever discover in nature . . ." (EHU 30), which is to say that these seem to be among the basic
types of causal mechanisms whereby all uniformities in nature are generated,
and that any attempt to reduce this number will probably be unsuccessful.
These principles are "powers and energies" whose "essence is incomprehensible" and whose "manner of operation" is "totally unknown" (D 178).
In what way, if any, we can know anything about the internal fabric and
structure of objects (which is what a principle is) will be considered in Section II. In addition, the role of principles or general causes as vehicles of
explanation will be dealt with in Section III. However, before we leave this
part of the problem, one additional facet of principles or powers needs to
be mentioned.

In a number of places, Hume claims that powers or forces are inconceivable (EHU 67) or incomprehensible (EHU 69, 72). By these terms he does
not mean that powers are logically impossible or that the notion of such
things is senseless or unintelligible. Rather, to say that a power is incomprehensible is to say no more than that it is something of which we have no
idea, in the Humean sense of idea, i.e., a perception which copies what is
presented in impressions. To talk about powers is to talk about the structural features of objects, which features, not being given to the senses or reason, are things of which we can form no impressions and hence no ideas.
Making this claim does not commit Hume to the position that any talk
about powers is senseless, any more than Hume's claim that causes are not
called such in virtue of the unknown features which make them causes commits him to the position that talk of causes is senseless. All that Hume requires to make talk of both powers and causes intelligible is that there be
empirical criteria for the application of the terms "power" and "cause." In
the case of both these terms the criteria coincide. We call an object a cause,
not because of its intrinsic features, but because of its effects, the other observable objects to which it is related via constant conjunctions. Similarly,
we ascribe a power to an object, again not because of its intrinsic features,
but because of the observed effects of that type of object. A power is what
makes an object a cause, and we identify an object as a cause when we
identify it, by its effects, as having a certain kind of power. Hence, it is
quite proper for Hume to say that powers or forces are inconceivable or incomprehensible, and, yet, that talk about them is meaningful because something is conceivable and comprehensible: the effects of the objects which are
bearers of powers:

> We find by experience, that a body at rest or in motion continues for ever in
> its present state, till put from it by some new cause; and that a body impelled
> takes as much motion from the impelling body as it acquires itself. These are
> facts. When we call this a *vis inertiae*, we only mark these facts, without pre-
> tending to have any idea of the inert power; in the same manner as, when we
> talk of gravity, we mean certain effects, without comprehending that active
> power [EHU 73, note].

We shall return to this notion on the incomprehensibility of powers when
we consider the nature of God in Section IV.

II

Thus far we have ascertained that Hume holds that causality depends on the fact that particular objects have certain structural features which, when sorted into kinds as powers, provide the generative mechanisms or principles which account for all observable changes. Because these principles are not particular objects, but rather generative mechanisms of certain kinds, Hume calls them "general causes" (EHU 30). They are called "general" because they exemplify kinds of powers, and are called "causes" because they bring about changes. Principles or general causes are not themselves particular objects. Gravity, for example, is not one particular object among others, but rather the power or nature which is common to a plurality of objects. Hence, we could justifiably say that Hume thinks that there are two types of causes: the particular and the general. This would not be a misleading characterization as long as we keep clear the distinction between an object and its nature or structure, between a particular object we call a cause, and its nature in virtue of which it is a cause. With this in mind, let us consider how principles or general causes could be known, in comparison to how particular causes are known.

Hume allows that we learn what the causes (or effects) of things are in two ways: from the senses and memory, and from reason or causal inference on the basis of things perceived or remembered (T 87). Causal inference presupposes not only previous experience of constant conjunctions of two types of objects, but also a present impression of the memory or senses which serves as the foundation of the inference from something perceived or remembered to that which is neither. Now, it follows from this account of how we learn what are the causes (or effects) of things that we do not, indeed cannot, come to know powers by means either of the memory or senses, or of causal inference (reason). The "powers, by which all natural operations are performed, never appear to the senses . . ." (EHU 42), and so we could not perceive them. Similarly, we could not come to know these powers by causal inference, because all such inference presupposes previous experience of constant conjunctions and we have no experience of powers at all, much less experience of them as constantly conjoined with anything else. Consequently, Hume concludes, powers or principles are known by neither sense nor reason (causal inference). How then are they known?

We should have great difficulty in answering this question were we to take a principle to be an entirely new type of object, one which we were never directly acquainted with, and whose existence we could fathom only in some indirect way. We should have this difficulty because any inference from the existence of one object to the existence of another presupposes, according to Hume, the observation of constant conjunctions:

> It is only when two *species* of objects are found to be constantly conjoined, that we can infer the one from the other . . . [EHU 148].

Principles, however, as has been shown, are not objects, and hence the task of distorting Hume's theory of causal inference to cover knowledge of these "secret causes" is one which we are thankfully spared. Still, this brings us no nearer an answer to our question: How are principles or powers known?

I do not think that there is any mystery here. We know what powers or nature a given object has in the same way in which we know that that object is a cause, viz., from its effects:

> When we consider the *unknown* circumstance of an object, by which the degree or quantity of its effect is fixed and determined, we call that its power: And accordingly, it is allowed by all philosophers, that the effect is the measure of the power [EHU 77, note].

The same point is again made in the *Treatise*:

> For to me it seems evident, that the essence of the mind being equally unknown to us with that of external bodies, it must be equally impossible to form any notion of its powers and qualities otherwise than from careful and exact experiments, and the observation of those particular effects, which result from its different circumstances and situations [T xxi].

Finally, the claim that principles are known by their effects is reiterated in the *Dialogues*:

> In this little corner of the world alone, there are four principles, *reason, instinct, generation, vegetation*, which are similar to each other, and are the causes of similar effects. . . . The effects of these principles are all known to us from experience: But the principles themselves, and their manner of operation, are totally unknown . . . [D 178].

We have in experiment and observation one of the factors which enable us to know the powers of objects. By observation we know what effects various objects have. But because principles are not merely powers but powers of various *kinds*, something in addition to observation is necessary to inform us that powers fall into kinds. To ascertain this we must make comparisons of the effects produced by various causes in order to see if there are any relevant resemblances among them. If such a resemblance is found upon comparison of numerous effects, we attribute a power of a certain kind to their causes. Hume calls this whole procedure "reasonings from analogy, experience, and observation" (EHU 30) and gives us a classic example of its implementation:

> Why do philosophers infer, with the greatest certainty, that the moon is kept in its orbit by the same force of gravity, that makes bodies fall near the surface of the earth, but because these effects are, upon computation, found similar and equal? [EPM 236].

The inference mentioned is not one of probable reasoning or causal inference. Rather, it is an inference of demonstrative reasoning of the following sort: (since forces are identified by the effects of their bearers,) if the effects are similar and equal, then (necessarily) the forces must also be similar and equal. In other words, if we attribute the force of gravity to one object on the basis of its effects, we must attribute the same (qualitatively identical) force to any other object with like effects.

The answer, then, to our question "How are principles known?" has now been arrived at. We know them by means of the senses and reason, which, I grant, sounds remarkably like what Hume has denied is a possible means, but with this notable difference. Hume denies that the senses and reason can give us any insight into powers or principles if they scrutinize only the objects we call causes. Yet he never denies (and, in fact, claims) that the senses and reason can give us knowledge of powers if they concern themselves with observing and comparing the effects of those objects. Sense and reason brought to bear on the effects of objects yield knowledge of principles.

III

It is a widely held opinion that Hume would explain the occurrence of a given event B by saying that B was preceded by event A and all B-like events have been preceded by A-like events. According to this opinion, causal explanations of events involve reference to other events, to certain laws, and to certain assumed permanent conditions as expressed in a statement about background conditions or in a *ceteris paribus* clause. Hume, it is believed, subscribed to this "covering-law" model of explanation. In this section, I shall attempt to show that this opinion is incorrect, that Hume never used or endorsed the pattern of explanation here described. I shall do this by indicating, briefly, how this opinion arose from some misconceptions about Hume's view of causality, and then by exhibiting what he takes the correct model of causal explanation to be.

Perhaps the most fertile source of this erroneous interpretation is an uncritical reliance on Hume's two definitions of cause as an indication of his views about causal explanation. Specifically: it is assumed that because we tell that something is a cause (or effect) by appeal to observed regularities obtaining between species of objects, we must also make mention of these regularities (as expressed by laws) whenever we causally explain the occurrence of some event. In other words, it is assumed that what is contained in the definition of cause (especially the first definition) must somehow be mentioned whenever a causal explanation is produced. But, as far as I can tell, no argument is presented to persuade us that this assumption is correct, or even plausible. There is, though, a reason why this assumption has been commonly thought to need no argument. Philosophers have assumed that Hume has denied the existence of powers, and if he has done so, no mention of powers could possibly be used in providing causal explanations. Hence, they continue, all that is left which could be used in such explanations is what we know of causes by observation, viz., what is included in the definitions of a cause. However, as we have discovered, Hume does not deny the existence of powers, and so it remains an open question whether Hume uses powers to provide causal explanations.

Although the assumption that Hume uses a covering-law model is unsupported by argument, there is one distinctive passage which could be taken as providing evidence that this is Hume's model:

It is confessed, that the utmost effort of human reason is to reduce the principles, productive of natural phenomena, to a greater simplicity, and to resolve the many particular effects into a few general causes, by means of reasonings from analogy, experience, and observation. But as to the causes of these general causes, we should in vain attempt their discovery; nor shall we ever be able to satisfy ourselves, by any particular explication of them. These ultimate springs and principles are totally shut up from human curiosity and enquiry. Elasticity, gravity, cohesion of parts, communication of motion by impulse; these are probably the ultimate causes and principles which we shall ever discover in nature; and we may esteem ourselves sufficiently happy, if, by accurate enquiry and reasoning, we can trace up the particular phenomena to, or near to, these general principles [EHU 30–31].

It should be sufficiently obvious at this stage that this passage can be taken to support the "covering-law" interpretation only if one mistakenly takes the terms "general causes" and "principles" to mean "general *laws*." But, as has been shown, general causes or principles are kinds of generative mechanisms, and as such are things which are "productive of phenomena," not descriptive of them as are laws. Consequently, this passage not only does not support the "covering-law" interpretation, but also is inconsistent with it.

We are now ready, in light of the above passage, to give a positive account of Humean causal explanation. One ingredient of it is surely that any causal explanation, if it is to be a genuine explanation at all, must make some reference to a generative mechanism of some kind, i.e., to a principle or general cause. Thus, according to Hume, if we were to give an explanation of why some phenomenon, say the motion of object B, took place, it would not be adequate to say that the motion of object A caused it because no mention is made of a principle. However, to say that B moved because a moving object A *collided* with it is to allude to a principle, viz., communication of motion by impulse. Or, alternatively, we might say that B moved because it was *attracted by* A, and in so doing make reference to the general cause, gravity. In Newtonian mechanics, with which Hume had some acquaintance, gravity and impact (communication of motion by impulse) would be the general causes or two basic principles which accounted for all changes of motion. Because the effects of these two principles are different, impact requiring contact of bodies, gravity not, they were considered to be irreducible mechanisms of change of motion, which undoubtedly is unsatisfactory. For why should there be two principles and not one? As Hume points out (EHU 73, note), Newton himself found this arrangement unsatisfactory, and so he hypothesized the existence of the ether, which, if there were such a thing, would allow for contact between distant objects and thus enable us to reduce the number of principles to one: communication of motion by impulse. However, because we do not know of the existence of the ether, we need to acknowledge that these two principles are for us basic and ultimate at our present state of knowledge. We have, at least, reduced the number of generative mechanisms to two, Hume would argue, and with this we must be satisfied. The task of causal explanation, then, is to find the various generative mechanisms in nature by the careful comparison of the effects of objects, to reduce those mechanisms or principles to the smallest number we can and, after this process has been completed, to use principles to render intelligible the behavior of the particular objects in the world, this by showing that things act and interact as they do because of their intrinsic natures, the principles which govern their operation.

Let us now proceed to a related matter. In the *Dialogues*, Philo makes an important point about the logic of causal explanation which we should carefully consider. He says:

> Naturalists indeed very justly explain particular effects by more general causes; though these general causes themselves should remain in the end totally inexplicable: But they never surely thought it satisfactory to explain a particular effect by a particular cause, which was no more to be accounted for than the object itself [D 164].

This observation comes at the end of Part IV after a lengthy discussion between Philo and Cleanthes on the logic of causal explanation. Cleanthes has suggested that we explain the order in the universe (a particular effect) by appeal to the mind of God (a particular cause). Philo counters that if we explain the effect by an object of the same type, i.e., explain particular effect by particular cause (material world by world of ideas), then we are committed either to an infinite regress of causes or to an arbitrary stop at some particular cause. Now, in the passage quoted above, Philo is arguing that it is unsatisfactory to explain a particular effect by a particular cause of which no further explanation can be given, yet it is not unsatisfactory to explain a particular effect by a general cause, even though no further explanation of the general cause can be given. The question which naturally suggests itself is: "Since neither the particular cause nor the general cause can be given any further explanation, why is it satisfactory to stop at a general cause when it is not satisfactory to stop at a particular one?"

The answer to this question lies, I believe, in recalling the distinction between general causes (or principles) and particular causes. The former are the natures of objects, whereas the latter are the objects which have these natures. This distinction is relevant to the problem of causal explanation insofar as Hume thinks that only general causes can, in principle, terminate the regress of explanation. The reason for this is that particular causes or Humean causes are causes precisely because they are effects of some precedent cause which in turn is caused in the same way (D 190; T 76). Hence, it is arbitrary to stop at any particular cause in the series and say that this is *the* cause of a given effect, because, being of the same logical type as all other members of the series, there is nothing about it to explain its privileged status. Now, it is, indeed, the case that we must as a matter of contingent fact stop somewhere in our enquiries about particular causes when our cognitive powers have reached their limits. In this sense, it is not arbitrary that we stop at a given cause. However, that our enquiries are terminated at that point is not due to any logically distinctive features of the cause. In other words, that we stop at a given point is due to facts about us and not about the object. The regress of particular causes goes on and on;

we just cannot follow it. It is considerably different in the case of the regress of principles or general causes. When we explain particular effects by principles, we are explaining a thing of one logical type, a particular, by a thing of a different logical type, a power. It is well known that, historically, regresses of causal explanation have been terminated by moving from an effect of one logical type, say a contingent being, to a cause of a different logical type, a necessary being. Hume's point, however, is not that, when one moves from particular effect to general principle, one terminates the regress of explanations by moving from a thing of one logical type to a thing of a different logical type. The reason I say this is that Hume regards general causes as also being inexplicable, which I take to mean that we are as a matter of fact unable to explain them, but not that it makes no sense to ask for an explanation of them. This reading of "inexplicable" is confirmed by a passage in the *Enquiry*:

> But as to the causes of these general causes, we should in vain attempt their discovery; nor shall we ever be able to satisfy ourselves, by any particular explication of them. These ultimate springs and principles are totally shut up from human curiosity and enquiry [EHU 30].

In speaking of the "causes of these general causes," Hume is clearly allowing the possibility of a cause of general causes. If so, it also makes sense to ask for a causal explanation of general causes, even though we cannot provide one because of the weakness of the human intellect. The question is, then, "Has not Hume left himself open to the charge that it may be the case that one general cause depends on another and it on a third and so on *ad infinitum*?" I think not. General causes are not objects which may or may not be related to other objects in the way in which particular causes and effects may be. General causes are the *natures* of various objects whereby they enter into regular relations with one another. They are structural features of objects. As such, each object must have a determinate and basic nature or structure. When we reach that basic nature of things we have found the ultimate cause. Since there must be a basic nature of things if things are to have any nature whatsoever, this basic nature is what in principle terminates the regress of general causes, and it is that to which one must allude when one provides an ultimate causal explanation. In this sense of ultimate causal explanation, we never do provide any, since we do not have more than an indirect access to the powers of objects, i.e., by means of their effects. Hence, the principles we discover are ultimate *for us* and are of the right *type*, i.e., involving the natures of objects to provide a model of the ultimate principle of explanation, whatever it may turn out to be.

IV

We turn, finally, to the main topic of this paper: the existence and nature of God in Hume's theism. I call his position "theism," not because of any historical claim that this is the most fitting title for it, but rather because it is what Hume himself calls it (see NHR 21, 75). My intention is not to spell out all aspects of Hume's theism, for that is a task considerably beyond the scope of this paper. Instead, I shall examine the allegation, which Philo makes in the *Dialogues*, that the existence of God is self-evident, but that his nature is incomprehensible. I shall argue that this is Hume's position also, and that it is not only consistent with his general philosophical position expressed elsewhere, but is also a direct consequence of it. Lastly, I shall attempt to indicate in part what can be known about the nature of God in spite of the fact that it is incomprehensible, i.e., it is something of which we can have no idea.

Philo's claims about the existence and nature of God are expressed early in Part II of the *Dialogues*:

> But surely, where reasonable men treat these subjects, the question can never be concerning the *being*, but only the *nature* of the Deity. The former truth, as you [Demea] well observe, is unquestionable and self-evident. Nothing exists without a cause; and the original cause of this universe (whatever it be) we call GOD; and piously ascribe to him every species of perfection. . . . But let us beware, lest we think, that our ideas any wise correspond to his perfections, or that his attributes have any resemblance to these qualities among men [D 142].

He argues for the incomprehensibility claim in this way:

> Our ideas reach no farther than our experience: We have no experience of divine attributes and operations: I need not conclude my syllogism: You [Cleanthes] can draw the inference yourself. And it is a pleasure to me . . . that just reasoning and sound piety here concur in the same conclusion, and both of them establish the adorably mysterious and incomprehensible nature of the supreme Being [D 142–43].

There are three interesting points raised by Philo in these passages: (1) that nothing exists without a cause; (2) that there is an original or ultimate cause; and (3) that the nature of this ultimate cause is incomprehensible because we can have no idea of it. I shall argue that all three points are made by Hume himself and that once it is shown why Hume accepted the first two doctrines it will also be clear that and why he accepted the third.

Hume agrees that nothing exists without a cause and takes an assertion of this fact to be equivalent to a denial of the existence of chance:

> It is universally allowed that nothing exists without a cause of its existence, and that chance, when strictly examined, is a mere negative word, and means not any real power which has anywhere a being in nature [EHU 95].

Likewise, according to Hume, to assert that something happened by chance is to deny that it happened of necessity, and to deny the latter is to deny it had a cause since "necessity makes an essential part of causation . . ." (T 407). But Hume goes even further than this to claim that "chance is commonly thought to imply a contradiction, and is at least directly contrary to experience . . ." (T 407). He does not elaborate on these points, but the following may be what he has in mind. When a person says that something happened by chance or as the result of chance, he purports to be providing a *causal* explanation of an occurrence. But it is logically impossible to provide such an explanation by advertence to chance because it implies a "negation of necessity and causes" (T 407). Hence the expression "to explain as a chance occurrence" would be, for Hume, self-contradictory. On the other hand, Hume may mean that people think of chance as a power in nature, and since powers are causes of regularities while chance implies irregularity, the notion of chance as a kind of power is absurd. The second charge, that the existence of chance is contrary to experience, means no more than that our experience of nature is of something constant and regular in its operation and not the reverse as alleged by those who ascribe chance to nature. Hume does, indeed, allow that there are irregularities in nature, but ascribes them, as he thinks do all natural philosophers, to the "secret operation of contrary causes" (EHU 87). For him, "chance" refers to nothing real in nature; it has only an epistemic use to mark our relative ignorance of the real causes in nature. Consequently, Hume would argue, when philosophers say that something happened by chance, they are not asserting that something happened which had no cause. They mean only that something happened for which they cannot discern the cause. The doctrine that nothing exists without a cause is axiomatic for all philosophers. It is a commitment to the view that the things which occur in nature are intelligible and capable of explanation, even if we cannot provide one at the moment. It is a view to which Hume himself is committed.

Given Hume's subscription to this view, must not he also be of the opinion that there is an infinite series of causes? For, if each thing has a cause of its existence, must not each cause have a cause and so on *ad infinitum*? Is not the doctrine that nothing exists without a cause incompatible with the doctrine that there is an original or ultimate cause? It would be were we to construe "cause" here as Humean or particular cause and not as general cause or principle. As we have already seen, one cannot, except arbitrarily, call a halt to a regress of particular causes and effects. But there must be an end to a regress of general causes in the form of the basic nature of objects. Hence, if there is a basic nature of objects in terms of which they interact with one another to produce all observable changes, then there must also be an ultimate general cause, for Hume takes these to be equivalent. If it is self-evident that there is such a thing as a basic nature, then it is also self-evident that there is an ultimate cause. It is clearly Hume's view, then, that nothing exists without a cause and that there is an ultimate cause, that being a principle. Both claims depend on recognizing the subsidiary nature of particular causes vis-à-vis general causes. It is, I believe, only by recognizing this fundamental distinction which Hume makes that one can understand why he thinks that there is an ultimate cause and that this fact is self-evident. Moreover, we can only tell that Philo represents Hume in the *Dialogues* by identifying his position as the distinctive one Hume maintains. Cleanthes begins and operates throughout the *Dialogues* only with the notion of particular cause. Because he does not recognize principles as causes he is totally unable to explain (as in Part IV) why we should consider any particular being as an ultimate cause. Indeed, if he is working only with

Humean causes, it is impossible, according to Hume, to terminate a regress of such causes in a satisfactory way. There can be no first Humean cause. Philo, though, has no such problem because he considers ultimate causes to be principles. Philo's view, then, that it is self-evident that there are ultimate causes, is a direct consequence of Hume's view, expressed throughout his works, that it is self-evident that there is no such thing as chance and that, consequently, everything happens through causes and necessity. But to say that things happen of necessity is merely another way of saying that things happen because of the natures or structural features of objects. To know those natures or essences, which we cannot do, is to know why things *must be* as they are. Necessity is grounded in the natures of objects. This is exactly the position which Philo takes:

> Chance has no place, on any hypothesis, sceptical or religious. Every thing is surely governed by steady, inviolable laws. And were the inmost *essence* of things laid open to us, we should then discover a scene, of which, at present, we can have no idea. Instead of admiring the order of natural beings, we should clearly see, that it was absolutely impossible for them, in the smallest article, ever to admit of any other disposition [D 174–75; emphasis added].

He repeats the same point in a slightly different way in Part IX. Using as an example the fact that "the products of 9 compose always either 9 or some lesser product of 9; if you add together all the characters, of which any of the former products is composed," he concludes:

> To a superficial observer, so wonderful a regularity may be admired as the effect either of chance or design; but a skilful algebraist immediately concludes it to be the work of necessity, and demonstrates, that it must for ever result from the *nature* of these numbers. Is it not probable, I ask, that the whole œconomy of the universe is conducted by a like necessity, though no human algebra can furnish a key which solves the difficulty? And instead of admiring the order of natural beings, may it not happen, that, could we penetrate into the intimate *nature* of bodies, we should clearly see why it was absolutely impossible, they could ever admit of any other disposition? [D 191; emphasis added].

Philo is arguing here that the order in the universe follows necessarily from the natures of the bodies in it, just as the regularities of numerical relations follow from the natures of numbers. One who discerned the natures of numbers and of bodies would have insight into mathematical and natural necessity. He would see that neither chance nor design can ultimately provide an explanation of why things are as they are.

We are now in a position to sum up the issue. The claims that nothing exists without a cause and that there is an ultimate cause are intimately related. The former denies the existence of chance and this affirms the existence of causes and necessity. But both causality and necessity are grounded in the natures of objects. Hence, to deny the existence of chance is to maintain that there is a basic nature of objects, or a basic principle or order. In fact, we could say that the two claims are just two sides of the same coin, and both Philo and Hume have latched on to it.

Moving on to the third problem, concerning the incomprehensibility of this first or ultimate cause, it is evident why Philo adopted this position. We noted earlier that it is a mark of a principle or general cause that it is incomprehensible, by which is meant that it is something of which we can have no idea. If we allow, as Philo does, that the ultimate cause must be a principle, then we must also allow that it is something incomprehensible. In fact, it becomes very difficult to explain why Philo considered the ultimate cause to be incomprehensible if we do not take the ultimate cause to be, for him, a principle. In addition, we also noted that Philo's explanation of why God's nature is incomprehensible is the same as that which Hume gives about principles, viz., that we have no experience of the nature of ultimate causes, and consequently no ideas of them, since ideas are derived from experience (impressions) (D 142–43; EHU 67, 68–69). However, we must not make the mistake of thinking that because both Philo and Hume advocate the incomprehensibility thesis, they think nothing can be known of the nature of the ultimate cause. They do think that we can have an indirect knowledge of the first cause, even though no direct knowledge of it is available by means of the senses or reason. In what does this indirect knowledge consist?

Again, it should be apparent that the ultimate principle is known in the same way in which any cause is: by its effects. By means of "reasonings from analogy, experience, and observation," we learn the effects of various objects and sort out those effects into kinds which, in turn, determine the kinds of powers or principles which exist. Since the matter of which principles exist is a matter of fact, it can be determined, as can any other matter of fact, only by reasoning from experience. Experience and reasoning of a comparative type (which enables us to discover resemblances among effects and kinds of effects) give us knowledge of the powers which exist in nature. Consequently, if we discover that "the effects resemble each other, we are led to infer, by all the rules of analogy, that the causes also resemble . . ." (D 143). In other words, Hume thinks that arguments from analogy not only are proper, but are the only way in which the nature of principles can be established. Because this is Hume's stance, he could not in general be opposed to the argument from design insofar as it proceeds to compare like effects and to argue that like effects have like causes. He would only say that, if the argument from design is used to identify the ultimate cause of order in the universe, then it has not found one if it identifies that ultimate cause as some particular being, i.e., as something other than a principle. But if the argument of design is used only as a means to "resolve the many particular effects into a few general causes" (EHU 30), it is a perfectly proper argument to the ultimate cause of order of the universe, subject, of course, to a critical examination of its success as a reductive measure.

What Philo tries to bring Cleanthes to recognize is that, in searching for an *ultimate* cause, we must have recourse to principles, for these are the only causes which are of the right type to play that role. This, I take it, is Philo's purpose in Part IV. Yet Cleanthes never really does grasp the distinction between the two kinds of causes, and, hence, he never does understand how Philo can accept the argument from design as methodologically sound without agreeing with the conclusion Cleanthes derives from it: that the ultimate cause is a particular mind.

Now, if we agree that the method of analogy is used by Philo to identify the ultimate cause of order, what does Philo identify as being that ultimate principle? In the case of other principles we have considered, e.g., gravity and communication of motion by impulse, Hume took these to be, for us, the ultimate principles productive of change of motion. A reductive account of such change he apparently ruled out because of a difference in the effects, a notable one being that impact seems to require contact of objects. However, there is no evidence that there is such a thing as the ether and so a successful reduction of the mechanisms of change of motion from two to one is precluded. Philo suggests that there are four principles (among an indefinitely large number which may exist elsewhere) with which we are familiar which could serve as the basis for reductive accounts of the order in the universe: reason, instinct, generation, and vegetation (D 178). By reason he means "that principle, by which our own minds operate" (D 178), and not the mind itself. It is to this principle, ultimately, that Cleanthes must appeal if he is to terminate the regress of explanations at the designing mind. Instinct is the mechanism which explains why spiders build webs, bees beehives, etc. Generation and vegetation explain the order and production of animals and vegetables, respectively. Each of these principles could serve as the foundation of a system of cosmogony, and Philo does invent, in Parts VI, VII, and VIII, theories based on instinct, generation, and vegetation without coming up with a convincing account. This is not to concede, as Philo notes, that Cleanthes' account based on mind is successful, for it, too, is subject to great difficulties:

> In all instances which we have ever seen, ideas are copied from real objects, and are ectypal, not archetypal, to express myself in learned terms: You reverse this order, and give thought the precedence. In all instances which we have ever seen, thought has no influence upon matter, except where that matter is so conjoined with it, as to have an equal reciprocal influence upon it. No animal can move immediately any thing but the members of its own body; and indeed, the equality of action and re-action seems to be an universal law of nature: But your theory [i.e., Cleanthes'] implies a contradiction to this experience [D 186].

In short, Cleanthes' designing mind hypothesis also fails because it assumes the existence of principles not only for which there is no evidence but against which there is definite evidence. Thus, Cleanthes must assume a mechanism to generate ideas without the use of the senses; all evidence shows no such mechanism. He must assume that a mind can act immediately on things other than its own body; all evidence shows a mind can operate immediately only on its own body, i.e., that mind–body interaction is a basic mechanism or principle. Moreover, even the principle of reason, which Cleanthes needs to end the regress at the mind of God (reason being that which orders God's mind), is argued by Philo to be derivative in nature:

> Reason, in innumerable instances, is observed to arise from the principle of generation, and never to arise from any other principle [D 180].

The point is, surely, that reason is known to depend on the organization of the biological organism in which it exists. Reason, as we know it, is a subsidiary principle insofar as it depends on generation, and so the evidence suggests that it is not the basic source of order in the universe.

The conclusion which Philo draws is that "we have no *data* to establish any system of cosmogony" (D 177). In other words, neither the four principles, nor any others we have ready to hand, are capable of providing an acceptable account of the order in the universe, of showing the ultimate principle of order. This, of course, does not mean that there is no ultimate principle, but only that the evidence we have leads us to conclude that it is none of these principles. These are principles which *for us* are ultimate, since we are unable, as Hume puts it, to discover "the causes of these general causes" since they are "totally shut up from human curiosity and enquiry" (EHU 30). Nevertheless, by comparing the effects of all these principles we are led to believe that, because the effects are so strikingly similar, there must be a common basis in all the causes to account for the likeness of the effects. This common basis is the most basic principle of order, the general cause which is the source of the four principles of reason, instinct, generation, and vegetation. It is like all these principles, but identical with none of them. This first principle is what Hume considers to be God. Philo makes this point nicely in Part XII:

> No man can deny the analogies between the effects [of art and of nature]: To restrain ourselves from enquiring concerning the causes is scarcely possible: From this enquiry, the legitimate conclusion is, that the causes have also an analogy: And if we are not contented with calling the first and supreme cause a GOD or DEITY, but desire to vary the expression; what can we call him but MIND or THOUGHT, to which he is justly supposed to bear a considerable resemblance? [D 217].

It should be evident that the only type of cause which Hume could take to be a first and supreme cause is principle. As such, God may be called "Mind" but not "a mind" since the latter refers to a system of perceptions, a particular being. No argument from analogy could be successful in showing a first cause to be a particular being, given the mechanics of Humean causal explanation, which requires reference to principles as ultimate causes. Nevertheless, we can call God "Mind" because of the resemblance he bears to the principle of order in our minds, and because of the honorific connotations of the term which serve to "express our adoration of him" (D 142). God, however, is not matter, not a mind. He is the most basic essence of things in terms of which all order arises.[2]

Hume is quite careful to exclude from God's nature any moral attributes as such since the recognition of moral good and evil by a moral agent presupposes, according to Hume's account, the possession not only of a mind but of sentiments of approbation and blame. This point is made indirectly by Philo in Parts X and XI, but was anticipated by Demea at the end of Part III. Demea argues there that neither the materials nor the manner of thought which is distinctive of our minds can be appropriate to the divine mind;

and were we to remove these circumstances, we absolutely annihilate its essence, and it would, in such a case, be an abuse of terms to apply to it the name of thought or reason. At least, if it appear more pious and respectful (as it really is) still to retain these terms, when we mention the supreme Being, we ought to acknowledge, that their meaning, in that case, is totally incomprehensible; and that the infirmities of our nature do not permit us to reach any ideas, which in the least correspond to the ineffable sublimity of the divine attributes [D 156–57].

It seems safe to conclude from this that both Demea and Philo share the incomprehensibility thesis and thus that they share the view that God is no mind in the usual sense of that term. Of course, the two still differ fundamentally in that Demea does, but Philo does not, think that the ultimate cause is a particular. In this respect, Demea and Cleanthes agree; but they disagree about the intelligibility of God, Cleanthes thinking the nature of God to be comprehensible. It is only Philo who maintains that God is neither a particular being nor a comprehensible one, an opinion which exactly echoes Hume's views on the nature of ultimate causes. Philo's conclusion about the attributes of God can only be that they are unknown and unintelligible, except insofar as we call him intelligent because of his similarity to the principle by which our own minds operate. Nothing else of the nature of God can be known. This is the conclusion which Philo sums up in the proposition *"that the cause or causes of order in the universe probably bear some remote analogy to human intelligence . . ."* (D 227). This analogy, he continues, "can be carried no farther than to the human intelligence; and cannot be transferred, with any appearance of probability, to the other qualities of the mind . . ." (D 227). In other words, God is similar to the human mind insofar as he, qua *power*, resembles its *power* of intelligence. Nothing else which characterizes minds can in seriousness be attributed to him.

Hume, of course, is not attempting to develop a new theology. He sees the task of natural religion to be to content itself with "instructing us in the nature of superior powers" (T xix). But a certain species of natural religion cannot contain itself and "carries its views farther, to their [the superior powers'] disposition towards us, and our duties towards them" (T xix). When natural religion exceeds its proper limits it becomes superstition:

'Tis certain, that superstition is much more bold in its systems and hypotheses than philosophy; and while the latter contents itself with assigning new causes and principles to the phænomena, which appear in the visible world, the former opens a world of its own, and presents us with scenes, and beings, and objects, which are altogether new [T 271].

Philosophy or metaphysics concerns itself with causes or principles which are explanative of natural phenomena. Since it deals only with principles, it cannot extend our knowledge beyond the sensible realm, except to say that there are causes of certain observable effects, of which causes little more can be said than simply that they produce those specific effects. Superstition, though, believes that it can gain access to suprasensible objects, and for this reason, especially, it recommends itself to the mind of man which cannot confine itself to the common course of experience since it is vitally concerned to know the nature of the secret causes responsible for the changes of human fortune. Hume not only recommends philosophy as preferable to superstition (T 271) but also thinks that it alone can conquer the terrors of superstition because "superstition being founded on false opinion, must immediately vanish when true philosophy has inspired juster sentiments of superior powers" (*Essays* 585). It is already clear in what sense Hume understands philosophy to provide juster sentiments of superior powers: it shows that the superior powers are just that, powers or principles and not personal beings threatening all manner of ills or promising all manner of goods to anxious mortals. In place of this superstitious scheme of things philosophy substitutes a sane one.

A question may arise at this point as to how Hume's theological position should be characterized. Should we call it deism, or atheism, or theism, the title which Hume himself deemed most fitting? Despite the rather jejune appearance of this question, some interesting aspects of Hume's theology may be revealed by considering it.

Certainly, Hume's views *could* be considered atheistic for he thinks that the ultimate cause is a principle and thus not a person, and the claim that God is a person is thought to be an essential ingredient in traditional theism. Note, however, that Hume need not deny the existence of the theistic God. He is saying, or need say, only that should there exist such a being he could not be considered the ultimate cause because he is a particular being and, as such, unfit for the role. The existence of a theistic God ultimately does not provide a proper explanation. But it does not at all follow from any of this that Hume denied the existence of the theistic God, a claim, I take it, central to atheism, but only that he thought that the supposition of such existence was methodologically wrongheaded and unsupported. I do not think this is atheism in the strict sense. Moreover, Hume would not have considered himself to be an atheist since he labels as such only those who "acknowledge no being, that corresponds to our idea of a deity" (NHR 33). Atheists, then, acknowledge "No first principle of mind or thought: No supreme government and administration: No divine contrivance or intention in the fabric of the world" (NHR 33). Since Hume definitely does think that God is a first principle of mind or thought, as we have seen, he is far from thinking of himself as an atheist. Rather, he seems to be distinguishing between views of God as a supreme person and other views, like his own, which construe God as being the supreme *intelligent*, but not personal, source of order in the universe. What Hume seems to see himself as doing is purifying the conception of God from the anthropomorphic accretions which have been attached to it by the speculations of philosophers and theologians who have attempted to form, not a rational, but an imaginative, picture of the deity. "Genuine Theism," or Hume's own position, is an attempt to preserve what is sound in traditional theism, its emphasis on the intelligent and supreme causality of the deity, a position which is rationally supported, and, at the same time, to illustrate that the conceptual move from God's intelligence to God's personhood is supported only by imaginative construction, not philosophical argumentation: "By degrees, the active imagination of men, uneasy in this abstract conception of objects . . . begins to render them more particular, and to clothe them in shapes more suitable to its natural comprehension" (NHR 47). Hence, Hume's expression "genuine Theism" is coined to signify that he has in his philosophy returned to what he considers to be essential to the theistic tradition, a judgment on his part with which we may well disagree. But a simplistic labelling of Hume as atheist contributes little to an understanding of his position.

Could Hume be considered a deist? This is somewhat harder to answer since the deism of the period was not a single uniform phenomenon but rather a tendency. Some deists were pantheists, some believed in a personal God, some saw morality as the essence of religion, some were extremely rationalistic, some agnostic about the nature of God, etc. In essence, deism did not constitute a philosophical doctrine but rather an attitude which emphasized the approach of reason and natural religion at the expense of faith and revealed religion. But even this generalization is an oversimplification. However, if we let it stand and consider Hume in terms of it, there is no doubt that Hume held a deistic attitude. Yet because deism is not a worked out, philosophically rigorous viewpoint, Hume suffers unfavorably by being linked with what are, to my mind, mostly second-class thinkers. It is surely preferable to discern the uniqueness of Hume's theological views rather than the sometimes remote analogies they may have to others'. Perhaps, too, it is easier to discover what Hume's views are than what constitutes theism, atheism, and deism. I have operated in this essay on the assumption that this is so.

NOTES

1. The notable exception to this rule is, of course, the term "general causes."

2. Resemblance among principles is ascertained by noting the resemblances among their effects. Thus two principles, say, reason and instinct, can be said to resemble if the effects which are ascribed to them resemble. The reason for this is that all knowledge of principles is indirect (viz., through their perceived effects), and hence all claims about the resemblance of principles derive, not from acquaintance with their intrinsic characteristics, but from the things to which they are related, the effects produced. By the same token, any higher level principle which explains a derivative principle will also resemble that derivative principle since both are the sources of similar effects. The higher level principle is more general than the derivative because its effects include but are more extensive than those of the derivative principle which it explains. Consequently, because the four principles of reason, instinct, generation, and vegetation have resembling effects, they are all resembling. Because they are resembling we suppose there to be a more basic principle to account for this resemblance. This more basic principle, the basic nature of the plurality of objects explained by the four principles, is identified by Hume as God. Since God and the four principles are the ultimate and derivative sources, respectively, of similar effects, they are all resembling. As a result, although it would be a mistake to suppose that a general cause or principle can resemble a particular effect or set of such effects, it is necessarily the case that any ultimate principle resembles any derivative one it explains, precisely because of the way in which principles as such are identified. That God is to be called "Mind" is due in part to the fact that his effects resemble the effects of mind, or more precisely, of human intelligence. Yet since God also resembles the principles operative in, for example, animals, this could not be the sole reason for the use of the term. It is also used because of its religious suitability.

III

7

The Location, Extension, Shape, and Size
of Hume's Perceptions

ROBERT F. ANDERSON
University of Nebraska
Lincoln

I

A CERTAIN PASSAGE OF ABOUT FIVE PAGES in the section "Of the Immateriality of the Soul" in Hume's *A Treatise of Human Nature* (T 232ff.) raises a question which seems to me important in his philosophy; yet it is a question which has largely been overlooked in writings on Hume. Norman Kemp Smith considers the passage more fully than do other scholars, I believe, devoting five pages of his own to it in an appendix; [1] yet he skirts the question which naturally arises in the context. The answer to this question, when elicited fully from Hume's text, reveals a good deal of his view concerning how perceptions exist, what sorts of things perceptions represent, and how perceptions represent them. But the answer also discloses, I regret to note, an inconsistency in Hume's account.

Early in this section of the *Treatise* Hume finds that the question of the substance of the soul, whether it be material or immaterial, cannot be answered since the question itself remains unintelligible, and he concludes:

> Thus neither by considering the first origin of ideas, nor by means of a definition are we able to arrive at any satisfactory notion of substance; which seems to me a sufficient reason for abandoning utterly that dispute concerning the materiality and immateriality of the soul, and makes me absolutely condemn even the question itself [T 234].

He takes note of a related argument, however, and chooses to pursue it in the hope that it will reveal something more worthwhile.

> This argument affects not the question concerning the *substance* of the soul, but only that concerning its *local conjunction* with matter; and therefore it may not be improper to consider in general what objects are, or are not susceptible of a local conjunction. This is a curious question, and may lead us to some discoveries of considerable moment [T 235].

Hume explains that one party to this dispute, whom he identifies only as "theologians," hold that the soul must be immaterial. He states their argument:

> Whatever is extended consists of parts; and whatever consists of parts is divisible, if not in reality, at least in the imagination. But 'tis impossible any thing divisible can be *conjoin'd* to a thought or perception, which is a being altogether inseparable and indivisible [T 234];

and reports their conclusion:

> Thought, therefore, and extension are qualities wholly incompatible, and never can incorporate together into one subject [T 234–35].

The opposing "materialist" group, he says, believe that all thought is compatible with extension—that is, that all thought is capable of conjunction in place with extension—and, hence, apparently, that the soul itself is material. Hume finds reason to reject both these views:

> But tho' in this view of things we cannot refuse to condemn the materialists, who conjoin all thought with extension; yet a little reflection will show us equal reason for blaming their antagonists, who conjoin all thought with a simple and indivisible substance [T 239].

In contending against both positions, Hume will offer several assertions of his own about objects and about perceptions and about their respective properties and ways of existing.

He observes that the question of what sorts of entities may have conjunction in place is really much broader and more commonplace than the immediate question:

> It may be better worth our while to remark, that this question of the local conjunction of objects does not only occur in metaphysical disputes concerning the nature of the soul, but that even in common life we have every moment occasion to examine it [T 236].

In keeping with this observation Hume previously offered a principle concerning the location of objects:

> 'Twill not be surprizing after this, if I deliver a maxim, which is condemn'd by several metaphysicians, and is esteem'd contrary to the most certain principles of human reason. This maxim is *that an object may exist, and yet be no where*: and I assert, that this is not only possible, but that the greatest part of beings do and must exist after this manner [T 235].

He explains what is meant in saying an object may exist without location:

> An object may be said to be no where, when its parts are not so situated with respect to each other, as to form any figure or quantity; nor the whole with respect to other bodies so as to answer to our notions of contiguity or distance [T 235–36].

His chief example of this sort of thing is flavor. We commonly suppose that the taste of any fruit is in the fruit itself; but Hume treats this opinion as a natural illusion, and he offers an explanation (T 237–38) of how we commonly acquire it. He then goes on to point out why this must be found unsatisfactory:

> But whatever confus'd notions we may form of an union in place betwixt an extended body, as a fig, and its particular taste, 'tis certain that upon reflection we must observe in this union something altogether unintelligible and contradictory. For shou'd we ask ourselves one obvious question, *viz.* if the taste, which we conceive to be contain'd in the circumference of the body, is in every part of it or in one only, we must quickly find ourselves at a loss, and perceive the impossibility of ever giving a satisfactory answer [T 238];

and he finds the only tenable conclusion to be that some objects (such as tastes) exist without any location:

> For we have only this choice left, either to suppose that some beings exist without any place; or that they are figur'd and extended; or that when they are incorporated with extended objects, the whole is in the whole, and the whole in every part. The absurdity of the two last suppositions proves sufficiently the veracity of the first. Nor is there any fourth opinion [T 239].

Now Hume applies the maxim "that an object may exist, and yet be no where" to perceptions as well as to objects. Immediately after offering his explanation of how "an object may be said to be no where," he says, "Now this is evidently the case with all our perceptions and objects, except those of the sight and feeling" (T 236), and the examples he provides include perceptions, indeed, and objects:

> A moral reflection cannot be plac'd on the right or on the left hand of a passion, nor can a smell or sound be either of a circular or a square figure. These objects and perceptions, so far from requiring any particular place, are absolutely incompatible with it, and even the imagination cannot attribute it to them [T 236].

Norman Kemp Smith rightly observes here the distinction Hume has indicated between objects and perceptions. He says that Hume's dual phrase "perceptions and objects" reflects his "fidelity to a realist standpoint." [2] He maintains that Hume holds to a distinction between " 'objects [meaning "bodies" in the widest sense, as including men and animals] and perceptions.' " [3] I find that Hume *regularly* distinguishes objects from perceptions, so that Kemp Smith's particular notice of it here seems to me needless; and I believe that the opinion, rather widespread among other scholars, that Hume does not distinguish objects from perceptions, probably arises from their failure to notice the various senses in which he employs "object." [4] I would differ with Kemp Smith, further, regarding what Hume here intends by "object." As the context shows, objects include not only bodies, but also qualities commonly attributed to bodies, e.g., flavors and odors.

Since Hume has now shown, to his own satisfaction, that perceptions such as those of tastes, odors, and sounds can have no location, he is in a position to show that the view of the "materialists" is mistaken; for if these perceptions can have no location at all, then surely they can have no local conjunction with matter:

> those perceptions, which are simple, and exist no where, are incapable of any conjunction in place with matter or body, which is extended and divisible; since 'tis impossible to found a relation but on some common quality [T 236].

Thus he concludes that the "materialist" view must be rejected: ". . . we cannot refuse to condemn the materialists, who conjoin all thought with extension . . ." (T 239).

In a parallel argument Hume now turns against the contention of the "theologians" that the soul is simple and indivisible. He continues:

> yet a little reflection will show us equal reason for blaming their antagonists, who conjoin all thought with a simple and indivisible substance [T 239].

Although "the greatest part of beings" exist without location, according to Hume, we have seen that he explicitly excepts "those of sight and feeling," and that his maxim "that an object may exist, and yet be no where" is applied to perceptions as well as to objects. Apparently, then, objects which we may see or touch do have location; and apparently our visual and tactual perceptions also have location. We shall see that they possess other properties in common as well.

Hume says the senses of vision and touch provide us with the idea of extension, as he has explained at length in Book I, Part II, "Of the Ideas of Space and Time." He reminds the reader of this, in the present context:

> The first notion of space and extension is deriv'd solely from the senses of sight and feeling; nor is there any thing, but what is colour'd or tangible, that has parts dispos'd after such a manner, as to convey that idea [T 235].

Later he adds that anything extended must have shape, thereby indicating that this will hold not only for visible and tangible objects but also for visual and tactual perceptions:

> What is extended must have a particular figure, as square, round, triangular; none of which will agree to a desire, or indeed to any impression or idea, except of these two senses above-mention'd [T 235].

Since ideas are copies of their impressions, according to Hume, any idea derived from a visual or tactual impression must of course also have extension and a particular shape. Toward the end of this discussion, he provides, as example, our perception of a table:

> That table, which just now appears to me, is only a perception, and all its qualities are qualities of a perception. Now the most obvious of all its qualities is extension. The perception consists of parts. These parts are so situated, as to afford us the notion of distance and contiguity; of length, breadth, and thickness. The termination of these three dimensions is what we call figure. This figure is moveable, separable, and divisible. Mobility, and separability are the distinguishing properties of extended objects [T 239].

It is obvious that Hume considers his discovery that perceptions have extension, shape, etc. as a strong point on the side of the free-thinker (apparently the "materialist") in his contention against the "theologians":

> The free-thinker may now triumph in his turn; and having found there are impressions and ideas really extended, may ask his antagonists, how they can incorporate a simple and indivisible subject with an extended perception? All the arguments of Theologians may here be retorted upon them [T 240].

The triumph of the "free-thinker" here, of course, is overshadowed by Hume's double victory over both parties in the dispute on the local conjunction of the soul with matter. For just as he holds that the position of the "theologians" is destroyed because there are some perceptions which have extension and location, so he holds that the position of the "materialists" is destroyed because there are other perceptions which have no extension or location.

We have found thus far that Hume has distinguished *objects* which have location, extension, and figure from objects which have none of these. It is more significant to my present purpose that Hume has further distinguished, among *perceptions*, those which have location, extension, and figure from those which have not. We can see that it is important to Hume, in his contentions against both the "theologians" and the "materialists," to draw this distinction. We cannot as easily perceive, I think, the ground on which this distinction is made. Thus, it seems to me, the question has naturally arisen: *Why do some perceptions have location, extension, and figure while other perceptions lack them?* Hume has provided no straightforward explanation, here or elsewhere; but I am inclined to believe that he is deriving this distinction among perceptions from two premisses found elsewhere in his writings.

II

First, I observe that Hume holds *that some perceptions represent external objects.* This is a view which, I fear, many students of Hume do not share. For example, John Laird says:

> The best known and probably the most important part of Hume's contentions in this matter was that all impressions were "compleat in themselves." Our senses, he said (189), "convey to us nothing but a single perception, and never give us the least intimation of anything beyond." . . . In other words, his doctrine was that impressions were *non-representative*, and *atomic*.[5]

In his summary of what he takes to be Hume's doctrine, D. G. C. MacNabb largely agrees with Laird's conclusion:

> First, we cannot form an idea of anything specifically different from ideas and impressions. The representative theory of perception is therefore nonsensical, for it maintains that the ideas in the mind represent material substances specifically different from them.[6]

On the other hand, we find John Passmore asserting that Hume grants that perceptions represent objects:

> If we ask what Hume believed, what view he committed himself to in his scientific work, the answer is that he believed in the existence both of mate-

rial objects *and* of perceptions, and thought that perceptions were "appearances of" material objects.[7]

The passage which Passmore quotes in support of his conclusion appears in *An Enquiry Concerning Human Understanding* in a discussion in which Hume has set forth at length the two main views of men with respect to objects and perceptions and their relations. He begins by describing the primordial conviction, common to men and animals, that there are external objects:

> It seems evident, that men are carried, by a natural instinct or prepossession, to repose faith in their senses; and that, without any reasoning, or even almost before the use of reason, we always suppose an external universe, which depends not on our perception, but would exist, though we and every sensible creature were absent or annihilated. Even the animal creation are governed by a like opinion, and preserve this belief of external objects, in all their thoughts, designs, and actions [EHU 151].

He continues, explaining that men (again apparently like the animals) naturally believe they are regarding directly the external objects themselves, not guessing that it is really impressions which they apprehend immediately:

> It seems also evident, that, when men follow this blind and powerful instinct of nature, they always suppose the very images, presented by the senses, to be the external objects, and never entertain any suspicion, that the one are nothing but representations of the other. This very table, which we see white, and which we feel hard, is believed to exist, independent of our perception, and to be something external to our mind, which perceives it [EHU 151–52].

Hume then describes how reflection leads men to distinguish perceptions from objects, and to recognize that the perceptions represent the objects:

> But this universal and primary opinion of all men is soon destroyed by the slightest philosophy, which reaches us, that nothing can ever be present to the mind but an image or perception, and that the senses are only the inlets, through which these images are conveyed, without being able to produce any immediate intercourse between the mind and the object [EHU 152].

His example, again, is the table:

> The table, which we see, seems to diminish, as we remove farther from it: but the real table, which exists independent of us, suffers no alteration: it was, therefore, nothing but its image, which was present to the mind [EHU 152].

This conclusion, he thinks, is both manifest and easily obtained:

> These are the obvious dictates of reason; and no man, who reflects, ever doubted, that the existences, which we consider, when we say, *this house* and *that tree*, are nothing but perceptions in the mind, and fleeting copies or representations of other existences, which remain uniform and independent [EHU 152].

This lengthy passage is sufficient to make clear, I maintain, that Hume believes that the theory that some perceptions represent objects is held by nearly every human. Furthermore, it is clear that Hume himself holds this theory. He has excepted himself neither in this statement nor elsewhere in the context. Moreover, he implies that those who have not reached this conclusion cannot have done even the least philosophical reflection—a class in which Hume is not likely to include himself.

Although one might urge that Hume, in writing his *Enquiries*, may have been endeavoring to soften or conceal his doctrines to make them more widely appealing than was his *Treatise*, so ill-regarded in his own time, and, hence, that the view expressed in the *Enquiry Concerning Human Understanding* cannot be accepted as Hume's true one unless it also be found in the *Treatise*, I find that such remarks on the topic as Hume does supply in the *Treatise* are in complete agreement with this passage from the *Enquiry*. For example, he says briefly:

> We may observe, that 'tis universally allow'd by philosophers, and is besides pretty obvious of itself, that nothing is ever really present with the mind but its perceptions or impressions and ideas, and that external objects become known to us only by those perceptions they occasion [T 67].

Or the more succinct expression:

> The most vulgar philosophy informs us, that no external object can make itself known to the mind immediately, and without the interposition of an image or perception [T 239].

These two remarks parallel very closely the longer statement in the first *Enquiry*. Not only has Hume clearly implied in both that some of our perceptions represent external objects, he has taken care in both to emphasize as well that this view is one easily arrived at, obvious, and widely accepted. Again, Hume has not excepted himself from those who hold this view.

Something of the seriousness with which Hume himself entertains this view is shown in his further remarks in the *Treatise* on the adequacy of representation which perceptions may enjoy in relation to external objects. He says, for example, that

> WHEREVER ideas are adequate representations of objects, the relations, contradictions and agreements of the ideas are all applicable to the objects . . . [T 29].

He continues, finding that our ideas do adequately represent even the smallest objects:

> But our ideas are adequate representations of the most minute parts of extension; and thro' whatever divisions and subdivisions we may suppose these parts to be arriv'd at, they can never become inferior to some ideas, which we form. The plain consequence is, that whatever *appears* impossible and contradictory upon the comparison of these ideas, must be *really* impossible and contradictory, without any farther excuse or evasion [T 29].

Hume is aware, of course, of the sceptical implications of much of his doctrine; and he freely admits, in the *Enquiry*, that reason is powerless to oppose scepticism regarding the external world. He rehearses both "popular" and "philosophical" objections to belief in external objects, then vigorously attacks "excessive scepticism" on other grounds.[8] For one thing, it is without purpose or benefit:

> For here is the chief and most confounding objection to *excessive* scepticism, that no durable good can ever result from it; while it remains in its full force and vigour. We need only ask such a sceptic, *What his meaning is? And what he proposes by all these curious researches?* He is immediately at a loss, and knows not what to answer [EHU 159–60].

Indeed, it seems that excessive scepticism can have only evil consequences. He continues:

> On the contrary, he must acknowledge, if he will acknowledge anything, that all human life must perish, were his principles universally and steadily to prevail. All discourse, all action would immediately cease; and men remain in a total lethargy, till the necessities of nature, unsatisfied, put an end to their miserable existence [EHU 160].

Even though it be dangerous to men, and even though it be irrefutable, excessive scepticism can never be taken seriously for long, since it is destroyed by everyday concerns:

> The great subverter of *Pyrrhonism* or the excessive principles of scepticism is action, and employment, and the occupations of common life. These principles may flourish and triumph in the schools; where it is, indeed, difficult, if not impossible, to refute them. But as soon as they leave the shade, and by the presence of the real objects, which actuate our passions and sentiments, are put in opposition to the more powerful principles of our nature, they vanish like smoke, and leave the most determined sceptic in the same condition as other mortals [EHU 158–59].

Hume expresses the same view in other terms only shortly afterward, indicating, it seems to me, both the importance he attaches to this matter, and the strength of his conviction:

> Nature is always too strong for principle. And though a Pyrrhonian may throw himself or others into a momentary amazement and confusion by his profound reasonings; the first and most trivial event in life will put to flight all his doubts and scruples, and leave him the same, in every point of action and speculation, with the philosophers of every other sect, or with those who never concerned themselves in any philosophical researches. When he awakes from his dream, he will be the first to join in the laugh against himself . . . [EHU 160].

Those accustomed to reading Hume's philosophical prose will recognize in these passages a rather unusual length and vehemence in expression—further evidence, it seems to me, of Hume's firmness in rejecting "excessive scepticism."

Some scholars of Hume dealing with this topic have, however, largely ignored the *Enquiry* and have devoted their attention instead to the section entitled "Of scepticism with regard to the senses" in the *Treatise.* H. H. Price, in particular, in his book, *Hume's Theory of the External World,* says:

I wish to examine Hume's theory of Perception and the External World upon its own merits, as it stands in the section on *Scepticism with regard to the Senses* (*Treatise*, Book I, Part iv, Section 2). It will be necessary to refer occasionally to two other sections of Part iv—Section 4, *Of the Modern Philosophy*, and Section 5, *Of the Immateriality of the Soul*—since these add some finishing touches without which the argument of Section 2 cannot be fully understood.[9]

The *Enquiry* is, however, dismissed:

> When he came to write the *Inquiry concerning Human Understanding*, which professes to be the definitive reformulation of his theory of knowledge, he reduced these sections of the *Treatise* to a brief and sketchy summary, and omitted the most interesting passages altogether.[10]

In thus omitting the *Enquiry* from consideration, Professor Price here seems unaware that Hume disowned the *Treatise* in his Advertisement to the posthumous edition of his *Enquiries* and asked us all to read only this collection of his later writings, saying:

> *Most of the principles, and reasonings, contained in this volume, were published in a work in three volumes, called* A Treatise of Human Nature: *A work which the Author had projected before he left College, and which he wrote and published not long after. But not finding it successful, he was sensible of his error in going to the press too early, and he cast the whole anew in the following pieces, where some negligences in his former reasoning and more in the expression, are, he hopes, corrected. Yet several writers, who have honoured the Author's Philosophy with answers, have taken care to direct all their batteries against that juvenile work, which the Author never acknowledged, and have affected to triumph in any advantages, which, they imagined, they had obtained over it: A practice very contrary to all rules of candour and fair-dealing, and a strong instance of those polemical artifices, which a bigotted zeal thinks itself authorized to employ. Henceforth, the Author desires, that the following Pieces may alone be regarded as containing his philosophical sentiments and principles* [EHU (2)].

Some have suggested that we ought not to take this Advertisement seriously, since he wrote it on his deathbed in 1776 and was, perhaps, not wholly clear in his mind. This same assessment of the *Treatise* was expressed many years earlier, however, in his letter of April 1751 to his friend, Gilbert Elliot of Minto:

> I believe the philosophical Essays contain every thing of Consequence relating to the Understanding, which you woud meet with in the Treatise; & I give you my Advice against reading the latter. By shortening & simplifying the Questions, I really render them much more complete. *Addo dum minuo.* The philosophical Principles are the same in both: But I was carry'd away by the Heat of Youth & Invention to publish too precipitately. So vast an Undertaking, plan'd before I was one and twenty, & compos'd before twenty five, must necessarily be very defective. I have repented my Haste a hundred, & a hundred times [LDH 1 158].

There appears to remain no reason, therefore, not to take seriously Hume's disowning of his *Treatise*. Hence, if we are to respect his wishes, we should take the *Enquiry* over the *Treatise* in case of any apparent difference between them.

So far as I can discern, however, the section "Of Scepticism With Regard to the Senses" does not differ substantially from Hume's contentions which we have observed in the *Enquiry* and elsewhere in the *Treatise*. At worst, I think, Hume is guilty of an overstatement of his view; for he says, at the beginning of this section:

> Thus the sceptic still continues to reason and believe, even tho' he asserts, that he cannot defend his reason by reason; and by the same rule he must assent to the principle concerning the existence of body, tho' he cannot pretend by any arguments of philosophy to maintain its veracity. Nature has not left this to his choice, and has doubtless esteem'd it an affair of too great importance to be trusted to our uncertain reasonings and speculations. We may well ask, *What causes induce us to believe in the existence of body?* but 'tis in vain to ask, *Whether there be body or not?* That is a point, which we must take for granted in all our reasonings [T 187].

This passage clearly is largely a brief, earlier version of Hume's scornful attack on sceptics and excessive scepticism which we have already noted in the *Enquiry* (EHU 158–60). Hume here has also carelessly implied, however, that it is psychologically impossible not to believe in external objects. H. H. Price rightly finds fault with this contention.[11] I am inclined to consider this one of those "negligences in expression" which Hume hoped to correct, for it is clear from the *Enquiry* that Hume believes we *can* doubt the reality of external objects, although not for long. At the end of "Of Scepticism With Regard to the Senses," indeed, Hume offers a passage which both agrees with the *Enquiry* and clarifies, it seems to me, his intention in this section:

> 'Tis impossible upon any system to defend either our understanding or senses; and we but expose them farther when we endeavour to justify them in that manner. As the sceptical doubt arises naturally from a profound and intense reflection on those subjects, it always encreases, the farther we carry our reflections, whether in opposition or conformity to it. Carelessness and in-attention alone can afford us any remedy. For this reason I rely entirely upon them; and take it for granted, whatever may be the reader's opinion at this present moment, that an hour hence he will be persuaded there is both an external and internal world . . . [T 218].

Many scholars, among them most recently Jonathan Bennett,[12] hold that "Of Scepticism With Regard to the Senses" nevertheless contains a good deal of argument on the topic of reasons for believing in the existence of external objects, and that the indicated conclusion is scepticism. I have provided a number of texts, from both the *Enquiry* and the *Treatise*, which support the contrary view: that Hume holds that there are external objects and that some perceptions represent them. Furthermore, Hume explicitly states that it is not his purpose in this section to discuss whether there are external objects or not, but only the causes of our belief in them:

> We may well ask, *What causes induce us to believe in the existence of body?* but 'tis in vain to ask, *Whether there be body or not?* That is a point, which

we must take for granted in all our reasonings. The subject, then, of our present inquiry is concerning the *causes* which induce us to believe in the existence of body . . . [T 187–88].

All arguments in this section, I submit, should therefore be understood in the light of this expressed intention. A thorough examination of all parts of "Of Scepticism With Regard to the Senses," and of the differing interpretations of these parts by various scholars, would, of course, require a great deal more space than this paper affords. At most, however, Professor Bennett and scholars of like persuasion can show only an inconsistency between the *Enquiry* and "Of Scepticism With Regard to the Senses" on the question of whether there are external objects. Even if such an inconsistency were shown, we must surely respect Hume's implicit request that the *Enquiries* be taken over the *Treatise* in any case of apparent difference. So I think it cannot be questioned that Hume holds that there are external objects and that some of our perceptions represent them. And this, I believe, is all I need show for my purpose in this paper.

III

A second premiss which I find in Hume's account is *that representation requires resemblance between that which represents and that which is represented*. This is most clear, of course, in Hume's numerous and emphatic remarks on the relation of simple ideas to their impressions. On the first page of the *Treatise* he says that ideas are *images* of impressions:

> Those perceptions, which enter with most force and violence, we may name *impressions*. . . . By *ideas* I mean the faint images of these . . . [T 1].

As frequently, he says that ideas are *copies* of impressions: "all our ideas or more feeble perceptions are copies of our impressions or more lively ones" (T 72; see also T 96). Hume often says that ideas are *derived* from impressions (T 4, 7, 19, 33, 37, 161, 243) and occasionally, more loosely, he says that they are *borrowed* from impressions (T 34, 319, 634). Such images thus borrowed, derived, or copied, must, in Hume's view, *resemble* their impressions: "impressions can give rise to no ideas, but to such as resemble them" (T 63; see also T 3, 66). Furthermore, ideas resemble impressions *exactly*: "every idea is deriv'd from some impression, which is exactly similar to it . . ." (T 33; see also T 319).

Since ideas are borrowed, derived, or copied from impressions, they *represent* their impressions:

> Ideas always represent the objects or impressions, from which they are deriv'd, and can never without a fiction represent or be apply'd to any other [T 37; see also T 7, 34, 157, 161].

And it is apparently by virtue of the *resemblance* which ideas bear to their impressions, inasmuch as they are images or copies of them, that ideas represent their impressions:

> We have no idea of any quality in an object, which does not agree to, and
> may not represent a quality in an impression; and that because all our ideas
> are deriv'd from our impressions [T 243; see also T 19].

Since Hume holds, as we have seen, that simple ideas resemble their impressions exactly, it follows *that simple ideas represent their simple impressions exactly*. Hume offers this general proposition regarding simple perceptions:

> *That all our simple ideas in their first appearance are deriv'd from simple
> impressions, which are correspondent to them, and which they exactly represent* [T 4].

Hume has said that ideas have less force and vivacity than do the impressions from which they are borrowed. But he does not understand this difference in force and vivacity to reduce the resemblance of idea to impression:

> Now since all ideas are deriv'd from impressions, and are nothing but copies
> and representations of them, whatever is true of the one must be acknowl-
> edg'd concerning the other. Impressions and ideas differ only in their strength
> and vivacity [T 19; see also T 3, 5, 319].

Thus if the force and vivacity of an idea is altered, it will still represent the same impression; but if it is altered in any other respect, it will cease to represent the impression from which it was derived.

> Our ideas are copy'd from our impressions, and represent them in all their
> parts. When you wou'd any way vary the idea of a particular object, you can
> only encrease or diminish its force and vivacity. If you make any other change
> on it, it represents a different object or impression [T 96].

D. W. Hamlyn has suggested Hume's reasons for holding so strongly for this correspondence of idea to impression:

> The principle that every simple idea must correspond to an impression is vital
> for a delimitation of the understanding and as a weapon against rationalism.[13]

B. M. Laing observes, however, that Hume's view regarding correspondence conflicts with his account of the imagination:

> it must be noted that Hume limited himself unnecessarily by accepting the
> view that an idea must be a copy of an impression, for what he is asserting
> about the imagination really involves a rejection or at any rate a considerable
> mitigation of that view.[14]

Farhang Zabeeh thinks Hume has, in fact, been heedless in his many statements on exact resemblance and correspondence:

> Hume quite carelessly describes the relation between the members of the two
> classes of impressions and ideas in terms of the exact resemblance—copying,
> derivability of ideas from impressions, priority of impressions to ideas, con-
> stant conjunction of the two, etc.[15]

Later, Zabeeh concludes that Hume has not really intended to say that ideas are exact resemblances of impressions:

At this point, I want to assert that despite Hume's statement that "all ideas are copy'd from impressions," we find that he does not really care whether ideas in fact are the exact copies of impressions. . . . All that Hume cares to establish is the fact of priority of impressions to ideas, and the derivability of the latter from the former, and not the thesis that ideas are copies of impressions.[16]

I do not find, however, that Professor Zabeeh has provided any texts which support this opinion. On the contrary, it seems to me, the number and emphases of Hume's remarks on this topic stand strongly against it. I think we must accept Hume's own statements as straightforward expressions of his views: that simple ideas exactly resemble and hence exactly represent the simple impressions from which they are derived.

It is an additional question, of course, whether representation of an external object also requires exact resemblance between that object and the perception of it. Now we have already observed that Hume says that ideas may be adequate representations of objects. I take such adequate representation to consist at least in such resemblances as Hume himself instances: it is a house which our perception of a house represents, and not a tree; it is a tree which our perception of a tree represents, and not a house (EHU 151–52). We must inquire, however, what further elements of exactness Hume expects in the representation of external objects by perceptions.

A part of the answer to this has already been touched on in our earlier examination of Hume's discussion of our perception of the table. He here concludes that our perception of an extended object is itself extended:

That table, which just now appears to me, is only a perception, and all its qualities are qualities of a perception. Now the most obvious of all its qualities is extension. . . . And to cut short all disputes, the very idea of extension is copy'd from nothing but an impression, and consequently must perfectly agree to it. To say the idea of extension agrees to any thing, is to say it is extended [T 239–40].

Hume goes on to tell us, as we have already noted, that this amounts to a discovery that "there are impressions and ideas really extended." I suggest that Hume intends that just as an idea, being copied from an impression, must "agree to" or resemble that impression, so also that impression, being copied from and representing an object, must "agree to" or resemble that object. Thus the impression of an extended object, such as a table, must itself be extended, and the idea derived from that impression must also be extended.

Furthermore, Hume maintains that the origin of impressions of sensation may be explained by "the constitution of the body, . . . the animal spirits, or . . . the application of objects to the external organs" (T 275). Accordingly, the extension of our perceptions of visible objects is to be explained by the ways perceptions are copied from these objects. Thus Hume says of visual perceptions:

When an object augments or diminishes to the eye or imagination from a comparison with others, the image and idea of the object are still the same, and are equally extended in the *retina*, and in the brain or organ of perception. The eyes refract the rays of light, and the optic nerves convey the images to the brain in the very same manner, whether a great or small object has preceded . . . [T 372].

The extension of our perceptions of extended objects, then, appears to result from the physics of light and the physiology of visual perception, according to Hume's account. The impression or idea of the extended object apparently is quite literally an image of that object, and hence, resembles it in that sense. Since Hume had said that what is extended must have a particular figure (T 235), we may infer that the perception also must have some shape; and since it is an image of the object, we may infer that its shape will be the same as, or very like, that of the object.

In a passage which we have already observed, Hume implies that ideas which are adequate representations of small objects will resemble them in having size:

> But our ideas are adequate representations of the most minute parts of extension; and thro' whatever divisions and subdivisions we may suppose these parts to be arriv'd at, they can never become inferior to some ideas, which we form [T 29].

Fortunately, our power to form small ideas is equal to the task:

> This however is certain, that we can form ideas, which shall be no greater than the smallest atom of the animal spirits of an insect a thousand times less than a mite . . . [T 28].

These passages on the extension and size of perceptions are sufficient, I think, to show that Hume goes a considerable way toward requiring an exact resemblance between a perception and the object it represents. It is now a simple matter to explain his remark, applying his maxim, "that an object may exist, and yet be no where" (T 236), as well to perceptions. If adequate representation requires the perception of an extended object to be itself extended, and if adequate representation requires the perception of an object having size itself to have size, then adequate representation would seem to require the perception of an object having location itself to have location. And if we grant Hume his conclusion that there are some objects, such as flavors, which have no location, then it seems clear that perceptions adequately representing these objects must themselves lack location. Moreover, we know the location of those perceptions which have location. They are in the brain where, so Hume tells us, they possess extension (T 372).

We have perhaps encountered, as well, some hint of the limits of Hume's principle that adequate representation requires resemblance. While some perceptions have location, they cannot have the same location as the objects they represent. Instead, they are in the brain. Furthermore, while they have size, some clearly cannot have the same size as their objects, yet exist within the spatial limits of the brain. Hume seems to have an awareness of this in his additional remarks on the size of certain perceptions:

This however is certain, that we can form ideas, which shall be no greater than the smallest atom of the animal spirits of an insect a thousand times less than a mite: And we ought rather to conclude, that the difficulty lies in enlarging our conceptions so much as to form a just notion of a mite, or even of an insect a thousand times less than a mite. For in order to form a just notion of these animals, we must have a distinct idea representing every part of them . . . [T 28].

Perhaps Hume is suggesting that perceptions of visible and tangible things must all be much smaller than their objects. As long as the relative proportions of the perceptions are correct, perhaps, the adequacy of representation is sufficiently preserved.

Finally, we should observe that Hume employs his principle that representation requires resemblance in a negative way to deny that we have certain ideas. Thus, in opposing the claim that we each possess an idea of self, he says:

If any impression gives rise to the idea of self, that impression must continue invariably the same, thro' the whole course of our lives; since self is suppos'd to exist after that manner [T 251].

That is, since the self is said to exist throughout a lifetime and to remain unchanged through that period, a perception which would represent this alleged self must itself exist lifelong and unchanging. As we know, Hume here denies that he has any such impression. His negative use of the principle is even more clear when he attacks the allegation that there is an idea of the mind as a substance:

As every idea is deriv'd from a precedent impression, had we any idea of the substance of our minds, we must also have an impression of it; which is very difficult, if not impossible, to be conceiv'd. *For how can an impression represent a substance, otherwise than by resembling it?* And how can an impression resemble a substance, since, according to this philosophy, it is not a substance, and has none of the peculiar qualities or characteristics of a substance? [T 232-33; emphasis added].

Hume is implying that if there *were* a perception representing a substantial mind, that perception must itself *be* a substance. The question which I have italicized in the above passage is not, I think, a merely rhetorical question for Hume.

IV

A lengthy paragraph in the *Treatise* appears to offer strong support to my conclusion above regarding the location of perceptions in the brain. In a discussion concerning the associating qualities of the imagination, Hume reminds us that he had originally said that the causes of these associating qualities "must be resolv'd into *original* qualities of human nature," and that he did not pretend to explain them (T 13). He now gives a reason:

When I receiv'd the relations of *resemblance, contiguity* and *causation,* as **principles** of union among ideas, without examining into their causes, 'twas more in prosecution of my first maxim, that we must in the end rest contented with experience, than for want of something specious and plausible, which I might have display'd on that subject. 'Twou'd have been easy to have made an imaginary dissection of the brain, and have shewn, why upon our conception of any idea, the animal spirits run into all the contiguous traces, and rouze up the other ideas, that are related to it [T 60].

Some have advised me that this account of the brain and the associating qualities ought immediately to be dismissed as trifling, since Hume has admitted that it is specious. I observe, however, that "specious" has had several definitions, not all of them indicating what is deceptive, false, or lacking in merit. Samuel Johnson's dictionary was compiled in Hume's own time; and the first meaning of "specious" given therein is, merely, "Showy; pleasing to the view." [17] In at least one passage, moreover, Hume appears clearly to *distinguish* the false from the specious. Consider the following sentence from *An Enquiry Concerning the Principles of Morals*:

> We may conclude, therefore, that, in order to establish laws for the regulation of property, we must be acquainted with the nature and situation of man; must reject appearances, which may be false, though specious; and must search for those rules, which are, on the whole, most *useful* and *beneficial* [EPM 194–95].

I submit, therefore, that Hume's use of "specious" in the *Treatise* passage just cited may not be taken to indicate his rejection of this mode of explanation.

On somewhat different grounds, B. M. Laing implies that Hume is not in earnest in proposing an account in terms of the brain and its animal spirits:

> Malebranche makes use of a conception of animal spirits and of *traces*, and a doctrine of *natural* relations which have *effects*. . . . Hume's theory is similar, except that, apart from a reference to the notion of animal spirits (*Treatise* I, Part II, Sect. v) as a possible means of explanation, he drops this notion as an unverifiable assumption.[18]

I find, however, that Hume employs explanation in terms of animal spirits in other contexts as well. When he is explaining what occurs when we experience difficulty in concentrating on a topic, for example, he writes:

> The attention is on the stretch: The posture of the mind is uneasy; and the spirits being diverted from their natural course, are not govern'd in their movements by the same laws, at least not to the same degree, as when they flow in their usual channel [T 185].

And in his "A Dissertation on the Passions," Hume similarly explains the behavior of passions which we are experiencing at the same time:

> The predominant passion swallows up the inferior, and converts it into itself. The spirits, when once excited, easily receive a change in their direction; and it is natural to imagine, that this change will come from the prevailing affection.[19]

I conclude, therefore, that Hume by no means drops explanation in terms of animal spirits and traces in the brain, but is willing to employ it wherever it seems required.

In any case, Hume proceeds to reveal that he is here serious in this kind of account, since he needs it in order to explain error:

> But tho' I have neglected any advantage, which I might have drawn from this topic in explaining the relations of ideas, I am afraid I must here have recourse to it, in order to account for the mistakes that arise from these relations. I shall therefore observe, that as the mind is endow'd with a power of exciting any idea it pleases; whenever it dispatches the spirits into that region of the brain, in which the idea is plac'd; these spirits always excite the idea, when they run precisely into the proper traces, and rummage that cell, which belongs to the idea. But as their motion is seldom direct, and naturally turns a little to the one side or the other; for this reason the animal spirits, falling into the contiguous traces, present other related ideas in lieu of that, which the mind desir'd at first to survey [T 60–61].

Thus Hume's explanation of the operations of the natural relations, and his explanation of error, depend upon the location of perceptions in the brain. Unless ideas related by resemblance, contiguity, or causation in our experience are spatially near one another in the brain the animal spirits could not "rouze up" both, and so these associating qualities of the imagination would not function or, perhaps, would not exist. And it is scarcely possible to exaggerate the importance of these qualities in Hume's account. Similarly, unless related ideas are located near one another in the brain, the errant animal spirits could not produce mistakes by rummaging an adjacent cell and presenting a different idea. Thus a great deal which is fundamental in Hume's epistemology depends upon perceptions' having location.

Yet a difficulty appears in this connection. Hume has said that certain perceptions, like certain objects, have no location:

> A moral reflection cannot be plac'd on the right or on the left hand of a passion, nor can a smell or sound be either of a circular or a square figure. These objects and perceptions, so far from requiring any particular place, are absolutely incompatible with it . . . [T 236].

Indeed, he has said that all our perceptions, except those of vision and touch, exist "no where." If this is true, then Hume's explanation of the associating qualities, and his explanation of error, can apply only to ideas of vision and touch. Yet it seems obvious that we do associate odors and sounds, and other non-visual and non-tactual ideas, by resemblance, by temporal contiguity, or by cause and effect. Even ideas of passions and moral reflections might be associated in these ways, as Hume supposes in his writings on passions and on morals. And surely errors may occur in our thoughts employing such ideas. Must not these errors also be explained in the same general way?

A possible resolution of this apparent inconsistency comes readily to mind. We may note that the first description of the location of perceptions

(T 60–61) is provided as an explanation of only the associating qualities, memory and error. But the second account (T 234–40), as I have argued, pertains to the representation of objects by perceptions. This suggests that the location of perceptions which Hume is discussing in the later passage, as well as their extension, shape, and size, are but "representational" kinds of location, extension, shape, and size. There would be nothing inconsistent in an idea of a taste or emotion containing no representation of location, yet itself having a location in the brain, hence, being subject to the operations of memory and the associating qualities. At worst, it may be argued, Hume has merely employed "location," "extension," "figure," and "size" equivocally in widely separated passages in the *Treatise*, and a bit of indulgence on our part will set straight the account.

I believe that it does not appear in any of the passages we have examined in this investigation, however, that Hume employs these terms other than univocally. Were it Hume's intention that there be a second, "representational," sense in which these terms are to be applied to perceptions, particularly in the later passage, there has surely been ample opportunity to make this clear; and I know of no remarks in which he does so. Indeed, Hume is emphatic that "there are impressions and ideas really extended . . ." (T 240). Since he has already told us that whatever is extended must also have figure (T 235), we may infer the emphasis also applies to figure. I need scarcely add that entities having real extension and real figure must have real location and real size as well.

The quarrel between "theologians" and "materialists," moreover, into which Hume here inserts himself, concerns the compatibility or incompatibility of thought with real extension. "Theologians" hold that thought and extension are wholly incompatible; "materialists" hold that all thought is compatible with extension. Hume rejects both, arguing that some perceptions have extension and location and some do not. Were Hume understanding "extension" and the other terms only in a "representational" sense, I suggest, he would be making no point at all against either "theologians" or "materialists." I conclude, therefore, that Hume employs these terms univocally throughout, and that an inconsistency remains in his account of the location, extension, shape, and size of perceptions.

NOTES

1. Norman Kemp Smith, *The Philosophy of David Hume* (New York, 1960), 319–24.
2. Ibid., p. 321.
3. Ibid., p. 323; see also p. 512.
4. I have endeavored to sort these out in chap. 5 of *Hume's First Principles* (Lincoln, 1966), pp. 39–47.
5. John Laird, *Hume's Philosophy of Human Nature* (London, 1932), pp. 29–30.
6. D. G. C. MacNabb, "David Hume," *The Encyclopedia of Philosophy*, ed. Paul Edwards, 8 vols. (New York, 1967), IV 78.
7. John Passmore, *Hume's Intentions*, rev. ed. (New York, 1968), p. 90.
8. Hume's other term for "excessive scepticism" is "Pyrrhonism." For a thorough discussion of this and related topics, see Richard H. Popkin's "David Hume: His Pyrrhonism and His Critique of Pyrrhonism," *Philosophical Quarterly*, 1, No. 5 (October 1951), 385–

407 (repr. in *Hume: A Collection of Critical Essays*, ed. V. C. Chappell [Garden City, 1966], pp. 53–98).

9. H. H. Price, *Hume's Theory of the External World* (Oxford, 1940), p. 10.

10. Ibid., p. 1.

11. Ibid., pp. 11–12.

12. Jonathan Bennett, *Locke, Berkeley, Hume* (Oxford, 1971), pp. 313ff.

13. D. W. Hamlyn, "History of Epistemology," *Encyclopedia of Philosophy*, III 26.

14. B. M. Laing, *David Hume* (New York, 1932), p. 151.

15. Farhang Zabeeh, *Hume: Precursor of Modern Empiricism* (The Hague, 1960), pp. 68–69.

16. Ibid., pp. 72–73.

17. Samuel Johnson, *A Dictionary of the English Language* (London, 1755; repr. Hildesheim, 1968).

18. Laing, *David Hume*, p. 83.

19. "A Dissertation on the Passions," *Essays Moral, Political, and Literary*, edd. T. H. Green and T. H. Grose, 2 vols. (London, 1875), II 163; see also T 99, 123.

8

Hume's Theory of the Passions

Nicholas Capaldi
Queens College
The City University of New York

INTRODUCTION

THE GENERAL NEGLECT [1] OF HUME'S THEORY OF THE PASSIONS has always puzzled me, especially in view of the fact that without understanding that theory one cannot understand the structure and main theme of the *Treatise*, one cannot understand Hume's analysis of belief, the function of the discussion of scepticism, the sympathy mechanism, and hence the whole of Hume's moral theory, and one cannot understand Hume's conception of the self. In short, the failure to comprehend fully the theory of the passions detracts from any attempt to comprehend the most significant issues in Hume's philosophy. Hence, I shall concern myself with explicating Hume's theory of the passions both narrowly and as it operates within the broader context of his entire philosophy. What I should like to think I am doing is presenting an hypothesis which conveys a glimpse of the richness, profundity, and coherence of Hume's philosophy.

I suspect that part of the reason for the general neglect of Hume's theory of the passions can be found in examining the present state of the secondary literature on Hume. A good deal of it, both on Hume's philosophy in general and on the passions in particular, seems plagued by a recurrent malady. To a large extent, Hume's older and less sympathetic commentators seemed content to expose apparent contradictions in his work. On reflection, these contradictions always turn out to be conflicts between what Hume said and what he should have said if he would remain consistent with his commentator's preconceptions. One may view these lapses, as is usually done, as regrettable, or one may view these alleged contradictions as invalidation of the standing preconceptions about Hume. I shall take the latter path. In so doing, I do not wish to give the impressions that everything said by Hume's commentators to date is false, or that I agree with everything Hume says.

PRESENT STATE OF THE LITERATURE

Let us review some of the major preconceptions, and in chronological order. The oldest and most unsympathetic view of Hume is to be found in the work of Thomas Reid. Among other things, it was Reid who first accused Hume of advocating a form of irrational hedonism. According to Reid, "Mr. Hume gives the name of passion to every principle of action in the human mind; and, in consequence of this maintains, that every man is and ought to be led by his passions." [2] In one form or another, this view has been echoed by others.

T. H. Green, for example, assumed that Hume is a psychological hedonist. Therefore, when he came across Hume's statement that some of the direct passions do not operate on the anticipation of pleasure and pain, Green accused Hume of being inconsistent. [3] It never occurred to him that Hume might not be a psychological hedonist after all.

B. M. Laing, in his book on Hume, offered a useful summary of the historical influences on Hume's treatment of the passions, including that of Crousaz, Descartes, and Malebranche. Moreover, Laing was among the first, but not the first if we count Kemp Smith's 1905 article, to point out that Reid had misinterpreted Hume. Further, and most interesting, Laing raised the issue of whether Hume's treatment of the passions was consistent with what Hume had said earlier about the self. [4] Because of the scope of his treatment, Laing never developed the point about the difficulty of Hume's theory of the self.

John Laird's analysis of Hume, written in 1932, the same year in which Laing's book was published, reverted to the position of T. H. Green. Laird charged Hume with being an inconsistent hedonist. [5] He also repeated the Reid charge by claiming that Hume's position on the relation between reason and passion is trivially true in that it follows from the definitions Hume gives of these factors. He goes on to construe Hume's position as sheer counteraffirmation and not argument: "Hume's opponents affirmed that the apprehension of duty and of the fitness of things pertained to reason and *did* affect conduct." [6] Furthermore, Laird charged that the discussion of the relationship between ideas and impressions at the beginning of Book II conflicts with the discussion at the beginning of Book I. [7] But this, in fact, is just a part of his more general charge that Hume's phenomenalism and associationism, understood in a phenomenalistic sense, are inconsistent with some of the things Hume says about the passions. [8] Finally, in mentioning Hume's discussion of sympathy, Laird claimed that on Hume's view sympathy with someone else's toothache required us to feel a toothache as well. [9] It is tacitly assumed that this constitutes a *reductio* of Hume's position.

One of the most influential discussions of Hume's philosophy has been Norman Kemp Smith's, written in 1941. Although he is generally considered to have refuted the traditional Reid–Green interpretation, and although he recognized that Hume is in no way a hedonist, Kemp Smith nevertheless perpetuated one of Reid's worst errors. To be precise: he reasserted that for Hume "reason is and ought to be the slave of the passions," [10] and, like

Reid, he incorrectly quoted Hume, omitting the crucial word "only" (see T 415). That this misleading quote gives rise to or, alternatively, exemplifies a distorted view of Hume on the relation of reason to passion had already been pointed out in 1932 by Laird,[11] who was then criticizing Kemp Smith's original article in *Mind* in 1905. Much more extended critiques of the same point were later given by Albert Glathe and by Richard H. Popkin.[12]

Of greater interest is the fact that Kemp Smith restates the charge, which he had originally made in his 1905 article and which was repeated by Laing, that Hume's treatment of the passions contradicts earlier statements in the *Treatise* about the self. Kemp Smith's own elaborate interpretation of the *Treatise*, including speculation about the order of the composition of its Books, hinges upon this alleged contradiction; if there is no such contradiction, then his major theses are vitiated. And, finally, Kemp Smith maintains that the treatment of the passions, all difficulties aside, is largely irrelevant to what he considers to be the main argument of the *Treatise*.

In 1950, Albert Glathe published a pioneering, serious treatment of Hume's discussion of the passions in a book entitled *Hume's Theory of the Passions and of Morals*. Glathe carefully attempted to summarize the main doctrines in the order in which they appeared. His main positive contribution was in the detailing of the importance of the transfer of vivacity; negatively, he undermined the so-called Hutchesonian-origin thesis propounded by Kemp Smith. He thus settled once and for all the importance of the missing "only" in the discussion of the relation between reason and passion. Nevertheless, Glathe's preoccupation was with Book III, not Book II, and he hardly considered Book I at all. Furthermore, his study of the passions was, and rightly for his time, expository and not critical. As a result, some of the serious criticism of Hume's theory of the passions was never considered. Finally, there are those who would seriously disagree with Glathe's interpretation of Hume's moral theory and would therefore conclude that important elements about the passions had been overlooked.

John Passmore, writing in 1952, acknowledged the influence of Kemp Smith, Green, and Laird, but he apparently had not read Glathe. Although he recognized that Hume was not a hedonist, Passmore repeated the charges that (a) Hume had contradicted himself on the nature of the self, (b) associationism was compromised as was Hume's pheomenalism, and (c) sympathy with someone else's toothache required us to have a toothache as well. In addition, he claimed that what Hume did with sympathy violated the argument about the existence of other minds. Passmore's general conclusion was that "Hume, it must again be emphasized, had a quite extraordinary insensitivity to consistency. . . ." [13]

In 1963, P. L. Gardiner wrote a brief essay on Hume's theory of the passions for the Pears anthology. Gardiner perceptively noted that Hume did not, as James Mill did, seek to derive all passions through association.[14] But Gardiner was to restate a recurrent criticism of Hume: namely, that "Hume's entire treatment of the passions as the isolable contents of a direct introspective awareness" was problematic.[15]

The most serious treatment of the passions to date is Páll Árdal's *Passion and Value in Hume's Treatise* (1966). Passmore had emphasized the connection between Books I and II, and had thereby ignored Book III. Like Glathe, Árdal emphasized the connection between Books II and III, and therefore had little to say about the difficulties previously cited. As I shall show below, the failure to consider all three books together has obscured much of Hume's position.

Árdal rightly took Kemp Smith to task for claiming that the discussion of the passions was irrelevant. He also made clear that Hume was not an egoist, and that Hume's theory of sympathy did not extend to toothaches, rather we pity someone who has a toothache.

Árdal's interest was primarily in the moral theory of Hume. The same point made against Glathe could be repeated here, namely, that if someone disagreed about Árdal's interpretation of Hume's moral theory, it could also be claimed that important elements in the theory of the passions had been overlooked or misconstrued.

CRUCIAL ISSUES IN THE PASSIONS

The foregoing survey raises a number of issues either on which Hume's commentators do not agree or which appear problematic in Hume's theory of the passions. Those issues may be summarized as follows:

1. What is the overall relationship of Book II of the *Treatise*, in which Hume discusses the passions, to Books I and III? Do we need an overall theory about Hume's philosophy in order to understand properly the theory of the passions? More specifically: is there a rationale for the order in which Hume presents his theory in the *Treatise*?

2. In what way does Hume identify the passions, and how are they related to the other entities in his universe?

3. Does Hume give a purely phenomenalist analysis of the passions, and does this analysis lead to contradictory remarks about the functioning of the passions?

4. What is the precise role of associationism in the theory of the passions? How is this role related to Hume's alleged phenomenalism?

5. What is the role of the self in Hume's theory of the passions, and does it contradict what he said about the self in Book I?

6. What is the role of sympathy?

7. What is the relationship between reason and passion?

8. How are the passions related to moral sentiments and moral judgments? In short, what is the relationship between the passions and Hume's moral theory?

GENERAL ORIENTATION

In the light of what I have said about the reason for most misconceptions about Hume's philosophy, it becomes necessary to sketch at least in a general way some overall view of Hume's philosophy. As I have argued elsewhere, Hume is a common sense philosopher whose world is made up of physical objects and other people, a world which is both public and social: [16] "philosophical decisions are nothing but the reflections of common life, methodized and corrected" (EHU 162). Hence, Hume is not a Cartesian, not a clumsy pre-Kantian, not a failed idealist, and not a precursor of either positivism or phenomenalism. For him, the test of all philosophical speculation is its relevance to our common experience (T 270–71). Common sense is not something to be explained away but something which calls for explanation.[17]

In this assumption, what Hume cannot abide is a view of human life which he finds in direct conflict with common experience, a view which is totally preposterous and yet to which most of previous Western philosophy pays lip service. That view consists of three parts: (a) a belief in the fundamental conflict between reason and passion; (b) a narrowly rationalistic conception of reason; and (c) a recommendation that we join the conflict on the side of reason (T 413). Such a view not only is alien to our experience but leads to absurd consequences. In a very important sense, Hume's philosophy is a standing refutation of this rationalist model. The refutation takes the following form:

1. If reason operated solely in terms of the rationalist model (mathematical–deductive), and
2. If men were guided solely by reason, then
3. Men would not act.
4. This is equivalent to the truth of extreme scepticism.
But
5. Men do act.
6. Therefore, extreme scepticism is untenable.
7. Therefore, *either* reason does not operate solely by means of the rationalist model
   or
   men are not guided solely by reason.

With regard to (7), Hume will argue throughout the *Treatise* that reason does not operate solely in terms of the rationalist model, so that we have to have a much broader conception of reason. And he will argue that men are guided not solely by reason but by the passions as well. This explains the overriding importance of the passions in Hume's philosophy.

On the positive side, Hume's aim is to carry out the Enlightenment program of constructing a science of man, that is, of extending the scientific model to human behavior. The philosophical rationale for this extension is a belief that the cosmos is uniform and that Newtonian science is the model for comprehending it. Specifically: Hume believes that even the categories of the human understanding can be explained, not explained away, by that model. Thus, the *Treatise* is what Hume says it is and not a clever *reductio* of Locke and Berkeley; and it is not just a prelude to an ethical theory, but a highly ambitious attempt to present a total view of man. Hence, the elaborate discussion of the passions is not an irrelevant and lengthy addition but an integral part of the *Treatise*.[18]

HUME'S METHODOLOGY

In the *Treatise* Hume presents a unified interpretation of every aspect of human nature in terms of three principles, but before we can discuss these three basic explanatory principles, we must say something about his method. Hume adopts the Newtonian precepts of universality, simplicity, the empirical criterion, and the rejection of occult hypotheses. Consequently, he must offer as his thesis a theory which is universal, simple, and experimentally confirmable, and which stops short of going beyond what is *currently* observable. Since Hume believes in a public and social world, he has no doubt about the existence of physical objects, human bodies, and physiological processes. He is as aware as everyone else in the seventeenth and eighteenth centuries that external stimuli on the bodily organs in some way account for our experience (T 7, 13, 190, 212, 239, 242, 248, 340–41). Hence, he is not reconstructing the whole of reality in phenomenal terms.[10] At the same time, he knows that the exact nature of the physiological process is still a matter of speculation so that the demand for empirical confirmation cannot be extended into that discipline *yet* (T 13, 275–76). Nevertheless, he is confident that *we* can still empirically confirm the presence of certain operations of the human mind. Thus, we may describe Hume's methodology as an appeal to a kind of introspection (which he calls his *experiments*), duly supplemented by the observation of other people and of animals, an introspection which *confirms* the presence of universal principles which operate on a physiological level. Hume is both optimistic of the possibility of confirmation and never confuses the present empirical confirmation with the actual physical–biological reality. He repeatedly reminds us that even his own principles will eventually be explained, but not in the present state of our knowledge. In short, Hume's experiments are invitations to the reader to see whether the presence of these operations can be confirmed (EHU 10).

The physiological basis of Hume's theory of the passions has not entirely escaped the notice of his commentators. That Descartes and Malebranche had treated the passions with reference to the body is common knowledge. B. M. Laing has pointed out the similarity of Hume's treatment to that of Crousaz in the latter's *A New Treatise of the Art of Thinking*, which was translated into English in 1724. Crousaz had interpreted the mind as a mechanism "manifested in the train of ideas and in the succession of desires and passions."[20] This is precisely what Hume is arguing. John Laird claims, on the one hand, that Hume's treatment of the passions has a tacit physiological basis somewhat similar to the psycho-physical dualism of Descartes and Malebranche,[21] and, on the other, accuses Hume of invoking the existence of "an impression which secretly attends every idea" (T 375), which, Laird says, should have been anathema to a sound phenomenalist.[22] Well, it is perfectly clear that secret impressions are inconsistent with phenomenalism, and it is equally perfectly clear that Hume's physiological references are not tacit but rather explicit. Hence, the only conclusion is that

Hume is offering, not a phenomenal analysis, but the conscious confirmation of processes which are essentially physiological.

It may very well be that psycho-physical interactionism is an untenable epistemological position, and that Hume himself was largely responsible in the long run for showing that dualism was untenable, but it is still the case that Hume's own philosophy is based upon such a dualism. At the same time I note that the problems of dualism do not vitiate everything which Hume says. Moreover, once this dualism is noted, certain other aspects of Hume's treatment become clear.

For example, I have already mentioned that Hume has been chastised for seemingly asserting that passions can be identified as the "isolable contents of a direct introspective awareness." [23] This seems overly artificial and incompatible with the common sense notion of the passions as dispositional. But if we recognize that such feelings are only the conscious tip of a more basic physiological process, Hume's analysis will no longer seem artificial, and it will allow for the dispositional analysis not only built-in to the common sense view but actually manifested in Hume's own theory.

We may now turn to the three principles which form part of Hume's grandiose scheme for explaining human nature. First, Hume declares that impressions cause ideas, or, more accurately, that every idea or simple idea in its first appearance is caused by an impression. This accounted for the representative function of ideas. Laird has challenged this first principle on the ground that the impressions of reflection, which include the passions, were derived from other impressions—that is, followed them in our train of awareness—but were not said to be representative of them. Laird claims that this shows the "bankruptcy of the theory that what was *derived* from impressions necessarily 'copied' impressions." [24] In rebuttal of Laird's point we might suggest that it was never Hume's position to claim that what follows an impression always and necessarily copies it. Rather, Hume's position is that ideas copy impressions, and it is a position requiring some way or ways of identifying or distinguishing between ideas and impressions; Hume provides several. But the most important consideration is that impressions are caused by external objects or internal physiological processes operating upon the nervous system. In short, once more we see how the presumption of phenomenalism obscures Hume's real meaning. Once we understand that impressions are perceptions either of the external world or of the internal operations of our body and that ideas are afterthoughts of these original perceptions, the distinction between impressions and ideas is consistent with Hume's common sense position and one we still use today.

Second, Hume argues that whatever the imagination finds distinguishable is capable of existing separately. Third, and most important, there is the communication of vivacity between impressions and ideas. It is this principle which explains, at least on the conscious level, belief in Book I, the passions and sympathy in Book II, and through sympathy the moral theory in Book III. This is the key explanatory principle in Hume's *Treatise*, and it is what holds the *Treatise* together. The failure to see this is the result of analyzing only Books I and II as Passmore did or just Books II and III as Glathe and Árdal did.

Since the communication of vivacity is best seen in the operation of the passions, and since impressions precede ideas, we may well ask why Hume begins the *Treatise* with a discussion of ideas and belief before moving on to the passions.[25] I remind the reader that since Hume is not phenomenalistically reconstructing reality but presupposes the common sense framework, he is not under any logical obligation to begin with impressions. But Hume answers the question himself at the beginning of the *Treatise*. He has distinguished between impressions and ideas, between impressions of sensation and impressions of reflection, and it is among the latter that he finds our passions. He claims that these deserve our greatest attention, but because it is ideas which cause impressions of reflection, he proposes to X study ideas first and to see in what way they can give rise to these special impressions (T 8). In short, the discussion of belief is a prelude to the discussion of the passions, and it is the passions which constitute Hume's central concern. In addition, as we shall see below, the rationalist model of reason fails to account for belief, and it is only by relating belief to passions that we can make sense of belief. However, it is first necessary to convince the reader of the failure of the rationalist model before he can appreciate Hume's theory of the passions.

BELIEF AND PASSIONS

The largest part of Book I is concerned with Hume's analysis of causality and belief. Negatively, Hume argues that if causal reasoning operates by means of *a priori* conceivability, and if we can always conceive of the future's not repeating the past, we never have any reason to believe a causal inference. On the positive side, Hume offers a theory of belief in which a causal inference is believed because *"when any impression becomes present to us, it not only transports the mind to such ideas as are related to it, but likewise communicates to them a share of its force and vivacity"* (T 98). Even more important is the influence of belief: "The effect, then, of belief is to raise up a simple idea to an equality with our impressions, and bestow on it a like influence on the passions. This effect it can only have by making an idea approach an impression in force and vivacity" (T 119). The mechanism of the transfer of vivacity, Hume tells us, will explain the rest of the *Treatise* (T 118–24).

Causal reasoning is the most important kind for human behavior, and it is clear that Hume does not wish to challenge the rules of causal reasoning. What he does wish to challenge is the explanation of those rules by the rationalist model. The influence of causal reasoning would be incomprehensible on the rationalist model. Not content with just this victory, Hume presses his case against the "several systems of philosophy" (T 263). If we should take (seriously) the rationalist model or explanation of how reason operates, our beliefs in the external world and in ourselves would dissolve, and we would be paralyzed. The consummation of the rationalist model is scepticism. But there is no question of whether an external world exists for "That is a point, which we must take for granted in all our reasonings" (T 187). Again the real question is not how to refute scepticism, for that cannot be done; rather we must ask *"how it happens, that even after all we retain a degree of belief, which is sufficient for our purpose, either in philosophy or common life"* (T 185). The question is not do-we or should-we have these beliefs but why-do-we have these beliefs. Hume's deliberately paradoxical tone of voice is meant to drive home this point.

To sum up: Part IV of Book I is a prelude to the passions because in demolishing the rationalist model, in showing its failure to account for the world of our common experience, in showing the standing contradiction between our actual behavior and the paralysis that model would inflict upon us, Hume has offered the only kind of refutation one can offer of an empirical hypothesis: its failure to fit the facts. This is not how men operate. This is not how men ought to be said to operate. Well, then how do men operate? This brings us to the passions in Book II.

PASSIONS

The passions are an interesting topic in themselves. From at least Descartes on, philosophers had attempted to explain the passional life of men. Thus in examining the passions Hume is not breaking new ground, but he is offering a new theory about them.

Hume distinguishes between the primary impressions of sensation and the secondary impressions of reflection. Among these secondary impressions he is interested in those which are secondary because they are aroused by an idea. Here is where he locates the all-important indirect passions. Hume stops to remind us that of course there is an anatomical explanation for all this, but he plans to present his theory by an introspective appeal which everyone can follow (T 275–76), especially by examining those transitions from idea to impression. Again *contra* Laird we note that Hume's reference to the assumed underlying physiological explanation is not tacit but rather explicit.

The passions are further subdivided into the direct and the indirect. The direct arise from the idea of pleasure and pain; the indirect require the additional presence of other qualities. Later Hume will qualify his first remark by stating that some of the direct passions do not proceed from good and evil but actually produce them. Among these special direct passions are the desire for the punishment of our enemies and benevolence (T 439). This rules out hedonism, a heresy with which many Englishmen and Scotsmen are charged but few convicted.

The indirect passions, which are the focus of Hume's analysis, pose the special problem of the relationship between the arousing ideas and the subsequent impressions or passions. To explain that relationship, Hume introduces the *double association theory of ideas and impressions.* According to this theory, each indirect passion has two referents or temporal accompaniments, an object and a cause. The cause is that idea which precedes and arouses the passion, and the object is that idea toward which the passion is directed. In the case of pride and humility the object is the "self, or that succession of related ideas and impressions, of which we have an intimate memory and consciousness" (T 277). In love and hatred the object is another self. The causes of the passions, the arousing ideas, possess two general characteristics: they produce pleasure or pain, and they have a reference either to ourselves or to others. The passions have two corresponding properties: they are either pleasant or painful impressions, and they are always oriented toward other persons or to ourselves.

THE SELF

Since a number of commentators have raised questions about Hume's treatment of the self, this is a good point at which to explain the nature of the self. Hume makes a number of statements about the self in a variety of contexts, each with a specific purpose. Yet there is a consistent point of view behind his remarks, a negative and a positive side to his theory. The negative view is given in the discussion of thought in Book I; the positive, in the discussion of the passions in Book II. As Hume puts it, "we must distinguish betwixt personal identity, as it regards our thought or imagination, and as it regards our passions or the concern we take in ourselves" (T 253). Both the negative and the positive views still reflect Hume's common sense position. He already believes in the self, so the only question is how we are to understand it.

The negative side seems pretty clear. Hume's first mention of the problem of the self (T 14) comes in the discussion of relations. There Hume introduces the important distinction between philosophical relations, which include identity, "in its strictest sense," which means "constant and unchangeable objects," and natural relations, which include resemblance and causality. It is there that Hume tips his hand that he is going to understand personal identity as a natural relation and not as a philosophical relation. Failure to have noted this early discussion casts some doubt on the Penelhum thesis that Hume fails to distinguish the two senses of identity. The distinction seems to me to be what Hume is establishing.[26]

Hume never denies either that there is a self or that there is an idea of the self. What he does deny, at least in the *Treatise*, is the existence of a simple and individual substance of the Cartesian variety. He also denies the Lockean view of consciousness as reflected thought (T 635). He concludes by saying that what we can discover by the introspection of ourselves is only a particular perception, such as love or hatred, for example (T 252), or a composite of perceptions (T 634). In making these statements Hume is already presupposing that we in some sense know what the self is. In fact, in both the *Treatise* (T 298, 303) and the later "Dissertation"[27] he asserts that our notion of the self includes a reference to our bodies as well as to our minds. Thus, it is not the self which is a fictitious entity but the continuous identity which we ascribe to the mind. It is not the case that men are bundles of perceptions but only that when each man examines his "mind" all that he finds is a bundle of perceptions (T 252).

To what does the idea of the self refer? If the idea of the self does not refer to a simple impression, might it refer to something else? Hume distinguished between impressions of sensation and impressions of reflection. The latter arise in the following manner:

> An impression first strikes upon the senses, and makes us perceive heat or cold, thirst or hunger, pleasure or pain of some kind or other. Of this impression there is a copy taken by the mind, which remains after the impression ceases; and this we call an idea. This idea of pleasure or pain, when it returns upon the soul, produces the new impressions of desire and aversion, hope and fear, which may properly be called impressions of reflexion, because derived from it. These again are copied by the memory and imagination, and become ideas; which perhaps in their turn give rise to other impressions and ideas. So that the impressions of reflexion are only antecedent to their correspondent ideas; but posterior to those of sensation, and deriv'd from them [T 7–8].

Ideas which refer to impressions of reflection are the products of a series consisting of (*a*) impressions, (*b*) ideas, and (*c*) impressions again. Thus it would seem that if there is an idea of the self, it must be derived from an impression of reflection, and that it would thereby refer to an entire previous series, and in some way be related to pleasure and pain. Finally, since it derives from an impression of reflection, it would be the product *either* of the memory or of the imagination.

This is precisely what Hume claimed. First he tells us "They are the successive perceptions only, that constitute the mind . . ." (T 253) and " 'Tis the composition of these [perceptions], which forms the self" (T 634); then he stresses that it is the memory and the imagination which are responsible for discovering personal identity. Finally, when discussing identity with regard to the passions, he indicates that such an identity gives us "a present concern for our past or future pains or pleasures" (T 261).

The idea of the self is derived from impressions of reflection and, hence it refers to a series or set of perceptions. But we should stress that it is not the self which is a set of perceptions, but the idea of the self which refers to a set of perceptions.

This is yet another instance of the way the presupposition that Hume is a phenomenalist leads his readers to ignore some of his statements. As persons or selves, we are bodies as well as minds; we have characters and dispositions as well as impressions and ideas. The relation of cause and effect holds not only among our perceptions but between our perceptions and our bodily actions. What memory discovers is precisely this causal chain of all our "parts," and it is in this sense that memory does not produce our identity but discovers it. Without action and the causal connections in our action it is difficult to see how we could ever have an idea of ourselves. We are obviously more than just our perceptions. We must therefore distinguish not only between ourselves and the idea of ourselves, but also between the question of what constitutes the idea of ourselves and the question of how we discover the idea of our continuous identity.

All our perceptions are, obviously and tautologically, our perceptions, but they are not all perceptions *of* ourselves. They may be impressions and ideas of other selves or of other external objects. For an idea or an impression to be *of* ourselves, it must be causally connected to ourselves, to our bodies, or to our other perceptions. Our passions, which are impressions of reflection, have causal connections both with other perceptions and with the actions of our bodies. As Hume puts it, "our identity with regard to the passions serves to corroborate that with regard to the imagination, by the making our distant perceptions influence each other, and by giving us a present concern for our past or future pains or pleasures" (T 261). This connection between the passions and action is brought out again when Hume says of the will that it is "*the internal impression we feel and are conscious of, when we knowingly give rise to any new motion of our body, or new perception of our mind*" (T 399). The will is not a passion but every passion which motivates us gives rise to the impression of will.

When Hume comes to discuss his positive theory of the self in the passions, we realize that what he is saying is that we discover ourselves not as disembodied intellects but as beings motivated by the passions. We see ourselves as creatures who act because of what we feel. This is personal identity as it regards the passions. Here Hume can freely say that "the idea, or rather impression of ourselves is always intimately present with us . . ." (T 317). By seeing the *idea of the self as the object of a passion* which is itself an impression, and by noting the all-important notion of the transfer of vivacity from impressions to ideas, we can come to understand why the idea of the self acquires the vivacity of an impression. Finally, the idea of the self refers to a series of other ideas and impressions, and it can in turn communicate its vivacity to them.

To sum up: (1) as selves, we are composites of minds and bodies; (2) our minds consist of a series of isolable perceptions, both impressions and ideas; (3) the idea of the self is the idea of the set or of the series considered as related by resemblance and causation, and the relation of causation extends to our bodies as well; when we discover this idea of the self in retrospect, we have our identity in thought; (4) the very idea of the self can be, on occasion, one of the ideas in the mind; (5) when the idea of the self is produced by a passion, we have a vivid conception of ourselves, and this is identity as it concerns our passions.

Kemp Smith argued that the introduction of "the impression of the self" signaled Hume's awareness of a difficulty in distinguishing between ideas and impressions.[28] My explanation avoids any notion of a difficulty. Passmore claimed that Hume is not entitled to talk about an idea of ourselves.[29] My explanation shows that Hume has every right. Laird recognized Hume's distinction between the concept of self in thought and in the passions but claimed that Hume never develops it.[30] On the contrary. The discussion of the passions in Book II is precisely where Hume develops the distinction. There are difficulties with Hume's theory of the self, difficulties which he gradually came to realize. We cannot discuss them here, but suffice it to say that Hume's difficulties with the self are not the ones noted by his critics, and are not in any way relevant to his analysis of the passions or of sympathy; they involve, rather, the concept of substance, and derive from his dualism of matter and mind.

PASSIONS, SELF, AND SYMPATHY

The important element which Hume introduces into his discussion of the passions is the association of passions. It should be recalled that ideas are associated by the imagination in three ways and that Hume has already claimed that some ideas can cause passions. He also specifically claims that passions cause their ideas and as such can transfer vivacity to these ideas (T 78). In Book II, he claims that as impressions the passions can be associated with other passions only by resemblance. In order for there to be movement from one passion to another we need resemblance between the passions or an intervening idea. Hence, it is necessary for the idea of the self, which is caused by one passion, itself to be a cause of other passions. This subtle process is missed completely by Passmore who chided Hume by arguing that if the passions are to "be subject to the laws of association, the passions must stand to the imagination as raw material to an artificer." [31] But the imagination, as Hume makes clear, deals only with ideas and not with impressions. As impressions, the passions cannot be material for the imagination, and therefore mere reason cannot move us to action. What ideas influence us can be discovered only empirically by seeing which ideas trigger the mechanism of the passions. There are definite limitations to this process, and Hume is attempting to show those limitations and how they depend upon the transfer of vivacity.

It is rather odd for Passmore to describe the imagination as an artificer, but this charge actually stems from his insistence upon interpreting Hume as a phenomenalist. When Passmore did recognize the limitations which Hume places on the various processes which he is trying to describe, he asserted that these supplements were "modestly, almost surreptitiously, introduced" because Hume wanted to "represent himself as a great simplifier, in the style of Newton and Copernicus." [32] On the same page, Passmore interpreted Hume's associationism as the basis for the Humean claim to be the Newton of the moral sciences. If, contrary to Passmore, we do not interpret Hume as a phenomenalist but as one engaged in describing the conscious counterparts of physiological processes, the mystery disappears. Whatever the imagination is, it is not an artificer. Since the major physiological processes are not directly analyzable, it is not a subterfuge on Hume's part to claim that he can describe only a limited amount. Moreover, with respect to the passions Hume claims to be only its Copernicus and not its Newton (T 282). Hume modestly claims only to be simplifying the material involved and not offering any final explanation. This same modest claim is found not only in the *Treatise* but also in the closing statement of the "Dissertation."

Let us now return to the correspondence between the properties of the causes of the passions and the properties of the passions themselves. Hume's theory is a working out of the laws of association as exemplified in this correspondence. The direction which the cause of the passion takes is the same as the idea of the object toward which the passion itself is directed: the self or some other self. By the same token, the impression which is produced independently by the cause of the passion is pleasant or painful just as the passion itself is. These two associative bonds among all ideas and impressions mutually reinforce each other and account for the double impulse which the mind experiences under such circumstances. This explains the passional strength of all objects which are pleasant or painful and which bear a reference either to ourselves or others. Finally, an easy transition can be made from one idea to another, once the idea in question acquires the vivacity of the associated impression, and thus a transition from one passion to the next. The arousal of a passion causes a whole series of similar ones to follow.

When examining the causes of pride and humility, the last cause Hume mentions is reputation, and to account for it, he invokes the process of *sympathy*. Sympathy is an instance of the double association of ideas and impressions. It begins with a belief about the affections of some other person, a belief derived by inference from "those external signs in the countenance and conversation" (T 317) which are customary effects of the affection in question, and is converted into the very impressions it represents. This conversion requires a source of vivacity, and Hume finds that source in the impression of the self.

The idea which is the cause gives rise to an independent impression of pleasure or pain; this first impression is associated with other impressions which are pleasant or painful such as pride and humility; the impression of pride or humility then gives rise to the idea of the self. The transition is thus from an idea to an impression; from the first impression to the second resembling impression; from the second impression to a second idea. In sympathy, the second idea—namely, the idea of the self—acquires the vivacity of the second impression, thereby arousing the corresponding affection within ourselves.

Our fame or infamy, resulting from praise or blame, produces pleasure or pain in us. The exact relationship of this praise or blame to pride and humility can be understood only in terms of sympathy. When we are pleased by the praise of others, it is only because we observe the admirer and feel his pleasure, a pleasure produced by qualities in us which are the objects of his admiration. In other words, our idea of his emotion becomes an emotion or impression directed toward the same qualities. To experience one's own infamy is to feel, through sympathy, the displeasure of one's detractor.

It should be noted that Hume insists that we can never directly inspect someone else's passion, even though sympathy allows us to feel it because of the outer resemblance between other human beings and ourselves. Passmore did not miss the opportunity to point out that this cannot be acceptable as a proof of other minds because Hume's general theory of causality relies upon the observed past conjunction, and of course we could not have directly observed the emotions of others.[33] Hume, no doubt, would be delighted by the prospect of pointing out to Professor Passmore that what reason is incapable of doing, namely, to get us to believe in the emotions of others, nature has provided for in the sympathy process. Not only do we believe in the minds of others, we feel the analogous emotion in certain specific cases. This merely reinforces Hume's whole critique of the rationalist model.

Again and again Hume shows that his theory of the passions with respect to sympathy is analogous to his explanation of belief. Sympathy, says Hume, is "exactly correspondent to the operation of our understanding; and [it] contains something more surprising and extraordinary" (T 320): namely, the impression of the self. Belief is the conversion of an idea into an impression by means of vivacity, and for that reason belief has such an influence upon behavior. Since the causes of the passions are ideas, these ideas can affect us only by becoming like impressions.

Hume's explanation of action is the obvious consequence of his previous conclusions. There is no self-consciousness which sits in judgment on the rest of our experience. There are direct passions which do not respond to expectations of pleasure and pain but instead are the original drives on which all subsequent action is based (T 280, 439). All subsequent action depends upon ideas which trigger the indirect passions. Is it any wonder that Hume concludes that reason is and ought only to be understood as the slave of the passions?

A number of critics beginning with Reid and including Laird among the moderns have argued that Hume's seemingly paradoxical conclusions are mere consequences of his definitions of reason and passion. As Laird contended, "Hume's opponents affirmed that the apprehension of duty and the fitness of things pertained to reason and *did* affect conduct." [34] But if we re-examine a number of Hume's arguments we shall see that Hume's case is really much stronger. To begin with, Hume is offering an empirical hypothesis. Moreover, he is taking the analysis of reason given by various rationalists, of both the Platonic and the Aristotelian persuasions, and is showing that on the very conception they advocate it is impossible for reason to move us. Scepticism is the only consistent position of those who follow out all the implications of the rationalist model. Hence, despite what they may say, it would be internally inconsistent to argue that reason does guide us. Secondly, when we examine the actual words of Hume's critics we find that they qualify their assertion in a manner which totally undermines their position. Reid, for example, asserts that reason influences our behavior by making us see our long-range interest. This is perfectly compatible with Hume's assertions about reason's maximizing our interest or our most important passions. Moreover, Reid admits "men's passions and appetites, too often draw them to act contrary to their cool judgment and opinion of what is best for them." [35] If the passions can divert us, then reason cannot act automatically. Either the passions really lead, or there is a third faculty which adjusts passion and reason, and this Reid neither explains nor can he if he is to remain consistent with the view that reason is supreme.

When this same doctrine is worked out with respect to morality, we see that Hume's position is even stronger. When we morally blame others, we do so not because they failed to see what was moral but because they did see what was morally right and ignored it. The fact of life with which moralists deal is this ignoring of what we know to be right. That is why, in part, the concept of the moral "ought" was invented. Hume's position is that if the most reason can do is to tell us what we "ought" to do, and if the "ought" is not hypothetical and tied in some manner to the passions, then morality as thus understood is useless. Yet common sense tells us that we go to a great deal of trouble to inculcate moral principles because such principles can and do influence us. Therefore, morality must be intimately tied to the passions.) As in his earlier argument with respect to determinism, Hume is saying that no matter to what we may pay lip service, in practice we assume that determinism in some sense is the case. The same is true with respect to morality, for in practice we assume that there is some way to move people. Thus, Hume's conclusions with respect to the relationship between reason and passion are not the mere consequences of definitions but follow from his critique of the rationalist model of reason and his earlier arguments on the determinants of the will.

SYMPATHY AND MORALITY

When we examine Hume's moral theory, we discover the crucial role of sympathy in Book III of the *Treatise*. Sympathy is the general principle of morals (T 618). Thus does Hume emphasize the continuing importance of the communication of vivacity.

A few general assertions are necessary here. First, as a number of us have shown on repeated occasions,[36] there is a clear distinction in Hume between a moral judgment and a moral sentiment, wherein the former reports or describes the latter. This automatically eliminates all subjective interpretations of Hume's theory of moral judgment. Moreover, it is the failure to see and to emphasize that sympathy is a form of inference "exactly correspondent to the operation of our understanding" which obscures this point in the minds of some. Second, for Hume, moral sentiments are not different in kind from non-moral sentiments; therefore we may dismiss all deontologized moral sense theories. If this is true, then moral sentiments may be described in non-moral terms, and if this in turn is true, then we may infer moral judgments as a special sub-class from the more general class of non-moral judgments.

Sympathy is the psychological process which Hume introduces precisely in order to account for the conversion of non-moral characteristics into peculiarly moral sentiments. The importance of sympathy is that it involves, as part of the conversion, a form of inference from the presence of non-moral characteristics to the existence of moral sentiments.

The first distinguishing characteristic of a moral sentiment is that it is the result of a general social view, a disinterested perspective (T 371, 551, 583, 586). If anything, Hume has a tendency in Book III to overemphasize the presence of general rules. Since it is this general view which allows for the confirmation of moral judgments, we may say that the disinterested perspective accounts for the social objectivity of such judgments. But since it is possible to have disinterested judgments about a great many things, most of which are not moral, we need another distinguishing property for the moral sentiments reported in moral judgments.

The second distinguishing property of moral sentiments is that such sentiments produce the indirect passions of pride and humility, love and hatred (T 473). The production of the indirect passions is the most considerable effect which virtue and vice have upon the human mind. Previously, Hume had criticized alternative accounts of morality for being unable to explain the influence of moral sentiments upon behavior and for making morality applicable to animals and inanimate objects (T 465; EPM 213, note). If moral sentiments produce the indirect passions of love and hatred, then such sentiments will also influence behavior. It should be made very clear here that the moral sentiments are not themselves passions.[37] Finally, since the indirect passions involve only human beings, Hume's view avoids applicability to animals and inanimate objects. On the other hand, Hume recognizes that not every indirect passion is related to a moral sentiment. We may be proud of our wealth or humiliated by our poverty without thereby experiencing a moral sentiment. It is only when the indirect passions are involved with the interests of society that such passions are the result of a moral sentiment. Thus there are two distinguishing properties of a moral sentiment: disinterestedness and the production of the indirect passions.

In Book I, Hume explained the logic of causal inference and belief by means of a present impression communicating vivacity to an inferred idea. In Book II, he explained the operation of the passions by means of the double association of ideas and impressions, which included as part of its function the communication of vivacity from impressions to ideas. One example of this process was sympathy. In Book III, he explained beauty, morals, and politics by means of sympathy. Association and the communication of vivacity are obviously the cement of Hume's *Treatise* and constitute both his originality and genius. He himself put it best in the *Abstract*:

> THRO' this whole book, there are great pretensions to new discoveries in philosophy; but if any thing can intitle the author to so glorious a name as that of an *inventor*, 'tis the use he makes of the principle of the association of ideas, which enters into most of his philosophy. . . . 'Twill be easy to conceive of what vast consequences these principles must be in the science of human nature, if we consider, that so far as regards the mind, these are the only links that bind the parts of the universe together, or connect us with any person or object exterior to ourselves. For as it is by means of thought only that any thing operates upon our passions, and as these are the only ties of our thoughts, they are really *to us* the cement of the universe, and all the operations of the mind must, in a great measure, depend on them [A 31, 32].

THE PASSIONS AFTER THE *Treatise*

I wish that I might have concluded this essay with the previous quotation, but the story continues. When Hume rewrote and further developed his thoughts, he did so in a number of separate works instead of in the unity presented in the *Treatise*. There are many reasons for this, but for our purposes I shall mention just one. Toward the end of the *Treatise*, in the course of noting and answering objections to his theory, Hume was forced to recognize the possibility of moral judgments which referred to no actual moral sentiment (T 603). It is ironic that the philosopher so often represented as a subjectivist is, when forced to choose, totally committed to the objectivity of moral judgment.

The real source of Hume's difficulty can be found earlier in the discussion of the passions. Hume had consistently argued that when the self is involved sympathy cannot operate to produce the double relation of impressions and ideas. "But when self is the object of a passion, 'tis not natural to quit the consideration of it, till the passion be exhausted; in which case the double relations of impressions and ideas can no longer operate" (T 341).

As a result, when Hume rewrote Book III as the later *Enquiry Concerning the Principles of Morals*, he rejected the sympathy mechanism:

> It is but a weak subterfuge, when pressed by these facts and arguments, to say, that we transport ourselves, by the force of imagination, into distant ages and countries, and consider the advantage, which we should have reaped from these characters, had we been contemporaries, and had any commerce with the persons. It is not conceivable, how a *real* sentiment or passion can ever arise from a known *imaginary* interest; especially when our *real* interest is still kept in view, and is often acknowledged to be entirely distinct from the imaginary, and even sometimes opposite to it [EPM 217].

Although he still retains the word "sympathy," it is now identified with the sentiment of humanity or the extended benevolence which Hume had earlier rejected in the *Treatise* as the general principle of morals.

When he surrendered the sympathy mechanism, Hume also surrendered the communication of vivacity as the connecting link of the three books of the *Treatise*. Though I would not deny the continuing importance of association or of the communication of vivacity, it is still the case that a major reason for presenting all of Hume's views as part of a single work had been lost. More important, the rejection of sympathy severs one of the important connecting links between the theory of the passions and Hume's moral theory. This even explains, in part, why Hume discarded the idea–impression apparatus when he wrote the second *Enquiry*. Finally, I should note that the lack of enthusiasm which permeates the later "Dissertation" on the passions is no doubt a result of the changes in Hume's view. In conclusion, I hope that I have shown not only how important the passions were for Hume but even why problems in the theory of the passions necessitated some of the later revisions in his thought.

NOTES

1. The most recent general anthology of commentary on Hume (*Hume: A Collection of Critical Essays*, ed. V. C. Chappell [Garden City, 1966]) contains not a single essay on the passions.

2. T. Reid, *Essays on the Active Powers of the Human Mind*, 3.3.1 (Cambridge, Mass., 1969), pp. 200–203.

3. T. H. Green, *Hume and Locke* (New York, 1968), pp. 332–33.

4. B. M. Laing, *David Hume* (London, 1932), p. 161.

5. John Laird, *Hume's Philosophy of Human Nature* (London, 1932), p. 191.

6. Ibid., p. 204.

7. Ibid., p. 190.

8. Ibid., pp. 191, 197.

9. Ibid., p. 197.

10. Norman Kemp Smith, *The Philosophy of David Hume* (London, 1941), p. 11.

11. Laird, *Hume's Philosophy of Human Nature*, pp. 185–86.

12. A. B. Glathe, *Hume's Theory of the Passions and of Morals* (Berkeley, 1950), chap. 1; see also Richard H. Popkin, "David Hume: His Pyrrhonism and His Critique of Pyrrhonism," *Philosophical Quarterly*, 1, No. 5 (October 1951), 385–407; repr. in *Hume*, ed. Chappell, pp. 53–98, at 76n44.

13. John Passmore, *Hume's Intentions* (Cambridge, 1952), p. 131.

14. P. L. Gardiner, "Hume's Theory of the Passions," in *David Hume: A Symposium*, ed. D. F. Pears (London, 1963), p. 38.

15. Ibid., p. 39.

16. See my *David Hume: The Newtonian Philosopher* (Boston, 1975).

17. Ibid., chap. 1.

18. "More than a third of Book II is employed in the treatment of four passions which have no direct bearing upon Hume's ethical problems, and play indeed no really distinctive part in his system . . ." (Kemp Smith, *Philosophy of David Hume*, p. 160).

19. Robert F. Anderson in his *Hume's First Principles* (Lincoln, 1966), has argued brilliantly for the materialist foundations of Hume's philosophy.

20. Laing, *David Hume*, p. 160.

21. Laird, *Hume's Philosophy of Human Nature*, p. 207.

22. Ibid., p. 197.

23. Gardiner, "Hume's Theory of the Passions," p. 39.

24. Laird, *Hume's Philosophy of Human Nature*, p. 190.

25. Kemp Smith, *Philosophy of David Hume*, pp. 112–13.

26. Terrence Penelhum, "Hume on Personal Identity," *Philosophical Review*, 64, No. 4 (October 1955), 571–89; see also James Noxon, "Senses of Identity in Hume's *Treatise*," *Dialogue*, 8, No. 3 (1969), 367–84.

27. "A Dissertation on the Passions," in *Essays Moral, Political, and Literary*, edd. T. H. Green and T. H. Grose, 2 vols. (London, 1898), II 148.

28. Kemp Smith, *Philosophy of David Hume*, pp. 171–73.

29. Passmore, *Hume's Intentions*, p. 126.

30. Laird, *Hume's Philosophy of Human Nature*, pp. 160–61.

31. Passmore, *Hume's Intentions*, p. 128.

32. Ibid., p. 131.

33. Ibid., p. 129.

34. Laird, *Hume's Philosophy of Human Nature*, p. 204.

35. Reid, *Essay on the Active Powers*, 3.3.2; p. 209.

36. Nicholas Capaldi, "Some Misconceptions About Hume's Moral Theory," *Ethics*, 76, No. 3 (April 1966), 208–11; Ronald Glossop, "The Nature of Hume's Ethics," *Philosophy and Phenomenological Research*, 27 (1966–67), 527–36.

37. Páll Árdal, *Passion and Value in Hume's Treatise* (Edinburgh, 1966), pp. 109, 126.

9

Strains in Hume and Wittgenstein

PETER JONES
University of Edinburgh

IN THE FIRST PART OF THIS PAPER, I shall show that in Hume's view the place and nature of philosophy must be characterised in the light of the fundamental fact that man is a social animal. In the second part, I shall show that a parallel view is prominent in the later work of Wittgenstein. These two sections are intended to mirror each other, and I shall provide only the barest commentary. Finally, in the third part, I shall comment briefly on some of the strains to which the views in the first two parts seem to be subject, and suggest directions for further enquiry.

I

For Hume, communication presupposes shared sets of judgments and experiences. In his view, knowledge is essentially a social phenomenon. He holds that human beings, like other animals, learn in the first place by means of reaction, imitation, and re-inforcement; in this way certain natural habits are built up which can be displaced only partly by subsequent formal education. Doubt and scepticism cannot precede initial training, because they are attitudes which logically presuppose a natural background. Although he never tried to work out a full-blown theory of language, Hume clearly regards language as a conventional activity founded upon certain natural expressions. The main point of his famous method of searching for the impression from which a puzzling idea may have been derived was to discover the foundations of particular judgments, and that included finding out how they were acquired and the roles they played. A broad notion of tradition permeates the foundations of Hume's philosophy, although the word itself hardly appears. In his view, to establish that "We are determined by CUSTOM alone to suppose the future conformable to the past" (A 16) is to establish an essential feature of inductive arguments, and, thus, of their justification. He believes that philosophical problems often arise from misunderstanding our language, and that we easily succumb to illusions or make use of faulty analogies. In addition to recognising the complexities of language, we should recognise that language is only one mode of human behaviour. Consideration of what men do, in the widest sense of "do," must form the foundation for any "science of *man*" (A 6), and reference to tradition will occur here.

I shall now begin the detailed discussion. Hume lists four ways in which knowledge may be acquired: instinct, education, experience, and abstract reasoning. He does not formally define any of these notions, but characterises them only in a general way, and like Hume himself I shall omit discussion of abstract reasoning here. In line with his classical predecessors, Hume often compared man's capacities and instincts with those of other animals. In his essay "Of the Dignity or Meanness of Human Nature," he remarks that in such comparisons one often makes "an unfair representation of the case" (*Essays* 84), especially if one stresses only the extremes. For then we might describe man as

> a creature, who traces causes and effects to a great length and intricacy; extracts general principles from particular appearances; improves upon his discoveries; corrects his mistakes; and makes his very errors profitable. On the other hand, we are presented with a creature the very reverse of this; limited in its observations and reasonings to a few sensible objects which surround it; without curiosity, without foresight; blindly conducted by instinct, and attaining, in a short time, its utmost perfection, beyond which it is never able to advance a single step [*Essays* 83].

Hume wants to stress, however, that man is an animal, and differs from other animals, as men differ among themselves, only in degree. All derive "many parts" of their knowledge "from the original hand of nature": "These we denominate Instincts, and are so apt to admire as something very extraordinary, and inexplicable by all the disquisitions of human understanding" (EHU 108). There are, of course, many instincts with which we are familiar, although some strike us as more extraordinary than others; we find a dog's avoidance of fire or precipices less remarkable than a bird's "art of incubation" (T 177; EHU 108). But the dog's behaviour proceeds "from a reasoning, that is not in itself different, nor founded on different principles, from that which appears in human nature" (T 177); indeed, "the experimental reasoning itself, which we possess in common with beasts, and on which the whole conduct of life depends, is nothing but a species of instinct or mechanical power, that acts in us unknown to ourselves; and in its chief operations, is not directed by any such relations or comparisons of ideas, as are the proper objects of our intellectual faculties" (EHU 108). It is to this latter type of comparative reasoning that Hume refers when he denies that neither animals nor children, neither philosophers nor "the generality of mankind, in their ordinary actions and conclusions" (EHU 106) are guided by "any process of argument or reasoning" by means of which they conclude "that like events must follow like objects, and that the course of nature will always be regular in its operations" (EHU 106). Hume acknowledges that "even brute beasts, improve by experience" (EHU 39), but stresses that " 'Tis . . . by means of custom alone, that experience operates upon them" (T 178).

Hume is eager to classify as instincts both the nesting habits of birds—not to mention the social habits of animals generally (EPM 307–308, note)—and the inferential reasoning about matters of fact in which all animals, including man, engage. Generally, in Hume the ascription of an instinct to an animal is a description of what it does, rather than a putative explanation of the action; often, indeed, the occurrence of the term denotes the point at which philosophical enquiry may appropriately stop. The following passage illustrates the move:

> It is needless to push our researches so far as to ask, why we have humanity or a fellow-feeling with others. It is sufficient, that this is experienced to be a principle in human nature. We must stop somewhere in our examination of causes . . . [EPM 219–20, note].

It may be true, Hume thinks, that experimental reasoning is an instinct which "arises from past observation and experience; but can any one give the ultimate reason, why past experience and observation produces such an effect, any more than why nature alone shou'd produce it?" (T 179). Hume is not looking for ultimate explanations, in the rationalists' sense; for him it suffices that philosophy has foundations in what happens and in what animals do, and for this reason reference may be made to instincts. Hume would be happy to concede that the notion of an instinct constitutes a problem for specialist scientists; it is enough for him to disavow its use as an explanation.

At this early stage of the discussion it is worth comparing with Hume's views on instincts Wittgenstein's claim that in the earliest learning processes man may be regarded as "a primitive being to which one grants instinct but not ratiocination" (OC 475):[1] "The squirrel does not infer by induction that it is going to need stores next winter as well. And no more do we need a law of induction to justify our actions or our predictions" (OC 287).

Presumably it is because we detect certain regularities in behaviour that we designate the pattern as a whole, or its constituent elements, as "instinctive" or "natural" (see EHU 22, note; EPM 307–308, note). Even if some beliefs can be analysed in terms of knowing what to do, in contrast to knowing what is the case or that something is the case—in such a way a "natural belief" in the regularity of nature might be ascribed to a non-articulate animal—Hume does not think that this accounts for all of man's beliefs. On the contrary, "more than one half of those opinions, that prevail among mankind, [are] owing to education, and . . . the principles, which are thus implicitely embrac'd, over-ballance those, which are owing either to abstract reasoning or experience" (T 117). Education, in Hume's view, "is an artificial and not a natural cause . . . built almost on the same foundation of custom and repetition as our reasonings from causes and effects" (T 117). We can see its "artificial" character most clearly "from the effects of discipline and education on animals, who, by the proper application of rewards and punishments, may be taught any course of action, and most contrary to their natural instincts and propensities" (EHU 105). Since Hume "attribute[s] all belief and reasoning" to custom (T 115), it is inevitable that he should treat education as the inculcation of habits. Now, it is a fundamental tenet in Hume that "No man can have any other experience but his own. The experience of others becomes his only by the credit which he gives to their testimony; which proceeds from his own experience of human nature" (LDH I 349). Clearly, then, one cannot discuss education without discussing the role of testimony. There "is no species of reasoning more common, more useful, and even necessary to human life, than that which is derived from the testimony of men, and the reports of eye-witnesses and spectators" (EHU 111), but testimony, like experience itself, "is not altogether infallible, but in some cases is apt to lead us into errors" (EHU 110). The reason why such deviant cases cannot be the norm is that man is a social being—a point to which I shall return shortly. A second observation about testimony must be made. If the earliest stages of education are conceived as habit-training, then a passive element must predominate:

> As to the youthful propensity to believe, which is corrected by experience; it seems obvious, that children adopt blindfold all the opinions, principles, senti-ments, and passions, of their elders, as well as credit their testimony; nor is this more strange, than that a hammer should make an impression on clay [LDH I 349].

Hume holds, then, that only after I have accepted certain things am I in a position to reflect on the nature of the testimony and to question it. A par-allel remark by Wittgenstein may be quoted here: "The child learns by be-lieving the adult. Doubt comes *after* belief" (OC 160). "I learned an enor-mous amount and accepted it on human authority, and then I found some things confirmed or disconfirmed by my own experience" (OC 161).

Although he hardly mentions memory, Hume assigns it a central role in the acquisition of knowledge, since we must remember what we are told as well as what happens to us—"animals, as well as men, learn many things from experience. . . . The ignorance and inexperience of the young are here plainly distinguishable from the cunning and sagacity of the old, who have learned, by long observation, to avoid what hurt them, and to pursue what gave ease or pleasure" (EHU 105). Hume here refers to the "conjec-tures" of a greyhound, but his emphasis is quite clearly on the passive ele-ment in learning, with particular stress on conditioning. He devotes so little attention to what we can learn by ourselves because he is intent on his cen-tral tenet that knowledge is a social phenomenon: to this I now turn.

(I have already stated that I shall not discuss Hume's fourth source of knowledge, abstract reasoning. It would be compatible with his view that many instincts and propensities are species-relative to claim that this source is unique to man.)

It is in connection with testimony that the social nature of man first becomes apparent. Four points should be noted. First, men "are necessarily born in a family-society, at least; and are trained up by their parents to some rule of conduct and behaviour" (EPM 190). Indeed, "Men cannot live without society . . ." (T 402; see also T 493, 363; EPM 205); a hypotheti-cal, self-sufficient being who had lived cut off from all others "would be as much incapable of justice, as of social discourse and conversation" (EPM 191). Secondly, "our opinions of all kinds are strongly affected by society and sympathy, and it is almost impossible for us to support any principle or sentiment against the universal consent of every one." [2] This fact is connected with the public dimension of most claims. When someone talks about the world, "the course of nature lies open to my contemplation as well as theirs" (EHU 142). This is not to deny that an individual or even a whole community might be justified in their claims, but mistaken; over the disposition of the planets (*Essays* 166–67), for example, or in the way the Indian prince was mistaken about ice (EHU 113–14). The third point about the social nature of man is that he exhibits "an inclination to truth and a principle of probity" (EHU 112); in due course we discover these qualities to be "inherent in human nature" (EHU 112), but initially we simply assume it. And the assumption is appropriate, in Hume's view, because it is a condition of the possibility of communication. The fourth point also concerns communication. Hume holds that languages are "gradually establish'd by human conventions" (T 490), where a convention is taken to be a set of shared attitudes or procedures, not necessarily articulated or formalised, which enable members of a community to achieve common, determinate goals (see EPM 306). Certain activities are intelligible only on assumptions about social groups and conventions; thus, "a promise is not intelligible naturally, nor antecedent to human conventions . . ." (T 516). And conventions, of course, are an important contributory factor to that "uniformity in human actions" without which "it were impossible to collect any general observations concerning mankind . . ." (EHU 85). It is clear, then, that if the "mutual dependence of men is so great in all societies that scarce any human action is entirely complete in itself, or is performed without some reference to the actions of others, which are requisite to make it answer fully the intention of the agent" (EHU 89), "the science of *man*" (A 6) must take proper account of the social nature and context of man.

What consequences for philosophical method, and for the nature of philosophy, would such emphasis have? Hume is quite explicit on the point. "[P]hilosophical decisions are nothing but the reflections of common life, methodized and corrected" (EHU 162). How does one decide which of those reflections need correction? We "find what are the proper subjects of science and enquiry" (EHU 163) once we have made "an accurate scrutiny into the powers and faculties of human nature" (EHU 13). It should then become apparent to us that "knowledge and probability are of such contrary and disagreeing natures, that they cannot well run insensibly into each other . . ." (T 181), and "that the only objects of the abstract sciences or of demonstration are quantity and number, and that all attempts to extend this more perfect species of knowledge beyond these bounds are mere sophistry and illusion" (EHU 163). The greatest difficulty is to recognise and accept the "narrow limits of human reason" (D 131). Hume draws a double distinction between kinds of evidence and kinds of certainty, on the one hand, and between degrees of certainty within each kind of evidence, on the other (e.g., T 131; EHU 110): "There are many different kinds of

Certainty; and some of them as satisfactory to the Mind, tho' perhaps not so regular, as the demonstrative kind" (LDH 1 187). The crucial point is that it is not demonstrative reasoning, but "other measures of evidence on which life and action intirely depend, and which are our guides even in most of our philosophical speculations" (A 8). Reasoning about matters of fact is called "probable reasoning," but "all probable reasoning is nothing but a species of sensation. . . . When I am convinc'd of any principle, 'tis only an idea, which strikes more strongly upon me. When I give the preference to one set of arguments above another, I do nothing but decide from my feeling concerning the superiority of their influence" (T 103). This is why Hume holds that "Our reason must be consider'd as a kind of cause, of which truth is the natural effect . . ." (T 180), and that *belief is more properly an act of the sensitive, than of the cogitative part of our natures"* (T 183).

Once we grasp the role of natural, instinctive behaviour, and the effects of education, we shall see, in Hume's opinion, that sceptical questioning is justifiable only as a device for instilling *"Modesty . . .* and *Humility,* with regard to the Operations of our natural Faculties," "a Kind of *Jeux d'esprit"* (L 19). No one ever sincerely held "that all is uncertain" (T 183). Hume always argued against "universal Doubt, which it is impossible for any Man to support" (L 19), and his two main logical reasons are important. First, Pyrrhonist scepticism is "founded on this erroneous maxim, that what a man can perform sometimes, in some dispositions, he can perform always, and in every disposition" (D 133)—a view powerfully endorsed by Wittgenstein's attack on the similar proposition that "What sometimes happens might always happen" (PI 345). The second reason concerns the nature of evidence and certainty. The test of whether a man "really" doubts is whether he can "make it appear in his conduct for a few hours" (D 132); but it is "impossible" for a man to pass this test—he will either be dead ("If [sceptics] be thoroughly in earnest, they will not long trouble the world with their doubts . . ." [D 132]), or no longer human (since his scepticism will "have totally destroy'd human reason" [T 187]). Further, it is not "only probable the sun will rise tomorrow, or that all men must dye . . ." (T 124); it is not only probable that my friend will refrain from holding his hand in the fire "till it be consumed"; "I know with certainty" these things, and no "suspicion of an unknown frenzy can give the least possibility" to such events (EHU 91). Ultimately, one is entitled to ask any excessive sceptic *"What his meaning is?"* (EHU 159), for if there is no state of affairs in which what he says could be true, his position is neither pointless nor mistaken, but incoherent. Such sceptical philosophy, perhaps, qualifies for consignment "to the flames: for it can contain nothing but sophistry and illusion" (EHU 165).

One proper task for philosophy is to detect and prevent the operation of certain illusions to which we all may be subject from time to time: illusions caused by imagination (T 267), by our passions (*Essays* 182, note), by our "partiality in our own favour" (D 148), by scepticism (EHU 159–60), or by "religious superstition or philosophical enthusiasm" (EPM 343). To avoid such illusions we should search for "a natural unforced interpretation of the phenomena of human life" (EPM 244). This will help us to achieve "an easy sympathy" (T 354) with others, and our own "peace and inward satisfaction" (T 620). Then, at least, philosophy will pose no threat, since "every thing remains precisely as before" (T 251). The close parallel between this characterisation of philosophy and Wittgenstein's views will become clear shortly. We have already seen that, in Hume's view, a man's knowledge has sources in his instincts as a human animal, in his education, in his own experience, and in his abstract reasoning. It is important to note, therefore, that the appropriate method for dispelling a particular illusion will depend on its source and on the context; there is not just one proper procedure covering all subjects. Some methods, indeed, even those established within a tradition, might be misguided. For example, introspection might be the wrong way to grapple with a "question concerning liberty and necessity" (EHU 93); a demand for simplicity in physical explanations might be "the source of much false reasoning" (EPM 298). Again, one might conflate procedures proper to different disciplines; thus, it is not the task of moral philosophy to engage in "the examination of our sensations" (T 8), for the procedures in moral philosophy are "not the same . . . as in physics" (EPM 299). In these last cases it would be a useful task for philosophers to point out the use of misleading analogies; for although all "our reasonings concerning matter of fact are founded on a species of Analogy . . ." (EHU 104), nevertheless suppositions of resemblance are "the most fertile source of error" (T 61).[3] Philosophers, moreover, like other men, are likely to misconceive the nature of their own activities. It is their task to point out where "subtle or ingenious" "hypotheses and systems" (EPM 175) in natural philosophy and ethics rest on mishandling language, but, on the other hand, it is not "for philosophers to encroach upon the province of grammarians and to engage in disputes of words . . ." (EPM 312; see also EPM 314). Certainly it is "worth while to consider what is real, and what is only verbal" (Essays 82) in a dispute, but no special philosophical knowledge or acumen is needed to realise, for example, that a "moral reflection cannot be plac'd on the right or on the left hand of a passion . . ." (T 236), or that the criteria for speaking of the "same church" differ from those for speaking of the "same sound" and "same river" (T 258).

Hume holds that the science of man must be founded "on experience and observation" (T xx). "Man is a reasonable . . . a sociable . . . an active being . . ." (EHU 8), but the domain in which he may properly expect to be reasonable is narrow—especially if this notion is used only for deductive arguments. When we ask for the impression behind a supposed idea (e.g., EHU 18), we are seeking the sources of a man's knowledge in instinct, education, his own experience, or abstract reasoning; in establishing the source, Hume believed, we would determine the conditions under which a particular claim was learned, and thereby grasp not only its meaning but also the type of justification appropriate to it. Now a philosopher "must act . . . and live, and converse like other men; and for this conduct he is not obliged to give any other reason than the absolute necessity he lies under of so doing" (D 134). According to this criterion "excessive" scepticism is at once ruled out, since "all human life must perish, were [such] principles universally and steadily to prevail" (EHU 160). "Nature is always too strong for principle" (EHU 160); sceptical philosophy, indeed, is a paradigm case of a human activity which is unnatural, since it contravenes or seeks to contravene man's essential nature as a social animal.

II

I have discussed only one, albeit central, element in Hume's philosophy. For comparison, I turn now to just one, albeit central, element in Wittgenstein's philosophy. I shall preface my discussion with an advance summary of the main points. Wittgenstein holds that if we recognise the fundamental role of training in the acquisition of beliefs and capacities, we shall see that such education presupposes certain ranges of natural or instinctive behaviour which, so to say, it sometimes codifies, sometimes extends. Training is a social activity, requiring the acquiescence of the participants; this is one reason why a different education may well lead to the acquisition of different concepts. Many philosophical muddles can be traced to misconceptions about the nature of the behaviour which education codifies, or to mishandling of the codification. In his view, philosophical problems are not empirical but what he calls "conceptual," and in many cases the proper philosophical method is "description," not explanation. Our linguistic behaviour has roots in primitive behavioural activities, and changes in our linguistic performances entail changes in our concepts, and thus in the meanings of the words we use. Scepticism of a Cartesian variety is ultimately incoherent, not just mistaken, because it fails to take account of how man, as a social animal, acquires cognitive attitudes. The anxieties felt by post-Cartesian empiricists over their failure to "justify" inductive arguments rested on misconceptions about the nature and varieties of justification. Wittgenstein claims that philosophers should examine the grounds of beliefs, not their causes; and the ultimate ground is what a man does.

Wittgenstein wrote: "I really want to say that scruples in thinking begin with (have their roots in) instinct. Or again: a language-game does not have its origin in *consideration*. Consideration is part of a language-game. And that is why a concept is in its element within the language-game" (Z 391). Many language-games are extensions of primitive behaviour (see Z 545), and it is often misleading to apply to primitive reactions terms which imply the learning and application of rules—it might be wrong, for example, to speak of "understanding" in connection with a particular "primitive language-game" (PI 146). In Wittgenstein's view, "Any explanation has its foundation in training. (Educators ought to remember this.)" (Z 419); very often what we teach is a *"capacity"* (Z 421). In teaching a child to talk, for example, "the teaching of language is not explanation, but training" (PI 5), and during the process the child "learns to react in such-and-such a way; and in so reacting it doesn't so far know anything. Knowing only begins at a later level" (OC 538). The following paragraphs, also from *On Certainty*, are important:

> When a child learns language it learns at the same time what is to be investigated and what not. When it learns that there is a cupboard in the room, it isn't taught to doubt whether what it sees later on is still a cupboard or only a kind of stage set [OC 472].

> Just as in writing we learn a particular basic form of letters and then vary it later, so we learn first the stability of things as the norm, which is then subject to alterations [OC 473].

> This game proves its worth. That may be the cause of its being played, but it is not the ground [OC 474].

> I want to regard man here as an animal; as a primitive being to which one grants instinct but not ratiocination. As a creature in a primitive state. Any logic good enough for a primitive means of communication needs no apology from us. Language did not emerge from some kind of ratiocination [OC 475].

Three points from these quotations are germane to our inquiry. To the first two points, concerning the contexts in which one learns to doubt, and concerning a distinction between "the cause" and "the ground" of an activity, I shall return shortly. Further, however, we should note the claim that at least at the outset of his learning we should think of man as an animal with instincts, but not with ratiocination—the latter will be a capacity to be taught and developed. Initially, an animal learns and is taught what to do; children, for example, "do not learn that books exist, that armchairs exist, etc. etc.,—they learn to fetch books, sit in armchairs, etc. etc." (OC 476). Now, if it is inappropriate to ascribe to children, at this stage of their learning, theories and presuppositions about what they are doing, or knowledge of rules which could codify their activities, there may be ranges of adult behaviour which would be better understood if described as "primitive" or "natural" or "instinctive." Thus Wittgenstein observes that "our naïve, normal way of expressing ourselves, does not contain any theory of seeing—does not show you a *theory* but only a *concept* of seeing" (Z 223); or, again: "Being sure that someone is in pain, doubting whether he is, and so on, are so many natural, instinctive, kinds of behaviour towards other human beings, and our language is merely an auxiliary to, and further extension of, this relation. Our language-game is an extension of primitive behaviour. (For our *language-game* is behaviour.) (Instinct)" (Z 545).

By emphasising the central place of *doing* in the acquisition of knowledge, at least in the early stages, Wittgenstein shows the degree of acquiescence, if not pure passivity, which must prevail. "We do not learn the practice of making empirical judgments by learning rules: we are taught *judgments* and their connexion with other judgments. *A totality* of judgments is made plausible to us" (OC 140). "When we first begin to *believe* anything, what we believe is not a single proposition, it is a whole system of propositions. (Light dawns gradually over the whole.)" (OC 141). Now, although "What we believe depends on what we learn" (OC 286), and although "Bit by bit there forms a system of what is believed . . ." (OC 144), Wittgen-

stein holds that the system itself "is something that a human being acquires
by means of observation and instruction. I intentionally do not say 'learns' "
(OC 279). Sometimes the conditions required for conveying and acquiring a
particular capacity are complex; for example, to grasp what "expressive
playing" in music is, a pupil may need knowledge and experience of a
whole culture (Z 164). But even here, perhaps, as in the case of judgments of
colour, and also in mathematics, "if there were not complete agreement,
then neither would human beings be learning the technique which we
learn. It would be more or less different from ours up to the point of un-
recognizability" (PI p. 226). That is why "an education quite different from
ours might also be the foundation for quite different concepts" (Z 387).

If our grasp of concepts has its roots in what we are taught and learn to
do, it is clearly important to understand the methods appropriate for characterising what we do:

> How could human behaviour be described? Surely only by sketching the ac-
> tions of a variety of humans, as they are all mixed up together. What deter-
> mines our judgment, our concepts and reactions, is not what *one* man is doing
> *now*, an individual action, but the whole hurly-burly of human actions, the
> background against which we see any action [Z 567].

> Seeing life as a weave, this pattern (pretence, say) is not always complete and
> is varied in a multiplicity of ways. But we, in our conceptual world, keep on
> seeing the same, recurring with variations. That is how our concepts take it.
> For concepts are not for use on a single occasion [Z 568].

Wittgenstein would accept Hume's claim that suppositions of resemblance
are "the most fertile source of error" (T 61). Because of their re-applicability,
concepts may overemphasise similarities, and blind us to the nature of the
particular case. Wittgenstein remarks that some of our misunderstandings
over "the use of words" are caused by "certain analogies between the forms
of expression in different regions of language"; sometimes these misunderstandings "can be removed by substituting one form of expression for another . . ." (PI 90). Sometimes, he claims, when we are "impressed by the
possibility of a comparison, we think we are perceiving a state of affairs of
the highest generality" (PI 104). We must always ask ourselves whether a
putative similarity is *important* for our purposes (Z 380); and this may help
us see that we do not always have "a single concept everywhere where there
is a similarity" (Z 380). Furthermore, we cannot justifiably assume that the
recurrence of a proposition ensures that it is being used in the same way or
for the same purposes. On the contrary, "the same proposition may get
treated at one time as something to test by experience, at another as a rule
of testing" (OC 98); "our empirical propositions do not all have the same
status, since one can lay down such a proposition and turn it from an empirical proposition into a norm of description" (OC 167, qualified in
OC 321). It is worth noting, here, an excellent example of a proposition
treated in quite different ways. Hume's "first proposition" (A 9) that there
are no ideas without impressions is sometimes treated as a testable empirical
claim, sometimes as a methodological device for establishing the meaning
of puzzling expressions, and sometimes as an unquestioned "general maxim"

(e.g., T 5; A 9; T 6). The proper way to take the proposition depends not only on the needs of the context, but on the stage reached in the developing structure of the overall argument. These matters raise the issue of the rhetoric of presentation, on which I shall comment briefly later.

What consequences do Wittgenstein's remarks have for the characterisation of his own philosophy? Although, in one place, he says that "What we are supplying are really remarks on the natural history of human beings . . ." (PI 415), this quite clearly is not his view of philosophy. On the contrary, when pointing out that his interest is not in the causal explanation of the formation of concepts, he writes: "Our interest certainly includes the correspondence between concepts and very general facts of nature. (Such facts as mostly do not strike us because of their generality.) But our interest does not fall back upon these possible causes of the formation of concepts; we are not doing natural science; nor yet natural history—since we can also invent fictitious natural history for our purposes" (PI p. 230). Philosophical investigations, in Wittgenstein's view, are not factual or causal but "conceptual investigations" (Z 458). Now, the dismissal of causal inquiry is crucial in his account of the limits of philosophy, as it becomes clear from his discussions of the justification and grounds of belief. "The causes of our belief in a proposition are indeed irrelevant to the question what we believe. Not so the grounds, which are grammatically related to the proposition, and tell us what proposition it is" (Z 437): "Giving grounds, however, justifying the evidence, comes to an end;—but the end is not certain propositions' striking us immediately as true, i.e., it is not a kind of *seeing* on our part; it is our *acting*, which lies at the bottom of the language-game" (OC 204). It is of the utmost importance to realise that even the notion of justification has boundaries; indeed, "Justification by experience comes to an end. If it did not it would not be justification" (PI 485). "At the end of reasons comes *persuasion*" (OC 612). "If I have exhausted the justifications I have reached bedrock, and my spade is turned. Then I am inclined to say: 'This is simply what I do.' " (PI 217). In so far as philosophical problems are concerned with those human activities which form the bedrock of our language-games, "problems arising through a misinterpretation of our forms of language" and whose "roots are as deep in us as the forms of our language" (PI 111), the proper philosophical method is "description":

> we may not advance any kind of theory. There must not be anything hypothetical in our considerations. We must do away with all *explanation*, and description alone must take its place. And this description gets its light, that is to say its purpose, from the philosophical problems. These are, of course, not empirical problems; they are solved, rather, by looking into the workings of our language, and that in such a way as to make us recognize those workings: *in despite of* an urge to misunderstand them. The problems are solved, not by giving new information, but by arranging what we have always known [PI 109].

Although it is perfectly possible to reform language "for particular practical purposes" (PI 132), that is not a task for philosophers; their work "consists in assembling reminders for a particular purpose" (PI 127). "Philosophy may in no way interfere with the actual use of language; it can in the end only describe it. For it cannot give it any foundation either. It leaves everything as it is" (PI 124). Much of what we say will then have the form "This is how things are" (PI 134) or *"this language-game is played"* (PI 654). Wittgenstein emphasises that "There is not *a* philosophical method, though there are indeed methods, like different therapies" (PI 133) —although, presumably, most fall under the general classification of "description"—and this is connected with the fact that, because of the interconnectedness of human activities, it will not be "a *single* problem" which is solved, but rather "problems" (PI 133). In Wittgenstein's view, the "confusions which occupy us arise when language is like an engine idling, not when it is doing work" (PI 132); by reminding ourselves of its essential roles in human activities, in what we do, we can set it back to work. This is one consideration behind the remark that the "real discovery is the one that makes me capable of stopping doing philosophy when I want to.—The one that gives philosophy peace, so that it is no longer tormented by questions which bring *itself* in question" (PI 133).

Once we begin to grasp the connections between "the concept of teaching and the concept of meaning" (Z 412), and realise that "a great deal of stage-setting in the language is presupposed . . ." (PI 257) in our linguistic activities, many issues come into focus but none more clearly than traditional philosophical speculations on doubt. Wittgenstein holds that a "person can doubt only if he has learnt certain things; as he can miscalculate only if he has learnt to calculate. In that case it is indeed involuntary" (Z 410). Thus, "If you tried to doubt everything you would not get as far as doubting anything. The game of doubting itself presupposes certainty" (OC 115); this means that, *pace* Descartes, our "first attitude of all" could no more be one of doubting than it could "be directed towards a possible disillusion" (Z 415). It is easy to misrepresent the case here, so that doubt is dismissed merely on pragmatic grounds: "But it isn't that the situation is like this: We just *can't* investigate everything, and for that reason we are forced to rest content with assumption" (OC 343). On the contrary: "the *questions* that we raise and our *doubts* depend on the fact that some propositions are exempt from doubt, are as it were like hinges on which those turn" (OC 341); "That is to say, it belongs to the logic of our scientific investigations that certain things are *in deed* not doubted" (OC 342). We must recognize that "about certain empirical propositions no doubt can exist if making judgments is to be possible at all" (OC 308). A child, for example, "learns by believing the adult. Doubt comes *after* belief" (OC 160); and a teacher would be quite right to reprimand a pupil who "continually interrupts with doubts," because at that stage his "doubts don't make sense at all" (OC 310). Thus, a pupil who "cast doubt on the uniformity of nature, that is to say on the justification of inductive arguments . . . has not learned how to ask questions. He has not learned *the* game that we are trying to teach him" (OC 315). Some putative expressions of doubt simply would not be understood, such as a doubt "whether the earth had existed a hundred years ago" (OC 231). "I shall get burnt if I put my hand in the fire: that is certainty. That is to say: here we see the meaning of certainty. (What it amounts to, not just the meaning of the word 'certainty.')" (PI 474); someone who argued that "it is *only in the past* that I have burnt myself" has failed to grasp the "character of the belief in the uniformity of nature" (PI 472). Philosophical sceptics, of a Cartesian variety, say, subscribe to "a false picture of *doubt*" (OC 249); they assume, falsely, that "we are in doubt because it is possible for us to *imagine* a doubt" (PI 84), and fail to see that they "have no system at all within which" their "doubt might exist" (OC 247). The trouble is that it "may easily look as if every doubt merely *revealed* an existing gap in the foundations; so that secure understanding is only possible if we first doubt everything that *can* be doubted, and then remove all these doubts" (PI 87). Such a view ignores the crucial fact that doubting is a practice we are taught; and we are also taught the places, within the system of beliefs we acquire, where the exercise of doubting is proper. We learn that a "doubt without an end is not even doubt" (OC 625), that at "the foundation of well-founded belief lies belief that is not founded" (OC 253).

Wittgenstein emphasises the interconnectedness of our beliefs. Our convictions, doubts, knowledge, methods of verification are all said to form systems (OC 102, 126, 410, 279): "All testing, all confirmation and disconfirmation of a hypothesis takes place already within a system. . . . The system is not so much the point of departure, as the element in which arguments have their life" (OC 105). It is essential, in each case, to ask how doubt is "introduced into the language-game" we are examining (OC 458), because "Doubting has certain characteristic manifestations, but they are only characteristic of it in particular circumstances" (OC 255). One problem is that there exists "no clear boundary" between "cases where doubt is unreasonable" and "others where it seems logically impossible" (OC 454). Of course, where "a doubt would be unreasonable, that cannot be seen from what *I* hold" (OC 452) since it is not "just *my* experience, but other people's, that I get knowledge from" (OC 275). We shall have to examine the system of beliefs in which the doubt is supposed to occur; it might then turn out that a doubt is possible only if a proposition is isolated from its natural surroundings (see OC 274). Eventually we must recognise that the "reasonable man does *not have* certain doubts" (OC 220), that "rational suspicion must have grounds" (OC 323), and that most inquiries properly end with the observation: "Any 'reasonable' person behaves like *this*" (OC 254; see also OC 39, 47, 620).

We must also recognize that "my picture of the world . . . is the inherited background against which I distinguish between true and false" (OC 94). My world-picture is, so to say, "the substratum of all my enquiring and asserting" (OC 162); hence one can say that at the end of the grounds is "not an ungrounded presupposition: it is an ungrounded way of acting" (OC 110). If we want to speak of certain propositions which "seem to underlie all questions and all thinking" (OC 415), propositions which "form the foundation of all operating with thoughts (with language)" (OC 401), then we might well come to "speak of fundamental principles of human enquiry" (OC 670). We should note that although most of my convictions are "anchored in all my *questions and answers*" (OC 103), they have not been "consciously arrived at." "I do not explicitly learn the propositions that stand fast for me" (OC 152); they are acquired in acquiring the whole system of beliefs—Hume's description of the law of induction as a "natural belief" is appropriate, since it is generally "not an item in our considerations" (OS 135). We may discover the nature and scope of our most basic convictions only when the whole system in which they function is challenged. That is why something like "conversion" (OC 92, 612) may be necessary to overthrow my beliefs, to change my *"way of looking at things"* (PI 144).

Wittgenstein held that "If language is to be a means of communication, there must be agreement . . . in judgments" (PI 242). Since "we belong to a community which is bound together by science and education" (OC 298), we can even say that "Knowledge is in the end based on acknowledgement" (OC 378). This means that "In order to make a mistake, a man must already judge in conformity with mankind" (OC 156). "Sure evidence is what we *accept* as sure, it is evidence that we go by in *acting* surely, acting without any doubt. What we call 'a mistake' plays a quite special part in our language games, and so too does what we regard as certain evidence" (OC 196). To survive as social animals we have to do what we have been taught to do; the non-conformist always risks being branded as insane. Thus, where we cannot fit a man's strange utterances into a framework of what we think he knows, such that we can say he is merely mistaken, we may doubt his sanity (OC 74, 465–69). This is another place where the philosophical sceptic goes wrong. Most of our remarks will not bear the weight of what we might call "metaphysical emphasis" (OC 482); the fact that I use all the "words in my sentence without a second thought, indeed that I should stand before the abyss if I wanted so much as to try doubting their meanings —shews that absence of doubt belongs to the essence of the language-game . . ." (OC 370). Our ordinary certainty is "something that lies beyond being justified or unjustified"; rather, it is "something animal" (OC 359).

III

I shall now indicate, briefly, some of the strains to which the views above seem subject.

Wittgenstein claims that "The philosopher's treatment of a question is like the treatment of an illness" (PI 255), and that "In philosophizing we may not *terminate* a disease of thought. It must run its natural course, and *slow* cure is all important" (Z 382). Even where this is an appropriate method—and the scope of the claim is unclear—no reason is given for denying philosophy a preventive function over and above its diagnostic and therapeutic functions. Elsewhere, he remarks that when a philosopher "give[s] the circumstances in which [an] expression functions" he is not making "an observation about English grammar" (OC 433); rather, "everything descriptive of a language-game is part of logic" (OC 56). Now, "a language-game is something that consists in the recurrent procedures of the game in time . . ." (OC 519), but it is unclear whether every practice without exception counts as a language-game, because we are given no clear criteria of individuation and identity. Since Wittgenstein conceded that "a language game does change with time" (OC 256), that what counts as reasonable alters (OC 336), and that some systems of beliefs are better than others (OC 286), it must be asked who judges the efficacy of a language-game or its need for revision. Although Wittgenstein gives no explicit reply to the question (OC 326), it is clear that the answer must be: the qualified practitioners in the particular field. Other practitioners learn who these are in learning the practice in question. Earlier we saw how Hume emphasised the dominance of instinct and education over the formation of our beliefs. By so doing, he sought to establish the narrow domain of rational thought and inquiry—especially if "rational" is taken to cover only the moves permitted by traditional logic. Both Hume and Wittgenstein, by stressing the influences on our attitudes and beliefs of what we have been taught and what we have imbibed unconsciously from our environment, face the problem of explaining the possibility of revision, extension, and overthrow of our position. Their fundamental views are essentially conservative, grounded in the past and in the preservation of its traditions. Wittgenstein claims that, in the end, we must resort to conversion or persuasion to change a person's views, devices as markedly devoid of rationality in the narrow sense as the means by which our basic convictions were themselves acquired. It is as if only re-training can modify in any radical degree what we have been taught previously.

These last points require amplification. An egocentric epistemology was a consequence of the Cartesian insistence that one must first doubt in order to understand. In contrast, both Hume and Wittgenstein hold that one must first believe in order to understand—believe one's teachers and accept the traditions they convey; one cannot otherwise achieve identity within one's social context. Amongst the teachers of the community at large will be found the philosophers. And here, in advance of a detailed study elsewhere, it is important to comment briefly on the tone and style of both authors—on what may be called their "rhetoric of presentation." Apart from an obvious similarity in tone between St. Augustine's *Confessions* and Wittgenstein's *Philosophical Investigations*, one should also notice in Wittgenstein's work a tone redolent of Tolstoy's prophetic writings, which we know he admired. Two features of prophetic writings may be underlined. Because they often see themselves as articulating the very grounds of beliefs and institutions, grounds beneath which there are no further grounds, prophets rarely engage in ratiocination; the basic truths and values can only be stated or described, and they cannot be explained in terms of something yet more basic. A common device for presenting such grounds consists in the assembling of "reminders." An auditor trained within a particular social tradition, it is assumed, need only be reminded of the constitutive conditions for the existence and membership of that tradition in order to defend it and to seek to rectify deviations. By trading on his good-will and covertly re-defining the central claims, the device can be used, of course, to alter an auditor's attitude. Galileo exemplifies this move in his *Dialogue Concerning the Two Chief World Systems*. If philosophy is conceived as concerned essentially with ultimate grounds and values, we might expect to find not only the device of "reminders," but also the view that if the reminding is efficacious the philosophical task is concluded. If the social context has attained or been restored to equilibrium, and the machinery of thought functions properly, because all have been properly "reminded" of the constitutive conditions of these phenomena, peace will reign and prophets perhaps become redundant. Because it would be contingent, however, that at a particular time no philosophical tasks remained, a prophet might wish to guard against disorder and misunderstanding by re-iterating the traditions. Furthermore, such philosophers might disdain those who, whilst claiming to be philosophers, did not centre their activities upon the articulation of ultimate grounds and values; those other "philosophers" might be deemed to be doing something as un-natural as it is unnecessary, and most likely to misconceive the nature and domain of rationality.

The tenets of Hume and Wittgenstein, as well as their mode of presentation, have something in common with the prophetic, as here characterised. For both, the terms "reasonable" and "rational" have a social dimension, and thereby an ethical dimension. A "reasonable" man is not one who merely performs certain formal moves; rather, he is to be defined in terms of what he has learned and been taught to do in particular social contexts. Hume makes quite clear in his discussion of aesthetics, for example,[4] that reasoning is possible only in contexts where man is considered as a social being; expressions of our preferences which are based on private sensations or upon our more general psychological make-up are not open to discussion or assessment in terms of rationality, although they may serve some personal ends. One task for reasoning in aesthetics is to remind us of the tradition of judgments which constitute any context and which ground the intelligibility of what we say in a given context. At the outset of his aesthetic, as of his epistemic, career, an individual is taught and learns within a tradition, and can be neither very self-conscious nor self-critical. Although the conventions are neither absolute nor unchallengeable, their authority is sufficient to discourage egocentricity until it becomes acceptable to, or at least can survive alongside, the tradition itself. Although he is opposed to any *a priori* account of standards, values, laws, or institutions, Hume gives to conventions, in terms of which all social phenomena are defined, an authority which might be called "the secular *a priori*."

In addition to the occurrence of the prophetic and the secular *a priori* in Wittgenstein, we should also notice the central place of passivity in the learning of the traditions. It is worth asking whether passivity must play a central role in any view of knowledge as a social phenomenon, as opposed to an individualistic enterprise; and also what social consequences follow from a refusal to ground epistemology (and centre education) on the traditions of the community. (Wittgenstein is generally held to have overthrown the allegedly egocentric epistemologies of Locke and Hume, both of whom are also accused of allowing passivity to dominate their theories. But, as I have tried to show, Hume stressed the social dimension as much as Wittgenstein, and Wittgenstein is committed to as much passivity as Hume.) It is also worth contrasting Wittgenstein's rarely expressed views on ethics and aesthetics with those of Hume. In about 1929 Wittgenstein wrote: "although all judgments of relative value can be shown to be mere statements of facts, no statement of fact can ever be, or imply, a judgment of absolute value"; further, "Ethics so far as it springs from the desire to say something about the ultimate meaning of life, the absolute good, the absolute valuable, can be no science. What it says does not add to our knowledge in any sense. But . . . I would not for my life ridicule it." [5] And in 1938 he wrote: "The words we call expressions of aesthetic judgement play a very complicated rôle, but a very definite rôle, in what we call the culture of a period. To describe their use . . . you have to describe a culture. . . . What belongs to a language game is a whole culture." [6] Now, to locate a social event, whether a particular utterance or an institution as a whole, within a culture, requires a broader notion of context than is often used by philosophers. And a philosopher who advocates or who is committed to such a notion may expect to be understood, himself, in a relatively broad context. Notwithstanding the importance of being able to formalise a writer's arguments and assess them in the light of the canons of logic, it is notable that the writings of both Hume and Wittgenstein have yielded few fruitful results from such an approach. In Hume, it is said, inconsistencies are too easy to find, and in Wittgenstein arguments are too hard to find. There is, however, an integral relation between the basic tenets of these philosophers, and their rhetoric of presentation; the reminders, examples, conflicting considerations, apparently contradictory claims are often intelligible if read in a broader context than that of a paragraph, section, or chapter. Further, writers concerned with a large-scale map, and aware that few objections are properly treated as over-riding objections, are often constrained to attend to large-scale features at the expense of detail or consistency of detail. For example, it seems to be Hume's view that a man's "natural beliefs," at least his beliefs in independent existence and causal dependence, do not conflict so long as they are taken in a general form; philosophical analysis of them, on the other hand, may result in conflict which then needs resolution. Perhaps an obscure remark by Wittgenstein also accords with this view: "It is always by favour of Nature that one knows something" (OC 505).

We have already noted two of the considerations which lay behind Wittgenstein's insistence on description as the proper philosophical method, not explanation—granting that what we call "description" may well serve different functions (see PI 291, 304). First, the fundamental principles of enquiry, or the substrata of thought, can only be described, because there is nothing in terms of which they could be explained. Thus, second, a characteristic remark at the end of philosophical investigation would be: "This is so." There may have been a third consideration, which we have also mentioned. In both Wittgenstein and Hume there is an occasional hint that there are no uniquely philosophical problems; what we call "philosophical" problems occur when the machinery of thought is idling, and this is one reason for the inconsequentiality of scepticism. The "everyday use" of language, however, when working properly, is generally clear (OC 347; see also OC 388). Now, the normative element in this characterisation of philosophy should not be overlooked, since both Hume and Wittgenstein seek to identify and rectify philosophical mistakes, even if "Not all corrections of our views are on the same level" (OC 300). For example, just as Hume rejects the views of both sceptics and dogmatists (T 187), so Wittgenstein rejects the views of idealists, solipsists, and realists (PI 402; see also OC 24, 59). Correction, of course, does not leave everything as it was, and, furthermore, correction will often be in accord with a view of what ought to be. It is therefore unclear in this context why, in Wittgenstein's view, philosophy should not advance theories designed to improve our understanding of puzzling phenomena. It may be that the main reason for contrasting the language-games of philosophy unfavourably with those of other activities, is that philosophy seems not to have helped in the practical life of man as a social animal. Such a claim, however, would be as empirically testable as the claim that the everyday use of language is generally clear; and the dismissal of philosophy on such a ground would be as pragmatic as dismissal of scepticism on grounds of inconsequentiality. But Wittgenstein, at least, is anxious that his "conceptual" remarks are not mistaken for pragmatic observations (e.g., see OC 422). Again, unless theorising is taken to impair every endeavour, no reason is given which would show the practical futility, say, of the philosophy of particular sciences, or philosophy of law, or moral philosophy—to take just three examples.

It may be contended that since scepticism was a common target for both Hume and Wittgenstein, it is easy to establish some parallelism between their views by means of careful selection, and by concentration on Wittgenstein's *On Certainty*. It would certainly be absurd to deny that there are major differences between Hume and Wittgenstein, at least if traditional interpreters are to be followed; indeed, it has been claimed that in his later philosophy Wittgenstein overthrew completely most of Hume's views. I contend, however, that most interpreters of Hume have overlooked a fundamental feature of his position—his emphasis on man as a social animal. The first Book of the *Treatise* does not epitomize Hume's philosophy; and although there is much in that book which conforms with the stress on the social nature of man and of knowledge, there is also much which seems to conflict with such tenets—which is surely sufficient reason for thinking that Book I was written [7] before the other Books, in which the tenets are more fully developed and assume ever greater prominence. Hume's insistence on what we *do* as a focus for our enquiries into the nature and scope of man's capacities as a social animal, especially into the relatively narrow domain of reason and reasons—a topic on which I have touched only briefly here— has much in common with Wittgenstein's similar insistence; and the consequences they draw in their view of the nature and role of philosophy are also parallel. If my contention has plausibility, however, there is much in

the writings of both philosophers which now calls for re-assessment. I hope
to contribute to that task on another occasion.

NOTES

1. Paragraph references to Wittgenstein's works are abbreviated as follows:
   OC *On Certainty*, edd. G. E. M. Anscombe and G. H. von Wright (Oxford, 1969)
   PI *Philosophical Investigations*, edd. G. E. M. Anscombe and G. H. von Wright (Oxford, 1953)
   Z   *Zettel*, edd. G. E. M. Anscombe and G. H. von Wright (Oxford, 1967).

2. "A Dissertation on the Passions," *Essays Moral, Political, and Literary*, edd. T. H. Green and T. H. Grose, 2 vols. (London, 1898), II 152.

3. For discussion of this in connection with the *Dialogues Concerning Natural Religion*, and Hume's notions of explanation and description therein, see my "Hume's Two Concepts of God," *Philosophy*, 47, No. 182 (October 1972), 322–33.

4. For the place of reason in Hume's aesthetics, see my "Another Look at Hume's Views of Aesthetic and Moral Judgments," *Philosophical Quarterly*, 20, No. 78 (January 1970), 53–59, and "Hume's Aesthetics Reassessed," ibid., 26, No. 102 (January 1976), 48–62. See also chap. 15 of this volume, "Cause, Reason, and Objectivity in Hume's Aesthetics."

5. "A Lecture on Ethics," *Philosophical Review*, 74, No. 1 (January 1965), 6, 12.

6. *Lectures and Conversations on Aesthetics, Psychology and Religious Belief*, ed. Cyril Barrett (Oxford, 1966), p. 8.

7. Although, as my argument shows, I agree with some of Norman Kemp Smith's claims in "The Naturalism of Hume" (*Mind*, 30, N.S. 14 [April and October 1905], 149–73, 335–47), I cannot agree with his contention there, and in *The Philosophy of David Hume* (London, 1941), that ". . . Books II and III of the *Treatise* are in date of first composition prior to the working out of the doctrines dealt with in Book I" (ibid., p. vi).

IV

10

Hume's Historical Theory of Meaning

Donald W. Livingston
Northern Illinois University

ALTHOUGH HUME CONSIDERED HIS THEORY OF MEANING one of his most important philosophical discoveries, his commentators are unanimous in holding the theory to be indefensible. As Church puts it: "It is a commonplace that Hume's confidence in the importance for philosophy of his first principle is indefensible." [1] And Broad writes: "Hume's general account of what is involved in having an idea of so-and-so is, and can be shown to be, rubbish." [2] However, even if a theory is false, it may, nonetheless, have an important idea behind it which is philosophically interesting. In what follows, I shall try to show that this is the case with Hume's theory of meaning. My main purpose, then, is not to defend the theory but to explore its rationale for whatever philosophical value it might have. In doing so, however, we shall find that in certain respects it is defensible and that in one important respect it is superior to the main alternative theories of meaning proposed in the empirical tradition. In passing, I shall offer an explanation why Hume's commentators have failed to appreciate the theory.

Hume's "first principle" is that *"all our simple ideas in their first appearance are deriv'd from simple impressions, which are correspondent to them, and which they exactly represent"* (T 4). Complex ideas are built up out of associations of simple ideas through the relations of resemblance, causality, and contiguity in space and time. Two empirical reasons are deployed in support of the theory: (1) "To give a child an idea of scarlet or orange, of sweet or bitter, I present the objects, or in other words, convey to him these impressions; but proceed not so absurdly, as to endeavour to produce the impressions by exciting the ideas"; (2) "where-ever by any accident the faculties, which give rise to any impressions, are obstructed in their operations, as when one is born blind or deaf; not only the impressions are lost, but also their correspondent ideas. . . . Nor is this only true, where the organs of sensation are entirely destroy'd, but likewise where they have never been put in action to produce a particular impression. We cannot form to ourselves a just idea of the taste of a pine-apple, without having actually tasted it" (T 5). (1) and (2) jointly entail that simple impressions are necessary and sufficient for their corresponding simple ideas. Having established his first principle on empirical grounds, Hume goes on to fix a rule for clarifying our ideas upon it: "When we entertain, therefore, any suspicion that a philosophical term is employed without any meaning or idea (as is but too frequent), we need but enquire, *from what impression is that supposed idea derived?* And if it be impossible to assign any, this will serve to confirm our suspicion" (EHU 22). Many commentators take this rule to be a sign of a logical mistake in Hume's procedure, namely that the first principle which is and was intended to be an empirical proposition is being illegitimately treated as an analytic truth. Flew writes that such shifting "manoeuvres have the effect of making it look as if the immunity to falsification of a necessary truth had been gloriously combined with the substantial assertiveness of a contingent generalization." [3] And Bennett asks: "Why can't his opponents say that these are precisely the classes of 'ideas' for which the theory is false?" [4] Basson goes further, claiming that Hume's principle has no empirical force at all: "No matter how he purports to prove his principle, the use he makes of it shows that for him an idea is by definition a copy of an impression." [5] We should note that these objections are not about the empirical evidence Hume uses to support his principle but about employing the principle to challenge the use of certain "philosophical" terms which purport to express ideas. But granting that (1) and (2) do lend empirical support to the first principle, there is nothing *formally* odd about using it to support a rule for testing ideas. Wittgenstein once remarked that "our empirical propositions do not all have the same status since one can lay down such a proposition and turn it from an empirical proposition into a norm of description." [6] In "Of Miracles," Section X of *An Enquiry Concerning Human Understanding*, Hume used the empirical regularities of nature as canons for ruling out testimony to miracles, i.e., purported counter-instances of those regularities. His procedure in restricting the range of philosophic discourse is essentially no different. Why some empirical propositions are nomological and can be used as norms of description and others not is a difficult question which cannot be considered here. But it is worth pointing out that having many positive instances and having withstood falsifying instances is not sufficient to confirm a general proposition much less to bestow nomological force on it. Indeed, as Nelson Goodman has shown, only nomological propositions can be confirmed by their instances. [7] One criterion for a nomological proposition is that it be connected in certain ways to other propositions in a theoretical framework. Hume, of course, does not explicitly introduce a theoretical framework in which to ground his first proposition. However, there are some important background considerations which lend support to Hume's nomic use of his first proposition and save it from being a mere isolated contingent generalization, devoid of all theoretical backing.

First, Hume does not follow the Cartesian method of supposing that all terms purporting to express ideas are meaningless unless there are conclusive reasons to think otherwise. His nomic use of the proposition is directed only against "philosophical" terms many of which are presystematically known to be semantically dubious and which are contrasted with terms used in the relatively non-controversial language of common life. So, at the outset, Hume is appealing to what we supposedly all know: that the language of common life, informing as it does a community of shared judgments, is a paradigm of non-controversial descriptive meaning whereas philosophical language is not. There may or may not be a phlogiston, vacua, or substantial selves, but there are dinner parties, taxes, and the New York Yankees. His strategy is to show why the descriptive language of common life has this special clarity by showing how it connects to the empirical world, and then, having accounted for this clarity, to argue that philosophical language should be reconstructed as much as possible to conform to the paradigm: "Here . . . is a proposition, which not only seems, in itself, simple and intelligible; but, if a proper use were made of it, might render every dispute equally intelligible, and banish all that jargon, which has so long taken possession of metaphysical reasonings, and drawn disgrace upon them" (EHU 21).

It is best, then, to treat Hume's first principle as an articulation of that special sort of clarity which the descriptive language of common life embodies and as a canon for disciplining philosophical language. It is then appropriate to ask: (1) how well does Hume's theory account for the descriptive clarity of common language, and (2) to what extent can it be used as a standard for judging philosophical language? We have now to consider a well-entrenched criticism that Hume's theory is worthless in respect to both (1) and (2).

I

The criticism as Flew put it runs as follows: "The first thing to appreciate is that in Hume's official view . . . the meanings of words are ideas, ideas . . . being identified with mental images." But "the capacity to form mental images is neither a logically necessary nor a logically sufficient condition of understanding the meaning of a term. . . ." Flew grants that Hume often "says things which are hard or impossible to square with this official position." But "there is no doubt that this is his opinion when he is on guard." [8] We may call this the private language critique. It has been a popular criticism of Hume's first principle ever since Wittgenstein first formulated an argument to show that a private language is impossible. Behind it lies the much older interpretation of Hume as a phenomenalist, trying rationally to reconstruct the public world out of indubitable private mental images. In this section, I shall show that phenomenalism is a wrong reading of Hume and that, consequently, the private language critique fails to make contact with the theory of meaning Hume actually proposed.

Hume's explicit views on the status of the public world were first presented in Book I, Part IV, Section II of the *Treatise*. There he argues that belief in an external world is an ultimate belief which we all have and for which no evidence can be given since the very idea of evidence presupposes it. What Hume tries to do is to make clear what the belief is, specify the conditions under which it is logically necessary, and discover the causes which produce it. The analysis is presented dialectically. The idea of the public world common to us all, Hume calls the "popular" or "vulgar" system, the view that our perceptions are our "only objects" and that "the very being, which is intimately present to the mind, is the real body or material existence" (T 206). Moreover, "this very perception or object is suppos'd to have a continu'd uninterrupted being, and neither to be annihilated by our absence, nor to be brought into existence by our presence" (T 207). And the popular system is consistent: "The supposition of the continu'd existence of sensible objects or perceptions involves no contradiction" (T 208). This admission, alone, is sufficient to exclude Hume from the phenomenalist camp. For a phenomenalist analysis would have to define perceptions as wholly mind dependent, so that a perception existing independent of the mind would be not merely a false supposition but contradictory as well. Hume, however, is very careful to exclude this meaning from the term "perception": "as every perception is distinguishable from another, and may be consider'd as separately existent; it evidently follows, that there is no absurdity in separating any particular perception from the mind. . . ." Likewise, "objects" considered as mind-independent existences can be directly present to the mind: "If the name of *perception* renders not this separation from a mind absurd and contradictory, the name of *object*, standing for the very same thing, can never render their conjunction impossible" (T 207).

But though the popular system could be true, empirical reflection *appears* to provide some ground for doubting it. The experience of double images when "we press one eye with a finger" (T 210), "and an infinite number of other experiments of the same kind" convince us that "all our perceptions are dependent on our organs, and the disposition of our nerves and animal spirits" (T 211). To account for these purely empirical facts, philosophers have proposed a more sophisticated system which Hume calls the doctrine of "double existence," distinguishing "betwixt perceptions and objects, of which the former are suppos'd to be interrupted, and perishing, and different at every different return; the latter to be uninterrupted, and to preserve a continu'd existence and identity." Hume goes on to argue, however, that the philosophical system "contains all the difficulties of the vulgar system, with some others, that are peculiar to itself" (T 211).

(1) "We can never perceive any thing but perceptions." Consequently, the conception of an object independent of perceptions and resembling them is, in reality, just the conception of a perception. Thus the reason for rejecting the popular system (that the public world cannot be explicated in terms of perceptions) is a reason for rejecting the philosophical system which, in effect, has arbitrarily invented "a new set of perceptions" endowed with the properties requisite for a public world. The philosophical system, then, "must derive all its authority from the vulgar system; since it has no original authority of its own" (T 213). (2) The evidence for the dependent existence of perceptions which prompts the philosophical system is causal and depends upon the popular system for its possibility, since causal reasoning operates on what are thought to be continuously existing bodies: "what any common man means by a hat, or shoe, or stone, or any other impression, convey'd to him by his senses" (T 202; see also T 209, 210, 216).

Hume now claims that his analysis is exhaustive, that he has examined "all the systems . . . with regard to external existences." These reduce to two: the popular and the philosophical. Philosophical reflection reveals a false premiss in the popular system: that our "resembling perceptions are numerically the same" (T 217). On the basis of this error, the philosophical system attempts *totally* to replace the popular one, but, ironically, this and any other reflective total critique presupposes the popular system: the philosophical system has the same difficulties as the popular one, "and is over-and-above loaded with this absurdity, that it at once denies and establishes the vulgar supposition" (T 218). So here we have a kind of Humean "transcendental deduction" for belief in the popular conception of the public world: we absolutely believe the popular system, and no criticism of the whole or any part of it which does not presuppose that belief is possible. Nor can we ask whether there is any empirical evidence for the popular system, since that system is internal to the idea of empirical evidence.

Now, we must not confuse this purely *logical* justification of the popular system with the well-known psychological account of why we believe the false proposition that our "resembling perceptions are numerically the same." Hume explains this belief by reference to "the natural propensity of the imagination, to ascribe a continu'd existence to those sensible objects or perceptions, which we find to resemble each other in their interrupted appearance . . ." (T 210). Kemp Smith is one of a long line of commentators who take the psychological account to be Hume's only ground and "not a rational" one for accepting the popular system.[9] Behind Kemp Smith's interpretation is, presumably, the view that since the popular system contains what, from an empirical point of view, is admittedly a false premiss, it must be irrational and capable of only a brute psychological justification. Hume, however, was one of the first in modern times to appreciate the fact that the acceptability of a system is independent of the truth or falsity of its axioms. Considerations of the logical strength of the axioms to generate theorems within the system and of the system's relations, logical and otherwise, to other systems are more important than an isolated concern with the semantic properties of the axioms. These are just the sort of factors which Hume finds decisive: the popular system is consistent, is presupposed by any philosophical system, and is internal to the idea of empirical evidence.

The lesson to be learned from all this, in Hume's view, is that philosophy is parasitic upon the popular system, and although it can and must modify the system in part, this can be done only by accepting it as a whole: "philosophical decisions are nothing but the reflections of common life, methodized and corrected" (EHU 162). And this conclusion provides us with important theoretical backing for Hume's first principle which was not and could not have been introduced in the early pages of the *Treatise*. First of all, it is now clear that philosophical language is the result of critical reflection on the language of common life (the popular system) and must preserve in its meanings as much as possible the primordial language it is a reflection on. This point is crucial for appreciating how Hume uses the term "perception" and its species "impression" and "idea." Their introduction on the first page of the *Treatise* is disarmingly informal: "I believe it will not be very necessary to employ many words in explaining this distinction [between impressions and ideas]" (T 1), and it is not until Part IV of Book I that their full meaning is explicated. There we learn two crucial facts about perceptions which we must read back into the first pages of the *Treatise* where the theory of meaning is first presented. (1) Perceptions are not defined as logically private mental images. Perceptions can exist independent of any mind; whether they are private mental images or public objects is a contingent matter. (2) The evidence required to show that some perceptions are fleeting and perishing existences presupposes the popular system, and it is, therefore, logically impossible that there be evidence to show that *all* perceptions are fleeting and perishing existences. From (1) and (2), we get the principle that perceptions may be thought of as public existences unless there is some special causal reason to think otherwise. This principle operates in the early sections of the *Treatise*, enabling Hume to treat perceptions indifferently as public or private existences, relying on the context to make his meaning clear. And we may note here another reason why Hume does not give a rigorous definition of "perception" in the opening pages of the *Treatise*. Presumably, such a definition would make reference either to mind dependent existences or to public objects. But for Hume the concept of mind and the concept of a public object are *equally* problematic. Only by working through the dialectic of the popular and philosophical systems can we begin to appreciate the unexpected difficulties which lurk in the use of terms like "mind," "body," and "perception" and so begin to appreciate the sort of limit which must be placed on their meaning.

Hume's physicalistic use of the term "perception" and "impression" in contexts where the theory of meaning is being introduced has been recognized by Hume commentators and is usually viewed as the result of careless thinking. Kemp Smith finds that much of the wording "in these opening sections is loose" and laments Hume's "unfortunate" mode of exposition.[10] Passmore finds them due to "that insensitivity to consistency which Hume shares with Locke." [11] And Flew interprets them as the inevitable lapse of phenomenalists into physicalistic language which makes phenomenalism appear sound and hides its error: "It is only by a systematic failure to launch and to press home a really determined attempt to state the position consistently that its fundamental impossibility is concealed." [12] But, as we have seen, Hume is not a phenomenalist; the popular system (which is physicalistic) is presupposed by every philosophical system, including phenomenalism, which intends to replace it.

So the private language critique, insofar as it rests on a phenomenalistic interpretation of Hume, must be rejected. From the early pages of the *Treatise*, Hume's first principle is placed in the context of a public world, the understanding of which is supposed to deepen as the inquiry proceeds. Yet there is a way in which the private language critique points up an inadequacy in the theory. Although Hume does not think that having mental imagery is a sufficient condition for having an idea, he does think it is necessary. He takes it to be obvious, for instance, that those born blind do not enjoy visual imagery, and he concluded from this that in such cases "not only the impressions are lost, but also their correspondent ideas . . ." (T 5). But the meanings of color words can be understood by those born blind (and who are presumably without visual imagery) insofar as they can make the proper physical discriminations associated with the use of color words. Those who can use color words properly may be said to have an idea of color. (Hume, incidentally, was aware of this sense of "having an idea of something" through his friend the blind poet Blaklocke, and the physicalistic interpretation of perceptions urged above allows him to account for it [LDH I 201, 209]). Since imagery does seem superfluous for the purpose of communication about the public world, Hume's view requires explanation. A suggestion is given in the following passage: "We cannot form to ourselves a just idea of the taste of a pine-apple, without having actually tasted it" (T 5). A person who had never tasted a pineapple, but who could make the physical discriminations necessary for using the expression "taste of pineapple" would have an idea of the taste, but this would not be, in Hume's view, a "just idea" of what we mean by the expression. Now, there is a clear sense in which Hume is right. This same person could well say upon actually tasting the fruit and knowing that it is pineapple that for the first time he really understood what people mean when they speak of the taste of pineapple. We must keep in mind that the world Hume is explicating is the popular system which is very much a world rich in color and hue. He never doubted that physical discriminations were necessary to constitute a proper use of words in a public language, but he did not think that that condition was especially interesting. Given the proper physical discriminations, what really rounds off our understanding of a sensory expression is the sensuous experience itself or the memory of it. This is how Hume discusses the idea of extension. First he simply claims that we do have an idea of extension because we have learned to use the term: " 'tis certain we have an idea of extension; for otherwise why do we talk and reason concerning it?" (T 32). Having analyzed the idea of extension, along with showing on purely formal grounds that its parts cannot be infinitely divisible, he goes on to put the idea into canonical form by deriving it from past impressions. The same procedure is used to explicate the idea of time.

But though one might grant that sensory imagery is necessary to understand sensory terms *fully*, Hume often writes as if it were necessary to understand any descriptive term whatsoever, and that is surely wrong. Theoretical terms such as "infinity," "meson," "ego," and the like do not require mental imagery for their partial or full comprehension. Indeed, the whole order of theoretical language is purged from Hume's theory of meaning. Hume, of course, is not alone in this. The empirical tradition is littered with proposals for reducing theoretical language to sensory language. Braithwaite has shown, and I think conclusively, that scientific progress logically requires a class of predicates which fall outside the class of sensory predicates, so that if the empiricist reduction were accomplished and all theoretical predicates eliminated in favor of sensory ones, science would grind to a halt.[13] Hume's mistake, then, was the attempt to reduce theoretical language to the language of common life (especially sensory language). But there is a virtue in this mistake which is easy to overlook. It can best be brought out by contrasting it with the opposite and much more prevalent mistake of trying to reduce the language of common life to some favored theoretical language. This sort of reduction is usually also part of a program to *ontologize* the theoretical language and to hold that reality can be grasped by it alone, common language being, at best, an inadequate approximation. To many, this program appears analytic to the very idea of philosophy. And, indeed, much of the history of philosophy from Zeno's paradoxes to Russell's logical atomism can be viewed as an attempt to ontologize some favored theoretical language, and always with the result that the language or judgments of common life are seen to be inadequate as a *whole*. The most important case of this for our understanding of Hume is what he called the doctrine of "double existence," stated early in the modern period by Galileo and first systematically worked out by Descartes.

In this view, the whole of sensory language which we ordinarily take to describe the physical world is thought of as describing merely private mental images. Only the language of theoretical physics describes the physical world as it really is, and according to that description physical objects are thought of as having no sensory properties. Three centuries after Descartes, Sir Arthur Eddington could present virtually the same view. In a famous passage, he says he is writing at *two* tables: one is the richly colored table of common life, the other is the table described by theoretical physics and having no sensory properties. Only the latter table is real; the table of common life is a "strange compound of external nature, mental imagery and inherited prejudice." [14] Although the doctrine of double existence first arose in modern times from philosophical reflections on physics, it is the result of a quite general way of thinking, and by the eighteenth century had begun to make an appearance in social and political philosophy. Consider the thesis Rousseau seeks to demonstrate in *The Social Contract* that "Man is born free, but everywhere he is in chains." Or Proudhon's thesis that "Property is theft." Both of these paradoxical statements are parallel to Eddington's talk about a real but invisible table which stands before our very eyes. So theoretical alienation from tables can lead to alienation from the social and political structures of common life, which are then seen as a *total* illusion. By the nineteenth century the habit of ontologizing the theoretical language of social and political science had become established and with it a metaphysical longing for some sort of total revolution and liberation. Thus Charles Fourier who greatly influenced Marx and Engels and who claimed to be the first to have worked out the theoretical laws of history could write of the whole of human history: "The vice of our so-called reformers is to indict this or that defect, instead of indicting civilization as a whole, inasmuch as it is nothing but a vicious circle of evil in all its parts; one must get out of this hell." [15]

Hume's philosophical method, with the theory of meaning internal to it, is designed to check the tendency of philosophers to ontologize theoretical language and to rescue the language of common life from the category of illusion. Its weakness lies in its not being an adequate account of theoretical language; its strength lies in its being a better account of common language than the alternatives in the empirical tradition. In what follows, I shall argue that Hume's paradigm for understanding the language of common life is not theoretical inquiry but *historical* inquiry. It is a currently fashionable dictum that all language is "theory-laden." No doubt part of common language is theory-laden, but if Hume is right, the greater part is *story-laden*. We shall now see what these claims come to.

II

Theoretical thinking is non-temporal, refers to universal structures (if it refers at all), and has lawlike form. By contrast, historical thinking is tensed, is about individuals, and has narrative form. Hume's first principle requires reference to past individual impressions and so satisfies the first two conditions for historical thinking. In the final section, I shall show that it also satisfies the narrative requirement. But we should begin with the objections Hume commentators have raised to the past tense structure of the theory.

Perhaps the most obvious objection is that ideas cannot be derived from past impressions because past impressions cannot be recalled for comparison with present ideas. Thus Russell writes: "How, then, are we to find any way of comparing the present image and the past sensation? The problem is just as acute if we say that images differ from their prototypes as if we say that they resemble them; it is the very possibility of comparison that is hard to understand." [16] And Church: "For as no prototype of any memory may be revived so no original of any primary idea may be recalled. In no case, then, can an idea be known to be a copy." [17] Laird offers a similar criticism: "Yet the mere fact (if it were) that ideas are derived from impressions surely does not prove, or even suggest, that every idea is so very wise as to know its own father, or even as to know that it has a pedigree of any kind." [18] Price makes the same criticism along with a recommendation for improving the theory: "The idea is present to the mind now; the impressions from which it is supposed to have been derived are past and gone. If he can no longer inspect the past impressions, how is he to tell whether the present idea was or was not derived from them? What can even lead him to suspect that it was derived from anything at all? He ought to have made memory a third species of *acquaintance*, alongside of sensation and introspection." [19]

These objections presuppose the principle that no resemblance comparisons are possible unless the objects compared are available for inspection in the present. Since it is conceptually impossible for past impressions to be present, they cannot be compared with any present existent, and so the theory fails. The application of this principle to Hume's theory is part of the phenomenalistic interpretation of his work. But it should be noted that the principle itself is quite general and, if correct, would rule out any theory which tied meaning to past existences. The snows of yesteryear are not private mental images, but can no more be brought into the present for comparison than private mental images can. What the above critics find objectionable about Hume's theory is not that it is grounded in private mental images (though they believe so) but that it is grounded in *past* existences.

But Hume is not a phenomenalist; nor did he accept the principle that resemblance comparisons hold only between present existences. In the *Treatise*, after asserting that ideas resemble past impressions, he goes out of his way to point out that it is "impossible to recal the past impressions, in order to compare them with our present ideas . . ." (T 85). Passmore takes this passage to be fatal: Hume "never realizes the full implications of this admission. Taken seriously, it would destroy his positivist method. There is now no way of discovering whether a supposed idea in fact derives from an impression." [20] But the passage is fatal only if one is justified in reading into the text the phenomenalist principle that resemblance comparisons hold only between present existences. Reading Hume as a phenomenalist, Passmore cannot appreciate the fact that the passage provides good reason *not* to read the text that way. In the same strained way, Zabeeh takes the passage to support the claim that "Hume realizes that no correspondence theory of truth could be stated in his system," [21] in spite of the fact that Hume explicitly affirms the correspondence theory (T 458, 448).

The criticism that Hume has no way of comparing past impressions with present ideas must be rejected since it is based on a principle which is neither asserted nor implied by the text. Nor does the principle appear to be true so that we could use it to show that Humean doctrines inconsistent with it are false. If we cannot compare a past impression with a present idea because the impression is "past and gone," then, presumably, we cannot compare any past existent with any present existent. And this certainly appears wrong. We can compare contemporary political institutions with medieval institutions, and we can compare the pain of a present toothache with one of last year. Indeed, if this objection against Hume's first principle should be taken seriously, historical knowledge would be impossible, for if we could ever know anything about past existences, the object of that knowledge could be compared to whatever we know of the present. But if the latter is impossible, then, presumably, the former is also. So we cannot reject Hume's first principle for the reason given without embracing historical scepticism. Why have Hume's commentators failed to appreciate this fairly obvious fact about the theory?

One reason, perhaps, is that virtually every empirical theory of meaning entails that expressions supposedly about the past be meaningless. (1) Most forms of phenomenalism explicate descriptive meaning by reference to actual or possible present experiences. Thus Ayer writes that "propositions referring to the past . . . can be taken as implying that certain observations would have occurred if certain conditions had been fulfilled." [22] Expressions supposedly about the past are either meaningless or must be taken as referring to sets of actual or possible present experiences, in which case they are no longer about the past. (2) Likewise, pragmatism holds that the meaning of descriptive expressions is grounded in reference to the present and future. C. I. Lewis writes: "To ascribe an objective quality to a thing means implicitly the prediction that if I act in certain ways, specifiable experiences will eventuate." And the "whole content of our knowledge of reality is the truth of such 'If–then' propositions." [23] If this account were right, then expressions purportedly about the past would have to be either meaningless or recast somehow into expressions about the present and future. In neither case could any expression be about the past. (3) Phenomenalism and pragmatism are *tensed* theories of meaning insofar as they require the use of tensed expressions. But not all forms of empiricism employ tensed expressions. Various forms of logical empiricism explicate descriptive meaning by reference to tenseless expressions. Again, expressions thought to be about the past must either be recast into some tenseless idiom or be judged meaningless. So again no expression can refer to the past.[24] We may note here that absolute idealism and logical empiricism share common ground in the view that reality can be understood only through tenseless language and that, consequently, statements purportedly about the past are philosophically defective. For this reason Bosanquet writes that history is "a hybrid form of experience, incapable of any considerable degree of 'being or trueness.' "[25] And Oakeshott writes that "no fact, truth or reality is, or can be, past. . . ." And again, "there are no facts at all which are not present absolutely."[26] More recently, Jack Meiland has defended a version of the idealist view of statements about the past which he calls the "construction" theory of history. On this theory historians should not be thought of as making statements about the past because there is no past reality for their statements to be *about*. Rather, history should be thought of as a study of the *present* understood in a tenseless way. The task of history, Meiland says, is "to give a coherent account of the present world as a whole."[27]

The views expressed in (1)–(3) are not forms of *scepticism* about the past. They do not purport to show that sentences about the past cannot be true or that we cannot know them to be true. They purport to show, rather, that we cannot say anything *about* the past at all, that any attempt to speak about the past must either turn out to be a way of talking about something else or a way of talking about *nothing* at all. Accordingly, we may call this view historical *nihilism* rather than historical scepticism. Given the well-entrenched position of historical nihilism in contemporary philosophy, it is perhaps not surprising that Hume commentators would have *conceptual* difficulties in appreciating a theory of meaning based on relations between present and past existences. It is largely for this reason that phenomenalism has been read persistently into Hume's theory of meaning despite the brutish inconsistencies it sometimes leaves in the text. We have also insight into why, caught in the coils of his own phenomenalism, Russell found the theory not only false but "hard to understand," and why Price was reduced to the high phenomenalistic emendation of the theory that Hume "ought to have made memory a third species of *acquaintance*, alongside of sensation and introspection" because comparison between past and present existences "requires an immediate apprehension of past impressions themselves." But Hume is surely right: it is "impossible to recal the past impressions, in order to compare them with our present ideas." There is no way to inspect past existences in the present, and there is no phenomenalistic acquaintance with the past.

But having rejected this objection to Hume's theory, one might still want to ask how *can* Hume compare a past existence with a present existence?

The question, however, is inappropriate insofar as it rests on the assumption that the past is a strange or dubious sort of reality requiring *special* explanation. Hume takes past existence and knowledge of it as primitive to the language of common life, just as phenomenalists and pragmatists take experience of the present and reference to the future as primitive. Any theory of meaning must take some concepts as basic in terms of which other concepts are explicated. So we must reply to this challenge that Hume can account for comparisons between past and present existences in whatever way phenomenalists can account for the possibility of experience of the present or in whatever way pragmatists can account for the possibility of comparisons between present and future existences.

III

We have now to consider an objection which, in effect, grants that comparisons between past and present existences are possible but holds that reference to the past is not part of the meanings of terms. We can begin with a comment by MacNabb: "The mysterious 'past reference' of an idea of memory is mentioned by Hume in the passage about the memory of a past idea (*Treatise*, Book I, Part III, Section VIII); but no attempt at clarification is made." [28] MacNabb gives no reason why the "past reference" of ideas should be "mysterious." It is not that mental images are logically incapable of referring to the past, for although MacNabb thinks Hume has confused mental images with ideas, that is, he says, a point "in addition to the mysteriousness of past reference." It appears, then, that some form of historical nihilism is behind MacNabb's perplexity—in this case, the presumption that past references are in some way conceptually odd. But one could just as well say that references to the present or to the future, or to non-temporal structures, are equally mysterious. Indeed, if it comes to that, there is something of a mystery that anything can *refer* to anything at all. So unless some special argument is given, there is no reason to find past reference mysterious.

Jonathan Bennett also finds Hume's past referential theory of meaning conceptually odd: "But if it really does matter now whether a given expression makes sense, then its making sense or not ought to show *now*: we ought to be able to settle the question by attending to the present and the future. Yet Hume, in trying to answer the question through his theory, implies that it is best answered by looking to the past." [29] Like MacNabb, Bennett betrays no need to explain why Hume is wrong in thinking that the question of determining meaning is "best answered by looking to the past"; much less does he try to determine emphatically how Hume could have made such a disastrous mistake. He is content simply to point out the supposed conceptual strangeness of the theory.

A more suggestive criticism offered by Bennett is the following: "What someone understands now is not logically tied to what he underwent earlier: the account of 'newly born' adults in Shaw's *Back to Methuselah* is a perfectly consistent fantasy." [30] With certain restrictions the fantasy is, indeed, consistent, and it will be instructive for an understanding of Hume's theory to see what these restrictions are.

It is logically possible for a being suddenly to appear before us having all the observation and disposition properties of an adult male. Upon inspection, he would look like an ordinary adult male; his organs would act normally, and his mind would be programed with a coherent set of thoughts about the past, all of which would be false. In fact, what is in general true of any adult male is true of him except that he has no past. Could we call him a man? In one sense we would have to; a thing is a man if it looks and functions like one. The fact that it lacks certain temporal properties should no more tell against its humanity than should a lack of spatial or color properties. Likewise, something could appear before us which has all the observation and disposition properties of a house but which has no past, and we would have to call it a house. It would, of course, be a strange house, but given a little time the usual questions of who owns the house, who should maintain it, and the like would arise. Indeed, it appears that anything with observation and disposition properties can be thought of as, logically, not requiring a past. The reason for this is that many concepts are atemporal and do not require reference to the past as a condition of their instantiation. Sensory concepts, concepts structured by atemporal scientific laws, theories, moral principles, mathematical principles, aesthetic principles, and the like are all atemporal. The entities instantiated by these concepts may be thought of as having no past, though they may in fact have one. And it is this logical fact about a very large and important class of concepts which has enabled Hume's commentators to find his past referential theory conceptually perplexing. But not all concepts are atemporal.

Consider again our man without a past which was designed to fit Bennett's objection to Hume's theory.[31] Although we may call him a man, a rational agent, a moral agent, a person, we cannot call him a father, priest, friend, senator, police officer, or lover. The reason is that these are, logically, past-entailing concepts which apply to the present on condition that certain statements about the past are true. We cannot apply the concept "is a priest" to an entity on the basis of observation and disposition properties alone. Indeed, there are no priest-like properties to be observed, the reason being that reference to the past is logically built into the concept of a priest, and the past is unobservable *in principle*. So we cannot observe an entity under the concept "is a priest" in the way we can observe an entity under the concept "is a man." Modern philosophers from Descartes on have found exciting and problematic the theoretical language of science because it appears to pick out explanatory entities which are unobservable in principle. Reflections on the meaning of theoretical language have spawned a plethora of epistemological and metaphysical doctrines to account for these exotic entities, the most prominent of which is the doctrine of double existence with its real invisible tables and illusory colored ones. But we need not have recourse to anything so remote as theoretical physics to find explanatory entities unobservable in principle. Common life provides us with ample material to marvel over. Part of the necessary conditions and all the sufficient conditions for someone's being a senator, friend, or priest are unobservable in principle. A priest *qua* priest looks like anybody else. Indeed, it is because the properties of being a priest are unobservable that vestments and clerical collars were devised: they are symbols of the past which structures the entity before us.

We should notice, however, that past-entailing concepts contain an atemporal element. If it is true that x is a priest, it follows (a) that x is a man, and (b) that certain obvious sentences about x's past are true; (a) is a tenseless truth condition, whereas (b) is a tensed one. It is important also to see that the relation between (a) and (b) is *analytic*. Athena *could* have been born full grown from the head of Zeus, and God could have created Adam out of the dust without a past, but not even God could create a nephew or a U. S. senator without a past. There cannot be any U. S. senators without a past stretching back at least to 1789 when the U. S. Constitution was ratified, and the concept of a U. S. senator is *logically* unintelligible without some concept of U. S. constitutional history.

What of future-entailing concepts? Are there any concepts which apply to the present on condition that statements about the future be true? Consider the following past-entailing concept applied to a present existent: (1) Here is the man who pitched two no-hitters in the 1970 World Series. The parallel application of a future-entailing concept to the present would be: (2) Here is the man who pitched two no-hitters in the 1989 World Series. Both (1) and (2) are false, but for different reasons: (1) is false because there is *in fact* no one who answers the description, (2) is false because there *cannot be* anyone who answers the description. If (2) were true, the 1989 World Series would already have occurred before it had in fact occurred. So (2) can be true only if fatalism is true. In general, no future-entailing concept can apply to the *present* unless fatalism is true. I shall assume the relatively non-controversial thesis that fatalism is false. If so, then, future-entailing concepts are impossible since they require a condition which cannot be satisfied. This does not mean, of course, that we cannot make rational predictions about the future. But one must note that the predicates in a sentence of the form S will be P are either atemporal or past-entailing: we make predictions about what will happen to men and senators, but we do not or should not make predictions about what will happen to the man who pitched two no-hitters in the 1989 World Series before the event occurs. Even concepts such as "is the heir-apparent" and "is condemned by law to death," which in some obvious way refer to the future, do not require true statements about the future (or even rational predictions) as a condition for their application to present existences. Hume's theory of meaning is a theory of how *terms* expressing ideas are meaningful, not a theory of how sentences, individually, or systems of sentences, are meaningful, and this is no doubt a limitation. But in this case, it is an illuminating one, for it points up the fact that we have only two sets of terms with which to describe the world: atemporal terms and past-entailing terms. However important the future might be, it does not semantically constitute our understanding of the world, whereas the past does:

this is the fundamental truth in Hume's past-entailing theory of meaning. If the future should somehow be cut away, all concepts which can properly be applied to the present would still apply; but if the past should be cut away, the present would be virtually *unintelligible*, for only atemporal concepts would remain. We would have the concept of men, women, and trees, but no concept of fathers, senators, Rembrandts, friends, no concept of the Bill of Rights; indeed, no concept at all of the world of common life which has reference to the past built into it. Without the past, common life would disintegrate into a state of nature with atemporal individuals pursuing atemporal goals disconnected from each other and from preceding generations like "the flies of a summer."

The language of common life, then, is constituted by past-entailing concepts; and since phenomenalism and pragmatism rule out past-entailing concepts, they are inadequate accounts of the language of common life. Whether they are adequate accounts of theoretical language, we cannot consider here. But it is important to observe that their failure to account for past-entailing concepts is due to an extravagant extension of an analysis of theoretical language into the language of common life. Consider Professor Murphy's recent defense of the high pragmatic explication of statements about the past: "George Washington enjoys at present the epistemological status of an electron: each is an entity postulated for the purpose of giving coherence to our present experience, and each is unobservable by us." [32] Like an electron, George Washington is, indeed, unobservable in principle, but if we must "postulate" this entity to account for present experience (understood in a temporally neutral sense), then we shall also have to postulate aunts, priests, friends, and police officers as theoretical entities; for, as we said earlier, these too are unobservable in principle and are necessary to account for the temporally neutral properties of present experience. But this is surely to twist theoretical language out of shape and to bloat theoretical entities beyond necessity.

Having rejected the tensed empirical theories of meaning (phenomenalism and pragmatism), we turn to the tenseless ones. If tensed expressions could be reduced to tenseless expressions, then Hume's past-entailing theory would have to be abandoned. Arthur Danto has argued, however, and I think conclusively, that no such reduction is likely. If we try to recast the sentence "Brown died at t" in the usual way as (1) "Brown dies at t" and (2) the utterance of (1) occurs after t, we still do not have the information that Brown's death is in the *past*, but only that it occurs prior to the utterance of (1). Similarly, 1984 is prior to 1985 but neither is past. [33]

We may conclude, then, that the main theories of meaning in the empirical tradition are inadequate insofar as they cannot account for past-entailing terms which are an all-pervasive part of the language of common life. Since Hume's past-entailing theory does allow for such terms, it is superior to the alternative accounts and should be taken seriously as a contribution to the theory of meaning.

I turn now to what is perhaps the most problematic part of Hume's theory. Past-entailing concepts such as "is a senator" presuppose atemporal concepts such as "is a man" as a condition of their intelligibility. How, then, can a past-entailing theory of meaning account for atemporal terms? Having worked through this question, we shall be in a position to appreciate the philosophical significance of a point made earlier: that Hume's theory has narrative form.

IV

The first problem is that Humean simple ideas such as "is red" do not seem to be past-entailing, and this has led some commentators to read Hume's theory as a tenseless one. Basson distinguishes two forms of theory: (1) that ideas resemble impressions, and (2) that ideas are derived from past impressions. As we saw earlier, he takes (1) to be analytic. But (2) is held to be "of subsidiary importance only, in so far as it lends a certain additional force to the principle of correspondence between simple impressions and simple ideas. The latter is Hume's chief analytical tool." [34] This enables Basson to graft Hume's theory onto logical empiricism, to read it as a tenseless theory, and thereby avoid its troublesome past-entailing character. Similar interpretations of Hume's theory as a prototype of logical empiricism have been put forth by MacNabb,[35] Flew,[36] Bennett,[37] and, more recently, by Noxon.[38] As charitable interpretations they are surely misplaced, for it is precisely the past-entailing character of the theory which makes it interesting and the lack of which makes logical empiricism uninteresting as an account of common language. But however this may be, Hume did think, rightly or wrongly, that expressions such as "is red" are past-entailing. He insists, as we saw, that mental imagery is a necessary condition for understanding the meaning of sensory terms and his paradigm for a sensory image is the *after*-image which may be thought of as analytically past-entailing. If Hume is right, then, what appear to be tenseless expressions such as "is red" have, logically, a past-entailing content.

Indeed, we may, if we wish, go on to read (2) as analytic in the same way as Basson reads (1) as analytic, and the interpretation of Hume's first principle urged earlier would give support to that move. But whether (2) is analytic or whether it just has a high degree of nomological force, it is an essential part of Hume's theory and has a much better claim to be his chief "analytical tool" than (1). As Zabeeh has argued: "All that Hume cares to establish is the fact of the priority of impressions to ideas, and the derivability of the latter from the former, and not the thesis that ideas are copies of impressions." [39] Hume is mainly concerned with examining complex ideas, especially complex ideas of reflection which constitute the objects of moral philosophy, and these complex ideas, though past-entailing, need not copy the impressions from which they are derived: "I observe, that many of our complex ideas never had impressions, that corresponded to them, and that many of our complex impressions never are exactly copied in ideas" (T 3; see also T 8). Thus "is a senator" is a complex past-entailing idea which does not copy the impressions from which it is derived. So even if we rejected (1) altogether, the most important part of Hume's theory would survive. Failure to appreciate this fact about the theory has led not only to misplaced charity but to misplaced criticism as well. Consider Frege's remarks: "Do the concepts as we approach their supposed sources, reveal themselves in peculiar purity? Not at all; we see everything as through a fog, blurred and undifferentiated. It is as though everyone who wished to know about America were to try to put himself back in the position of Columbus, at the time when he caught the first dubious glimpse of his supposed India." [40] Hume is certainly not committed to the view that a concept like "America" is a vague idea corresponding in some way to vivid past America-like impressions. "America" is a complex idea and need not correspond to any set of past impressions. Moreover, the concept of "America" is an unhappy choice for the kind of criticism Frege wants to make, for it is also a past-entailing concept. Frege considered all meaning to be tenseless, but if all past-entailing language were eliminated, expressions such as "is an American," "is the American Ideal of life," "is the American anthem" would be unintelligible.

But to return to our main question: how do atemporal concepts fit into Hume's past entailing theory? We shall begin with Hume's analysis of the idea of time. The account is first presented in Book I and further developed in Book II. No commentator has discussed the latter account, and many who have examined the former consider it disastrous. Laird found that it "deserves some of the very hard things that have been said of it," [41] and Kemp Smith found it "very bewildering." [42] But if both of Hume's accounts are considered, we have an analysis of time which despite its inadequacies is philosophically insightful and interesting.

The account in Book I yields two main conclusions. (1) Hume does not introduce the idea of time by deriving it from past impressions; instead he presents a purely formal analysis of the idea in the process of examining the question whether time is infinitely divisible. His conclusion is that our idea of time is the idea of an order of objects in succession, the simple parts of which are moments having no duration and so are not infinitely divisible. He then goes on to certify this conception of time by deriving it from past impressions. The example which corresponds to his formal account is "five notes play'd on a flute" which gives us "an impression and idea of time" (T 36). (2) Hume next draws ontological implications from his analysis, concluding that time (and space) not only can but " 'tis certain they actually do exist conformable to" the idea he presents of them (T 39). What is important about this analysis is that the idea of time is an *untensed* idea: it does not entail the ideas of past, present, and future. And since *real* time is said to conform to this idea, there is no past, present, or future in real time.

Since the idea of the past is not entailed in the idea of time (real time being untensed), Hume is not begging the question by explaining the idea of time by reference to past impressions. However, it does appear that the idea of the past entails the idea of untensed time, in roughly the same way that the past-referring concept "is a father" entails the atemporal concept "is a man." Taking this suggestion, we shall examine Hume's account of the idea of the past and its relation to untensed time. The idea of the past is, of course, a primitive idea in Hume's theory and cannot be explained by deriving it from past impressions. But from this it does not follow that the idea of the past is unanalyzable. Granting we have the idea, it is possible to examine its structure by comparing it with other ideas. This Hume does in Book II, Part III, Sections VII and VIII where he examines the influence of the ideas of space and time on the imagination.

The problem is why do we think about the past and future differently. If our only idea of time is the untensed idea of Book I, the problem could not even arise. So in explaining why we think differently about past and future, Hume is also explaining what we mean by *tensed* expressions. His analysis runs as follows. The focal idea for understanding what we mean by past and future is the idea of the present. What do we mean when we say that something is happening *now*? Hume's answer can be inferred from the following passages: "Ourself is intimately present to us, and whatever is related to self must partake of that quality" (T 427). " 'Tis obvious, that the imagination can never totally forget the points of space and time, in which we are existent; but receives such frequent advertisements of them from the passions and senses, that however it may turn its attention to foreign and remote objects, it is necessitated every moment to reflect on the present" (T 427–28). The present is not experienced as an objective feature of real time but as a certain relation of real time to self-awareness. Hume seems to be saying that by the present we mean the self-awareness that what we are experiencing is occurring at the same time as our experience of it. Or as he metaphorically puts it: our position in the present is derived from the "advertisements" of our position in time given by the "passions and senses" and not from any perception of a present tense structure in time itself. And since "there is a continual succession of perceptions in our mind; so that the idea of time [is] for ever present with us," we always have a self-reflective idea of the present (T 65).

Given this analysis of the idea of the present, definitions of the past and future come easy. Past events are just those occurring earlier than now, and future events are just those occurring later than now. Recall that although Hume ontologized the untensed idea of time introduced in Book I, he does not ontologize the tensed idea of time introduced in Book II. The ideas of tensed time are ideas of reflection and so are ideas of passions. As such they are structures of the imagination and not of time as it is in itself. Tensed ideas make possible what might be called tensed passions such as the past-referring passion of veneration and the future-referring passion of anticipation. But what is most important for our purposes is that the ideas of these tensed passions function also as categories of narrative understanding, a point which will be developed shortly.

We turn now to Hume's account of the tensed passions. The first question raised is why, all things being equal, do we have a more lively conception of objects removed in the future than we do for those removed an equal distance in the past? Hume's answer is derived from three properties of the fancy.

(1) The imagination is essentially present-oriented: "however it may turn its attention to foreign and remote objects, it is necessitated every moment to reflect on the present" (T 428).

(2) In reflecting on temporally remote objects, "we take them in their proper order and situation, and never leap from one object to another, . . . without running over, at least in a cursory manner, all those objects, which are interpos'd betwixt them. When we reflect, therefore, on any object distant from ourselves, we are oblig'd not only to reach it at first by passing thro' all the intermediate space betwixt ourselves and the object, but also to renew our progress every moment; being every moment recall'd to the consideration of ourselves and our present situation" (T 428). This certifies the view that the idea of any past tense or future tense object is a temporally complex idea entailing: (a) the temporally distant object along with (b) the awareness of the self's present temporal location as explained above, and (c) the idea of what is thought to be the correct temporal order between (a) and (b). We have seen how on Hume's theory of meaning all ideas have a past-referring content; we now see that ideas of the past and future refer to the self's recognition of its place in the present and to the untensed order of time. Neither of these points could have been brought out in the early pages of the *Treatise* because Hume had not yet introduced the idea of time, and the idea of the self is not introduced as a category of explanation until Book II.

(3) "Besides the propensity to a gradual progression thro' the points of . . . time . . . We always follow the succession of time in placing our ideas, and from the consideration of any object pass more easily to that, which follows immediately after it, than to that which went before it. We may learn this, among other instances, from the order, which is always observ'd in historical narrations" (T 430). The view here is that time as an order of succession has a direction or "arrow" which is causally reflected in a propensity of the imagination. Again, the direction of time itself is not from past to future, but the real direction of time, reflected in the imagination and anchored on our self-awareness of the present, yields what we call a direction from past to future.

Using propensities (1)-(3), we can now state Hume's explanation why we have a more lively conception of future objects than of those removed an equal distance in the past. The "present situation of the person is always that of the imagination, and . . . 'tis from thence we proceed to the conception of any distant object" (T 430). When the object is past, the progression of thought in passing to it from the present "is contrary to nature, as proceeding from one point of time to that which is preceding, and from that to another preceding, in opposition to the natural course of the succession." But when we turn our thought to the future object, the "fancy flows along the stream of time" and arrives at the object by an order which seems natural "passing always from one point of time to that which is immediately posterior to it." This "*easy* progression of ideas" gives us a stronger conception of future tense ideas than we have of past tense ideas where we "are oblig'd to overcome the difficulties arising from the natural propensity of the fancy." Moreover, this future-referring propensity of the fancy is brought into play, to some degree or other, upon the conception of any temporally disposed object. Past and present objects are always conceived in association with some idea of the future: "The fancy anticipates the course of things, and surveys the object in that condition, to which it tends, as well as in that, which is regarded as the present." In thinking this way, we "advance, rather than retard our existence. . . . By which means we conceive the future as flowing every moment nearer us, and the past as retiring" (T 430, 431, 432). In this way Hume provides a ground for explicating such future-directed passions as anticipation, hope, anxiety, destiny, and fate. Whitehead once remarked that if the future is cut away, "the present collapses, emptied of its proper content." [43] But if Hume's theory of meaning is right, the present would lose none of its semantic content. It would, however, lose its "life" or, in Hume's terms, the idea that our present is "continually encreasing" as opposed to "continually diminishing" (T 432).

The second question to be considered is why do we have a greater veneration and esteem for an object in the remote past than for one in the remote future. To answer this question, Hume uses the three propensities mentioned above along with two more.

(4) " 'Tis a quality very observable in human nature, that any opposition, which does not entirely discourage and intimidate us, has rather a contrary effect, and inspires us with a more than ordinary grandeur and magnanimity" (T 433).

(5) " 'tis evident that the mere view and contemplation of any greatness, whether successive or extended, enlarges the soul, and give it a sensible delight and pleasure. A wide plain, the ocean, eternity, a succession of several ages; all these . . . excel every thing, however beautiful, which accompanies not its beauty with a suitable greatness" (T 432). Now, although it is difficult to conceive of a past object because of the propensity of the imagination to conceive of future objects which extend our existence, this propensity can be overcome. The "difficulty, when join'd with a small distance, interrupts and weakens the fancy: But has a contrary effect in a great removal. The mind, elevated by the vastness of its object, is still farther elevated by the difficulty of the conception; and being oblig'd every moment to renew its efforts in the transition from one part of time to another, feels a . . . vigorous and sublime disposition" which by association is transferred to the idea of the distant past object and "gives us a proportionable veneration for it" (T 436). It is "as if our ideas acquir'd a kind of gravity from their objects" (T 435), so that the remote past is seen as a realm of monumental greatness, a source of authority and standards: "Hence we imagine our ancestors to be, in a manner, mounted above us, and our posterity to lie below us" (T 437). On this rudimentary passion of temporal piety are grounded the passions of veneration, love of antiquity, and, most important, the purely temporal standards framed in traditions, customs, precedent, and prescription. Indeed, even the standards of causal inference derive much of their authority from this normative manner of conceiving the past.

It should be stressed that the greatness and normative character of the past is determined *a priori* by an original propensity of the mind and not as the result of applying any temporally neutral standard. We may, of course, take a temporally neutral stance and find our ancestors to be inferior to us in many ways, e.g., in matters of health and scientific knowledge; but in Hume's view, this can never lead to a *total* rejection of the normative past unless we are prepared to think *only* in a temporally neutral way but at the cost of eliminating all past-entailing expressions and, with them, virtually everything we consider important in common life. This specifically Humean conclusion can be easily underrated and so needs further comment.

Entire social and political orders are grounded in traditions, and at the root of these traditions are what might be called normative institutions and individuals: the Magna Carta, the Bill of Rights, the Last Supper, the Founding Fathers, the Church Fathers, and so on. For these events and individuals men have a temporal affection and piety, and it is this *passion* of reflection which transforms them into normative entities from which flow a great variety of religious, legal, political, and social standards of varying degrees of authority. To operate in common life, these standards, logically, and in fact, need have no temporally neutral justification such as a utilitarian or moral justification. Hume did not deny the existence of temporally neutral standards nor the possibility of using them to evaluate the traditions which constitute common life. But he recognized that the authority of the past is internal to every institution and individual in common life and that the social and political critic who applies temporally neutral standards to society must not make the mistake of ontologizing them and inferring that the entities he is evaluating are themselves temporally neutral existences. So even if we apply temporally neutral standards to society, there will always be a purely temporal authority to tradition which must be recognized and which constitutes both a limit within which the evaluation must operate and a barrier to any temporally neutral total critique of the tradition. In this way Hume's past-entailing theory of meaning provides broad conceptual support for his social and political conservatism. But Hume's account of the authority of tradition differs from that of most conservatives. The oldest theory is that the Founders received their wisdom from a divine authority, a theory defended by Burke and many later conservatives, making the tradition a sacred one. For Hume, however, the authority of tradition lies not in a divine origin but in an original "property of the fancy" (T 431). The individuals and institutions of common life are the products of *thought* and in particular of temporal associations. As long as the imagination remains the same, there will be tensed language and so Founders, traditions, prescriptive rules, relics, and all the other past-entailing structures of common life.

We are now in a position to answer the question of how atemporal concepts can be worked into Hume's past-entailing theory of meaning. Although Hume does not try to reduce tenseless expressions to tensed expressions, he does think that we understand tenseless expressions only in a tensed context. The most striking case of this is deriving the untensed idea of time from past impressions. The procedure is paradoxical for the following reason. Tensed concepts, as we saw, entail untensed concepts, but untensed concepts do not entail tensed concepts, e.g., "is past" entails "before and after" but the latter does not entail the former. Now, if in understanding a tensed concept we are logically committed to understanding a tenseless concept, why does Hume require that we view the latter in a tensed light as a condition of understanding it? This brings us to the rationale of Hume's historical theory of meaning and the final assessment of its value.

Theories of meaning in the empirical tradition have functioned more like *metaphysical* theories than like analyses of how words actually have meaning. In some form or other, they have been referential theories and have always generated some line marking off the distinction between reality and illusion. And it is their purported power to govern ontological decisions which has been their most interesting and controversial feature; for instance, if the phenomenalistic and pragmatic theories of meaning are right, there are no facts about the past because there is no past *reality*. And like metaphysical systems, they are modeled on structures of significance which are thought to be paradigmatic for an explication of the nature of understanding and reality. The phenomenalist finds a paradigm in immediate sense experience and from that generates categories of meaningful discourse, understanding, and reality. In the same way, the pragmatist finds instrumental activity paradigmatic, and the logical empiricist finds systematic activity paradigmatic. Hume, we may say, finds the *narrative* structure of historical inquiry paradigmatic and from it generates categories of meaning and understanding. To have value, it is enough that these theories uncover some aspect of understanding and reality which would otherwise have remained obscure. And this is the value of Hume's historical theory of meaning. It brings into focus what the other theories had obscured: the importance of past-entailing language, narrative thought as a form of understanding, and the past as a category of reality.

Arthur Danto, who has done more than any other contemporary philosopher to explicate the logic of narrative thinking, has proposed what he calls "narrative sentences" as the basic logical unit of narrative significance. "Their most general characteristic is that they refer to at least two time-separated events though they only *describe* (are only *about*) the earliest event to which they refer." [44] Narratives reveal the meanings of past events by viewing them in the light of temporally later events. In a clear non-linguistic sense of meaning we may ask for the meaning of an event in a story. Thus Lincoln's birth, which at the time of its occurrence had no special meaning, can be seen to have meaning in the light of later events as in the narrative sentence: "In 1809 the man who issued the Emancipation Proclamation was born." It is on this narrative structure of significance that Hume tries to ground a theory of meaning and understanding. Impressions on their first appearance are unintelligible and have no meaning for us. It is only *after* they have occurred that we have an idea of them. So the meaning structure of a simple Humean idea is narrative in form: a past impression is viewed in the light of a later event which conveys significance to it and, because of that fact, is called an idea. After we have acquired a simple idea, we can, by attending to those aspects in which it resembles other ideas, and ignoring their differences, form an idea of its universal significance. And this universal significance would, of course, be tenseless.

Given this tenseless information, we can then see for the first time that our narrative perceptions of the world presupposed all along a tenseless structure. It is then we recognize that impressions are in themselves tenseless and that real time is tenseless.

Given the idea of universal meanings, we can form general rules and standards which give us a temporally neutral perspective from which to evaluate the various temporally provincial narrative orders which the imagination has woven. So not all relations founded by association of ideas are narrative, or, to recast a dictum of Kant's: although all our knowledge begins in narrative form, it is not determined by narrative form. Of the seven philosophical relations mentioned in the *Treatise*, only causality (which is the only relation capable of determining matters of fact) is necessarily narrative in form. When we say that A caused B, whatever else we are doing, we are judging A to be significant in the light of a temporally later event, and that is a narrative relation. Nor can we say that all narrative relations are causal. To say that Hume is a precursor of modern empiricism is to assert a narrative relation but not, presumably, a causal one. In the Christmas story, King Herod sought to kill a child under the narrative description of one born King of the Jews, but the description is not a causal one; indeed, it is a description of a *fated* birth, which is why Herod's act appears hopelessly impotent. When Marx says that all history is the history of class struggle, he is asserting a narrative relation which is projected onto the whole of history, including the future. But it is not clear that this description is a causal one. Indeed, it appears to be a fated description very much like the King Herod case. Even the problem of induction as Hume formulated it has narrative form. To ask whether the future will be like the past is to put the causal relation in a tensed and narrative context. It is at the very least an attempt to understand *now* the significance of present and past events in the light of future events. The question seems to be motivated by a desire to project narrative forms into the future, and this comes very close to the desire for fated knowledge of the present. But the whole problem of induction changes if we recast it into a tenseless idiom. For then, our knowledge of the past is seen to be as problematic as our knowledge of the future, or, rather, no logical weight can be given to the one over the other. But it is not clear that inductive thinking *can* be emancipated from its narrative roots.

All of this is intentionally sketchy, but enough has been said, perhaps, to suggest that narrative structures are philosophically interesting and deserve more attention than they have received. To say that x caused y, x is a precursor of y, x is a founder of y, x is in the vanguard of y, x is fated to be y, x is more progressive than y, is to make narrative assertions. But these assertions make different claims and have different truth conditions. Until we have a clear idea of the nature and limits of narrative significance, we may easily take one assertion to have the logic of the other, saying one thing when we must be meaning something else.

Although Hume's theory of meaning and understanding is narrative in structure, he did not work out a systematic theory of the nature and limits of narrative thought; nor, for that matter, has any such theory been worked out since. Yet there are scattered hints throughout the *Treatise* and other works, and it is significant that the chapter "Of the Association of Ideas" in the Hendel edition of the first *Enquiry* is devoted almost entirely to a discussion of the nature of narration in history and epic poetry as a way of explaining the theory of association. But perhaps Hume's most suggestive contribution to the analysis of narrative thinking is in the sections of Book II we have examined, where we find that tensed structures are mind dependent which entails that narrative structures are also. Yet Hume holds at the same time that the narrative pattern is a form of *understanding*. The suggestion, then, is that the narrative form of the imagination is brought in to structure an essentially tenseless reality in order to understand it. This is certainly true of the individuals and institutions of common life which, being past-referring and *constituted* by the narrative imagination, are usually understood only in the narrative way (we can, of course, always adopt, for limited purposes, a temporally neutral view of common life).

Hume, in these sections, is aware that he is breaking new ground and senses that his readers may grow impatient; he appears to cut his treatment short, and pleads as his excuse for continuing at all "the curiousness of the subject" (T 432). The reason the subject is only "curious" and not "serious" is that history (and other narrative forms of inquiry such as evolutionary biology) had not yet begun to challenge theoretical physics as the paradigm of inquiry. But already in Hume's time metaphysical philosophies of history were being presented as ultimate forms of inquiry more profound than theoretical physics. The third edition of Vico's *Scienza nuova* appeared in 1744, the year of his death. In it he argued that only God can ultimately understand nature since He alone made it. But man has made history and so can have an ultimate understanding of it. History, therefore, and not physics must be for man the paradigm of inquiry.[45] Turgot, Condorcet, Kant, and Fichte, following Vico, worked out sketches of a progressive metaphysical history which includes the whole of man's past and future. It is with Hegel, however, that history first takes on full metaphysical form. Certainly Hegel was the first to ontologize the narrative form of thought rigorously and to hold that reality must be conceived to have *narrative* structure and so must be conceived as spiritual activity. Parallel to Hume's semantic thesis that all our ideas have a past-entailing content is Hegel's remark on how the deepest sort of inquiry, now conceived in narrative form, proceeds: "When philosophy paints its gray in gray, a form of life has become old, and this gray in gray cannot rejuvenate it, only understand it. The owl of minerva begins its flight when dusk is falling." [46]

Following Hegel, a plethora of metaphysical histories was developed in the nineteenth century by such men as Comte, Fourier, Buckle, and Marx, all comprehending, in concept, the past and future of man's history and all following in their own way Hegel's dictum that "Philosophy concerns itself only with the glory of the Idea mirroring itself in the History of the World." [47] We saw that ontologizing the tenseless theoretical language of physics leads to the doctrine of "double existence" and a consequent alienation from common life. But there is a parallel doctrine of double existence which comes from ontologizing *narrative* language. There is, on the one hand, the category of reality: the real movement of history which is typically a struggle of some favored class, race, group, or idea directed toward an inevitable fulfillment or liberation which is seen as a demand of history itself. On the other hand, there is the category of illusion: the parallel class, race, group, or idea which obstructs, is oppressive, and yet necessary for the dialectical movement of history toward its fulfillment. Progressive metaphysical philosophies of history preside over the large ideological issues of today, and the doctrine of double existence peculiar to them has informed many mass social and political "movements" in the twentieth century. The empirical tradition, with the exception of Hume, has been profoundly ahistorical and, consequently, has not developed the conceptual tools for a just and searching criticism of *historical metaphysics*. In Hume's historical theory of meaning, however, and the narrative pattern of understanding he built upon it, we find an appreciation of the importance of narrative thought *and* a recognition of its limits. On these two insights, one can see dimly a form of empiricism, historically oriented, and in the Humean spirit logically capable of placing a check on the intrusion of this new doctrine of double existence into common life.

NOTES

1. Ralph W. Church, *Hume's Theory of the Understanding* (Ithaca, 1935), p. 27.

2. C. D. Broad, "Hume's Doctrine of Space," Dawes Hicks Lecture on Philosophy, *Proceedings of the British Academy*, 47 (1961), 165.

3. Antony Flew, *Hume's Philosophy of Belief* (New York, 1969), p. 26.

4. Jonathan Bennett, *Locke, Berkeley, Hume* (Oxford, 1971), p. 229.

5. A. H. Basson, *David Hume* (Baltimore, 1958), p. 37.

6. Ludwig Wittgenstein, *On Certainty*, edd. G. E. M. Anscombe and G. H. von Wright (Oxford, 1969), paragraph 167; see also paragraphs 98, 321.

7. Nelson Goodman, *Fact, Fiction, and Forecast* (Indianapolis, 1965), chaps. 3–4.

8. Flew, *Hume's Philosophy of Belief*, pp. 22–23.

9. Norman Kemp Smith, *The Philosophy of David Hume* (New York, 1964), p. 485; see also p. 482.

10. Ibid., p. 212.

11. John Passmore, *Hume's Intentions* (London, 1952), p. 93.

12. Flew, *Hume's Philosophy of Belief*, p. 47.

13. R. B. Braithwaite, *Scientific Explanation* (New York, 1960), chaps. 1–4.

14. Arthur Eddington, *The Nature of the Physical World* (Ann Arbor, 1968), p. xiv.

15. Charles Fourier, *Œuvres complètes*, 6 vols. (Paris, 1846–48), VI xv.

16. Bertrand Russell, *The Analysis of Mind* (London, 1924), p. 159.

17. Church, *Hume's Theory of the Understanding*, p. 27.

18. John Laird, *Hume's Philosophy of Human Nature* (London, 1932), p. 32.

19. H. H. Price, *Hume's Theory of the External World* (Oxford, 1948), p. 5.

20. Passmore, *Hume's Intentions*, p. 94.

21. Farhang Zabeeh, *Hume: Precursor of Modern Empiricism*, 2nd rev. ed. (The Hague, 1973), p. 57.

22. A. J. Ayer, *Language, Truth and Logic* (London, 1946), p. 19.

23. C. I. Lewis, *Mind and the World Order* (New York, 1956), pp. 140, 142.

24. A. J. Ayer, *The Problem of Knowledge* (Baltimore, 1956), p. 160; Willard Van Orman Quine, *Word and Object* (Cambridge, 1960), pp. 170–73.

25. Bernard Bosanquet, *The Principle of Individuality and Value* (London, 1912), pp. 146–47.

26. Michael Oakeshott, *Experience and Its Modes* (Cambridge, 1933), p. 108.

27. Jack Meiland, *Scepticism and Historical Knowledge* (New York, 1965), p. 192.

28. D. G. C. MacNabb, *David Hume* (Hamden, 1966), p. 42.

29. Bennett, *Locke, Berkeley, Hume*, pp. 229–30.

30. Ibid., p. 228.

31. The examination of temporal concepts which follows is based on Arthur Danto's profound analysis of historical language in *Analytical Philosophy of History* (Cambridge, 1965). See esp. chaps. 4–6.

32. Murray G. Murphy, *Our Knowledge of the Historical Past* (New York, 1973), p. 16.

33. Danto, *Analytical Philosophy of History*, pp. 53–62.

34. Basson, *David Hume*, p. 37.

35. MacNabb, *David Hume*, pp. 23–32.

36. Flew, *Hume's Philosophy of Belief*, pp. 29–30.

37. Bennett, *Locke, Berkeley, Hume*, p. 231.

38. James Noxon, *Hume's Philosophical Development* (Oxford, 1973), p. 150.

39. Zabeeh, *Hume*, p. 55; T 634.

40. Gottlob Frege, *The Foundations of Arithmetic* (Oxford, 1950), p. viii.

41. Laird, *Hume's Philosophy of Human Nature*, p. 77.

42. Kemp Smith, *Philosophy of David Hume*, p. 310.

43. Alfred North Whitehead, *Adventures of Ideas* (New York, 1933), p. 246.

44. Danto, *Analytical Philosophy of History*, p. 143.

45. *The New Science of Giambattista Vico*, trans. Thomas Goddard Bergin and Max Harold Fisch (Ithaca, 1968), para. 331, pp. 52–53.

46. G. W. F. Hegel, *Philosophy of Right and Law, or Natural Law and Political Science Outlined*, trans. J. M. Sterret and C. J. Friedrich in *The Philosophy of Hegel*, ed. Carl J. Friedrich (New York, 1954), p. 227.

47. G. W. F. Hegel, *The Philosophy of History*, trans. J. Sibree (New York, 1944), p. 457.

11

Hume and Conservatism

SHELDON S. WOLIN
Princeton University

ALTHOUGH DAVID HUME'S STATURE AS A PHILOSOPHER has rarely been questioned, his claims as a political theorist have fared less well. Jefferson showed deep hostility toward Hume's ideas, while John Adams could find agreement with only a few points.[1] Later opinion has been less vehement but still reserved. Thomas Huxley thought Hume's political writings suggestive, but on the whole marred by an unabased desire for literary success.[2] In Sir Leslie Stephen's judgment Hume was guilty of a "cynical conservatism" which was at once superficial and unhistorical.[3]

Studies, such as those of Sabine and Halévy, have established more securely Hume's place in political thought but have left certain ambiguities. Sabine has coupled Hume with Burke as an opponent of eighteenth-century rationalism, while Halévy viewed him as a forerunner of the "philosophical radicalism" of Bentham, Adam Smith, James Mill, and Ricardo.[4] To have fathered squabbling children is always something of an embarrassment, but particularly so when one is, like Hume, temperamentally averse to taking sides. It is true, nonetheless, that if a temporary distinction is made between Hume's doctrine and his influence, it is possible to maintain that his influence worked in two quite different directions. His inquiries into causation, the role of reason, and the nature of moral judgments helped eventually to undermine the natural law structure of eighteenth-century liberalism, while his emphasis on utility as the test of institutions contributed an important ingredient to Benthamite liberalism. On the other hand, his attack on reason and its claims to universal truths helped to relieve eighteenth-century conservatives of a potent enemy and prepared the way for the authority of sentiment and feeling. Hume's labors, then, worked to alter the future course of both liberalism and conservatism.

This double aspect of Hume's influence, however, has served to obscure his own political doctrines. The latter warrant some attention because in

An earlier version of this essay appeared in the *American Political Science Review*, 48, No. 4 (December 1954), 999–1016; permission to reprint has been obtained from the Editor of that journal.

doctrine, as well as in personal inclination, he was a conservative, but of a distinctive kind. While the character of his conservatism was somewhat colored by its being formulated in the more placid era which preceded the French Revolution, its distinctiveness had its roots in Hume's peculiar relationship to the Enlightenment. Later conservatives tended to lump together the Enlightenment with the Revolution and to damn the former because of its presumed relation to the latter. Rationalism and *sans-culottism* were viewed as two sides of the same coin. "The eighteenth century," declared De Maistre, "which distrusted itself in nothing, hesitated at nothing."

The so-called "crisis of the eighteenth century," when the full impact of seventeenth-century rationalist and scientific modes of thought was felt, constituted a watershed for modern political thought. And the attack on the authority of accepted ideas was soon accompanied by an attack on the legitimacy of accepted institutions. "Rude establishments," wrote Bentham, must be brought "to the test of polished reason." Under the impress of revolutionary events set in motion in America and in Europe, modern conservatism was formed. In its origins, conservatism was not so much a defense of the existing order, which had been breached by the establishment of revolutionary regimes, as a sustained attack on the rationalist currents which had come to dominate much of European thinking since the days of Hobbes, Descartes, and Newton. Whatever else may be said of the conservative response, it cannot be held to have disagreed about the identity of its enemy. Burke's strictures against "men of theory," Hegel's condemnation of the "abstract reason" of the French revolutionaries, and Metternich's sarcasms about the "presumptuous man" were all testimony to an almost unanimous rejection of the claims of reason to be the ultimate arbiter in political questions. According to the conservative indictment, the Enlightenment, inspired by a destructive rationalism, had succeeded in loosening the cohesive ties of society; it had insisted that slumbering beliefs and institutions, which men had unthinkingly and naturally "accepted," be made to undergo the ordeal of conscious, rational acceptance.

Given this view of the Enlightenment as a kind of extended orgy of rationalism, conservatives were irresistibly drawn to some form of political supernaturalism. For, as De Maistre put it, the rationalist has engaged in "an insurrection against God" whereby "the trowel believes himself the architect." The political community, according to the conservatives, was part of the time dimension of history to which "political geometry" could never do justice. History, in turn, was "the great drama of an ever-unfolding Providence," [5] or, in Burke's phrase, an expression of the "divine tactic" which men could only faintly comprehend. Of the political community, men could only know that it was part of a providential pattern; they could not know its ultimate basis. The last resort of conservatism, then, was to invoke a veil of mystery and to warn that men plumb the origins of society at their peril; the "natural" forces of society, in response to a divine imperative, worked in a wondrous fashion beside which the cleverest political contrivances stood as pale imitations.

These constitute some of the main elements in the conservative tradition as it developed near the end of the eighteenth century. It is against this background that the earlier conservatism of Hume assumes some significance. The first fundamental respect in which his position differed from that outlined above was that his was a conservatism without benefit of mystery. There was no recourse to a "divine tactic," a *Weltgeist*; nor any disposition, such as displayed by Coleridge, to revive Scripture as a "statesman's manual." Hume's conclusions were stubbornly rooted in a strictly secular analysis, with experience as the final court of appeal. Secondly, Hume's conservatism was constructed from the very materials of the Enlightenment: its quest for objective analysis, its distrust of obscurantism, its faith in empirical data, its disdain for the *a priori*, and its strong emphasis on the criterion of utility. He employed the Enlightenment methods of analysis to probe the roots of established pieties and institutions, and he carried it out with the sort of dispassion which Coleridge was to call "cold-blooded." Thirdly, his was a conservatism which owed no inspiration to catastrophe, impending or past, but rather reflected the "peace of the Augustans." Consequently, Hume exhibited none of the heightened sensitivity of later conservatives to the necessity for strong authority as the main guarantor of unity. Where later De Bonald was to assert that "outside religious and political unity man can find no truth and society no salvation," Hume was content with the matter-of-fact judgment that society was a product of human interests whose satisfaction provided the requisite amount of social cohesion.

Nevertheless, Hume was something more than the Enlightenment incarnate, for his significance is that he turned against the Enlightment its own weapons. And herein lies his importance as a conservative thinker. His starting point is to be found in *A Treatise of Human Nature* (1739–40) which bears the subtitle "An attempt to introduce the experimental method of reasoning into moral subjects." The first book illustrates Hume's tactic: to whittle down the claims of reason by the use of rational analysis. Reason, he contended, was admittedly an instrument for advancing our knowledge, but it was an instrument with a circumscribed sphere of activity:

> Reason is the discovery of truth or falsehood. Truth or falsehood consists in an agreement or disagreement either to the *real* relations of ideas, or to *real* existence and matter of fact. Whatever, therefore, is not susceptible of this agreement or disagreement, is incapable of being true or false, and can never be an object of reason [T 458].

The consequence of this conclusion was to stake off an important realm either impervious to reason or within which reason played only a derivative role. Thus what men described as cause and effect was not a deductive conclusion of reason but the product of experience: we have become accustomed to seeing a certain effect follow from a given cause, but, strictly speaking, there existed no logically necessary connection between the two.

Facts were derived from observation, not from reason; hence reason could not be employed to prove or disprove the existence of a fact. Human behavior, in turn, was governed largely by unanalyzed experience or habits. "Custom," Hume concluded, "is the great guide of human life" (EHU 44).

The significance of Hume's argument was not merely that it greatly extended the reign of custom at the expense of reason, but that it undercut the whole idea of an underlying rational harmony in nature, a harmony from which eighteenth-century rationalists had deduced the existence of universal moral imperatives. Hume destroyed this assumption, not by a frontal assault, but by the contention that the external order was not a discovery of reason but was rooted in "the principles of human nature." The "order" which we attribute to the phenomenal world rests really on a conviction and not on a process of logical validation; it is the "force and vivacity" which the idea of an "order" exerts on our imagination which explains its hold (T 94–106).

Equally modest was the role assigned reason by Hume in matters of morals. Reason functioned as a calculator, an instrument of analysis. It was "perfectly inert" in the sense that it provided neither the springs of human action nor the final judgment in questions of moral controversy. In Hume's view, human actions were stimulated initially by the passions, which were a response to a direct emotional experience. The passions, in short, were the active, generating factor in human behavior. Consequently, they could not be yoked or restrained by reason, as the rationalists maintained, because this would be to argue that an inert principle could control an active one. Hence the famous conclusion: "Reason is, and ought only to be, the slave of the passions, and can never pretend to any other office than to serve and obey them" (T 415). Passions were thus outside the range of rational criticism, except as they might be based on a false supposition about objects which had no existence, or as the passions selected inadequate means for the fulfillment of their ends. Reason could indicate the tendencies and consequences of certain actions, but sentiment or feeling alone could actively stimulate us to follow one choice rather than another. Again, reason dealt with facts and relations, but moral concepts, such as "crime" or "ingratitude," were not analyzable as facts or relations except by ignoring the original source of the concept itself in our sentiments or feelings. For example, certain elements of a "crime" could be analyzed by the understanding into components, but the totality of these did not equal a "crime"; it was only as our feelings affixed such a designation that certain actions took on a moral meaning. "The approbation or blame which then ensues, cannot be the work of the judgement, but of the heart . . ." (EMP 290). Thus, since morals were linked to the passions or feelings, and since reason was unable to master the latter, it followed that morals could never be designated true or false, reasonable or unreasonable.

The net effect of this argument was, of course, to undermine the whole theory of natural law with its immutable values discoverable by rational inquiry. Having withdrawn morals from the jurisdiction of reason, Hume was prepared to maintain that morality was "more properly felt than judg'd of"

(T 470).[6] Morality derived from a moral sense which received impressions; these might be either pleasing or displeasing. Actions or situations which cause pleasing impressions men have identified as good or virtuous, their contraries as bad. When it is asked, what is it which renders some impressions pleasurable and others painful, Hume's reply was that in some instances it was "natural" for men to feel delight or aversion; in other cases the response was due to habit or conditioning. Morals were, then, a product of nature *or* convention, but, as Hume pointed out in his discussion of justice:

> Mankind is an inventive species; and where an invention is obvious and absolutely necessary, it may as properly be said to be natural as any thing that proceeds immediately from original principles, without the intervention of thought or reflexion. Tho' the rules of justice be *artificial*, they are not *arbitrary* [T 484].

Thus art could be fused with nature, and when innovation became overlain with habit, the distinction between the artificial and the natural vanished.

There existed, in this line of argument, a subtle difference between Hume and later conservatives. Some conservatives, Sir William Blackstone for example, were to maintain that a rational institution or law could be declared "natural" on the grounds that its long existence demonstrated its rationality and naturalness. Hume, however, in denying the relationship between the rational and the natural, was asserting quite another basis for the validity of institutions: an arrangement might, through usage, become habitual and therefore "natural," but this had nothing to do with its rationality and rationality had nothing to do with it.

The full implications of Hume's analysis were not to be realized until after the revolutionary events in America and France had made their mark. Prior to that time little difference existed between conservative and radical theorists in the approach taken to political problems. The points of disagreement between John Adams and Jefferson in America, Blackstone and Priestley in England, or D'Argenson and Diderot in France were less striking than the degree to which they shared a common premiss that the test of a political system or a particular policy was a matter of rational demonstration. The influence of Hume's iconoclasm, however, was to dissolve this area of agreement by showing that ultimate truth could not be proven by rational methods. And after 1789 both sides were to become increasingly preoccupied with ultimate truths. By restricting reason to a narrow zone between experience and the passions, Hume cleared the way for political romanticism. "Nothing is more free," he wrote, "than the imagination of man. . . ." The "difference between *fiction* and *belief* lies in some sentiment or feeling, which is annexed to the latter, not to the former, and which depends not on the will, nor can be commanded at pleasure" (EHU 47, 48).

In fairness to Hume it should be noted that his remarks cannot be turned into a justification for some of the later extravagances of the romantics. Habit, emotion, and imagination did not constitute political values in his system, but belonged to the catalog of descriptive facts concerning human behavior. They might, and often did, have valuable consequences, yet they were not values in themselves. It was true that on occasion Hume might casually remark that in philosophy, as in music and poetry, "we must follow our taste and sentiment" (T 103), but he was aware that this might prove too much. After all, he cautioned, there was a clear difference between "a poetical enthusiasm" and "a serious conviction" resting on "reflexion and general rules." [7] Negatively, however, Hume's labors worked towards the alteration of the future course of conservatism. With reason discredited, new premisses could be fashioned from custom and sentiment.

II

The quest for a science of politics was one of the great intellectual adventures of the Enlightenment.[8] It was believed, perhaps not logically, that a science of this kind would be a natural ally of reform and progress. It was almost inevitable, given the cautious disposition of conservatives toward political and social change, that a deep hostility toward a science of politics should color conservative thought of the late-eighteenth century. Here again Hume took a different tack. While sharing the conservative distrust of reform, he was still convinced that the study of politics could achieve the status of a science. At the same time, he demonstrated that there was no inherent necessity that such a science led to radical conclusions.

Although Hume remarked in one place that "the world is still too young to fix many general truths in politics, which will remain true to the latest posterity" (Essays 89), his works were studded with references to "causes and principles eternal and immutable" and to "universal axioms." While he admitted that social sciences, dealing as they did with matters of fact, could not aspire to the same degree of certitude as mathematics, dealing as it did with relations between ideas, Hume did go so far as to assert that the social sciences were capable of the same degree of certitude as the physical sciences. He further maintained that "politics, natural philosophy, physics, chemistry, etc.," which employ "moral reasoning," were more securely grounded than the study of morals or aesthetics; the latter were "not so properly objects of the understanding as of taste and sentiment." This was not to imply that politics, any more than the other sciences, could transcend experience or explain "ultimate principles" (T xxii). Nor was it meant to deny that "irregular and extraordinary appearances" might defy attempts to reduce political phenomena to near-mathematical axioms (Essays 372).

Despite these qualifications, Hume's conviction remained unshaken that, as the title of one of his essays suggested, "politics may be reduced to a science" if it adheres to "experimental" procedures rather than the methods of traditional logic. Logic, which relied on demonstrations founded on the understanding, was useless for dealing with the probabilities which were of the essence of man's actual life in society. A science of politics, therefore, must be grounded in experience supplied by historical inquiry and observation of existing societies. Essentially, it was to be an investigation into the interaction between institutions and human nature. From an historical point of view, the function of political institutions had been to channel and control human behavior. Institutions were, in short, artificial contrivances which exerted an independent force and were not merely a reflex or simple reaction to human drives. "So great is the force of laws, and of particular forms of government, and so little dependence have they on the humours and tempers of men, that consequences almost as general and certain may sometimes be deduced from them, as any which the mathematical sciences afford us" (*Essays* 14).

Hume's method of political analysis, as noted earlier, was grounded in the typical Enlightenment technique of "analytic dissection," which, to borrow Cassirer's description, "dissolves everything merely factual . . . and everything believed on the evidence of revelation, tradition and authority" as preliminary to the ultimate goal of "synthetic reconstruction." [9] Hume pressed this approach with devastating effect against the state-of-nature hypothesis present in some social contract theorizing. He pointed out the slippery logic which sought to justify rebellion against authority on the basis of a "mere philosophical fiction" like the state of nature; he denied that society was simply the product of a voluntary agreement aimed at eliminating certain "inconveniences" present in the pre-social condition. The arrangement called society represented an accumulated set of responses to human needs and drives: to the "natural appetite betwixt the sexes" and to man's oscillation between altruism—which diminishes in force as it is extended through the concentric circles of self, family, friends, and strangers —and selfishness—which increases as societal demands become more abstract and remote. Furthermore, as man found himself situated amid circumstances of material scarcity his insecurity deepened, leading him to invade the material possessions of his fellows. This "natural" condition could be overcome by artificial arrangements which would restrain man's "heedless and impetuous passion" and gratify his instinct for self-interest (T 484–501). "After that interest is once establish'd and acknowledg'd, the sense of morality in the observance of these rules follows *naturally* and of itself . . ." (T 533).

In his explanation Hume made no sharp distinction between government and society. Government was viewed as the instrument whereby society's arrangements were protected and society's purposes executed. Consequently, when Hume came to discuss the problem of political obligation, his argument paralleled to a large extent his explanation of society. His aim, in both cases, was to demonstrate that neither society nor government had emerged full-blown from a sudden agreement. The basis of government was traceable to consent only in the sense that every government required that its subjects agree to its existence. To label this obvious truism a contractual agreement only worked to distort the element of truth contained in the idea of contract, namely, that "it is . . . on opinion only that government is founded . . ." (*Essays* 29). "Opinion," in turn, was composed of several aspects. First, there was "opinion of interest" which referred to the "sense of the general advantage which is reaped from government, together with the persuasion that the particular government which is established is equally advantageous with any other that could easily be settled." Second, there was "opinion of right" which comprehended (*a*) the "right to power" or the prevalent disposition of men to believe that governments which have endured over a long period of time were legitimate governments; and (*b*) the "right to property" or the general desire of men to secure their possessions.

Such were the "principles" which supported government. Viewed from this perspective, the "ought" element in political obligation was reduced to a secondary consequence following from certain naturalistic considerations. Men obeyed because the interests which they sought to protect and promote necessitated obedience to authority. "Society could not otherwise subsist" (*Essays* 468).

According to Hume's view, all the rules of society were "artificial" in that they represented conscious contrivances designed to meet human needs and problems. As rules of convenience they could not be expected to satisfy the demands of morality or strict logic. For example, the rules of justice might result in a wicked miser's winning a legal judgment against a virtuous peasant, yet the necessity and value of a general rule excludes consideration of the "fitness or unfitness of objects to particular persons" (T 502). The essential point was that there was no sharp contrast between an "artificial" rule and a "natural" one. Through the passage of time men became accustomed to social expedients, and what was once artificial soon became natural. It followed that the "natural" was not necessarily the primitive or the original condition. Hume strongly inferred that the opposite was more likely: that the truly unnatural situation was to be found in the state of nature.

The significant element in Hume's political ideas lies not so much in the particular arguments employed, but rather in the sensitivity displayed toward the workings of actual institutions. Like his contemporaries, he appeared to use the analytical method to dissect institutions, to peel off layer after layer of historical accretion. Yet, unlike that of many of his contemporaries, Hume's method proceeded on the belief that a particular institution was to be viewed as a whole possessing subtle interconnections with other institutional wholes.

Implicit in this approach were two ideas which were to play a central role in later conservative thinking in England. Institutions were to be understood in terms of human needs, but institutions were not merely the product of human needs. The two elements became intertwined and inseparable by virtue of their common root in historical time. It followed that there was no necessary opposition between what was useful and what existed; the desirable and the factual were not out of joint. In this way Hume indicated to later conservatives that the strongest arguments for the existing order were to be found within the facts of that order; that under an empirical approach utility could be located as an immanent value dwelling within the interstices of actual social arrangements, not as a grim measuring rod contrived to reveal the shortcomings of institutions.

Moreover, institutions were developments over a period of time. Their purpose and nature could not be correctly understood without a sense of time. The concept of time, then, was closely associated with the blending of fact and utility. Historical time imparted to social arrangements a qualitative element. Time implied experience, and experience in turn provided the motive for gradual adjustment. Conversely, the greatest calamity was violent change, which worked to snap the close union which history had fashioned between an institution, its utility, and its duration. In contradicting the nature of time and experience, sweeping change could not adapt institutions according to utility; for utility, in political matters, was inseparable from time and experience.

Students of political theory have, as yet, paid insufficient attention to the concept of time and the part which it has played in the shaping of political theory. To the eighteenth-century liberal reformer, time appeared as a kind of quantitative duration, a series of succeeding points without any particular value, except of a negative character. Future time alone held the promise of a qualitative character. To the conservatives who followed Burke, however, time lent an essentially qualitative element to existing arrangements. Past time had not really been superseded, but merged into the present in the form of institutions and values. Drastic change, in the same way it had contradicted utility, contradicted time. In seeking to sever past time from present and future time, in order to impute a negative value to the past and a positive value only to the present or future, drastic change stood condemned of being unhistorical and therefore unavailing.

While it would be claiming too much to attribute the whole of the conservative conceptions of time and utility to Hume, it is important to recognize that, within the limits imposed by his own methods and temper, he had glimpsed something of the conservative case.

III

Hume's conservatism was given more concrete expression when he turned from his philosophical writings to his informal essays on society, government, and economics. His detachment was, if anything, reinforced by the complexities which he pronounced present in any political question (*Essays* 487–88).

Although his temperament made him unwilling to join in the party battles of the period, it did not prevent him from making thrusts at both sides, at Tory sentiments about divine right and the royal prerogative, as well as at the precious tenets of Whiggism. But in common with the conservatives of the period Hume had a hearty disdain for that type of radical reformer who thought that every morning the world was an open question:

> Did one generation of men go off the stage at once, and another succeed, as in the case with silkworms and butterflies, the new race, if they had sense enough to choose their government, which surely is never the case with men, might voluntarily, and by general consent, establish their own form of civil polity, without any regard to the laws or precedents which prevailed among their ancestors. But as human society is in perpetual flux, one man every hour

going out of the world, another coming into it, it is necessary, in order to preserve stability in government, that the new brood should conform themselves
to the established constitution, and nearly follow the path which their fathers,
treading in the footsteps of theirs, had marked out to them. Some innovations
must necessarily have place in every human institution . . . but violent innovations no individual is entitled to make . . . [*Essays* 463].

Hume's scorn of "novelties" also rested on the conviction that settled forms
and institutions carried a momentum which often nullified the efforts of
evil men and happily compensated for the meager talents of others:

In the smallest court, or office, the stated forms and methods by which business must be conducted, are found to be a considerable check on the natural
depravity of mankind. . . . And so little dependence has this affair on the
humours and education of particular men, that one part of the same republic
may be wisely conducted, and another weakly, by the very same men, merely
on account of the differences of the forms and institutions by which these
parts are regulated. . . . Good laws may beget order and moderation in the
government, where the manners and customs have instilled little humanity or
justice into the tempers of men [*Essays* 22–23].

But where Burke would have looked for some divine cunning to account for
these phenomena, Hume was content to point out the utilitarian basis of
institutions and the strong support which they found in human habits. He
was at one with Burke in being sceptical of man's ability to effect reforms
which would be both widesweeping and beneficial, but where Burke, at the
time of the French Revolution, inveighed against "men of theory" who
sought political solutions by "geometrical demonstration," [10] Hume, writing during the calm of the Augustan age, reserved his contempt for what
the age called "enthusiasm." In his eyes religious "enthusiasm" or fanaticism
had split seventeenth-century England into warring sects and had paved the
way for rebellion, a state of affairs which Hume abhorred even more than
tyranny (*Essays* 51–52).

This fear and distrust of violent antagonisms underlay Hume's analysis of
party politics, for this analysis was motivated by a practical purpose: to
prevent in his time the recrudescence of the seventeenth-century struggles by
showing the many points of agreement between Tories and Whigs, or, as he
more accurately called them, the "court" and "country" parties. Although
the method which he adopted, which was to apportion praise and blame
impartially to both sides, rested on the hope that sweet reasonableness
would prevent both parties from adopting mutually exclusive positions, this
was of less significance than the realistic analysis of the nature of parties
which preceded his conclusions. To be sure, earlier political writers, like
Halifax, Bolingbroke, Swift, and Defoe, had all been aware of the increasingly important role played by "factions" or parties in the constitutional system. Yet among these writers there remained a lingering reluctance
to accept "party" as anything but a distasteful necessity. "The best Party,"
wrote Halifax, "is but a kind of Conspiracy against the rest of the Nation." [11]

In his discussion of parties or factions—the terms were used interchangeably—Hume began from a position similar to that of James Madison in Number 10 of the *Federalist Papers*: [12] since it was not possible to eliminate parties under a free government, some means must be found of limiting their disruptive and predatory tendencies. It was necessary, then, to draw a distinction between those parties which posed a threat to the very existence of a political system and those whose activities, while not always salutary, were confined within reasonable bounds. In the former category Hume placed the fanatical group with uncompromising tenets, a type which had been spawned in abundance during the bitter religious controversies of the last century. Extremist groups, reflecting the dogmatic tempers of their members, were perfectly willing to sacrifice peace and order for the achievement of their objectives: *fiat justitia, ruat caelum*. Furthermore, the tendency to exaggerate principles into unyielding absolutes was a peculiarly modern phenomenon: "Parties from *principle*, especially abstract speculative principle, are known only to modern times, and are, perhaps, the most extraordinary and unaccountable *phenomenon* that has yet appeared in human affairs" (*Essays* 58). Although such parties constituted the exception, they represented a pathological condition to which all parties were susceptible. Traces of these symptoms could be found in both the Whigs and the Tories. Hume, writing in a period when the uproar over the Hanoverian succession had not completely died down and when Jacobite memories and hopes were still strong, repeatedly warned of the consequences which would follow if party distinctions were allowed to harden. That this eventuality need not come about was the whole lesson of Hume's analysis of parties.

In his dissection of the anatomy of party, Hume found a compound of interests, principles, and sentimental attachment to certain leaders. Two broad types of parties existed: those founded on the personal attraction of a particular leader or group of leaders, and those founded on "real" differences of opinions or of interests (*Essays* 56–58). Most parties were a compound of the two and this was fortunate, for it meant that principles, interests, and personal ambitions tended to offset each other. In particular, the tugs of personal rivalry and economic interests lessened the possibility of conflicts over questions of political or religious principles. To a sceptic and a moderate like Hume, the disputes over principle were largely meaningless, because the historic quarrels which had given birth to the conflicting ideas had long since been settled. The Whigs, Hume noted, regarded themselves as the sole heirs of the revolutionary traditions of 1688, and their arguments implied that the revolutionary settlement stood in constant danger of being overthrown. The Tories, on the other side, responded in the opposite vein: they represented the sole defenders of a monarchy which had been temporarily abolished by the forerunners of the Whigs; it was the Tory mission to insist on the primacy of the allegiance owed by subject to sovereign. In actuality, Hume commented, these antics were largely absurd because of the fundamental similarity between both parties. Both had accepted the results of 1688; neither wanted to abolish the monarchy. The division between them rested on a matter of emphasis. It lay in the shades of meaning which each side attached to certain accepted fundamentals. "A TORY, therefore, since the *Revolution* . . . [is] a *lover of monarchy, though without abandoning liberty, and a partisan of the family of Stuart*: as a Whig may be defined to be a *lover of liberty, though without renouncing monarchy, and a friend to the settlement in the Protestant line*" (*Essays* 70). His advice to both parties was to be moderate, accept the present situation, and pursue the public good. There were, he remarked dryly, "enow of zealots on both sides . . ." (*Essays* 23–24).

In emphasizing that a substantial area of agreement existed between the two parties Hume put his finger on the most singular aspect of the modern British party system. From it he drew the conclusion that it was both desirable and possible to create "a coalition of parties" which would govern England with a minimum of discord. "The transition from a moderate opposition against an establishment, to an entire acquiescence in it, is easy and insensible" (*Essays* 485). "Coalition" thus implied an agreement between the parties to exclude the fundamentals of the system from the range of controversy. As Hume acutely noted, the "only dangerous parties are such as entertain opposite views with regard to the essentials of government . . ." (*Essays* 478). His hope was that the area of friction between the parties could be reduced once they had recognized their agreement on fundamentals. When this actually became the case in Britain a century and a half later, Hume would have welcomed Balfour's remark that the nation "is so at one that we can safely afford to bicker."

IV

From the death of Queen Anne in 1714 until the outbreak of the American Revolution, England enjoyed a period of comparative harmony unruffled by any deep antagonisms or sharp controversies. The Jacobite uprisings were the only major exceptions. The stability of England had become one of the wonders of Europe, for such had not been her reputation in the preceding century, when the turmoil of revolutionary events had made her name a byword for political instability. The era of good feeling prevalent at this time received its intellectual expression in the admiration for balance and proportion. The classic lines with which Newton had sketched in his picture of an harmonious universe were duplicated in the ordered couplets of Pope. English political writers, not unmindful of the almost universal praise for their institutions, explained that the key to the riddle of stability was in the balanced nature of the system. The idea of balance became the central starting point, the key concept in British constitutional thought until the appearance of Bentham's *Fragment on Government* in 1776.[13] Its classic formulation was to be found in Blackstone's *Commentaries*:

> And herein indeed consists the true excellence of the English government, that all the parts of it form a mutual check upon each other. In the Legislature the people are a check upon the nobility, and the nobility a check upon the people; by the mutual privilege of rejecting what the other has resolved: while the king is a check upon both, which preserves the executive power from

encroachments. . . . Thus every branch of our civil polity supports and is supported, regulates and is regulated, by the rest: for the two houses naturally drawing in two directions of opposite interest, and the prerogative in another still different from them both, they mutually keep each other from exceeding their proper limits; while the whole is prevented from separation, and artificially connected together by the mixed nature of the Crown, which is a part of the legislative, and the sole executive magistrate. Like three distinct powers in mechanics, they jointly impel the machinery of government in a direction different from what either, acting by itself, would have done; but at the same time in a direction partaking of each, and formed out of all; a direction which constitutes the true line of the liberty and happiness of the community.[14]

Although the importance of the concept of balance might be admitted for the realm of constitutional theory, the query arises: how much was this idea a creation existing solely in the minds of closet philosophers and how closely did it correspond to the actual workings of the constitution of the time? Although the dominant theme of parliamentary supremacy was obtrusive at certain times,[15] there was, by and large, an implicit cooperation between the various branches of government. Hence, there is no paradox in the statement by Sir William Holdsworth that during the period of Whig supremacy from roughly 1720 until 1760 the constitutional system resembled a partnership, but not on equal terms, of King, Lords, and Commons.[16]

When it is asked, by what means was this semblance of balance maintained, the answer is to be found largely in the conventions interwoven in the general constitutional fabric.[17] As contemporary British historians, under the inspiration of Sir Lewis Namier, have demonstrated, the nucleus about which these conventions clustered was the system of "influence," that is, the ties of family, patronage, contracts, bribes, and corruption through which the King and his ministers managed the parliamentary machinery.[18] This system, developed by Walpole and Newcastle and perfected later by George III, was not incidental to the politics of the period, but was a crucial element. Without it, the British constitution would have too closely resembled the nicely compartmented separation of powers which Montesquieu imagined in his *Esprit des Lois*. The conventions of the period, including the system of "influence," supplied the lubrication necessary to ensure that the machinery of government would work in coordinated fashion and with a degree of central direction provided by the Crown.

Although many writers and politicians were aware of the part played by "influence" in preserving an area of royal initiative, Hume, perhaps alone, had grasped the tactical role of this system in preserving the constitutional balance.[19] He began by raising doubts about the validity of Harrington's widely accepted thesis that political stability depended upon a coincidence between property and political power.[20] The paradox of the British system, Hume contended, was that although property and power had gravitated from the King to the House of Commons, there was no evident disposition on the part of the House to usurp all the powers of government so as to leave the King helpless. It was apparent that the House could not be considered as a kind of passive funnel through which the propertied interests exerted overwhelming mastery. The question then became: what were the means by which the dominant partner of the constitution was confined within its proper limits? His answer was that

the interest of the body is here restrained by that of the individuals, and that the House of Commons stretches not its power, because such an usurpation would be contrary to the interest of the majority of its members. The crown has so many offices at its disposal, that, when assisted by the honest and disinterested part of the House, it will always command the resolutions of the whole, so far, at least, as to preserve the ancient constitution from danger [*Essays* 45].

Rail as men may at the "invidious appellations of *corruption* and *dependence*," it must not be forgotten, as men are apt to do in the heat of party strife, that "some degree and some kind of it are inseparable from the very nature of the constitution, and necessary to the preservation of our mixed government" (*Essays* 45). The proper course for the zealots of liberty and parliamentary independence was not one of demanding a root-and-branch extirpation of patronage and its attendant evils, but of exercising prudent vigilance over "the proper degree of this dependence, beyond which it became dangerous to liberty" (*Essays* 45).

More than any other observer, Hume saw that whatever balance there was in the constitution resembled less the mechanical equipoise of Newtonian forces than a restless equilibrium whose components were hidden from the prevailing formal and legalistic types of analysis. It followed that it was unrealistic to define rigidly the boundaries of power between the three main participants of the constitutional system (*Essays* 46). Custom and expediency, not speculative reason, had shaped the constitution. Accordingly, these highly artificial political arrangements could not be measured by the rigors of abstract theory. Furthermore, as the system had demonstrated its ability to combine both liberty and order and had behind it the inertia of the settled habits of a nation, it was folly to "tamper, . . . or try experiments merely upon the credit of supposed argument and philosophy. . . ." The "wise magistrate, . . . though he may attempt some improvements for the public good, yet will he adjust his innovations as much as possible to the ancient fabric, and preserve entire the chief pillars and supports of the constitution" (*Essays* 499).[21]

V

Hume's "analytical conservatism" prepared the way for Burke in many respects. Although the latter possessed a conviction and passion which Hume lacked, many of the same materials had been worked over in Hume's writings. The emphasis on traditionalism, the importance of habit and sentiment, a disdain for "political projectors" (as Hume called them), and a fine feeling for the complexities of government were all to be found in Hume. Yet Hume's true uniqueness rested on his analysis of parties and the hidden conventions of the constitution. It was by far the keenest discussion of the century and far overshadowed in insight the partisan tracts of Bolingbroke and Burke. At the same time, his critique struck a note of realism which contributed in an important way to the decline of Locke's influence. Hume saw clearly, as the later philosophic radicals did not, that the arena of practical politics was not peopled by individuals pursuing their own aims in the splendid isolation of self-interest. Rather, the basic elements were political groups held together by individual leaders and by the cement of common interests and professed principles. This approach, reminiscent of the sociological methods of Montesquieu, also differed significantly from the legalism which pervaded the political thought of England at that time. The dominant tendency was to argue issues like electoral reform, representation, and colonial matters on the basis of law and precedent. The influence of Hardwicke, Mansfield, and Blackstone symbolized the alliance which had sprung up between law and politics.

Although Hume's appreciation of existing institutions and his realization of the long, painful, and largely unconscious process by which society is shaped led him in the same general direction as the lawyers, the journey was accomplished by his effecting a minor revolution in political thought. Politics was now to be conceived in psychological rather than juridical categories. Earlier writers, like Locke and Hobbes, while emphasizing the importance of human nature for the understanding of politics, had nevertheless approached this element as preliminary to the central juridical concept of contract. In this way, the political categories of allegiance, obligation, and justice assumed the status of logical derivatives from the basic concept of sovereignty (or as Locke preferred to call it, "supreme power") established by the contract. Hume, on the other hand, turned the procedure around: justice, obligation, and authority were consequences of human attitudes and expectations. These concepts were to be explained on psychological, not juridical, grounds.

The psychologism of Hume was part of his general legacy to later conservatism, a legacy of empiricism in which the useful and the factual were made to cohere in subtle fashion. Yet it was also a legacy which later events superseded. Hume, appropriately enough, died in 1776, and from this point on revolutionary events worked to make a mockery of Hume's comfortable conclusions. The realm of fact provided cold comfort for conservatives; it was now controlled by the revolutionaries. The central fact of revolution could not be explained away, although a Burke might attribute it to intellectual perversity and a De Maistre to an avenging deity. But if it could not be ignored, it could be transcended. So it was that conservatives began to turn to transcendental norms in order to combat the revolutionary appeal to reason; to weave from the diverse elements of irrationalism, romanticism, religion, and history a new vision of an older order; to replace an analytical conservatism with a metaphysical conservatism. In so doing they rejected much of Hume's naturalistic approach and substituted in its stead a philosophy of history, the idea that history had a "course" whose main outlines were determined by a divine hand operating from outside the confines of human time.

The final assessment of Hume raises certain difficulties. In some respects he typified conservatism, in others liberalism, and in still others he belonged to no school but his own. His conclusions in political matters carried strong overtones of conservatism, yet most conservatives of the period felt too uncomfortable with Hume's scepticism to welcome him as one of their own. Nevertheless, his conclusions were conservative for the reason that Hume never probed past a certain point nor carried his scepticism to its ultimate conclusions. He held too much respect for custom and tradition, and for their importance as social cements, to subject them to the kind of devastating critique which Voltaire and his allies were employing in France. With later conservatives he shared a distrust of reform, an hostility toward abstractions, and a scepticism of the claims of reason.

On the other hand, Hume stood close to the liberals of the century in the respect he accorded to liberty and property, and in his decided coolness toward religion and anything bordering on obscurantism. Above all, his political thought contained no traces of the particularist bent which was to play such an important role in later conservative thought. National history, national peculiarities and values had not yet replaced the universalist or European assumptions of seventeenth- and eighteenth-century rationalism.[22]

It would be easy to conclude from these remarks that the categories of "liberal" and "conservative" were irrelevant when applied to Hume. But this would be misleading. The significant point is that Hume's position was symptomatic of the change which was taking place in English liberalism around the middle of the eighteenth century. Liberalism was becoming conservatized. Seventeenth-century liberalism, which had been compounded from the criticisms and protests of the Civil War period and then reshaped in more moderate fashion by the Glorious Revolution, had been transformed. It had lost its status as a challenge to the established order and had become the order itself. By the beginning of the eighteenth century, England was committed to the idea of government under law, the superiority of Parliament, and the rights of Englishmen. The incorporation of liberal elements into the political structure worked to rid liberal thought of one of its central themes: its revolt against the idea of the organic community. The idea of a corporate society—compact, graded, deeply-niched by place and privilege—had been a commonplace in Tudor thought, as well as in the royalist doctrines of the seventeenth century.[23] The reaction to this belief in a close community, with all that implied in social and political policies, can be traced not only in the radical doctrines of the Civil War, but also in such diverse thinkers as Hobbes and Locke. The systems of Hobbes and Locke began with abstractions which cut through the communal bonds of class, status, and hierarchy, leaving only unattached and undifferentiated individuals. In neither system was there a "sense of community."

Once English society was modified by the revolutionary changes of the seventeenth century, the theme of revolt was gradually replaced by a growing "sense of society," a quickening appreciation of the extent to which the values established by protest and revolt had become deeply dependent on communal arrangements of an unwritten and informal nature. Hume was representative of this changing temper, which prized the gains made possible by the upheavals of the previous century, and sought to preserve both the institutional achievements and their social undergirding. In this way, the assumption of an organic community, which had been cast aside during the seventeenth century, was being recaptured.

The developments form a background for Hume, as well as for English conservatism. For the uniqueness of this form of conservatism lies in the extent to which it had incorporated the results of the revolutionary experience of the seventeenth century. The master example here was Burke's pamphlet, *An Appeal from the New to the Old Whigs*; in it he conservatized the revolution of 1688, while at the same time liberalizing conservatism.

NOTES

1. *The Works of John Adams*, ed. Charles Francis Adams, 10 vols. (Boston, 1865), IV 466–68; *Selected Writings of John and John Quincy Adams*, edd. Adrienne Koch and William Peden (New York, 1946), p. 120; *The Writings of Thomas Jefferson*, edd. Andrew A. Lipscomb and Albert E. Bergh, 20 vols. (Washington, 1903), XI 223, XII 405–407, XVI 44, 125–26. John Stuart Mill declared Hume to be "the profoundest negative thinker on record" (*Mill on Bentham and Coleridge*, ed. F. R. Leavis [New York, 1950], p. 43).

2. Thomas Huxley, *Hume* (New York, n.d.), pp. 10–11.

3. Sir Leslie Stephen, *History of English Thought in the Eighteenth Century*, 3rd ed. (New York, 1949), II 181. .

4. George H. Sabine, *A History of Political Theory*, 2nd ed. (New York, 1950), pp. 597–606; Elie Halévy, *Growth of Philosophic Radicalism* (London, 1934), pp. 9–13, 42–45, 131–33; John Plamenatz, *The English Utilitarians* (Oxford, 1949), pp. 22–44; *Hume's Moral and Political Philosophy*, ed. Henry D. Aiken (New York, 1948), Introduction; *David Hume: Theory of Politics*, ed. Frederick M. Watkins (Edinburgh, 1951), Introduction.

5. *The Political Thought of Samuel Taylor Coleridge*, ed. R. J. White (London, 1938), p. 93.

6. See the discussion in D. G. C. MacNabb, *David Hume: His Theory of Knowledge and Morality* (London, 1951), pp. 159ff.

7. John Passmore, *Hume's Intentions* (Cambridge, 1952), p. 10.

8. On this point see John H. Randall, *The Making of the Modern Mind*, 2nd ed. (Boston, 1940), pp. 334ff., and Ernst Cassirer, *The Philosophy of the Enlightenment* (Princeton, 1951), pp. 253ff.

9. Cassirer, *Philosophy of the Enlightenment*, pp. 13–16.

10. Edmund Burke, *Reflections on the French Revolution*, ed. Ernest Rhys (London, 1910), pp. 38, 170.

11. *The Complete Works of George Savile, First Marquis of Halifax*, ed. Walter Raleigh (Oxford, 1912), p. 225.

12. For a discussion of Hume's influence on James Madison, see chap. 19 of this volume, "'That Politics May Be Reduced to a Science': David Hume, James Madison, and the Tenth *Federalist*."

13. Examples of this concept can be found in the following: *The Prose Works of Jonathan Swift*, ed. Temple Scott, 12 vols. (London, 1898), I 231–35; Chancellor Hardwicke in Lord John Campbell, *Lives of the Lord Chancellors*, 7 vols., 2nd ed. (Philadelphia, 1851), V 127; *Parliamentary History of England*, ed. William Cobbett (London, 1813–20), Vol. 15, cols. 481–82, 506; Vol. 66, cols. 43–44.

14. William Blackstone, *Commentaries on the Laws of England*, ed. Edward Christian, 4 vols., 12th ed. (London, 1793), I 154–55.

15. E.g., the Act of Settlement, the Regency Bill (1788–89), and the dispute over parliamentary privileges during the Wilkes affair.

16. William Holdsworth, *A History of English Law*, 12 vols., 3rd ed. (London, 1922–38), x 55; Sir David Keir, *The Constitutional History of Modern Britain*, 3rd ed. (London, 1948), pp. 293–99.

17. Holdsworth, *History of English Law*, 464.

18. Sir Lewis B. Namier, *The Structure of Politics at the Accession of George III*, 2 vols. (London, 1922); and *England in the Age of the American Revolution* (London, 1930); *The Parliamentary Papers of John Robinson, 1774–1784*, ed. William T. Laprade (London, 1922); Richard Pares, *King George III and the Politicians* (Oxford, 1953); George H. Guttridge, *English Whiggism and the American Revolution* (Berkeley & Los Angeles, 1942).

19. In this connection it should be noted that Burke, for all his concern for the "nice equipoise" of the constitution, was unaware of the degree to which the system of "influence" contributed toward that result. See his proposals for "economical reform" designed to implement Dunning's resolution of 1780, which warned against the Crown's system of "influence" (*Works*, 12 vols. [London, 1815], II 69–70).

20. Hume's criticisms of Harrington are scattered throughout the following essays: "Idea of a Perfect Commonwealth," "On the Independence of Parliament," and "Whether the British Monarchy inclines more to Absolute Monarchy, or to a Republic."

21. Hume was careful to preface his "Idea of a Perfect Commonwealth," the admittedly utopian essay from which this quotation is taken, with several remarks intended to underline his own affection for an established system which worked tolerably well.

22. The exception to this point was Hume's interest in "national character." Although he suggested that certain common traits, such as similar manners and habits, could be discovered in a people who had been associated over a long period of time, this idea was not employed to prove any qualitative differences among peoples. Note also the statement in the first *Enquiry*: "Would you know the sentiments, inclinations, and course of life of the Greeks and Romans? Study well the temper and actions of the French and English: You cannot be much mistaken in transferring to the former *most* of the observations which you have made with regard to the latter. Mankind are so much the same, in all times and places, that history informs us of nothing new or strange in this particular" (EHU 83).

23. John W. Allen, *A History of Political Thought in the Sixteenth Century*, 2nd ed. (London, 1940), pp. 134ff.; Christopher Morris, *Political Thought in England: Tyndale to Hooker* (London, 1953), pp. 68–126; Sheldon S. Wolin, "Richard Hooker and English Conservatism," *Western Political Quarterly*, 6, No. 1 (March 1953), 28–47; Francis D. Wormuth, *The Royal Prerogative, 1603–1649* (Ithaca, 1939), pp. 83ff.

12

Infinite Divisibility in Hume's *Treatise*

Antony Flew
University of Reading

1. "Think of all the sections which are seldom discussed in Book I of the *Treatise*. Hardly anyone is familiar with Hume's work on space and time." [1] These words from the Introduction to a recent study of *The Moral Philosophy of David Hume* strike near the mark. And, furthermore, it might easily be argued that there is no very good reason why anyone should struggle to gain such familiarity—except, of course, simply in order better to understand Hume and to appreciate his weaknesses as well as his strength. However, it will be time enough to think about the question whether there has been or could be any further profit in the exercise when we have first mastered what Hume's problems were and how he believed that he had solved them. The aim of the present paper is to contribute towards that mastery of what is, by common consent, one of the least satisfactory Parts of the whole *Treatise*.

The title of Part II of Book I is, of course, not "Of Space and Time" but "Of the Ideas of Space and Time." From this title, and from its position immediately following a discussion "Of ideas; Their Origin, Composition, Abstraction, Connexion, &c.," we should expect that Hume's first concern here would be to try to develop some account of the origin and composition of these particular ideas consistent with his fundamental principles, especially: *"That all our simple ideas in their first appearance are deriv'd from simple impressions, which are correspondent to them, and which they exactly represent"* (T 4). After that we might expect, remembering the hopes of the Introduction, that Hume would go on to display some alleged consequence for Mathematics, Natural Philosophy, or Natural Religion: for " 'Tis impossible to tell what changes and improvements we might make in these sciences were we thoroughly acquainted with the extent and force of human understanding, and cou'd explain the nature of the ideas we employ, and of the operations we perform in our reasonings" (T xix).

Certainly we do in fact find Hume trying to do both these expected things in this Part. For in Section III he enquires after "the model, from which

Reprinted by permission from the *Rivista Critica di Storia della Filosofia*, 4 (1967).

the idea of space is derived" (T 33), and having found a solution which satisfies him, he proceeds to present an analogous answer to the parallel question about the idea of time. Then in Section IV, under the heading "Objections Answer'd," he sketches a consequential account of the nature and limitations of geometrical thinking, before, as "The Same Subject Con-tinu'd," attempting to meet three objections to the implication "that we can form no idea of a vacuum, or space, where there is nothing visible or tangi-ble" (T 53). But what should be surprising is that, instead of plunging straightway into the search for the impression or impressions from which each of these fundamental and rather special ideas may be derived, Hume starts by examining "the doctrine of infinite divisibility" (T 26), and that the account which he later gives of these ideas is presented as a consequence of his conclusions about infinite divisibility: "The other part of our system is a consequence of this" (T 39). We shall be dealing here primarily with what Hume has to say about "the doctrine of infinite divisibility," and with the other themes of the Part only secondarily and in so far as they bear on our primary interest.

2. To Hume, any suggestion of the infinite divisibility of anything, or at least of any finite thing, was in itself scandalous. But, as we have urged else-where, he had two for him compelling reasons for wanting to remove this particular scandal.[2] First, what he took to be the absurdities and contradic-tions of and arising from this doctrine had, especially through the Port-Royal *Logic*, become a stock weapon for taming the presumption of secular reason in order to open the gates to religious faith; and Hume was utterly opposed to obscurantism. Second, if the doctrine is indeed thus contradic-tory and absurd, this must put geometry in jeopardy; and Hume, as he has suggested in his Introduction, wants to do all he can to remedy "the present imperfect condition of the sciences" (T xvii).

Unless we recognize these two powerful motives we shall not understand why the Part "Of the Ideas of Space and Time" starts from, and gives so much attention to, questions about infinite divisibility. Similarly, and more importantly, we must realize that Hume saw his accounts both of the ideas of space and time, and of the nature of geometrical thinking, as—whatever their other merits or demerits—corollaries of what seemed to him to be the only possible escape from these disastrous contradictions and absurdities. This is necessary if we are fully and sympathetically to appreciate how Hume was able to present such incredibilities so confidently in the *Treatise*; and, furthermore, why although he later sketches a far better account of both pure and applied geometry in the first *Enquiry*, he still has back-slidings towards the view outlined in the *Treatise*.[3]

After a prefatory paragraph, on how "philosophers and their disciples" are inclined greedily to embrace "Whatever has the air of a paradox, and is contrary to the first and most unprejudic'd notions of mankind," Hume opens his argument by laying down two fundamental principles (T 26). Both he mistakes to be obvious: although one is true, surely, only in his own highly artificial interpretation, the other is without qualification false. Certainly both are fundamental.

(a) The first is "that the capacity of the mind is limited, and can never attain a full and adequate conception of infinity . . ." (T 26). This principle, as Laird reminds us,[4] is kin to the ninth axiom given in Chapter VII of Part IV of the Port-Royal *Logic*: "Il est de la nature d'un esprit fini de ne pouvoir comprendre l'infini." And that, so far from being as Hume has it "universally allowed," was, as "Mens nostra, eo quod finita sit, nihil certi scire potest de infinito," on the list of Cartesian propositions condemned by the Jesuits. In Hume's formulation, straightforwardly interpreted, it is surely untrue. For there is no insuperable difficulty about learning the ordinary uses of the words "infinite" and "infinity," and we can perfectly well understand what is meant by talk of a series' being infinite or going on to infinity. But, of course, Hume is not construing the expression "attain a full and adequate conception" in any such studiously simple-minded way. For he equates conceiving with imagining, and mistakes it that to imagine —or at any rate to be able to imagine—is always to form—or at any rate to be able to form—the appropriate mental image or images.[5]

Thus Hume tells us: " 'Tis an establish'd maxim in metaphysics, *That whatever the mind clearly conceives includes the idea of possible existence, or in other words, that nothing we imagine is absolutely impossible.* We can form the idea of a golden mountain, and from thence conclude that such a mountain may actually exist" (T 32; emphasis added).[6] Earlier he had spoken of "one image or idea" (T 22) in a way which makes it clear that for him "image" and "idea" refer here to the same thing; and he will later desire "our mathematician to form . . . the ideas of a circle and a right line; and . . . ask, if upon the conception of their contact he can conceive them as touching in a mathematical point, or if he must necessarily imagine them to concur for some space" (T 53). Since conceiving is thus identified with imagining, and since both are always thought of in terms of forming mental images, to "attain a full and adequate conception of infinity" would be to have a clear and distinct idea, or image, of infinity. And from here it is scarcely a step to that equation of an idea of infinity with an infinite idea which makes it seem to Hume just obvious that since "the capacity of the mind is limited," we "can never attain a full and adequate conception of infinity."

(b) The upshot is that the first thing which Hume wants to lay down as fundamental and obviously true surely is, for the reason he gives, true; but that he certainly has not, by pointing to the fact that our capacities to form mental images are in this way limited, made out the entirely different contention that we cannot "attain a full and adequate conception of infinity"— a conclusion which, it should at least be noticed, ought to embarrass someone who proposes to develop an extensive argument around that selfsame supposedly inadequate notion of infinity.

The second of Hume's fundamentals, thought allegedly obvious, is in fact false. He says: "whatever is capable of being divided *in infinitum*, must consist in an infinite number of parts . . ." (T 26). This, though it struck him, and has struck many others, as a self-evident truth, is mistaken twice over. First, and less importantly, to say that something is divisible into so many parts is not to say that it consists of—that it is, so to speak, already divided into—that number of parts. A cake may be divisible into many different numbers of equal slices without its thereby consisting in, through already having been divided into, any particular number of such slices. Second, and absolutely crucially, to say that something may be divided *in infinitum* is not to say that it can be divided into an infinite number of parts. It is rather to say that it can be divided, and sub-divided, and sub-sub-divided as often as anyone wishes: infinitely, without limit. That this is so is part of what is meant by the saying: "Infinity is not a number!"

The contradictions and absurdities, whether real or only apparent, which make the doctrine of infinite divisibility scandalous to Hume spring from precisely this proposition "that whatever is capable of being divided *in infinitum*, must consist in an infinite number of parts." Indeed this obnoxious doctrine just is that there are some finite things which are infinitely divisible—construing "infinitely divisible" in this supposedly correct and only possible way; and what, in Hume's view, is wrong with this assertion is that it implies that these finite things are constituted of infinite collections of other finite things, which in turn are constituted of infinite collections of infinitely smaller finite things, and so on, *ad infinitum*. The most vivid and forceful statement is found in the first *Enquiry*:

> No priestly *dogmas*, invented on purpose to tame and subdue the rebellious reason of mankind, ever shocked common sense more than the doctrine of the infinitive divisibility of extension, with its consequences; as they are pompously displayed by all geometricians and metaphysicians, with a kind of triumph and exultation. A real quantity, infinitely less than any finite quantity, containing quantities infinitely less than itself, and so on *in infinitum*; this is an edifice so bold and prodigious, that it is too weighty for any pretended demonstration to support, because it shocks the clearest and most natural principles of human reason [EHU 156].

3. Hume, therefore, proposes to start from two fundamental principles, one of which is the very misconception which generates the paradoxes he wishes to remove. After such a beginning we cannot but fear as bad or worse later; and we are not disappointed. However Hume's next step is, as an argument, sound; and his immediate conclusion, surely, true. He proceeds to deduce from his ruinous premises that there must be experiential minima, particularly in our ideas or images. Since the capacity of the mind is finite, and since nothing finite can be infinitely divisible (because an infinite number of parts must make something infinite), there must be mental elements which are not further divisible: "In rejecting the infinite capacity of the mind, we suppose it may arrive at an end in the division of its ideas; nor are there any possible means of evading the evidence of this conclusion" (T 27).

" 'Tis therefore certain," Hume continues, "that the imagination reaches a *minimum*, and may raise up to itself an idea, of which it cannot conceive any sub-division, and which cannot be diminished without a total annihilation" (T 27). The conclusion that there are such minima at the thresholds of discernment is one which Hume might have rested on a direct appeal to experience. Thus Berkeley had urged, in Section LIV of the *New Theory of Vision*, that: "There is a 'minimum tangible' and a 'minimum visible,' beyond which sense cannot perceive. This everyone's experience will inform him." But having distinguished two categories of experience Hume reserves the direct appeal as his case for minima in impressions.

Laird makes extraordinarily heavy weather of this. Hume says: "Put a spot of ink upon paper, fix your eye upon that spot, and retire to such a distance, that at last you lose sight of it; 'tis plain, that the moment before it vanish'd the image or impression was perfectly indivisible" (T 27). Laird asks: "What is *the* 'spot' if the 'impressions' form a series?" [7] Quite clearly the spot is the spot of ink, which is the cause of the whole series of impressions; and the minimum is the last impression in that series. Laird goes on: "If the 'image or impression' were perfectly indivisible, how could a pair of binoculars 'spread' it?" [8] Certainly Hume does talk of how the use of "A microscope or telescope . . . gives parts to impressions, which to the naked eye appear simple and uncompounded . . ." (T 28), but his previous sentence should have made it perfectly clear that he does not really mean that these physical instruments operate directly upon the individual impression, but rather that by spreading rays of light "which always flowed" they make visible things which would not otherwise have succeeded in causing even a minimum impression: " 'Tis not for want of rays of light striking on our eyes, that the minute parts of distant bodies convey not any sensible impression; but because they are remov'd beyond that distance, at which their impressions were reduc'd to a *minimum*, and were incapable of any further diminution" (T 27).

What does present difficulties is the concluding paragraph, where Hume draws the moral that "common opinion" is in error in thinking "that the capacity of the mind is limited on both sides." "Nothing can be more minute," he tells us, "than some ideas, which we form in the fancy; and images, which appear to the senses; since there are ideas and images perfectly simple and indivisible." ("Images" is being used here, presumably for stylistic reasons, as a synonym for "impressions.") It might perhaps be suggested that Hume intended this claim to apply only to the minima in ideas and impressions, were it not that he goes on, in his next sentence but one, to rebuke those who, "taking the impressions of those minute objects, which appear to the senses, to be equal or nearly equal to the objects, and finding by reason, that there are other objects vastly more minute, . . . too hastily conclude, that these are inferior to any idea of our imagination or impression of our senses" (T 28).

These statements raise two important questions. First, how is it supposed to make sense to compare the relative sizes of ideas and impressions, on the one hand, with those of physical objects, on the other? To this objection Hume provides no answer, although it gains special pertinence from his own later claim that "the notion of any correction beyond what we have instruments and art to make, is a mere fiction of the mind, and useless as well as incomprehensible" (T 48). Second, why does Hume think it quite "certain, that we can form ideas, which shall be no greater than the smallest atom of the animal spirits of an insect a thousand times less than a mite . . ." (T 28), and so on?

Kemp Smith, in what is certainly the fullest and surely also the most helpful commentary on these Sections, answers that since the minima are "minima . . . having no size whatsoever, nothing can possibly exist of a more minute character." [9] The objections to this an interpretation of the present passage are two: first, that Hume has not yet said anything even to suggest that his minima themselves are supposed to be unextended; and, second, that the reason which Hume himself offers here is "since there are ideas and images perfectly simple and indivisible."

This is one of the places where Kemp Smith's treatment suffers from his not having started by noticing and examining Hume's two stated fundamentals. See 2 (a) and 2 (b), above. For the crux is that Hume equates conceiving something with forming a mental image of it, and that he thereby collapses in this case the distinction between contingent and necessary impossibility. A minimum image, being as such "perfectly simple and indivisible" in fact, is, by the same token, of the minimum size conceivable. The conclusion is then, presumably, in default of any relevant dissimilarity between the two categories, extended from ideas to impressions. On Humean principles such simple ideas must be derived from appropriate antecedent impressions. Both minima being at the threshold of discernment are taken to be in the same case. And so, since the idea is in fact indivisible, nothing could conceivably be smaller. Hume therefore points out and accepts the implication that "the difficulty lies in enlarging our conceptions so much as to form a just notion of a mite, or even of an insect a thousand times less than a mite" (T 28).

4. In Section I, "Of the Infinite Divisibility of Our Ideas of Space and Time," Hume in fact says nothing at all about time; and, although he uses as examples such spatial representations as "the idea of a grain of sand" (T 27), the only actual mention even of the notion of space is in the statement that he is going to begin the subject of the whole Part "Of the Ideas of Space and Time" with an examination of "the doctrine of infinite divisibility." Section II, "Of the Infinite Divisibility of Space and Time," begins and ends with the application to (spatial) extension of the principles laid down in the first, although a couple of parenthetical paragraphs notice that "All this reasoning takes place with regard to time . . ." (T 31). It is only in Section III, "Of the Other Qualities of Our Ideas of Space and Time," that Hume attempts—what we might have expected to be his prime objective—the uphill task of applying in this pair of recalcitrant cases his own doctrine "that every idea, with which the imagination is furnish'd, first makes its appearance in a correspondent impression" (T 33). So little has the application and defence of this doctrine been in his mind that he is able to begin the penultimate paragraph of Section II with what should have been to him the altogether obnoxious claim: "Now 'tis certain we have an idea of extension; for otherwise why do we talk and reason concerning it?" (T 32).[10]

(a) The first thing worth noticing about what Section II does, as opposed to what it does not, contain is that both the two fundamental principles of the first are employed and that either separately would be sufficient to yield Hume's conclusion. For if we were to allow that "Every thing capable of being infinitely divided contains an infinite number of parts . . . ," and if the expression "an infinite number of parts" is to be construed as Hume would wish, then clearly it is a contradiction "to suppose, that a finite extension contains an infinite number of parts . . . ," and it must follow that "no finite extension can be infinitely divisible" (T 29). Indeed, what Hume here presents as the conclusion of a demonstrative argument might better be offered as a definition or an axiom: "that the idea of an infinite number of parts is individually the same idea with that of an infinite extension . . ." (T 30).

What is perhaps less obvious is that the same conclusion can be independently derived from the various notions involved in the first of Hume's fundamentals here. See 2 (a), above. For if a spot at the threshold of discernment in one of those mental images which are ideas must as such be something which could not conceivably be smaller, then surely there must be a bottom conceivable limit to size. But, if that is so, then nothing (finite) can even in theory be infinitely divisible. Any process of division must if not, as Hume curiously says, "immediately" at least in the end "be stopt short by the indivisible parts": parts which it would not even make sense to talk of dividing further (T 29). Although Hume chooses, as we have seen, to present the conclusion "that the imagination reaches a minimum" as following "with scarce any induction" from the conjunction of his two supposedly truistic first principles, there seem to be no reasons—if we discount possible considerations of literary elegance—why it should not have been established by the same sort of direct appeal to experience as he employs to buttress the parallel thesis about impressions. See 3, above.

(b) The importance of the point made in our previous paragraph begins to appear when we look at the note appended to the conclusion from which we quoted in our last paragraph but one. Hume writes:

> It has been objected to me, that infinite divisibility supposes only an infinite number of *proportional* not of *aliquot* parts, and that an infinite number of proportional parts does not form an infinite extension. But this distinction is entirely frivolous. Whether these parts be call'd *aliquot* or *proportional*, they cannot be inferior to those minute parts we conceive; and therefore cannot form a less extension by their conjunction [T 30, note].

Here, clearly, the argument which is to Hume's mind decisive depends directly upon his equation of conceiving with imagining, and of his identification of imagining with forming mental images.

Laird speaks of Hume's dismissing this objection "very cavalierly"; and he proceeds to quote from a mathematical commentary among the Hume papers in Edinburgh some acute remarks about lines and points, none of which appears to bear directly upon precisely the matter here at issue.[11] Laird entirely fails to appreciate that for Hume any minimum in image must be the minimum conceivable; even Kemp Smith surely underrates Hume's reply by presenting it as based upon the contention that the idea of extension "as conceived by the imagination, does not consist of an infinite number of parts, since that exceeds our limited powers of comprehension." [12] Nevertheless, when all due allowance has been made, Hume's handling of this objection certainly is far too cavalier. For, even though it does nothing to meet the case against infinite divisibility based upon the first of Hume's two fundamentals, it does constitute a direct challenge to the second. That this is so is, however, not at all obvious until we can discover, what Hume does nothing to explain, the nature of this "entirely frivolous" distinction.

Thanks to Kemp Smith, we can now recognize that the background to Hume's consideration "Of the Ideas of Space and Time" was provided by Hutcheson and Bayle.[13] It is most probable, though it cannot be proved, that the present objection was not put to Hume by a contemporary but found by him in Bayle's article on "Zeno." It derives, as Bayle says, from Aristotle; and the prime source, as it is high time that somebody should say in this context, is Book VI of the *Physics*. Bayle offers the substance of the objection—apparently without intentional irony—"with the perspicuity which the Coimbrian commentaries have given it," in his Note F, although it is only in Note G that he mentions, but despises to explain, what he regards as the factious distinction between "parts . . . proportional and aliquot." If we now at last turn to the Aristotelian original, it becomes clear both what the objection is and that it is decisive:

> For there are two senses in which length and time and generally anything con-
> tinuous are called "infinite": they are called so either in respect of divisibility
> or in respect of their extremities. So while a thing in a finite time cannot
> come in contact with things quantitatively infinite, it can come in contact
> with things infinite in respect of divisibility: for in this sense the time also is
> infinite.[14]

(c) An oddity of Section II is the inclusion of the "very strong and beautiful argument" explicitly attributed to M. Malazieu.[15] This piece of *a priori* ontologizing is so incongruous with both the general temper and the stated object of this "attempt to introduce the experimental method of reasoning into moral subjects," and so reminiscent of the sort of positive natural theology for which Hume had least respect, that he surely ought to have asked himself whether its aptness here is not an indication that something is going badly wrong; which it is. The argument starts: " 'Tis evident, that existence in itself belongs only to unity, and is never applicable to number, but on account of the unites, of which the number is compos'd" (T 30). If this involves only that, for instance, a collection of ten bottles of Chianti consists of nothing more or less than ten bottles of Chianti, and that no such collection could exist without these constituent bottles of Chianti (or similar substitutes), then no doubt it is evident. But from so uncontentious a premiss it is impossible to deduce that "the unity, which can exist alone, . . . must be perfectly indivisible . . ." (T 31). For this premiss refers only and in particular to what are already described as collections, which must as such be—at least theoretically—divisible into their members. It says nothing in general about any practical or theoretical limit to divisibility. Alternatively, if the premiss is to be so construed that it does entail the conclusion suggested, then that it is true is certainly no longer evident.

(*d*) The first of the two parenthetical paragraphs urging the applicability of "All this reasoning . . . to time" is remarkable for the introduction of a fresh fallacy. Hume offers as "an additional argument" that "if in time we could never arrive at an end of division, . . . there would be an infinite number of co-existent moments, or parts of time; . . . an arrant contradiction" (T 31). Certainly the conclusion is contradictory. But it simply does not follow from the premiss. Possibly Hume was misled into thinking that it did because, being stubbornly convinced that finite periods could not be infinitely divisible into shorter periods all of which would either precede or succeed any one of the others, it seemed to him that any sub-division of one of his postulated minimum durationless moments could only be into moments which were at the same time both different and simultaneous; which is indeed absurd. But, since this reconstruction presupposes the conclusion it is supposed to prove, it scarcely provides "an additional argument . . . proper to take notice of" (T 31).

5. In the remainder of Section II Hume first insists that "A demonstration, if just, admits of no opposite difficulty . . ." (T 31), and then recapitulates his argument for conceivable minima as a demonstration of the impossibility of proving the impossibility of mathematical points—an expression which he has not employed previously, and which, notwithstanding that the use he proposes is idiosyncratic, is not here explained. It is in Section III, "Of the Other Qualities of Our Ideas of Space and Time," that Hume actually presents his account of the ideas of (spatial) extension and of time. It must have been the preferred reading of those who, in earlier generations, used to describe and dismiss all Hume's philosophy as atomistic. Anyone familiar with the theories and the paintings of Seurat might also mischievously characterize the Hume of this Section as "the Father of Pointillisme": "my senses convey to me only the impressions of colour'd points, dispos'd in a certain manner. . . . we may conclude . . . that the idea of extension is nothing but a copy of these colour'd points, and of the manner of their appearance" (T 34).

Towards the end of this Section Hume asks us to consider "one of those simple indivisible ideas, of which the compound one of *extension* is form'd . . ." (T 38). This last must, upon Humean principles, be formed of elements: both because, generally, anything divisible is composed of as many parts as it is divisible into, and because, particularly, "*all ideas, which are different, are separable*" (T 24). The elements have, again on Humean principles, got to be simple and "indivisible": both because, generally, no finite extension—including the area of a mental image—can be infinitely divisible, and because, particularly, there are in fact minima in "the perceptions of the mind"—spots at the threshold of discernment. Finally, and perhaps most paradoxically, these ultimate constituents of the idea of extension cannot themselves be extended: "For the idea of extension consists of parts; . . ." whereas its elements must be "perfectly simple and indivisible" (T 38).

It now becomes easy for Hume, thinking in this way of ideal spots deprived of area, to identify them in some way with mathematical points. He therefore asks: not, what is "the nature of mathematical points?": but—and he believes "the question itself has scarce ever yet been thought of"—"*What is our idea of a simple and indivisible point?*" (T 38). Granted always the Humean equation between conceiving and forming mental images, and granting too that both spatial ideas and "The idea of space" are "conveyed to the mind by two senses, the sight and touch . . . ," the answer comes pat and easy: "There is nothing but the idea of their colour or tangibility which can render them conceivable by the mind" (T 38). The idea of space is therefore composed of simple, indivisible, and extensionless mathematical points, while mathematical points have to be endowed with the essential characteristic of colour or tangibility. For good measure similar conclusions, not precisely specified, must apply both to the idea of time and to the presumably durationless moments of which it must ultimately be composed.

6. (*a*) Under the disarming title "Objections Answer'd," Section IV begins with a suggestion that Hume's conclusions, which he has so far confined largely to the realm of ideas, must have drastic applications to the physical world. Since "*whatever the mind clearly conceives includes the idea of possible existence . . .*" (T 32), it must be "possible for space and time to exist conformable to this idea: And if it be possible, 'tis certain they actually do exist conformable to it; since their infinite divisibility is utterly impossible and contradictory" (T 39).

It is perhaps difficult nowadays to grasp what is to be meant by a claim, not about the ideas or concepts of space and time, but about space and time themselves. But we must not permit any hesitations on this score to stop us from recognizing that Hume is absolutely right in thus claiming that his thesis of the impossibility of the infinite divisibility of any finite thing does have ontological implications, and at fault only in not spelling out just what and how wide these implications are. For this thesis is the thesis that continuous magnitudes are impossible, and, hence, that any divisible finite existent must consist of a finite number of elements. This is indeed a very drastic and pervasive form of atomism. Furthermore, Hume is presumably also committed generally by the same thesis to insisting that the ultimate elements constituting any particular sort of magnitude cannot themselves possess whatever is the characteristic in question: the indivisible points composing space cannot themselves have extension; the atomic moments of time must themselves be without duration; and so on.

These are very high, wide, and handsome metaphysical findings; and they scarcely consist with any stock pictures of Hume—including his own. They must, if correct, require extremely extensive "changes and improvements" even in "Natural Philosophy" (T xix). We need not be surprised if it seems that Hume, the admirer and would-be imitator of Newton, is a little reluctant to expatiate upon—or even to notice—the full extent of such ontological implications. Certainly he contrives not to draw what would appear to be the clear consequences of his saying "that we can form no idea of a vacuum . . ." (T 53), although he seems well content with the implications for geometry of his fundamental principles. These he develops in the latter half of Section IV, and in the *Abstract* he draws attention to the resulting account as the second "of two opinions which seem to be peculiar to himself . . ." (A 24). But where, as in the case of vacua, the implications threaten to touch physics, even the Hume of the *Treatise* becomes cautious.

The same principles which commit him to requiring "a full and adequate conception of infinity" to be an infinite idea must similarly demand that an idea of a vacuum would have to be an idea of nothing, and hence no idea at all. See 2 (*a*), above. In both cases there not merely are not, there surely could not be, impressions from which appropriately "full and adequate ideas" may be properly derived. It will not do to refer to a totally black visual image field, and to offer that as the idea of a vacuum. It will not do since, precisely because this is an image, it is not the idea of nothing, which must be no idea at all.

It is this difficult, but within the official *Treatise* framework compulsive, point which Hume is striving to make in his confused and confusing discussion of "the idea of darkness." Hume writes: " 'Tis evident the idea of darkness is no positive idea, but merely the negation of light, or more properly speaking, of colour'd and visible objects" (T 55). Kemp Smith comments: "This, surely, is a very strange and perverse way of asserting that 'darkness' is being taken as signifying simply the absence of *any* type of visual experience, and therefore of *any* apprehension of extension. . . .[16] Yet this is still too charitable. For Hume goes on in his next sentence to show that he is not fully master of his own point: "A man, who enjoys his sight, receives no other perception from turning his eyes on every side, when entirely depriv'd of light, than what is common to him with one born blind; and 'tis certain such-a-one has no idea either of light or darkness" (T 55–56). But, and this is crucial for Hume's argument, to have a black visual image is not the same as not to have any visual image at all; and it is the latter which would be the idea of a vacuum which we do not (and cannot) have.

If, therefore, we do not (and cannot) have this idea which is not an idea, it would seem to follow on Humean principles that when the physicists talk about vacua they must be talking nonsense, and that when they purport to demonstrate to us the evacuation of vessels these pretended vacua must really be plena. But these conclusions—both so embarrassing to anyone raised in Britain under the enormous shadow of Newton, and so apparently inconsistent with experience—are not drawn. Instead, while insisting that "natural philosophy . . . lies without our present sphere" (T 55), Hume struggles to meet three objections, and to do it in a way which does not obviously demand either a denial or even a reinterpretation of any physical fact.

The vital distinction, he thinks, is between sensed and inferred gaps: "betwixt that distance, which conveys the idea of extension, and that other, which is not fill'd with any colour'd or solid object" (T 59). It is with this distinction in mind that we must approach both the theorizings and the demonstrations of the physicists:

> When every thing is annihilated in the chamber, and the walls continue immoveable, the chamber must be conceiv'd much in the same manner as at present, when the air that fills it, is not an object of the senses. This annihilation leaves to the *eye*, that fictitious distance, which is discover'd by the different parts of the organ, that are affected, and by the degrees of light and shade; and to the *feeling*, that which consists in a sensation of motion in the hand, or other member of the body [T 62].

And, furthermore, "experience comes in play to persuade us" that such inferred space does really possess "a capacity of receiving body" (T 63).

This is no doubt all very well, and most ingenious. But we must not fail, as Hume did, to notice that the price for thus accommodating the facts and theories of physics is an implicit abandonment of his principles, that to be able to conceive is to be able to form a mental image, and hence that it cannot make sense to talk about anything of which there cannot be a mental picture—and that too a picture of which at least the simplest elements "are copied from our impressions." Hume certainly anticipated that there would be further new objections and difficulties. But all he mentions is the complaint which he is explaining—he should have said *describing*— "the manner in which objects affect the senses, without endeavouring to account for their real nature and operations" (T 63). This he takes as an occasion for disclaiming any "intention . . . to penetrate into the nature of bodies, or explain the secret causes of their operations. . . . such an enterprize is beyond the reach of human understanding . . ." (T 64).

(*b*) Finally we must notice Hume's treatment of what he presents in Section IV as the first objection to "the finite divisibility of extension." This is one of the passages which suggests most strongly that Hume had Bayle's article on "Zeno" in mind throughout the first five Sections of the Part "Of the Ideas of Space and Time." For in that article Bayle argues that there are three and only three possible views about the constitution of space and time; all three of which are equally impossible, because they are self-contradictory. This paradoxical conclusion was, for reasons indicated already— see 1, above—altogether unacceptable to Hume. He now presents his own resolution of the trilemma in terms borrowed from Bayle. First, the notion of the infinite divisibility of any finite thing really is, for reasons now sufficiently familiar, absurd. Second, actually a corollary of the first, the "system of physical points" is equally absurd: "A real extension, such as a physical point is suppos'd to be, can never exist without parts. . . ." Third, the option of mathematical points is equally absurd: "because a mathematical point is a non-entity, and consequently can never by its conjunction with others form a real existence." But then, in the fifty-ninth minute of the eleventh hour, the hero arrives to save the situation by "bestowing a colour or solidity on these points" (T 40).

To do this is, of course, to put an altogether new construction upon the expression "mathematical points"; and this, as Kemp Smith remarks, may be misleading. But it is not so clear, *pace* Kemp Smith, that the terminological change in the first *Enquiry* constitutes an improvement.[17] For the points, or spots, which Hume has in mind are ideal and not physical; and, although they are the constitutive elements of the idea of extension, they are—unlike physical points—specifically not supposed to be themselves extended. The second thoughts which are really needed would take the strange conclusions as reasons for reversing the whole argument. One wishes Hume had thus been led to challenge the questionable fundamentals on which depend both the atomistic ontology which he only suggests and the bizarre first account of geometry which he presents so proudly.[18]

NOTES

1. R. D. Broiles, *The Moral Philosophy of David Hume* (The Hague, 1964), p. 3.

2. See Antony Flew, *Hume's Philosophy of Belief* (London, 1961), pp. 255–56; and compare Norman Kemp Smith, *The Philosophy of David Hume* (London, 1941), pp. 284–90.

3. Flew, *Hume's Philosophy of Belief*, chap. 3; and compare pp. 255–63, especially pp. 259–60.

4. John Laird, *Hume's Philosophy of Human Nature* (London, 1932), p. 67.

5. For an excellent account of the various relevant distinctions, see Annis Flew, "Images, Supposing, and Imagining," *Philosophy*, 28, No. 106 (July 1953), 246–54.

6. Parenthetically, one is tempted to suggest that whenever Hume links two clauses with the expression "or, in other words," they will be, at least in the ordinary acceptation of their component terms, crucially not equivalent! Compare Flew, *Hume's Philosophy of Belief*, pp. 129ff.

7. Laird, *Hume's Philosophy of Human Nature*, p. 68.

8. Ibid., pp. 68–69.

9. Kemp Smith, *Philosophy of David Hume*, p. 277.

10. Contrast, for instance, Hume's insistence in Section V that "The frequent disputes concerning a vacuum . . . prove not the reality of the idea . . ." (T 62).

11. Laird, *Hume's Philosophy of Human Nature*, p. 67.

12. Kemp Smith, *Philosophy of David Hume*, p. 296.

13. Ibid., chap. 14, especially its Appendix C. Compare Laird, *Hume's Philosophy of Human Nature*, pp. 78–79.

14. Aristotle, *Physics*, trans. R. K. Gaye (Oxford, 1930), pp. 23–29.

15. Kemp Smith, *Philosophy of David Hume*, chap. 14, Appendix D.

16. Ibid., p. 309.

17. Ibid., pp. 286–87.

18. I should like to end by generally thanking those who have joined with me in various seminars on Hume, but specially two graduate students at the University of Pittsburgh in the Summer Trimester of 1965, Messrs. R. Schuldenfrei and R. Goodwin.

13

Remembering and Imagining the Past

JAMES NOXON
McMaster University

IN THE SPRING OF 1974, it was reported in the press that a British journalist had been sentenced in a Rhodesian court to two years of imprisonment at hard labour for violating an Official Secrets Act. His wife, then five months pregnant with their first child, was interviewed on international radio. She expressed concern for her husband's health, which, she said, had deteriorated during forty-seven days of detention and a trial held *in camera*. She said that he had lost twenty pounds in weight and was "losing his sense of reality." To illustrate this loss of a sense of reality, she reported that her husband thought he remembered her having been involved in a car accident which had resulted in a traumatic abortion. She had found it virtually impossible, during the weekly half-hour visits permitted, to persuade him that there had been no such accident and that she was still carrying the child.

No doubt the phrase "loss of a sense of reality" appropriately describes a wide range of mental disturbances. It applies in the present case to a man's believing that an event which he had imagined had actually happened. The imprisoned journalist held his belief with such conviction that even the principal in the imaginary event failed repeatedly to persuade him that his belief was false. His loss of a sense of reality consisted in a sudden failure of the normal capacity to distinguish between imagining and remembering with respect to a particular event. Less acute delusions about the past, at least about the details of actual events, are experienced from time to time by most of us, perhaps by all. This case of a man under stress taking a wholly fictitious event invented by himself for an historical fact recalled dramatically raises the question of how we ordinarily discriminate between our imaginings and our memories. It is with this question, or, more precisely, with the answer which Hume gives to it in *A Treatise of Human Nature* that I shall be concerned throughout this paper.* By taking up this

* This paper was written during the course of a sabbatical leave from McMaster University which was made possible by a Canada Council Leave Fellowship awarded for 1973–74. Since public acknowledgement of the Council's grant would otherwise have to await completion of the longer work promised, I welcome this earlier opportunity to express my appreciation of its generous support.

question about memory and imagination, another one, about history and fiction, is made unavoidable, as Hume himself found. An event imagined to have happened in the past is fictional, one remembered to have happened is historical—or so, at least, Hume supposed. If he should be right about this, there must be a conceptual connexion between remembering and historical truth and between imagining and historical falsity, and it would seem to be important to elucidate this connexion.

"Memory" and "imagination" are both words which may appropriately denote a wide range of diverse phenomena. Both are used here in restricted senses. I am not, for example, concerned with habit memory, or with unconscious memory, but almost exclusively with experienced memory, with the retrieval in imagery or in words, or in some combination of the two, of persons, places, and events with which the individual who is remembering was once personally acquainted. By "imagination" I mean the faculty or act of inventing characters, scenes, and episodes which are like those which are remembered, except that they did not exist or take place, or are not believed by the person imagining them to have existed or taken place. One can imagine future events as easily as past ones, of course, and it may be proper to assign imagination as prominent a role in musical composition or architecture as in the writing of fiction. For an examination of Hume's theories of imagination and memory, however, it is indicated that discussion be restricted to those uses of the imagination which can be appropriately compared with remembering.

In the present state of Hume scholarship there is no need of an extended argument merely to prove that these theories are defective. Several eminent commentators have reserved space for displaying their flaws, and no one has defended them as adequate. D. G. C. MacNabb showed Hume greater leniency than he is usually accorded by graciously remarking "that if he has failed to produce an intelligible account of memory no other philosopher has done so either." [1] John Passmore's verdict that, in his attempt to distinguish between remembering and imagining, "Hume's inconsistencies reach epic proportions" [2] is more typical of the severity with which these theories have been commonly judged. This judgement against Hume's perplexed analyses of memory and imagination has been upheld by epistemologists recently concerned with these concepts,[3] and there is no more hope of reversing the judgement now than there is point in adding new arguments to sustain it. What is possible, and perhaps not without point, is to show what initial mistake impaired Hume's treatment of these concepts and consequently damaged his account of historical belief. My argument to this purpose moves through the following six stages:

I. *Hume's double standard*: Hume introduces two logically independent criteria for distinguishing between ideas of memory and ideas of imagination. His first criterion ("phenomenal") distinguishes them in terms of introspectible differences in intrinsic nature. His second criterion ("epistemic") distinguishes them on the basis of their respective truth values.

II. *Hume's causal account of historical beliefs*: Although the phenomenal criterion of memory experiences and the epistemic criterion of memory claims are logically independent, Hume takes the marks of memory experiences as signs of true recall. It is consistent with a causal theory of memory to claim that the distinguishing features of memory experiences are attributable to the past events which memories represent, and that by learning to recognize those features men acquire contingent grounds to warrant memory beliefs. Hume's attempt to encompass historical beliefs within this same causal framework yields an incoherent account of them.

III. *Hume's distinction between historical and fictional narrative*: Hume extends his psychological theories of memory and imagination to account for our believing historical narratives but not fictional ones. But his theory is over-strained, for the source of historical ideas is not analogous to that of ideas of memory. Hume is left with the trivial but interesting proposition intact that we believe historical statements to be true because we believe them to be historical statements. By inappropriately contrasting imagination and memory with respect to belief, Hume misconstrues the role of imagination and thus misdescribes the experience of the reader of fiction.

IV. *Hume's theory of belief*: Hume's misrepresentation of the experience of imaginative literature is indicative of the limited range of applicability of his doctrine of natural belief. His definition of belief in terms of the introspectible features of credible ideas yields no criterion for distinguishing between fictional and historical ideas, or between ideas of memory and of imagination.

V. *Hume's conception of recollection*: Hume's failure to find satisfactory phenomenal criteria to distinguish between remembering and imagining reflects the realities of mental life, in which these functions are normally collaborative, not antithetical or mutually exclusive. The temptation to divide them sharply stems from the epistemological demand to distinguish clearly between historical truths and literary fictions.

VI. *Conclusion*: In accordance with his usual policy of resolving epistemological problems by psychological theories, Hume attempted to define the truth conditions of historical assertion in terms of the phenomenal features of memory experiences. Recognizing the logical independence of phenomenal and epistemic criteria of remembering which ensured Hume's failure provides the basis for resolving his problem of how a man can tell whether he is remembering or imagining an event of the past.

I

Hume's first attempt to distinguish between ideas of memory and of imagination, in Book I, Part I, Section I of the *Treatise*, is notoriously unconvincing. When remembering an event, Hume says, one's ideas are much more vivacious, lively, and strong, than ideas entertained when imagining an event. His observation that the memory "paints its objects in more distinct colours" than does the imagination, whose ideas are "faint and languid" (T 9), suggests that we should find history books livelier than fiction. He later confirms the impression given here that such was his eccentric verdict on these two sorts of literature (T 97–98).[4]

However implausible Hume's way of distinguishing memory from imagination, his strategy in this early section shows clearly enough when viewed in the light of the theory of belief developed later in the *Treatise*. He is looking to the intrinsic properties of ideas (imagery and thoughts) for the "sensible difference" between ideas of actual events recalled and ideas of fictitious events imagined. Undoubtedly there is a felt difference between true recollection and pure fantasy, but this difference is hard to capture in phenomenal descriptions of the two sorts of experience. Hume later admits that the vivacity criterion will fail when applied to cases of faded memories and to imaginings of hallucinatory intensity. But this failure is not fatal to his theory of belief, which holds strength of conviction to vary proportionally with the liveliness of the idea entertained; for, as Hume says later (Book I, Part III, Section V), memory ideas may become so faded that all belief in their truly representing a real event of the past is lost. And, as he also says, ideas of imagination sometimes "acquire such a force and vivacity" as to pass for memories and to "counterfeit" belief. Thus, Hume's theory of belief can accommodate those failures of memory and deceptions of imagination which are known to occur. Even so, the phenomenological problem of distinguishing between paradigmatic ideas of memory and imagination in terms of their respective intrinsic properties remains unsolved.

Nor is it evident that an explanation of the felt difference between remembering and imagining can be extracted from Hume's quasi-empirical theory of the causes and association of ideas. Ideas of memory and imagination have a common source in impressions. A complex idea of memory is a fair copy of the previous complex impression, from which the vivacity of the memory idea is derived. A complex idea of imagination is composed of simple ideas arranged with indifference to previous combinations and sequences of simple impressions. But each of the simple ideas of an imaginative complex has its quota of intensity imparted to it by the simple impression which it copies. The complex idea should be expected to display vivacity commensurate with the combined force of its constituent parts. Why these ideas should be faint and languid, compared with ideas of memory, since both are composed of simple ideas having the same copying relation to simple impressions, is not, so far as I can see, explicable on Hume's principles.

Relative vivacity is not the only criterion proposed by Hume for distinguishing between ideas of memory and of imagination. In this same very early section of the *Treatise* (Book I, Part I, Section III), it already appears that problems of memory and of history were associated in Hume's thinking. Historical narrative and personal recollection alike are required to preserve the true "order and position" of the events recalled. Memory is bound by the past. The imagination is free to alter ideas and to play them out at will. This difference between memory and imagination Hume illustrates here, as he will do again later (Book I, Part III, Section IX), by contrasting historian and poet.

This second criterion differs in type from the first, involving a relation between idea and event. Relative intensity of ideas can only be determined introspectively. The congruity of a sequence of ideas with a past series of events obviously cannot be determined simply by contemplating the ideas alone. When a man is correctly remembering an event which he witnessed, his ideas are faithful copies of the impressions he had at the time of the event, occurring in "the same order and position" as did his original impressions. This observation might serve as a crude preliminary to defining "memory," in the limited sense of the recall of personally observed events. Fidelity to the past is, in some sense which need not be refined here, a defining feature of memory as here considered, and of history as well. It is what distinguishes memory from fantasy, and histories from works of the literary imagination. But it is not an introspectible feature of ideas, or an intrinsic property of historical prose; hence it does not explain a man's tacit belief that he is remembering and not inventing, or that he is reading an historical rather than a fictional narrative. Leaving history aside for the moment, how can we account for the familiar, recurrent belief, supposition, or assumption that what we have "in mind" on certain occasions is a memory of an actual event rather than an imagined fiction? The fact that we *are* remembering rather than imagining does not in itself explain our *believing* that we are remembering.[5] The problem of fixing the connexion between the psychological peculiarities of memory experiences and the relevant historical facts cannot be evaded by shifting back and forth from a subjective, phenomenal criterion for distinguishing between remembering and imagining to an objective, epistemic one. For that expedient merely generates further perplexities, as I now shall show.

II

The double standard for distinguishing between memory and imagination introduced into Hume's *Treatise* (Book I, Part I, Section III) gives rise to paradoxes. Phenomenal and epistemic differentia are set down there end to end, as if they were correlative. A phenomenal criterion applies, of course, to inner, private experiences, and is tacitly relied upon to discriminate between two sorts of mental acts directed toward the past. An epistemic criterion applies to statements about the past and is relied upon to distinguish history from fiction. The phenomenal criterion is abstracted from the differing descriptions of remembering and imagining. These descriptions derive from introspection, and the criterion which they yield can be applied to any single, given case by one person only, viz., by the subject, who alone can be aware of the intrinsic character of his mental activity. The phenomenal criterion is in every sense subjective. The epistemic criterion is abstracted from rules of evidence used to determine the truth value of statements about the past. These rules derive from the procedures which have evolved for sifting truth from error in historical assertion; they are common property, and have to do with evidence in the public domain. The epistemic criterion is in every sense objective.

Interpreting Hume's phenomenal criterion in the light of his subsequent theory of belief, we may say that if a man believes that his mental picture or inner speech correctly depicts or describes an actual event of the past, he is remembering. If, on the other hand, he has no disposition to believe that what he has in mind represents a past event as it happened, he is imagining. According to Hume's epistemic criterion, what validates the claim of a witness to remember is the truth of his testimony, his having preserved "the original form, in which [his] objects were presented . . ." (T 9). Narratives which are historically false are attributed to the imagination, which "is not restrain'd to the same order and form with the original impressions . . ." (T 9).

It is obvious that the occurrence of belief does not guarantee the truth of recollection. Nor, and this is less obvious, does the absence of belief ensure the historical falsity of imagined fictions. Belief and disbelief in representations of the past are logically independent of their truth value. When belief and truth, or disbelief and falsity, coincide, no problem appears about distinguishing between memory and imagination. When memory beliefs are falsified, or imagined fictions confirmed, the conflict of phenomenal and epistemic criteria generates paradoxes. Cases will arise of people imagining actual historical events, which seems a little odd, and of remembering events which never happened, which seems distinctly odd, indeed absurd. To sharpen the paradox, we will have cases which are at once instances of remembering and of not remembering.

If we retain either the phenomenal or the epistemic criterion and discard the other, the paradoxes can be resolved. But both these obvious ways of satisfying the law of the excluded middle with respect to cases of remembering and of imagining entail unacceptable consequences. One implication of using the phenomenal criterion exclusively would be that introspective discriminations between these mental acts are incorrigible; whereas, in fact, memory claims are sometimes withdrawn in the face of contrary evidence. If memory is to be rightly taken as a source of knowledge about the past— as, indeed, the prime source of historical knowledge—its deliverances must be assessed for coherence and put to whatever corroborative and verifying tests are available. Even so, because a phenomenal criterion is not universally sufficient alone, it does not follow that it can be dispensed with altogether. Although we usually do apply whatever objective tests of the truth of memory claims are at hand, sometimes there are none available; and then we can only decide, as judges, jurors, or newspaper readers, whether the witness or journalist is honest and undeluded. The presupposition of questioning the reliability of a witness speaking from memory is that most probably he can tell whether he is remembering the incident which he relates or imagining it. If this presupposition were denied, the possibility of insincerity in witnesses would have to be denied also, which would surely be unacceptable.

In sum, it is quite proper to appeal to an epistemic criterion to distinguish within testimony between memories and fabrications. However, to insist that witnesses must rely upon this same criterion in order to discriminate between their memories and their fantasies is false as a psychological statement of fact and wholly impractical as a recommendation.

Phenomenal and epistemic criteria of memory, each of which is needed for a different purpose, are logically independent of one another. At the root of the paradoxes propounded above is the tacit assumption that inferences can be made in either direction between experiences of certain descriptions (remembering, imagining) and the truth value of statements about the events concerned (historical, fictional). It is assumed that if a mental act is correctly described with respect to a certain event as one of remembering it, then the statements about the event issuing from that experience are true, or approximately true; whereas, if the event is imagined, statements about it have no literal truth value. And it is also assumed, of course, that in both cases the direction of inference is reversible. Although these assumptions are unwarranted, it would be preposterous to deny connexions of every kind between memory and confirmed testimony and between imagination and acknowledged fiction. It is enough to deny a conceptual connexion between remembering as a psychological fact (an experience) and a verified historical claim (confirmed testimony), and similarly for imagination. What must be allowed is a contingent relation between remembering and asserting historical truths. In the beginning was the event; it was witnessed; the information was stored, retrieved, and reported. Here are four steps in a causal sequence, which, if fully understood, would explain (psychologically and physiologically) the possibility of historical knowledge.

Regarding autobiographical ideas, a man stakes his claim that something happened upon his memory of it, as he does his claim that something is happening upon his perception of it. Upon what does he stake his claim to remember? Upon nothing, of course; his claim to remember something is groundless, because his memory is itself the ground of his claim. Scepticism about other people's memories can be reasonable to a degree that scepticism about one's own memory cannot. To refuse the evidence of one's own memory because of a general mistrust of testimony would imply that each man stands in the same relation to the memories of others as to his own, which is, of course, untrue. His mistrust of witnesses, unless it is perfectly gratuitous, must be based upon his memory of their past failings; since in order to be rationally sceptical of the memories of others, he cannot be sceptical of his own, a total scepticism about memory is incoherent.[6]

Although memory is the only immediate source of knowledge of the past, it does not follow that memory claims are incorrigible. Distorted pictures of past events can be corrected through the sort of concerted effort to recall which retrieves temporarily forgotten names or melodies or telephone numbers. Sometimes memories can be tested against the recollections of others, or against hypotheses required to account for present states of affairs, or against records preserved in letters or diaries of the time. But each of these procedures presupposes a degree of reliance upon memory in general. Although the implications of memory beliefs can be tested against present evidence, one cannot get back of the memories themselves, so to speak, to find a surer basis in the past for beliefs about it. But even if a particular memory claim can be given no deeper or firmer grounding than a particular act of remembering, a quite general endorsement of the capacity of memory to recover the past can be tendered. A causal theory like Hume's, which explains the occurrences of memory ideas as effects of past impressions, provides such a warrant for memory beliefs in general. If our ideas of past events are caused by the impressions which we formerly had of those events, then our memory ideas do have the grounding in the past which is required to explain and justify our guarded trust in memory. Since the original impressions are irrecoverable, the theory is not directly verifiable; but it is indirectly verified whenever memory beliefs are confirmed by such corroborative tests as I mentioned above.

It is true that a confirmed idea of memory might have as its cause, not the original impression which it supposedly reproduces, but a reminder of later date. But such deviant cases cannot seriously damage the causal theory, since, to deal with one sort of case, we cannot be reminded of what we cannot remember. There may also be cases of men supposing that they are remembering a thing or event when in fact they are recalling an idea induced in the past by some memento of it.[7] However, it does not follow from the fact that occasionally we may be in doubt or error about whether an apparent memory is a genuine one that in cases where we are sure and correct the original experience can be dispensed with as a necessary condition of recall. Again, the standing causal condition of remembering that something existed or happened may be the last in a series of recollections; but, in such a case, the causal chain is nonetheless fastened to original impressions entertained during our immediate acquaintance with the thing or event.

Historical beliefs are not adequately covered in a Humean context by the same causal theory. Our ideas of whatever existed beyond the range of our own experience are not grounded in impressions, but in ideas drawn from books and lectures and conversations. Through one of the most bizarre arguments which Hume ever penned we get an oblique view of his failure or refusal to recognize the logical independence of remembering and making true historical judgements. In the course of his analysis of causality in Book I, Part III of the *Treatise*, Hume wants to make the point that causal inference must start from hard empirical data. In Section IV ("Of the Component Parts of Our Reasonings Concerning Causes and Effects"), he tells us that prediction must be ultimately grounded in "an impression of the memory or senses" (T 83), and no doubt he would say the same of explanation. He chooses a very curious instance to illustrate this need of the individual to tie chains of inference to immediate data of his sense or memory. He cites the fact "that CÆSAR was kill'd in the senate-house on the *ides* of *March*," and asks "for what reason we either believe or reject it." We believe it, he says, "because this fact is establish'd on the unanimous testimony of historians." The cause of our belief resides in the text of the history book where we read of Caesar's assassination: "Here are certain characters and letters present either to our memory or senses; which characters we likewise remember to have been us'd as the signs of certain ideas . . ." (T 83).[8] The explanation of our belief terminates in our reading, but such a psychological explanation would serve as well to account for our credulous acceptance of an apocryphal story as for our belief in a well-attested historical fact. Besides, many people may have heard of Caesar's murder only from the pages of Shakespeare, and yet believe it. A legend and an historical fact differ because the causes of each differ in kind. A legend is made up in someone's imagination and is likely to be embroidered as it is passed down. The testimony of the witness who remembered the historical event is accepted and preserved in the annals of history. There is, I suppose, some sort of causal connexion between the observations of the eyewitness of the attack upon Caesar and our belief in the dictator's murder. But such a tenuous causal chain hardly allows us to ground our historical belief in this contemporary witness's impressions of sense and memory. What seems to be required for Hume's instance of this historical belief to illustrate his point about empirically grounding factual knowledge is that our ideas about Caesar's death be enlivened by the centuries-old impressions of some Roman's sense and memory. Although this might seem too farfetched a notion to attribute to Hume, he does in fact immediately go on to say, in the same sentence in which he spoke of the historical text as the source of our ideas, that

> these ideas were either in the minds of such as were immediately present at that action, and receiv'd the ideas directly from its existence; or they were deriv'd from the testimony of others, and that again from another testimony, by a visible gradation, 'till we arrive at those who were eye-witnesses and spectators of the event [T 83].

True ideas about the remote past may be causally dependent upon the sense and memory impressions of contemporary witnesses of events; but the student of history must depend upon books for his ideas, and it does not follow from his truly remembering what he read in them that what he remembers is true. A causal explanation of an historical belief need not include any reason for believing it. The actual occurrence of the appropriate event will be the most remote cause cited in any such explanation; but the statement that the event happened will be hypothetical, its truth conditional upon the truth of his belief in it. In other words, one cannot cite as evidence for belief in an historical fact the occurrence of the event needed to explain the belief (if true), because the evidence would be identical with what it is supposed to be evidence for. Regarding the next link in the causal chain of explanation, the eyewitnessing of the event, as Professor Anscombe has remarked about the case of Julius Caesar, it is more likely that we believe that his murder was witnessed because we believe that he was murdered than that we believe he was murdered because we believe his murder was witnessed.[9]

When Hume says in the following passage, "without the authority either of the memory or senses our whole reasoning wou'd be chimerical and without foundation," we must ask whose memory or senses are in question: the historian's or the eyewitnesses's?

> 'Tis obvious all this chain of argument or connexion of causes and effects, is at first founded on those characters or letters, which are seen or remember'd, and that without the authority either of the memory or senses our whole reasoning wou'd be chimerical and without foundation. Every link in the chain wou'd in that case hang upon another; but there wou'd not be any thing fix'd to one end of it, capable of sustaining the whole; and consequently there wou'd be no belief nor evidence. And this actually is the case with all *hypothetical* arguments, or reasonings upon a supposition; there being in them, neither any present impression, nor belief of a real existence [T 83].

Hume's statements give no unequivocal answer to our question of whose impressions are being talked about. He is unintentionally evasive here, I think, because he has it so fixed in his mind that remembering and true historical assertion are conceptually tied that he supposes either can be inferred from the other, even in the case of historical claims based upon ancient testimony. Our ideas of whatever existed beyond the range of our own experience are not grounded in impressions (inferences aside), but in ideas drawn from books and lectures and conversations. And yet numerous such ideas are as confidently believed as any turned up in personal reminiscence. Hume allows this fact, and his problem is to explain why we do believe that the heroes of history really existed, performing the deeds of which historians write, and do not believe that the characters of fiction ever really existed, or that the events related by novelists actually took place.[10]

III

Why do we believe that Hannibal and Napoleon and Joan of Arc really existed, and that Don Quixote, Prospero, and Anna Karenina did not? Hume's first answer to this question is that ideas picked up from historical writing about people who once existed are more vivid than any ideas of fictional characters evoked by imaginative literature. And belief, of course, is proportional to the vivacity of an idea. Although beliefs about the past based upon memories of firsthand experiences are generally recognized as fallible, it might be expected that they would have a greater authority for us than beliefs instilled by others. It might be supposed harder to doubt what we remember having witnessed than what we remember of what we have been taught. Such is not the case, however, according to Hume, who depicts personal memories and reported facts as residing equally comfortably and unquestioned in the consciousness of each of us. Reflection proves Hume right, I think; at least I have never felt more prone to doubt Caesar's crossing of the Rubicon in 49 B.C. than my own crossing of the Atlantic in 1973. Perhaps because believing is a more passive state than Hume's theory implies, when there is no incentive or demand for proof, we acquiesce in a host of historical claims as readily as in our memories. Whether we have equal title to our historical beliefs as to our convictions based upon memory is a question which draws Hume onto dangerous ground.

He attempts (in Book I, Part III, Section IX) to fuse his theories of memory and history. Of the two "systems . . . of reality" which are the objects of a man's belief, one is made up of distinct memories, and the other of ideas inferred from those memories. Present impressions often evoke associated ideas of things once directly experienced; these ideas have that peculiar vividness which characterizes sense impressions and ensures (or rather constitutes) belief. It is the different feel of memories, their intensity, which distinguishes them "from the mere fictions of the imagination." Sometimes remembering involves more than entertaining ideas of persons and places, of episodes and emotions, which earlier were objects of acquaintance. Fair copies of past impressions are the substance of autobiography, but standing alone they would make up only a fragmented narrative. However, these same ideas also provide grounds for the causal inferences needed to fill out the story and to render reflection on a past experience coherent. In recollection we regularly believe that things which we did not observe did exist or happen, because other things which we observed and remember would otherwise be unaccountable. Such inferred ideas of things past make up that system of realities which is the object, not, strictly speaking, of memory, but, Hume says, "of the judgment" (T 108). Their credibility is conferred by association with ideas of memory, whose intensity approximates or equals that of impressions.

Scattered amongst autobiographical ideas are ideas of historical events in which the subject did not participate. Just as he becomes used to things happening in a certain way, and therefore believes that they will continue to do so in the future, so he becomes accustomed to hearing that certain things happened in the past, and therefore comes to believe that they really did happen. Men are equally coerced by reiterated testimony as by personal memory. When ideas taken from histories are remembered, they serve as cues for the imaginative reconstruction of the remote past, as do personal memories for the recovery of past experiences. When an historical narrative is created within consciousness, the imagination (judgement) works by causal inference, paying deference to the usual considerations of probability. Hume contrasts the poetic imagination (fancy), in which fictions are freely spawned, with the historical imagination (judgement), as the source of credible conceptions of things past:

> 'Tis this latter principle which peoples the world, and brings us acquainted with such existences, as their removal in time and place, lie beyond the reach of the senses and memory. By means of it I paint the universe in my imagination, and fix my attention on any part of it I please. I form an idea of ROME, which I neither see nor remember; but which is connected with such impressions as I remember to have received from the conversation and books of travellers and historians. The idea of *Rome* I place in a certain situation on the idea of an object, which I call the globe. I join to it the conception of a particular government, and religion, and manners. I look backward and consider its first foundation; its several revolutions, successes, and misfortunes.

All this, and every thing else, which I believe, are nothing but ideas; tho' by their force and settled order, arising from custom and the relation of cause and effect, they distinguish themselves from the other ideas, which are merely the offspring of the imagination [T 108].

It will be noticed that Hume speaks here of historians providing their readers with impressions of persons and places of the past. This proposal is contrary to expectations built up by Hume's account of the respective origins of impressions and ideas. It introduces into his discussion of history and fiction the same inconsistency which plagued his theories of memory and imagination and of which John Passmore complained.[11] On the very first page of the *Treatise*, following the Introduction, Hume illustrated his distinction between impressions and ideas by pointing out that what one may expect to receive from reading his book is ideas. The only impressions involved in the experience will be visual and tactual ones made by examining a copy (open or closed) and handling it and whatever feelings of "immediate pleasure or uneasiness it may occasion." Accordingly, anyone starting on Hume's *History of England* should expect from his reading—visual impressions of printed pages aside—ideas of persons and places and events of the past, not impressions of them.

On reflection, it is easy enough to understand how pressure exerted by Hume's theory of belief forced his surprising choice of term when he came to perceptions invoked by the reading of history. If the student of history is to acquire any beliefs about the past at all, some of his ideas must have the required relation to vivifying impressions. Sense impressions registered when observing and handling volumes of history are useless here, and so are impressions of excitement or boredom, delight or exasperation, felt while reading them. Only impressions of memory are left; and it is true that Hume has consistently given memories equal standing with sense perceptions as a source of belief. He is able to do this because, on the scale of intensity by which he discriminates perceptions, fresh and vivid memories fall alongside or adjacent to the original impressions which they copy. But the vividness of memory images, which warrants Hume's frequently speaking of impressions of memory, is borrowed from the original sense impressions. Consequently, if the memory of what was read in a history book is to generate belief, the theory requires that the reader has acquired impressions, not ideas, from the book. But what would be required for him to get an impression, rather than an idea, of Hannibal or ancient Rome or the Battle of Trafalgar through reading? It would be necessary that he believe that the general or the city existed as stated or that the battle took place as reported. If the claim were that the reader believed in any such existence or occurrence because his idea of it had a vividness tantamount to that of an impression, Hume would now be completely encircled. But he has prepared his escape by reversing for historical beliefs the sequence which terminates in natural ones. The courses of events move in opposite directions in the two sorts of situation, as appears in the following pair of examples.

1. I feel the glass slip from my fingers. Instantly, spontaneously, the idea of its falling and shattering on the tile presents itself. My predictive image

is a summation of many experiences of unsupported heavy bodies and of the effect of impact upon brittle objects. My idea of its imminent destruction is as irresistible as my tactual impression of having lost my grip on it. The idea carries conviction because I have not feigned or manipulated it. Like my impression of its leaving my hand, the associated idea of its breaking presents itself vividly as a fact which I am powerless to alter. In such a case, the psychic current—the vivifying charge—runs from impression to idea; and the same will be true for my host, who observes the fragments of crystal at my feet upon re-entering the room, and infers the cause of the damage. The associative mechanism upon which prediction and explanation depend would be inoperable in a lawless universe. I need not understand gravity or the mechanics of fracture to predict the results of my carelessness, but if results were random—if physical laws of which I may be ignorant did not steadily obtain nonetheless—I would not be able to predict, for I would not have built up any expectations. A long run of successes in predictions of various kinds, after careful observations, may inspire in a reflective man a conception of the uniformity of nature. This principle is not one which he need invoke when settling his common sense or scientific beliefs, but at a relatively late stage he may recognize it as one upon which he tacitly relies when he puts his confidence in experience.

2. I open *The History of England* and read the following:

> Prince Henry . . . retired to St. Michael's Mount, a strong fortress on the coast of Normandy, and infested the neighbourhood with his incursions. Robert and William with their joint forces besieged him in this place, and had nearly reduced him by the scarcity of water; when the elder, hearing of his distress, granted him permission to supply himself, and also sent him some pipes of wine for his own table. Being reproached by William for this ill-timed generosity, he replied, *What, shall I suffer my brother to die of thirst? Where shall we find another when he is gone?* [12]

Hume's words provide me with an idea of the fact they state. I have what Hume calls a "strong and steady conception" of the idea; in its "firmness and solidity," in its compelling force, it *feels* like an impression of memory, and I acquiesce in its truth as I do in that of vivid memories. By my manner of conceiving this idea, I charge it with the irresistible vividness which forces it toward the end of the continuum of perceptions where impressions of sense and memory fall. And my manner of conceiving this idea is dictated by my awareness that it has been stated in a history book. When I take up a work of history, I am disposed to believe that the people who will be named in it once existed, actually doing the deeds to be related, in such real places as will be mentioned. I do not come gradually to the conviction that an historical work is true by accumulating beliefs in its particular ideas. I believe the particulars because I tacitly believe that historians, generally and on the whole, tell the truth about the past, and this unexamined article of faith determines the way I feel about the ideas which they present to me. My historical beliefs, my impressions of persons, places, and events of the past, are generated by ideas—a reversal of the sequence which begins with an impression and ends in a natural belief. In relying upon recorded history for beliefs about a past I do not remember, I am in no stronger position rationally than I am when depending upon the principle of the uniformity of nature for my predictions and explanations of natural phenomena. In both cases, the only defense lies in a necessity imposed by the lack of alternatives. The determined historical sceptic must renounce all sense of a past beyond the scope of his personal memory. He lives in an intellectual world where no distinction is recognized between fact and fable, like a physicist in a lawless universe.

Hume's own view, that our habit of trusting historians' accounts for our believing in the particular figures and incidents portrayed in historical literature, may itself seem to be a sceptical one. There is a semblance of paradox in the implication that a single book will yield one experience to a man who reads it as a history and a very different one to another who takes it as fiction. Although I do not think that Hume's words capture this difference, I believe that he is right in his main contention about there being one, and that it is attributable to the readers' differing preconceptions about the type of literature they are engaged with:

> If one person sits down to read a book as a romance, and another as a true history, they plainly receive the same ideas, and in the same order; nor does the incredulity of the one, and the belief of the other hinder them from putting the very same sense upon their author. His words produce the same ideas in both; tho' his testimony has not the same influence on them. The latter has a more lively conception of all the incidents. He enters deeper into the concerns of the persons: represents to himself their actions, and characters, and friendships, and enmities: He even goes so far as to form a notion of their features, and air, and person. While the former, who gives no credit to the testimony of the author, has a more faint and languid conception of all these particulars; and except on account of the style and ingenuity of the composition, can receive little entertainment from it [T 97–98].

Only the most indifferent reader of fiction would recognize his literary experience in Hume's description. All that is said here about the response to historical writing fits the experience of any receptive reader of imaginative literature. It is not the reader of a romance which Hume has succeeded in contrasting with the confident reader of a history, but, contrary to his intent, it is the incredulous reader of a history. The languid reader "who gives no credit to the testimony of the author" is reading (God knows why) a history book of some sort which he does not believe to be true. If Hume's misdirected comparison expressed merely an incidental bit of thoughtlessness, it would not be worth mentioning. But readers of the *Treatise* will recognize it as typical of his way of dealing with history and poetry up to this point. Although Hume will shortly try to correct his focus on aesthetic experience, it is worthwhile looking into the distorted view of it which was imposed by his initial mismanagement of the concepts of memory and imagination.

It is sometimes appropriate to contrast memory and imagination and sometimes not. Consider the situation of two men sitting down to narrate independently some episode in which they both participated. One recalls it in vivid detail, without doubt or hesitation writing the report which his memory dictates. The other (having been in a state of shock at the time, let us say) has only a shadowy recollection of a few particulars. Working uncertainly with this sparse assortment of dim memories, he pieces together a coherent report by imagining what seems likely to have happened during each interval from which his memory draws a blank. It is virtually a truism to maintain, as Hume would, that the first man will believe more firmly in his own testimony than will the second in his. And it is at least plausible to suggest that the first account will have a ring of authority which will be missing from the second. Where memory and imagination have undertaken a common task, a comparison of their performances has some point. But it is not the fate of imagination to work only at making good memory's losses. Suppose the second man to be asked to take some such episode as the first is chronicling as the theme and starting point of a story. He is instructed to make his story as exciting as he can, and to make only such use of historical facts as suits that purpose. We must infer from this hypothetical situation and Hume's theory that the ideas and images of this man, who is firing his imagination to make up a lively story, will be more "faint and languid" than those of the author of the factual report. If the fiction writer's conception acquired the vividness of the reporter's, he would be deluded by his own imagination, and take himself to be remembering. Neither this inferred conclusion about the relative intensity of the two writers' thoughts and imagery, nor our own suspicion that it may be false, is testable. But it can be argued that the comparison is a pointless one, drawn through a misapplication of Hume's theory of belief. It is because Hume has made vivacity of conception the essence of belief that he would feel compelled to characterize the undeluded fiction writer's ideas and images as pale shadows of the reporter's memory impressions. But the comparison should never have been drawn.[13] It is not that the imaginative writer falls far down on a scale of belief which gives the author of a memoir a splendidly high rating. This scale simply does not apply to imaginative conceptions. When historical facts are irrelevant, and there is no question of believing or disbelieving, it makes no sense to apply one's gauge to find out just how weak the belief really is. Nor will the work of fiction be comparable with respect to belief to the work of reportage. It may be credible as a story, a believable piece of fiction. But whoever reads it as a work of the imagination, and finds it believable as such, does not find it believable because it impresses him as a reliable historical narrative.

IV

It is doubly regrettable that Hume did not work his ideas about aesthetics into theories as elaborate and finished as those he developed for ethics and politics. His discussion of artistic verisimilitude in the *Treatise* (Book I, Part III, Section X) starts a line of investigation which one might wish he had pursued for its inherent interest. During the course of such an extended inquiry, moreover, Hume might have been alerted to a major flaw in his theory of belief.

Hume makes a point of the extent to which the credibility of fiction derives from strands of literal truth running through imaginative writing:

> 'Tis evident, that poets make use of this artifice of borrowing the names of their persons, and the chief events of their poems, from history, in order to procure a more easy reception for the whole, and cause it to make a deeper impression on the fancy and affections. The several incidents of the piece acquire a kind of relation by being united into one poem or representation; and if any of these incidents be an object of belief, it bestows a force and vivacity on the others, which are related to it [T 122].

Hume's point is, I suppose, obvious enough, once stated; but it is a fundamental point about literary credibility, one well worth making and capable of extension beyond the historically based tragedies to which he refers. The suspension of disbelief in a fictional event is fostered, for instance, by depicting it as taking place in a faithfully described setting with which readers are familiar. When the factual details in a work of fiction go pointlessly wrong, the disposition to acquiesce in the imaginary as real is disturbed.

What belief as constitutive of aesthetic experience has in common with belief in certain other contexts is passivity. It seems to me that often, contrary to Hume, believing is a negative condition, a state of inertia preserved by the absence of doubting. It is doubting rather than, as Hume would have it, believing which is an intellectual activity requiring a dynamic explanation. What is peculiar to aesthetic belief is that what is accepted as credible is tacitly recognized as untrue. The paradox of aesthetic illusion is that whoever undergoes it fails to be deceived. What would otherwise be a self-contradictory state of consciousness is tenable because the object of the imagination is not used as a basis of inference to facts outside the imaginative invention, or of belief about them. Hume seems to have supposed that all literary art aspires to the condition of history, and that the explanation of the credibility of fiction can be found in his account of how beliefs about the external world and the historical past are acquired. However, a believable fiction does not masquerade as history, successfully disguised as literal truth. Nor does a man believe that the people and events in a believable story really existed and happened as he believes what he reads in a believable history or remembers from personal experience. The belief—or lack of disbelief—attending the experience of compelling fiction is *sui generis*. It is not a degenerate form of the natural or conditioned beliefs which Hume's theory is suited to explain. It is not, like the self-deception of the habitual liar or the delusions of the insane, an aberrant form of belief which can be covered by a consistent development of Hume's theory of natural belief.

In the section immediately preceding this discussion "Of the influence of belief," Hume had insisted that vivacity of conception does not cause belief but constitutes it: "Here we must not be contented with saying, that the vividness of the idea produces the belief: We must maintain that they are individually the same" (T 116). But here he claims that beliefs instilled by educators and poets are causes of the vivification of ideas: "The effect, then, of belief is to raise up a simple idea to an equality with our impressions. . . . This effect it can only have by making an idea approach an impression in force and vivacity" (T 119). In order to satisfy the conditions imposed by this second account, a belief would have to obtain prior to the effect (the vivification) it is said to produce; but imposing this requirement is inconsistent with defining belief in terms of vivacity of conception.

A credible idea is attended by a certain feeling, according to Hume. Evoke a belief ("by making an idea approach an impression in force and vivacity"), and the feeling occurs. Alternatively, induce this feeling toward an idea, and it will be vivified and thus believed. Except for cases of poetic delusion, credible fictions fail to produce this feeling, and therefore the ideas induced by a "poetical description," however vivid, fail to command belief: "But still the ideas it presents are different to the *feeling* from those, which arise from the memory and the judgment. There is something weak and imperfect amidst all that seeming vehemence of thought and sentiment, which attends the fictions of poetry" (T 631). It may seem that there is or ought to be this felt difference between entertaining a factual idea and a fictional one. The difficulty is that Hume's theory has provided nothing but varying degrees of intensity to account for it. To be credible as a fiction, an idea must approach an impression in intensity; in order not to be mistaken for a factual idea, it must recede from that same level of intensity. These inconsistent demands imposed by Hume's theory raise suspicions about its adequacy to account for artistic verisimilitude. These suspicions tend to be confirmed when one considers his description of aesthetic belief as a degenerate variant of natural belief.

At the root of Hume's problem is his univocal sense of belief. He has taken as a paradigm of belief the situation in which the perception of an object or event evokes an associated idea of its cause or effect. When belief occurs as a sudden realization, the idea embodying it often appears in consciousness as a dominating presence with all the force and vivacity in terms of which Hume defines belief. But conscious believing often takes the form of a far less sharply defined experience, one appropriately described as a passive attitude of acceptance. Far from giving way before the irresistible force of a vivid idea, the believer is often in a tranquil state of intellectual resignation in which rather vague and hazy conceptions pass unchallenged. If this is so, we should not expect to find in the intrinsic properties of conceptions the features which distinguish remembering from imagining. Between uncritically trusting memory during an interlude of reminiscence and indulging in a fanciful reverie there is no doubt a difference with respect to belief. But that difference is not describable in terms of the relative intensity of the conceptions involved. Nor can the difference between the experiences of the student of history and those of the student of imaginative literature be described appropriately in these terms.

If Hume's decision to make an introspectible feature of memory impressions the basis for distinguishing them from imagined ideas is revoked, his question remains. How is a present conception recognized as representing something experienced in the past? The matching of present conception with past experience justifies belief in the memory, but does not explain it, for only one of the terms in this relation is available in consciousness at the time of remembering. If the problem is conceived according to a model of pictures fitting things, Hume's solution may appear to be the only one available. For much experienced memory, however, this model is not at all suitable; it suggests a much closer resemblance in form between originals and copies than is needed or usual. Even predominantly visual or auditory experiences may be recalled mainly in words—in the form of mental notes, so to speak. Although memory paraphrase is still not well understood,[14] it is at least safe to say that often what one has in mind when remembering is less similar in form or structure to what is remembered than is a picture to its subject. Even for cases most favourable to Hume's picture theory, those in which an image of something formerly seen appears, the model is misleading. It suggests that a man remembering is like a policeman with an unlabelled identity photograph and no suspect with which to match it. What is involved in recognizing a memory image as representing a familiar person, for example, is better understood by considering what happens when one recognizes an acquaintance or a picture of him. In such a case there is opportunity for comparison (of present perception with memory image), but it does not take place. What happens is that the sight of one's acquaintance or of his picture directly elicits some appropriate response: calling his name in greeting, ducking into a doorway to avoid him, or whatever; saying, aloud or to oneself, "Old Grindthorpe's got his picture in the paper again," or something of the sort. All that operates to produce behaviour manifesting (or, better perhaps, constituting) recognition is no doubt very complicated, but its description is the responsibility of psychologists and physiologists, not of philosophers. What philosophers can understand at this stage is that the explanation of recognition in these familiar situations will include factors of which no one is aware in the ordinary course of experience. I am sure that the same is true in the case of recognizing a memory image as representing whatever it does represent. Hume proceeded as if he really supposed that because remembering is a conscious act, performing it depends only upon factors present in consciousness. He concluded therefore that memory impressions must reveal themselves for what they are, and he conferred upon them the spurious distinguishing characteristic which suited his theory of belief.

v

The psychology of disembodied man practised by Hume is a science of limited capability. Presumably it may be said, without betraying an eccentric metaphysical bias, that for purposes of perceiving, thinking, believing, remembering, and imagining, a body is indispensable. The human body is not placed at the centre of Hume's theories of mental life, and he was more diffident than was Hobbes about speculating on questions of physiology. There is, however, considerable textual evidence, impressively assembled by

Robert Anderson, of Hume's conviction that the deep explanation of such mental phenomena as remembering is to be given in terms of "material processes in the brain." [15] Hume clearly distinguished his role as a moral philosopher concerned with phenomenological descriptions of conscious experiences from that of the natural philosophers who might be expected to discover someday the anatomical structures and physiological processes underlying mental phenomena. It is with a correct description and classification of conscious experiences which are prerequisite to their experimental investigation that philosophers can provide anatomists and physiologists as a starting point for their difficult, technical work. From analyses based upon what Hume calls experience, restricted, in other words, to data accessible to introspection, answers to such questions as how men can distinguish their memories from their imaginings can only be, in the literal sense, superficial.

Hume says that the ideas of memory and imagination differ "in the manner of their conception" (T 629). If force or vivacity does not make the difference, what does? What is the noticeable difference between remembering an event in which one took part and imagining a similar event which one does not believe ever took place? It may at first prove tempting to say that when remembering, but not when imagining, a man believes that his conceptions truly represent a past event; if this were so, the object of his memory belief would be a relation of correspondence between conception and event. But this account surely misrepresents his memory experience in a way which can be brought out if one considers an analogous case of perceiving. If a man sees a tree (as opposed to wittingly imagining one), he does *not* believe that his visual image truly represents the physical tree. He does not entertain as an object of belief a relation of correspondence between image and tree; for, when perceiving, he is not aware of any distinction between what is in his perceptual consciousness and what is in the external world. Such a distinction is an analytical one drawn within a certain theory of perception. Similarly, the distinction between a memory impression and the event represented by it is never thought of when one is simply remembering an event. This distinction, too, is an analytical one, drawn for theoretical purposes, usually of an epistemological kind.

The distorting effect of theory upon introspection is difficult to avoid. Even the apparently trivial statement "When I remember an event, I believe that it took place, but when I imagine one, I do not" is misleading. It suggests that recollection consists of at least two distinct performances: remembering and believing, as if one first attempts the feat of recall, and then makes a reflective decision about the credibility of the result. Such a description does not fit countless familiar instances, although it may do for some cases in which, for whatever reason, the advent of the memory impression is followed by an interval of uncertainty. The inseparability of believing from remembering normally experienced is reflected in the presupposition of ordinary usage that "believing" is part of the meaning of "remembering." If "I remember his firing into the crowd, but I do not believe that he did" is absurd, the affirmation of belief in "I remember his firing into the crowd, and I believe that he did" is redundant: redundant because remembering an event entails believing that it happened, without there being any further mental exercise required. Remembering an event does not provide a man with evidence from which he infers that the event took place. Remembering is a way of believing about the past—the only direct way. In effortless recall, consequently, believing is not a feature which could distinguish remembering from any other mental activity, because it is not distinguishable from remembering itself. Since remembering is a specific way of believing, the question of why we believe what we remember and not what we imagine is illicit. It mistakenly presupposes that believing and disbelieving are mental acts or attitudes supervening upon the primary acts of remembering and imagining. It is one of a kind with the obviously trivial question "Why do we feel what we touch, but not what we see at a distance?"

Just as one is not usually aware of a distinctly experienced state or activity of believing when remembering, so one is not usually conscious of disbelieving one's own imaginings. When a person is imagining, he is not, normally, overtly acknowledging to himself the historical falsity of his conceptions. The words "usually" and "normally," which seem bound to recur in any such discussion as this of introspectible features distinguishing remembering from imagining, point to an apparently insoluble problem. Whatever feature one hits upon turns out to do at best for a certain range of cases, but not for all. It might be said that what distinguishes these two kinds of performances within consciousness is that the man remembering experiences a sense of effort "to get it right," or at least awareness of the possibility of making a mistake; whereas the man imagining experiences a sense of freedom "to make it up" as he goes along, quite unhampered by the prospect of falling into error. But these descriptions are not universally true of either sort of performance. Some remembering is effortless, with no thought of error occurring. While indulging in extravagant fantasy, the imagination may have unlimited freedom from fact and reality; but in many exercises of the imagination, the subject, once decided, imposes restraints.

After much searching I have failed to find in my imagery, thoughts, or inner speech any introspectible feature which could serve for all occasions to inform me of whether I am remembering or imagining. This failure, I have decided, points to the banal truth of the matter. I recognize certain images and thoughts as memories because I am engaged in remembering, other images and thoughts as imaginings because I am engaged in imagining. I know what I am about, and it is by virtue of my chosen project, to remember an actual event of the past or to imagine a fictitious one, that I spontaneously confer the appropriate status upon my conceptions. The analogies between these performances and readings of history and fiction are obvious. How I take ideas currently in consciousness is a function of what I understand myself to be engaged in doing.

The need or wish to treat memory schematically results in a picture which, by over-simplifying, suggests, curiously, that remembering is a richer experience, more replete with detail, than it usually is. One speaks of recollection in terms of recalling scenes once observed, episodes witnessed, conversations overheard, and the like. Thus it is suggested that recollection is similar to watching a documentary film or to reading a memoir. It is suggested that past experiences, when truly remembered, present themselves full-blown before the inner eye. When we remember an event, we are again aware of its happening, as we were when first we experienced it. Our tacit belief in the fidelity of our reproduction to the original excludes for us the possibility that we are imagining—"making it up." This conception of remembering is surely idealized. What is usually present in consciousness when an event is recalled are fragments of the original. Occasionally, it is true, events are recalled intact, the original experience of most of these exceptions having been highly charged with emotion. Except for these rare, peculiarly significant, or traumatic events of short duration, whose recall may be of hallucinatory vividness, what is present to a person remembering is not a fair copy of the original but a token of it.

To reconstruct an episode from memory requires an effort which we often have no incentive to make, and hence we make do with memory tokens. Such tokens are, like photographs, cues for reconstructing the past, pegs upon which are fastened threads of reminiscence. By evoking a sense of recognition, they confer verisimilitude upon reminiscence. Spanning the gaps between tokens, when composing a coherent historical narrative, is work which is left to the imagination.

It may seem to be a harmless falsification to present in theory as re-enactments of past experiences what in reality are usually recoveries of memory tokens of those experiences. But this particular distortion is symptomatic of a general tendency in philosophy to misrepresent the psychological facts of remembering and imagining. The hard line drawn in the conceptual distinction between memory and imagination has no counterpart in experience. Abstractly considered, an imagined fiction is at the opposite pole from a remembered fact. However, many of our experiences belong at neither pole; they fall upon middle ground. We do sometimes present as actual events what we are aware of as being pure fantasies; we fabricate the past, as liars and as novelists. Occasionally, on the other hand, we do report a distinctly remembered fact in statements which we believe, and rightly believe, to be literally true—as accurate in detail as a contemporary account by a reliable observer. But often—more often than not, I should think—our memories are inadequate to the task of composing a full and coherent narrative, and imagination collaborates unnoticed.

Thus memory claims commonly go beyond the evidence provided by hard memory data. Narratives based upon recollection usually include some features which were not actually observed, and which must, therefore, be put down to imagination. Imaginative material which fills gaps in the original experience, or others made by forgetting, is so completely assimilated into the memory process that it is not distinguished in the ordinary course of experience from true memories. The corollary that imaginative invention needs the support of memory is perhaps even more obviously true. A man without memories would lack material for his imagination to work upon. When a man is imagining, he does not, I think, notice the difference between what he invents and what he recalls; he regards a fusion of mixed materials simply as the fiction which he understands himself to be imagining. This last, speculative, point I would not insist upon. What seems to me true and important is that in experience memory and imagination are not antithetical, as they appear to be when abstractly considered in relation to historical fact.

Correspondence between a narrative and an historical fact is not precluded by imposing coherence upon recollection by imaginatively supplementing memory data. One point of stressing the role of imagination in recollection is the insistence that on the face of ideas pointing to past events there is often nothing noticeable marking some as true copies of actual impressions and others as inventions which fill observational gaps or replace lost memory tokens. Another point is that the confirmation by evidence that a particular idea does correspond to some feature of a witnessed event does not certify it as an idea of memory. The epistemic distinction between recall and invention, following the division between fact and fiction, is too coarse to separate remembered from imagined elements in most cases of recollection. Here, as elsewhere, conceptualization is tidier than experience.

It is not implausible to suppose that the imaginative amplification of memory data sometimes yields misrepresentations of the past. Misdating, reversed sequences, transposed identifications, inferences mistaken for observations (especially in the case of motives: "I remember how resentful she was," for example) are only a few of the familiar errors which memory is heir to. If we grant these pitfalls, we find that errors transferred to historical narratives are, in principle, corrigible. Historians, journalists, judges, and other professional and private persons use a variety of means for corroborating and correcting eyewitness reports, and Hume worked at systematizing these in his discussion "Of Miracles" in *An Enquiry Concerning Human Understanding*. The personal histories men compose privately for themselves elude many of these objective, public controls, and it is in this circumstance, surely, that we should look for a solution to the perplexed problem of self-deception.

A false assumption underlies the temptation to say that the sincere author of an untrue report from memory must have been imagining, not remembering, and this way of speaking has an awkward consequence. The assumption is that remembering and imagining are psychologically disparate activities, which I have argued is, even in the case of true reports, mistaken. The consequence is to nullify "wrongly remembered" and cognate terms.[16] Both the assumption and the consequence could be accommodated by legislating new conventions for the use of the two key terms. We might agree to use "memory" to designate the retentive faculty,[17] putting the burden both of retrieval and of fabrication upon what we would call "imagination." However, philosophers' attempted reforms of everyday speech seldom "take," and from a philosophical vocabulary out of step with common usage we may expect merely verbal solutions to real problems. It is less tidy, but truer, I think, to acknowledge the regular collaboration of memory and imagination in both recollection and invention, and to distinguish between remembering and imagining teleologically, in terms of the main objectives of their respective exercises.

VI

It is not surprising that a philosopher concerned with the conditions of factual knowledge imposed by human nature should oppose memory and imagination when considering historical truth and error. Since clearly defined concepts and sharp distinctions are desirable in epistemology, it is tempting to draw comparably firm boundaries and stark contrasts when mapping the intellectual processes from which various kinds of assertion are delivered. Rigidity and simplicity, however, are rarely compatible with fidelity to the facts of mental life; nor is the epistemologist disposed by his preoccupation with truth conditions to do justice to the complexity of the psychological aspect of those same facts. Hume seems at times to have regarded imagination as a degenerate form of memory; when comparing the two, the highest compliment he found to pay imagination was to admit that it may sometimes pass with deluded subjects as memory. But feats of imagination are not, after all, aberrations of memory. A theory which condones equating failure at "getting it right" with success in "making it up" is in need of refinement.

By invoking the distinction between the phenomenal and the epistemic senses of memory and imagination, the question of how a man can tell whether he is remembering or imagining is easily disposed of. The question is ambiguous, open to two interpretations which should be separately put as follows:

1. How can a man undertaking to recall an event tell whether or not what he currently has in mind truly represents what actually happened?
2. How can a man tell whether he is engaged in recalling an actual event or in inventing a fictitious one?

1. The proper answer to this first question is that a man *cannot* tell at the time of his attempt whether or not his memories match the past event. There is nothing in the intrinsic character of his experience, no discernible feature of imagery or thought which provides an infallible indicator of success. The inexplicable feat is never performed, and the tantalizing question therefore vanishes.

2. What makes this second question as nonsensical as it appears to be is its supposition that people awaken to the realization that they are engaged in one or the other of two similar mental activities and then try to discover which one it is. Such situations are conceivable; a person reviving from a drugged or drowsy state might be thus momentarily perplexed. What we called at the beginning "a sense of reality," in so far as it involves discriminating between remembering and imagining, consists in using a set of skills in which training by parents and natural consequences begin early. Its exercise, like that of many other learned skills, may be expected to deteriorate when corrective influences are removed from the environment.

Thus, a prisoner who is cut off from the steady flow of information against which men normally test their ideas may persist in deluding himself about which performance he is conducting. Apart from such atypical cases, about which the question is not specifically asked, people normally engage in remembering or imagining in full awareness of what they are setting out to do from the start.

The original question appeared to be both answerable and important because it traded on the ambiguity of "remembering" and "imagining," retaining both their epistemic and phenomenal connotations. Of course, it is important to distinguish between true and false reports about the past; but the epistemological question of how it is done bears upon objective evidence, upon various corroborating and verifying tests publicly available for evaluating testimony. What determines the correct ascription of memory and imagination as epistemic concepts is the correspondence or not of conceptions to historical facts; but this relation is no part of the experience of the subject, who cannot, therefore, base his discriminations between experiences upon the truth value of the assertions to which they give rise. The psychological question is answerable, but quite as trivial as "How can a man tell whether he is engaged in whistling a familiar tune or in humming an original one of his own?" People can tell what they are doing because they have decided what to do; from which it does not follow, of course, that they always succeed in doing what they are attempting to do. The psychological question seemed important only because its key terms smuggled in the epistemic connotations which make it unanswerable.

NOTES

1. D. G. C. MacNabb, *David Hume: His Theory of Knowledge and Morality* (Oxford, 1966), p. 42.

2. John Passmore, *Hume's Intentions* (Cambridge, 1952), p. 94; see also Norman Kemp Smith, *The Philosophy of David Hume* (London, 1941), chap. 11, where it is suggested that difficulties in Hume's analyses are matters of presentation rather than of substance.

3. See, e.g., R. F. Holland, "The Empiricist Theory of Memory," *Mind*, 63, No. 252 (October 1954), 464–86 (repr. in *Human Factual Knowledge*, ed. Mark Levensky [Englewood Cliffs, 1971], pp. 13–34), which opens with a quotation from the *Treatise* and concludes by denying the possibility of distinguishing on Humean lines between ideas of memory and ideas of imagination. Holland's criticism is re-affirmed by D. W. Hamlyn, *The Theory of Knowledge* (London, 1970), chap. 7, especially p. 192; see also B. S. Benjamin, "Remembering," *Mind*, 65, No. 259 (July 1956), 312–31 (repr. in *Essays in Philosophical Psychology*, ed. Donald F. Gustafson [Garden City, 1964], pp. 171–94): "Hume's theory of remembering is the purest example of what I might call the mental datum theory. . . . I wish now to show that it is an impossible thesis to maintain in any form" (in *Human Factual Knowledge*, p. 174).

4. See Section III of Editions K, L, and N of *An Inquiry Concerning Human Understanding*, where Hume appears to express a contrary view. Applying his associationist theory to the analysis of the concept of unity, he says of epic poetry: "The imagination both of writer and reader is more enlivened, and the passions more inflamed than in history, biography, or any species of narration that confine themselves to strict truth and reality" (ed. Charles W. Hendel [Indianapolis, 1955], p. 35).

5. In "Remembering" (*Philosophical Review*, 75 [1966], 161–96, at 161), a paper intended "to define what it is to remember," C. B. Martin and Max Deutscher argue that

believing is not a necessary condition of remembering. They claim to show that it is logically possible for a man to remember a scene or event whilst not believing that it existed or happened, or even whilst believing that it did not exist or happen. The possibility of such atypical experiences may be admitted, and so may the need to re-examine the relations between belief and memory. If believing is not a necessary condition of remembering, it is (in some sense which needs elucidation) a feature which is in fact common to numerous instances of remembering; and it is such typical cases, rather than deviant ones, which are relevant to the purposes of this paper. When attempting to answer the question of how men can tell that they are remembering when they are, it would not be helpful to dwell upon cases of men who cannot tell that they are remembering when they are.

6. See H. H. Price, "Memory–Knowledge," *Proceedings of the Aristotelian Society*, Suppl. Vol. 15 (1936), 16–33; and E. J. Furlong, "Memory," *Mind*, 57, No. 225 (January 1948), 16–44, repr. in *Human Factual Knowledge*, ed. Levensky, pp. 56–83.

7. Graham Greene considers such a possibility in the following passage of his autobiography, *A Sort of Life* (London, 1971), p. 15: "In all these early years I am uncertain what is genuinely remembered. For example, I think I can remember a toy motor-car, which now surely—a 1908 vintage toy—might be worthy of a sale at Sotheby's, but since it appears in a photograph of myself and my brother Raymond, this may not be a true memory."

8. Hume has not overlooked the point that we can remember a fact although we have forgotten the occasion on which we read of it. In the next, final paragraph of this section, he writes: "I need not observe, that 'tis no just objection to the present doctrine, that we can reason upon our past conclusions or principles, without having recourse to those impressions, from which they first arose. For even supposing these impressions shou'd be entirely effac'd from the memory, the conviction they produc'd may still remain . . ." (T 84).

9. See G. E. M. Anscombe, "Hume and Julius Caesar," *Analysis*, 34, No. 1, N.S. 157 (October 1973), 1–7. Professor Anscombe's thesis—that by regarding the existence of Caesar as an hypothesis which may be doubted, Hume committed himself to radical historical scepticism—is contested by Donald W. Livingston in a reply article, "Anscombe, Hume and Julius Caesar," *Analysis*, 35, No. 1, N.S. 163 (October 1974), 13–19.

10. My statement of the problem may seem to presuppose an invariable alignment of belief and history, and of unbelief and fiction, which, I am aware, does not obtain, and which, since there are errors in history, and incidental truths in fiction, would not be warranted. Many people apparently believe that Sherlock Holmes actually existed, and many others, presumably believing that he does exist still, post hundreds of letters each year to his Baker Street address, often, as in the recent case of an American corporation, to engage his professional services (retainer enclosed). There are deviations on the other side as well. For example, Thucydides mentions Achilles on an early page of *The History of the Peloponnesian War* (trans. Richard Crawley [London, 1910], p. 3), implying that he accepts Homer's authority for the existence of Achilles. Considering what Thucydides says later about "the lays of a poet displaying the exaggeration of his craft . . . the subjects they treat of being out of the reach of evidence, and time having robbed most of them of historical value by enthroning them in the region of legend" (ibid., p. 14), I am not sure whether I do or should believe that Achilles ever really existed. Although scholars are similarly in doubt or disagreement about King Arthur, I think that most of them would concede that if King Arthur ever did exist, there is as much truth—or no more untruth—about him to be found in Thomas Malory's poem as in the history of Geoffrey of Monmouth. Neither these deviant cases, nor the seams of imaginative invention in historical writing ("At this point Frederick the Great knocked out his pipe") or of factual reporting in fiction ("Two mountain chains traverse the republic roughly from north to south, forming between them a number of valleys and plateaux") defuse Hume's problem. The general tendency to believe that statements with past reference made in one sort of literature are, on the whole, literally true, and those made in another are not, still needs, even in the face of exceptions, to be explained and justified.

11. In *Hume's Intentions*, Passmore writes of "the change which gradually comes over

Hume's theory, as a result of which ideas of memory are transformed into impressions. On this matter (and this is no accident or fit of carelessness) Hume's inconsistencies reach epic proportions; within a few pages of the *Treatise* he describes ideas of the memory as 'equivalent to impressions' (T, 82), speaks of 'an impression of the memory' (T, 84), contemplates 'a repetition of that impression in the memory' (T, 86), and yet never ceases to emphasize that memory presents us with ideas (T, 85). Unless memory presents us with actual impressions, Hume's theory of belief collapses; and yet, if it does, impressions are no longer 'original existences,' with the comforting solidity and actuality that phrase suggests. And also, if both remembering and 'feeling' (observation) consist in our having impressions, Hume cannot possibly explain in the language of perceptions how one can be distinguished from the other or—if he was prepared to argue that they are in fact identical—how anyone ever came to believe that certain of our perceptions have a special relation to the past, that they are 'remembered' " (pp. 94–95).

12. Ed. T. Cadell, 8 vols. (London, 1778), I 290.

13. See Holland, "Empiricist Theory of Memory": "In the case of Hume, an immediate difficulty arises from the fact that each of the contrasts in terms of which he proposes to differentiate between ideas of the memory and ideas of the imagination seems to be utilized already for the purpose of distinguishing some imaginings from others, or for the purpose of distinguishing some rememberings from others, or for both of these purposes. One may have recollections that are clear or unclear, faint or strong, more vivid or less vivid; one's imagination also may be vivid or not vivid, lively or not lively, weak or powerful. The suggestion that the haziest of recollections must be somehow clearer and more vivid than the most powerful products of a lively imagination seems implausible, if not senseless" (*Human Factual Knowledge*, ed. Levensky, p. 15).

14. The classic work in this field is F. C. Bartlett's *Remembering* (Cambridge, 1932). For a detailed review of recent empirical investigations of this subject ("coding"), see Peter Herriot, *Attributes of Memory* (London, 1974).

15. *Hume's First Principles* (Lincoln, 1966), p. 132.

16. This consequence is accepted by some writers as being conformable to common usage. A. H. Bassoon remarks: "On Hume's definition of a memory we can have false memories as well as true ones. . . . Other people would define a memory as an idea of something that really happened . . ." (*David Hume* [Harmondsworth, 1958], p. 38). See Benjamin, "Remembering": "If one proffers information accompanied by the formula 'I remember (that) p' or 'I know (that) p,' then, should p turn out to be false, to be misinformation, one is forced not merely to admit the falsity of the information, but also that one did not remember, that one did not know. One is forced by the rules of language formally to eat one's words" (*Essays in Philosophical Psychology*, ed. Gustafson, p. 189).

17. Precisely this view is attributed to Hume by Jan Wilbanks in *Hume's Theory of Imagination* (The Hague, 1968), p. 76: "As far as Hume's general conception of memory is concerned, I am convinced that he conceived this faculty to be essentially retentive in character." Although Wilbanks is able to quote two statements consistent with this interpretation, it is not clear how he could accommodate other statements such as Hume's first one on the subject: "The faculty, by which we repeat our impressions . . . is called the MEMORY . . ." (T 8).

14

Economics and the Mechanism of Historical Progress in Hume's *History*

Constant Noble Stockton
The University of Wisconsin
River Falls

I · THE "SCIENCE OF MAN" AND THE *History of England*

In the past fifteen years it has ceased to be necessary to argue against the previously received opinion that Hume's *History of England* is an aberration of no relevance to his philosophical writings.[1] From one recent perspective, on the contrary, it is viewed as the logical culmination of his life's work. According to this perspective, developed in the writings of E. C. Mossner[2] and others, the central of Hume's several intentions was to set forth the roots and branches of a "science of man," to do for "moral philosophy" what Newton had done for "natural philosophy."[3] In Hume's terminology, "moral philosophy" included not only the chief subdivisions of what we today call "philosophy" but also what we today would call the "human sciences." The obvious difficulty with this perspective is that it makes Hume's sceptical epistemology and *its* implications, which many of us regard as the most important part of his work, appear less than central to his intentions, a kind of inconvenient by-product. Perhaps it was; this consideration would account for a possible inconsistency in Hume, that so much of his work seems to assume the possibility of the very kind of knowledge which his sceptical epistemology seems to have proved unjustifiable. The virtue of this perspective is that it unifies Hume's efforts in such disparate fields as epistemology, moral theory, psychology, aesthetic criticism, political theory, economics, anthropology of religion, and British constitutional history into an intelligible whole.

This "science of man" is essentially historical. The point here is not that Hume's epistemological work and his practice as a historian yield valuable suggestions for the analytical philosophy of history, although that is true.[4] My point is that the "science of man" is empirical, grounded in human experience, and that this experience for Hume includes historical experience.

History, therefore, is a source both for many of the principles of this "science of man" and for their verification. Thus, historical materials appear sometimes in the *Treatise*, very frequently in the *Essays*; the whole of *The Natural History of Religion* is history of a sort. It is not surprising, therefore, that Hume concluded his lifelong effort to develop the "science of man" by writing a long work which was explicitly a history of the traditional sort.

What is the *History of England* really about? It pursues so many topics that it is hard for the commentator to say, "Hume's central theme is so-and-so" without either vagueness or the exclusion of some purposes which Hume himself deemed important.[5] In some passages, especially in the earlier volumes, the *History* indeed seems to consist merely of a disconcertingly perfunctory political chronicle with no theme at all. After one such passage, Hume interrupts himself with an outburst which itself is instructive as well as entertaining:

> It is almost impossible, and quite needless, to be more particular in relating the transactions of the East Angles. What instruction or entertainment can it give the reader, to hear a long bead-roll of barbarous names, Egric, Annas, Ethelbert, Ethelwald, Aldulf, Elfwald, Beorne, Ethelred, Ethelbert, who successively murdered, expelled, or inherited from each other, and obscurely filled the throne of that kingdom? [6]

The phrase "instruction and entertainment" appears repeatedly in Hume's *History of England* [7] as well as in his suppressed essay "Of the Study of History" (*Essays* 558) as a description of the historian's proper aim. Instruction in what? The several threads which Hume weaves into his account of English history are for the most part theories which he had presented more abstractly in his non-historical writings. For example, the hypotheses of the essay "Of Superstition and Enthusiasm" and to a much lesser extent of *The Natural History of Religion* are illustrated and perhaps modified in the passages in the *History* which treat religion. One could take elements in his political theory and his views about the British government and show how these are developed in the *History*.[8] Some of the principles of his psychological theory find expression in the *History* in his character sketches of famous figures and his explanations of their motivation.[9] His views on aesthetics and criticism could be compared with his treatments of literature and the arts in his *History*. The aim of this paper is to do the same for his work in political economy. In short, the *History of England* embodies Hume's own application of his frequently quoted dictum in the *Enquiry Concerning Human Understanding* that the "chief use" of history

> is only to discover the constant and universal principles of human nature, by showing men in all varieties of circumstances and situations, and furnishing us with materials from which we may form our observations and become acquainted with the regular springs of human action and behaviour. These records of wars, intrigues, factions, and revolutions, are so many collections of experiments, by which the politician or moral philosopher fixes the principles of his science, in the same manner as the physician or natural philosopher becomes acquainted with the nature of plants, minerals, and other external objects, by the experiments which he forms concerning them [EHU 83–84].

We can restate the assumption and aim of this paper in the terminology of Hempel's theory of scientific explanation. The "instruction" in Hume's *History* often takes the form of deductive nomological explanation, its covering laws usually having been set forth in his earlier writings.[10] This paper will show how the covering laws which he presents in his economic essays are exemplified in his *History*.

In one way this characterization of the *History of England* is too generous; in a related way it is not generous enough. In his efforts to work out the principles of his "science of man" in an historical context, Hume met with uneven success. The writing of history before him (if we eliminate the work of Vico, which he apparently did not know, and that of Voltaire, which appeared at about the same time as his own) had been either political or ecclesiastical. The attempt to integrate the principles of "moral philosophy" into the framework of political history was new. Hume's own attempts at integration are often far from satisfactory. In the first place, he is given to sprinkling the *History* with maxims which have less the tone of empirical demonstration than the aura of armchair "philosophizing" at its worst. For instance: "Where ambition can be so happy as to cover its enterprises, even to the person himself, under the appearance of principle, it is the most incurable and inflexible of all human passions." [11] Many such *obiter dicta* are so obvious that they seem hardly worth saying; some of them are inconsistent; some of them may not even be altogether true. In the second place, some of the more general theories of Hume's "science of man" find application in systematic digressions of two kinds. Four long appendices, appearing after the discussions of the reigns of Edward the Confessor, John, Elizabeth, and James I, treat at length the constitution, laws, fiscal affairs, economic life, "manners," and "learning and the arts" for the previous period. Lists of "miscellaneous transactions," appearing at the end of Hume's chronicle of almost every important reign, treat similar topics in a more haphazard way. Hume repeatedly emphasizes the importance of these digressions:

> The rise, progress, perfection, and decline of art and science, are curious objects of contemplation, and intimately connected with a narrative of civil transactions. The events of no particular period can be fully accounted for, but by considering the degree of advancement which men have reached in those particulars.[12]

These somewhat disjointed digressions, although intrinsically more substantial than the occasional maxims, are hardly integrated into the course of his narrative. On the other hand, Hume's more successful efforts at integration are less conspicuous precisely because integration so often succeeded. In particular his treatment of constitutional and religious developments in the *History* unobtrusively support, illustrate, and expand upon his treatment of the same topics in the essays. This method serves to enrich a history already valuable as history, a synthesis of more limited and often objectionably partisan sources into a detailed general history of England which remained unrivaled among historical works in its field for a century.[13]

This paper will first discuss Hume's relationship to the origin and development of the discipline of economic history, his own practice of that discipline, and his sources. It will then show how several of the themes in Hume's economic essays are reflected in the *History*, incidentally casting light on several ambiguities within his economic theory itself. Lastly, it will show how Hume uses economic development as a causal factor to explain political development—a causal theory almost Marxist in several respects.

II · HUME—PIONEER ECONOMIC HISTORIAN

The many-sided Hume appears to be the only figure in the whole of intellectual history who first made a substantial contribution to the development of economic theory and who then turned to write an important historical work. Indeed, in the order of Hume's publications most of the economic essays immediately precede the *History of England* and one crucial essay, "Of the Jealousy of Trade," appearing in 1758 or 1759,[14] must have been written about the time that Hume was finishing the Tudor volumes of his *History*. The central theme of the present study is to show how Hume the economic theorist is reflected in Hume the historian. But, first, a wider context for this study of Hume will be suggested.

Although much has been written on the history of economic theory, there have been few secondary studies on the history of the writing of economic history.[15] The discipline of economic history, like several other social sciences, took on recognizable form in the age of Enlightenment. In the seventeenth century, both the partisans of particular economic policies and other men of a somewhat more disinterested viewpoint wrote pamphlets and books about what they called "commerce." In the late-seventeenth century, in France, Germany, and England, these writings on "commerce" began sometimes to contain historical materials, treating such topics as the economic life of classical antiquity and why the Dutch had been able to rise so quickly to a position of economic power. In the eighteenth century, specialized studies in what we would call economic history began to appear. Bishop William Fleetwood's *Chronicon preciosum* (1707, expanded edition 1745) treated the history of prices, wages, and money, with tables of prices running back to the eighth century.[16] Thomas Maddox published his *History of the Exchequer*[17] in 1711 and other works on medieval government, feudal institutions, and corporations between 1702 and 1736. Although his main interest was in political rather than economic institutions, his works nonetheless provided a mine of fiscal and other economic data for historians of the next generation. The first historical study of what had been Britain's first major commercial product was published in 1747 by Rev. John Smith—*Chronicon rusticum commerciale, or, Memoirs of Wool.*[18] This two-volume compendium contained every public paper relating to wool, and an account of every other English publication concerning wool which Smith could lay his hands on, the whole arranged in chronological order. The first substantial work devoted to a more generalized economic history was written by a Scot employed at the South Sea House, Adam Anderson's *Historical and Chronological Deduction of the Origins of Commerce* (1764), which treated trade and manufacturing from Creation to the end of the Seven Years' War.[19] In this sequence, Hume's *History of England* (first edition 1754–62) comes just before Anderson and after the others. In his contribution to this new discipline of economic history, as in his contribution to the writing of political history,[20] Hume's principal achievement was to utilize previously published materials in a new and creative synthesis.

What type of economic historian was Hume? In the past generation the discipline of economic history has experienced a crisis of self-definition. The new "Cliometricians" reject the earlier style of economic history on the ground that it was not really economic history at all, but rather a kind of social history.[21] What economic history ought to be doing, according to partisans of the new viewpoint, is economic analysis in historical context—applying the hypotheses of economic theory in the dimension of time. For instance, if economists have developed a theory which fits recent periods of inflation, then economic historians should see whether the same theory, appropriately modified, explains the inflations of the sixteenth and eighteenth centuries. If the current theory fails to explain the earlier experience, then there are potentially fruitful opportunities for improving the theory. In the *History of England* Hume practiced, in his way, both kinds of economic history. On the one hand, although Hume's own economic theories differed in content from the theories of today's "Cliometricians" and although he lacked the quantitative data and the mathematical techniques which they use, he shared their basic methodological assumption: he, too, sought to verify the laws of economic theory in the dimension of time. And, on the other hand, Hume found an even greater interest in the area where economic history and social history intersect. A recurring theme of his *History* is how medieval economic and social conditions fostered ignorance, barbarism, and the political alternatives of feudal despotism or feudal anarchy, and how progress in economic and social conditions led to learning and civility which, in turn, provided the conditions for political and constitutional liberty.

III · HUME'S SOURCES OF ECONOMIC DATA

It is reasonable to inquire whether Hume had sufficient quantitative data to enable him to practice economic history in a systematic way. In fact, he had some data and applied it with great ingenuity. In the first place, Hume used Fleetwood, Maddox, and Smith, and incorporated material from Anderson into later editions of his *History*. In the second place, he made much use of the earlier literature of economic theory. From the brief and often obscure polemics out of which British economic theory developed, he extracted information concerning economic conditions at the time in which the various works were written. In the *History* he cites works by Thomas Mun, Edward Misselden, Lewes Roberts, Sir Joseph Child, Sir William Petty, and Charles Davenant, as well as several anonymous tracts. He praises "the judicious author" of *A Compendious or Brief Examination of Certain Ordinary Complaints of Divers of our Countrymen* but judiciously refrains from identifying it with William Shakespeare, under whose name it had been republished in 1751.[22] It is a little surprising that Hume does not cite John Graunt, whose computations of the population of seventeenth-century London, for instance, would have fascinated him. Nor does he refer to Gregory King, whose work was known in Hume's day (to Sir James Steuart and to Adam Smith, among others) through references and excerpts in several works by Charles Davenant including the one which Hume cites.[23] Neither does Hume cite Richard Cantillon, although Cantillon's work must have been known to Hume—at least after 1756, when Eléazar de Mauvillon, having published in 1754 a probably unauthorized French translation of Hume's *Political Discourses* at Amsterdam,[24] published Cantillon's *Essai sur la nature du commerce en général* in its French version in a third volume of the same set. It is less surprising that Hume makes no use of Sir Dudley North, whose work was unknown to economists in the eighteenth century.[25] Moreover, Hume studiously ignores Malachy Postlethwayt, whose *Universal Dictionary of Trade and Commerce* (1751) had plagiarized Cantillon at length.[26] In general, while by no means ignorant of eighteenth-century economic theorists whose work he synthesized in his own economic theory,[27] in the *History of England* Hume rarely cites economic theorists who published after 1688, the date at which his *History* ends.

Third, Hume inferred a good deal of economic and social information from the primary and secondary sources of English law and government. For the age of feudalism he often used Sir Henry Spelman and occasionally the continental writers François Hotman and Nicholas Brussel. He cited Sir Edward Coke and Sir John Fortescue, although he appears to have known their work very imperfectly. He often derived economic data from the texts of laws and statutes, beginning with the collections of Anglo-Saxon laws published by Lambarde (1568) and David Wilkins (1727). He cites such works as the *Dialogus de Scaccario* and John Cotton's abridgement of the Tower of London records with William Prynne's preface. He makes much use of the *Parliamentary History* (1751–63) and often finds items of economic relevance in the published journals of the House of Commons and in the private parliamentary journal kept by Simonds D'Ewes during the reign of Elizabeth.

Fourth, Hume gleaned bits of economic data from the ordinary primary and secondary sources of English history which he used. Archives and collections of original manuscripts were not normally open to historians in the eighteenth century,[28] although Hume eventually gained access to some important materials and even saw the memoirs of James II in Paris. But for the most part he had to write his *History* from published sources. He used medieval writers from Gildas and Bede to Matthew Paris and Froissart; such chroniclers as Camden and Stow, whose *Survey of London* (1598) yielded several economic items; the historical writings of such figures as Raleigh, Bacon, Clarendon, and Burnet; collections of materials published by such scholars as Wharton, Hearne, Rushworth, Rymer, Strype, and Birch; and the works of such historians as Brady, Carte, and Rapin de Thoryas.[29]

Fifth, Hume found fragments of economic information in a remarkable variety of miscellaneous sources. He cites a line by Sir John Falstaff concerning the price of Holland cloth [30]—carefully attributing the price to Shakespeare's time rather than to the age of Henry IV and commenting that the price was high. He cites an oration of Cicero's to substantiate his contention that Roman agricultural science was as bad as that of medieval England. In other places he refers to a letter of Erasmus, to More's *Utopia*, and to Sir James Harrington's praise of the commercial regulations of Henry VII. He devotes extensive quotation and analysis to the privately published account book of the fifth Earl of Northumberland in the sixteenth century.[31]

Hume is almost always sceptical about the reliability of quantitative data reported by earlier historians and even by firsthand sources. In his essay "Of the Populousness of Ancient Nations," arguing for the necessity of the criticism of numbers reported even by respected sources, he offers a striking example of seemingly authoritative data which proved to have been quite wrong. Sir William Temple, in his *Memoirs*, described a conversation with Charles II in which Temple, mentioning the size of Cromwell's army, overestimated its size by more than double but was not contradicted by the king —who surely, Hume suggests, had been in a position to know its true size (*Essays* 422–23, note). A similarly constructive scepticism is usually found in the *History of England*. Thus, for example, Hume records that historians had asserted that in two years Richard I received from England, over and beyond the costs of the English government, a sum of one million, one hundred thousand marks; Hume rejects this sum as "quite incredible" for three reasons. First, it would have meant a "thorough dilapidation" of the royal demesnes, which is unlikely in itself and improbable on other grounds. Second, if Richard had possessed such wealth, he easily could have paid his own ransom of a hundred and fifty thousand marks and would not have endured fourteen months of captivity. And, finally, "the prices of commodities in this reign are also a certain proof that no such enormous sum could be leavied on the people." [32] Why are such errors likely to appear in the historian's sources? Sometimes Hume blames the quirks of earlier historians.[33] For instance, Gervase reported that Henry II had imposed a scutage of £180,000 on knights' fees. But this, Hume calculates, "would amount to much above half the rent of the whole land." How is the exaggeration to be explained? "Gervase is indeed a contemporary author," Hume continues, "but churchmen are often guilty of strange mistakes of that nature, and are commonly but little acquainted with the public revenues." [34] In another place he interjects, "The sums mentioned by ancient authors, who were almost all monks, are often improbable and never consistent." [35] Yet not all of the errors are to be blamed on such "monkish historians," for public officials themselves were sometimes at fault. Speaking of the great overestimation of the revenues to be derived from the Black Prince's hearth tax in Aquitaine, Hume notes that "such loose conjectures have commonly no manner of authority, much less in such ignorant times." [36] Hume is even aware that the copyists of manuscripts, before the invention of printing, were especially likely to err in transcribing numbers, for "Any alteration in other places commonly affects the sense of grammar, and is more readily perceived by the reader and transcriber" (*Essays* 418); hence, he notes, "the numbers in Cæsar's Commentaries can be more depended on than those of any other ancient author, because of the Greek translation, which still remains, and which checks the Latin original" (*Essays* 446, note). At his best, Hume shows a noteworthy ingenuity in inferring from diverse sources what the quantitative data must really have been—as, for instance, in attempting to correct Knighton on the quantity and value of wool exported under Edward III,[37] and in correcting Strype by D'Ewes on the debt of Elizabeth.[38] Yet on the other hand our historian still occasionally lets pass a statistic which he ought to have questioned. For example, in contemptuously describing the ignorance of geography in the fourteenth century, despite the supposedly flourishing condition of the universities, he seems to accept the assertion of Speed's *Chronicle* that there were then thirty thousand students at Oxford alone.[39]

IV · HUME'S USE OF ECONOMIC MATERIALS IN THE *History*

Hume's *History of England* reflects his interests in historical demography, in theory of money, in the fiscal history of the English government (problems of taxation, national expenditures, national debt, and the like), in his theories on the question of mercantilism *vs.* economic liberty, of prices, of interest, of economic cycles, and of the relation between a nation's economic development and its social and political development. Limitations of space do not permit detailed analysis of everything which Hume says in his *History* concerning all these topics. But a few instructive and entertaining points can be indicated concerning each of them.

1. *Historical demography.* Nowhere in the *History of England* does the reader find such an elaborate exercise in historical demography as in Hume's earlier essay "Of the Populousness of Ancient Nations." In the *History* most of his treatments of population problems occur in the context of a discussion of the military strength available at a particular place, or available to the realm as a whole. But scattered through the *History* are many such calculations, some of them very ingenious in their critical utilization of contradictory or seemingly irrelevant data. Noteworthy in this respect, for instance, is his critical treatment of inconsistent evidence concerning the size of the militia and the total population of England under Elizabeth.[40]

2. *Money.* The *History of England* provides no suitable occasion for Hume to repeat the theory of the fictitious nature of money which he develops in such essays as "Of Money." But he records the amount of money circulating in England at the end of Elizabeth's reign and the increasing quantities of money coined during the seventeenth century.[41] He notes with disapproval several measures increasing the number of shillings to the pound and the repeated coining of base money,[42] pointing out that relatively sounder money would be hoarded or driven out of the kingdom, while the resulting inflation would cause hardship in the short run and would be of little benefit to the kingdom in the long run.[43] Hume is almost always careful to con-

vert sums of money mentioned for earlier periods into the equivalent sum of money in his own time, taking into consideration not only the changing weight of the shilling and the penny and the increasing number of shillings per pound, but also "the greater plenty of money" in England and the increase of population and prosperity which would make a given sum of money dearer in the earlier periods.[44]

3. *Government finance*. Hume devotes systematic attention to the financial situation of almost every reign, usually recording the amount and sources of revenue and typical items of expenditure. Often such treatments cast light on one of Hume's favorite historial themes—the struggle between liberty and authority in English history. Henry V, for example, was driven to arbitrary measures by his financial difficulties.[45] On the other hand, it was the financial independence of the Anglo-Norman kings and the relative financial independence maintained by Elizabeth which freed those monarchs to make their rule arbitrary if never quite absolute.[46] Hume analyzes the causes of the Stuarts' financial difficulties very fully. Noting the increasing prosperity of the people, especially of the middle class, in contrast to the increasing poverty of the crown, he develops the Harringtonian thesis that where the wealth is, there the power is or soon will be.[47] Hume concludes:

> Could the Parliaments in the reign of Charles I have been induced to relinquish so far their old habits, as to grant that prince the same revenue which was voted to his successor, or had those in the reign of Charles II conferred on him as large a revenue as was enjoyed by his brother, all the disorders of both reigns might easily have been prevented, and probably all reasonable concessions might peaceably have been obtained from both monarchs.[48]

Whatever the student of Hume's sceptical epistemology might think of the logical status of such counterfactual conditional propositions, Douglass North's manifesto of the new style of economic history in the *International Encyclopedia of the Social Sciences* argues that an important part of the work of the economic historian consists in the attempt to verify propositions that are logically similar.[49]

4. *National Debt*. Comparison of the first and last editions of Hume's *History* shows the same change in his attitude toward national debt which is revealed in his revision of his 1752 essay "Of Public Credit." The first edition of that essay, like his first edition of the *History*, shows a temperate disapproval of England's policy of financing her national emergencies by increasing her public debt. But as he grew older his revisions of that essay, his letters,[50] and his revisions of the *History* show an increasingly querulous preoccupation with that issue. In the first edition of the *History*, for example, he reports without any comment that "the first instance of debt contracted upon parliamentary security occurs" in the reign of Henry VI. But in a later edition Hume inserted strong words condemning "a practice the more likely to become pernicious, the more a nation advances in opulence and credit," the "ruinous consequences" of which "are now become apparent, and threaten the very existence of the nation."[51] The first edi-

tion, in treating the financial history of the reign of Elizabeth, notes without extensive comment that she paid the "incredible sum" contracted under her three predecessors [52] and praises the work of Sir Thomas Gresham in re-establishing the royal credit.[53] In the last year of his life—the note bears the date 1776—Hume inserted a long footnote containing an almost ludicrous diatribe against the public debt of his own time:

> Our late delusions have much exceeded any thing known in history, not even excepting those of the crusades. For I suppose there is no mathematical, still less an arithmetical demonstration, that the road to the Holy Land was not the road to paradise, as there is, that the endless increase of national debts is the direct road to national ruin. But having now completely reached that goal, it is needless at present to reflect on the past. . . . No imagination can figure a situation which will induce our creditors to relinquish their claims, or the public to seize their revenues. So egregious indeed has been our folly, that we have even lost all title to compassion in the numberless calamities that are awaiting us.[54]

5. *Mercantilism* vs. *economic liberty: an inconsistency in the* Essays *clarified.* Hume, like several other non-Whig predecessors of Adam Smith,[55] often manages to sound like a nineteenth-century advocate of *laissez-faire.* Just such a passage opens Hume's remarkable argument in favor of ecclesiastical establishment:

> Most of the arts and professions in a state are of such a nature, that, while they promote the interests of the society, they are also useful or agreeable to some individuals; and, in that case, the constant rule of the magistrate, except, perhaps, on the first introduction of any art, is to leave the profession to itself, and trust its encouragement to those who reap the benefit of it. The artisans, finding their profits to rise by the favor of their customers, increase as much as possible their skill and industry; and as matters are not disturbed by any injudicious tampering, the commodity is always sure to be at all times nearly proportioned to the demand.
>
> But there are also some callings which, though useful and even necessary in a state, bring no particular advantage of pleasure to any individual; and the supreme power is obliged to . . . give them public encouragement. . . .[56]

Hume goes on to argue that the former principle must not be allowed to function in religion, since "this increased diligence of the clergy" brings pernicious consequences. Hence the wise magistrate should "bribe their indolence" by supporting an established church.[57]

Regarding the question of Hume's position regarding *laissez-faire,* the *History* helps to clarify an ambiguity in the economic essays. In "Of the Balance of Trade" he attacks those who still sought, like the later bullionists, to maintain a favorable balance of trade for the purpose of preventing the nation's wealth from leaving it. Near the end of this essay, however, Hume endorses a reasonable tariff for revenue and even for protection (*Essays* 331–33). According to Eugene Rotwein, the latter position is "pointedly repudiated" [58] in Hume's later essay "Of the Jealousy of Trade," which appeared in 1758 or 1759.[59] To be sure, we might question whether the contradiction between the two essays is quite as great as Rotwein has suggested. The later essay is directed against the "narrow and malignant policies" of "states which have made some advances in commerce" which erect trade barriers for the purpose of depressing the prosperity of their economic rivals (*Essays* 334–38). It does not argue against tariffs for revenue, and it does not necessarily rule out protective tariffs for less economically developed nations. Nevertheless, the fact that Hume's position on governmental regulation of commerce is complex and may have changed makes it worthwhile for us to see what light the *History of England* casts upon it. Chronology suggests that "Of the Jealousy of Trade," appearing about 1758, may have been a by-product of his studies for the Tudor volumes of the *History of England*, the manuscript of which was sent to the printers in August 1758, as well as being Hume's own reaction to the war against France in those years.

In the *History of England* Hume's official position is this: since a nation benefits in many ways from a flourishing foreign and domestic commerce, government should lay upon the natural flow of trade only those restrictions which will in fact stimulate the prosperity of the nation. This means that in most instances, but not in all, foreign and domestic trade should have been more free than they were. Thus, from his careful analysis of the economic measures of Henry VII Hume concludes, "If we may judge by most of the laws enacted during his reign, trade and industry were hurt rather than promoted by the care and attention given to them." [60] When the Czar revoked the monopoly of the Muscovy Company, Hume sees in his letter to Elizabeth an anti-mercantilist lecture. "So much juster notions of commerce were entertained by this barbarian," he points out, "than appear in the conduct of the renowned Queen Elizabeth!" [61] But, in keeping with the latter part of his essay "Of the Balance of Trade," Hume in his *History* is not a consistent advocate of completely free trade. For example, he praises an arrangement with Gustavus Ericson whereby Sweden was given special trading privileges in exchange for bullion which enabled a reformation of English coin and consequently encouraged English commerce.[62] Similarly, in the *History* Hume almost always deplores whatever inhibits English exports. Yet he still suggests the possibility that some inhibitions on exports can be beneficial, speaking gently of the "premature" measures of James II which sought to encourage English woolen manufacture by forbidding export of unprocessed wool to the Dutch.[63] Hume argues repeatedly that governmental attempts to fix prices and wages "only aggravate the evil, by cramping and restraining commerce." [64] Perhaps the economic lesson taught most forcefully by history is the ill effect of monopoly. Monopolies of foreign trade conferred by the crown upon exclusive trading companies, "by which almost all foreign trade, except that of France, was brought into the hands of a few rapacious engrossers, and all prospect of future improvement in commerce was forever sacrificed to a little temporary advantage in the sovereign" were an "enormous grievance, one of the greatest which we read of in English story," [65] "diametrically opposite to all the principles of free government." [66] Domestic monopolies proved even worse, "grievances, the most intolerable for the present, and the most pernicious in their consequences, that ever were known in any age or under any government." [67]

6. *Prices.* Especially in the four earlier volumes of the *History*, Hume records the changing prices of such commodities as grains, horses, cattle, poultry, wool and woolen cloth, foodstuffs, and the rent and sale prices of land and houses. He is aware that individual prices usually are of less significance than "an estimation of the middling prices for a series of years" [68] but that sudden fluctuations of prices can also be significant.[69] He remarks that prices often differed from place to place [70] and that in the early modern period some prices were as high as if not higher than in his own day, if adjustment be made for the changing value of money.[71]

Hume's *History*, like several of his essays, contains unsystematic comments on the factors which determine prices. He is of course aware of the fundamental importance of supply and demand, including demand abroad.[72] Difficulties of transportation between producing and consuming areas significantly raised prices, especially in the earlier periods of history.[73] Prices were reduced by the decline in the percentage of profit at the end of the Middle Ages.[74] Hume is especially interested in the ways in which prices are affected by the level of commerce and of technological development. But, unlike such more present-minded preclassical economists as Gregory King—Hume makes no mention of "King's Law" [75]—our historian is in general less interested in using social and technological factors to explain prices than in using his price data to illuminate the social and technological situation of earlier periods.

Specifically, what does Hume do with his lists of prices? Sometimes his purpose seems merely to report quaint social history. More often he uses these statistics as evidence in developing a broader hypothesis concerning the economic, social, or political life of the past. Alluding by implication to the agricultural revolution of his own time, he repeatedly argues that his price data demonstrate a deplorable lack of agricultural skill in earlier periods. Thus the great variations in the price of bread in the Middle Ages are a proof of "bad tillage," although similar fluctuations of grain prices in ancient Rome show that Roman agricultural skill was no better.[76] Relatively high rent in comparison with low commodity prices is, for Hume, another "presumption of the bad husbandry in that age." [77] Another favorite argument of Hume's is that in the Middle Ages the relative costliness of grain, in contrast to the relative cheapness of meat, proves "that, in all uncivilized nations, cattle, which propagate themselves, bear always a lower price than corn, which requires more art and stock to render it plentiful than those nations are possessed of." [78] And the fact that in the Middle Ages ale was cheaper in the country, although later it became cheaper in the city, is evidence of poor communication within England during the earlier period.[79] From such hypotheses about early English society, hypotheses concerning politics can follow. For example, Hume cites household accounts and other quantitative data to demonstrate the uncultivated life-style of the late-medieval nobility, who competed with one another in the number and ferocity of their retainers rather than in luxury, and who were therefore a continuing danger both to the liberty of lesser men and to the security of the state.[80]

7. *Interest and profit.* In his fine essay "Of Interest," Hume argues that

"interest is the barometer of the state, and its lowness is a sign, almost infallible, of the flourishing condition of a people" (*Essays* 312). In this context Hume often treats the level of profit and the level of interest together, holding "that low interest and low profits of merchandise, are two events that mutually forward each other, and are both originally derived from . . . extensive commerce . . ." (*Essays* 311). Conversely, as he remarks in another essay, "Great interest of money, and great profits of trade, are an infallible indication, that industry and commerce are but in their infancy" (*Essays* 414). This is one of the economic hypotheses which Hume sees illustrated in the course of English history. Thus, in treating commerce in the reign of Henry III, he writes, "Interest had in that age mounted to an enormous height, as might be expected from the barbarism of the times and men's ignorance of commerce. Instances occur of fifty per cent paid for money." [81] Although our historian reports Maddox's assertion that mention is made of ten-per-cent interest in the tenth year of Richard I, Hume adds that the Jews frequently exacted much higher interest.[82] Of a heavy tax "upon the whole stock and moneyed interest of the kingdom" enacted by Parliament in 1549, he writes:

> These exorbitant taxes on money are a proof that few people lived on money lent at interest; for this tax amounts to half of the yearly income of all money-holders, during three years, estimating their interest at the rate allowed by law; and was too grievous to be borne, if many persons had been affected by it. . . . The profits of merchandise were commonly so high, that it was supposed it could bear this imposition.[83]

It is not surprising that Hume sympathizes with the Jews of medieval England, victims of "the most barefaced acts of tyranny and oppression." [84] He criticizes their expulsion under Edward I on economic as well as humanitarian grounds:

> As it is impossible for a nation to subsist without lenders of money, and none will lend without a compensation, the practice of usury, as it was then called, was thenceforth exercised by the English themselves upon their fellow-citizens, or by Lombards and other foreigners. It is very much to be questioned, whether the dealings of these new usurers were equally open and unexceptionable with those of the old. By a law of Richard, it was enacted, that three copies should be made of every bond given to a Jew; one to be put into the hands of a public magistrate, another into those of a man of credit; and the third to remain with the Jew himself. But as the canon law, seconded by the municipal, permitted no Christian to take interest, all transactions of this kind must, after the banishment of the Jews, have become more secret and clandestine, and the lender, of consequence, be paid both for the use of his money, and for the infamy and danger which he incurred by lending it.[85]

Hume points out the danger and futility of such measures as the "severe laws" of Henry VII "against taking interest for money, which was then denominated usury." These measures not only forbade all profits from the loan of money, even indirectly, but even "the profits of exchange were prohibited, as savoring of usury, which the superstition of the age zealously proscribed." "It is needless to observe," he comments, "how unreasonable and iniquitous these laws, how impossible to be executed, and how hurtful to trade, if they could take place." [86] In 1546 a statute of Henry VIII fixed interest at ten per cent, "the first legal interest known in England. . . . The preamble of this law treats the interest of money as illegal and criminal; and the prejudices still remained so strong, that the law permitting interest was repealed in the following year." [87] It was in approximately the age of Elizabeth, according to Hume, when "by a lucky accident in language, which has a great effect on men's ideas, the invidious word *usury* which formerly meant the taking of any interest for money, now came to express only the taking of exorbitant and illegal interest. An act passed in 1571 violently condemns all usury, but permits ten per cent interest to be paid." Hume notes that about the same time Henry IV of France reduced interest to six and a half per cent, "an indication of the great advances of France above England in commerce." [88] In England, interest was reduced from ten to eight per cent in 1624, but still "this high interest is an indication of the great profits and small progress of commerce." [89] It was reduced to six per cent in 1650.[90]

8. *Inflation: An ambiguity in the* ESSAYS *clarified.* Hume's essays offer treatments of inflation which may be inconsistent. In one famous passage in "Of the Balance of Trade," he seems to argue, against mercantilist exponents of the balance-of-trade theory, that "treasure" and monetary inflation, by themselves, are of no long-range effect at all for a nation (*Essays* 318–19).[91] In his essay "Of Money" (*Essays* 293–97), on the other hand, he traces the short-run consequences of an increase in money upon a nation, pointing out that the consequent inflation will diffuse itself through the economy gradually and unevenly while giving to the economy as a whole what John Laird called a "temporary filip." [92] As Eugene Rotwein has pointed out, "there is no obvious reason" why the allegedly short-term results "should be wholly ephemeral." [93] In a letter to James Oswald of Dunnikier, Hume himself grants this possibility, conceding "that the increase of money, if not too sudden, naturally increases people and industry, and by that means may retain itself; but if it do not produce such an increase, nothing will retain it except hoarding." Hume added, "My expression in the Essay needs correction, which has occasioned you to mistake it" (LDH I 143), although in fact he revised neither essay. Rotwein argues that the last sentences in "Of the Balance of Trade," interpreted in this light, do reveal the same qualification.[94] At any rate, the qualification which Hume made explicit in his letter to Oswald has important consequences. If, as Hume puts it, under certain conditions "the increase of money . . . may retain itself," then there is at least a possibility that his short-term argument undercuts and refutes the long-term argument. It is because of this ambiguity, Rotwein suggests, that the short-term argument has been widely misinterpreted. Rotwein goes on to attack, as an example of such misinterpretation, Sir Eric Roll's comment that Hume's short-term argument describes a profit inflation "which was taking place at the expense of labor—a fact about which Hume was quite happy." [95]

The *History of England* exhibits Hume's final position. Nothing like the long-term argument appears in the *History*, unless it be his demonstrations that increasing the number of shillings in relation to the pound and the coining of base money were of no long-range benefit to the nation.[96] The fact is that Hume's long-term argument is a construct which describes a hypothetical situation lacking several factors which would have altered a real situation. The short-term argument, as Hume amended it in his letter to Oswald, describes what did happen in England. In the *History* Hume shows exactly how a gradual increase of money did indeed affect "people and industry, and by that means retain itself":

> Labor and commodities have certainly risen since the discovery of the West Indies; but not so much in every particular as is generally imagined. The greater industry of the present time has increased the number of tradesmen and laborers, so as to keep wages nearer a par than could be expected from the great increase of gold and silver. And the additional art employed in the finer manufactures has even made some of these commodities fall below their former value. Not to mention, that merchants and dealers, being contented with less profit than formerly, afford the goods cheaper to their customers.[97]

A noteworthy theme of the *History of England* is the concrete and lasting benefits of inflation, which not only quickens commerce but also raises society to new levels of civilization and liberty. But as the foregoing quotation makes clear, this progress was to an extent at the expense of the working class, who found prices rising faster than their wages and who therefore were forced to increase their "industry"—a fact which Hume did view with equanimity.

Three periods of rising prices are described in the *History*—in the fourteenth, sixteenth, and eighteenth centuries. Hume's treatment of sixteenth-century inflation and its consequences is the fullest and most instructive, but before turning to it, we shall mention his references to the other two periods. His comments on these, inserted into later editions of his *History*, are not entirely consistent.

Hume's sole mention of the inflation of the fourteenth century occurs in a footnote which does not appear in the first edition. At the passage describing Parliament's "impracticable scheme" for reducing wages after the black death, Hume inserted a footnote asserting that although at the Norman conquest prices were perhaps ten times cheaper than "at present," by the reign of Edward III they were only three or four times cheaper. "This change seems to have taken place," he adds, "in a great measure since Edward I." He offers an illustration instead of an explanation of the cause of this change.[98]

His treatment of inflation in the eighteenth century offers several minor historiographical problems. Neither of the two passages in which he speaks of it appears in the first edition.

One of these passages is a footnote appended to Hume's assertion, in speaking of commerce and prices in the reign of James I, that "the chief difference in expense between that age and the present consists in the imaginary wants of men, which have since extremely multiplied." In the first posthumous edition of the *History* (1778) and in the American editions which follow it, a footnote at this point reads: "This volume was written above twenty years before this edition of 1778. In that short period, prices have perhaps risen more than during the preceding hundred and fifty." [99] Two nineteenth-century English editions which I have consulted contain the same footnote but with the date 1786 instead of 1778.[100] In the last year of his life Hume occupied himself with final revisions of the *History* which did not appear until the first posthumous edition of 1778.[101] No doubt Hume's English publishers updated the footnote for the third posthumous edition, 1786, but did not do so thereafter, while American publishers continued to follow the wording of the 1778 edition. But did Hume write the footnote himself? Its wording is not quite in Hume's usually felicitous style. However, other stylistic imperfections appear in his last letters.

The second passage which speaks of rising prices in the eighteenth century is written in a style more typical of Hume's but is open to question on another ground. In an appendix describing England at the end of the reign of Elizabeth, we read, "There seem . . . to have been two periods in which prices rose remarkably in England; namely that in Queen Elizabeth's reign, when they are computed to have doubled, and that in the present age." Between the two periods, our author continues, "industry . . . increased as fast as gold and silver, and kept commodities nearly at a par with money." [102] But either Hume had forgotten the price rise of the fourteenth century or he did not consider it "remarkable" in comparison with the inflations of the sixteenth and eighteenth centuries.

At least two other passages do not refer to this inflation of the eighteenth century when they should have. First, near the end of his treatment of the Anglo-Saxon period, in a passage which does appear in the first edition, Hume mentions in passing that "money" in Queen Elizabeth's reign "was nearly of the same value as in our time." [103] This inconsistency can be explained by assuming that Hume neglected to correct the earlier passage in the light of his later realization of the rising prices in his own lifetime. The second passage cannot be explained in that way, for it occurs in a footnote which bears the date 1776 (the year of Hume's death) and which clearly reflects the pessimistic and anti-English viewpoint of Hume's last years. In a diatribe against the Seven Years' War and the national debt, Hume asserts that "money . . . was in most particulars of the same value" in Elizabeth's day and at the time of "the war begun in 1754." As an example he refers to the wages of footsoldiers, but he means to enforce the general point that Elizabeth's government, despite the real dangers which it faced, was wisely frugal, while in recent years the English government, despite "the extreme frivolous object of the late war," had been ruinously lavish.[104] This passage can be rendered consistent with the *History*'s two references to rising prices in "our own time" only by the assumption that the current inflation had not commenced until "the war begun in 1754."

The inflation of the sixteenth century is the only one which Hume treats carefully and it is the only one mentioned in the first edition of his *History*. His analysis offers, moreover, a clear illustration of his theory of short-term inflation, complete with explanations of why and how the social changes which resulted became permanent.

The rise of prices began, he suggests, under Henry VII, occasioning the statutes fixing prices and wages which Hume criticized, we have seen, as incorrect and ineffectual.[105] Prices continued to rise gradually in the first half of the sixteenth century and then doubled under Elizabeth,[106] finally attaining "in England, as well as in the rest of Europe, . . . a height beyond what had been known since the declension of the Roman empire." [107]

As if in illustration of his short-term theory, Hume observes that the inflation was not equally distributed throughout the economy. For example, in 1544 a piece of land in Cambridgeshire was let at a price ten times cheaper than "at present," while "commodities were not above four times cheaper; a presumption of the bad husbandry of that age." [108] In the Middle Ages, Hume had pointed out, grain was dear in comparison with meat because its production required more agricultural skill.[109] Now in the age of the Tudors the largest price increase was exhibited by those commodities, such as meat and fish, "which cannot be much augmented in quantity by the increase of art and industry." [110] The price of grain rose more slowly, presumably because the supply of grain increased as the agricultural revolution began to stir. The prices of "the finer manufactures," such as clothing, remained stationary or even dropped a little, both because of the decreasing percentage of profit and because the "additional art employed in their manufacture led to an increasing supply." [111] Wages rose, "but not so much in every particular as generally imagined." Hume offers two reasons why the rise in wages was not greater. His first reason, rendered slightly ambiguous to us by his use of the word "industry," is that the labor supply increased: "The greater industry of the present time has increased the number of tradesmen and laborers, so as to keep wages nearer a par than could be expected from the great increase in gold and silver." [112] His second reason is that the growing demand raised fastest the prices of those commodities which could conveniently be transported to where the demand was; "but in England, the labor of men, who could not so easily change their habitation, still remained nearly at the ancient rates, and the poor complained that they could not gain a subsistence by their industry." [113] Rents of land let on long leases did not rise at all, of course; the fact that this was especially true of crown lands contributed to the poverty of the crown as the costs of commodities and provisions rose.[114]

Concerning both the causes of this inflation and its results, Hume is explicit. One cause was the Tudors' debasement and "tampering" with the coin.[115] Of greater significance to Hume was that "after the discovery and conquest of the West Indies, gold and silver became every day more plentiful in England, as well as in the rest of Europe." [116] Yet it was not only a money inflation. Hume suggests that the increase of navigation and commerce throughout Europe led to a similar quickening in England: "While money thus flowed into England, we may observe, that at the same time, and probably from that very cause, arts and industry of all kinds received a mighty increase; and elegance in every enjoyment of life became better known and more cultivated among all ranks of people." [117] Thus an increased demand for goods, especially for luxuries, was both a result and a further cause of the inflation and of the economic growth which accompanied it.[118] And as the "art and industry" of labor increased,[119] the English economy was permanently transformed. The change in "manners" meant an improvement in the public morality; extensive consequences for England's government and constitution eventually followed. Hume's treatment of this "secret revolution" [120] will be discussed in the next section.

V · THE MECHANISM OF HISTORICAL PROGRESS

At several places in his various writings, Hume invokes the ancient theory that history follows a cyclical pattern. In the *Natural History* he describes a perpetual alternation between polytheism and monotheism, each tending to develop within the theory which officially teaches the other. In the *History of England* he repeatedly refers to a perpetual oscillation between the ascendancy of liberty and authority. And in general, Hume says, the rise and decline of civilization is cyclical:

> Those who cast their eyes on the general revolutions of society will find that, as almost all improvements of the human mind had reached nearly to their state of perfection about the age of Augustus, there was a sensible decline from that point or period; and men thenceforth relapsed gradually into ignorance and barbarism. . . . But there is a point of depression, as well as of exhaltation, from which human affairs naturally return in a contrary direction, and beyond which they seldom pass either in their advancement or decline. The period in which the people of Christendom were the lowest sunk in ignorance, and consequently in disorders of every kind, may justly be fixed at the eleventh century, about the age of William the Conqueror; and from that era the sun of science, beginning to reascend, threw out many gleams of light, which preceded the full morning when letters were revived in the fifteenth century.[121]

In practice, however, most of the six volumes of Hume's *History of England* treat the period of ascent, from the ages of "ignorance and barbarism" to 1688. Our question is how Hume explains the mechanism of that linear ascent.

In this mechanism, several factors are involved—alterations of national constitution and political institutions, of social institutions and "manners" and public morality, and of commerce and what he calls the "arts" (including technology). But as to the causal order of changes among these factors, Hume appears to have changed his mind, in the *Essays* offering what a Marxist would call a more idealist analysis and in the *History of England* offering a more materialist analysis. In such essays as "Of the Rise and Progress of the Arts and Sciences" and "Of Refinement in the Arts," Hume seems to mean that the political structure of a community is the cause, or at least provides the condition, of its social as well as its cultural development (*Essays* 115–26, 280). But in the *History of England*, as John Laird pointed out,[122] Hume seems to take a contrary position. First, changes in economic life begin to transform social behavior and "manners," these changes hastening in turn the economic changes which had begun them. As people's patterns of behavior change, society changes. And these changes

in the social, cultural, and moral level of a community are in the cause, or
at least the condition, of its political and constitutional development.

Let us examine Hume's treatment of this upturn. At its beginning, liberty
existed nowhere in Europe:

> Every one that was not a noble, was a slave; the peasants were sold along
> with the land; the few inhabitants of cities were not in a better condition;
> even the gentry themselves were subjected to a long train of subordination
> under the greater barons or chief vassals of the crown; who, though seemingly
> placed in a high state of splendor, yet, having but a slender protection from
> law, were exposed to every tempest of the state, and, by the precarious condi-
> tion in which they lived, paid dearly for the power of oppressing and tyran-
> nizing over their inferiors.[123]

Social changes preceded the political ones. Commerce began to develop.
The people of England, fortunately situated on an island, were able to devote less than total attention to war, and "civil employments and occupa-
tions" soon became honorable among them. The nobility began to lead
more civilized lives. This encouraged the development of commerce and,
hence, of cities. Political liberty appeared first, Hume informs us, in the
form of immunities granted to incorporated communities and other groups;
second, in a modification of feudal tenures, together with a more regular
recognition of the rights of vassals; and, finally, in a loosening of the bonds
of serfdom for the peasants as well. According to Hume the revival of commerce and improvement of "manners" led to a mitigation of the burdens
of the serfs in the following way. In the feudal period, barons preferred to
employ their free vassals in their personal retinues and to employ their serfs,
who were less warlike, in farming. The serfs, in this earlier period, paid their
traditional rents in agricultural produce. But "in proportion as agriculture
improved and money increased, it was found that these services, though
extremely burdensome to the villain, were of little advantage to the master." [124] With the gradual shift to a monetary economy, consequently, "personal freedom became almost general in Europe." [125] (One wonders whether
Hume was aware of the continuing rigor of serfdom in central and eastern
Europe, and even in parts of France, at the time he was writing.) And,
finally, the rise of personal freedom "paved the way for the increase of
political or civil liberty, and which, even where it was not attended with
this salutary effect, served to give the members of the community some of
the more considerable advantages of it." [126]

Feudalism typically meant a relatively weak king whose regime was
perpetually threatened by many relatively autonomous local tyrants. The
increase in commerce and the increase of monetary wealth both among
many of the rural magnates and among new men caused, Hume repeats, an
increase in "luxury." To some social commentators of Hume's day and
earlier this change signified moral decay. To Hume this "secret revolution"
signified the opposite. The nobility, in turning to a more magnificent style
of living, not only encouraged commerce and the arts but also, in expending
so large a part of their wealth upon consumption, sank as a group to a

lesser significance in the new nation. Men of less wealth, while contributing to the growing economy by their own style of life, increased in relative influence. Even during the rule of the House of Tudor, when according to Hume the new monarchy made itself "almost absolute," [127] the middle class grew in significance, cultivating habits of industriousness and bourgeois civility. In this way the spread of commerce and "luxury" led to a more moral society. "It must be acknowledged," Hume writes, "in spite of those who declaim so violently against refinement in the arts, or what they are pleased to call luxury, that as much better as an industrious tradesman is both a better man and a better citizen than one of those idle retainers who formerly depended on the great families, so much is the life of a modern nobleman more laudable than that of an ancient baron." [128]

Moreover, political power inevitably shifted to the new classes and to the institutions which they controlled. The constitution, after painful struggles, was altered accordingly. Thus the growth of commerce and luxury was an essential cause of the growth of a wider and more secure liberty. As Adam Smith wrote in *The Wealth of Nations*:

> Commerce and manufacturing gradually introduced order and good government, and with them, the liberty and security of individuals, among the inhabitants of the country, who had before lived almost in a continual state of war with their neighbors, and of servile dependency upon their superiors. This, though it has been the least observed, is by far the most important of all their effects. Mr. Hume is the only writer who, so far as I know, has hitherto taken notice of it.[129]

Thus Hume offers an almost Marxist dialectic—a first stage of early medieval society, in which there was little commerce, barbarism reigned, and there was little civil liberty for anyone; a second stage, in which economic development transformed the structure of society and enabled the Tudors to make themselves "almost absolute"; and a third stage in which the further development of the economy and "manners" led to a shift of power to the gentry. The footnotes to *Das Kapital* show that Marx studied Hume's economic essays thoroughly; it is amusing to speculate whether Marx knew Hume's *History of England* as well. In one obvious respect Hume's viewpoint differs from the Marxist one. Hume sees the struggles between the old nobility and the new middle class and clearly sympathizes with the latter, although he has no use for the "enthusiastic" Puritans who put Charles I to death. But, like most writers of his day and class, he felt less sympathy for the common people. Assuming that they are naturally lazy and need the threat of imminent starvation to goad them into increased productivity, Hume concluded that the sufferings of the poor during this period of economic growth were beneficial to the nation as a whole. But a Marxist would find no difficulty in explaining Hume's viewpoint in relation to the economic class with which Hume himself was identified and which made up the greater part of his literary audience.

Hume's work in the substance of economic history—monetary history, history of prices, and the like—is noteworthy as a pioneering effort, but it offers only limited instruction and entertainment to us who have seen the same kind of work done more fully, reliably, and systematically. The most valuable aspect of Hume's contribution to the discipline of economic history is not so much his economic history itself but rather what he does with it, the use he makes of it. There are several respects in which Hume's work in political economy shows him a precursor of the classical economists. But typically such figures as Ricardo aimed to describe a static situation, lacking the dimension of time. Hume, like some very early economists and some very recent ones, is a student of economic growth. For his combining of economic theory with historical analysis, and for his tracing the consequences of economic change in the non-economic sectors of a changing society, he deserves an honored place in the history of the beginnings of economic history.

NOTES

1. Constant Noble Stockton, "David Hume among the Historiographers," *Studies in History and Society*, 3, No. 2 (Spring 1971), 14–24.
2. Ernest Campbell Mossner, "An Apology for David Hume, Historian," *PMLA*, 56 (1941), 657–90.
3. See, for instance, Mario Dal Pra, *Hume e la scienza della natura umana*, Biblioteca di cultura moderne, No. 749 (Rome & Bari, 1973); and Nicholas Capaldi, *David Hume: The Newtonian Philosopher* (Boston, 1975).
4. See, for instance, *David Hume: Philosophical Historian*, edd. Richard H. Popkin and David Fate Norton (Indianapolis, 1965); and Donald W. Livingston, "Hume on the Problem of Historical and Scientific Explanation," *The New Scholasticism*, 47 (1973), 38–67.
5. John Laird, *Hume's Philosophy of Human Nature* (London, 1932), pp. 267–68; and Thomas Preston Peardon, *The Transition in English Historical Writing, 1760–1830* (New York, 1933), p. 22, who find Hume's *History* lacking in thematic definition.
6. David Hume, *History of England from the Invasion of Julius Caesar to the Abdication of James the Second, 1688*, 6 vols. (New York, 1850), I 36; hereafter cited as *History*.
7. *History*, I 1, 2, 22, 36, 278; II 507; IV 41; V 519.
8. Constant Noble Stockton, "Hume—Historian of the English Constitution," *Eighteenth-Century Studies*, 4, No. 3 (1971), 277–93.
9. This view is developed in an unsympathetic way by J. B. Black in *The Art of History* (London, 1926), pp. 96–103.
10. For a concise definition of these terms, see Carl G. Hempel, *Philosophy of Natural Science*, Foundations of Philosophy Series (Englewood Cliffs, 1966), p. 51.
11. *History*, I 198–99.
12. Ibid., II 508. See also IV 496.
13. Concerning Hume's synthesizing of historical sources, see Sir Charles H. Firth, "The Development of the Study of Seventeenth-Century History," *Transactions of the Royal Historical Society*, 3rd series, 7 (1913), 25–40. Concerning the popularity of Hume's *History of England* for a century, see William Cortez Abbott, *Adventures in Reputation* (Cambridge, Mass., 1935), pp. 118–30.
14. T. E. Jessop, *A Bibliography of David Hume and of Scottish Philosophy from Francis Hutcheson to Lord Balfour* (New York, 1966), p. 6, says that this essay and another were printed and circulated separately between 1758 and 1760, although paginated for inclusion in the 1758 edition of the *Essays*. T. H. Grose, in his "History of the Editions" in *Essays Moral, Political, and Literary* (edd. T. H. Green and T. H. Grose, 2 vols. [London, 1875]), I 72, says that these two essays, arriving too late to be inserted into the contents of the 1758 edition, were nevertheless bound up with at least some copies of it. In

LDH I 317n3, Grieg says that the two essays, printed and paged separately, were bound up with later copies of the edition of 1759. Hume sent the manuscript of the two Tudor volumes of his *History* to the printer in August 1758.

15. J. H. Clapham, *The Study of Economic History: An Inaugural Lecture* (Cambridge, 1929), pp. 10–17; N. S. B. Gras, "The Rise and Development of Economic History," *Economic History Review*, 1 (1927–28), 12–34.

16. William Fleetwood (subsequently Bishop of Ely), *Chronicon Preciosum: or, an Account of English Gold and Silver Money; the Price of Corn and other Commodities; and of Stipends, Salaries, Wages, Jointures, Portions, Day-labour etc. in England, for Six Hundred Years—shewing from the Decrease of the value of Money, and from the Increase of the value of corn and other commodities that a Fellow, who has an Estate in Land of Inheritance or a perpetual Pension of Five Pounds per Annum, may conscientiously keep his Fellowship . . . though the Statutes of his College (founded between the years 1440 and 1460) did then vacate his Fellowship on such condition* (London, 1707).

17. Thomas Maddox, *History and Antiquities of the Exchequer of England (1066–1327)* (London, 1711).

18. (Rev.) John Smith, *Chronicon rusticum commerciale, or, Memoirs of Wool*, 2 vols. (London, 1747).

19. Adam Anderson, *An Historical and Chronological Deduction of the Origin of Commerce . . .* , 2 vols. (London, 1764).

20. Firth, "Development of the Study of Seventeenth-Century History," 38.

21. For statements of the new viewpoint, see Douglass C. North, "Economic History," *International Encyclopedia of the Social Sciences*, ed. David Sills (New York, 1968), VI 468–74; and John R. Meyer and Alfred H. Conrad, "Economic Theory, Statistical Inference, and Economic History," *Journal of Economic History*, 17 (1957), 524–53.

22. The 1751 edition of this work was a republication of the edition of 1581 which had ascribed authorship to "W. S., Gentleman." Apparently written in 1549, it has been twice republished under the title, *A Discourse of the Commonweal of This Realm of England*, with authorship attributed to Sir Thomas Smith in the edition by Mary Dewar (Charlottesville, 1969) and to John Hales in the edition by Elizabeth Lamond (Cambridge, 1893).

23. Concerning Gregory King in general, see D. V. Glass, "Two Papers on Gregory King," with introductory note, in *Population in History*, edd. D. V. Glass and D. E. C. Eversley (Chicago, 1965), pp. 159–220. King is mentioned in Charles Davenant's *Discourses on the Publick Revenues and on the Trade of England*, 2 vols. (London, 1698), which Hume cites (*History*, V 506). For Steuart's use of King, see Edgar A. J. Johnson, *Predecessors of Adam Smith* (New York, 1937), pp. 77, 196.

24. That this translation was unauthorized is argued by Grieg (LDH II 343).

25. William Letwin, *Origins of Scientific Economics* (Garden City, 1964), pp. 274ff.

26. Concerning Malachy Postlethwayt in general, see Johnson, *Predecessors*, chap. 10. Hume must have known of Postlethwayt, whose *Dictionary* was going through three editions at London while Hume was writing his *History* and afterward residing for a time in London. But he pointedly fails to mention it when, in a letter to the Abbé Morellet in 1767, he is discussing the difficulties of compiling such a dictionary of commerce (LDH II 158n1).

27. The synthetic element in Hume's economic theory is emphasized by Johnson, *Predecessors*, pp. 163ff. This interpretation is criticized by Eugene Rotwein in his introduction to *David Hume: Writings on Economics* (Madison, 1955), p. xxv.

28. Firth, "Development of the Study of Seventeenth-Century History," 29.

29. The fullest treatment of Hume's general sources is in two somewhat unfriendly articles by Sir Francis Palgrave, both published originally as anonymous book reviews in the *Quarterly Review*: "Anglo-Saxon History," a review of an 1825 republication of Hume's *History* (34 [June–September 1826], 248–89); and "Hume and his Influence upon History," supposedly a review of Augustin Thierry's *Histoire de la conquête de l'Angleterre par les Normands* (73 [March 1844], 536–92). The two articles were republished in Sir Francis Palgrave's *Collected Works*, 10 vols. (Cambridge, 1922), IX 375–428 and 535–98, respectively.

30. Shakespeare, *2 Henry IV*, III.iii.82.

31. *The Regulations and Establishment of the Household of Henry Algernon Percy, the Fifth Earl of Northumberland, at his Castles of Wresill and Lekinfield in Yorkshire, begun Anno Domini MDXII*, privately published at London in 1770 by the antiquarian Bishop Thomas Percy. Bishop Percy was unhappy with the use which Hume made of it; see his letters of January 5 and January 22, 1773 to Hume (*Letters of Eminent Persons Addressed to David Hume*, ed. John Hill Burton [Edinburgh, 1849], pp. 317–24) and Hume's reply of January 16, 1773 (NLDH 197–99; see also NLDH xvii–xviii). In Hume's *History*, the book is quoted and analyzed in note C, III 453–56.

32. *History*, I 391–92.

33. See, for example, ibid., I 213.

34. Ibid., I 481, note P, in reference to I 293.

35. Ibid., II 26n.

36. Ibid., II 260n. See also II 273–74.

37. Ibid., II 373–74.

38. Ibid., IV 361n. For another good example, see VI 80.

39. Ibid., II 277.

40. Ibid., IV 368–69.

41. Ibid., IV 371; V 526; VI 370.

42. Ibid., I 175; II 373; III 291, 355; IV 332, 364.

43. Ibid., III 355–56. See also III 372n and IV 332.

44. Ibid., I 174–76; II 373; III 291; IV 364.

45. Ibid., II 372–73.

46. Ibid., I 460–69; IV 360–61.

47. Ibid., IV 414.

48. Ibid., VI 367.

49. North, "Economic History," *International Encyclopedia*, ed. Sills, VI 470.

50. "Of Public Credit" appears in *Essays* 355–71. Pages 356–65 of this edition indicate Hume's extensive revisions of the essay. For his later opinions on the issue, see his letters to William Strahan of March 11, March 25, June 25, and August 19, 1771 (LDH II 237, 242, 245, 248).

51. David Hume, *The History of England, under the House of Tudor . . .* , 2 vols. (London, 1759), II 384. The same passage, with the strong words added, appears in the last edition, *History*, II 444.

52. David Hume, *The History of England, under the House of Tudor . . .* (1795), II 729; last edition, *History*, IV 361.

53. David Hume, *The History of England, under the House of Tudor . . .* (1759), II 731; last edition, *History*, IV 364.

54. *History*, IV 363n.

55. See Sir William J. Ashley, "The Tory Origins of Free Trade Policy," reprinted from *Quarterly Journal of Economics* in Ashley's *Surveys, Historic and Economic* (London, 1900), pp. 268–303.

56. *History*, III 128.

57. Ibid., 129.

58. *David Hume: Writings on Economics*, ed. Rotwein, p. 76n; see also pp. lxxvii–lxxviii.

59. See note 14.

60. *History*, III 72.

61. Ibid., IV 366.

62. Ibid., III 372.

63. Ibid., IV 515.

64. Ibid., II 172; see also II 275; III 73, 316–17.

65. Ibid., IV 394, 295.

66. Ibid., IV 417.

67. Ibid., IV 336; see also III 446–47; IV 364.

68. Ibid., II 64.

69. Ibid., I 176; II 172–73.

70. Ibid., II 64.

71. Ibid., II 73; IV 511.

72. Ibid., II 173; III 355.

73. Ibid., II 64.

74. Ibid., III 73.

75. See Joseph A. Schumpeter, *History of Economic Analysis* (New York, 1954), p. 212, regarding "King's Law."

76. *History*, II 63–64.

77. Ibid., II 317; see also III 448.

78. Ibid., II 64–65; see also I 176; II 172–73; III 73–74, 75.

79. Ibid., II 64.

80. Ibid., III 453–56, note C.

81. Ibid., II 65.

82. Ibid., I 483, note S.

83. Ibid., III 463–64, note T.

84. Ibid., I 366–67, 469–70; II 65–66, 73.

85. Ibid., II 74.

86. Ibid., III 72.

87. Ibid., III 318.

88. Ibid., IV 369–70.

89. Ibid., IV 509.

90. Ibid., V 526.

91. See also Hume's letter of April 10, 1749 to Montesquieu (LDH I 137). This letter has been translated in *David Hume: Writings on Economics*, ed. Rotwein, pp. 188–89.

92. Laird, *Hume's Philosophy of Human Nature*, p. 254.

93. *David Hume: Writings on Economics*, ed. Rotwein, p. lxv.

94. Ibid., p. lxv, note.

95. Ibid.; Sir Eric Roll, *A History of Economic Thought*, rev. ed. (New York, 1942), p. 123. Roll's most recent edition (3rd ed. [1964]), p. 119, omits the last phrase.

96. *History*, I 175; II 373; III 291, 355–56; IV 332, 364.

97. Ibid., III 73.

98. Ibid., II 275n. The passage concerning the wage-fixing statute appears, without the footnote, in the first edition, *The History of England, from the Invasion of Julius Caesar to the Revolution in 1688*, 6 vols. (London, 1762), II 239; hereafter cited as first edition.

99. *History*, IV 511n. The footnote does not appear in the first edition at V 128.

100. *History of England from the Invasion of Julius Caesar to the Abdication of James the Second, 1688*, 8 vols. (London, 1822), VI 118, note *u*; 5 vols. (London, 1865), IV 113, note *m*. The elaborate edition in six folio volumes (London, 1806), III 802, note *z*, contains a singularly irrelevant citation of Rymer's *Foedera* at just that point.

101. Jessop, *Bibliography of David Hume*, p. 30.

102. *History*, IV 371. This and several other paragraphs do not appear at the corresponding place in the first edition: IV 735.

103. *History*, I 176; first edition, I 162.

104. *History*, IV 367n. The corresponding place in the first edition is IV 731.

105. *History*, III 73–74.

106. Ibid., IV 371.

107. Ibid., IV 413.

108. Ibid., III 317.

109. Ibid., I 176; II 64–65, 172–73; III 75.

110. Ibid., III 73–74.

111. Ibid., III 73; IV 516.

112. Ibid., III 73.

113. Ibid., III 355.

114. Ibid., IV 413.

115. Ibid., III 291, 355; IV 332, 364.

116. Ibid., IV 413; see also III 75, 317, 354–55.

117. Ibid., IV 413–14.

118. Ibid., III 355.

119. Ibid., III 71, 73, 355; IV 371, 414.

120. The phrase "secret revolution" appears at ibid., IV 375.

121. Ibid., II 508.

122. Laird, *Hume's Philosophy of Human Nature*, p. 269.

123. *History*, II 511.

124. Ibid., II 512.

125. Ibid., II 513.

126. Ibid.

127. Ibid.

128. Ibid., III 71–72.

129. Smith, *The Wealth of Nations* 3.4 (New York, 1937), p. 385.

v

15

Cause, Reason, and Objectivity in Hume's Aesthetics

PETER JONES
University of Edinburgh

HUME'S SCATTERED BUT COMPREHENSIVE OBSERVATIONS ON AESTHETICS reward careful scrutiny, and throw light on his other doctrines. Although Hume never published his promised treatise on "criticism" (T [xii], xx),[1] it is essential to realise that it would have been a contribution to his "science of *man*" (A 6; T xix). Such a task required consideration of all the variables, including the propensities of the observer as well as the properties of the observed. As part of his sustained attack on the rationalist view that human nature is governed essentially by "reason" and *a priori* tenets, Hume's remarks on aesthetics are unashamedly, and self-consciously, focused on the causes of certain human responses. It must be stated emphatically that in these contexts, as in others, Hume does not confuse questions of psychology and questions of logic.

Under the heading of "aesthetics" I include discussions of beauty, as well as discussions of art and of criticism. In this essay I shall restrict myself to consideration of Hume's views on three topics:

1. the nature of beauty (Section I);
2. the nature of judgments of beauty (Section II);
3. the conditions for a proper response to works of art (Sections III and IV).

I shall conclude with a list of important issues which require discussion, and which I shall study on another occasion. I also amplify the preliminary summary of my argument with which I now begin.

Hume holds that objects of certain sorts, if perceived in definable ways, cause normal people to have sentiments of certain sorts; he says that "The very *feeling* constitutes our praise or admiration" (T 471). Our verdicts on the objects presuppose such feelings. The sentiment of beauty is a particular kind of inner feeling; it is a calm passion or secondary impression, pleasurable but otherwise indefinable. The objects which cause such sentiments, by courtesy and through association of ideas, are themselves called beautiful. It is pointless to try to change by argument the physiological mechanisms which enable a man to feel the sentiments he does. By a "figurative" way of speaking (T 459), however, "affection can be call'd unreasonable . . . [w]hen a passion . . . is founded on the supposition of the existence of objects, which really do not exist" (T 416). Reasoned discussion can focus, therefore, on the putative causes of a man's sentiments, and by altering his perception set off a new causal chain, as a result of which he experiences different sentiments. In this way perceptual judgments may be said to be *mediate* causes of our sentiments (T 462), in contrast to perceptions themselves, which are *immediate* causes. Hume regards discussion of beauty as thoroughly objective; that is, beautiful objects have properties, which may be difficult to perceive or describe, but whose characterisation can be achieved within conventions necessary for communication. Sometimes the conditions for determining such characterisations are complex, and sometimes they are satisfied by, and known to, only a minority in a given community. It should be clear, already, why Hume's main arguments in aesthetics occur in contexts where man is considered as a social being, for only there is reasoning requisite and, indeed, possible. And we shall soon see, also, why he holds that one can neither make a judgment of beauty without some concept of the object to which beauty is ascribed, nor justify such a judgment without appeal to the type of beauty in question. Excluding those rare cases of natural beauty which *command* (EPM 172–73; cf. Kant) our approbation, we have to learn what objects can cause pleasure; socially, our verdicts on the mere form of something are relatively uninteresting, precisely because reasoned discussion seems out of place.

In Hume's view, an effective social institution presupposes the possibility of communication between its members. The conventions and rule-governed nature of language secure the intelligibility and objectivity of such communication. These allegedly empirical claims, together with the further empirical claims that certain causal connections and psychological phenomena are wide-spread, if not universal, are central to Hume's attempt to introduce a non-rationalist, non–*a priori* objectivity into the realms of morals and aesthetics. In his view, pleasure and pain are the principal motives to action, and all men share a ready, even natural, interest in anything which is found to please (EPM 294; see T 574). Such views lie behind his contention that sensibility to poetry is itself a beauty of character (*Essays* 173; EPM 261). As social beings we are ready to search for publicly shareable viewpoints of whatever can give pleasure, and reference to such viewpoints is necessary whenever we try to resolve conflicts in judgments of taste. Justification of judgments of taste is possible, in part, at least, because men's internal sentiments are much the same in similar circumstances (*Essays* 107–108, 166–67, 168, note; but see LDH 1 40); and they are similar because, physiologically, men's minds function in the same way. The assumed stability and universality of these functions make possible other capacities which Hume requires, such as the capacity to learn and to improve by practice.

I

Hume distinguishes between beauty, perception of beauty, and judgments of beauty. Beauty "is not, properly speaking, a quality in any object, but merely a passion or impression in the soul" (T 301); as such, it "cannot be defin'd" (T 299). Hume is quite clear on the point:

> Beauty is not a quality of the circle. It lies not in any part of the line, *whose* parts are all equally distant from a common centre. It is only the effect, which that figure produces upon a mind, whose particular fabric or structure renders it susceptible of such sentiments. In vain would you look for it in the circle, or seek it, either by your senses, or by mathematical reasonings, in all the properties of that figure [*Essays* 167–68; repeated, but with variants, in EPM 291–92].

Shortly before, there occurs a passage of equal importance in this context:

> the case is not the same with the qualities of *beautiful and deformed, desirable and odious,* as with truth and falsehood. In the former case, the mind is not content with merely surveying its objects, as they stand in themselves: it also feels a sentiment of delight or uneasiness, approbation or blame, consequent to that survey; and this sentiment determines it to affix the epithet *beautiful or deformed, desirable or odious.* Now, it is evident, that this sentiment must depend upon the particular fabric or structure of the mind, which enables such particular forms to operate in such a particular manner, and produces a sympathy or conformity between the mind and its objects. Vary the structure of the mind or inward organs, the sentiment no longer follows, though the form remains the same. The sentiment being different from the object, and arising from its operation upon the organs of the mind, an alteration upon the latter must vary the effect; nor can the same object, presented to a mind totally different, produce the same sentiment [*Essays* 166–67].

The distinction between beauty and perception of beauty comes out in a further passage:

> It is on the proportion, relation, and position of parts, that all natural beauty depends; but it would be absurd thence to infer, that the perception of beauty, like that of truth in geometrical problems, consists wholly in the perception of relations, and was performed entirely by the understanding or intellectual faculties [EPM 291].

These remarks also show how Hume treats beauty as a dependent property, and this move enables him to provide a focus for reasoned discussion, since there can be public argument over the properties on which the sentiment of beauty depends. Hume is anxious to stress that "the reality" of beauty is in no way diminished as a result of the claim that beauty lies not in bodies "but merely in the senses," and that critics and moralists need be no more worried by such claims than are natural philosophers by parallel claims about colours (*Essays* 168, note)—"the appearance of objects in daylight, to the eye of a man in health, is denominated their true and real colour, even while colour is allowed to be merely a phantasm of the senses" (*Essays* 238–39).

Hume holds that "the beauty of all visible objects causes a pleasure pretty much the same, tho' it be sometimes deriv'd from the mere *species* and appearance of the objects; sometimes from sympathy, and an idea of their utility" (T 617). In an earlier passage, Hume asserts that "both these causes are intermix'd in our judgments . . ." (T 590). One implication of these quotations is that the species of pleasure we experience depends on some conceptual judgment; we shall find that this interpretation can be confirmed. An even earlier passage should be noted first, however. Since beauty "is discern'd only by a taste or sensation," Hume claims that "the power of producing pain and pleasure make in this manner the essence of beauty and deformity . . ." (T 299). Since Hume has already said that beauty is not a property discoverable by the senses, whilst yet being something whose detection requires the occurrence of a sentiment (and also a proper viewpoint, as we shall see), it is easy to grasp why he claims that the essence of beauty is a "power." We can also see why he calls beauty the "effect" of the interaction of an object with certain properties, and a properly tuned mind; the sentiment *of* beauty, of course, is the calm passion announcing the presence of beauty, but must not be identified as beauty itself.

Hume distinguishes different "kinds" (T 298) of beauty: beauty of "form," which would contribute to the "intrinsic worth and value" of something (T 593); beauty of "interest"; beauty according to "species." The point of the distinction is to show that variations in our sentiments of pleasure can be traced to discernible variations in the perceptions and perceptual judgments which function as their immediate and mediate causes, respectively. This part of the discussion is best carried on under the heading of judgments, therefore, and to that topic I now turn.

II

Hume gives two closely related examples of intrinsic beauty, perception of which is mediated by conceptual judgment only minimally, if at all—we must remember that, from now on, Hume constantly adopts the courtesy-use of the term "beauty," applying it to objectively discernible properties. First, he says that we might attend to the beauty of "form" of "some senseless inanimate piece of matter" (T 363). Second, some "species of beauty, especially the natural kinds, on their first appearance, command our affection and approbation; and where they fail of this effect, it is impossible for any reasoning to redress their influence, or adapt them better to our taste and sentiment" (EPM 173). The references here to nature and natural kinds as the objects of non-comparative judgments of beauty are, of course, echoed in Kant. Kant claimed that "the empirical interest in the beautiful exists only in *society*," and that interest can combine with a judgment of taste "after it has once been posited as a pure aesthetic judgment." [2]

Aside from intrinsic beauty, Hume asserts that two important "principles" operate in judgments of beauty. The first, comparison, functions in our classification of objects into kinds: "We judge more of objects by comparison, than by their intrinsic worth and value; and regard every thing as mean, when set in opposition to what is superior of the same kind" (T 593; see also

T 375, 557, and *Essays* 82–83). The second (which Hume, in fact, treats as "the *first*" principle [T 592]), is sympathy (T 576, 618): "tho' our first object be some senseless inanimate piece of matter, 'tis seldom we rest there, and carry not our view to its influence on sensible and rational creatures" (T 363). Our sympathy with the owner of a house enables *us* to derive pleasure from the "convenience" of *his* house; his own sentiment of pleasure, of course, is a mixture of beauty of utility and "beauty of interest, not of form" (T 364). In this same passage, Hume claims that sentiments of pleasure derived from the utility of objects concern "only the owner, nor is there any thing but sympathy, which can interest the spectator." The beauty of "tables, chairs, scritoires, chimneys, coaches, sadles, ploughs, and indeed . . . every work of art . . . is chiefly deriv'd from their utility, and from their fitness for that purpose, to which they are destin'd" (T 364).

At this point we begin to see how the justification appropriate to judgments of beauty depends both on the kind of beauty and on the concept of the object to which beauty, by courtesy, is ascribed. If "nothing renders a field more agreeable than its fertility, and . . . scarce any advantages of ornament or situation will be able to equal this beauty" (T 364), it is clear that to describe a stretch of land as a "field" is *ipso facto* to limit what can be beautiful about it. Hume holds that in any social community there are agreed descriptions of the phenomena which most concern that community; any deviation from the conventions governing such descriptions requires explanation, but no special mystery surrounds the conventions themselves, although philosophers of the science of man may seek for their historical and psychological origins. One cannot predicate beauty of something already described as an overgrown plain because of the conventions governing the denotation of "overgrown" and "plain"; what counts as a beautiful plain depends on a given community's concept of a plain. Hence, "a plain, overgrown with furze and broom, may be, in itself, as beautiful as a hill cover'd with vines or olive-trees; tho' it will never appear so to one, who is acquainted with the value of each. But this is a beauty merely of imagination, and has no foundation in what appears to the senses" (T 364). One can think of the overgrown plain as beautiful only by thinking of it under another description, one "merely of the imagination," and one which is, in fact, false. There are other important cases, however, in which, although imagination has to operate, it is justifiable to predicate beauty of the phenomena in question. An empty but well-designed house, an uninhabited but fertile land, an imprisoned athlete, may be justifiably judged to be beautiful, because "where any object, in all its parts, is fitted to attain any agreeable end, it naturally gives us pleasure . . ." (T 584); in these cases the "imagination adheres to the *general* views of things . . ." (T 587) so that the "*seeming tendencies* of objects affect the mind . . ." (T 586). We are entitled to call these things beautiful "even tho' some external circumstances be wanting to render it altogether effectual" (T 584). In other words, the plain is overgrown and not ready for use, whereas the house is well-designed and is ready for use; the latter is therefore beautiful, and the former is not. Utility is often treated as a potential (T 299, 311), as here.

Beauty of utility is always relative to species, whether the utility is of benefit to the animal itself or to the owner of an object (T 299, 483, 615): "The same degree of beauty in a woman is called deformity, which is treated as real beauty in one of our sex" (*Essays* 85). The conventions which govern the attribution of beauty of utility differ between cultures, of course, but that is quite consistent with everything Hume has said: "in countries where men's bodies are apt to exceed in corpulency, personal beauty is placed in a much greater degree of slenderness, than in countries where that is the most usual defect" (EPM 264). Hume is at pains to insist that the "more we converse with mankind, and the greater social intercourse we maintain, the more shall we be familiarized to these general preferences and distinctions, without which our conversation and discourse could scarcely be rendered intelligible to each other" (EPM 228).

The importance of the descriptions under which we see something becomes even more obvious in Hume's accounts of beauty in art and of criticism in general, with his special emphasis on appropriate viewpoints as a condition of proper response. To these matters I now turn.

III

A proper moral verdict and, we may suppose, a proper aesthetic verdict, presuppose special viewpoints; central factors in such viewpoints are the beliefs and attendant attitudes we have towards the phenomena in question. Furthermore, particular points of view are necessary conditions for the causal relations to obtain between the phenomena and the observer. Finally, without publicly attainable and discernible viewpoints no social communication can take place; they are conditions of objectivity for judgments in the empirical world.

Hume writes: " 'Tis only when a character is considered in general, without reference to our particular interest, that it causes such a feeling or sentiment, as denominates it morally good or evil" (T 472). Of course, not "every sentiment of pleasure or pain, which arises from characters and actions, [is] of that *peculiar* kind, which makes us praise or condemn" (T 472); but after practice, a man "who has command of himself, can separate these feelings, and give praise to what deserves it" (T 472). Such skills, as we shall see again later, explain how he is able to praise wine for its flavour and music for its harmony, even when both "equally produce pleasure" (T 472). Although the "approbation of moral qualities most certainly is not deriv'd from reason, or any comparison of ideas; but proceeds entirely from a moral taste, and from certain sentiments of pleasure or disgust, which arise upon the contemplation and view of particular qualities or characters" (T 581), and although these sentiments "must vary according to the distance or contiguity of the objects" (T 581), we can nevertheless, "arrive at a more *stable* judgment of things" by trying to "fix on some *steady* and *general* points of view; and always, in our thoughts, place ourselves in them, whatever may be our present situation" (T 581–82). Hume insists that " 'twere impossible we cou'd ever make use of language, or communicate our sentiments to one another, did we not correct the momentary appearances of things, and overlook our present situation" (T 582). Strictly speaking, the adoption of a "general" viewpoint enables us to correct our language (T 583, 582; see also T 375, 594) rather than our sentiments. Firstly, "our passions do not readily follow the determination of our judgment" (T 583), and change more slowly than the operations of the imagination as it functions in the general viewpoint (T 441); secondly, our sentiments are caused by the interaction of properties in the perceived object and the particular physiological constitution of our brain, and, as such, are not influenced immediately, but only mediately, by judgments. The facts as Hume finds them, however, are more complex than this latter point implies:

> though the value of every object can be determined only by the sentiment or passion of every individual, we may observe, that the passion, in pronouncing its verdict, considers not the object simply, as it is in itself, but surveys it with all the circumstances which attend it. A man, transported with joy on account of his possessing a diamond, confines not his view to the glittering stone before him. He also considers its rarity; and thence chiefly arises his pleasure and exultation. Here, therefore, a philosopher may step in, and suggest particular views, and considerations, and circumstances, which otherwise would have escaped us, and by that means he may either moderate or excite any particular passion [*Essays* 174–75].

Two important points in this loosely worded passage become clearer if we first juxtapose it with another quotation: "in many orders of beauty, particularly those of the finer arts, it is requisite to employ much reasoning, in order to feel the proper sentiment; and a false relish may frequently be corrected by argument and reflection"; "in order to pave the way for such a sentiment, and give a proper discernment of its object, it is often necessary, we find, that much reasoning should precede, that nice distinctions be made, just conclusions drawn, distant comparisons formed, complicated relations examined, and general facts fixed and ascertained" (EPM 173). The two points are these. First, the proper sentiment depends on the proper discernment, and the latter may involve many complex factors. Second, discussion can bring about a different survey of an object, and thus a different causal sequence, and thus a different sentiment, and thus a different verdict. The importance of the descriptions under which we view phenomena is clear. So also is the fact that " 'tis impossible men cou'd ever agree in their sentiments and judgments, unless they chose some common point of view, from which they might survey their object, and which might cause it to appear the same to all of them" (T 591).

The major medium of communication, of course, is language, a complex set of conventional devices developed by humans to satisfy their particular needs. To secure effective communication, Hume contends, language "must invent a peculiar set of terms, in order to express those universal sentiments of censure or approbation, which arise from humanity, or from views of general usefulness and its contrary" (EPM 274). It is an empirical question to determine what these terms are, in any given community, and their conditions of application. Our own language is full of clues about our evaluations (EPM 174–75, 242–43), some of which are clearly expressions of self-interest

(EPM 272), and some of which influence us in unsuspected ways. Hume suggests that we reserve the term "beautiful" for exceptional cases determined by comparative judgment (*Essays* 85–86); that if we think of a work as a forgery we may discern no merit in it at all (LDH 1 399),[3] as indeed happened in connection with the so-called Ossian poems; [4] and that if our descriptions arouse unfulfilled expectations, our consequent disappointment may be disproportionate to the facts (EPM 253–54, note). Our aversion to a city may change into "the opposite passion" (T 354) when familiarity provides us with more accurate descriptions of the city than those based on the uncertainties of our "first perusal" (see T 446).

The general viewpoint is the source of the "general inalterable standard, by which we may approve or disapprove of characters and manners. And tho' the *heart* does not always take part with those general notions, or regulate its love and hatred by them, yet are they sufficient for discourse, and serve all our purposes in company, in the pulpit, on the theatre, and in the schools" (T 603). Such standards, of course, are revisable, since they serve the needs of a community, and those needs may change (EPM 229 and note); furthermore, "*General rules* are often extended beyond the principle whence they first arise . . ." (EPM 207), and only a sharp historical sense will enable us to distinguish between the origins of a principle and its present foundations (*Essays* 455–56). It should be noted, however, that although it is contingent which standards are judged sufficient—since the judgment is made on grounds of utility—it is *necessary* that there be standards.

Before turning from Hume's general account of evaluation to his specific observations on art and criticism, three points should be made.

(*a*) The sentiment of beauty is a calm passion, or secondary impression:

> Our affections, on a general prospect of their objects, form certain rules of conduct, and certain measures of preference of one above another: and these decisions, though really the result of our calm passions and propensities, (for what else can pronounce any object eligible or the contrary?) are yet said, by a natural abuse of terms, to be the determinations of pure *reason* and reflection [EPM 239; see T 417].[5]

I cannot explore here the mechanisms of sympathy as Hume understands the notion, although I have mentioned already that sympathy is one of the two "principles" governing judgments of beauty.

(*b*) Although "precept and education" have some influence, our most general sentiments of "approbation or dislike" (EPM 214) have a natural foundation; this explains why any tolerable representation of a passion arouses a sympathetic response, because there are no passions "of which every man has not, within him, at least the seeds and first principles" (EPM 222).

(*c*) Hume also claims that certain fundamental "rules of art are founded on the qualities of human nature; and the quality of human nature, which requires a consistency in every performance, is that which renders the mind incapable of passing in a moment from one passion and disposition to a quite different one" (T 379). This observation is crucial to Hume's emphasis on *moderation*, throughout his works—a quite neglected aspect of his philo-

sophical method and tenets which I have discussed elsewhere.[6] It is sufficient here, however, to notice that the requirement for consistency is said
to have its foundations in nature, understood in this case to be certain
physiological capacities of the mind. Hume gives another example: "An
heroic and burlesque design, united in one picture, wou'd be monstrous;
tho' we place two pictures of so opposite a character in the same chamber,
and even close by each other, without any scruple or difficulty" (T 380).
Hume argues that because a spectator can consider the two pictures *as* two,
"this break in the ideas, breaks the progress of the affections . . ." (T 380);
furthermore, "the want of relation in the objects or ideas hinders the natural
contrariety of the passions . . ." (T 380). It is important to notice Hume's
remark that what he is here claiming for the *passions* "is analogous to what
we have observ'd . . . concerning the *understanding* . . ." (T 380); in both
cases, he is concerned to describe the mechanisms at work, whether they be
best classified as physiological or psychological. His explicit analogy also
allows us to introduce a broader term to embrace the notion of "consistency"
as it functions in connection with the passions and with the understanding:
intelligibility. I shall elaborate on that notion, shortly. Two more points
must be made about the passages above, however.

First, it is clear that the description offered of an object is crucial, as the
example of the two pictures shows; since, by design or accident, we may
establish a relation between two items "which may cause an easy transition of
the ideas, and consequently of the emotions or impressions, attending the
ideas . . ." (T 380). Many of our responses have a natural foundation, as we
have seen; our descriptions of them, and of their putative causes, however,
are governed by the linguistic conventions which operate in our particular
community, and which have to be learned by members of that community.
As I showed in my earlier essay in this book,[7] Hume places great weight on
the importance of education, alongside our natural instincts, as a source of
our knowledge. Complex conventions, therefore, govern our criteria of
identity and individuation, and determine whether we have given one description of two pictures or two descriptions of one picture. It is not relevant
to Hume's argument in this context, that he should spell out these assumptions; it is only important that a reader should not foist on Hume absurd
views about language and meaning which he never held, and which make
nonsense of what he actually said. Precisely because he is not talking about
language here, Hume does not use any linguistic labels. "Description" is a
term which *I* have been using; but from Hume's references to comparisons,
and from his examples of plains, diamonds, and forgeries, we might equally
use the term *interpretation*, with its emphasis on dimensions of meaning.

The second point may be mentioned briefly. In so far as the calm passions
which have to do with beauty are natural responses to certain situations, so
far may they be termed "involuntary" (T 608); and Hume tells us that the
reasoning posited as the associative link between the attendant ideas may
be termed "implicit" (T 553). He suggests that our displeasure at a figure
interpreted as off-balance is caused by our sympathy for something which we
believe will fall and will suffer pain (T 364); now he concedes that discussion

might persuade us that our relatively immediate interpretation of the situation is mistaken, although he adds, as we have seen, that sometimes the verdicts of our heart may outlive the judgments of our head—as when we say "I know it is (meant to be) a man just beginning to move forward, but it still looks to me like a man falling over." The important point is that our sentiments are caused directly by our perceptions, and only in a mediate fashion by our perceptual judgments; it is quite possible, therefore, for a man to express perceptual judgments which, in fact, do not match his perceptions. In such a case, the public may be satisfied with the judgments whilst remaining ignorant of the fact that the man harbours his old sentiments.

IV

"Of the Standard of Taste" is Hume's most sustained and subtle essay on aesthetics, although its complexities are easily missed by readers unfamiliar with his other work. A brief examination of the essay will enable us to focus and extend our discussion.

The aim of the essay is to prove "that the taste of all individuals is not upon an equal footing" (*Essays* 248), and to characterise the nature of the procedures which enable us to confirm or condemn men's sentiments (*Essays* 233–34) Hume says that "it is natural for us to seek" such a rule. He recognises that at least two problems confront "those who found morality on sentiment." First, if "no sentiment represents what is really in the object," then "a thousand different sentiments, excited by the same object, are all right," and it would be fruitless to "seek the real beauty, or real deformity" (*Essays* 234, 235). Second, by thus implying that "the difference among men is really greater than at first sight it appears" (*Essays* 232), such a view seems unable to explain why, in fact, no one accepts "the principle of the natural equality of tastes" (*Essays* 235). Hume wants to establish that there are general rules of art, although they "are founded only on experience, and on the observation of the common sentiments of human nature" (*Essays* 237); such "rules" are "general observations, concerning what has been universally found to please in all countries and in all ages" (*Essays* 236); they are most definitely not "fixed by reasonings *à priori*" (*Essays* 235); nor do they have the form of geometrical prescriptions, for such rules would certainly produce "insipid and disagreeable" works. Hume's reference to all countries and ages needs interpretation. The dramatic wording is designed to show rationalists that empirically grounded rules have a scope of sufficient generality to be genuine substitutes for the *a priori* standards which are being challenged—however difficult it may be to establish empirically grounded rules; further, the wording is designed to re-enforce Hume's view that genuine causal connections have a certain character of necessity—although not of the kind postulated by rationalists.

Hume proceeds to make a long list of empirical claims. For example: "Some particular forms or qualities, from the original structure of the internal fabric are calculated to please, and others to displease; and if they fail of their effect in any particular instance, it is from some apparent defect or imperfection in the organ" (*Essays* 238). Further:

> Those finer emotions of the mind are of a very tender and delicate nature, and require the concurrence of many favourable circumstances to make them play with facility and exactness, according to their general and established principles. The least exterior hindrance to such small springs, or the least internal disorder, disturbs their motion, and confounds the operations of the whole machine. When we would make an experiment of this nature, and would try the force of any beauty or deformity, we must choose with care a proper time and place, and bring the fancy to a suitable situation and disposition. A perfect serenity of mind, a recollection of thought, a due attention to the object; if any of these circumstances be wanting, our experiment will be fallacious, and we shall be unable to judge of the catholic and universal beauty. The relation, which nature has placed between the form and the sentiment, will at least be more obscure; and it will require greater accuracy to trace and discern it. We shall be able to ascertain its influence, not so much from the operation of each particular beauty, as from the durable admiration which attends those works that have survived all the caprices of mode and fashion, all the mistakes of ignorance and envy [*Essays* 237].

The causal relation between objective properties and our calm passions is established only when the machinery of the mind is tuned in appropriate ways. As social beings, however, we often already know the repute of certain works, and this serves the double purpose of alerting us to the need for special attitudes to the works in question, and of allowing us to check upon the presence and nature of any sentiment of pleasure we may happen to feel. We should notice, also, the reference to "the force of any beauty"; this should be understood, of course, as a reference to the vivacity of the secondary impression, or calm passion. Hume adds that "If, in the sound state of the organ, there be an entire or a considerable uniformity of sentiment among men, we may thence derive an idea of the perfect beauty . . ." (*Essays* 238). Now, Hume always recognised that different problems confront an agent himself, and a spectator, when both are trying to estimate the agent's performances. The agent, obviously, is likely to be too involved with the object estimated (see note 19, below; EHU 94, note), but he may possess knowledge difficult for the spectator to attain. In art the problem is acute: "In order to judge aright of a composition of genius, there are so many views to be taken in, so many circumstances to be compared, and such a knowledge of human nature requisite, that no man, who is not possessed of the soundest judgment, will ever make a tolerable critic in such performances" (*Essays* 5).[8] Hume's procedure at this stage of "Of the Standard of Taste," is instructive: he examines several "cause[s] why many feel not the proper sentiment" (*Essays* 239) and suggests some "condition[s]" (*Essays* 245) which must be satisfied by "a true judge in the finer arts" (*Essays* 247).

Hume lists three causes of failure to feel the proper sentiment, two of which are especially important since they refer to definite capacities: want of "*delicacy* of imagination" (*Essays* 239), "*prejudice*" (*Essays* 244), and lack of "*good sense*" (*Essays* 245). The last refers to discriminating thought;

"prejudice," of course, refers to a viewpoint, in a literal and a metaphorical sense; and "delicacy of imagination" refers to discriminating perception, which is said to depend, ultimately, on "the organs of internal sensation" (*Essays* 247). For the improvement of our perception two procedures are said to be essential ("requisite"; "impossible . . . without" [*Essays* 243]): "*practice*" (*Essays* 242) and the forming of "*comparisons*" (*Essays* 243). *Practice* is necessary because "There is a flutter or hurry of thought which attends the first perusal of any piece, and which confounds the genuine sentiment of beauty. . . . Not to mention, that there is a species of beauty, which, as it is florid and superficial, pleases at first . . ." (*Essays* 243). Any "very individual performance [should] be more than once perused by us, and be surveyed in different lights with attention and deliberation" (*Essays* 243), for only in this way can we determine "the relation of the parts" and their respective merits. *Comparison* between "the several species and degrees of excellence" and "the different kinds of beauty" is essential, because "By comparison alone we fix the epithets of praise or blame, and learn how to assign the due degree of each" (*Essays* 243). The reference here to "learning how to" is important, and I shall return to it. A *prejudiced* critic fails to place "himself in that point of view which the performance supposes" (*Essays* 245). Hume claims that "every work of art, in order to produce its due effect on the mind, must be surveyed in a certain point of view, and cannot be fully relished by persons whose situation, real or imaginary, is not conformable to that which is required by the performance" (*Essays* 244). It must be remembered that this rule is an empirical generalisation based on the observation of causal connections between observer and work of art, under certain conditions; as a rule, of course, it can guide an artist's intentions as well as a spectator's attitudes. The chief task of *good sense*, Hume tells us, is to guard against prejudice, "and in this respect, as well as in many others, reason, if not an essential part of taste, is at least requisite to the operations of this latter faculty" (*Essays* 245). Hume indicates four aspects to which such thought should attend:

(*a*) a critic's thought must be "capacious enough" to comprehend the "mutual relation and correspondence of parts," and to "compare them with each other, in order to perceive the consistence and uniformity of the whole";

(*b*) "Every work of art has also a certain end or purpose for which it is calculated; and is to be deemed more or less perfect, as it is more or less fitted to attain this end. The object of eloquence is to persuade, of history to instruct, of poetry to please, by means of the passions and the imagination. These ends we must carry constantly in our view when we peruse any performance;"

(*c*) "and we must be able to judge how far the means employed are adapted to their respective purposes";

(*d*) further, "every kind of composition, even the most poetical, is nothing but a chain of propositions and reasonings"; and the "persons introduced in tragedy and epic poetry must be represented as reasoning, and thinking, and concluding, and acting, suitably to their character and circumstances . . ." (*Essays* 246).

It is surely reasonable to classify these tasks under the heading of *inter-pretation*, and to identify their goal as the understanding or *intelligibility* of works of art—the two notions I introduced at the end of Section III. In support of this move, we may cite Hume's observations from the long, and subsequently suppressed, footnote to Section III of *An Enquiry Concerning Human Understanding*. There, Hume insists that "As man is a reasonable being . . . he seldom acts or speaks or thinks without a purpose and intention." [9] "In all compositions of genius, therefore, it is requisite that the writer have some plan or object; . . . there must appear some aim or intention in his first setting out, if not in the composition of the whole work. A production without a design would resemble . . . the ravings of a madman. . . ." [10] In "narrative compositions," Hume argues, it is a rule which "admits of no exception," that the narrated events "must be connected together by some bond or tie," must "form a kind of *unity* which may bring them under one plan or view, and which may be the object or end of the writer in his first undertaking." [11] Again, in epic and narrative poetry, it "is incumbent on every writer to form some plan or design before he enter on any discourse or narration, and to comprehend his subject in some general aspect or united view which may be the constant object of his attention." [12] It is a necessary requirement that such works "have a sufficient unity to make them be comprehended. . . ." [13] Hume concludes the passage: "the three connecting principles of all ideas are the relations of *resemblance, contiguity,* and *causation*." [14] A little earlier he had observed that the unity of action "which is to be found in biography or history differs from that of epic poetry, not in kind, but in degree"; [15] in all these endeavours, "By introducing into any composition personages and actions foreign to each other, an injudicious author loses that communication of emotions by which alone he can interest the heart and raise the passions to their proper height and period." [16] Three observations should be made at this stage of the argument.

1. We saw above, in Section III, that consistency of ideas allegedly ensures their "easy transition . . . and consequently of the emotions or impressions, attending the ideas . . ." (T 380); the natural requirement for such easy transitions lies behind demands for consistency of tone in literature (T 379–80) and for balanced figures in painting and statuary (T 364; EPM 245–46). The matter can now be clarified further. The "designs, and projects, and views of men are principles as necessary in their operation as heat and cold, moist and dry . . ." (T 474); in other words, these "principles" are conditions of human agency, and knowledge of them is a condition of the intelligibility of what a man does. It is precisely because art is a human activity that the requirement of intelligibility arises, in Hume's view; indeed, sustained pleasure from a work depends on our understanding it in some way. Our attitudes to animate and inanimate objects are different (EPM 213, note), and Hume constantly insists on differences within the species of art itself; there will thus be differences in our attitudes towards different arts. We may now see why Hume says that "There is something approaching to principles in mental taste; and critics can reason and dispute

more plausibly than cooks or perfumers" (*Essays* 165). Critics can reason more *plausibly* because discriminating thought (*good sense*) is necessary to determine the intelligibility (*consistency*) of an intended human performance; but, of course, cooks and perfumers *can,* and do, reason, as Hume himself shows in the example of "the leathern thong" from *Don Quixote* (*Essays* 239–40).

2. We should notice that Hume discusses, in the present context, three separable though related issues: the artist and the conditions of creation; the work or art product; the audience and the conditions of response. It is a fundamental tenet of Hume's that causation is a condition of intelligibility in the empirical world, and Hume asks causal questions about all three issues. When a work of art is representational in a broad sense—and Hume's interest centers on such works—he asks causal questions of the items represented in order to determine the consistency of the content of the work. There are, so to say, external and internal causal questions, the former concerning the relations between the work and other things (the artist, the audience, society, morality), the latter concerning the internal consistency of the work itself; the detection of a work's consistency, however, presupposes a certain viewpoint, and that is an external causal question. "[J]udgment on any work of art" (*Essays* 246–47) involves much more than a mere verdict, even if the "final sentence depends on some internal sense or feeling, which nature has made universal in the whole species" (EPM 173). Judgment requires the perception and delineation of the causes of the calm passion, and the causes are objective properties internal to the work itself, but discernible only from certain viewpoints. A man of taste must have the internal sentiment, or at least *an* internal sentiment, of course, since this is the effect whose cause he seeks; his judgments are *objective triadic relational judgments*—"triadic" because they depend on the work, the critic, and the viewpoint.

3. Quotation (*b*) above, with its references to the different objects or ends of eloquence, history, and poetry serves to remind us, again, that Hume distinguished between different *genres,* and that his general account in no way confines the field of art. He tells us, for example, that the story of a poem is "the least essential part of it," [17] a remark which underlies his view of fiction (see *Essays* 235–36) and his explanation of why tragedy pleases (*Essays* 221–30; EPM 259–60). In contrast to these forms, the judges of eloquence must be the public at large (*Essays* 107–108) since its end is to persuade such a public.

Whilst outlining causes of failure to feel the proper sentiment, Hume raises two important questions, although he directly answers only one of them. First, he asks how we should "silence the bad critic, who might always insist upon his particular sentiment, and refuse to submit to his antagonist" (*Essays* 241). His answer is that we must appeal to consistency and acknowledged parallel cases:

> when we show him an avowed principle of art; when we illustrate this principle by examples, whose operation, from his own particular taste, he acknowledges to be conformable to the principle; when we prove that the same prin-

ciple may be applied to the present case, where he did not perceive or feel its influence: he must conclude, upon the whole, that the fault lies in himself, and that he wants the delicacy which is requisite to make him sensible of every beauty and every blemish . . . [*Essays* 241].

This answer shows clearly that Hume is eager to "modify and restrain" (*Essays* 235) the view that "a thousand different sentiments, excited by the same object, are all right; because no sentiment represents what is really in the object" (*Essays* 234). The whole discussion about feeling the *proper* sentiment is designed to establish that only certain sentiments are appropriate to certain objects. Two aspects of this point must be emphasised. It is an empirical fact that certain particulars are causally related; it is a linguistic convention which determines the correct designation of these particulars. The appropriate sentiments are those which have been found, empirically, to result from *discriminating* attention; and there are both psychological and social reasons why these sentiments are especially rewarding or worthwhile. Discussion must focus upon the causes of such sentiments, however, because only the causes are open to public scrutiny. It may be argued that no man can establish even *that* he has experienced an inner sentiment, or calm passion, let alone any more precise description of it, without the aid of publicly learned and rule-governed concepts; this being so, reference to any internal sentiments in discussions of art or beauty in general could be dropped. This is no objection against Hume's position, however. Hume is quite insistent upon the fact that publicly available viewpoints are conditions of objectivity, and publicly ascertainable conventions conditions of discussion and judgment. His reference to causes is part of an argument with a quite different point: namely, to explain why certain people behave as they do.

The second question Hume raises during his discussion of failure to feel proper sentiments, and which he does not directly answer, concerns the detection of pretenders. In contrast to the *bad critic* who insists on his own sentiment, the *pretender*, presumably, issues judgments which are in line with the established critical standards in his community, and need never reveal the absence of the proper sentiment.[18] Hume's subtle question (*Essays* 247) forces us to clarify the role of calm passions in his theory. Because a pretender could remain undetected by restricting himself to the already current judgment of his peers, the only way to establish the insecurity of his verdicts is to see how he deals with new or non-standard cases, where he needs to modify existing criteria. As Hume insists, everyone in this situation "must produce the best arguments that their invention suggests to them . . ." (*Essays* 248), and then appeal to their peers as jurymen. Only time will tell which arguments achieve authority, and this is one reason why Hume places such weight on the longevity of a work's reputation (*Essays* 136, 237–38). It is quite possible that a pretender's judgments gain acceptance; and they do so, be it noted, in the absence, by definition, of his own inner sentiments. His converts, however, on Hume's account, do have sentiments whose objective causes they take him to have isolated. Two points emerge. A man's internal sentiment is of interest primarily to him; in the arts, at least, its occurrence is often the occasion of his trying to find its cause (*pace* Hume's denial of this fact [T 471]). Hume contends that the imagination enables a man to distinguish feelings having different sources (T 587, 472). To others, however, what matters is the articulation of viewpoints from which objective properties of a work may be discerned. And the procedures for this articulation have to be learned. Hence Hume's remark that by comparison we "learn how to" assign the epithets of praise and blame (*Essays* 243). Even the pretender, at the outset of his sad career, must learn the same conventions as his peers, whether the conventions cover physical viewpoints or linguistic behaviour. Hume held that a "very small variation of the object, even where the same qualities are preserved, will destroy a sentiment" (EPM 213, note); he also held that "In changing the point of view, tho' the object may remain the same, its proportion to ourselves entirely alters . . ." (T 390). In the light of my earlier essay in this book we now know that Hume regarded knowledge as an essentially social phenomenon, and that he wished to insist upon the passive aspects of our early learning alongside our basically instinctive or natural responses. There certainly can be agreed descriptions of states of affairs, although it is an empirical fact whether a given community possesses the conventions to achieve them; wherever we detect causal relations, we can reach agreement over their description. When Hume asserts, therefore, that a calm passion "marks a certain conformity or relation between the object and the organs or faculties of the mind; and if that conformity did not really exist, the sentiment could never possibly have being" (*Essays* 234)—when Hume makes this bold assertion, we can be certain that he believes in the possibility of agreed refinements in our descriptions of the objects.

What sort of man, then, is the pretender? If the presence of a certain inner sentiment is of concern only to the man who experiences it, and if it plays no role at all in discussions of the publicly discernible objects we call works of art, a pretender must be one who wishes to be esteemed for his judgments of those works even though he lacks the normal sentiments of pleasure derived from attending to them. A pretender intends to deceive us about his own states, not about public objects, and his motives for such deception may vary. In Hume's view the most general reason why men want to agree is that they are social beings. He himself confesses his distress at being unable to change his sentiments to accord with those of men he respects; he hopes that the long-term verdict of posterity will vindicate him (LDH II 133). As social beings, in any case, it is almost impossible for men to hold out against the general opinion of others.[19] Moreover, "the happiness and misery of others are not spectacles entirely indifferent to us . . ." (EPM 243), and most of what is naturally approved of is beneficial (T 579). As social beings we begin by learning what to say, and only subsequently may we discover internal associations for such utterances, or even question their full meaning and import. Someone thrust into a new culture and society would not know what judgments it was appropriate to make, and at first would not even know what descriptions to offer of the phenomena at issue. Of course, education can lead to purely mechanical reactions (EPM 214–15,

202–203), which, in this case, might mean judgments made in the absence of the inner sentiments which are their proper liegemen. A man will become a pretender only when he discovers that his internal life differs from those of his peers, although, by then, he may well have established alternative associations which act as cues—like those who are colour-blind. Hume's pretender, indeed, has much in common with a colour-blind man. Both, for the most part, can get by with their learned responses; both, in his view, suffer from a defect in their mental constitution, as a result of which they are lacking in certain basically natural reactions (*Essays* 140–41).

Hume contends that there "remain two sources of variation" which are sufficient "to produce a difference in the degrees of our approbation or blame," although not "to confound all the boundaries of beauty and deformity" (*Essays* 249): "The one is the different humours of particular men; the other, the particular manners and opinions of our age and country" (*Essays* 249). Psychological facts about individuals, and social facts about communities explain variations within generally agreed evaluations. Thus, Ovid, Horace, and Tacitus are all worthy of esteem, although at different times of his life a man may prefer one above another (*Essays* 250); such preferences are "innocent" and "can never reasonably be the object of dispute," since "it is almost impossible not to feel a predilection for that which suits our particular turn and disposition" (*Essays* 251). Again, although it requires "some effort," we should not judge the representations of other ages and cultures as deformities, even if "we are not so sensibly touched with them" (*Essays* 251): adverse judgment of alien and unfamiliar works must be restricted to those which confound the limits of vice and virtue. But when men in a given community differ in their judgments "from prejudice, from want of practice, or want of delicacy . . . there is just reason for approving one taste, and condemning another" (*Essays* 250). It is an empirical question, of course, who the arbiters of taste are at a given time, and how they achieve recognition; in fact, Hume believes that most men "are apt to receive a man for whatever he has a mind to put himself off for . . ." (*Essays* 547–48), and he could argue, with plausibility, that arbiters of taste are usually self-proclaimed people with special interests and goals in the context. The notion of qualified observers poses no problems to one, such as Hume, who insists that we all begin by learning the established conventions; whilst doing this, we learn, also, who count as the master practitioners of our time, just as we learn what counts as an objective fact. Hume claims that "few are qualified to give judgment on any work of art, or establish their own sentiment as the standard of beauty" (*Essays* 246–47) because the "joint verdict" of strong sense and delicate sentiment, "improved by practice, perfected by comparison, and cleared of all prejudice" (*Essays* 247), is rarely found.

It is clear that Hume distinguishes expressions of preference from the objective critical judgments whose nature he has been discussing, but it is also clear that there can be no absolute distinction between them. There is a sense in which a man himself needs no reason for the pleasure he experiences from a work of art; Hume says that "our approbation is imply'd in the immediate pleasure . . ." (T 471) the works cause in us. As a social being, however, he wishes to communicate his pleasure, and to seek re-assurance that he does not deviate markedly from his peers; these aims can be achieved only by reference to the putative causes of his experience, and if no one endorses his causal claims he has grounds for anxiety. Hume remarked, in a letter (LDH 1 30), that we often conceal our dislike of something because of our inability to give reasons for our verdict. To express our dislike is often to publicise our deviation from the accepted evaluation, and, as such, our judgment calls for explanation. We can retreat, of course, in the direction of our psychological idiosyncrasies, but in so doing we withdraw our original verdict from public discussion; but if we advance towards a view-point available to others, we proceed towards objective verdicts. Likes are always personal, though many are shared. It is a social fact, and Hume was well aware of it, that we all like to like what we know is good; and some of us claim to. The old pretender lurks in us all.

V

To conclude this brief paper I shall indicate topics for future discussion.

1. For an adequate understanding of Hume's aesthetics, his concepts of *pleasure, sympathy,* and *imagination* require closer scrutiny than they have yet received.

2. Hume's views on *tragedy, rhetoric,* and *the sublime* need patient attention.

3. A study of his own modes of presentation (which partly falls under the heading of "rhetoric") and his own critical judgments will throw light on his views about language and meaning.

4. Analysis of what he says about the relations between art and morality, politics and society will enhance our understanding of Hume's philosophy as a whole.

5. An attempt to establish Hume's views on aesthetics, involving, as it does, a study of his complete *oeuvre,* illuminates the relative importance of Hume's central philosophical concepts; and it calls for adjustment in their traditional interpretation. Many of the views on epistemology, the philosophy of mind, the passions and morality, attributed to Hume, have been mis-attributed.

6. Students of Kant will benefit from reflection upon Hume's aesthetics, against which Kant, so often, seems to be arguing. On the one hand, there are remarkable parallels between their views, especially when Kant discusses judgments of dependent beauty, and taste; on the other hand, they differ sharply in their moral and metaphysical commitments. In both cases, however, their views on aesthetics are integral to their over-all philosophy, and a contemporary student will want to decide whether this must be so for any aesthetic doctrine.

7. Further clarification is needed of Hume's notions of *viewpoint* and *natural foundation,* and of the two notions I introduced on his behalf, *interpretation* and *intelligibility.*

Compared with the absolute necessities of life, art, along with much else is one of life's "superfluities" (*Essays* 279); in this sense it is "gratuitous" (D 198). Nevertheless, Hume holds that the habit of conversing together, and of contributing to each other's pleasures, increases the level both of knowledge and of humanity (*Essays* 278–79). Art is an important factor in these matters, for it is a human practice whose principal goal is the provision of pleasure—unlike all those other phenomena whose aesthetic dimension is, so to say, inessential and accidental.

A summary of our discussion can be provided by sketching a characteristic sequence of events, as Hume sees them. A man becomes conscious of his pleasure from a certain object; he may have only the vaguest awareness of the object's characteristics, although enough to individuate it for further scrutiny. Hume constantly warns readers against the inaccuracies of first appearances (e.g., EPM 242–43; T 47, 132, 446). In order to discern more precisely the cause of his present pleasure, the man attends more closely to the object (it must be asserted that Hume's distinction "betwixt the cause and the object" of a passion [T 278] has nothing to do with contemporary discussions of intentionality). The attention requires all his perceptual and intellectual faculties, and it is a fact of nature that these faculties seek a state of rest, equilibrium, balance, consistency: the terms Hume most often uses are *consistency* and *unity*. In so far as the work of the mind is involved, we could call the search a search for *intelligibility*. If a man achieves this, in some measure, his former sentiments of pleasure will be enhanced; or, rather, he will now experience new sentiments, resulting from his closer attention, but sentiments which are in accord with his first reactions. In so far as he has been seeking causes, however, a man needs confirmation of parallel instances; here he must appeal to publicly accessible phenomena and criteria, using the conventions of his community. These conventions secure inter-subjective agreement in judgments. Furthermore, as a social being he wishes to check that his responses are similar to those of his neighbours, and share the pleasures he experiences; this he can do only by making known their causes.

NOTES

1. In this paper I have re-worked and developed some of the themes from two earlier articles of mine: "Another Look at Hume's Views of Aesthetic and Moral Judgments," *Philosophical Quarterly*, 20, No. 78 (January 1970) 53–59, and "Hume's Aesthetics Reassessed," ibid., 26, No. 102 (January 1976), 48–62. I am grateful to the Editor of that journal for permission to make use of that material.

2. Kant, *The Critique of Judgment*, trans. James Creed Meredith (Oxford, 1952), pp. 154–55.

3. See *Critique of Judgment*, pp. 158 and 162, for Kant's attitude on discovering that flowers or bird songs are fakes; he is peculiarly worried about being duped in the realm of aesthetics.

4. "Of the Authenticity of Ossian's Poems," in *Essays: Moral, Political, and Literary*, edd. T. H. Green and T. H. Grose, 2 vols. (London, 1898), II 415.

5. "A Dissertation on the Passions," ibid., 161.

6. See my "'Art' and 'Moderation' in Hume's *Essays*" in the forthcoming *Proceedings of the McGill Bicentennial Hume Congress* (1976).

7. See chap. 9 of this volume, "Strains in Hume and Wittgenstein."

8. Hume's first essay in the 1742 volume of essays, from which this quotation comes, was entitled "Of the Delicacy of Taste and Passion." He tells us that he never intended to publish (LDH II 253) "Of the Standard of Taste," although it appeared, by chance, in 1757. Apart from the forced ending, it is one of his best essays, and it is interesting to speculate on why he did not intend to publish it.

9. There are several passages important to the thesis of this paper which do not appear in the Selby-Bigge edition of the first *Enquiry*. They are included in *An Inquiry Concerning Human Understanding*, ed. Charles W. Hendel (Indianapolis, 1955). Hendel, p. 33.

10. Ibid.

11. Ibid.

12. Ibid., p. 37.

13. Ibid., p. 39.

14. Ibid.

15. Ibid., p. 35.

16. Ibid., p. 39.

17. "Letter to the Authors of the Critical Review Concerning the Epigoniad of Wilkie," *Essays*, edd. Green & Grose, II 433.

18. When I discussed this issue in "Understanding a Work of Art" (*The British Journal of Aesthetics*, 9 [1969], 128–44) and in *Philosophy and the Novel* (Oxford, 1975), I did not realise that the modifications which I proposed represented Hume's own position more accurately.

19. "Dissertation on the Passions," 152.

16

The Place of the Language of Morals in Hume's Second *Enquiry*

JAMES T. KING
Northern Illinois University

THIS ESSAY EXAMINES the method and point of departure for the *Enquiry Concerning the Principles of Morals* and explores what is involved in the guidance which "the very nature of language" (EPM 174) gives to that inquiry. The method of the third Book of the *Treatise* is also discussed, and some reasons for thinking that of the *Enquiry* to be philosophically superior are offered.

I · THE POINT OF DEPARTURE FOR THE *Enquiry*

Toward the end of the first Section of the *Enquiry* Hume explicitates what he had in mind in setting forth to examine morality. He locates morality in language, advising the reader that the "very nature of language guides us almost infallibly in forming a judgement of this nature" (viz., relative to the objects of praise and blame); he continues:

> and as every tongue possesses one set of words which are taken in a good sense, and another in the opposite, the least acquaintance with the idiom suffices, without any reasoning, to direct us in collecting and arranging the estimable or blameable qualities of men. The only object of reasoning is to discover the circumstances on both sides, which are common to these qualities; to observe that particular in which the estimable qualities agree on the one hand, and the blameable on the other; and thence to reach the foundation of ethics, and find those universal principles, from which all censure or approbation is ultimately derived [EPM 174].

It is taken for granted that anyone possessing "acquaintance with the idiom" has the object of inquiry before him in an appropriate manner. Understanding and using the language forms, "without any reasoning," a kind of immediacy which, while familiar and accessible to any inquirer, still relates to a reality which is public and common. Being *at hand* in the common language of morals, the moral distinctions are readily analyzed—and perhaps more readily than when the distinctions are approached as elements of perception or experience.[1] As given in language, morality appears more stable, definite, and regular than it does when presented as a matter of the passions or the sentiments of the individual, and since it is independent of the experience of the single individual (though, of course, not independent of the experience of individuals generally), it comprises standards against which the sentiments and judgments of the individual may be measured. It appears, as a result, that the point of departure for Hume's *Enquiry* is a most promising one, and one whose far-reaching implications deserve to be explored.

II · FACT AND NORM IN THE LANGUAGE OF MORALS

1. As Hume declares in the continuation of the text last cited, the starting point for his inquiry about morality has the status of *fact*, and is something whose existence is evident in usage; the question with which Hume begins is "a question of fact, not of abstract science" (EPM 174). It would appear that the very nature of language is capable of guiding the inquiry concerning the principles of morals inasmuch as: (*a*) we engage with familiarity in the practice of praising and blaming; and (*b*) we commonly do so relative to roughly standardized objects ("mental qualities" or active dispositions of character) according to regular patterns of approval or disapproval such as result in a shared language of morals. This language of morals is an historical fact about men in society, something *positive* [2] and unproblematical. It should not be overlooked that Hume's strategy in establishing moral language as something already constituted, a *fait accompli*, is thoroughly in line with his avowed methodological inclination to ground inquiry in existence and fact (see T 415).

2. Inasmuch as morality or the moral distinctions are available to inspection and analysis in the common language men speak, it is a fact, furthermore, of a *social* or *public* character. Since the moral distinctions have an existence independent of the approvals and disapprovals of any given individual, the language of morals is readily seen not only to encompass approvals but to provide as well a *standard* as to what formally constitutes a proper approval or disapproval and *principles* according to which we may evaluate approvals and disapprovals. Thus there is no question in the *Enquiry* that morality is not tied through a one-to-one correspondence to the sentiments of the individual, but being locatable in a common language, stands forth as something against which the sentiments of the individual may be measured. Morality is not a private matter discovered through introspection or the analysis of perceptions, or something variable according to personal taste. Its positive, public reality vanquishes any suggestion of moral scepticism.

3. At the same time, the language of morals is neither a formal or ideal system nor the mere statistical convergence of a plurality of individual responses; rather, it is a language *in use*—the living moral language of common life which both reflects the appropriate perspective in which actions and characters are to be viewed and expresses the common sentiments of right and wrong. To Hume it is inconceivable that we should use this language without participating in its approvals with some genuine feeling of our own (EPM 226–27); the existence of the language would be incomprehensible, in fact, unless men had sentiments conformable to it.

It would not be inappropriate to ascribe to Hume some sensitivity to the factors which H. L. A. Hart brings together under his notion of what is involved in having the "internal point of view" to a normative system, viz. (a) recognizing that the system engenders obligations, (b) accepting these obligations as binding on oneself and on others, and (c) finding in the system reasoned justification for pressing conformity to those obligations.[3] The moral language which serves as a starting point for the *Enquiry* is moral language to which the inquirer is assumed to have, to some measure, attitudes and commitments like those involved in Hart's "internal point of view" to law.

It is assuredly part of the genius of the *Enquiry* that moral language as there depicted has both a public status, such that its existence may be said to be a matter of fact, and a normative status, such that it embodies a system of *oughts*. It follows that the recognition of the existence of the common language of morals is not like the recognition of plain matters of fact; it is the recognition which belongs precisely to the user of that language who, by participating in a set of approvals and disapprovals, finds therein something to which, by the constitution of his nature, according to Hume, he subscribes. There is no contradiction in affirming that the language of morals is both normative and factual, so long as it is understood that the kind of facticity in question is consequent upon the fact of common participation in the moral language as a normative system.

In the claim that moral language in common use is the point of departure for the *Enquiry*, "using moral language" is understood to involve being on the inside of patterns of evaluation and acknowledgments of obligation; from this it follows that moral language is a presupposition for the philosophical project of the *Enquiry*; but if this is the case, then in inquiring about morals Hume would seem to maintain that we cannot stand outside moral language so as to identify as conditions of its possibility factors which are independent of this presupposition. Those committed to upholding the viability of ethical naturalism in its *strictest* form, therefore, ought perhaps to reconsider whether the *Enquiry* may be appealed to as an instantiation of that particular meta-ethical stance.[4]

III · POSSIBLE DIFFICULTIES IN THE *Enquiry* APPROACH TO MORALS

The shift of focus of inquiry from sentiments to language signals another respect in which Hume is a thoroughly modern philosopher, deserving of the attention which is currently accorded him. This approach may involve certain difficulties, however, for if morality is located in the common language of morals and is acknowledged to have a public existence, then it might appear to be related only contingently to any given individual's sentiments, thus failing to be practical, and to possess a fixity at odds with the actual variability we recognize in moral language.

Undoubtedly Hume held certain opinions about man and morals which we may not share, and among such distinctively eighteenth-century beliefs must be numbered his conviction of the uniformity of human nature and his estimate that the language of morals is more stable than the language of science (*Essays* 253). But even if we do not subscribe to such beliefs, it is not clear that the fact that any given individual may fail to participate appropriately in the language of morals constitutes a difficulty for Hume's *Enquiry* approach to morality, since he is quite deliberate about making moral principles "universal," "general," and "abstract" (EPM 174, 274) and about removing them from the contingency which belongs to impressions and feelings. The very notion that the language comprises standards against which the sentiments of the individual may be measured presupposes the possibility that individual sentiment does not correspond perfectly to the language.[5]

More serious, it appears, is the possible objection that moral language, in having the status of public fact, cannot display the flexibility and openness to controversy which seem to the twentieth-century mind inseparable from morality. This objection appears to overlook the fact, however, that the common language of morals to which Hume appeals at the outset of the *Enquiry* is the living language of a people which involves, not an absolute consensus relative to a fixed set of approvals and disapprovals, but rather a general consensus relative to what we might term an open-ended core of shared approvals and disapprovals, such as to constitute the corpus of the language of morals and to provide a source for the examples on which Hume draws throughout the *Enquiry*. Using this language, moreover, is not simply a matter of engaging oneself in approvals and disapprovals but also of grasping and employing the principles governing our approvals and disapprovals. Thus for Hume the language of morals is flexible, and there is indeed a method and structure to its variability and openness to dispute and differences of opinion (*A Dialogue*: EPM 324–43).

Hume, in fact, identified two types of second-order principles of morality: (*a*) material principles relating to pleasure or benefit to self or others, and (*b*) formal principles of the moral judgment, relating to generality and objectivity;[6] both types of principle, being, as one would expect, quite general,[7] are not impediments to moral controversy but its very avenues. Since the set of approvals and disapprovals which constitutes the core of the common language of morals is open-ended, and since the second-order principles of the language are general, it is not at all surprising that moral language as envisioned in the *Enquiry* should accommodate controversy.

Thus it should be concluded that the *Enquiry* offers a philosophical and not a merely sociological account of morality. Inasmuch as Hume does not maintain that a character is worthy of approval because most men approve of it, the fact that there may be disagreement about approvals and disapprovals is not a criticism of his position. On the contrary. By affirming in his philosophical analysis of morality that approval is tied to pleasure or benefit to self or others, disapproval to their opposites, Hume presents a structure capable of accommodating an indefinitely large extent of dispute about morals, and thus can not only claim that, but also explain how, moral language has room for controversy.[8]

Finally, although Hume is not as critical as we might perhaps wish in affirming that men do participate in moral language to some extent, his is decidedly not a doctrine about moral behavior. Hume says little about how men in general behave; he offers a theory based on an analysis of language, not on a survey of practices. Hume, in short, would admit that, relative to any given individual and any particular approval or disapproval, it is contingent whether the individual engages himself in that approval or disapproval; but he would deny that the relationship of the individual to moral language may be described as contingent in this same sense.[9] The one sort of failure of men to participate in moral language which would be bothersome to Hume's theory is a failure to participate at all—but, of course, such a failure would devastate moral theories at large, and not simply Hume's.

Another possible objection against the *Enquiry* approach might be that once morality is given as a positive *fait accompli*, it ceases to evoke speculative interest, for if we are all familiar users of moral language, what remains to be discovered about it? Inasmuch as Hume presents morality as already constituted in its fundamentals, is his philosophical endeavor not subsequently limited to mere descriptive exposition?

While Hume does characterize the *Enquiry* as following a "very simple method" (EPM 173), he considers this method to be of great import and superior to any other. He describes it as an inductive or experimental approach which proceeds from fact and observations, and arrives at the foundations of ethics; but it may be asked whether this method possesses any genuine explanatory power. Does it not tell us only what we knew all along, that pleasure or benefit to self or to others—principles which we are accustomed to using in our daily judgments—are the source from which all approval is derived?

I believe that such an objection springs from failing to see what the *Enquiry* is about, and reading it as a continuation or a condensation of the *Treatise*. In the *Treatise* Hume posited certain doctrines about human nature and on the basis of these sought to explain the very "constitution" of morality. In the *Enquiry* human nature is no longer the *explanans*—it has become the *explanandum*; moral language indeed is not that about which conclusions are drawn, but the starting point which provides the source and impetus for the explanatory endeavor culminating in conclusions about something else, something non-normative, viz., human nature. It is true that, since morality is being taken as already constituted, there is little in it, as such, which has to be accounted for, but to treat this as a fault is to fail utterly to appreciate the sense in which the *Enquiry* transcends the problematic of the *Treatise*. Given his assumption that language, like other institutions and practices, tells us something about its users, Hume is able to *conclude* to what human nature must be like if men find it natural to use the language of morals. As a result, it is a methodological principle of the *Enquiry* that no trait may be attributed to human nature which would render unintelligible men's use of the common language of morals.[10]

IV · THE EXPLANATORY FOCUS OF THE *Enquiry*

The conclusions about human nature which this new method permits are of the highest moment. First, the selfish hypothesis is vanquished, since the view that benevolence is not a natural human characteristic would render simply incomprehensible how men could participate in a system of approving what pleases or benefits others. Second, the denial of any place to reason in morals must be false, for men approve of benefits which are not immediately in view, and commonly reckon the long-term consequences of actions and habits; moreover, the proper estimate of a character or deed depends on satisfying conditions (objectivity, generality, and so forth) which are commonly associated with "reason." Third, men must be capable of correcting the momentary appearances of things, not only the easy corrections which relate to visual perception, but particularly the much more demanding corrections which relate to the passions and interests of the individual; were this not the case, there would be no such thing as a common moral language comprising approvals and disapprovals deemed worthy of endorsement by the generality of men.

What is important to recognize about the *Enquiry* is not simply that there Hume espouses doctrines more or less the same as he had in the *Treatise*, or that his vision of moral values is more or less the same as that developed in the *Treatise*, but that the status of those doctrines *in his theory* is altogether different. Since the *Treatise* is, by Hume's own admission (T xx), the application of general principles from the Science of Man to the task of explicating, on what might be termed a causal-generative method,[11] the *constitution* of morality, and since Hume's effort is largely determined by his presuppositions, themselves frequently extra-theoretical, about self-love, reason and passion, the possible causes of corrections of the judgment, and so on, the entire project is in danger of misdirection and possible sceptical conclusion. In the *Enquiry* the passages dealing with self-love, reason and passion, the equivalent of correction of the judgment, and so on, do not dictate conclusions; rather, they are determined, both in their status as evidenced findings and in the precise nuance of the modality in which they are affirmed, by considerations involved in the common language of morals. No theoretical assumptions stand in the way of Hume's arriving at factually well-grounded conclusions about human nature.

That moral language plays the role of *explanans* in the *Enquiry* and is a presupposition of reflection on morality—so that one cannot stand outside the language of morals and explain it in terms independent of this presupposition—is not to deny that in some (though not, I submit, the strictest) sense Hume is a naturalist in ethics. Clearly, the *Enquiry* evinces no enthusiasm on its author's part for deducing or deriving morality from a set of propositions descriptive of human nature. The sense in which Hume is a naturalist refers to a version of naturalism which would not reduce the moral order to non-moral facts, but instead would use the moral order to confirm the attribution of certain properties to human nature.[12]

V · COMPARISONS WITH THE THIRD BOOK OF THE *Treatise*

Since what is distinctive about Hume's approach to the moral distinctions in the *Enquiry* may be better appreciated by seeing this study in contrast to Hume's earlier work, a few remarks on Book III of the *Treatise* may be in order. The topic of the relationship of the *Treatise* to the *Enquiries* is so controversial, however, that it would be wise to preface some cautionary observations.[13] First, Hume's own remarks on the relationship between the *Treatise* and the *Enquiries* are, in my judgment, ambiguous, and certainly do not decide the main questions. Second, because of the extensive overlap in the contents of the two works, it would be foolhardy to suggest that either could ever be rejected as on the whole unrepresentative of Hume's moral thinking. Moreover, it follows from the view that the *explanans* and *explanandum* of *Treatise* III and the *Enquiry* are said to be reciprocally related that any intimation that either method is utterly wrongheaded should not be tolerated. Of course, with regard to establishing that the method and explanatory objective of one or the other of these works is philosophically superior, it is not necessary to engage in consideration of all the respects in which they differ. On the contrary. What is interesting about how a philosopher might shift his position is found in looking not so much at the discreet propositions he affirms or denies, but at the logical and epistemic ordering of the propositions he affirms or denies. (Thus, it would be as much a mistake to claim that the discreet propositions which occur in the earlier theory should not appear as well in the later as it would be to think one could refute the claim that the two works are significantly different by adducing all manner of parallel texts.) Accordingly, the sort of shift in Hume's reflection on morality which, given a certain reciprocity between the moral distinctions as they are given in the language of morals and the principles of approval and disapproval which reside in human nature, is a systematic and not a random shift. If it is true that in the *Enquiry* Hume explored this correlativity by positing the former and concluding to the latter, it can scarcely be said that what he had done in the *Treatise*, positing the latter in an effort to arrive at the former, was utterly without merit, for the relation which exists *in re* is the same, whichever way it is approached.

Finally, the difficulty we encounter in charting and measuring a significant shift in the thinking of any philosopher (exaggerated, perhaps, in the case of so accomplished a stylist as Hume) is complicated by the fact that we have not yet developed a general theory of change and revolution in philosophical theory parallel to the work which has been done, for instance, on revolution in scientific theory.

I shall sketch briefly what I take to be the method and explanatory objective of *Treatise* III; I shall then offer an estimate of Hume's success in achieving the kind of account of morality he sought to give; and I shall conclude this section by describing certain respects in which the *Enquiry* approach to morals seems philosophically superior to that of the *Treatise*.

1. *Treatise* III is an endeavor to account for moral distinctions on the basis of a theory of human nature.[14] The elements of the explanation are, generally, perceptions and, specifically, what Hume calls the passions or the "springs and motives"; these elements are tied together according to dynamic principles, such as sympathy and association, in such a fashion as to yield a causal account of the moral distinctions or moral sentiments. Hume described *Treatise* III as aiming to uncover the *constitution* of morality.

> An action, or sentiment, or character is virtuous or vicious; why? because its view causes a pleasure or uneasiness of a particular kind. In giving a reason, therefore, for the pleasure or uneasiness, we sufficiently explain the vice or virtue. To have the sense of virtue, is nothing but to *feel* a satisfaction of a particular kind from the contemplation of a character. The very *feeling* constitutes our praise or admiration. We go no farther; nor do we enquire into the cause of the satisfaction. We do not infer a character to be virtuous, because it pleases: But in feeling that it pleases after such a particular manner, we in effect feel that it is virtuous [T 471].

Showing how morality is *constituted* in the "springs and motives" of human nature would appear to offer an explanatory gain for at least two reasons. First, such an account would not only establish a simple correlation between the "springs and motives" and the moral distinctions but show that morality is the way it is just because the "springs and motives" are as, according to Hume, they are. Second, such an account represents a gain on the assumption, which evidently Hume held, that the "springs and motives" are more accessible, *qua* perceptions,[15] than are the matters to be explained through them. In sum, that there is a gain to be expected from this constitutive project is due, it seems, to the causal and epistemic priority of the "springs and motives" to the *explanandum*, the moral distinctions.

It must be admitted that, though a grand and ambitious undertaking, the project of *Treatise* III involves some risk, for by opening up the possibility that a theoretical account cannot be provided of the moral distinctions, it introduces the unpleasant specter of a *theoretical scepticism with regard to the moral distinctions*. The reason why this possibility is implicit in *Treatise* III follows from its explanatory objective, to explain the very *constitution* of morality, for should it fail of this objective, then moral scepticism might seem to be the appropriate attitude for the philosophically and scientifically sophisticated to adopt.

The success of Hume's project in *Treatise* III would appear to hinge on his offering a satisfactory causal-generative account of the *correction* of the sentiments. In his early work Hume seems to have been comfortable with adapting the general thrust of moral sense theory into his own system. He starts out by tying morality to certain pleasing/displeasing sentiments which by their presence (in actually being felt) signify that their object is virtue, that the opposite is vice, and he claims that this in principle is how the moral distinctions may be explained. "Thus we are still brought back to our first position, that virtue is distinguished by the pleasure, and vice by the pain, that any action, sentiment or character gives us by the mere view and contemplation" (T 475). The impressions in question are accounted for largely by sympathy, but the description provided of them is vague throughout and does not preclude their being confused with other feelings (even when the constitutive impressions are described as "calm"). But since the "moral distinctions *depend entirely* on certain peculiar sentiments of pain and pleasure . . ." (T 574; emphasis added) and must have, at least at some point a one-to-one correspondence with these impressions, Hume recognizes that he must explain how the natural sentiments are, as he puts it, *corrected* so as properly to inform a moral judgment—that is, a judgment which is general and capable of entering into a common language establishing norms to which men should pay heed in their judgments and their actions (as opposed, for instance, to corrections in judgments of beauty, which do not generate standards of conduct). This, of course, is a thoroughly appropriate move on Hume's part, and one so commonly reflected in the writings of moral philosophers that, were it not something for which a theoretical accounting is possible, moral scepticism might indeed be indicated.

The problem for Hume is how to offer an account of this correction in terms of the "springs and motives" of human nature. Since he had cut reason and imagination off from having an influence, of themselves, on the passions, it would appear that he might try to explain the needed correction in terms of the sympathy mechanism. This possibility must be discarded, however, for although sympathy certainly does enlarge the horizon of the affections (and thus provides something of a "correction" to the narrower sentiments), sympathy itself can be, as Hume points out (T 602), a source of bias, and thus, rather than the sought for origin of the correction, sympathy itself stands in need of correction.[16]

It might be thought that Hume would account for correction of the moral judgment in much the same way as he accounted for correction in judgments of size and distance or in judgments of beauty (T 603, 582). Such a strategy would not be particularly promising for Hume, however, for although the analogy does demonstrate that it is possible to formulate judgments according to rules, it seems to overlook the difference between modifying a belief and modifying a passion. Ordinarily in the correction of appearances or beliefs, the evidence of experience does not meet with resistance from a causal counter-force. The very concept of the correction of the sentiments, however, posits a passion in existence, and, according to Hume's principle that "Nothing can oppose or retard the impulse of a passion, but a contrary impulse . . ." (T 415), requires the existence of a second actual passion to modify the first. Correction of the sentiments, consequently, is problematical because there seems to be no element available among the "springs and motives" inventoried in Hume's Science of Man to cause the correction in question.[17]

Similarly, it would not do for Hume simply to adduce a general standard and then, by pointing to the gap between the natural sentiments and that standard, enumerate rules for the correction of the sentiments, as he had done for the causal judgment (T 173–76); [18] for, if he is to explain how morality is constituted (and if he is to avoid a *petitio*), it seems he must offer a causal account of the existence of the general standard itself. To affirm that men are affected through sympathy by the *moral* sentiments of others would be to abandon the effort to explain the constitutive principles of morality and would leave the concept of the moral sentiments practically as vague and indefinite as it was at the outset of *Treatise* III.

As a result, it seems Hume did not succeed in developing a causal explanation of the correction of the sentiments. In fact, what he did instead is scale down his objective. Speaking of the sources which would make correction of the sentiments at least possible, he says, " 'tis certain, they are not altogether efficacious, nor do our passions often correspond entirely to the present theory" (T 583). He goes on to say that what is "corrected" is our language, not our sentiments.

> The passions do not always follow our corrections; but these corrections serve sufficiently to regulate our abstract notions, and are alone regarded, when we pronounce in general concerning the degrees of vice and virtue [T 585].

Hume's point appears to be that as we become accustomed to thinking in ways corresponding to the common language, our imagination finds it easy to construe situations from a standardized common point of view; and that once this outlook has become habitual, we discover that a certain sort of feeling accompanies the contemplation of the characters and deeds which are termed good, and another sort of feeling accompanies those characters and deeds termed wicked (T 487; see T 472, 499). It must be noted that such "calm feelings" are, of course, not constitutive of the moral distinctions but rather presuppose the information that the sort of thing to which each is concomitant is, independently, a virtue or a vice, as the case may be.

Apart from the observation that Hume did not satisfy the project of accounting for the constitution of morality, the question which now becomes pressing is whether when addressing himself to the topic of the "moral judgment" in Parts I and III of *Treatise* III, Hume may be said to be talking about the same thing. His thrust in Part I was to show that morality cannot be derived from reason because morality is practical (T 457), and reason, as Hume described it, is not. "Morals excite passions, and produce or prevent actions," Hume wrote in Part I (T 457), but in Part III he stated that "these observations serve sufficiently to regulate our *abstract* notions, and are alone regarded, when we pronounce in general concerning the degrees of vice and virtue" (T 585; emphasis added). General pronouncements and abstract notions figure into the judgment; but since "our passions do not readily follow the determination of our judgment" (T 583), it appears Hume has not with this theory identified that which excites passions, and produces or prevents actions. In short, the principle that only a passion can affect a passion appears to have forced Hume to construe the correcting factor to be limited to the imagination, and severs the thus conditioned moral judgment from the "springs and motives" of human nature.

2. The constitutive project apparently did not yield a glowing success. First, Hume did not generate an account of the constitution of morality; second, he could not account for morality strictly on the basis of the "springs and motives" in human nature; and, third, in describing the moral judgment, he did not remain within the requirements of his avowed method. Reading Part III with a careful eye, we may say that Hume there introduced the notion of a standard of moral judgment by explicitly appealing to the common language, altered the notion of "morality" operative in *Treatise* III from one which is decidedly practical and motivational to one which is "abstract," and introduced into his theory factors for whose influence he had not accounted on his avowed method. These observations are not meant to suggest that Hume ought not to have avoided the possibility of moral scepticism at the expense, if need be, of consistency with his avowed method and objective. The reader of the *Treatise* should not underestimate the dimensions of Hume's difficulty, for if consistency would not allow a satisfactory account of the correction of the sentiments, certainly the door is open to scepticism, since moral distinctions condemned to indefinition, vagueness, and variability are practically the same as no moral distinctions at all. Unfortunately, however, the measures Hume took to avoid that outcome appear *ad hoc* and extra-theoretical. Hume could, of course, have reasoned that, even if his system did not adequately account for the moral distinctions, in quitting his closet for the company of his friends, he regained assurance of the existence of morals. Since this assurance would spring, not from seeing impressions in a different light, but from abandoning talk of impressions and recognizing that morality has an independent existence in a shared or public world, the appeal to common sense and the shared language, though perhaps extra-theoretical relative to *Treatise* III, was not for that consideration any the less reasonable or creditable.

Were this as far as Hume carried his reflections, the outcome of his moral philosophy would have been simply the lesson that an endeavor to explain the *constitution* of morality in such terms and on such principles as he had put forward in the *Treatise* is unlikely to succeed. There are certain interpretations of Hume's rejection of scepticism with regard, for instance, to the external world which have it that Hume simply realized that at a certain point men must put theory aside and engage themselves in the everyday world of passion and praxis. Perhaps something of value would have been achieved had Hume stopped his reflections on morals at that point, but from what has been said in the first three sections of this paper, it appears that Hume did not stop there, but turned reflection on the conditions of that assurance which he had fallen back on in Part III, and sought to extend the theory of morality to account for our having a standard implicit in our own thinking whereby we not only know the moral distinctions with familiarity but can think and judge about morality.

It should be emphasized that the somewhat negative estimate of Hume's effort to account for the correction of the sentiments which this paper offers is not meant to suggest that the project of *Treatise* III was altogether wrongheaded or that it is in principle impossible to provide, from the sort of data Hume called the "springs and motives" in human nature and according to a methodological approach like Hume's, an illuminating account of morality. The importance of noticing what went wrong in *Treatise* III is not to convict Hume of inconsistency but to observe by what measures, even if in that context they were extra-theoretical, he sought to locate morality on a more solid foundation. What emerges from this observation is that the notion of morality to which Hume appealed in Part III is continuous with the view of morality which serves as the presupposition and starting point for the *Enquiry*. As a result, it is here contended that what went wrong in *Treatise* III relates not so much to the elements of the endeavor or the method of seeking causal conditions as to the constitutive aim of attempting to account for morality *ab ovo* in terms deliberately naturalistic.

3. By contrast, Hume began the *Enquiry* by eschewing moral scepticism (EPM 169–70) and concluded Section I by adducing a revamped experimental method which starts from the public, social fact of men sharing a language of morals, and promises to arrive at the general principles of morals; once these are established, Hume can offer broad statements about human nature which occupy in his theory the position of conclusions governed by facts, rather than that of principles determining the causal conditions of morality.

This approach permits Hume to address the matter earlier referred to as the correction of the sentiments in an altogether different fashion. Given the positive fact that men use the language of morals, since this language comprises general standards against which the adventitious sentiments of the individual may be measured, it follows that men must be capable of laying aside their temporary interests and basing judgment on the common interests of mankind (as these are articulated in the material evaluations in the language of morals).[19] Acquaintance with the moral distinctions follows the development of a shared language expressive of the common sentiment of humanity and reflecting a standardized perspective on characters and deeds.

> Virtue and Vice *become then known*; morals are recognized; certain general ideas are framed of human conduct and behaviour; such measures are expected from men in such situations. This action is determined to be conformable to our abstract rule; that other, contrary. And by such universal principles are the particular sentiments of self-love frequently controlled and limited [EPM 274; emphasis added; see also EPM 228].

Here something parallel to the *Treatise* notion of correction stands forth as a plain fact of our common life,[20] and is in no way diminished by the fact that we may lack a satisfactory causal or psychological explanation for it.[21] By contrast, *Treatise* III, precisely because it failed to generate a satisfactory causal account of the correction of the sentiments, did not provide a locus for a standard for the moral judgment.[22]

It might also be noted that Hume no longer treats the "springs and motives" in human nature as a datum which is pre-eminently accessible, clear, and cognizable,[23] and no longer treats understanding the moral distinctions as equivalent to providing a causal accounting in terms of constitutive principles.[24] Interest in causal explanations is replaced in the body of the *Enquiry* by interest in normative principles and their presuppositions in human nature; the best of Hume's analytical and psychological work from *Treatise* III, serving now as explorations of those presuppositions, is located in the Appendices, as if to set abstract speculation off from the basic import of the *Enquiry* and to make it all the clearer that the non-problematical character of morality as a positive fact is not to be confused, *malgré les philosophes*, with engaging questions in the theory of human nature.

Perhaps it would not be too venturesome to suggest that it was precisely the method of *Treatise* III to which in the closing paragraphs of Section I Hume contrasted the method of the *Enquiry*.

> The other scientific method, where a general abstract principle is first established, and is afterwards branched out into a variety of inferences and conclusions, may be more perfect in itself, but suits less the imperfection of human nature, and is a common source of illusion and mistake in this as well as in other subjects [EPM 174].

Certainly *Treatise* III matches that "other method" where general principles are established and then branched out into a variety of inferences and conclusions.[25] Although it is not certain that Hume would describe the endeavor of the *Treatise* as dealing in "abstract" principles (he frequently used the term in a pejorative manner), it is rather clear that he intended to develop in the *Treatise* a method which could aptly be described as "scientific." At any rate, the critique he offers of the method is quite gentle, since he goes out of his way to praise it as "more perfect in itself," conceding that because of human debility it is potentially dangerous for its results. To read this text as referring to the method of *Treatise* III (which is in no way essential to the view of the relationship of the two works elaborated in this paper) does not require ascribing to its author the view that *Treatise* III is riddled with "illusion and mistake"; it would suffice to explicate what is meant in saying that such a method "suits less the imperfection of human nature." The reference, I suggest, is probably to men's cognitive abilities and the ways we ordinarily come to know. Thus, the method of the *Treatise* might be, in the order of explanation, more perfect, for it begins with principles, causes, and origins; but if we ask, "How is it that we *know* morality?" and "Are we acquainted with it in the guise of 'springs and motives' or in 'the estimable or blameable qualities of men'?" the method of the *Enquiry* emerges as superior in the order of discovery or knowledge. Finally, whether Hume had the *Treatise* in mind or some other method, the conclusion of the paragraph on method certainly sets the *Enquiry* off from Book III.

> Men are now cured of their passion for hypotheses and systems in natural philosophy, and will hearken to no arguments but those which are derived from experience [EPM 174–75; see also EPM 298, 269].[26]

There is a further consideration which is occasioned by these remarks about the method of the *Enquiry*. This consideration bears on the meaning of the term "moral," and takes the form of the question: what is the paradigm employment of this term? Narrowing the candidates to the two which figure predominantly in the *Treatise* and the *Enquiry* affords a different type of comparison which, even if it may not have occurred to Hume, further betokens the superiority of the *Enquiry* approach, and does so independently of reference to the "imperfection of human nature."

If one asks, "How is it that we know what 'moral' means?"—is it by reference to sentiments or by reference to approvals as given in the moral language?—the epistemic superiority of an approach which presupposes ordinary usage immediately emerges. Clearly, if one starts from the common language of morals, one has at hand the information necessary for identifying the "pleasing sentiment of approval" (for one is in a position to know that a judgment is a moral approval independently of knowing what sentiments are concomitant to it); but it is not at all clear, I submit, that one could identify an impression, an instance of sympathy, a sentiment, and so forth, as *moral* independently of participating in the common language of morals. That Hume did not explicitly pose such a transcendental question as "How is it that we can reflect on morality at all?" does not imply that he was insensitive to the sorts of considerations which would be brought to bear in answering it. How we get to the point that we can reflect on morality at all is understood (in part, at least) if we see ourselves using the language of morals. If, on the contrary, moral language is not acknowledged as a presupposition—or if we imagine that we can stand outside it and account for its very constitution *ab ovo*—then it is thoroughly problematic by what license we may subsequently introduce the adjective "moral" into our theory at all.[27]

In sum, a kind of progress or development in Hume's thinking about morality may be presumed: he originally believed that he could account for moral distinctions in terms of feelings through the use of a causal-generative model of explanation; when this failed to provide theoretical underpinning for the needed correction of the natural sentiments, he found himself appealing to the common language of morals in an effort to account for the existence of moral norms and standards; reflecting on the inconsistency between the source of the problem and his response to it could well have led him to discover his own presuppositions and to examine the implications of his earlier appeal to the common language of morals; by doing so Hume could draw on a different philosophical perspective and achieve a new assurance about the object of reflection on morals.[28]

The shift in Hume's thinking about morals toward a focus on language seems to signal the recognition that human nature may be understood as well, if not better, "writ large," so to speak, in institutions and practices, complete with their histories, than it can in the "springs and motives" found when the inquirer turns reflection back onto himself (see EHU 83–84). The reversal of *explanans* and *explanandum* between *Treatise* III and the *Enquiry* indicates a re-orientation which, once recognized as a systematic change,[29] affords a picture of the unity of Hume's authorship, from the phenomenalistic investigations of the earliest work to the essays, philosophical and cultural, and the monumental *History*. What is important to see about Hume is that, once he had lost his enthusiasm for producing a system of human nature like that which, as he understood it, Newton had discovered in physical nature, and once he had brought his method into conformity with his avowed principle of starting from facts and observations, there ensues a unified endeavor to expound the theme of man in culture, and to describe and explain the many facets of human experience as it is condensed and articulated in our historical development. Perhaps when seen as the basic systematic statement of the principles involved in this endeavor, the *Enquiry* may be deemed worthy of the praise Hume bestowed on it.

VI · SUMMARY

The project of the third Book of the *Treatise* led Hume into a quandary when he was unable to explain how morality is constituted, and the status of the moral judgment in that system may be described as problematical, at best. A chief difficulty with the *Treatise* approach was occasioned by the lack of a convincing and consistent causal explanation for the correction of the sentiments. In view of this difficulty, it appears that Hume shifted the sense of the term "moral" from something tied to feelings and passions to something "abstract" and detachable from the sentiments. The *Enquiry* takes morality as something already constituted, and the status of the moral judgment in the later work is that of an element of the common language of morals. Here Hume abandons the point of departure in the impressions, the constitutive project, and the causal-generative methodology which started from general statements about human nature and aimed to arrive at an identification of the sentiments by which the moral distinctions would be effected. Dismissing the theoretical assumptions about human nature which had shaped the project of the *Treatise*, Hume reversed the *explanans* and *explanandum*, relying on institutions and practices to shed light on a freshly conceived *cultural*, rather than natural, Science of Man. By reasoning from patterns in our approvals and disapprovals to their principles in pleasure and utility, Hume was able to arrive at well-grounded philosophical conclusions about human nature (notably about benevolence and self-love, reason and passion, and our ability to identify with the common interest) which go far beyond the *Treatise*. The starting point of moral language in use, which is neither "abstract" nor tied to individual sentiments, reveals standards implicit in our own thinking about morals whereby we can measure (not "correct" in the *Treatise* sense) any sentiment or judgment; the latter, then, would be termed *moral* not by origin but by reference to common standards and principles.

Moral language in use is the point of departure for the *Enquiry* because it is presupposed in any inquiry regarding morality and because, as a *fait accompli* readily accessible for examination, it is less nebulous than the problematical impressions and sentiments which figure centrally in *Treatise*

III. This starting point has the status of both fact and norm because it is language in use, and the use involves being on the inside, so to speak, not only of an open-ended core of common approvals and disapprovals, but also of principles of evaluation and judgment, both material and formal, which, because they are general, provide a logic whereby morality is open to controversy and change.

It has been argued, on grounds more meta-philosophical than moral, that the *Enquiry* is superior to *Treatise* III both for generating philosophical conclusions relative to its explanatory focus in human nature, and for its approach to morality, inasmuch as: (*a*) our acquaintance with the meaning of the term "moral" is readily understood once the use of the common language of morals is assumed as a non-problematical fact; and (*b*) moral language is a presupposition of inquiry about morals, and it would be a mistake to think that one can stand outside the language so as to account for the conditions of morality in terms independent of this presupposition. The *Enquiry* allowed Hume to retrieve what was of value in *Treatise* III and to advance philosophical speculation on morality by addressing the object of inquiry from a methodologically circumspect perspective.

NOTES

1. As Hendel notes (*An Inquiry Concerning Human Understanding*, ed. Charles W. Hendel [Indianapolis, 1955], p. 7), the passage in question was inserted in edition O (1764). Previously Hume's reference was to *experience* rather than to *language*. The difference was esteemed by Hume as important enough to warrant inserting the change.

2. Adapting Alan Gewirth's terminology to the present context, one might say that in the *Enquiry* Hume presented a theory of *positive* morality. See " 'Positive' Ethics and 'Normative' Science," *Philosophical Review*, 69 (1960), 311–30.

3. H. L. A. Hart, *The Concept of Law* (Oxford, 1961), pp. 53–56.

4. See the concluding paragraphs of Section IV of this paper.

5. Despite his rather cavalier attitude about the uniformity of human nature, Hume may certainly not be criticized for illicit transition from the defensible belief that there would be no common moral language unless most of the members of society do participate in it to the dubious belief that every member of society does participate in the common moral language. See EPM 169–70, 190, 221.

6. It appears perfectly compatible with the *Enquiry* approach to morality to ascribe to Hume the principle that a judgment can be moral only if it has a form such that it could be incorporated into the common language of morals. Thus moral language would be presupposed as the source even of these formal principles of morality.

7. Vagueness, it should be recalled, is a defect in rules, but not in principles (in fact, the generality which typically belongs to principles is inseparable from a certain degree of vagueness). See Ronald Dworkin, "The Model of Rules," *The University of Chicago Law Review*, 35 (1967), 22–40. It should be noted that the *Enquiry* allows that principles are specifiable through the same patterns of approval and disapproval which serve as the inductive basis for their being identified in the first instance.

8. Such an explanation, in fact, would be guided by knowledge of how moral judgments are made and of what are the properties of a well-formed moral judgment; this knowledge itself is readily accounted for once the use of a common moral language is assumed, but would be utterly problematical apart from this assumption.

9. See below, the concluding paragraphs of the fifth section of this paper.

10. In point of fact, Hume's method is not experimental, as he suggests, but presuppositional.

11. See James Noxon, *Hume's Philosophical Development* (Oxford, 1973), p. 6; and Nicholas Capaldi, *David Hume: The Newtonian Philosopher* (Boston, 1975), chaps. 2 and 3.

12. Noxon correctly notices that in the *Enquiry* Hume "proposes 'to reach the foundation of ethics' . . . by observing and comparing 'particular instances' of moral, not psychological, phenomena" (*Hume's Philosophical Development*, p. 23).

13. The principal proponents of the view that the *Enquiry* does not represent an advance in philosophical penetration over *Treatise* III are: L. A. Selby-Bigge, "Editor's Introduction," *The Enquiries* (Oxford, 1902); J. B. Stewart, *The Moral and Political Philosophy of David Hume* (New York, 1963); and, for an extremist position, F. V. Kruse, *Hume's Philosophy in His Principal Work and in the Enquiries*, trans. P. T. Federspiel (New York, 1939). Kruse's views were squashed by E. C. Mossner in *The Life of David Hume* (Austin, 1954). The defense of the *Enquiry Concerning the Human Understanding* has been undertaken by, in addition to Noxon (*Hume's Philosophical Development*) and Capaldi (*David Hume*), Antony Flew, *Hume's Philosophy of Belief* (London, 1961).

14. " 'Tis evident, that all the sciences have a relation, greater or less, to human nature: and that however wide any of them may seem to run from it, they still return back by one passage or another. . . . 'Tis impossible to tell what changes and improvements we might make in these sciences were we thoroughly acquainted with the extent and force of human understanding, and cou'd explain the nature of the ideas we employ, and of the operations we perform in our reasonings" (T xix).

15. "It has been observ'd, that nothing is ever present to the mind but its perceptions; and that all the actions of seeing, hearing, judging, loving, hating, and thinking, fall under this denomination. The mind can never exert itself in any action, which we may not comprehend under the term of *perception*; and consequently that term is no less applicable to those judgments, by which we distinguish moral good and evil, than to every other operation of the mind. To approve of one character, to condemn another, are only so many different perceptions" (T 456).

16. An excellent analysis of sympathy in the *Treatise* in its relevance for morality, particularly as it relates to Hume's statements on the correction of the sentiments, is to be found in Philip Mercer, *Sympathy and Ethics* (Oxford, 1972), chaps. 4 and 6. Páll Árdal provides a very thorough analysis of sympathy in relation to Books II and III in his *Passion and Value in Hume's Treatise* (Edinburgh, 1966).

17. The view that Hume acknowledged, in effect, that the moral judgment may correspond to no actual sentiment (as opposed to the statement at T 471) may be derived from remarks offered late in *Treatise* III. "This concern we readily extend to other cases, that are resembling; and when these are very remote, our sympathy is proportionably weaker, and our praise or blame fainter and more doubtful. . . . In like manner, tho' sympathy be much fainter than our concern for ourselves, and a sympathy with persons remote from us much fainter than that with persons near and contiguous; yet we neglect all these differences in our calm judgments concerning the characters of men. . . . And tho' the *heart* does not always take part with those general notions, or regulate its love and hatred by them, yet are they sufficient for discourse, and serve all our purposes in company, in the pulpit, on the theatre, and in the schools" (T 603). This interpretation is espoused by Capaldi who comments as follows. "However, toward the end of the *Treatise*, in considering objections to his theory, Hume recognized the possibility of moral judgments that could not be confirmed, that referred to no real sentiment" (*David Hume*, pp. 182–83).

18. I know of no abler effort to utilize such an approach to render *Treatise* III reasonable than that of Thomas K. Hearn, "General Rules in Hume's *Treatise*," *Journal of the History of Philosophy*, 8 (1970), 405–22. If it is the case that Hearn's observations are undercut by the fact that *Treatise* III provides no causal explanation for the operation of such rules, his remarks are nevertheless wholly vindicated in terms of the *Enquiry* approach to morality argued for in this paper.

Using such rules presupposes the information that the belief which, for instance, they serve to correct is erroneous, and this in turn presupposes the existence of unquestioned standard cases. Hume seems somewhat sensitive to this when he accounts for the existence of general rules by saying that, did we not rely on their corrections, the course of our judgment would be "destructive of all the most *established* principles of reasonings" (T 150; emphasis added).

19. The position defended here is midway between the *Treatise* view that at some point the moral distinctions must be determined by sentiments which are *actual* and the interpretation of Hume's moral philosophy as instantiating the "disinterested spectator" approach to ethics, a view which is tolerant of the possibility that moral sentiments may in some sense be ideal. See Ronald Glossop, "The Nature of Hume's Ethics," *Philosophy and Phenomenological Research*, 27 (1966–67), 527–36.

20. The *Enquiry* model of the moral judgment allows the juxtaposition of sentiments deriving from humanity and from "conversation and discourse" (EPM 228) with any other range of sentiments. The principles and standards comprised in moral language have a status and motivational force sufficient to overshadow or displace the other sentiments (EPM 274–75, note) and to be recognized as norms of conduct. Here "correction" is not a psychological concept so much as a normative one, meaning simply that standards are to be conformed to (see also EPM 226, 229). Hume can legitimately talk about correction because the *Enquiry* acknowledges an *established* paradigm by reference to which a comparison or correction might be made. In this relation between the sorts of sentiments envisioned in talk of correction and the principles prescribed in moral language, "correction" corresponds on the side of sentiment to what "ought" signifies on the side of the prescribed principles. Accordingly, the locus of talk about correction in the *Enquiry* approach to the moral judgment relates to the manner of the individual's participation in the common language of morals.

21. There is a striking passage in the *Enquiry* which suggests that Hume may quite possibly have been aware of the precise nature of the difficulty in *Treatise* III with respect to the correction of the sentiments. In Book III (T 582) an illustration (comparing the esteem one might feel for Brutus with that one might have for one's manservant) had been employed relating to the need to adjust judgment to take account of situation and circumstance. In what would seem to be a reference to cases like the Brutus–manservant example, Hume wrote in the *Enquiry* (EPM 217): "It is but a weak subterfuge, when pressed by these facts and arguments, to say, that we transport ourselves, by the force of imagination, into distant ages and countries, and consider the advantage, which we should have reaped from these characters, had we been contemporaries, and had any commerce with the persons. It is not conceivable, how a *real* sentiment or passion can ever arise from a known *imaginary* interest; especially when our *real* interest is still kept in view, and is often acknowledged to be entirely distinct from the imaginary, and even sometimes opposite to it." Capaldi construes this text as "a perfect description of the sympathy mechanism in the *Treatise*" (*David Hume*, p. 181), but however Hume's intention in this passage is to be interpreted, the point Hume makes is a cogent criticism of the *Treatise* attempt to account for correction of the sentiments. See EHU 15.

22. It would be erroneous to suggest that in the *Enquiry* Hume "solved the problem" of correction of the sentiments, for in the *Enquiry* there is no "problem" of correction of the sentiments. More accurately, Hume withdrew from the problematics of *Treatise* III and discovered a different approach, one which, if the present interpretation is accepted, may be judged superior to that of the *Treatise*.

23. In this connection Capaldi goes so far as to observe: "The passions are thus no longer needed for the exposition of Hume's moral theory" (*David Hume*, p. 185).

24. Noxon notes that "When the problems involved in his [Hume's] attempt to introduce the method of natural science into the study of human nature are raised in Part Three, however, the *Treatise* will appear as a work of unwarranted methodological optimism" (*Hume's Philosophical Development*, p. 3).

25. Noxon sees in this text a striking contrast "with the intention to create a unified system declared on the opening page of Book III of the *Treatise* . . ." (ibid., p. 24).

26. A propos of Hume's criticism of "that love of *simplicity* which has been the source of much false reasoning in philosophy" (EPM 298; see EPM 269), Capaldi remarks concerning the present text, "The reason for not mentioning simplicity is that Hume now considers his own first theory of the *Treatise* as unduly simplistic" (*David Hume*, pp. 184–85).

27. Even if the present interpretation of the project of *Treatise* III be questioned, it appears one would have to be committed to the view that in that work Hume always consciously presupposed the common meaning of the term "moral"; but if that is the case, it would seem one must also concede that, since the act of philosophical reflection could extend to this very presupposition, a more complete and profound philosophical study would be possible, one which goes beyond the *Treatise* and explores the conditions of that presupposition in the common language of morals; and, of course, such a work is the *Enquiry*.

28. The line of argument offered here parallels that which Noxon outlines early in his book on Hume's development: "The difficulties which he encountered forced a change of tactics which accounts for the main differences between his early and his mature philosophy" (*Hume's Philosophical Development*, p. xiv).

29. Noxon goes some way toward realizing the extent involved in this shift in remarking "When Hume in his search for the principles of human nature turns from the science of man to the history of man, the intentions which were to be realized through the system projected in the *Treatise* have altered" (ibid., p. 20).

17

Hume, Stevenson, and Hare
on Moral Language

Ronald J. Glossop
Southern Illinois University
Edwardsville

I

Two recent classics in ethics are C. L. Stevenson's *Ethics and Language* [1] and R. M. Hare's *The Language of Morals*, [2] the very titles of which indicate the focus on language which pervades contemporary philosophical inquiry. This focus on language is as typical of recent philosophy as the focus on ideas was typical of the period in which David Hume made his contributions to philosophical thought. But Hume was not inattentive to the matter of language, especially in his discussions of ethical issues. It is my intent in this essay to compare what Hume has to say about moral language with what has been said more recently by Stevenson and Hare.

A comparison of Hume's views with those of Stevenson and Hare seems especially appropriate since both of these contemporary writers claim that Hume not only addressed himself to the issues in which they are interested but also advocated views similar in some respects to their own. Stevenson says:

> Of all traditional philosophers, Hume has most clearly asked the questions that here concern us, and has most nearly reached a conclusion that the present writer can accept [EL 273; see also EL vii].

Hare includes Hume along with Aristotle and Kant as one of the "great writers" on ethics (LM 45). He also singles out what he calls "Hume's Law" for special commendation.

> In this logical rule [that the conclusion of an argument can be an imperative if and only if at least one premiss is an imperative], again, is to be found the basis of Hume's celebrated observation on the impossibility of deducing an "ought"-proposition from a series of "is"-propositions—an observation which,

as he rightly says, "would subvert all the vulgar systems of morality," and not only those which had already appeared in his day [LM 29].[3]

By citing these remarks, I do not intend to indicate that I agree with the interpretation of Hume's ethics adopted by either Stevenson or Hare. I make reference to them only to show that both believed Hume to be addressing himself to the same issues with which they are concerned and to be advocating views with which they in general agree. In view of these supposed similarities, a further examination of the relations between Hume's views and those of Stevenson and Hare seems appropriate.

II

When we turn our attention to Hume's ethical writings, it is surprising to note how contemporary his views are. For example, he is quite aware of the distinction between analyzing what is happening when people use moral language, on the one hand, and making his own recommendations, on the other. Furthermore, he sets himself to do the former rather than the latter. At one point in *An Enquiry Concerning the Principles of Morals*, having found himself praising the virtues of generosity and benevolence, Hume says:

> But I forget, that it is not my present business to recommend generosity and benevolence, . . . our object here being more the speculative, than the practical part of morals . . . [EPM 177–78].

Hume had earlier indicated in his Introduction to *A Treatise of Human Nature* that his purpose was "to explain the principles of human nature" (T xx) rather than to engage in a prescriptive account of what people *should* do.

Hume is also contemporary in his awareness of the existence of verbal disputes. Anyone who believes that Hume was concerned about ideas to the exclusion of linguistic issues should examine the Fourth Appendix of *An Enquiry Concerning the Principles of Morals*, entitled "Of Some Verbal Disputes" (EPM 312–23). His concern there is the possibility and desirability of distinguishing between "virtues" and "talents" or between "vices" and "defects." His sensitivity to issues of linguistic usage throughout the section is remarkable.

Of course, if Hume's only concern with language were in this Fourth Appendix of the *Enquiry*, an essay concerning his views on moral language would need to be very restricted. But the fact is that Hume's attention to language is evident in the most central aspects of his ethical theory. For example, his sensitivity to emotive or evaluative meaning is apparent in his basic procedure, which he describes as follows:

> we shall analyse that complication of mental qualities, which form what, in common life, we call Personal Merit: we shall consider every attribute of the mind, which renders a man an object either of esteem and affection, or of hatred and contempt; every habit or sentiment or faculty, which, if ascribed to any person, implies either praise or blame, and may enter into any panegyric or satire of his character and manners. . . . The very nature of lan-

guage guides us almost infallibly in forming a judgement of this nature; and as every tongue possesses one set of words which are taken in a good sense, and another in the opposite, the least acquaintance with the idiom suffices, without any reasoning, to direct us in collecting and arranging the estimable or blameable qualities of men. The only object of reasoning is to discover the circumstances on both sides, which are common to these qualities . . . [EPM 173–74].

That is, Hume will use the evaluative meaning, favorable or derogatory, of terms such as "benevolent," "just," "cheerful," "industrious," "selfish," "dishonest," "melancholy," and "lazy" in order to make lists of desirable and undesirable traits. Then he will attempt to discover what characteristics are common to all the traits described by those terms with favorable evaluative meaning. The common characteristics, it turns out, consist of being useful or agreeable to oneself or to others. Thus, Hume's conclusion with regard to the general principles of morals is:

> Personal Merit consists altogether in the possession of mental qualities, *useful* or *agreeable* to the *person himself* or to *others* [EPM 268].

But the whole process of discovering the general principles of morals begins with a linguistic exercise—making a list of qualities the names of which carry favorable evaluative meaning.

The statement of his procedure which is discussed above is not the only one which Hume provides. An alternative description appears in the First Appendix of the *Enquiry*:

> The hypothesis which we embrace is plain. It maintains that morality is determined by sentiment. It defines virtue to be *whatever mental action or quality gives to a spectator the pleasing sentiment of approbation*; and vice the contrary. We then proceed to examine a plain matter of fact, to wit, what actions have this influence. We consider all the circumstances in which these actions agree, and thence endeavour to extract some general observations with regard to these sentiments [EPM 289].

It is obvious that the second half of this procedure is the same as the second half of the preceding one: namely, finding the common ingredients among the qualities of character regarded as virtues. What differs is the first half. Now, Hume uses the sentiments of a disinterested spectator as his guide for determining which qualities of character are virtues, rather than being guided by the evaluative meanings of the terms referring to such qualities.

Hume also gives us another definition of virtue which can be taken as the basis of yet a third way of compiling the list of virtues which constitutes the first half of his procedure.

> It is the nature and, indeed, the definition of virtue, that it is *a quality of the mind agreeable to or approved of by every one who considers or contemplates it* [EPM 261, note].

Now, instead of relying on the sentiments of a single disinterested spectator to determine which qualities of character are virtues, Hume suggests that we can rely on the judgments of everyone.

With three different techniques being recommended concerning the method for constructing our list of virtues, I think we can complain that at best Hume is being rather sloppy in his statements about the technique to be used for the first half of his procedure. But three things can be said in his defense. (1) It is the second half of his procedure, the generalizing from the particular qualities which are considered virtues, which Hume regards as his innovation. It is this second part which introduces "the experimental method" in which one infers "general maxims from a comparison of particular instances" (EPM 174). (2) From Hume's perspective, it would make no difference whether one's list of virtues be compiled on the basis of the evaluative meanings of terms, the sentiments of a single disinterested spectator, or the moral judgments of all persons. The list of virtues would be the same. The favorable evaluative meanings of those terms which describe virtues is simply a reflection of the approbation which everyone feels toward these qualities, and everyone's approbation will be the same because it depends on an "internal sense or feeling, which nature has made universal in the whole species" (EPM 173). (3) If there were borderline cases of qualities which may or may not be virtues, one could just ignore them at this point in his inquiry. The ultimate aim is to discover the general principles of morals, and this can be done by examining paradigm cases of virtues. Once one discovers these general principles, one can return to the borderline cases armed with the knowledge that this particular quality is a virtue to whatever extent it embodies the general principles.

I believe that the second statement of Hume's procedure, where he refers to the single disinterested spectator, is the best, especially if one insists on dealing with borderline cases where differences of opinion may exist.[4] But since our present interest is Hume's sensitivity to the evaluative aspects of moral language, it is the first-mentioned statement of his procedure which warrants our attention. It suggests that we can adopt an inductive procedure for arriving at the general principles of morals, which begins by making a list of desirable traits on the basis of their being described by terms which carry favorable evaluative meaning. Those who have an aversion to the notions of qualified spectators and unanimous approbations can still proceed with Hume's inductive method for discovering "the general principles of morals." I find it hard to believe that anyone would object to starting his moral investigations with the premiss that terms such as "generous," "just," "cheerful," and "industrious" have favorable evaluative meanings, while terms such as "selfish," "dishonest," "melancholy," and "lazy" have derogatory evaluative meanings.

There is another important aspect of Hume's view in which he makes reference to language. Hume contends that when making moral judgments *all persons do in fact approve of whatever promotes the welfare of the human species.* He gives three arguments to support his contention, one of which is based directly on linguistic considerations. But let us first examine the other two. The first argument is based on the premiss that it is an essential part of human nature to sympathize with other humans.

If we consider the principles of the human make, such as they appear to daily experience and observation, we must, *a priori* [that is, without bothering to check our inferences by further observation], conclude it impossible for such a creature as man to be totally indifferent to the well or ill-being of his fellow-creatures, and not readily, of himself, to pronounce, where nothing gives him any particular bias, that what promotes their happiness is good, what tends to their misery is evil, without any farther regard or consideration [EPM 230; see also EPM 273].

Hume's second argument is actually a summary of the argument of *An Enquiry Concerning the Principles of Morals* as a whole. The common ingredient of all the virtues is that they directly or indirectly promote human happiness, either of the person himself or of others. Thus, it is an empirically verifiable proposition that human beings do in fact approve of those traits of character which promote the welfare of the species.

Were it doubtful, whether there were any such principle in our nature as humanity or a concern for others, yet when we see, in numberless instances, that whatever has a tendency to promote the interests of society, is so highly approved of, we ought thence to learn the force of the benevolent principle . . . [EPM 231].

But it is Hume's third argument which most requires our attention when we focus on his views about moral language. He points out that both stable thought for the individual himself and communication with others require that moral language be used to reflect a *general point of view* which includes a concern for the general welfare:

it is necessary for us, in our calm judgements and *discourse* concerning the characters of men, to neglect all these differences, and render our sentiments more public and social. Besides, that we ourselves often change our situation in this particular, we every day meet with persons who are in a situation different from us, and who could never *converse* with us were we to remain constantly in that position and point of view, which is peculiar to ourselves. *The intercourse of sentiments*, therefore, *in society and conversation*, makes us form *some general unalterable standard*, by which we may approve or disapprove of characters and manners. And though the heart takes not part entirely with those general notions, . . . yet have these moral differences a considerable influence, and *being sufficient, at least for discourse*, serve all our purposes in company, in the pulpit, on the theatre, and in the schools [EPM 229; emphasis added; see also EPM 274].

Lest one think that Hume's view expressed here that thought and communication require moral judgments to reflect a general point of view is found only in the *Enquiry*, let me quote a similar passage from the *Treatise*.

In general, all *sentiments* of blame or praise are variable. . . . But these variations we regard not in our general decisions. . . . Experience soon teaches us this method of correcting our sentiments, or at least, of *correcting our language*, where the sentiments are more stubborn and inalterable. . . . Such corrections are common with regard to all the senses; and indeed 'twere impossible we cou'd ever *make use of language, or communicate our sentiments to one another*, did we not correct the momentary appearances of things, and overlook our present situation [T 582; emphasis added; see also T 603].

Thus Hume concludes that even if our sentiments cannot be "corrected" to reflect a general point of view, still our linguistic formulation of moral judgments must reflect such a viewpoint. Otherwise stable thought and interpersonal communication about moral matters would become impossible.

This linguistic argument which Hume uses to show that people must approve (at least in their communicated judgments) whatever promotes the general welfare of society can stand independently of the first two arguments he uses to establish this point. Even if people felt no empathy with other persons, and even if there were no empirical evidence that people do in fact approve of what promotes human happiness, still it would be necessary that our ethical judgments reflect a common interest rather than a personal point of view. If our language did not reflect a common viewpoint, we would become confused whenever our own personal situation changed and we would find ourselves unable to talk with others about moral issues.

III

It is precisely this point about the requirements of communicating with others which distinguishes Hume's analysis of ethical language from that of Stevenson. Stevenson takes the expression "X is good" to be roughly synonymous with "I approve of X; do so as well" (EL 21–22). The term "approve" suggests some effort on the part of the speaker to attain a broader point of view than that of his own personal interests. That is one reason why Stevenson's analysis in *Ethics and Language* seems so much more plausible than his earlier suggestion that "X is good" means "I *do* like X; do so as well." [5] Stevenson himself, however, seems not to appreciate the fact that the term "approve" to some extent suggests a disinterested rather than a personal point of view. He recognizes that the term "approve" may be used at times to indicate what he calls a peculiarly moral attitude, but he never relates this attitude to disinterestedness. He suggests rather that a peculiarly moral attitude differs from other attitudes in being more intense (EL 90) [6] or in being an attitude directed toward other attitudes. [7] Hume, on the other hand, makes it quite clear that moral sentiment differs from other kinds of sentiment by virtue of its indicating a disinterested point of view.

'Tis only when a character is considered in general, without reference to our particular interest, that it causes such a feeling or sentiment, as denominates it morally good or evil [T 472].

Furthermore, as I have already noted, according to Hume, moral *judgments* should reflect a disinterested or general point of view even if we cannot get our actual sentiments to reflect such a viewpoint.

According to Hume's approach, it is a fundamental error on Stevenson's part not to distinguish between the personal point of view, on the one hand, and the general point of view suggested by ethical language, on the other. As Hume puts it:

> When a man denominates another his *enemy*, his *rival*, his *antagonist*, his *adversary*, he is understood to speak the language of self-love, and to express sentiments, peculiar to himself, and arising from his particular circumstances and situation. But when he bestows on any man the epithets of *vicious* or *odious* or *depraved*, he then speaks another language, and expresses sentiments, in which he expects all his audience are to concur with him. He must here, therefore, depart from his private and particular situation, and must choose a point of view, common to him with others. . . . . [EPM 272; see also EPM 228–29, T 582–83, 591].

Since moral language is taken by listeners to indicate a disinterested or general point of view, it is easy to see why it can be used persuasively as Stevenson claims it can. But the imperative force or emotive meaning of "X is good" does not depend on some mysterious attractiveness of the sound of g-o-o-d.[8] It depends on the listener's expecting the speaker to be expressing a disinterested point of view. If the speaker uses moral language to express a personal point of view, as suggested by Stevenson's analysis, he catches the listener off-guard. Of course, we learn from experience that propagandists, advertisers, and the like regularly *misuse* language in this fashion, and we gradually become able to protect ourselves. But if *everyone* came to use what are currently moral terms to indicate a personal point of view as Stevenson's analysis permits, we would need to develop some new terms to use whenever a general point of view is being expressed. Sometimes we want to indicate that we are claiming that something is desirable from a general point of view and not simply from our own personal point of view, just as we also need the term "true" to indicate that we are making a claim that a proposition deserves to be believed by everyone and not merely that we just now happen to believe it. If our present moral terminology should become useless for this purpose, some new moral terms would be required.

It is Stevenson's failure to see that moral language indicates a general or disinterested point of view which also distorts his interpretation of Hume's theory. He correctly sees that for Hume only the sentiments of *informed* spectators are trustworthy indicators of virtue and vice, but he fails to note that for Hume a distinct point of view is indicated by the notion of approbation. His paraphrase of Hume's view is:

> "X is a virtue" has the same meaning as "X would be the object of approbation of almost any person who had full and clear factual information about X" [EL 274].

But why has Stevenson inserted the term "almost" when, as we observed earlier, Hume's own statement says "every one" (EPM 261, note)? It seems to me that Stevenson's statement reflects his assumption that the spectators will be relying entirely on their own momentary personal feelings rather than trying to make judgments which reflect a general point of view. When the spectators try to reflect a general point of view in their judgments, any differences in their judgments would necessarily reflect what Stevenson calls disagreement in belief since the attitudes of all the spectators would reflect the same general or disinterested viewpoint. Stevenson is aware of Hume's view that there will be agreement in attitude among all persons,[9] but he treats it as an unwarranted assumption (EL 275) rather than a necessary consequence of the fact that moral language reflects a general point of view.

Stevenson's failure to grasp Hume's point about the general or disinterested point of view reflected in moral language is also apparent in his further remarks about Hume's view. He says:

> Hume's manner of defining the moral terms makes such a statement as "Anything is good if and only if the vast majority of people, on being fully and clearly informed about it, would have approbation for it" an analytic one. . . . It excludes any sense of "good" . . . with which one might *oppose* the vast majority of informed people's attitudes, and so is persuasive [EL 276].

If we realize that the term "approbation" in the analytic statement above refers to a *disinterested* attitude, we get a very different suggestion from what we get when the term "approbation" is used as Stevenson uses it: namely, to reflect some very strong second-level, personal attitude. Stevenson suggests that Hume is saying that whatever the majority *favor* (there is no indication that only *moral* attitudes of the majority are being considered) is good, but if my interpretation of Hume is correct, then an individual person might well use "good" to "oppose the vast majority of informed people's attitudes" on grounds that *their* attitudes are not disinterested, that they are not *moral* attitudes. On the other hand, if other people actually have taken a disinterested point of view and I disagree with them, it would seem a bit presumptuous of me to use *moral* language to express my *personal* point of view as Stevenson's analysis permits. Stevenson's goes on to say that Hume's analysis of moral language "is persuasive in a further respect: it reserves the emotive meaning of ethical terms for the *benevolent* attitudes of 'approbation,' as distinct from the selfish ones" (EL 276). But it is incorrect to speak of this as "a further respect"; it is the same point again. Also, Stevenson's choice of terms is inappropriate. Instead of "benevolent" he should have used the term "disinterested," and instead of "the selfish ones" he should have used "those which reflect a personal point of view." When we make these substitutions the question of whether Hume's analysis or Stevenson's yields a persuasive definition depends on whose analysis of moral language one accepts. From the Humean point of view Stevenson is giving a persuasive definition which allows moral language to be used to indicate a personal point of view.

The differing analyses of moral language presented by Stevenson and Hume have some interesting implications for the types of arguments which are appropriate when disagreements about moral issues occur. As Stevenson puts it:

> . . . Hume, like so many others, emphasized not disagreement in attitude but disagreement in belief. . . . By neglecting disagreement in attitude he oversimplifies and overintellectualizes the arguments that occur between people who are not yet factually informed. and provides no place for persuasive methods [EL 275–76].

Hume's analysis with its reference to the views of an informed and disinterested spectator implies that only two types of reasons are appropriate when there is a dispute about moral issues. One type consists of rendering the other spectator more informed by supplying additional information, especially concerning the probable consequences of a given type of action or a given trait of character. For example, one might note that giving alms to beggars encourages these persons to continue begging rather than to find alternative ways of providing for their needs (EPM 180). The second type, being addressed to the fact that the spectator's viewpoint must be disinterested, directs attention to the personal interests and prejudices of the participants in an effort to get them to make allowance for these distorting influences. For example, during the course of an ethical argument it might be appropriate for one of the disputants to note that a person is likely to have more empathy with persons closer to himself than with others who are more distant (EPM 227, 229).

On the other hand, Stevenson's whole approach to moral reasoning centers on the goal of getting one's "opponent" to adopt one's own view. Non-rational methods are not ruled out by Stevenson's view because there is no fundamental distinction between moral (disinterested) attitudes and personal attitudes as there is in Hume's view. For Stevenson the aim of "moral arguments" is to *get this particular opponent to agree on this particular issue at this particular moment,* while according to Hume's view the aim is to *discover what would be approved by an informed person who takes a disinterested point of view.* Whether one believes that Hume's view "oversimplifies and overintellectualizes" moral arguments or that Stevenson's view overpersonalizes and overpersuasivizes moral arguments depends again on what analysis of moral language one adopts: Is moral language an instrument of personal persuasion or a device for indicating what is desirable from a disinterested point of view? And again a Humean must ask Stevenson: If you use moral language for merely personal persuasion, what terminology would be left for indicating a disinterested point of view? How would I be able to say that someone is vicious and not merely my enemy at this moment (EPM 272)?

IV

While the difference between Hume and Stevenson is focused on the issue of what point of view is expressed by moral language, the difference between Hume and Hare is focused on the issue of the relation between facts and moral issues. Hare would not agree with this statement, however, because he interprets Hume as advancing the same view he himself holds: that there is a gap between statements of fact ("is"-statements) and value judgments ("ought"-statements). Furthermore, he views Hume as being among the first to note this gap and refers to the need to preserve the gap as "Hume's Law." [10] Consequently, the discussion of the relation between the views of Hume and Hare must begin with a consideration of Hare's interpretation of the crucial "is–ought" paragraph of Hume's *Treatise.*

It must be emphasized that Hare does not devote much effort to defending his interpretation of Hume and that Hare's position does not depend on his being correct in his interpretation of Hume. He argues for his own position independently and then simply points to Hume as an earlier philosopher who advanced the same principle. But the interpretation of Hume's ethical views is a central concern of the present essay, and, therefore, Hare's interpretation of Hume is important for me even if it was only a peripheral issue for Hare.

The key paragraph in Hume's *Treatise* reads as follows:

> I cannot forbear adding to these reasonings an observation, which may, perhaps, be found of some importance. In every system of morality, which I have hitherto met with, I have always remark'd, that the author proceeds for some time in the ordinary way of reasoning, and establishes the being of a God, or makes observations concerning human affairs; when of a sudden I am surpriz'd to find, that instead of the usual copulations of propositions, *is*, and *is not*, I meet with no proposition that is not connected with an *ought*, or an *ought not*. This change is imperceptible; but is, however, of the last consequence. For as this *ought*, or *ought not*, expresses some new relation or affirmation, 'tis necessary that it shou'd be observ'd and explain'd; and at the same time that a reason should be given, for what seems altogether inconceivable, how this new relation can be a deduction from others, which are entirely different from it. But as authors do not commonly use this precaution, I shall presume to recommend it to the readers; and am persuaded, that this small attention wou'd subvert all the vulgar systems of morality, and let us see, that the distinction of vice and virtue is not founded merely on the relations of objects, nor is perceiv'd by reason [T 469–70].

The correct interpretation of this paragraph has been a center of controversy during the last twenty years.[11] The "traditional" interpretation is that Hume is denying that it is ever appropriate to draw "ought"-conclusions from "is"-premisses. Hare accepts this interpretation (LM 29; FR 186). Opponents of the "traditional" interpretation claim that Hume is saying only that the move from "is" to "ought" is an important move which has not received sufficient attention from previous moralists, and that if they had paid more attention to it they would have become aware that morality cannot be based on reason alone. These opponents of the standard interpretation point to the last third of the last sentence in the paragraph cited above as well as to the last part of the paragraph which immediately precedes the famous is–ought paragraph. There Hume says:

> But can there be any difficulty in proving, that vice and virtue are not matters of fact, *whose existence we can infer by reason*? Take any action allow'd to be vicious: Wilful murder, for instance. Examine it in all lights, and see if you can find that matter of fact, or real existence, which you call *vice*. In which-ever way you take it, you find only certain passions, motives, volitions and thoughts. There is no other matter of fact in the case. The vice entirely escapes you, *as long as you consider the object.* You never can find it, *till you turn your reflexion into your own breast, and find a sentiment of disapprobation*, which arises in you, towards this action. *Here is a matter of fact; but 'tis the object of feeling, not of reason. It lies in yourself, not in the object.* So

that when you pronounce any action or character to be vicious, you mean nothing, but that *from the constitution of your nature* you have a feeling or sentiment of blame from the contemplation of it. *Vice and virtue, therefore, may be compar'd to sounds, colours, heat and cold, which,* according to modern philosophy, *are not qualities in objects, but perceptions in the mind*: And this discovery in morals, like that other in physics, is to be regarded as a considerable advancement of the speculative sciences; tho', like that too, it has *little or no influence on practice.* Nothing can be more real, or concern us more, than our own sentiments of pleasure and uneasiness; and if these be favourable to virtue, and unfavourable to vice, no more can be requisite to the regulation of our conduct and behaviour [T 468–69; emphasis added].

This paragraph suggests that Hume is indicating how we move from "is" to "ought" (by sentiment rather than by reason). Consequently, it is argued by the opponents of the "traditional" view, it is improbable that in the very next paragraph he would assert that it cannot be done.

At least two other considerations seem to count against the "traditional" interpretation of the is–ought paragraph. The first is the section in which it is located. The controversial paragraph is the last paragraph of Section I of Part I of Book III of the *Treatise*. Book III is entitled "Of Morals"; Part I is entitled "Of Virtue and Vice in General"; Section I, in which the is–ought paragraph occurs, is entitled "Moral Distinctions not Deriv'd from Reason." Furthermore, immediately after the is–ought paragraph we find Section II, which is entitled "Moral Distinctions Deriv'd from a Moral Sense," a strange title to be chosen by someone who (supposedly) has just denied that one can make *any* move from "is"-statements to "ought"-statements. The second consideration is that, when he rewrote Book III of the *Treatise* as *An Enquiry Concerning the Principles of Morals*, Hume made no mention of the is–ought matter. If he had been putting forward something like G. E. Moore's attack on "the naturalistic fallacy," it seems probable that he would have either reasserted such an important point or inserted a footnote indicating that the earlier view was mistaken (as he did with regard to his efforts to describe the mechanism by which we come to identify with the welfare of others [compare EPM 219–20, note, with T 317–20]). The fact that he did neither suggests that in the is–ought paragraph he is not making a separate point that one cannot move from "is" to "ought," but rather asserting only that some attention concerning how that move is made would provide an additional support for his own view that morality cannot be based on relations between ideas or matters of fact known by means of the perceptions of the external senses.

As I mentioned earlier, Hare's position does not depend on the correctness of the "traditional" interpretation of Hume's is–ought paragraph. Hare might admit that his interpretation of Hume's position was incorrect and that he should not have made any reference to "Hume's Law" as an earlier statement of the principle that one cannot derive "ought" from "is." What is important for Hare is the point that all naturalistic ethical theories (theories which claim that "ought" statements are equivalent to or reducible to some kind of "is" statements) are mistaken. He claims that the function of moral language is to guide conduct, and this means that such language must be prescriptive rather than descriptive (LM 1). Moral language must commend and not just describe (LM 84–93). Thus, according to Hare, if Hume did in fact advocate a naturalistic ethical theory, he made the same mistake all ethical naturalists make of paying too much attention to the descriptive function of moral language and thereby neglecting the commending or prescriptive function.

But, contrary to Hare's suppositions, it is possible that there is no more of a gap between the descriptive and prescriptive functions of language than the naturalist allows to exist between "is"-statements and "ought"-statements. Rather than arguing again for the correctness of my naturalistic interpretation of Hume's views,[12] I intend to present that interpretation in outline form and then to construct a response to Hare's attack on naturalism in ethics on the basis of what I take to be the Humean theory.

I believe that Hume's ethical theory consists of two parts, an analytic part in which the term "virtue" is defined and a synthetic part in which one draws a generalization concerning the common characteristics of all qualities of character called "virtues." As I indicated in Part ii, Hume actually states the analytic part of his theory in at least three different ways:

(1) A virtue is any quality of character the term for which carries a favorable evaluative meaning.
(2) A virtue is any quality of character which arouses a sentiment of approbation in an informed, disinterested spectator.
(3) A virtue is any quality of character which arouses judgments of approbation in all informed spectators.

In order to simplify my remarks, from here on I shall refer only to the second formulation of the analytic part of Hume's theory. Having constructed a list of virtues (benevolence or generosity, justice, loyalty to government, chastity, discretion, industry, frugality, honesty, prudence, dignity, courage, tranquillity, politeness, wit, and so on), one then notes what is common to all of them: namely, that they are useful or agreeable to oneself or to others. Though Hume suggests that he is following a Baconian approach of listing individual instances and then examining them for common characteristics, his actual procedure seems to have been more in accord with our contemporary view of scientific investigation: that is, he apparently formulated his hypothesis and then examined individual virtues to see if they all would fit into one or more of his four categories of being useful to others, being useful to oneself, being agreeable to oneself, and being agreeable to others.

Now, what would Hume say in response to Hare's claim that the naturalistic approach to ethics fails because it makes ethical judgments descriptive and consequently leaves out their commending function? One key passage in which Hare challenges the naturalistic approach is the following:

> If "P is a good picture" is held to mean the same as "P is a picture and P is C [where C refers to a characteristic or set of characteristics which contains only descriptive expressions]," then it will become impossible to commend pictures for being C; it will be possible only to say that they are C. . . . whatever de-

fining characteristics we choose, this objection arises, that we can no longer commend an object for possessing those characteristics [LM 85].

In order to relate this challenge to Hume's approach, I will use the value term "virtue" rather than "good." According to Hume, "Q is a virtuous quality of character" means "Q is a quality of character and Q is C, where C consists of being such as to arouse a sentiment of approbation in an informed, disinterested spectator." Hare's objection to defining "virtue" in this way is that we could then no longer commend a quality of character for being C (for arousing approbation in an informed, disinterested spectator) by saying "Q is a virtue." Rather than commending Q, we would only be saying something descriptive about Q: namely, that it is C.

But why can a description itself not be commendatory? Why must we do something *else* in order to commend? If, in saying "Generosity is a virtue," I am indicating that generosity is a quality of character which arouses approbation in an informed, disinterested spectator, it seems that I have already commended generosity without there being anything *else* required. In fact, it seems to perform the function of commending even better than my saying "I commend generosity" since this latter statement would express only my *personal* attitude, which may be uninformed or biased.[13] In other words, if we adopt the Humean definition of what it means to say that a quality of character is a virtue, we have a *descriptive* expression which is itself *commendatory*. In answer to Hare's charge that "we can no longer commend an object for possessing those characteristics" (LM 85), the Humean naturalist can respond that we no longer need to do something *else* to commend it; its possessing the characteristic of arousing approbation in an informed, disinterested spectator is already as much of a commendation as can be given. We do not need to commend Qs for being Cs; to say that they are Cs is already to describe them *and commend* them at the same time.

How would Hare respond to such a view? It is difficult to anticipate someone else's thoughts on philosophical issues, but Hare does provide

a simple procedure for exposing any new variety of it [ethical naturalism] that may be offered. Let us suppose that someone claims that he can deduce a moral or other evaluative judgement from a set of purely factual or descriptive premises, relying on some definition to the effect that V (a value-word) means the same as C (a conjunction of descriptive predicates). We first have to ask him to be sure that C contains no expression that is covertly evaluative (for example "natural" or "normal" or "satisfying" or "fundamental human needs"). Nearly all so-called "naturalistic definitions" will break down under this test—for to be genuinely naturalistic a definition must contain no expression for whose applicability there is not a definite criterion which does not involve the making of a value-judgement. If the definition satisfies this test, we have next to ask whether its advocate ever wishes to commend anything for being C. If he says that he does, we have only to point out to him that his definition makes this impossible, for the reasons given. And clearly he cannot say that he never wishes to commend anything for being C; for to commend things for being C is the whole object of his theory [LM 92–93].

My task will be to consider the Humean definition of "virtue" in terms of these two tests provided by Hare for proposed naturalistic definitions.

Before taking up that task, let me make some preliminary comments. For Hume, the ultimate aim of ethical inquiry was to discover the general principles which determine what qualities of character are virtues.[14] The analysis of the meaning of ethical terms was just a passing problem on the way to the resolution of this primary problem, rather than an end in itself, as is the case with many contemporary writers. Secondly, a central interest of contemporary ethical theorists is how to go about resolving differences in evaluation in borderline cases. Their analyses of ethical terms are significant because of what is implied about the justification of moral judgments when disagreement occurs. On the other hand, Hume's naturalistic definition was not meant primarily to assist in deciding borderline cases of virtue (see Part II of this essay). After discovering the general principles of morals (that qualities useful or agreeable to oneself or to others are virtues), one could presumably then use these general principles to determine whether under certain conditions a given quality of character would or would not be a virtue. For example, one could forecast that with the development of portable computers the ability to do mathematical computations will probably become much less useful and thus less of a virtue, just as having a good memory is no longer the important virtue it once was (EPM 241). Thus, in trying to defend Hume's definition of the term "virtue" in the context of contemporary issues, I shall need to introduce some refinements and emphases which I believe did not interest Hume. I shall be stretching his definition to make it adequate for tasks which he never considered. Nevertheless, I believe I am following in his footsteps and am preserving the spirit of his approach to ethical issues as I make these extensions for the purpose of addressing contemporary issues.

Hare's first test for Hume's proposed naturalistic definition is to determine whether all the terms in the *definiens* are purely descriptive. Recall that for Hume the value-term "virtue" is being defined as equivalent to the descriptive expression "quality of character which arouses a sentiment of approbation in an informed, disinterested spectator." The terms in this definition which might be challenged as not purely descriptive are "approbation," "informed," "disinterested," and "spectator." Hare wants the naturalist to provide for each of these terms some "definite criterion" for applying it "which does not involve the making of a value-judgement" (LM 92). Establishing definite criteria for applying terms is not easy to do, even with regard to such a familiar and concrete term as "pencil" (try to set up criteria which will include colored pencils but exclude crayons, which will include ballpoint-pen–type pencils with "liquid lead" but exclude ballpoint pens). But let us try.[15] "Approbation" refers to that kind of pro–attitude which is felt when one takes a disinterested point of view while attempting to evaluate something. Perhaps the term "disinterested" in this definition of "approbation" is evaluative, but that term will be discussed in connection with the definition of "virtue" itself below. It is introduced here to differentiate approbation from other kinds of pro–attitudes.

"Informed" indicates that the spectator must know about the matter being evaluated, and especially about the probable consequences for behavior of having certain traits of character and the probable consequences for other people of behaving in certain ways. But it seems difficult to specify exactly how much a spectator must know in order to be considered informed. It seems a bit much to say that he must be omniscient. I think the best we can do is to say that he must know all information *relevant* to the matter being judged and that the word "relevant" here indicates that it would have some causal influence on the spectator's sentiments of approbation and disapprobation toward the matter then being evaluated. But even though this discussion of what it means to be "informed" contains references only to descriptive considerations, the term "informed" still seems somewhat evaluative. It is, after all, obviously *better* to be "informed" than to be "uninformed." Are we then introducing *implicitly evaluative* expressions into our definitions of virtue? This raises an issue we will need to consider at greater length later—whether Hare's challenge to the naturalist assumes a descriptive–evaluative dichotomy which does not exist in language.

The term "disinterested" in the *definiens* is actually redundant if one is clear about the meaning of "approbation." But since some philosophers such as Stevenson do not treat disinterestedness as an essential ingredient in the attitude of approbation (see Part III), it seemed best to me to include the term "disinterested" explicitly in the definition. "Disinterested" means having *no personal stakes* in the outcome of one's evaluations. It also means *not having any personal prejudices* which would lead a person to give greater weight to the interests of those closer to himself or more like himself. But it certainly does not mean being "uninterested," that is, not caring about the matter at all. The disinterested spectator is "blind" in the way the goddess Justice is blind. She is concerned that issues be decided fairly, without regard to favoritism for those with power, wealth, or other advantages. Even though it seems that the criteria for being disinterested are descriptive, once again we run into the problem that the term "disinterested," especially in the context of moral evaluation, seems to have a favorable evaluative meaning while terms such as "interested" or "partial" or "prejudiced" have a derogatory evaluative meaning in this context.

The term "spectator" refers to a human being, but in the face of challenges from anti-naturalists such as Hare it would need to be qualified. For example, we would need to specify that the person is an adult rather than a small child, that he is not mentally retarded or psychotic, that he is not a psychopath, and so on. Trying to be specific in any great detail concerning exactly who could qualify as a spectator does not seem to be warranted in view of the effort required because there are so many people who would not ordinarily be classified as abnormal. It seems best simply not to rely on anyone who seems for any reason to be even a borderline case. In the selection of judges or jurors, for example, if there is any doubt about a person's being a normal human being we just eliminate him and rely on others. In actual situations, the problem of finding spectators who are *disinterested* seems so much greater than the problem of finding spectators who are *not abnormal* that efforts to specify the latter condition in any precise way seem foolish. But, once again, even if we could say precisely what "not abnormal" means in purely descriptive terms, the expression seems to have a favorable evaluative meaning while "abnormal" seems to have a derogatory evaluative meaning.

Hare has in fact pointed out that the terms "natural" and "normal" are "covertly evaluative" (LM 92) and that the expression "a competent and impartial judge" (which is not very different from "an informed, disinterested spectator") is a "value-expression" (LM 42). But if the naturalist can give *descriptive* accounts of what is meant by "approbation," "informed," "disinterested," and "not abnormal spectator," what does it matter that these terms are *also covertly evaluative*? Hare's challenge to the naturalist to show how value-terms can be reduced to non–value-terms is ambiguous. It can be interpreted in two different ways, one of which is a legitimate demand, the other is not. He may be challenging the naturalist to have a *definiens* for value-expressions in which all the terms can be defined in terms of descriptive criteria. Such a challenge is legitimate because if the naturalist does not meet it, he has not made good on his claim that he can derive "ought"-statements from "is"-statements. I believe I have shown that the Humean definition can meet this challenge.

But Hare's challenge can also be understood in a second way: namely, that all the terms in the *definiens* of the value-expression not only can be specified in descriptive terms *but also must lack any covert* (LM 92) *or implicit* (LM 46) *evaluative or prescriptive meaning.* This challenge is *not* legitimate because it forces the naturalist to accept Hare's own assumption that it is necessary to keep evaluative meaning completely distinct from descriptive meaning. The naturalist has some very good reasons for doubting the desirability of accepting Hare's assumption. First, if in our language evaluative meaning is always separable from descriptive meaning, we should be able to find some terms with evaluative meaning but no descriptive meaning just as we have terms with descriptive meaning but no evaluative meaning. (I have no doubt that Hare believes there are terms with descriptive meaning and no evaluative meaning whatever. But if he were to deny that there are such terms, this second interpretation of his challenge to the naturalist to produce a definition for value-expressions which does not contain any evaluative meaning, even implicitly, would become an *a priori* impossibility.) Even terms which are primarily evaluative, such as "good," are admitted by Hare always to have at least some descriptive meaning (LM 121–22). Furthermore, there is nothing about the sound of g-o-o-d or that of other value-terms which would lead them to have favorable evaluative meaning.[16] They seem to acquire their evaluative meaning because of their descriptive meaning. Consequently, there seems to be good reason for the naturalist to reject Hare's assumption that evaluative meaning must be kept entirely separate from descriptive meaning.

Secondly, the naturalist could point to the way in which descriptive terms acquire evaluative meaning so that the linguistic rules for using those terms come to include the evaluative aspect. Hare himself gives as examples the terms "tidy" and "industrious" (LM 121). These expressions are taken to be terms of commendation indicating that they have evaluative meaning as well as descriptive meaning. All the other terms for virtues such as "benevolent," "courageous," "generous" and so on could be cited as further examples. It is their favorable evaluative meaning, in fact, which according to Hume leads us to identify them as virtues. Consequently, it seems quite inappropriate for Hare to suggest that one must always distinguish between verbal matters on the one hand and value-issues which are matters of substance on the other (LM 46–47; FR 195, 198). Why think that evaluative attitudes cannot be incorporated into the rules of the language? Undoubtedly Hare can point to some instances where philosophers have improperly tried to resolve substantive issues by verbal maneuvers (LM 47–49), but the fact that some such mistakes have been made is hardly sufficient to conclude that our language rules *never* incorporate *any* evaluative commitments. In fact, Hare himself argues that with regard to the linguistic rules for "good" the evaluative meaning is more important than the descriptive meaning (LM 118–21). If the evaluative meaning of terms can be incorporated into the rules for using them, and some descriptive meaning is also incorporated into the rules for using these same terms (such as happens in terms describing some virtues), then it would seem that at least for some terms the rules of the language connect descriptive and evaluative meanings. In this way substantive evaluative matters may in some cases also be verbal matters. The Humean naturalist claims that this is exactly what has happened in the case of terms such as "informed" and "disinterested." The criteria for applying these terms can be formulated in descriptive expressions, but the terms themselves will also have the implicit evaluative meaning acquired from past usage. For Hare to rule out such implicit evaluative meaning is to force naturalists to accept his unwarranted either-descriptive-or-prescriptive assumption about language.

But there is something else wrong with Hare's challenge to the naturalistic ethical theorist to produce a definition for value-expressions which does not even implicitly have any evaluative meaning: it is *in principle* impossible for naturalistic ethical theorists to meet this challenge. As Hare recognizes, the naturalistic position is distinguished from those views which try to define evaluative expressions in terms of metaphysical or suprasensible characteristics (LM 82) precisely by its recognition that the path from "is" to "ought" lies through human nature and human interests. *The descriptive terms in the naturalist's definition will always have some "covert" or "implicit" evaluative meaning because they will necessarily have some connection with what people have come to recognize as desirable.* The only way the naturalist could meet Hare's challenge to eliminate all implicitly evaluative terms in the *definiens* would be to define value-expressions by means of terms which either (1) have no relation at all to human interests and sentiments or (2) have some relation to human interests which is thus far unknown. Using the second alternative would at best be a temporary solution to Hare's challenge: as soon as people become aware of the link between the terms and human interests, implicit evaluative meaning would come to be attached to the terms in the *definiens*, and Hare's challenge would be unmet. With regard to the first alternative, it is one of Hume's main points, as I noted at the beginning of this section in discussing the is–ought paragraph, that morals cannot be based on *a priori* knowledge or on information gathered through the external senses but can be based only on human interests and sentiments.[17] To Hare's challenge Hume would need to respond as follows. On this matter I agree with you. *If* the move from "is" to "ought" must be made in the absence of any connection with human interests and sentiments, *if* it must be made without using any terms connected with such interests and sentiments, then it cannot be made. But such a challenge is illegitimate. It eliminates the only kind of response the naturalist can make by invoking your unwarranted assumption that in any analysis of language descriptive and evaluative meaning must be kept absolutely distinct from each other.

Hare's second test for any proposed naturalistic definition consists of asking "whether its advocate ever wishes to commend anything for being C" (LM 93). For our proposed Humean definition, "C" consists of "being such as to arouse the sentiment of approbation in an informed, disinterested spectator." So Hare is asking the Humean whether he would ever wish to commend anything for being such as to arouse approbation in an informed, disinterested spectator. But the use of the word "for" here makes the question sound odd in relation to the present proposed definition. "For" seems to be synonymous with "because," and it seems strange to say that one would want to commend benevolence, for example, *because* it arouses approbation in an informed, disinterested spectator. To say that it arouses such approbation is in fact already to commend it. The only way that the term "because" will be appropriate here is if I limit my commendation to being a matter of my own personal feelings. Then I might say "I personally esteem benevolence because I believe it is a quality of character which arouses approbation in an informed, disinterested spectator." But in general the advocate of the Humean definition would *not* want to commend virtues *because* they arouse approbation in an informed, disinterested spectator. To note that they arouse such approbation is already to commend them. Hare is wrong in saying that "the whole object" of the naturalistic theory is "to commend things for being C" (LM 93). The object of this naturalistic theory is rather to capture the significance of ethical terms and the fact that humans can engage in a cooperative effort to discover what qualities of character are desirable and what characteristics these desirable qualities have in common. Thus the Humean naturalistic definition seems also to pass Hare's second test without stumbling.

v

It is possible that Hare would want to construct a third test for our proposed Humean naturalistic definition, one which is closely related to his first test already discussed. He might want to ask how we are going to be able to determine when any particular person has become a completely informed, completely disinterested, perfectly normal spectator. Only if we have such a test are we going to be able to get definitive answers on value questions. Let me remind the reader of what I said earlier: that Hume does not concern himself with the evaluation of specific borderline cases. Consequently, in dealing with this third test, I shall again be extending Hume's definitions to deal with issues which Hume himself did not consider.

In order to extend the range of application of the Humean approach, let us say that "X is *good*" or "X is *right*" or "X *ought* to be done" is equivalent to saying "X would arouse the sentiment of approbation in an informed, disinterested, not abnormal spectator." Then let us note the implications of this definition for that issue which is of central concern to Stevenson and which lies in the background of Hare's anti-naturalistic statements: namely, the issue of resolving disagreement on value-issues. The need to be able to determine when a given person is completely informed, completely disinterested, and perfectly normal is motivated by the desire to get a *decisive* answer to evaluative issues, the kind of answer for which we feel a special need when there is disagreement. But our Humean definition is not going to be able to meet this demand. All I can do is to show that the fact that it cannot meet this demand does not make it useless. Furthermore, the fact that the Humean definition cannot meet such a demand is actually an asset rather than a liability.

First, even though we cannot determine *exactly* when a person is completely informed, completely disinterested, and perfectly normal, we certainly can understand when one person is *better* informed than another, *more* disinterested than another, and *less* abnormal than another. This observation parallels Hare's point that "the comparative 'better than' is much easier to define than the positive" (LM 183). Consequently, even though our Humean definition cannot direct us to completely ideal persons whose judgments will settle value-issues once and for all, it does direct us toward certain persons whose judgments on value-issues are *more likely* to be correct. And it does tell us what we must do in order to *improve* our own judgments on value-issues. It also gives us a basis in analysis for doing what Stevenson's analysis fails to do, to indicate how ethical reasoning can be distinguished from other devices of persuasion (EL 139–51) and how moralists can be distinguished from propagandists on some basis other than whether one happens to agree with their conclusions or happens to like their methods of promoting their views (EL 243–52). For it follows from the Humean analysis that ethical reasoning consists either of informing the participants of relevant information or of pointing out to them ways in which they must take account of their own biases (see Part III).

In order to explain why not being able to determine when a person is completely informed, completely disinterested, and perfectly normal is an asset of this proposed definition, let me first note how a parallel problem exists for deciding in a decisive way what is true. There are, after all, factual issues where there is disagreement about what is true. Suppose we were to try to resolve such disagreements by finding some person who is "fully qualified" to render a final judgment. There would be something wrong with any view which permitted us to say that some particular individual is "fully qualified" so that if he said "p is true" he could not be mistaken. On the other hand, a definition of "fully qualified" which showed us in what direction we needed to go in order to be able more competently to decide which propositions should be called "true" would be very helpful. This sort of approach seems to be what Charles S. Peirce had in mind when he said, "The opinion which is fated to be ultimately agreed to by all who investigate, is what we mean by truth. . . ." [18] For Peirce, to be qualified to judge about what is true is to have investigated in accord with the techniques used by scientists. For him "p is true" means "p would be believed by anyone who had fully investigated the matter." This type of definition of truth was part of Peirce's fallibilism, the doctrine that any actual human judgment about what is true may turn out to be mistaken. The Humean definition for moral terms generates the same type of fallibilism with regard to ethical judgments.[19] There would be something *wrong* with any view which defines "X is good" in such a way that we could go to any actual individual at a particular moment and get a judgment from him which is infallible. Thus the failure to be able to do this on the basis of the Humean definition is an asset rather than a liability.

Still we do not want to put *too much* emphasis on the ideality of values. Peirce suggested that "true" could be used in a *second sense* to refer to what those who have most thoroughly investigated now believe.[20] In the same way the Humean could suggest that "good" or "right" or "ought" could be used in a *second sense*, not unlike the "inverted commas" use discussed by Hare (LM 124–25), to refer to what has been found to arouse approbation in those who are best informed and most disinterested. In situations where there is no disagreement about what is true or what is good, it is generally supposed that the second sense does not differ from the first or "ideal" sense of the term in question. Consequently, it is to be expected that Hume himself would not need to emphasize the distinction between the first and second senses of value-terms because he was not dealing with borderline cases where disagreement is common, but rather with paradigm cases of virtues where there would be little disagreement. Also, as I have indicated elsewhere,[21] Hume dealt with traits in general and with hypothetical situations, thus avoiding the issues of whether the spectator would be disinterested or informed. Under these circumstances it is not surprising that some interpreters of Hume such as C. D. Broad [22] and Stevenson (see Part III) would take this second sense of value-terms to be the only sense with which Hume was concerned and, consequently, would interpret him as affirming that any quality of character which is generally approved by informed persons is a virtue.

It is worth mentioning again that Hume's primary aim was to discover the general principles of morals rather than to work out a definition for moral terms which would be helpful in cases of ethical disagreement. This aim led him to concentrate his attention on those qualities of character which were generally agreed to be virtues. But I think it is unfair to Hume to take his remarks made in this context as indicating that he would say that whatever is widely accepted as virtuous *necessarily* is virtuous. His own attacks on the monkish virtues (EPM 270) and on the detrimental influence of theology on moral language (EPM 322–23) count against such an interpretation.

VI

In fact the notion of monkish virtues ("celibacy, fasting, penance, mortification, self-denial, humility, silence, solitude") which are "everywhere rejected by men of sense" and thus deserve to be placed "in the catalogue of vices" (EPM 270) raises an interesting problem for Hume. If "virtue" means "any quality of character which arouses approbation in an informed, disinterested spectator," and if the monkish virtues do not arouse such approbation, how did they ever come to be called "virtues"? Hume does not address himself to this problem. Nevertheless I think it is fairly easy to figure out what he should have said and that, furthermore, it would have been a desirable addition to his theory if he had said it.

Remember that for Hume virtues consist of qualities of character which are useful or agreeable to oneself or to others. It is not likely that anyone will make a mistake concerning whether a given quality of character is *agreeable* to oneself or to others, the only danger here being that a person's own feelings might somehow be overcome by social conditioning so that he believes that he likes what he really dislikes or that he dislikes what he really likes. But with utility a different situation exists. Utility refers to usefulness for some good end, and there may well be some disagreement about whether a certain goal is desirable. For example, suppose someone truly believes the "superstition" (as Hume calls it [EPM 270]) that there is a life after death which is especially blessed for those who during their earthly life have denied themselves the pleasures of sex, eating, companionship, and so on. Under those conditions the "monkish virtues" would be viewed as useful. That is why they would be considered virtues.

What Hume needs to do, then, is to recognize that one must distinguish between traits of character which truly are virtues and traits of character which are *believed* to be virtues. A little more disinterestedness on Hume's part might well have led him to be a bit more sceptical about his own naturalistic metaphysical beliefs and to see that, except in the case of an omniscient spectator, it would be necessary to limit oneself to what *seems* to be a virtue, *given his own view of the nature of reality*. What we *think* is a virtue depends on what arouses our approbation, which in turn depends on our *beliefs* about what is useful and agreeable. And our beliefs about utility (and perhaps even to some extent in the case of our beliefs about agreeableness) depend in turn on our beliefs about the nature of reality.[23] Such a modified version of Hume's view might find adherents even among those who do not accept his anti-supernaturalistic metaphysical views. Such a modified version would also be in line with the common-sense recognition that a person's ethical views usually are grounded in certain metaphysical views. Hume's general principle that virtues are related to utility and agreeableness from the point of view of a spectator would be preserved, but one would no longer feel bound to accept Hume's own metaphysical views as a basis for what is useful.

VII

In this essay I hope to have shown that David Hume's views on ethics written in the eighteenth century have much relevance for the language-oriented ethical theories of the twentieth century. Some of the more important points are: (1) Both Stevenson and Hare point to Hume as an ethical theorist who is like them in the issues with which he deals and the views which he advocates. (2) Hume's ethical theory shows a sensitivity to linguistic matters such as verbal disputes and emotive or evaluative meaning. (3) In contrast to Stevenson's analysis of moral terms, Hume notes that such terms must reflect a general point of view rather than a personal point of view and that consequently there is a necessary connection between moral language and the notion of promoting the general welfare. (4) In response to Hare's point that any naturalistic definition necessarily fails to convey the commending function of value-expressions, the Humean can show that his own definition is itself commendatory, so no additional device for commending is required. (5) Hume claims that the only way we can move from "is" to "ought" is through human sentiments and interests. Consequently, Hare's challenge to the naturalist to show how to make this move can be met if it is interpreted as a challenge to provide a naturalistic definition all the terms of which can be defined by means of descriptive criteria; but Hare's challenge is illegitimate if it is interpreted as a challenge to provide a naturalistic definition all the terms of which lack even some implicit evaluative meaning. (6) The Humean definition for value-expressions cannot be used to settle ethical disputes in a completely decisive way; nevertheless, it is useful in giving us guidance concerning how to go about resolving such disputes. Furthermore, the fact that it cannot be used to settle such disputes in a completely decisive way is an asset rather than a liability because any definition which could provide decisive settlements would by virtue of that very fact be incorrect. (7) The fact that the monkish virtues are called "virtues" even when Hume feels they are not useful or agreeable suggests that he could have improved the statement of his theory if he had expressed it in terms of a link between what is *believed* to be a virtue and what is *believed* to be useful and agreeable rather than in terms of what *is* a virtue and what *is* useful and agreeable.

Because of the relevance of Hume's views to the issues of contemporary ethics I believe that what he has to say about morals will come in for even more attention in the years ahead. And that is a development which, in view of the direction of Hume's own philosophical interests, would make him very happy.

NOTES

1. C. L. Stevenson, *Ethics and Language* (New Haven, 1944); hereafter referred to as EL.

2. R. M. Hare, *The Language of Morals* (New York, 1964); hereafter referred to as LM. This book was originally published in England in 1952.

3. In his later book *Freedom and Reason* (New York, 1965)—hereafter referred to as

FR—Hare says: "I have been in the past, and still am, a stout defender of Hume's doctrine that one cannot deduce moral judgments from non-moral statements of fact . . ." (FR 186).

4. See my "The Nature of Hume's Ethics," *Philosophy and Phenomenological Research*, 27 (1966–67), 527–36; repr. in *Philosophy Today*, No. 3, ed. J. H. Gill (London, 1970), pp. 197–211.

5. C. L. Stevenson, "The Emotive Meaning of Ethical Terms," *Mind*, 62, N.S. 46 (1937), 25.

6. See ibid., 26.

7. C. L. Stevenson, "The Emotive Conception of Ethics and Its Cognitive Implications," *Philosophical Review*, 59, No. 3 (July 1950), 294.

8. See my "A Dilemma for Stevenson's Ethical Theory," *Journal of Philosophy*, 59, No. 17 (August 16, 1962), 459–63.

9. Although Stevenson takes note of the fact that for Hume approbation is very different from other attitudes and that it is to be contrasted with self-love (EL 275n49), he still does not see the consequences of this fact for the analysis of moral language. His concern seems to be with the problem of persuading someone to act in accord with the moral point of view rather than with the need to adopt a disinterested point of view when making moral judgments.

10. R. M. Hare, "Universalisability," *Proceedings of the Aristotelian Society*, 55 (1954–55), 303.

11. A collection of several of the more important articles in this controversy is contained in *The Is/Ought Question*, ed. W. D. Hudson (London, 1969).

12. See my "Nature of Hume's Ethics."

13. Hare himself seems to be aware of the fact that moral terms appeal to "a principle that is in some sense there already" (LM 195) and do not reflect merely the speaker's own view of the situation. But Hare wants to explain this phenomenon on the basis of "the descriptive force which moral judgements acquire, through the general acceptance of the principles on which they rest . . ." (ibid.). Such an explanation fails to account for what is happening when an individual is trying to *discover* what he *ought* to do in a given situation: he is trying to determine not what has been approved or even what he himself approves but what a qualified spectator would approve. See my " 'Good,' 'Doog,' and Naturalism in Ethics," *Philosophy and Phenomenological Research*, 34 (1973–74), 437–49.

14. Although Hare indicates his agreement with Hume's view that a good act is an act which is indicative of the goodness of the person doing it and that we "talk about good men and good acts in a context of moral education and character-formation" (LM 186), still his primary concern about moral language is with regard to guiding conduct (LM 1).

15. For a similar and more extended effort to give criteria for a similar definition, see Roderick Firth, "Ethical Absolutism and the Ideal Observer," *Philosophy and Phenomenological Research*, 12 (1951–52), 317–45; repr. in *Readings in Ethical Theory*, edd. Wilfred Sellars and John Hospers, 2d ed. (New York, 1970), pp. 200–21. See also Firth's exchange with Richard Brandt concerning this matter: Richard B. Brandt, "The Definition of an 'Ideal Observer' Theory in Ethics," *Philosophy and Phenomenological Research*, 15 (1954–55), 407–13, and Roderick Firth, "Reply to Professor Brandt," ibid., 414–21.

16. Again, see my " 'Good,' 'Doog,' and Naturalism in Ethics."

17. Hare, like Hume, recognizes that the moral judgments which people make depend on "the desires and inclinations of the human race" (FR 195). But, unlike Hume, Hare insists that these desires and inclinations cannot become incapsulated into the very meanings of moral terms. Why not? Because, according to Hare, moral language can never logically compel us to make certain evaluations. But, the Humean replies, if someone admits that action A would be approved by an informed, disinterested spectator, then he would be logically compelled to say that action A is good. Moral language *by itself* cannot compel us to make certain evaluations, but certain facts plus the meanings of moral terms *can*. Furthermore, says the Humean, the facts in this kind of situation must be facts about or relevant to human sentiments.

18. *Pragmatism and Pragmaticism*, edd. Charles Hartshorne and Paul Weiss, *Collected

Papers of Charles Sanders Peirce v (Cambridge, Mass., 1934), 5.407. See also 5.408, 5.557, and 5.565. Peirce himself discusses the application of his principle to "the normative sciences" in 5.566.

19. It is of some interest to note that Peirce also said that "Esthetic good and evil . . . are what would be pleasure or pain to the fully developed superman" (ibid., 5.552).

20. See Justus Buchler, *Charles Peirce's Empiricism* (New York, 1939), pp. 72–74, 144–49.

21. "Nature of Hume's Ethics," 534; in *Philosophy Today*, ed. Gill, p. 208.

22. See C. D. Broad, *Five Types of Ethical Theory* (New York, 1930).

23. In *A Dialogue*, which is appended in the Selby-Bigge edition of the *Enquiries* (EPM 324–43), Hume recognizes that "Sometimes men differ in their judgment about the usefulness of any habit or action . . ." (EPM 336). Consequently, it may be that Hume did in fact maintain that what is believed to be a virtue is what is believed to be useful or agreeable. The only problem then is that the tolerance Hume displays toward Athenians, Frenchmen, and others in the *Dialogue* never gets extended to Christian "superstition."

VI

18

Hume and Jefferson on the Uses of History

CRAIG WALTON
University of Nevada
Las Vegas

IN 1775 DAVID HUME REJECTED THE REQUEST of the Baron Mure of Caldwell that he draft an appeal for greater discipline of the American colonies, countering that ". . . I am an American in my Principles, and wish we woud let them alone to govern or misgovern themselves as they think proper . . ." (LDH II 303).[1] Douglass Adair has shown that the Framers thought it proper to make Hume's principles fundamental to the structure of the new Constitution, and that Madison forged the tenth *Federalist* by close study of Hume's political essays. The theory of "interests" and the checking and balancing of "factions" through the division of powers are Humean contributions to Enlightenment "political science" vital to the American fathers.[2] Hume's works had begun to be available in the colonies at least as early as 1753 (*Political Discourses*),[3] the *History of England* as published,[4] *My Own Life* in 1778, the *Treatise* at least by 1790,[5] and an American edition of the *Works* by 1817.[6] Most widely read and cited, of course, were the *Essays Moral and Political and Literary*, of which numerous editions and selections appeared both in book form and in gazettes.[7]

Thomas Jefferson bought Hume's *History* for the first time in 1764, and when his library burned in 1770, he replaced the set.[8] In this period he lent Patrick Henry the two-volume Hume *Essays*,[9] and repurchased that set for his own library after each of two fires. Yet by 1807 Jefferson's admiration for Hume had changed to the most horrified disapproval, and this change gave rise to one of the darkest and most puzzling efforts at thought control and censorship to be disclosed in the life of America's first renowned "champion of the free mind." While he was still in the White House, Jefferson began coaxing publishers to bring out John Baxter's *A New and Impartial History of England* to replace Hume's, and at least until 1824 Jefferson sought to install this "editic expurgation" [10] as the official English history for use at the University of Virginia. Fortunately, all these efforts failed. But what had prompted them in the first place?

Apparently the cause of Jefferson's extensive efforts to stop the reading of

Hume's *History* was his apprehension that the infant republic was in grave danger, and that part of that danger was conspiratorial "toryism." The future of the republic would hinge on popular belief in historical precedent for republicanism and for popular sovereignty, such as was argued by the great Whig historians. After he returned from his ambassadorial duties in Paris in 1790, Jefferson increasingly encountered what he believed to be a new, "American toryism" threatening to establish the same corruption and privilege his French patriot friends were just then defeating. By contrast, Baxter had been tried at Old Bailey in 1794 as a member of the London Corresponding Society, and he thereby acquired excellent radical democrat credentials. After his acquittal, Baxter took up his pen to establish a "true" historical case for liberty and parliamentary reform. Jefferson had purchased Baxter's expurgation of Hume in 1805, and by 1807 he saw antidemocratic "factions" so virulent in New York and in England that he decided a cutting off of Hume's *History* would be one good halt to further decay of "republican principles" here at home:

> Baxter has performed a good operation on [Hume's *History*]. He has taken the text of H[ume] as his ground work, abridging it by the omission of some details of little interest, and wherever he has found him endeavoring to mislead, by either the suppression of a truth, or by giving it a false coloring, he has changed the text to what it should be, so that we may properly call it Hume's history republicanized. . . . [If Mrs. Macauley's and a few other histories are read along with it,] a sufficient view will be presented of the free principles of the English Constitution.[11]

As controversy has increased in recent years concerning the intellectual origins of the American Revolution and of the early years of the infant republic, Jefferson's attacks on Hume have received increasing attention.[12] Arthur Bestor calls it a "painful episode," but he is confident that Jefferson's general principles of tolerance prevailed.[13] Leonard Levy goes farther, finding material for an entire volume on Jefferson's "true believer" fanaticisms, most especially his notions of "verbal political crimes." But these are seen as moral "lapses" rather than as acts indicative of a philosophical position.[14] Trevor Colbourn not only examines the attack on Hume, but studied the Baxter volume itself; yet his conclusion is that Jefferson the *philosophe* used history in a proper "ideological" manner to promote a salutary and inspiring myth, without which America might have suffered the violence of the myth-less French radicals.[15] Meanwhile, the controversy over Hume's *History* is far from ended.[16] What makes the Jefferson attacks on Hume most interesting is that we are compelled to wonder whether, beneath a mound of ironies, there may lie buried some skeleton to account for how or why those ironies piled up here as they did. Did Hume the "philosophical historian" and foe of "metaphysics" violate his own philosophical logic and historical evidence in striking the balances offered in summary sections of his *History*? Did Jefferson the democrat despair of the people's ability to weather the onslaught of Hume's volumes? Was Baxter actually closer to Hume than to Jefferson? But—and this is of crucial importance— what are the deeper beliefs about human nature and the philosophic way of life from which the Hume and Jefferson positions emerge and collide? Recently Peter Gay has argued that, despite all differences, there is a "family" of traits characterizing one genus of Enlightenment man. He cites Hume as perhaps the single closest actual paradigm of those traits.[17] Yet something Hume took as central, his "mitigated scepticism" (EHU 161ff.; T 263ff.), was not merely peripheral to, but alien and anathema to, the *philosophes*, many American intellectuals, and, most notably, Jefferson.[18] Consequently, a study of Baxter's "editic expurgation" of Hume and of Jefferson's reasons for his campaign, followed by a consideration of Hume's philosophical–historical conclusions in the *History*, may lead to some insight beyond the "painful episode" or "moral lapse" views of Jefferson's actions. If the incident reveals two conflicting notions of the Enlightenment, warring on the common ground of the nature and use of history for purposes of life, then we must ask whether the conflict arose from deeply set and carefully developed positions. If so, suggestions of "lapses" or fits of pique will no longer serve as interpretations. In what follows I want to argue that Jefferson's attack on Hume, though the result in part of personal and national stress and of human fallibility, is also consistent with a particular notion of men, ideas, and their histories, and that Jefferson's position is one which Hume rejected. My theme might be caricatured as "history: *topoi* or *tropoi?*"

Little is known of John Baxter, except that after John Horne Tooke and Thomas Hardy, as leaders of the London Corresponding Society, were acquitted of charges of high treason, Baxter, a lesser officer of the Society, was also acquitted; and that when he desired to address the court, he was denied that privilege.[19] Two years later his *History* appeared in London.[20] It is largely a reprinting or paraphrasing of Hume's *History*. The allegedly false statements and conclusions have been eliminated, and "truth" has been supplied. Baxter provides a new preface and some chapters on the revolutions in France and Holland, and includes Jefferson's Declaration of Independence as an appendix. Most histories, Baxter writes, are intended to deceive rather than inform, and especially is this the case with "party writers" (p. v). Though partisanship is presumably to be avoided, Baxter acknowledges the principle that "no individual or body of men, exercising power of the government, could become tyrants at once; the people can only be prevailed upon to part with their liberty by degrees, either by force, or on pretence of some necessity" (p. vi). Therefore a history of England would show when and how "liberties were invaded," and, by examples of this sort, would discover how that evil is to be prevented. What follows, in the preface and throughout, might easily be predicted. Hume's considerations for Charles I are replaced with censure, his comments on popular excesses are replaced with praises, and in general Hume is rendered a democratic republican historian. Baxter disputes a caricature of Hume concerning the present, as well: "Neither can we agree with those who say, the constitution, as it exists at present, is the height of human perfection, improved by time, and sanctioned by experience; for we have pointed out a time when it existed in much greater perfection, and had the universal suffrage of the people" (p. ix).[21]

In view of Professor Colbourn's comment that Jefferson's method is Baxter's,[22] a few examples of Baxter's method deserve notice. As to the purpose of his history, Baxter observed that although "standing armies, bastiles, and barracks" have walled the people off from each other, and government chooses to prevent "public discussion, and dissolve popular societies," still a redress of grievances may be achieved by writing and reading history: "It is the duty of every true born Englishman, to read and imbibe the principles of his most worthy ancestors," and then to propagate these principles by word of mouth (p. x). A history, then, should supply truth where government will not and open meetings cannot (because forbidden).

Concerning the popular element in ancient Saxon councils, Baxter tacitly admits Hume's point, though censoring it, and finding it to be unimportant. True, the records are lost, and we do not know the social or economic status of our ancestral popular councillors, but the lack of records is no bar to a conclusion, because people do not willingly give up a right they once had. The Normans must have destroyed the records. "We are therefore obliged to reason from analogy, and the imperfect records which remain. From these it appears, the *people* were *represented* in the Wittena-gemote, by persons chosen by themselves . . ." (p. 74). If history cannot complete the reformers' case, *a priori* argument as to human nature and political principles supplies the gaps. This "method" recurs in Baxter. On the Magna Carta, Baxter alludes to Hume's (censored) appendix two concerning its sections sixteen and seventeen (on representation), and tries to refute Hume in that, though Hume is correct that no reference is made there to a commons, still section seventeen names earls, barons, and so on. "There is some ambiguity in the sixteenth article" (p. 134), but still "nothing is more incontestable that there was provision for [a commons'] attendance." On the controversy over Strafford's trial, Baxter sees Hume as wrongly lamenting the legal device used there since, even though there was no statute for crimes against the "rights of the people," there should be! Hence, punishment was justified (p. 425).

Either as a pang of conscience or as illustrative of his "method" in history, Baxter had noted that since the Magna Carta was based on a feudal order, it is not really a model for today (this from Hume). Its rules for securing liberty and happiness are so vague, he continues, that "it is not from them, but the common rights of mankind, and the customs of the Anglo-Saxons, that Englishmen must deduce their constitution and their liberties" (p. 134). Baxter does not indicate how we could discover those customs without evidence, though he may mean for us to do it by "analogy."

But then, turning sharply away from the Saxon *vs.* Norman "origins" controversy, Baxter argues that in fact the present constitution owes its "radical *rottenness* and *mischievous effects*" to the "ancient and glorious constitution" (p. 194), in that today's "trading interests" are deceived into believing they are represented, while "landed" interests prey upon them economically and by government control. To overcome this sort of present, and the past which produced it, a new theory of representation must be offered, "fair and equal," a universal suffrage but one guided by "the most intelligent part of the people" in instructing elected representatives and in "obliging" them to obey instructions or be recalled (p. 193). No historical precedent is claimed for radical democratic republicanism. But Baxter does note that Cromwell's commonwealth is not a counter-instance, for it was impure and, in fact, a military "tyranny" (p. 485).

After discussing Henry VIII, Baxter adds to the Hume text his own argument for religious toleration, one which might well have struck Jefferson since it so resembles his own: "Good government has nothing to do with speculations in theology; it ought only to distinguish between the good and the bad citizen, by cherishing virtue and punishing vice, but leave him to worship his Creator according to the dictates of his conscience, without prohibition or limitation" (p. 294).

Finally, after applauding the American Revolution and identifying George III as either weak or wicked, Baxter praises the Declaration of Independence as full of "great and useful principles of politics"; since "it would be inexcusable to withhold it from public observation" (p. 789), the text is appended.

In 1810, Jefferson wrote to the publisher William Duane that "when young" he had read Hume's *History* with enthusiasm; only a long purge of "research and reflection" has relieved him of its "poison." "It is this book which has undermined free principles of the English government, has persuaded readers of all classes that there were usurpations on the legitimate and salutary rights of the crown, and has spread universal toryism over the land. And the book will still continue to be read here as well as there [in England]. . . ." [23] "This single book," he told John Adams, "has done more to sap the free principles of the English Constitution than the largest standing army. . . . Hume has concentrated . . . all the arbitrary proceedings of the English Kings, as true evidences of the Constitution, and glided over its Whig principles as the unfounded pretensions of factious demagogues." [24] In an 1824 entry in his *Commonplace Books*, Jefferson is still preoccupied with Hume and Baxter. He lists eight places in Hume's *History*, presumably the most offending passages: note AA to ch. 42; ch. 53; note GG to ch. 56; ch. 57; ch. 59 that revolutions rarely benefit the people; ch. 59 that popular sovereignty is of "specious" lineage; ch. 59 that obedience alone needs to be inculcated, and ch. 61 on Cromwell. Jefferson's comment to the list (or indictment?): "In a debate in the H[ouse] of Commons Mar. 23. 24 Sᵣ James McIntosh quotes Burke as having said in some speech, 'I believe we shall all come to think, at last, with Mr. Hume, that an absolute monarchy is not so bad a thing as we supposed.' *The Globe*. Mar. 24. 1824." [25]

Jefferson's attacks are difficult to sort. At one point he seems to find toryism in Hume where Whig principles would be closer to truth. But then he favors Baxter who overthrows Whig *and* Tory appeals to precedent by arguing a natural and universal right of suffrage and representation. Again, Jefferson attacks Hume for doubting the Whig precedent, but endorses Baxter who opposes any past ("rotten") tie to the present and would reform whatever of the Whig precedent England did have (because illusory, a false representation). Jefferson apparently sees Hume in error about the chances of popular excesses, yet he himself deplored the "terror" in France. He scores Hume for the view that rights of rebellion need not be taught, though duties of obedience should, but he went far beyond Hume toward repression by acquiescing to the Alien and Sedition Acts while Madison fought them.[26] Perhaps it is most ironic of all that he focuses on Hume's judicious verdict on Charles I as evidence of anti-republican sentiment, although that same verdict, *mutatis mutandis*, might be applied to Jefferson's own presidency, with his use of embargo, censorship, and strong state power to save the republic as he knew it and to combat political dissent as he saw it threatening.

Another ironic aspect of the attack on Hume reveals still another dimension to our story. In a letter to Peter Carr in 1787, Jefferson expresses two philosophic principles of considerable bearing. First, he argues (with Destutt de Tracy) that there is no philosophical science of ethics, for if God had so intended, most men would never acquire a "sense of right and wrong" at all; yet they do. That "sense," then, is a natural endowment, not a construction of reason, and is "as much a part of man's nature, as the sense of hearing. . . . It may be strengthened by exercise, as may any particular limb of the body." [27] Reason is able to guide it, but very little reason is needed— less than we need to have "common sense." In fact, a "plowman" would probably resolve a moral case more soundly than a "professor," since the latter's mind will be "led astray by artificial rules." But, secondly, Jefferson also argues in the same letter that Carr should "fix reason firmly in her seat" concerning religion in order to avoid "the fears and servile prejudices, under which weak minds are servilely crouched." He does not explain why such prejudices cannot be combatted by "moral sense" alone, or (alternatively) what is to happen to those with insufficient "artificial rules" here where "nature" has made no provisions. Rather, Jefferson goes on to fix a rule for judging what to believe about religions—and it is Hume's rule, almost *verbatim* from the essay "On Miracles"! "Examine upon what evidence [a writer's] pretensions are founded, and whether that evidence is so strong, as that its falsehood would be more improbable than a change in the laws of nature, in the case he relates. . . . [Finally, y]our own reason is the only oracle given you by heaven, and you are answerable, not for the rightness, but uprightness of the decision." [28] Apparently the dangers of religious "fears and prejudices" cannot be avoided unless reason is "firmly in her seat," but natural endowments and experience can avoid dangers of false moral beliefs. Many writers suggest Jefferson backed away from the "natural rights" doctrine after the Revolutionary War, but he seems to have retained (or acquired) the "moral sense" doctrine at least into the period of the attack on Hume. Jefferson's Humean rule of proportioning belief to evidence and of always accepting the "lesser" miracle, is of special interest to us here. For, according to Hume, this "general rule" or artifice of reason holds as much for the study of secular or moral history as it does for alleged or veridical religious histories. It is a rule for assessment of any testimony whatever, and is so treated in the *History of England*. But, for example, though Jefferson rejected Hume's conclusion that revolutions rarely benefit the people and normally simply change the identities of the rulers, neither Jefferson nor Baxter offers a preponderance of evidence for his optimism.

Further ironies deserve to be noted. Either unknown to, or unrecognized by, Jefferson, Hume had taken a number of positions quite close to Jefferson's own. Though in the *History* he considered utopian writing the pursuit of a "chimera," [29] Hume wrote such a utopian essay in which he opted for a republic formed by "hundreds" remarkably similar to Jefferson's republic by "wards" (*Essays* 499–515).[30] As early as the *Treatise*, Hume argued the right of rebellion whenever government failed to preserve the public interest. And he made this *especially* applicable to countries with constitutional government, since there one would find fewer excuses for claims to obedience by virtue of possession or custom (T 563–67). Again, Adrienne Koch has noted that although Jefferson never developed a socialist theory of political economy, he did read the French socialist Mably and seemed sympathetic to an egalitarian approach to economic justice.[31] Yet as Marshall notes, Jeremy Bentham found Hume's treatment of justice in the *Treatise* to be perhaps the first time the case for a political economy of "the people" had been stated in terms of fundamental human needs and interests primitive to any subsequent governmental arrangement.[32] Again, as was true for Jefferson, Hume placed his hopes for improvement of the human condition, not upon some form of government or system of institutions, but upon the condition of education, laws, arts and sciences, and enlightened individual judgment (*The Federalist Papers*, No. 84, concludes with a long quote from Hume to this effect). Finally, on the matter of myth, Hume remarks, in a letter to Turgot, that though evidence does not reinforce belief in an ancient precedent for the principles of popular sovereignty, it would be to the good if such were the case, because the "Incitement" gained would strengthen the forces of liberty (LDH II 181). While we cannot conclude that Hume presented a full appreciation of the uses and abuses of myth as a social force, he did write a utopian plan in spite of its "chimerical" quality, and realized the value of the Whig "ancient origins" doctrine even though it, too, was a myth. He did not consider his own *History* to be myth in this sense, and apparently endeavored not to mix the two; but he gives myth some stature.[33]

If Jefferson's attack on Hume's *History* is not merely a "painful episode" or a moral "lapse," and if it cannot be understood as the straightforward collision of a democratic republican with an authoritarian monarchist, one further avenue remains to be explored. This is the examination of Jefferson's philosophical theories of human knowledge and of man's nature as adapted from Destutt de Tracy, and then as contrasted with Hume's.[34] Jefferson labored long and hard to translate and publish works of de Tracy, corresponded with him, and sang his praises to many correspondents. De Tracy's school of "Ideology" was founded in 1796 as *L'Institut National*, where philosophy was "the science of methods" (p. 72). De Tracy argues for a biological foundation for all feelings, and thence for all "ideas" as experiences of feeling, and he condemned Hume as too sceptical and Locke as too sensationalistic (pp. 65–79). His basic unit of judgment is a proposition, not a term or an "idea," for knowledge begins with a "grouped judg-mental action" rather than with isolated sense data.[35] Since thought and feeling are initially one whole and responsive experience, languages ex-pressing experience suggest a range of thought and actions from the least to the most sophisticated. Jefferson's study of ancient Saxon dialects and of more than thirty American Indian dialects is in accord with the scholarly interests of de Tracy's "ideological" program. In these and other empirical investigations, Jefferson shows a considerable sceptical reserve *as method*, as did Dugald Stewart and de Tracy. But, again in their manner, he rejected Hume's "pyrrhonism" [36] because, as Dugald Stewart had put it, we need a scientific basis for action which is reasonable, not merely Hume's "custom" (p. 102). Adrienne Koch notes that Jefferson's references to resting on " 'the pillow of ignorance' when confronted with questions which exceeded human knowledge at the time, may reveal a constitutional unwillingness to remain long in the sphere of sceptical doubt" (pp. 102–103, note 31).

But reference to a "constitutional unwillingness" is, at least to readers of Hume, a begging of the question. For in the manner of Pyrrho, Montaigne, Pascal, and Bayle before him, Hume admits it to be a constitutional (or "natural") propensity of all men to resolve doubts at the practical level and to "believe" when imperatives of survival or civility become pressing. It was not that Hume found his doubts "constitutionally" easy to manage, but that he saw the need for developing by philosophical art an ability to endure them long enough to discern how reason might (in Jefferson's phrase) be "fixed firmly in her seat," before beginning the rough ride of practical com-mitment to some course of action. That ability is a philosophical excellence, not a natural trait. Hume's question was never that of the (unmitigated) "rightness" or "wrongness" of the choice to be made, but rather (in Jeffer-son's phrase) the "uprightness" which would separate the "mitigated" sceptic from the (affirming or denying) "dogmatist." Time after time, Hume's philo-sophical dialectic distinguished and evaluated positive and negative instances until as much illusion and self-deception could be closely examined as he had the talents and reach to accommodate. No judgment of beliefs could be made "safely," free from the tensions of paradox, ambiguity, or partiality. But, more than that, Hume often indicated that at the peak of the suspen-sion of judgment regarding a particular issue, the general field within which these tensions are generated *could* be recognized by philosophic man to such an extent that wherever his experience might move him when time for action arrived, it would be taken in a temperate and modulated manner. Moral excellence and philosophic excellence sustain each other. A separate study would be required to illustrate this view in the *Treatise, Enquiries, Dialogues*, and *Essays*. But present purposes justify illustrations from his *History of England*.

Reflecting on the overthrow of James I, Hume observed that lovers of liberty acted as they did, not because of harsh tyranny (for men had borne that before), but because the tyranny was founded on arbitrary and danger-ous principles. Consequently, "the wise and moderate" tried to see both sides. The people were divided, and civil war was coming. Both sides would be to blame. Faced with these realizations, "the good and virtuous would scarcely know what views to form; were it not that liberty, so necessary to the perfection of human society, would be sufficient to bias their affections towards the side of its defenders." [37] However, the revolution of 1688 decided "many important questions in favor of liberty; . . . it gave such an ascendant to popular principles, as put the nature of the English constitution beyond all controversy," such that if England's is not now the best system of *government*, it is "at least the most entire system of liberty that ever was known amongst mankind." [38] With this shift in the balance toward liberty and away from "established government," however, new difficulties have arisen, chiefly the corruption among the Whigs and their party operatives, to the point where public offices and perquisites toward the arts are going to party hacks and mediocrity (a corruption reported to Jefferson by John Cartwright as a scandal to be avoided!). Hume now observes, "on forgetting that a regard to liberty, though a laudable passion, ought commonly to be subordinate to a reverence for established government,[39] the prevailing faction has celebrated only the partisans of the former, who pursued as their object the perfections of civil society, and has extolled them at the expense of their antagonist, who maintained those maxims that are essential to its very existence. But extremes of all kinds are to be avoided; and though no one will ever please either faction by moderate opinions, it is there we are most likely to meet with truth and certainty." [40] No matter which party governs, Hume's lifelong focus on the "balance" of the public interest, and hence the balance between government and the culture, require a fundamental civility to all vital claims. Those who claim priority for the "existence" of the government, its survival, will often oppose those emphasizing its "perfection"; but a wise governor will realize this tension to be vital, and will moderate his own partisanship toward the end of public well-being. He cannot avoid his own limits and inclinations, his own partisanship, but a "mitigated scepticism" would enable him so to moderate them as neither to corrupt his own followers nor to alienate his opposition. Either of these latter "extremities" weakens the "constitution." Real value differences are both predictable and salutary to the vitality of the people, their government, and their culture. Stewart has argued that the *History* was intended to reduce Whig–Tory animus, by showing each side's anachronisms, and to show each that "because of the mixed, and therefore uncertain constitution, the other party had a part to play in contemporary politics, and that each should play its part with sedate restraint so as not to endanger that fabric of vulgar opinion of which the constitution was chiefly composed." [41] In the *History* as in other works, Hume's philosophical dialectic sometimes arrives at fundamental differences no longer beclouded with deception or fallacious argument. When he reaches those differences, Hume strives to moderate and civilize their inevitable interplay rather than to suppress one or more. It is his philosophical wisdom which led Whigs to see him as "Tory," and Tories as "Whig."

Hume concluded the final volume of this work by noting that history affords only slight positive assistance from the past, and teaches us to expect little latitude for human wisdom in the future:

> A civilized nation . . . ought to be cautious in appealing to the practice of their ancestors, or regarding the maxims of uncultivated ages as certain rules for their present conduct. Any acquaintance with the ancient period of their government is chiefly *useful*, by instructing them to cherish their present constitution, . . . and it is also *curious*, by showing them the remote and commonly faint and disfigured originals of the most finished and most noble institutions, and by instructing them in the great mixture of accident, which commonly concurs with a small ingredient of wisdom and foresight, in erecting the complicated fabric of the most perfect government.[42]

Stewart has considered these sorts of observations in Hume to be "antihistorical," [43] but it seems difficult so to separate the philosophical from the historical. For the greater part, Hume's "lessons" or *obiter dicta* seem to be consistent with his more philosophical writings.[44] David Norton has argued that Hume is as much an historical philosopher as he is philosophical historian.[45] But, Norton continues, is Hume not equally vulnerable in both areas, since his scepticism can only be "mitigated" by "proportioning" belief to evidence, whereas what shall count as evidence, and how it shall count, is determined by limited and fallible personal experience? Is Hume not up against a hopeless puzzle? Surely such was the judgment of Reid, Stewart, and de Tracy, all Jefferson's mentors. They saw Hume's scepticism as "pyrrhonism" by which the "customs" one accepts are literally the prevailing political and moral arrangements of one's age, whether true or false, salutary or disastrous, and no scientific data could therefore resolve such philosophical conservatism. According to Sextus Empiricus, Pyrrho claimed that we cannot know such ultimates. There is no "natural existence of anything good or bad or (in general) fit or unfit to be done," so that suspension of judgment alone is warranted and sane.[46] Jefferson takes Hume's use of "custom" to be Pyrrhonian, from which the case for Hume as apologist for the *status quo* seems to follow.

Yet whether or not Hume succeeded in revising Pyrrho and Sextus, such was his attempt; his notion of "custom" is not theirs. For, in Hume, that word is a synonym for "the principle of belief," whose natural operation can never be halted for long. But its operation can be studied by reflection and dialectical inquiry, until enough suspension can be achieved through *tropoi*, to offer some distance from which to begin taking perspective and doing the needed "proportioning." There is little reason can do; but that little makes the difference we are able to make; it is the difference between "dogmatism" and moderation. Hume's "experience" is not merely "personal," for the entire process of moral and intellectual development is interpersonal and cultural, from top to bottom. Especially in the *History*, the experience on which he reflects and by which he reaches his "lessons" or *obiter dicta* are, for better or worse, offered on a basis of common (informed and criticized) English experience. In his "anonymous" review of his own "still-born" *Treatise*, Hume wrote:

AND as there is often a constant conjunction of the actions of the will with their motives, so the inference from the one to the other is often as certain as any reasoning concerning bodies: and there is always an inference proportioned to the constancy of the conjunction. On this is founded our belief in witnesses, our credit in history and indeed all kinds of moral evidence, and almost the whole conduct of life [A 30–31].

Hume's notion of the status of evidence, "our credit" in history, of its uses as both *topoi* and *tropoi*, its lessons for the "proportioning" of our lives as philosophic men, all require further study and criticism. But Jefferson and others sharing his notion of Enlightenment have made up their minds. As Lawrence Bongie tells it, the counter-revolution in France developed enthusiasm for some of Hume's doubts about popular excesses, and began to use those aspects of his *History* for rightist (and others even for moderate left) purposes.[47] Concomitantly "le Bon David" was abandoned by the *philosophes*. Such was the quickness of this shift, and such its severity, that by 1800 J. E. M. Portalis concluded that the Enlightenment of the *philosophes* had rejected religious superstitions only to replace them with modern political ones. Portalis specifically cited the two doctrines that any political act for "liberty" is good, and that history is to be made over into political propaganda.[48] Americans, and probably Jefferson, knew Baxter was reported to be a Jacobin, and that Hume was being used by the French right. And it is at just this time (1805) that Jefferson bought his copy of Baxter and began the attack on Hume's *History*. The doctrines of Reid, Stewart, and de Tracy provided the "method" for overcoming Hume's alleged "Pyrrhonism." Baxter provided the remedy for Hume's alleged "universal toryism"; the borrowing of Humean principles of 1787 is long forgotten. We might conjecture the same fate eventually befell Hume in Jefferson's mind, as Richard Popkin notices among the French *philosophes*: Hume's "fundamental challenge to human intellectual security and peace of mind," was rejected. "What was to be done was to discover, within the limits Locke [and, here, de Tracy] had prescribed, and with the method Newton used, what man could know about himself and nature, and to employ this knowledge to reform society, liberate man, and tame the future." [49] It is not that Jefferson's Enlightenment was naïvely optimistic; his great faith in the people had been shaken, though not broken, by their hearkening after "American tories." Nor was his ideology unchecked by any scholarly habits, for he continued careful research in areas of interest to him. But as Trevor Colbourn details, Jefferson held that in the writing and study of history for practical philosophical application one could be both scholarly *and* partisan.[50] Jefferson would utilize some histories for the *topoi* they supply to current argument, and condemn other histories which counter or question the former. Though he boosted Baxter and attacked Hume in this way, he apparently did not realize the folly of Baxter's eventual decision that history is of very slight use here anyway since the key issues are "natural" truths. To suggest that Jefferson's "method" here was Baxter's is of little help when Baxter claims and then abandons two distinct positions in sequence, only to settle on a third lacking entirely in "method." [51]

The saga of Jefferson, Baxter, and Hume is particularly poignant in view of the ironies that Baxter and Jefferson were championing the radical democratic republican "eighteenth-century commonwealthman's" views which Hume had shared before them. If we agree with all three that no institutional reforms can supply hope where civic virtue in the people is absent, that foundations for liberty and law must be laid in accordance with man's nature if his artifice is to endure, and that even some role for myth may be necessary to vitalize civic reform, at least one question remains: must the non-rational, the non-controllable, and the accidental in man be explained away before civilization can be reconstructed, or can they be admitted and "mitigated"? Hume's *tropoi* in the *History* confront both irreducible value differences between men, and non-rational or non-controllable features in all of history.[52] Baxter and Jefferson seek to use history as the great empirical commonplace-book of a people, as would Hume, but without the paradox, accidents, real value differences, and non-rational elements he confronted and retained (at the expense of a "system").[53] They could use philosophy as "method"; they could not see it as the art of dialectical search for a human wisdom never secure. Finally, there seems some relationship, perhaps connection between their notions of history and philosophy on the one hand, and their characterization of those they opposed as enemies of the party of mankind, and of some kinds of political thoughts as intolerable (irrespective of deeds). It seems especially important today to discover, if we can, whether the "lamp of experience" can guide us away from such civic vices as those, and whether our present wide varieties of parties and cultures can retain real differences yet be "mitigated" by artfully fashioning civil ways of co-existence.[54]

NOTES

1. An earlier version of this paper was published in *Philosophy and the Civilizing Arts: Essays Presented to Herbert W. Schneider on His Eightieth Birthday*, edd. Craig Walton and John P. Anton (Athens, O., 1975), pp. 103–25. I am grateful to Professor Ernest Campbell Mossner for pointing out several errors in that version.

2. Douglass Adair, " 'That Politics May Be Reduced to a Science': David Hume, James Madison, and the Tenth *Federalist*," *Huntington Library Quarterly*, 20 (1956–57), 343–60; this essay has been included, in a revised version, as chap. 19 of the present volume. Hume first offers his theory of balance and checking of interests in Book III, Part II, Section VII of the *Treatise* (T 534–39).

3. E. B. Braly, "The Reputation of David Hume in America" (University of Texas diss., 1955), p. 23.

4. Ibid., pp. 13ff.

5. Ibid., p. 22.

6. Ibid., pp. 13ff.

7. The *Essays Moral and Political and Literary* were published under that title until 1748. After that date, Hume included them in *Essays and Treatises on Several Subjects* (1753–6), published in four volumes. That collection was then published in a two-volume set in 1764, 1767, 1768, 1772, 1777, and so forth, and it would have been one of these latter two-volume sets which Jefferson purchased, as noted in note 9. The confusion resulting from the use of the title *Essays* for both the 1748 set and the quite expanded collection of 1753–6 and of subsequent years is a point which has frequently been overlooked by

philosophers, as I myself did in an earlier version of this paper. My thanks are due to Professor Ernest Campbell Mossner for this clarification.

8. Marie Kimball, *Jefferson: The Road to Glory—1743-1776* (New York, 1943), pp. 167, 101.

9. Phillips Russell, *Jefferson: Champion of the Free Mind* (New York, 1956), p. 16.

10. Letter to George Washington Lewis, October 25, 1825; quoted in *The Life and Selected Writings of Thomas Jefferson*, edd. Adrienne Koch and William Peden (New York, 1944), p. 726.

11. Letter to John Norvell, June 11, 1807; in *The Jefferson Cyclopedia*, ed. John P. Foley (New York & London, 1900), p. 406 (entry no. 3747).

12. Concerning the intellectual origins of the American Enlightenment era, I have drawn considerably upon Herbert W. Schneider, *A History of American Philosophy*, 2nd ed. (New York, 1963); Adrienne Koch, *Power, Morals, and the Founding Fathers* (Ithaca, 1961); Carolyn Robbins, *The Eighteenth-Century Commonwealthman* (Cambridge, Mass., 1959); Douglass G. Adair, "'Experience Must Be Our Only Guide': History, Democratic Theory, and the United States Constitution," *The Reinterpretation of Early American History: Essays in Honor of John Edwin Pomfret*, ed. R. A. Billington (San Marino, 1966), pp. 129-48; *Pamphlets of the American Revolution. I. 1750-1765*, ed. Bernard Bailyn (Cambridge, Mass., 1965), pp. viii-202; and R. M. MacIver, "The Philosophical Background of the Constitution," *Journal of Social Philosophy*, 3 (October–July 1937-38), 201-209.

13. Arthur Bestor, *Three Presidents and Their Books* (Urbana, 1955), p. 20. In his chapter on Jefferson, Bestor does not examine Baxter or Hume; nor does he discuss why Jefferson interpreted them as he did. Bestor takes the "painful episode" as an exception to Jefferson's rule of toleration, rather than as exhibiting a view of the uses of history.

14. Leonard Levy, *Jefferson and Civil Liberties: The Darker Side* (Cambridge, Mass., 1963), passim. Levy discusses Jefferson's bill of attainder against Josiah Philips, his hope for the University of Virginia as a true republican "seminary" combatting Harvard's American tories, his silence when others opposed the Alien and Sedition Acts, and his view of political dissent or opposition as conspiratorial or un-American. Levy examines the campaign to publish Baxter, but does not examine Baxter or Hume.

15. Trevor Colbourn, *The Lamp of Experience: Whig History and the Intellectual Origins of the American Revolution* (Chapel Hill, 1965). Colbourn indicates sympathy for Jefferson's views that Hume had "royalist" leanings and preferred established authority over liberty, and that history is a lamp of experience especially as it supports those myths which incite men toward bettering their condition. He argues, for example, that, although the myth of Saxon liberty has been dispelled, Jefferson and his English radical democratic predecessors used the myth to substantiate their radicalism, in such a way that less violence and greater stability resulted from their efforts than was the case with French revolutionaries of the same period, who argued without such myths (pp. 194-98). Jefferson and the English radicals before him had used history as a guide to a "perfectable future" by studying a "blemished past"; "it was Jefferson's ability to learn from and employ history for the present and future that contributed to his historical optimism" (p. 184). I am indebted to Professor Colbourn for his letters of encouragement for more than nine years and, in particular, for his help in finding a microfilm of Baxter's *History*. As he will doubtless recognize, what follows borrows from, but differs somewhat from, his valuable study.

16. See E. C. Mossner, "Was Hume a Tory Historian?" *Journal of the History of Ideas*, 2 (1941), 225-36, and "An Apology for David Hume, Historian," *PMLA*, 56 (1941), 657-90; Marjorie Grene, "Hume: Sceptic and Tory," *Journal of the History of Ideas*, 4 (1943), 338-48; Geoffrey Marshall, "David Hume and Political Scepticism," *Philosophical Quarterly*, 4, No. 16 (1954), 247-57; J. G. A. Pocock, *The Ancient Constitution and the Feudal Law* (Cambridge, 1957); H. R. Trevor-Roper, "David Hume as Historian," *The Listener*, 66 (December 18, 1961), 1103ff.; F. A. Hayek, "The Legal and Political Philosophy of David Hume," *Il Politico*, 28 (1963) (repr. in *Hume: A Collection of Critical Essays*, ed. V. C. Chappell [Garden City, 1966], pp. 335-60); Laurence L. Bongie, *David Hume: Prophet of the Counter-Revolution* (Oxford, 1965); John Benjamin Stewart, *The Moral*

and Political Philosophy of David Hume (New York, 1963), esp. chaps. 6 and 9; Richard H. Popkin, "Scepticism in the Enlightenment," *Transactions of the First International Congress on the Enlightenment* (1963), I 1321–45; *David Hume: Philosophical Historian*, edd. Richard H. Popkin and David Fate Norton (Indianapolis & New York, 1965), introductions (pp. ix–l) and bibliography on the Hume-as-historian controversy (pp. liii–lv); Constant Noble Stockton, "Hume—Historian of the English Constitution," *Eighteenth-Century Studies* 4, No. 3 (Spring 1971), 277–93.

17. Peter Gay, *The Enlightenment: An Interpretation*. I. *The Rise of Modern Paganism* (New York, 1966), "Overture," e.g., p. 13; see also "David Hume: The Complete Modern Pagan," pp. 401–19, esp. pp. 418ff.: "He was willing to live with uncertainty, with no supernatural justification, no complete explanations, no promise of permanent stability, with guides of merely probable validity. . . ."

18. See Bongie, *David Hume: Prophet*, Braly, "Reputation of David Hume," and Popkin, "Scepticism in the Enlightenment," for examples of attacks on Hume as "the Infidel," sceptic, etc.

19. *A Complete Collection of State Trials . . .*, edd. T. B. Howell and Thomas J. Howell, 33 vols. (London, 1818), XXIV 21–25; XXV 743–48.

20. *A New and Impartial History of England*. From the Most Early Period of Genuine Evidence to the Present Important and Alarming Crises; a Period Pregnant with the Fate of Empires, Kingdoms and States. . . . Including an History of the American War and Revolution, To which are added histories of the French Revolution, and the Revolution in Holland, etc. . . . interspersed with Remarks, Observations and Reflections: By which former Errors are corrected, Absurdities pointed out, fabulous Narrations expurged, Party Prejudices removed, & what has hitherto appeared obscure and doubtful authenticated from the most respectable Evidences. By JOHN BAXTER. Member of the London Corresponding Society, and one of the twelve indicted & acquitted of High Treason at the Old Bailey, assisted by several gentlemen, Distinguished Friends to Liberty & a Parliamentary Reform (London, 1796). Subsequent references appear in the text.

21. David Hume, *History of England from the Invasion of Julius Caesar to the Abdication of James the Second, 1688*, 6 vols. (Boston, 1852), II 514. This work is hereafter cited as *History*.

22. Colbourn, *Lamp of Experience*, pp. 178, 181.

23. Letter to William Duane, August 12, 1810; quoted in *Life and Selected Writings of Thomas Jefferson*, edd. Koch and Peden, p. 606.

24. Letter to John Adams, November 25, 1816; in *Jefferson Cyclopedia*, ed. Foley, entry no. 3749.

25. *The Commonplace Book of Thomas Jefferson*, intro. Gilbert Chinard (Baltimore, 1926), pp. 374–76 (entry no. 905).

26. See Levy, *Jefferson and Civil Liberties*, pp. 50–55, on John Thomson of New York, James Madison, and Tunis Wortman, all of whom argued that only deeds can count as treasonous, and compare their views with Jefferson's at the time; see also pp. 162ff.

27. Letter to Peter Carr, August 10, 1787; quoted in *Life and Selected Writings of Thomas Jefferson*, edd. Koch and Peden, pp. 429–34.

28. Ibid., pp. 432ff.; see EHU 109–31.

29. See *History* v 531–32 on Harrington and others who might write utopias: "The idea . . . of a perfect and immortal commonwealth, will always be found as chimerical as that of a perfect and immortal man."

30. Compare Hume's "hundreds" with Jefferson's "wards" as described in Adrienne Koch, *The Philosophy of Thomas Jefferson* (New York, 1943) pp. 162–65.

31. Ibid., p. 120n19.

32. Marshall, "David Hume and Political Scepticism," 250, cites Bentham's *Fragment on Government*, chap. 1, note to para. 35, on Hume's treatment of justice: "the cause of the people [is] the cause of virtue." See Book III, Part II, Sections I–III (T 477–513).

33. Hume considered "original contract" theories neither true nor false, but "philosophical fictions." See Book III, Part II, Section II of the *Treatise* (T 484–501), and, concerning Hume's wider notion of the place of "fictions" in philosophy, note Selby-Bigge's topical index, p. 662.

34. In this section, I rely on Koch's *Philosophy of Thomas Jefferson*. Additional references to her discussion appear in the text.

35. Koch notes that William James (in *Principles of Psychology*, I 247) found de Tracy's "ideology" as half-way between Lockean sensationalism and nineteenth-century "act philosophy" or voluntarism (*Philosophy of Thomas Jefferson*, p. 82n62).

36. Letter to John Adams, August 15, 1820 (in *The Writings of Thomas Jefferson*, edd. Andrew A. Lipscomb and Albert Ellery Bergh, 20 vols. [Washington, D.C. 1903], XV 275–76); cited in ibid., p. 102.

37. *History*, IV 468ff.

38. Ibid., VI 363ff.

39. The context here, and other passages (such as I 171 and II 510ff.) indicate that Hume means a reverence for government within the laws. The Whigs were the "established government," but went outside or scoffed at the laws for the sake of patronage and spoils.

40. Ibid., VI 365–66. See VI 364 for the attack on Whig corruption; see also NLDH 80–82.

41. Stewart, *Moral and Political Philosophy of David Hume*, pp. 298ff. See also Marshall, "David Hume and Political Scepticism," esp. 252–57.

42. *History*, II 154. As Jefferson said, Hume wrote the *History* "backwards": Volumes V and VI were published in 1754, III and IV in 1759; and I and II in 1762. Thus, in point of time, the conclusion to Volume II is Hume's summing-up.

43. Stewart, *Moral and Political Philosophy of David Hume*, p. 299.

44. See Stockton, "Hume—Historian of the English Constitution," 293, where Hume is considered as dropping intuitive maxims here and there, to such an extent that his *History* takes on an *a priori* cast.

45. *David Hume: Philosophical Historian*, edd. Popkin and Norton, pp. xxxii–l.

46. Sextus Empiricus, *Outlines of Pyrrhonism* 3.22, trans. R. G. Bury (London, 1933), p. 483. Sextus finds the sceptic concluding that therefore, too, there is no place for ethics in philosophy since there is nothing it could study and no method it could use to teach if it did have a subject matter. It is ironic that although the premises are the contrary of Jefferson's, the conclusion is the same: that philosophy does not study ethics.

47. See Bongie, *David Hume: Prophet*, pp. 168ff.

48. In *De l'usage et de l'abus de l'esprit philosophique durant le dix-huitième siècle* (written 1798–1800, published 1820); cited in ibid.

49. Popkin, "Scepticism in the Enlightenment," 1339.

50. Colbourn, *Lamp of Experience*, pp. 179, 181, 184, 193–98.

51. That is: (1) a nonpartisan history based on ancient evidence; then (2) characterization of what "must have happened" by "analogy" with what Baxter would have done; finally (3) urging what must be done, on humane and natural grounds, irrespective of the lack of precedent. See ibid., pp. 178, 181.

52. See Richard H. Popkin, review of George Boas's *Dominant Themes of Modern Philosophy* in *Journal of Philosophy*, 56, No. 2 (January 15, 1959), 67.

53. Jefferson's study of history did teach him that there are fundamental differences, but also that they are not equally human. Rather, for example, we find the "weakly" and corrupt *vs.* the healthy and virtuous (in a letter in 1823 to Lafayette); or (to Abigail Adams, 1804) that one natural sort fears the people as ignorant, another natural sort fears the powerful as selfish; and that history is useful chiefly to control future social programs by inculcating proper beliefs (Koch, *Philosophy of Thomas Jefferson*, pp. 122–26).

54. I should like to express my thanks to Herbert W. Schneider, Jean Faurot, James T. King, and Donald F. Koch for their discussions and close criticism of, and helpful suggestions concerning, an earlier version of this paper. At the least, they will barely recognize the present version.

19

"That Politics May Be Reduced to a Science": David Hume, James Madison, and the Tenth *Federalist*

The Late DOUGLASS ADAIR
Claremont Graduate School

IN JUNE 1783, the war for American independence being ended, General Washington addressed his once-famous circular letter to the state governors with the hopeful prophecy that if the union of the states could be preserved, the future of the republic would be both glorious and happy. "The foundation of our Empire was not laid in the gloomy age of Ignorance and Superstition," Washington pointed out,

> but at an Epocha when the rights of mankind were better understood and more clearly defined, than at any former period; the researches of the human mind after social happiness, have been carried to a great extent, the treasures of knowledge, acquired by the labours of Philosophers, Sages, and Legislators, through a long succession of years, are laid open for our use, and their collected wisdom may be happily applied in the Establishment of our forms of Government. . . . At this auspicious period, the United States came into existence as a Nation, and if their Citizens should not be completely free and happy, the fault will be intirely their own.

The optimism of General Washington's statement is manifest; the reasons he advances for this optimism, however, seem to modern Americans nearly two centuries later both odd and naïve, if not slightly un-American. For Washington here argues in favor of "the Progress of the Human Mind." Knowledge gradually acquired through "researches of the human mind" about the nature of man and government—knowledge which "the gloomy age of Ignorance and Superstition" did not have—gives Americans in 1783 the power to new-model their forms of government according to the precepts of wisdom and reason. The "philosopher" as sage and legislator,

An earlier version of this article appears in the *Huntington Library Quarterly* (20 [1956–57], 343–60); permission to reprint has been granted by the Henry E. Huntington Library and Art Gallery.

General Washington hopes, will preside over the creation and reform of American political institutions.

"Philosopher" as written here by Washington was a word with hopeful and good connotations. But this was 1783. In 1789 the French Revolution began; by 1792 "philosophy" was being equated with the guillotine, atheism, the reign of terror. Thereafter "philosopher" would be a smear-word, connoting a fuzzy-minded and dangerous social theorist—one of those impractical utopians whose foolish attempts to reform society according to a rational plan created the anarchy and social disaster of the Terror. Before his death in 1799 Washington himself came to distrust and fear the political activities of philosophers. And in time it would become fashionable both among French conservatives and among all patriotic Americans to stress the sinister new implications of the word "philosophy" added after 1789, and to credit the French philosophers with transforming the French Revolution into a "bad" revolution in contrast to the "good" non-philosophical American Revolution. But this ethical transformation of the word still lay in the future in 1783. Then "philosophy" and "philosopher" were still terms evoking optimism and hopes of the high tide of Enlightenment on both sides of the Atlantic.

Dr. Johnson in his *Dictionary* helps us understand why Washington had such high regard for philosophy as our war for independence ended. "Philosophy," according to the lexicographer, was "knowledge natural or moral"; it was "hypothesis or system upon which natural effects are explained." "To philosophize," or "play the philosopher," was "to search into nature; to enquire into the causes of effects." The synonym of "philosophy" in 1783 then was "science"; the synonym of "philosopher" would be our modern word (not coined until 1840) "scientist," "a man deep in knowledge, either moral or natural."

Bacon, Newton, and Locke were the famed trinity of representative great philosophers for Americans and all educated inhabitants of Western Europe in 1783. Francis Bacon, the earliest prophet of philosophy as a program for the advancement of learning, had preached that "Knowledge is power" and that truth discovered by reason through observation and free inquiry is as certain and as readily adapted to promote the happiness of human life, as truth communicated to mankind through God's direct revelation. Isaac Newton, "the first luminary in this bright constellation," had demonstrated that reason indeed could discover the laws of physical nature and of nature's God, while John Locke's researches into psychology and human understanding had definitely channeled inquiry toward the discovery of the immutable and universal laws of human nature. By the middle of the eighteenth century, a multitude of researchers in all the countries of Europe were seeking, in Newtonian style, to advance the bounds of knowledge in politics, economics, law, and sociology. By the middle of the century, the French judge and *philosophe* Montesquieu had produced a compendium of the behavioral sciences, cutting across all these fields in his famous study of *The Spirit of the Laws*.

However, Washington's assurance that scientific knowledge about government had already accumulated to such an extent that it could be immediately applied to the uses of "legislators" pointed less toward France than toward Scotland. There, especially in the Scottish universities, had been developed the chief centers of eighteenth-century social science research and publication in all the world. The names of Francis Hutcheson, David Hume, Adam Smith, Thomas Reid, Lord Kames, Adam Ferguson, the most prominent of the Scottish philosophers, were internationally famous. In America the treatises of these Scots, dealing with history, ethics, politics, economics, psychology, and jurisprudence in terms of "system upon which natural effects are explained," had become the standard textbooks of the colleges of the late colonial period. At Princeton, at William and Mary, at Pennsylvania, at Yale, at King's, and at Harvard, the young men who rode off to war in 1776 had been trained in the texts of Scottish social science.[1]

The Scottish system, as it had been gradually elaborated in the works of a whole generation of researchers, rested on one basic assumption, had developed its own special method, and kept to a consistent aim. The assumption was

> that there is a great uniformity among the actions of men, in all nations and ages, and that human nature remains still the same, in its principles and operations. The same motives always produce the same actions. The same events follow from the same causes. . . . Would you know the sentiments, inclinations, and course of life of the Greeks and Romans? Study well the temper and actions of the French and English . . . [EHU 83]

—thus David Hume, presenting the basis of a science of human behavior. The method of eighteenth-century social science followed from this primary assumption—it was historical–comparative synthesis. Again Hume:

> Mankind are so much the same, in all times and places, that history informs us of nothing new or strange in this particular. Its chief use is only to discover the constant and universal principles of human nature, by showing men in all varieties of circumstances and situations, and furnishing us with materials from which we may form our observations and become acquainted with the regular springs of human action and behaviour [EHU 83].

Finally, the aim of studying man's behavior in its comparative–historical manifestations was for the purpose of prediction—philosophy would aid the legislator in making correct policy decisions. Comparative–historical studies of man in society would allow the discovery of the constant and universal principle of human nature, which, in turn, would allow at least some safe predictions about the effects of legislation "almost as general and certain . . . as any which the mathematical sciences afford us" (*Essays* 14). "Politics" (and again the words are Hume's) to some degree "may be reduced to a science."

By thus translating the abstract generalizations about "philosophy" in Washington's letter of 1783 into the concrete and particular type of philosophy to which he referred, the issue is brought into new focus more congenial to our modern understanding. On reviewing the specific body of philosophical theory and writing with which Washington and his American contemporaries were familiar, we immediately remember that "the collected wisdom" of at least some of the Scottish academic philosophers was applied to American legislation during the nineteenth century. It is obvious, for example, that the "scientific predictions," based on historical analysis, contained in Professor Adam Smith's *An Inquiry into the Nature and Causes of the Wealth of Nations* (London, 1776), concerning the role of free enterprise and economic productivity, were of prime significance in shaping the relations of the state with the American business community, especially after 1828. Washington's expectations of 1783 were thus accurate in the long-run view.[2]

It is the purpose of this paper, however, to show that Washington's immediate expectations of the creative role of "philosophy" in American politics were also accurate in the period in which he wrote. It is thus the larger inference of the following essay that "philosophy," or "the science of politics" (as defined above), was integral to the whole discussion of the necessity for a *more* perfect union which resulted in the creation of the American Constitution of 1787.

It can be shown, though not in this short paper, that the use of history in the debates both in the Philadelphia Convention and in the state ratifying conventions is not mere rhetorical–historical window-dressing, concealing substantially greedy motives of class and property. The speakers were making a genuinely "scientific" attempt to discover the "constant and universal principles" of any republican government in regard to liberty, justice, and stability.

In this perspective the three hundred pages of comparative–historical research in John Adams's *Defence of the Constitutions of the United States* (1787), and the five-hour closely argued historical analysis in Alexander Hamilton's Convention Speech of June 18, 1787, were both "scientific" efforts to relate the current difficulties of the thirteen American republics to the universal tendencies of republicanism in all nations and in all ages. History, scientifically considered, thus helped *define* both the nature of the crisis of 1787 for these leaders and their audience, and also determined in large part the "reforms" which, it could be predicted, would end the crisis. To both Adams and Hamilton history proved (so they believed) that sooner or later the American people would have to return to a system of mixed or limited monarchy—so great was the size of the country, so diverse were the interests to be reconciled, that no other system could be adequate in securing both liberty and justice. In like manner Patrick Henry's prediction, June 9, 1788, in the Virginia Ratifying Convention, "that one government [i.e., the proposed constitution] cannot reign over so extensive a country as this is, without absolute despotism" was grounded upon a "political axiom" scientifically confirmed, so he believed, by history.

The most creative and philosophical disciple of the Scottish school of science and politics in the Philadelphia Convention was James Madison. His effectiveness as an advocate of a new constitution, and of the particular constitution which was drawn up in Philadelphia in 1787, was certainly based in large part on his personal experience in public life and his personal knowledge of the conditions of America in 1787. But Madison's greatness as a statesman rests in part on his ability quite deliberately to set his limited personal experience in the context of the experience of men in other ages and times, thus giving extra reaches of insight to his political formulations.

His most amazing political prophecy, formally published in the tenth *Federalist*, was that the size of the United States and its variety of interests could be made a guarantee of stability and justice under the new constitution. When Madison made this prophecy, the accepted opinion among all sophisticated politicians was exactly the opposite. It is the purpose of the following detailed analysis to show Madison, the scholar–statesman, evolving his novel theory, and not only using the behavioral science techniques of the eighteenth century, but turning to the writings of David Hume himself for some of the suggestions concerning an extended republic.

It was David Hume's speculation on the "Idea of a Perfect Commonwealth," first published in 1752, which stimulated James Madison's thought on factions.[3] In this essay Hume disclaimed any attempt to substitute a political utopia for "the common botched and inaccurate governments" (*Essays* 500) which seemed to serve imperfect men so well. Nevertheless, he argued, the idea of a perfect commonwealth

> is surely the most worthy of curiosity of any the wit of man can possibly devise. And who knows, if this controversy were fixed by the universal consent of the wise and learned, but, in some future age, an opportunity might be afforded of reducing the theory to practice, either by a dissolution of some old government, or by the combination of men to form a new one, in some distant part of the world? [*Essays* 500].

At the very end of Hume's essay was a discussion which could not help being of interest to Madison. For here the Scot casually demolished the Montesquieu small-republic theory; and it was this part of the essay, contained in a single page, which was to serve Madison in new-modeling a "botched" confederation "in a distant part of the world" (*Essays* 514).

Hume concluded his "Idea of a Perfect Commonwealth" with some observations on "the falsehood of the common opinion, that no large state, such as France or Great Britain, could ever be modelled into a commonwealth, but that such a form of government can only take place in a city or small territory" (*Essays* 513–14). The opposite seemed to be true, decided Hume. "Though it is more difficult to form a republican government in an extensive country than in a city, there is more facility when once it is formed, of preserving it steady and uniform, without tumult and faction" (*Essays* 514).

The formidable problem of first unifying the outlying and various segments of a big area had thrown Montesquieu and like-minded theorists off the track, Hume believed.

> It is not easy for the distant parts of a large state to combine in any plan of free government; but they easily conspire in the esteem and reverence for a

single person, who, by means of this popular favour, may seize the power, and forcing the more obstinate to submit, may establish a monarchical government [*Essays* 514].

Historically, therefore, it is the great leader who has been the symbol and engine of unity in empire building. His characteristic ability to evoke loyalty has made him in the past a mechanism both of solidarity and of exploitation. His leadership enables diverse peoples to work for a common end, but because of the power temptations inherent in his strategic position he usually ends as an absolute monarch.

And yet, Hume argued, this last step is not as rigid a social law as Montesquieu would have it. There was always the possibility that some modern leader with the wisdom and ancient virtue of a Solon or of a Lycurgus would suppress his personal ambition and found a free state in a large territory "to secure the peace, happiness, and liberty of future generations" (*Essays* 54). In 1776—the year Hume died—a provincial notable named George Washington was starting on the career which was to justify Hume's penetrating analysis of the unifying role of the great man in a large and variegated empire. Hume would have exulted at the discovery that his deductive leap into the future with a scientific prediction was correct: all great men who consolidated empires did not necessarily desire crowns.

Having disposed of the reason why monarchies had usually been set up in big empires and why it still was a matter of free will rather than of necessity, Hume then turned to the problem of the easily founded, and unstable, small republic. In contrast to the large state,

> a city readily concurs in the same notions of government, the natural equality of property favours liberty,[4] and the nearness of habitation enables the citizens mutually to assist each other. Even under absolute princes, the subordinate government of cities is commonly republican. . . . But these same circumstances, which facilitate the erection of commonwealths in cities, render their constitution more frail and uncertain. Democracies are turbulent. For, however the people may be separated or divided into small parties, either in their votes or elections, their near habitation in a city will always make the force of popular tides and currents very sensible. Aristocracies are better adapted for peace and order, and accordingly were most admired by ancient writers; but they are jealous and oppressive [*Essays* 514].

Here, of course, was the ancient dilemma which Madison knew so well, restated by Hume. In the city where wealth and poverty existed in close proximity, the poor, if given the vote, might very well try to use the power of the government to expropriate the opulent; while the rich, ever a self-conscious minority in a republican state, were constantly driven by fear of danger, even when no danger existed in fact, to take aggressive and oppressive measures to head off the slightest threat to their power, position, and property.

It was Hume's next two sentences which must have electrified Madison as he read them:

> In a large government, which is modelled with masterly skill, there is compass
> and room enough to refine the democracy, from the lower people who may be
> admitted into the first elections, or first concoction of the commonwealth, to
> the higher magistrates who direct all the movements. At the same time, the
> parts are so distant and remote, that it is very difficult, either by intrigue,
> prejudice, or passion, to hurry them into any measures against the public in-
> terest [*Essays* 514–15].

Hume's analysis here had turned the small-territory republic theory upside
down: *if* a free state could once be established in a large area, it would be
stable and safe from the effects of faction. Madison had found the answer to
Montesquieu. He had also found in embryonic form his own theory of the
extended federal republic.

Madison could not but feel that the "political aphorisms" which David
Hume scattered so lavishly in his essays were worthy of his careful study. He
re-examined the sketch of Hume's perfect commonwealth: "a form of government, to which I cannot, in theory, discover any considerable objection"
(*Essays* 502). Hume suggested that Great Britain and Ireland—"or any
territory of equal extent"—be divided into one hundred counties, and that
each county in turn be divided into one hundred parishes, making in all
ten thousand minor districts in the state. The twenty-pound freeholders and
five-hundred-pound householders in each parish were to elect annually a
representative for the parish. The hundred parish representatives in each
county would then elect out of themselves one "senator" and ten county
"magistrates." There would thus be in "the whole commonwealth, 100 senators, 1,100 [*sic*] county magistrates, and 10,000 . . . representatives." Hume
would then have vested in the senators the executive power: "the power of
peace and war, of giving orders to generals, admirals, and ambassadors;
and, in short, all the prerogatives of a British king, except his negative"
(*Essays* 502). The county magistrates were to have the legislative power; but
they were never to assemble as a single legislative body. They were to con-
vene in their own counties, and each county was to have one vote; and although they could initiate legislation, Hume expected the senators normally
to make policy. The ten thousand parish representatives were to have the
right to a referendum when the other two orders in the state disagreed.

It was all very complicated and cumbersome, but Hume thought that it
would allow a government to be based on the consent of the "people" and
at the same time obviate the danger of factions. He stated the "political
aphorism" which explained his complex system:

> The lower sort of people and small proprietors are good enough judges of
> one not very distant from them in rank or habitation; and therefore, in their
> parochial meetings, will probably choose the best, or nearly the best repre-
> sentative: but they are wholly unfit for country meetings, and for electing into
> the higher offices of the republic. Their ignorance gives the grandees an op-
> portunity of deceiving them [*Essays* 508].[5]

This carefully graded hierarchy of officials therefore carried the system of
indirect elections to a logical conclusion.

Madison quite easily traced out the origin of Hume's scheme. He found it in the essay entitled "Of the First Principles of Government." Hume had been led to his idea of fragmentizing election districts by his reading of Roman history and his contemplation of the historically verified evils incident to the direct participation of every citizen in democratical governments. The Scotsman had little use for "a pure republic," that is to say, a direct democracy.

> For though the people, collected in a body like the Roman tribes, be quite unfit for government, yet, when dispersed in small bodies, they are more susceptible both of reason and order; the force of popular currents and tides is in a great measure broken; and the public interests may be pursued with some method and constancy [*Essays* 33].

Hence, Hume's careful attempts to keep the citizens with the suffrage operating in thousands of artificially created electoral districts. And as Madison thought over Hume's theoretical system, he must suddenly have seen that in this instance the troublesome corporate aggressiveness of the thirteen American states could be used to good purpose. There already existed in the United States local governing units to break the force of popular currents. There was no need to invent an artificial system of counties in America. The states themselves could serve as the chief pillars and supports of a new constitution in a large-area commonwealth.

Here in Hume's *Essays* lay the germ for Madison's theory of the extended republic. It is interesting to see how he took these scattered and incomplete fragments and built them into an intellectual and theoretical structure of his own. Madison's first full statement of this hypothesis appeared in his "Notes on the Confederacy" written in April 1787, eight months before the final version of it was published as the tenth *Federalist*.[6] Starting with the proposition that "in republican Government, the majority, however composed, ultimately give the law," Madison then asks what is to restrain an interested majority from unjust violations of the minority's rights? Three motives might be claimed to meliorate the selfishness of the majority: first, "prudent regard for their own good, as involved in the general . . . good"; second, "respect for character"; and, finally, religious scruples.[7] After examining each in its turn Madison concludes that they are but a frail bulwark against a ruthless party.

In his discussion of the insufficiency of "respect for character" as a curb on faction, Madison again leans heavily upon Hume. The Scot had stated paradoxically that it is

> a just *political* maxim, *that every man must be supposed a knave*; though, at the same time, it appears somewhat strange, that a maxim should be true in *politics* which is false in *fact*. . . . men are generally more honest in their private than in their public capacity, and will go greater lengths to serve a party, than when their own private interest is alone concerned. Honour is a great check upon mankind: but where a considerable body of men act together, this check is in a great measure removed, since a man is sure to be approved of by his own party . . . and he soon learns to despise the clamours of adversaries [*Essays* 42–43].

This argument, confirmed by his own experience, seemed to Madison too just and pointed not to use, so under "Respect for character" he set down:

> However strong this motive may be in individuals, it is considered as very insufficient to restrain them from injustice. In a multitude its efficacy is diminished in proportion to the number which is to share the praise or the blame. Besides, as it has reference to public opinion, which, within a particular society, is the opinion of the majority, the standard is fixed by those whose conduct is to be measured by it.[8]

The young Virginian readily found a concrete example in Rhode Island, where honor had proved to be no check on factious behavior. In a letter to Jefferson explaining the theory of the new constitution, Madison was to repeat his category of inefficacious motives,[9] but in formally presenting his theory to the world in the letters of Publius he deliberately excluded it.[10] There was a certain disadvantage in making derogatory remarks to a majority which must be persuaded to adopt your arguments.

In April 1787, however, when Madison was writing down his first thoughts on the advantage of an extended government, he had still not completely thought through and integrated Hume's system of indirect elections with his own ideas. The Virginian, nevertheless, had not dismissed the subject from his thoughts. He had taken a subsidiary element of Hume's "Perfect Commonwealth" argument and developed it as the primary factor in his own theorem; but he was also to include Hume's major technique of indirect election as a minor device in the constitution he proposed for the new American state. As the last paragraph of "Notes on the Confederacy" there appears a long sentence which on its surface has little organic relation to Madison's preceding two-page discussion of how "an extensive Republic meliorates the administration of a small Republic."

> An auxiliary desideratum for the melioration of the Republican form is such a process of elections as will most certainly extract from the mass of the society the purest and noblest characters which it contains; such as will at once feel most strongly the proper motives to pursue the end of their appointment, and be most capable to devise the proper means of attaining it.[11]

This final sentence, with its abrupt departure in thought, would be hard to explain were it not for the juxtaposition in Hume of the material on large area and indirect election.

When Madison presented his thesis to the electorate in the tenth *Federalist* as justification for a more perfect union, Hume's *Essays* were to offer one final service. Hume had written a scientific analysis on "Parties in General" as well as on the "Parties of Great Britain." In the first of these essays he took the position independently arrived at by Madison concerning the great variety of factions likely to agitate a republican state. The Virginian, with his characteristic scholarly thoroughness, therefore turned to Hume again when it came time to parade his arguments in full dress. Hume had made his major contribution to Madison's political philosophy before the Philadelphia Convention. Now he was to help in the final polishing and elaboration of the theory for purposes of public persuasion in print.

Madison had no capacity for slavish imitation; but a borrowed word, a sentence lifted almost in its entirety from the other's essay, and, above all, the exactly parallel march of ideas in Hume's "Parties" and Madison's *Federalist*, No. X, show how congenial he found the Scot's way of thinking, and how invaluable Hume was in the final crystallizing of Madison's own convictions. "Men have such a propensity to divide into personal factions," wrote Hume, "that the smallest appearance of real difference will produce them" (*Essays* 56). And the Virginian takes up the thread to spin his more elaborate web: "So strong is this propensity of mankind to fall into mutual animosities, that where no substantial occasion presents itself, the most frivolous and fanciful distinctions have been sufficient to kindle their unfriendly passions and excite their most violent conflicts." [12] Hume, in his parallel passage, presents copious examples. He cites the rivalry of the blues and the greens at Constantinople, and recalls the feud between two tribes in Rome, the Pollia and the Papiria, which lasted three hundred years after everyone had forgotten the original cause of the quarrel. "If mankind had not a strong propensity to such divisions, the indifference of the rest of the community must have suppressed this foolish animosity [of the two tribes], that had not any aliment of new benefits and injuries . . ." (*Essays* 56). The fine Latinity of the word "aliment" [13] apparently caught in some crevice of Madison's mind, soon to reappear in his statement "Liberty is to faction what air is to fire, an aliment, without which it instantly expires." [14] So far as his writings show, he never used the word again; but in this year of 1787 his head was full of such words and ideas culled from David Hume.

When one examines these two papers in which Hume and Madison summed up the eighteenth century's most profound thought on party, it becomes increasingly clear that the young American used the earlier work in preparing a survey on faction through the ages to introduce his own discussion of faction in America. Hume's work was admirably adapted to this purpose. It was philosophical and scientific in the best tradition of the Enlightenment. The facile damnation of faction had been a commonplace in English politics for a hundred years, as Whig and Tory vociferously sought to fasten the label on each other. But the Scot, very little interested as a partisan and very much so as a social scientist, treated the subject therefore in psychological, intellectual, and socio-economic terms. Throughout all history, he discovered, mankind has been divided into factions based either on personal loyalty to some leader or upon some "sentiment or interest" common to the group as a unit. This latter type he called a "real" as distinguished from the "personal" faction. Finally he subdivided the "real factions" into parties based on "interest," upon "principle," or upon "affection." Hume spent well over five pages (*Essays* 55–60) dissecting these three types; but Madison, while determined to be inclusive, had not the space to go into such minute analysis. Besides, he was more intent now on developing the cure than on describing the malady. He therefore consolidated Hume's two-page treatment of "personal" factions, and his long discussion of parties based on "principle and affection" into a single sentence. The tenth *Federalist* reads:

A zeal for different opinions concerning religion, concerning government, and many other points, as well of speculation as of practice; [15] an attachment to different leaders ambitiously contending for pre-eminence and power; [16] or to persons of other descriptions whose fortunes have been interesting to the human passions,[17] have, in turn, divided mankind into parties, inflamed them with mutual animosity, and rendered them much more disposed to vex and oppress each other than to cooperate for their common good.[18]

It is hard to conceive of a more perfect example of the concentration of idea and meaning than Madison achieved in this famous sentence.

It is noteworthy that while James Madison compressed the greater part of Hume's essay on factions into a single sentence, he greatly expanded the quick sketch of the faction from "interest" buried in the middle of the philosopher's analysis. This reference, in Madison's hands, became the climax of his treatment and is the basis of his reputation in some circles as the progenitor of the theory of economic determinism. Hume had written that factions from interest

> are the most reasonable, and the most excusable. Where two orders of men, such as the nobles and people, have a distinct authority in a government, not very accurately balanced and modelled, they naturally follow a distinct interest; nor can we reasonably expect a different conduct, considering that degree of selfishness implanted in human nature. It requires great skill in a legislator to prevent such parties; and many philosophers are of opinion, that this secret, like the *grand elixir*, or *perpetual motion*, may amuse men in theory, but can never possibly be reduced to practice [*Essays* 58].

With this uncomfortable thought Hume dismissed the subject of economic factions as he fell into the congenial task of sticking sharp intellectual pins into priestly parties and bigots who fought over abstract political principles.

Madison, on the contrary, was not satisfied with this cursory treatment. He had his own ideas about the importance of economic forces. All that Hume had to say of personal parties, of parties of principle, and of parties of attachment, was but a prologue to the Virginian's discussion of "the various and unequal distribution of property," throughout recorded history.

> Those who hold, and those who are without property, have ever formed distinct interests in society. Those who are creditors, and those who are debtors, fall under a like discrimination. A landed interest, a manufacturing interest, a mercantile interest, a moneyed interest, with many lesser interests, grow up of necessity in civilized nations, and divide them into different classes actuated by different sentiments and views.[19]

Here was the pivot of Madison's analysis. Here in this multiplicity of economic factions was "the grand elixir" which transformed the ancient doctrine of the rich against the poor into a situation which a skillful American legislator might model into equilibrium. Compound various economic interests of a large territory with a federal system of thirteen semi-sovereign political units, establish a scheme of indirect elections which will functionally bind the extensive area into a unity while "refining" the voice of the people, and you will have a stable republican state.

This was the glad news which James Madison carried to Philadelphia. This was the theory which he claimed had made obsolete the necessity for the "mixed government" advocated by Hamilton and Adams. This was the message he gave to the world in the first *Federalist* paper he composed. His own scientific reading of history, ancient and modern, his experience with religious factions in Virginia, and, above all, his knowledge of the scientific axiom regarding man and society in the works of David Hume, ablest British philosopher of his age, had served him and his country well.

> Of all men that distinguish themselves by memorable achievements, the first place of honour seems due to LEGISLATORS and founders of states, who transmit a system of laws and institutions to secure the peace, happiness, and liberty of future generations [*Essays* 54].

NOTES

1. An examination of the social theory of the Scottish school is to be found in Gladys Bryson, *Man and Society: The Scottish Inquiry of the Eighteenth Century* (Princeton, 1945). Miss Bryson seems unaware both of the position held by Scottish social science in the curriculum of the American colleges after 1750—Princeton, for example, where nine members of the Constitutional Convention of 1787 graduated, was a provincial carbon-copy, under President Witherspoon, of Edinburgh—and of its influence on the revolutionary generation. For a brilliant analysis of Francis Hutcheson's ideas and his part in setting the tone and direction of Scottish research, as well as the trans-Atlantic flow of ideas between Scotland and the American colonies in the eighteenth century, with a persuasive explanation of why the Scots specialized in social science formulations which were peculiarly congenial to the American revolutionary elite, see Caroline Robbins, "When It Is That Colonies May Turn Independent," *William and Mary Quarterly*, 3d ser., 11, No. 4 (April 1954), 214–51.

2. The theoretical and prophetic nature of Adam Smith's classic when it was published in 1776 is today largely ignored by both scholars and spokesmen for the modern American business community. In 1776, however, Smith could only theorize from scattered historical precedents as to how a projective free enterprise system might work, because nowhere in his mercantilist world was a free enterprise system of the sort he described on paper actually operating.

3. Madison apparently used the 1758 edition of the *Essays Moral, Political, and Literary*, which was the most complete printed during the Scot's lifetime, and which gathered up into two volumes what he conceived of as the final revised version of his thoughts on the topics treated. Earlier versions of certain of the essays had been printed in 1742, 1748, and 1752; there are numerous modern editions of the 1758 printing.

4. Hume seems to be referring to the development in cities of a specialized product, trade, or industrial skill, which gives the small area an equal interest in a specific type of economic activity. All the inhabitants of Sheffield from the lowly artisan to the wealthiest manufacturer had an interest in the iron industry; every dweller in Liverpool had a stake in the prosperity of the slave trade. It was this regional unity of occupation which Hume was speaking of, not equality of income from the occupation, as is shown by the latter part of his analysis.

5. Hume elaborated his system in great detail, working out a judiciary system, the methods of organizing and controlling the militia, etc. The Scot incidentally acknowledged that his thought and theories on the subject owed much to James Harrington's *Oceana* (London, 1656), "the only valuable model of a [perfect] commonwealth that has yet been offered to the public" (*Essays* 501). For Hume thought that Sir Thomas More's *Utopia* and Plato's *Republic*, as well as all other utopian blueprints, were worthless. "All plans of government, which suppose great reformation in the manners of mankind," he noted, "are plainly imaginary" (*Essays* 500).

6. *The Federalist*, No. X, appeared in *The New York Packet*, Friday November 23, 1787. There are thus three versions of Madison's theoretic formulation of how a properly organized republic in a large area, incorporating within its jurisdiction a multiplicity of interests, will sterilize the class conflict of the rich versus the poor: (1) the "Notes" of April 1787; (2) speeches in the convention during June 1787; and (3) the final polished and elaborated form, in *The Federalist*, November 1787.

7. James Madison, *Letters and Other Writings*, 4 vols. (Philadelphia, 1867), I 325–26.

8. Ibid., 326.

9. Ibid., 352; to Thomas Jefferson, October 24, 1787.

10. In Madison's earliest presentation of his thesis, there appear certain other elements indicating his debt to Hume which have vanished in *The Federalist*. In the "Notes on the Confederacy," the phrase "notorious factions and oppressions which take place in corporate towns" (*Letters*, I 327) recalls the original starting point of Hume's analysis in the "Perfect Commonwealth." Also the phraseology of the sentence: "The society becomes broken into a greater variety of interests . . . which check each other . . ." (ibid.), varied in the letter to Jefferson to: "In a large society, the people are broken into so many interests" (ibid., 352), is probably a parallel of Hume's "the force of popular currents and tides is in a great measure broken . . ." (*Essays* 33).

11. *Letters*, I 328.

12. *The Federalist*, ed. Max Beloff (Oxford & New York, 1948), No. X, p. 43. Hereafter page references to *The Federalist* will be to this edition.

13. L. *alimentum*, fr. *alere*, to nourish. Food; nutriment; hence, sustenance, means of support. Syn. see pabulum. This word is not a common one in eighteenth-century political literature. Outside of *The Federalist* and Hume's essay, I have run across it only in Bacon's works. To the man of the eighteenth century even the cognate forms "alimentary" (canal), and "alimony," so familiar to us in common speech, were still highly technical terms of medicine and law.

14. *Federalist*, p. 42. Compare Hume's remarks: "In despotic governments, indeed, factions often do not appear; but they are not the less real; or rather, they are more real and more pernicious upon that very account. The distinct orders of men, nobles and people, soldiers and merchants, have all a distinct interest; but the more powerful oppresses the weaker with impunity, and without resistance; which begets a seeming tranquillity in such governments" (*Essays* 58). Also, see Hume's comparison of faction to "weeds . . . which grow most plentiful in the richest soil; and though absolute governments be not wholly free from them, it must be confessed, that they rise more easily, and propagate themselves faster in free governments, where they always infect the legislature itself, which alone could be able, by the steady application of rewards and punishments, to eradicate them" (*Essays* 55), and notice Madison's "The regulation of these various and interfering interests forms the principal task of modern legislation, and involves the spirit of party and faction in the necessary and ordinary operations of the government" (*Federalist*, p. 43).

15. This clause of Madison's refers to Hume's "parties from *principle*, especially abstract speculative principle," in the discussion of which he includes "different political principles" and "principles of priestly government . . . which has . . . been the poison of human society, and the source of the most inveterate factions. . . ." Hume, in keeping with his reputation as the great sceptic, feels that while the congregations of persecuting sects must be called "factions of principle," the priests, who are "the prime movers" in religious parties, are factious out of "interest" (*Essays* 58, 60–61). The word "speculation" which appears in Madison is rendered twice as "speculative" in Hume.

16. Here is Hume's "Personal" faction, "founded on personal friendship or animosity among such as compose the contending parties . . ." (*Essays* 55). Hume instances the Colonnesi and Orsini of modern Rome, the Neri and Bianchi of Florence, the rivalry between the Pollia and Papiria of ancient Rome, and the confused mass of shifting alliances which marked the struggle between Guelfs and Ghibellines (*Essay* 56).

17. This phrase, which is quite obscure in the context, making a separate category of a type of party apparently just covered under "contending leaders," refers to the loyal bitter-end Jacobites of eighteenth-century England. These sentimental irreconcilables of

the Squire Western ilk made up Hume's "party from *affection*." Hume explains: "By parties from affection, I understand those which are founded on the different attachments of men towards particular families and persons whom they desire to rule over them. These factions are often very violent [Hume was writing only three years before Bonnie Prince Charlie and the clans frightened all England in '45]; though, I must own, it may seem unaccountable that men should attach themselves so strongly to persons with whom they are nowise acquainted, whom perhaps they never saw, and from whom they never received, nor can ever hope for, any favour" (*Essays* 61–62).

The fact that Madison includes this category in his paper satisfies me that, when he came to write the tenth *Federalist* for publication, he referred directly to Hume's volume as he reworked his introduction into its final polished form. One can account for the other similarities in the discussion of faction as a result of Madison's careful reading of Hume's works and his retentive memory. But the inclusion of this "party from affection" in the Virginian's final scheme where its ambiguity indeed detracts from the force of the argument, puts a strain on the belief that it resulted from memory alone. This odd fourth classification, which on its face is redundant, probably was included because Hume's book was open on the table beside him, and because James Madison would leave no historical stone unturned in his effort to make a definitive scientific summary.

18. *Federalist*, pp. 42–43.

19. Ibid., p. 43.

Index

Adair, Douglass, 17–18, 389
Adams, John, 17, 239, 243, 393
Anderson, Adam, 299
Anderson, Robert F., 11–12, 288
Anscombe, G. E. M., 278
Árdal, Páll S., 8–9, 12–13, 175, 178, 190, 359*n*16
Argenson, (Marc Pierre de Voyer) Count d', 243
Aristotle, 81–82, 264, 362
Augustine, St., 12, 205
Ayer, A. J., 3, 80, 222

Bacon, Francis, 69, 84–86, 89, 301, 405
Balfour, Arthur James, 250
Basson, A. H., 214, 228, 295*n*16
Bauer, Bruno, 5
Baxter, John, 389–93, 395, 399–400
Bayle, Pierre, 264, 268
Beattie, James, 1
Bede, The Venerable, 301
Bennett, Jonathan, 162, 214, 224–25, 228
Bentham, Jeremy, 239–40, 250, 395
Berkeley, George, 260
Bernoulli, J., 68*n*12
Bestor, Arthur, 390, 401*n*13
Birch, T., 301
Blackstone, Sir William, 243, 250, 253
Bolingbroke, (Henry St. John) Viscount, 248, 253
Bonald, Louis Gabriel Ambroise de, 241
Bongie, Lawrence, 399
Bosanquet, Bernard, 223
Boyle, Robert, 28
Brady, Robert, 301
Broad, C. D., 7, 86, 213, 381
Brussel, Nicholas, 301
Bryson, Gladys, 415*n*1
Buckle, Henry, 236
Burke, Edmund, 233, 239–40, 248, 252–53, 255, 256*n*19
Burnet, Gilbert, 301

Camus, Albert, 5
Cantillon, Richard, 301
Capaldi, Nicholas, 10–12, 16
Carnap, Rudolf, 7, 53, 57, 63–65, 68*n*9, 80, 89*n*22
Carr, Peter, 394
Carte, Thomas, 301

Cartwright, John, 397
Charles I, 315, 394
Charles II, 302
Child, Sir Joseph, 300
Church, Ralph, 213, 221
Cicero, 302
Clarendon, (Edward Hyde) Earl of, 301
Clark, Samuel, 74
Coke, Sir Edward, 301
Colbourn, Trevor, 390, 392, 399
Coleridge, Samuel Taylor, 241
Comte, Auguste, 236
Condorcet, (Marie Jean Antoine Nicholas de Caritat) Marquis de, 236
Copernicus, 184
Cotton, John, 301
Cromwell, Oliver, 393
Crousaz, J. P., 173

Danto, Arthur, 227, 234
Davenant, Charles, 300
Defoe, Daniel, 248
Descartes, René, 2, 173, 177, 180, 202, 220, 225, 240
Destutt de Tracy, Antoine Louis Claude, 394–96, 398–99, 403*n*35
Deutscher, Max, 293*n*5
D'Ewes, Sir Simonds, 301, 303
Diderot, Denis, 243
Duane, William, 17, 393

Eddington, Sir Arthur, 220
Einstein, Albert, 57
Elizabeth I, 304–306
Elliot, Gilbert, 161
Engels, Friedrich, 220
Erasmus, 302

Feigel, H., 82
Ferguson, Adam, 18, 406
Feyerabend, Paul, 57
Fichte, Johann Gottlieb, 236
Fleetwood, (Bishop) William, 299–300
Flew, Antony, 13, 121*n*7, 214–15, 218, 228, 359*n*13
Fortescue, Sir John, 301
Fourier, Charles, 220, 236
Frege, Gottlob, 229
Freud, Sigmund, 58
Froissart, Jean, 301